Street by Street

SOUTH HAMPSHIRE
PLUS BOURNEMOUTH, CHRISTCHURCH, FERNDOWN, POOLE, SOUTHBOURNE, VERWOOD, WIMBORNE MINSTER
Enlarged Areas Fareham, Gosport, Havant, Portsmouth, Southampton, Winchester

Ist edition May 2001

© Automobile Association Developments Limited 2001

This product includes map data licensed from Ordnance Survey® with the permission of the Controller of Her Majesty's Stationery Office. © Crown copyright 2000. All rights reserved. Licence No: 399221.

Published by AA Publishing (a trading name of Automobile Association Developments Limited, whose registered office is Norfolk House, Priestley Road, Basingstoke, Hampshire, RG24 9NY.
Registered number 1878835).

Mapping produced by the Cartographic Department of The Automobile Association.

ISBN 0 7495 2360 3

A CIP Catalogue record for this book is available from the British Library.

Printed by G. Canale & C. s.p.a., Torino, Italy

The contents of this atlas are believed to be correct at the time of the latest revision. However, the publishers cannot be held responsible for loss occasioned to any person acting or refraining from action as a result of any material in this atlas, nor for any errors, omissions or changes in such material. The publishers would welcome information to correct any errors or omissions and to keep this atlas up to date. Please write to Publishing, The Automobile Association, Fanum House, Basing View, Basingstoke, Hampshire, RG21 4EA.

Ref: MX007

Key to map pages   ii-iii

Key to map symbols   iv-1

Enlarged scale pages   2-15

Street by Street   16-245

Index – towns & villages 246-247

Index – streets   247-278

Index – featured places   278-282

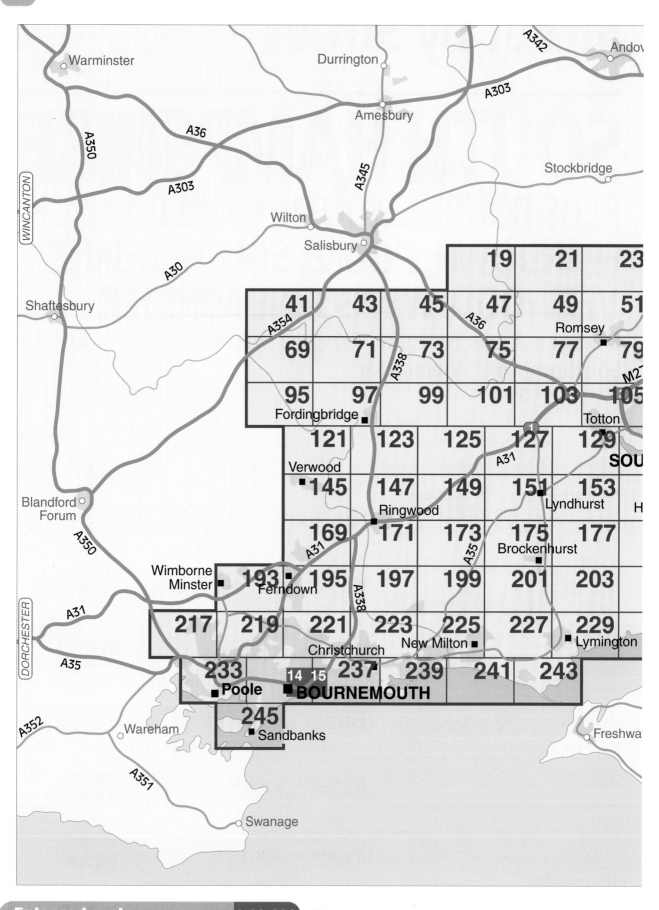

Warminster

Durrington

Andov

A342

A303

A36

A350

A303

A345

Amesbury

Stockbridge

Wilton

Salisbury

A30

Shaftesbury

| 19 | 21 | 23 |

A354

| 41 | 43 | 45 | 47 | 49 | 51 |

A36

Romsey

| 69 | 71 | 73 | 75 | 77 | 79 |

A338

M2

| 95 | 97 | 99 | 101 | 103 | 105 |

Fordingbridge

Totton

| 121 | 123 | 125 | 127 | 129 |

A31

Verwood

SOU

Blandford
Forum

| 145 | 147 | 149 | 151 | 153 |

Ringwood

Lyndhurst

H

A350

| 169 | 171 | 173 | 175 | 177 |

A31

A35

Brockenhurst

Wimborne
Minster

| 193 | 195 | 197 | 199 | 201 | 203 |

Ferndown

A338

DORCHESTER

A31

| 217 | 219 | 221 | 223 | 225 | 227 | 229 |

A35

New Milton

Lymington

Christchurch

| 233 | 14 | 15 | 237 | 239 | 241 | 243 |

Poole

BOURNEMOUTH

| 245 |

Wareham

Sandbanks

Freshwa

A352

A351

Swanage

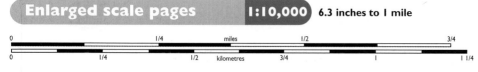

Enlarged scale pages   **1:10,000**   6.3 inches to 1 mile

| 0 | | 1/4 | miles | 1/2 | | 3/4 |
| 0 | 1/4 | | 1/2 | kilometres | 3/4 | | 1 | | 1 1/4 |

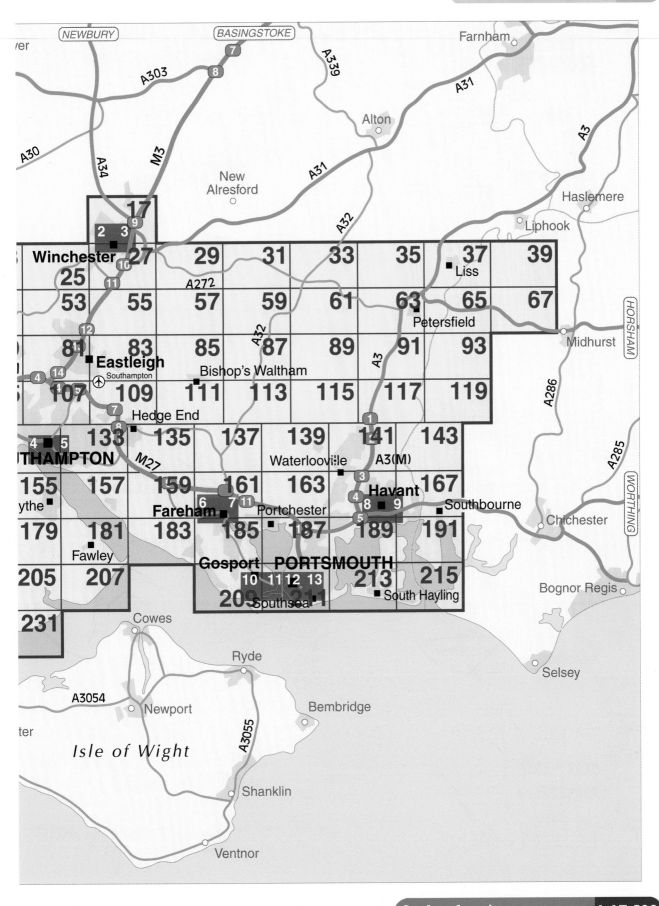

Junction 9	Motorway & junction
Services	Motorway service area
	Primary road single/dual carriageway
Services	Primary road service area
	A road single/dual carriageway
	B road single/dual carriageway
	Other road single/dual carriageway
	Restricted road
	Private road
← ←	One way street
	Pedestrian street
	Track/ footpath
	Road under construction
	Road tunnel
P	Parking

P+	Park & Ride
	Bus/coach station
	Railway & main railway station
	Railway & minor railway station
	Underground station
	Light railway & station
+++++++++++++	Preserved private railway
LC	Level crossing
•—•—•—•—•	Tramway
- - - - - - - - -	Ferry route
·············	Airport runway
— · — · — · —	Boundaries- borough/ district
▼▼▼▼▼▼▼▼▼	Mounds
93	Page continuation 1:17,500
7	Page continuation to enlarged scale 1:10,000

	River/canal lake, pier			Toilet with disabled facilities
	Aqueduct lock, weir			Petrol station
465 ▲ Winter Hill	Peak (with height in metres)		PH	Public house
	Beach		PO	Post Office
	Coniferous woodland			Public library
	Broadleaved woodland		i	Tourist Information Centre
	Mixed woodland		✗	Castle
	Park			Historic house/ building
	Cemetery		Wakehurst Place NT	National Trust property
	Built-up area		M	Museum/ art gallery
	Featured building		†	Church/chapel
	City wall			Country park
A&E	Accident & Emergency hospital			Theatre/ performing arts
	Toilet			Cinema

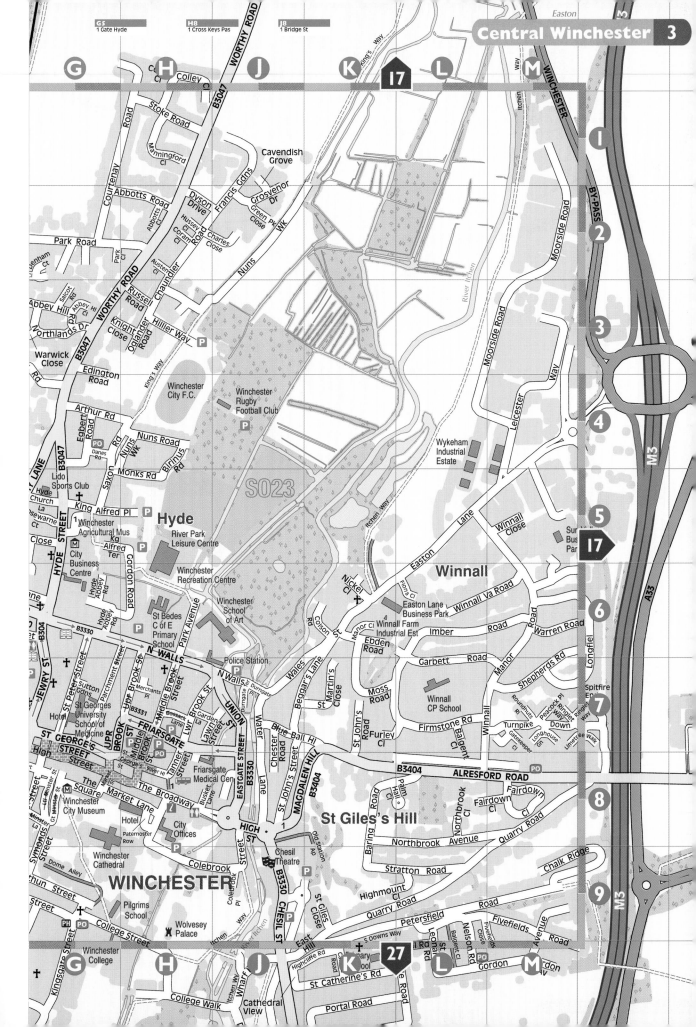

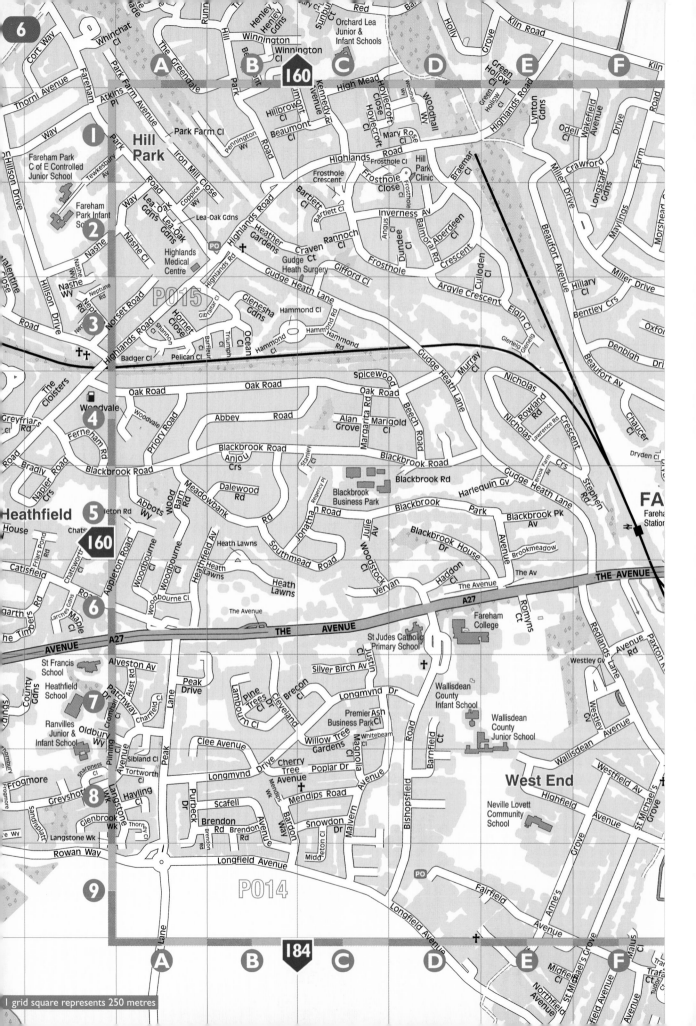

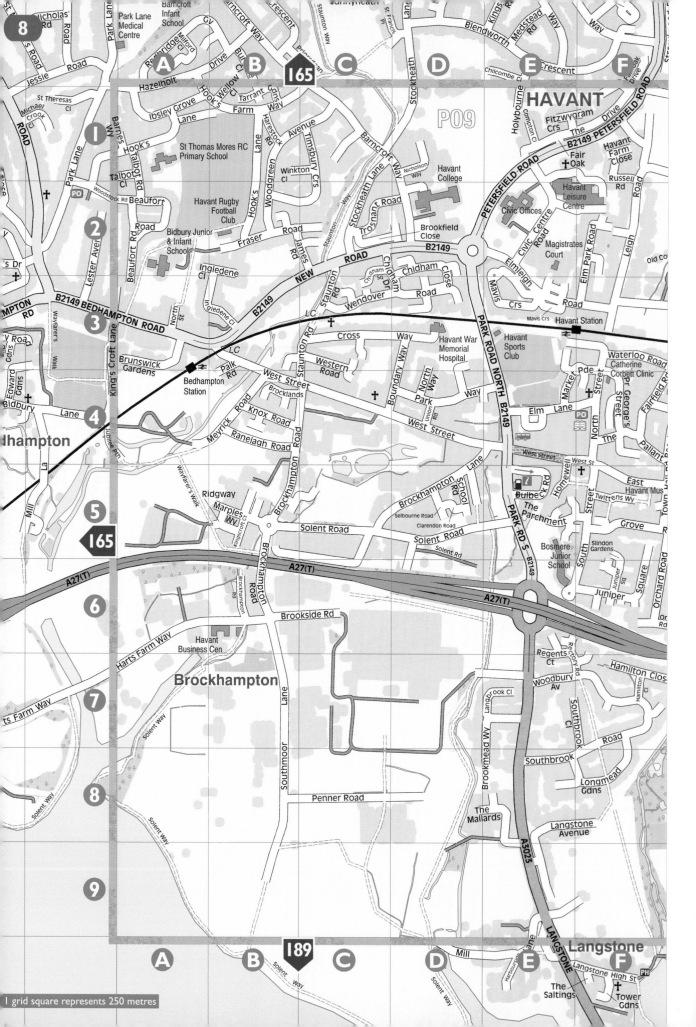

Central Havant map showing Denvilles and Warblington areas.

Grid references: G H J K L M across top and bottom; 1–9 down right side.

Map labels include:
Lockerley Road, St Albans C of E Prim Sch, Hayward Business Cen, Hayward Business Centre, Dunhurst Close, Crossland Drive, River Way, Lavant Dr, Lakeside Gdns, Old Fern Dr, Cedar Gdns, Eastern Road, New Lane, Oak Pk Dr, Anderson Cl, Burrows Close, Copse Rd, Nutwick Rd, Swallow Cl, Rowan, Elder Road, Hornbeam Rd, Hornbeam Road, Marlborough Park, Spindle Cl, Spindle Warren, Weavers Gn, Chartwell Dr, Bladon Cl, Blenheim, Fifth Avenue, Denvilles, Denvilles Cl, Carisbrooke Cl, Fourth Avenue, Second Av, Southleigh Rd, First Avenue, Hallett Road, Third Avenue, Grange Close, Glenleigh Park, Warblington Station, LC, St George's Avenue, Ryecroft, Fairfield Infant School, Montgomery Rd, Glenhurst School, Connaught Road, Warblington School, Oaklands Rd, Bellair Road, Oaklands Rd, Pine Gv, White Ladies Close, Emsworth Road, Meadowlands, Berkeley Square, Woodpecker Cl, Warblington Avenue, Castle Avenue, Nightingale Park, Castleway, Emsworth Rd, Green Pond Corner, Netherfield, Tavistock Gdns, The Gdns, Hampshire Co Council, Willow Cl, Granville Cl, Luard Ct, Bedford Cl, Lymbourn Rd, Lower Grove Road, Northup Close, Shawfield Rd, Pembury Road, Norris Gdns, Elm Road, South Cl, Wade, Havant Road, A27(T), Pook La, Pook Lane, Church Lane, Warblington, A27(T), A259, Havant Road, Nore Crs, Nore Fa, Hotel, Southleigh Fm, Southleigh Road, Christchurch Medical Centre, Nutwick Rd, Snowberry Crs, Camelia Cl, Bramble Cl, Solent Way, Cemetery, Conigar Point

Page references: 165, 166, 189

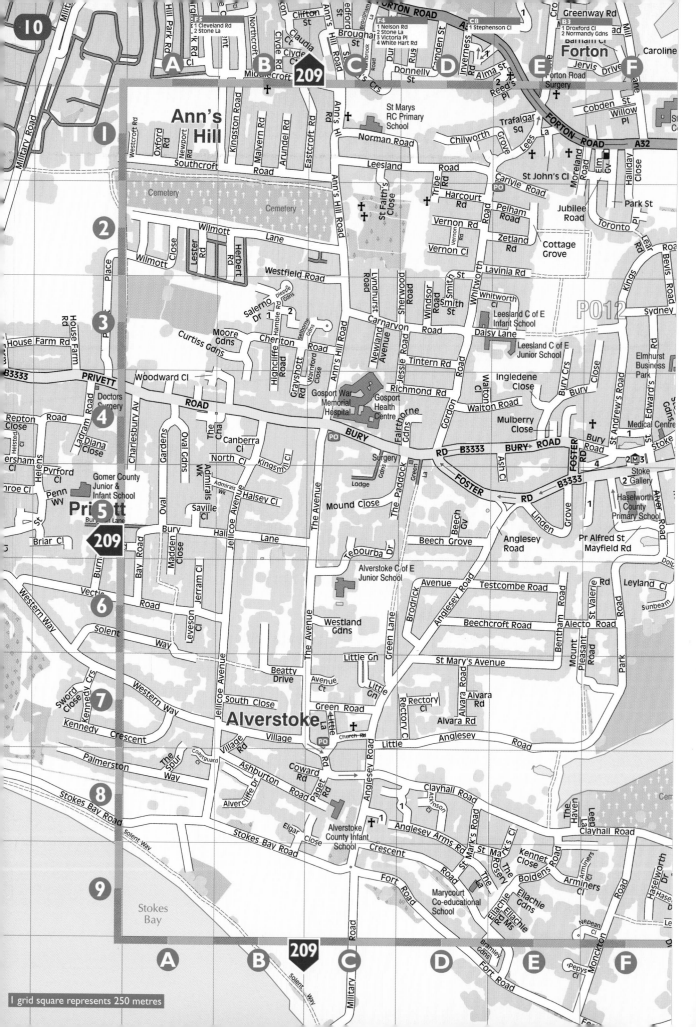

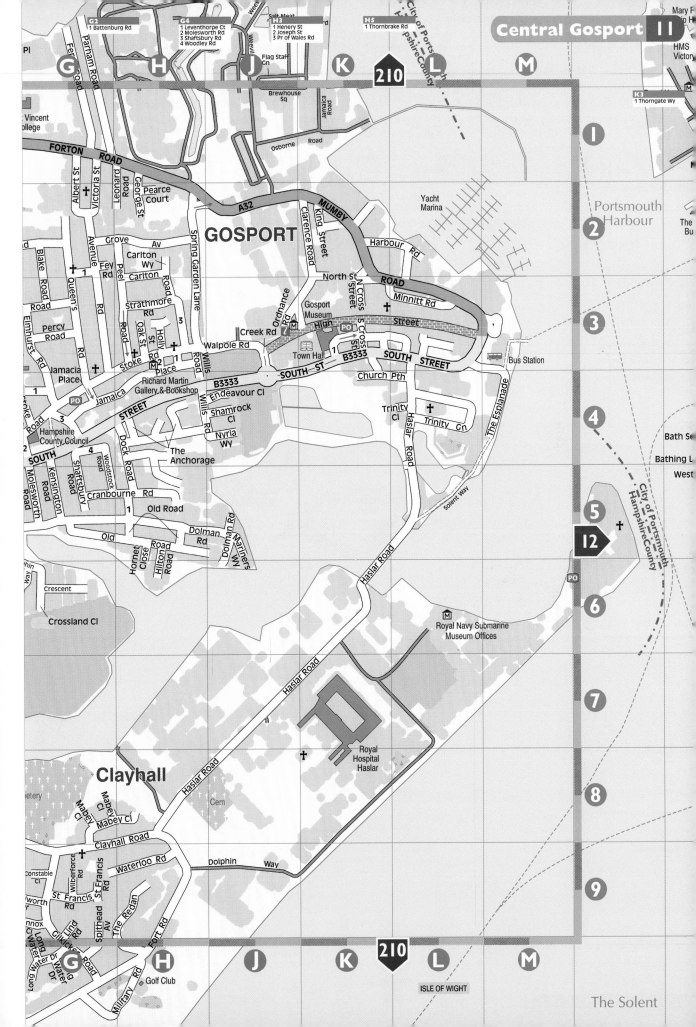

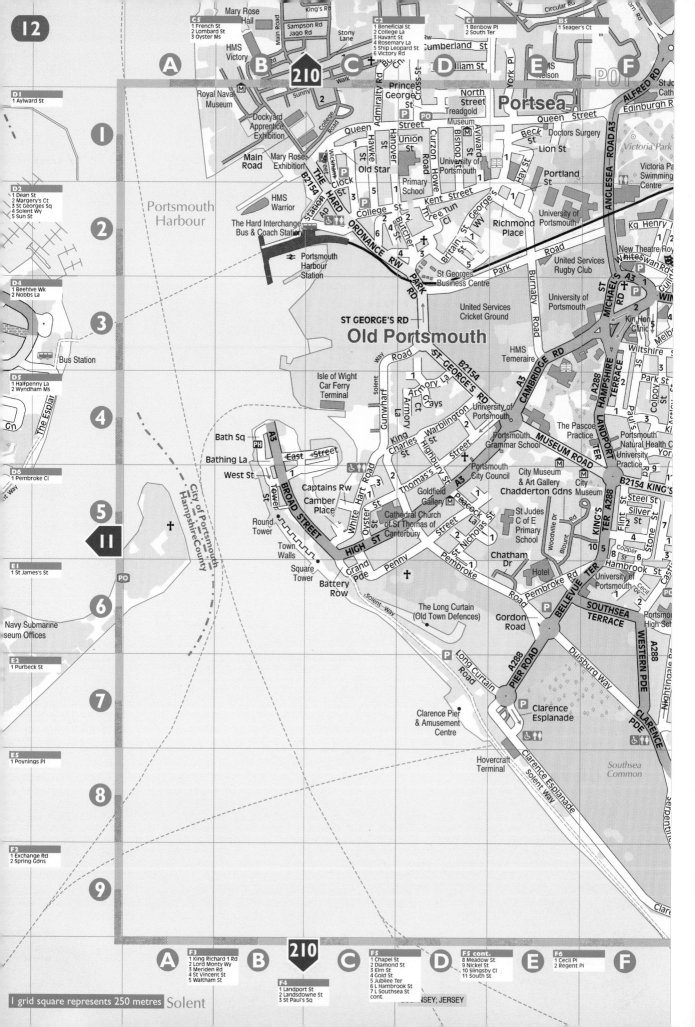

12

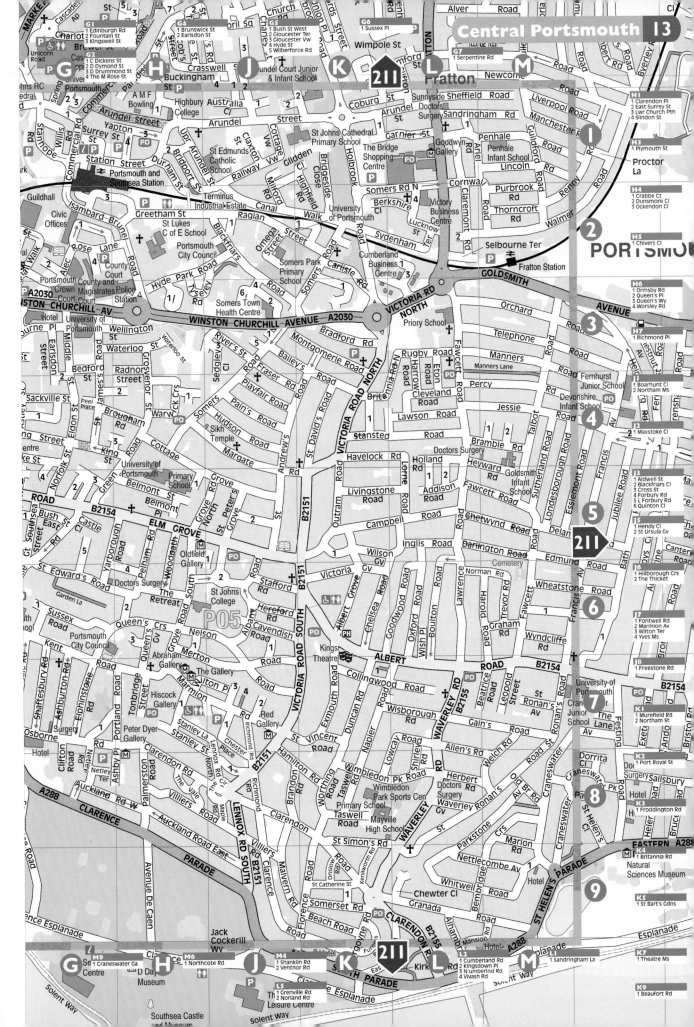

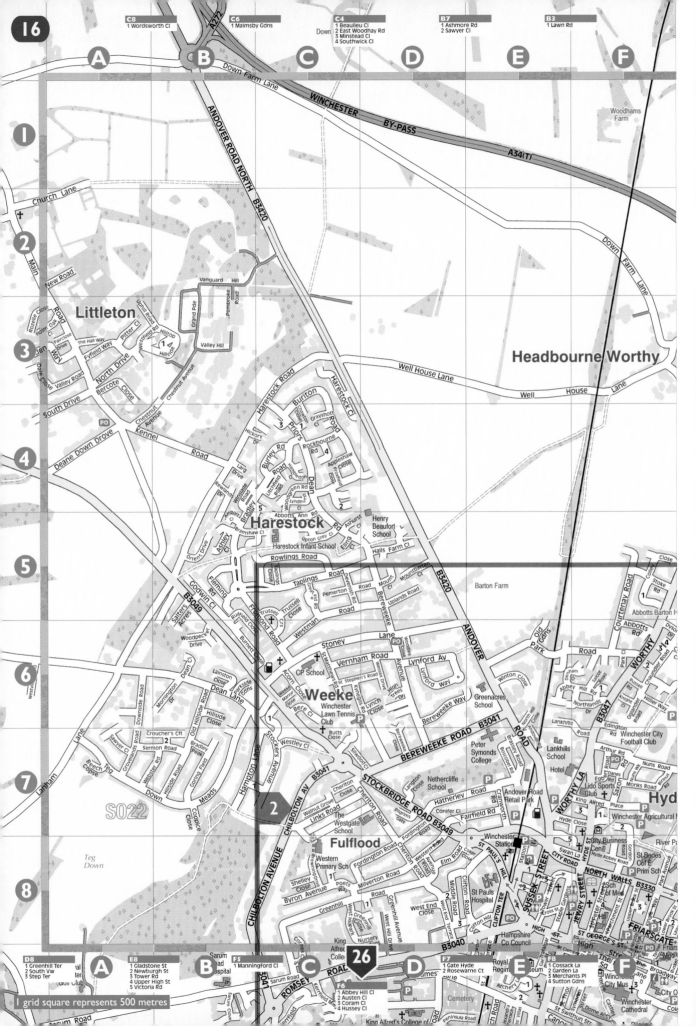

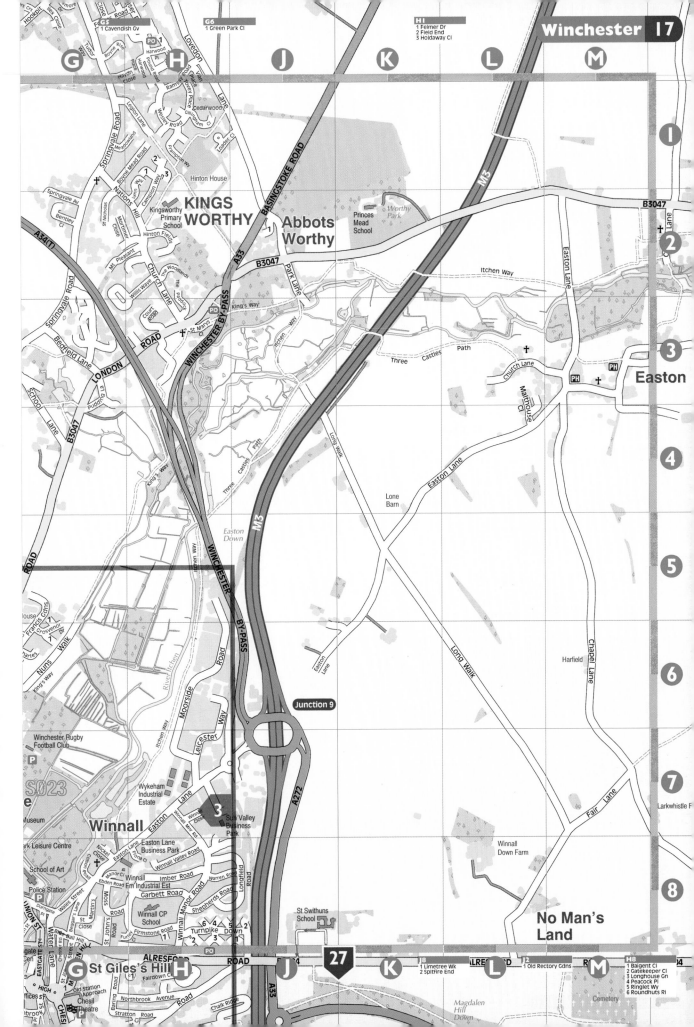

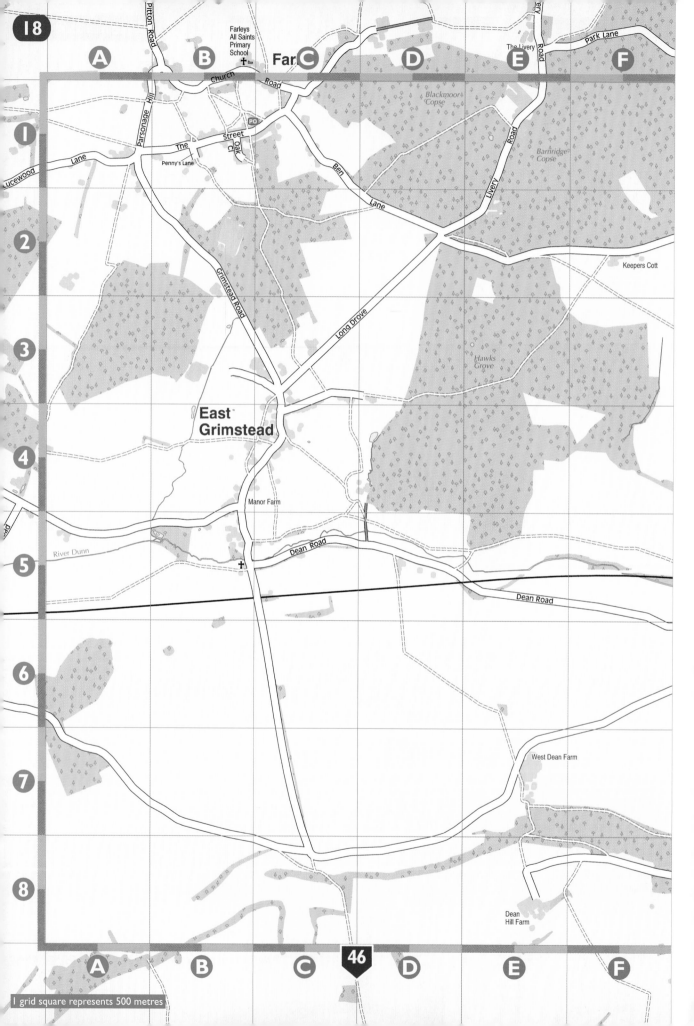

G   H   J   K   L   M

The
Gre

I

Howe
Copse
East

Park

Copse

Wiltshire County
Hampshire County

Dean Copse

Frenchmoor

Dean Road

Drove Farm Ho

Frenchmoor Lane

2

Drove

3

4

20

Pilgrims
Croft

PO

River Dunn

Rectory Hill

West
Dean

Park Farm

Frenchmoor La

5

Dean
Station

6

East
Dean

Glebe Mdw

Dean Road

Moody's Hill

Ashmore Lane

Hillside Close

7

Deanhill
Barn

8

Gatmore
Copse

Hampshire County
shire County

G   H   J   K   L   M

Mean
Wood

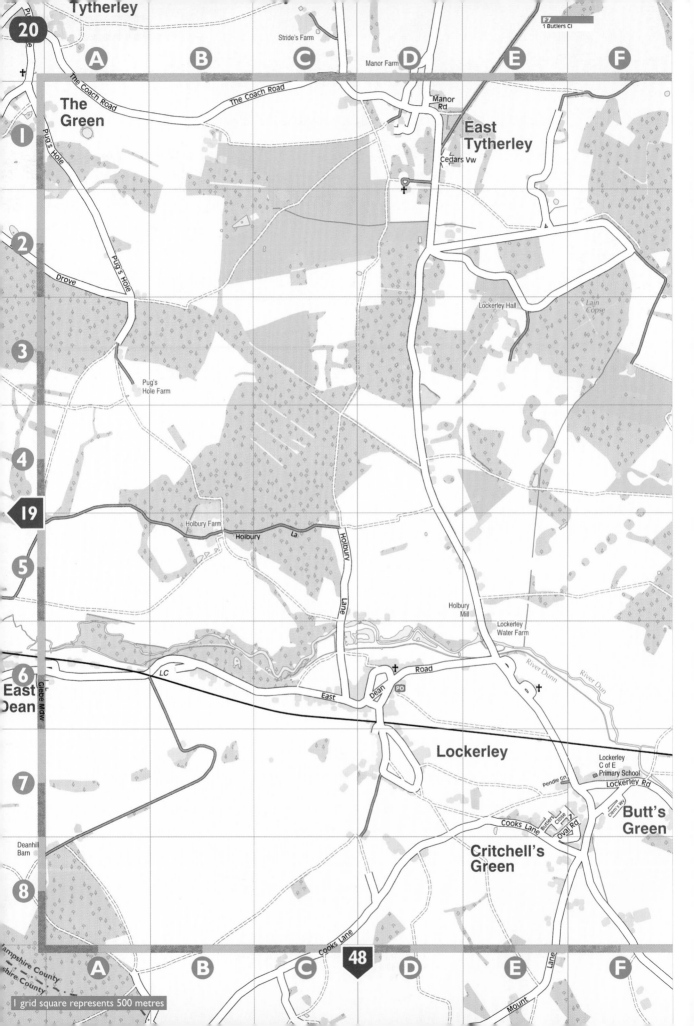

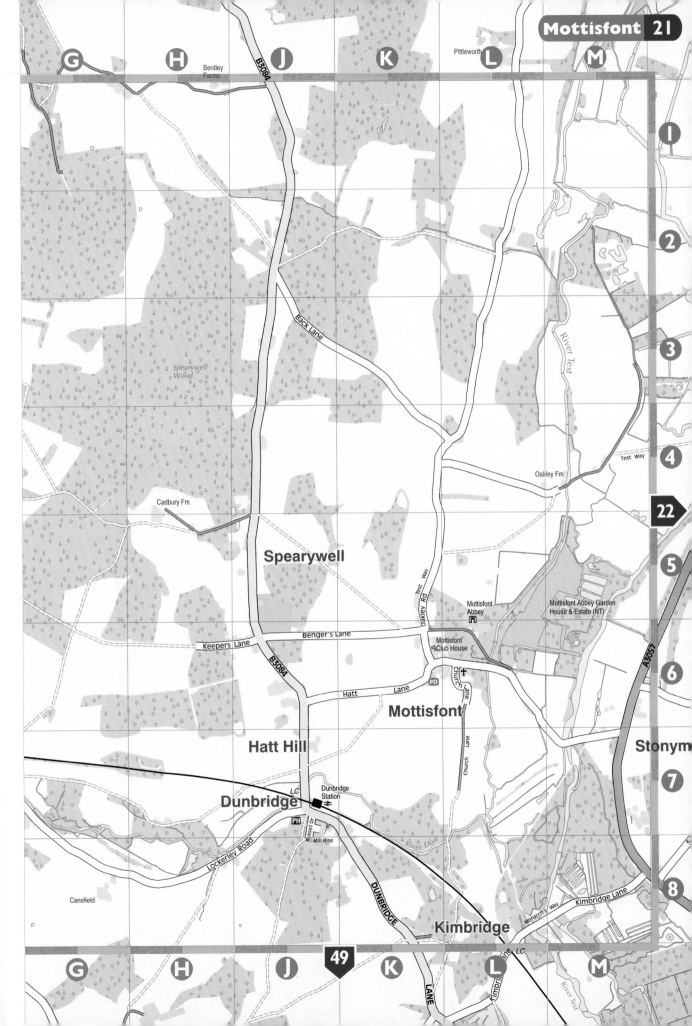

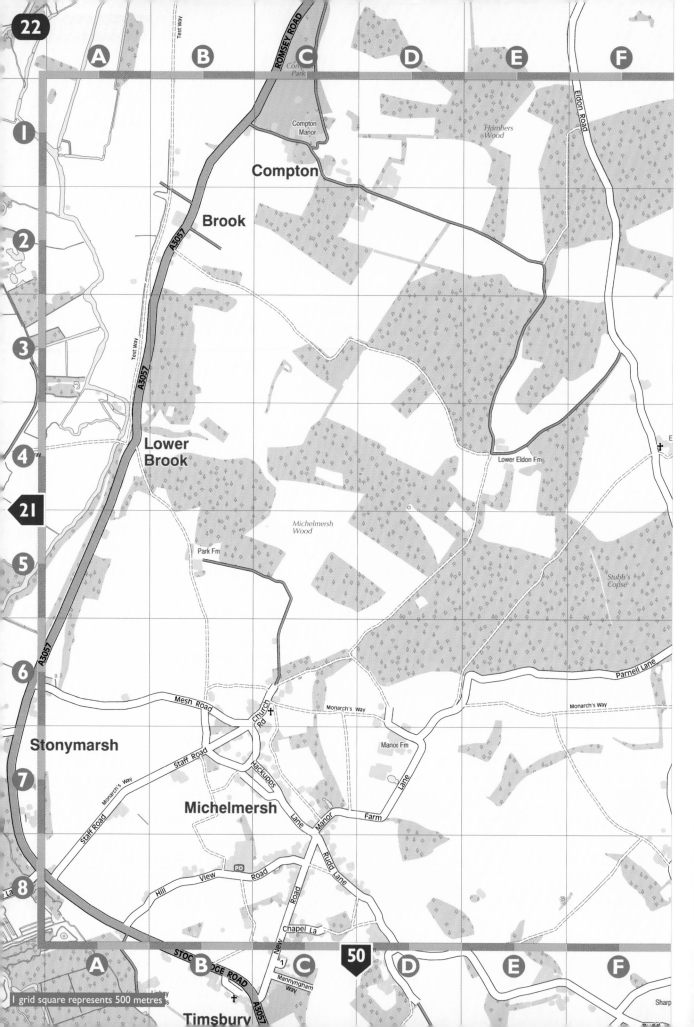

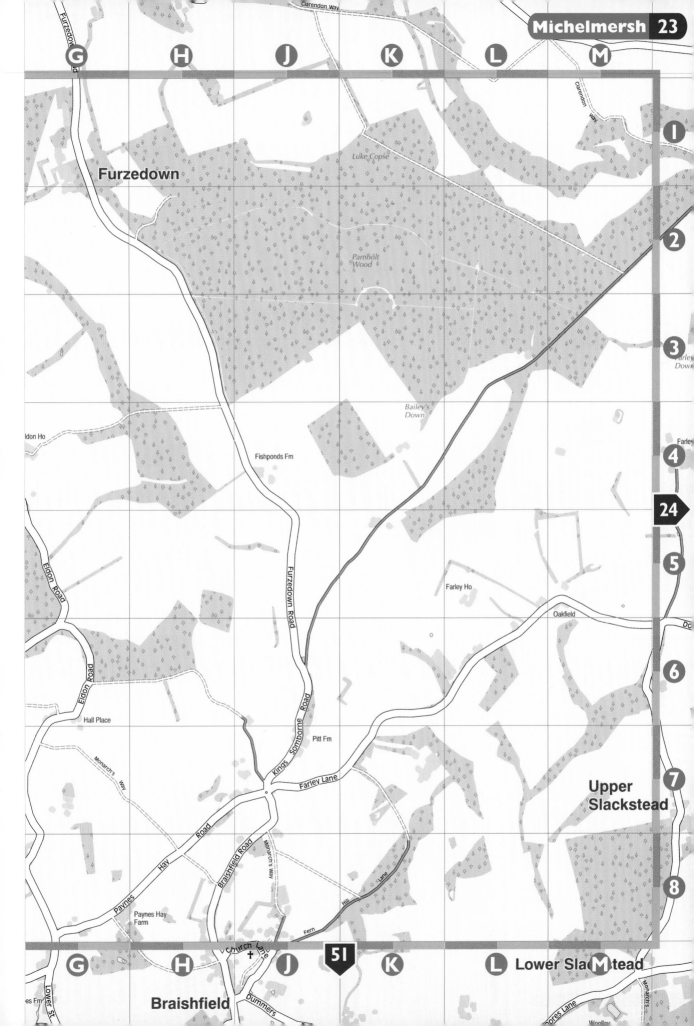

G   H   J   K   L   M

Furzedown

Clarendon Way

Luke Copse

Parnholt Wood

Bailey's Down

Eldon Ho

Fishponds Fm

Eldon Road

Farley Ho

Oakfield

Furzedown Road

Hall Place

Kings Somborne Road

Pitt Fm

Farley Lane

Monarch's Way

Upper Slackstead

Monarch's Way

Braishfield Road

Paynes Hay Road

Paynes Hay Farm

Hill Lane

Clarendon Way

Church Lane

Lower St

Braishfield

Dummers

G   H   J   **51**   K   L   **Lower Slackstead**   M

1
2
3
4
24
5
6
7
8

Clarendon Way

Farley Down

Farley

Do

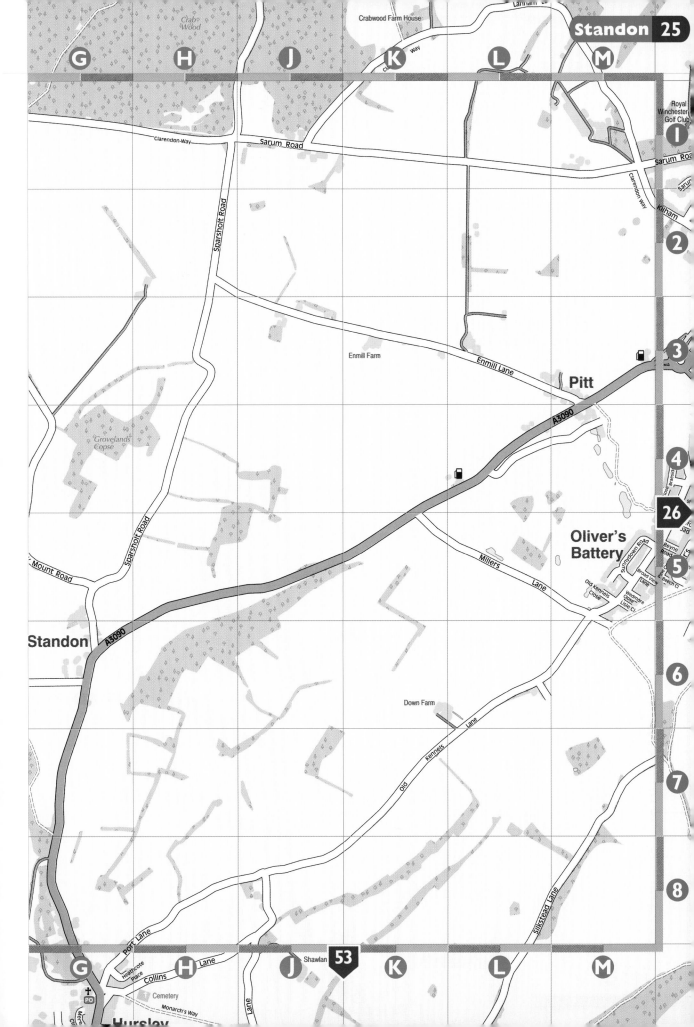

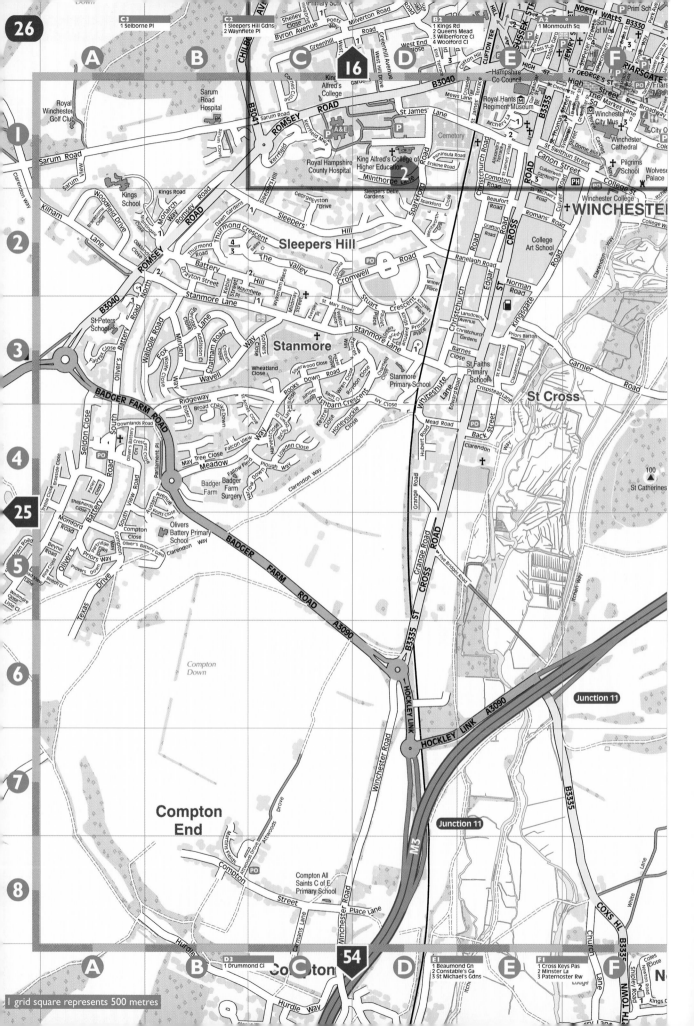

A B C D E F

B3404

A31

ALRESFORD ROAD

I

ETERSFIELD ROAD

A31

A272

*Chilcomb
Down*

King's Way

South Downs Way

2

3

*Temple
Valley*

South Downs Way

4

27

King's Way

5

King's Way

*Fawley
Down*

6

*Longwood
Warren*

7

Warren Lane

King's Way

8

Warren Farm

*Old
Down*

Honeyman Farm

Down

Old

A B C D E F

56

1 grid square represents 500 metres

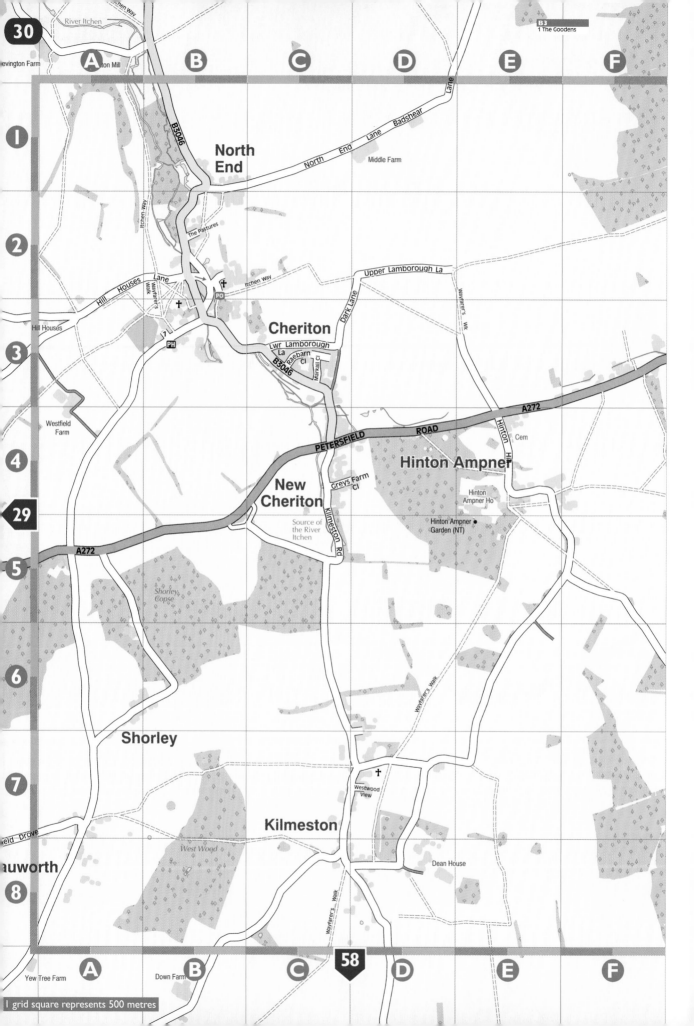

B3
1 The Goodens

A　B　C　D　E　F

1

River Itchen
Itchen Way

North End Lane
Badshear Lane
North End Lane
Middle Farm

B3046

North End

2

The Pastures

Itchen Way
Hill Houses Lane
Wayfarer's Walk
PO
Itchen Way

Upper Lamborough La

Dark Lane

Wayfarer's Wk

3

Hill Houses
PH
Cheriton
Lwr Lamborough La
Raeburn Cl
Markall Cl
B3046

A272

PETERSFIELD ROAD
Hinton Hill
Cem

Westfield Farm

4

Hinton Ampner

Greys Farm Cl
New Cheriton
Kilmeston Rd

Hinton Ampner Ho

29

A272

Source of the River Itchen

Hinton Ampner ●
Garden (NT)

5

Shorley Copse

6

Shorley

Wayfarer's Walk

7

field Drove

Westwood View

Kilmeston

auworth

8

West Wood

Dean House

Warfarer's Walk

Yew Tree Farm
A　Down Farm　B　C
58
D　E　F

1 grid square represents 500 metres

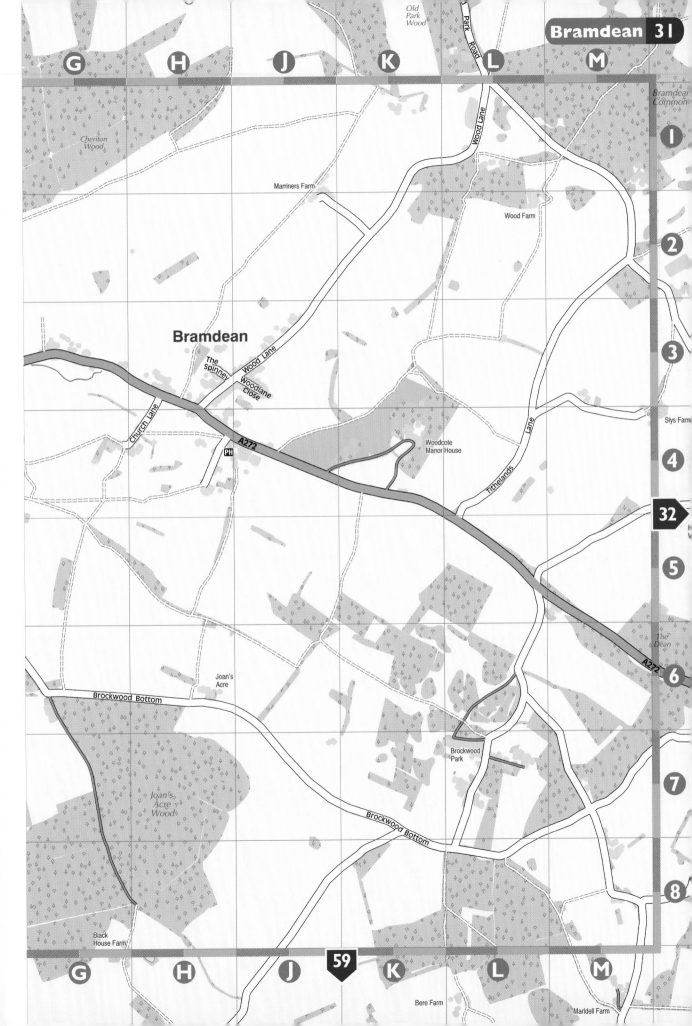

Old Park Wood

Park Road

Bramdean Common

Cheriton Wood

Marriners Farm

Wood Lane

Wood Farm

Bramdean

The spinney

Wood Lane

Woodlane Close

Church Lane

A272

PH

Woodcote Manor House

Titherlands Lane

Slys Farm

The Dean

A272

Joan's Acre

Brockwood Bottom

Joan's Acre Wood

Brockwood Bottom

Brockwood Park

Black House Farm

Bere Farm

Mardell Farm

G H J K L M

G H J K L M

I

2

3

4

32

5

6

7

8

59

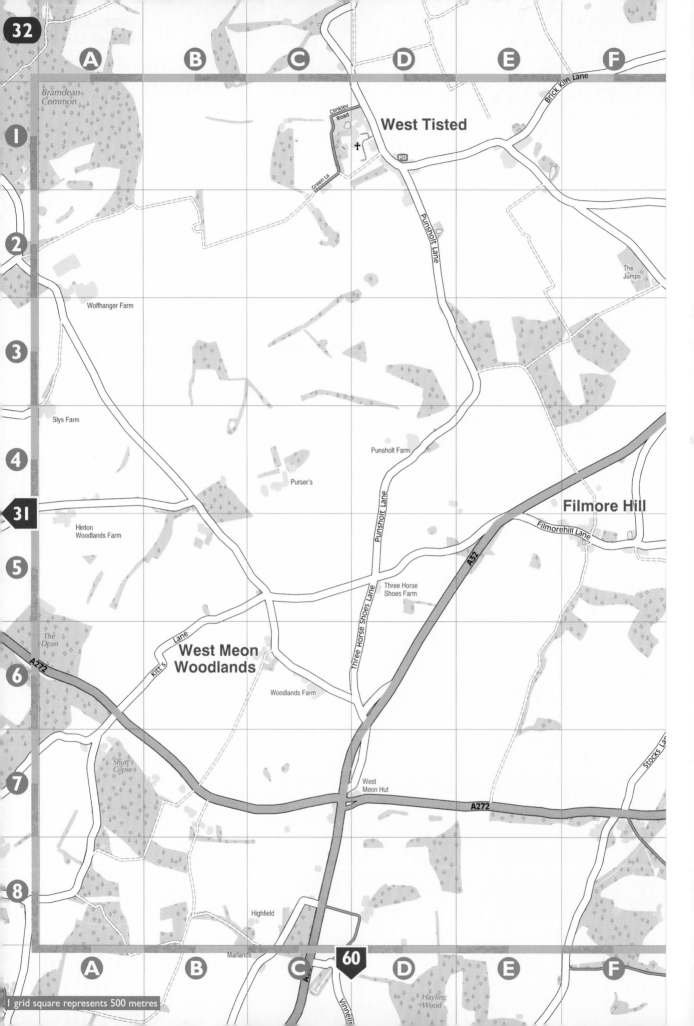

West Tisted

Brick Kiln Lane

Clinkley Road

Green La

PO

Bramdean Common

The Jumps

Punsholt Lane

Wolfhanger Farm

Slys Farm

Punsholt Farm

Purser's

Filmore Hill

Hinton Woodlands Farm

Filmorehill Lane

A32

Three Horse Shoes Farm

Three Horse Shoes Lane

The Dean

Kitt's Lane

West Meon Woodlands

A272

Woodlands Farm

Shutt's Copse

West Meon Hut

Stocks Lane

A272

Highfield

Marlands

Vinnells

Hayling Wood

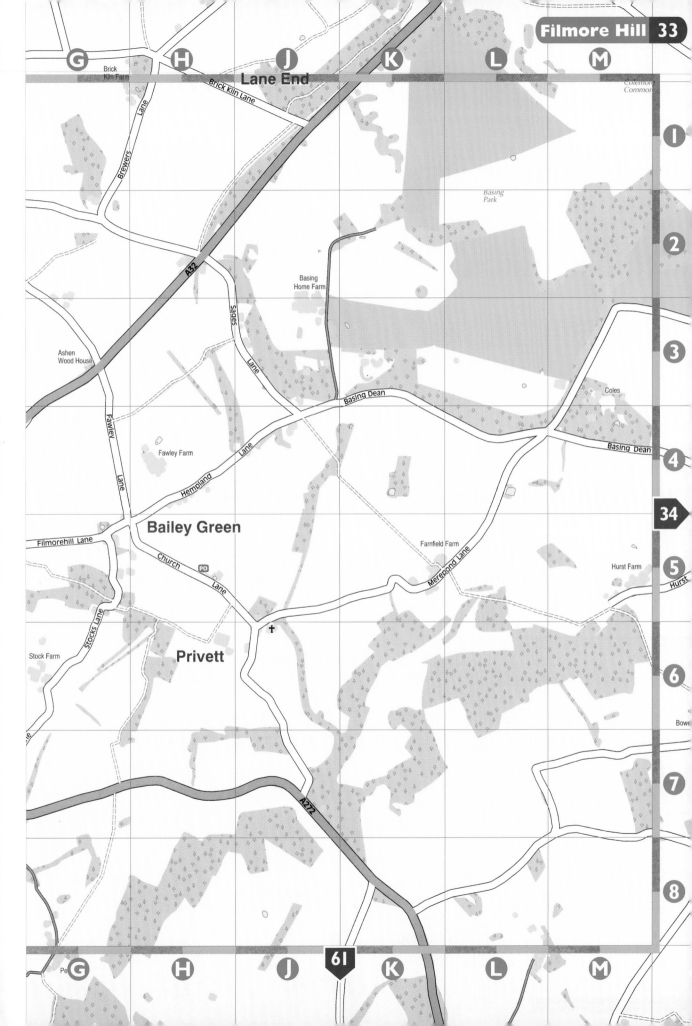

G   H   J   K   L   M

Lane End

Brick Kiln Farm
Brick Kiln Lane

Brewers Lane

Coleman Common

I

2

Basing Park

A32

Sages Lane

Basing Home Farm

3

Ashen Wood House

Coles

Basing Dean

Basing Dean

4

Fawley Farm

Hempland Lane

Fawley Lane

34

Bailey Green

Farnfield Farm

Filmorehill Lane

Church

PO

Lane

Merepond Lane

Hurst Farm

Hurst

5

Stocks Lane

Stock Farm

✝

Privett

6

Bowe

A272

7

8

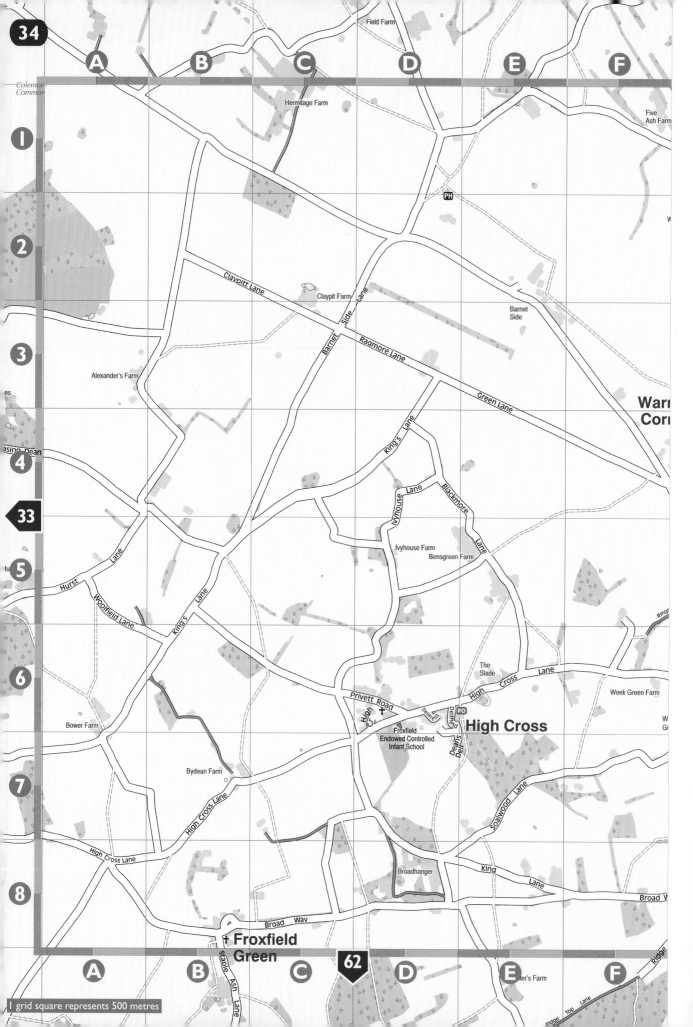

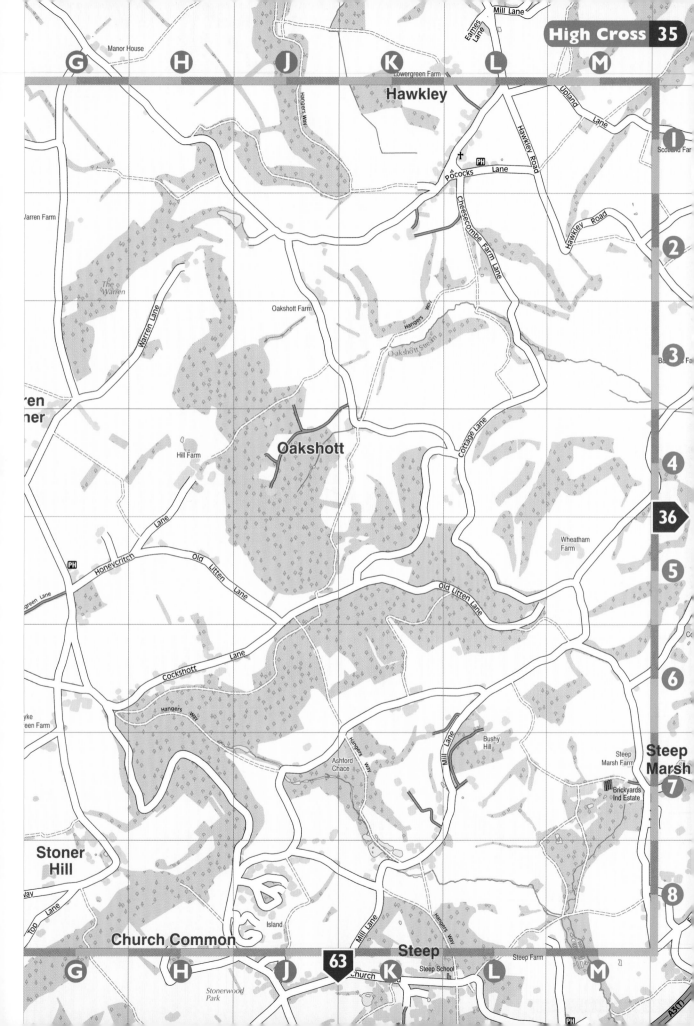

A   B   C   D   E   F

GU33

1   Scotland Farm

Liss Forest

Forest Road

Forest Corner

Briar Wood

Snailing Lane

Sherwood Close

Newfield

PO

Pine Walk

Temple Road

Road

Snailing Lane

2

Church St

Burgates

Rotherbank Farm Lane

Forest Rise

Forest Road

3   Barefoots Farm

Hawkley Road

Lyss Place

Kiln Field

Mead Hawks

West Liss

Liss Business Cen

Wylde

Farnham Road

Mill Road

Kelsey Close

St Mary's Road

Western Rd

Millbrook Cl

Kelseys Doctors Surg

4

A3(T)

Farnham Road

Mainline Business Cen

Riverside Close Surg

Balfour Drive

Tonkwood

Syers Rd

The Oval

Oak Tree Dr

Greenfields

Porter's Close

Patrick's Close

35

Batt's Brook

Limes Cl

Riverside Close

Liss Stn

PO

Station Rd

Rake Road

Moss Close

Chase Rd

Vinson Rd

5

Flexcombe

Longmead

Rushfield Road

Barnside Way

Upper Ash Mt

Nursery Field

Liss County Infant & Junior School

LISS

Dennis Way

Cardew Road

East Hill Drive

Coldhayes

B3006

HILL BROW ROAD

6

Farnham Road

A3(T)

LC

Andlers

Stodham Lane

Prince's Marsh

Stodham Lane

Pruetts Lane

Steep Marsh

Steep Sh Farm

7

B... Ind Estate

Bowyer's Common

Stodham Park

8

Tankerdale

Lane

Petersfield Golf Club

Farnham Road

ROAD

A   B   C   D   E   F

64

Upper Adhurst Farm

1 grid square represents 500 metres

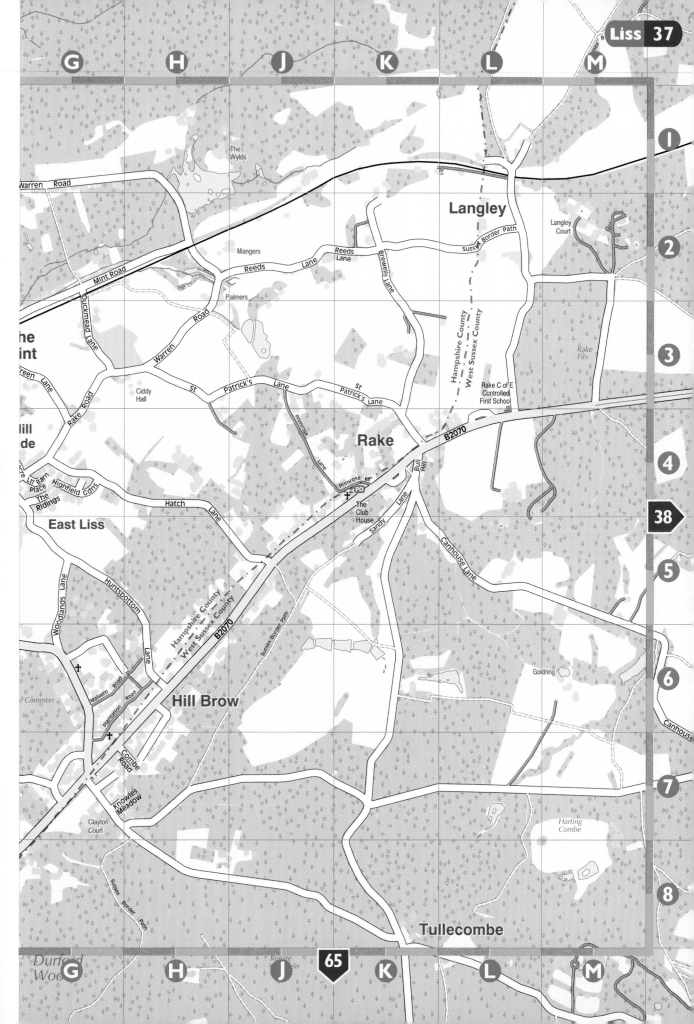

G   H   J   K   L   M

I
2
3
4
38
5
6
7
8

Warren Road

The Wylds

Mangers
Reeds Lane
Reeds Lane

Mint Road
Duckmead Lane

Palmers

Warren Road
Rake Road

Langley

Langley Court

Brewells Lane

Hampshire County
West Sussex County

Rake Firs

Sussex Border Path

Rake C of E
Controlled
First School

St Patrick's Lane
St Patrick's Lane

Ciddy Hall

Green Lane

Highfield Gdns
Lr Barn Place
The Ridings

Primrose Lane

Rake

B2070

Bull Hill

Hatch Lane

PO
The Club House

East Liss

Sandy Lane

Canhouse Lane

Woodlands Lane
Huntsbottom Lane

Hampshire County
West Sussex County
B2070

Sussex Border Path

Goldring

Canhouse

Common

Malvern Road
Plantation Road

Hill Brow

Combe Road

Knowles Meadow

Clayton Court

Harting Combe

Durford Wood

G   H   J   K   L   M

Rogate

65

Tullecombe

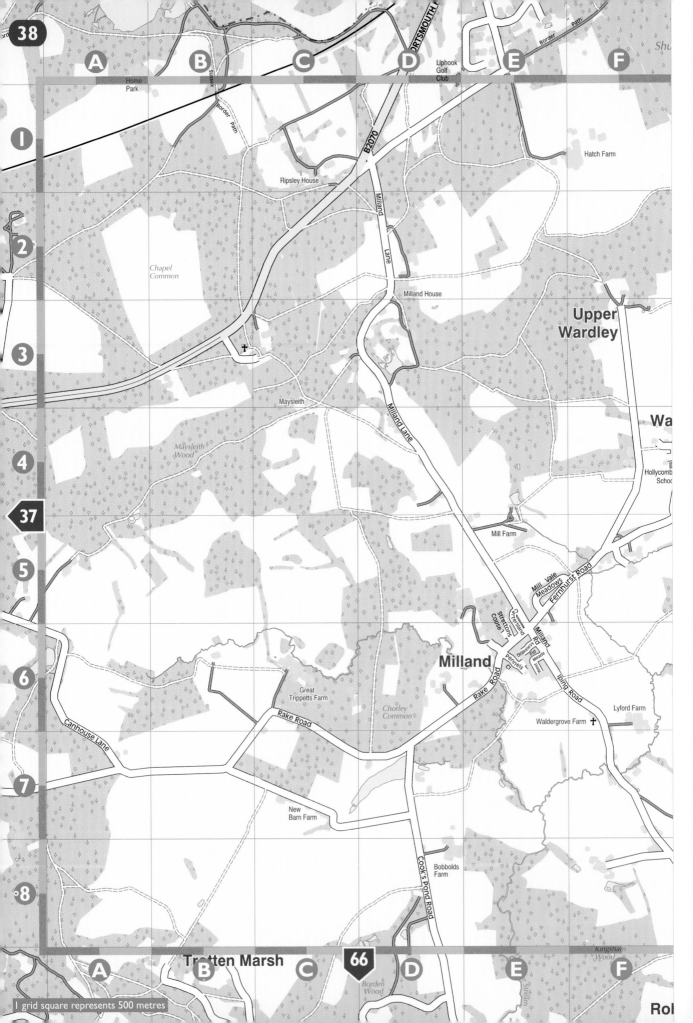

A B C D E F

RTSMOUTH

Liphook
Golf
Club

Home
Park

Border Path

Sussex

Hatch Farm

Ripsley House

B2070

Milland

Lane

Chapel
Common

Milland House

Upper
Wardley

Wa

✝

Maysleith

Milland Lane

Maysleith
Wood

Hollycomb
School

Mill Farm

Mill Vale
Meadows

Fernhurst Road

Strettons
Copse

Milland Rd

Milland
Meade

Pennels
Cl

Draxeneys

Milland

Canhouse Lane

Great
Trippetts Farm

Rake Road

Chorley
Common

Rake Road

Iping Road

Lyford Farm

Waldergrove Farm ✝

New
Barn Farm

Cook's Pond Road

Bobbolds
Farm

Kingsham
Wood

A B Tr tten Marsh C 66 D E F

Borden
Wood

Sussex

Rol

1 grid square represents 500 metres

G H J K L M

I
2
3
4
5
6
7
8

Hollycombe

Parkgate
Rough

fflesheeps

Minepit
Copse

Home
Farm

**Elmers
Marsh**

Elmers
Copse

rdley

Upper North
Park Farm

Northend Farm

✝

Woodmansgreen

Lambourne Lane

Linch Road

Redford

PO

Inholms
Copse

Lambourne Lane

Hurst
Farm

Woolbeding
Common

Iping Road

Titty Hill

**Queen's
Corner**

Linch Road

oins

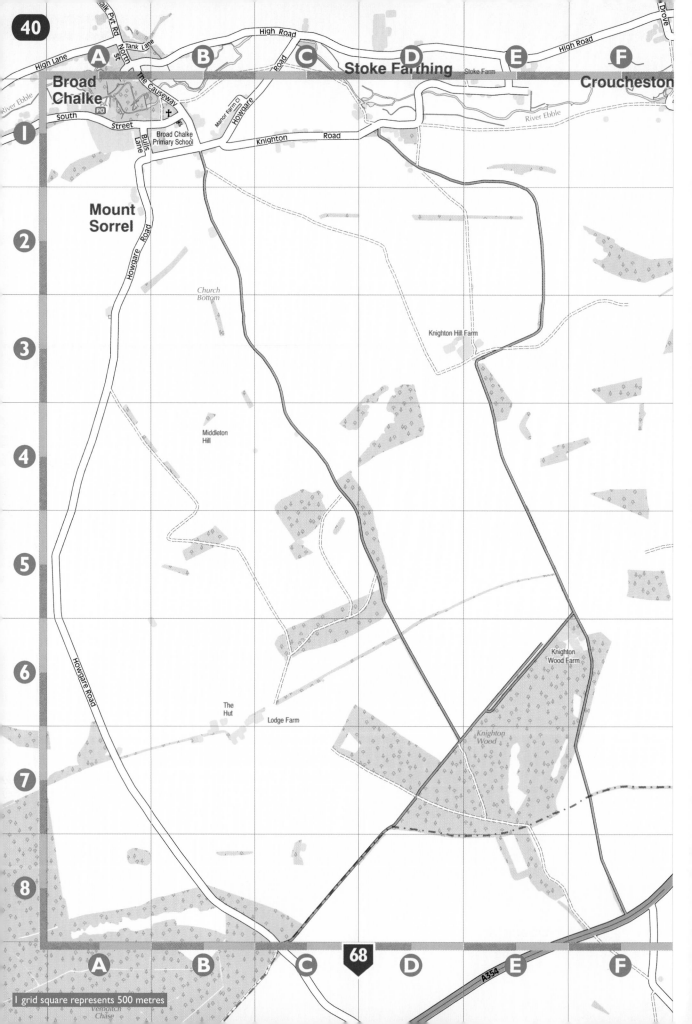

Broad Chalke

High Lane

High Road

Stoke Farthing

Croucheston

River Ebble

Tank Lane

The Causeway

North St

High Lane

South Street

PO

Bulls Lane

Manor Farm

Howgare Road

Stoke Farm

High Road

Broad Chalke Primary School

Knighton Road

River Ebble

Mount Sorrel

Howgare Road

Church Bottom

Knighton Hill Farm

Middleton Hill

Knighton Wood Farm

Howgare Road

The Hut

Lodge Farm

Knighton Wood

A354

Vernditch Chase

I grid square represents 500 metres

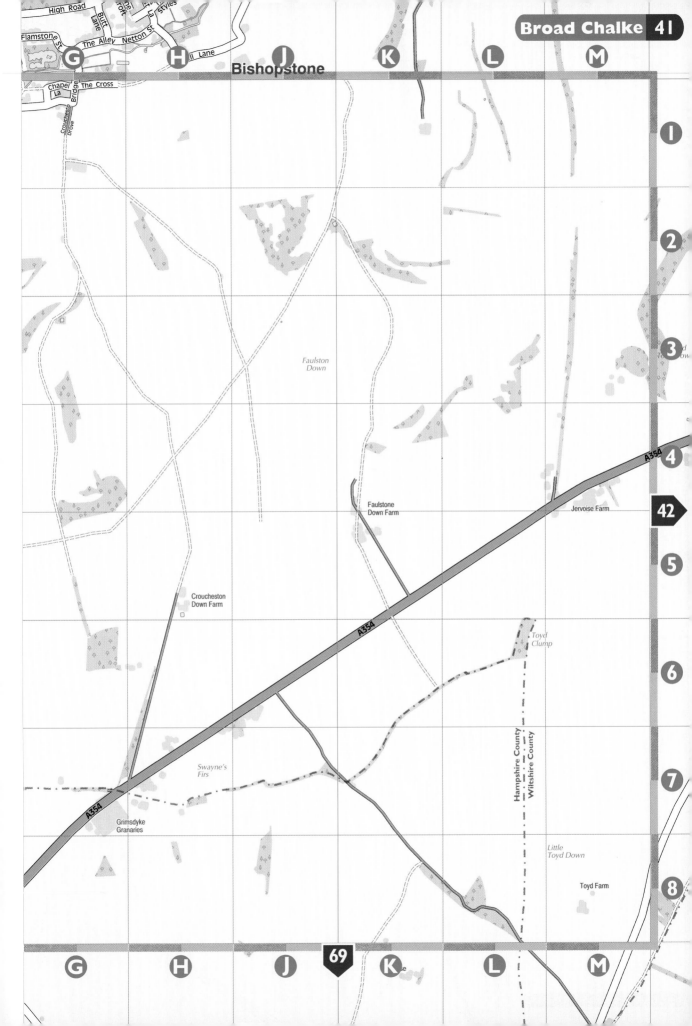

High Road
Butt
Lane
The Alley Netton St
Styles
Flamston St

G
H Hil Lane
J
K
L
M

Bishopstone

Chapel
La The Cross
Bridge
Croucheston Drove

1

2

3

Faulston
Down

A354
4

42

Faulstone
Down Farm
Jervoise Farm
5

Croucheston
Down Farm

A354
Toyd
Clump
6

Hampshire County
Wiltshire County

Swayne's
Firs
7

A354
Grimsdyke
Granaries

Little
Toyd Down

Toyd Farm
8

G
H
J 69
K
L
M

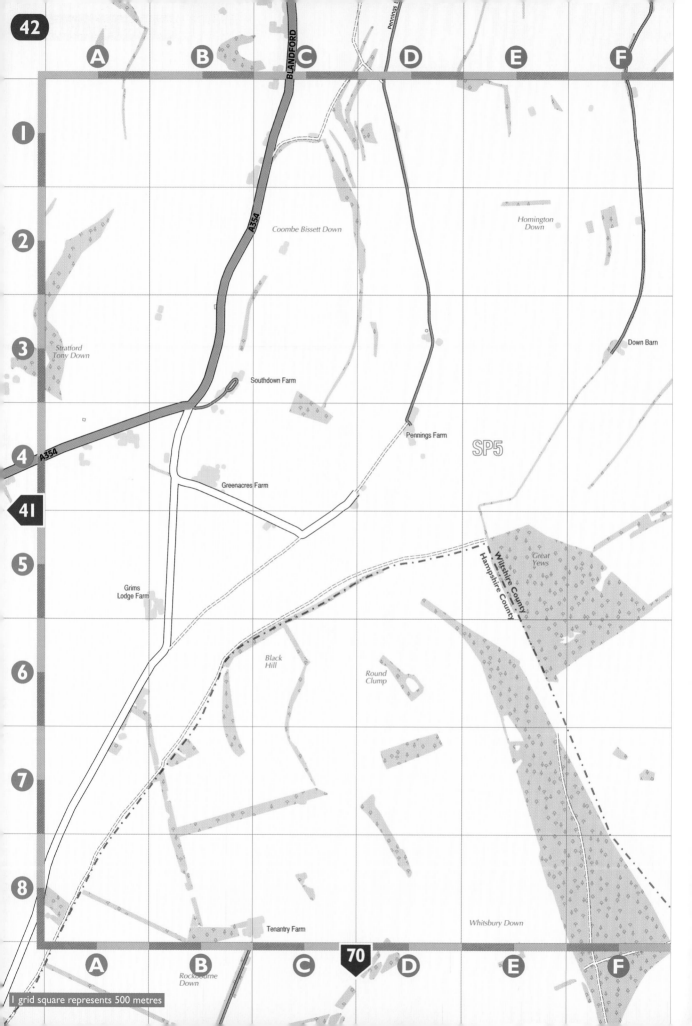

G H J K L M

Odstock

Odstock Down

Little
Yews

Nunton Drove

Yews Farm

New Court Down

New Court
Down Bar

Wick
Down

Wick Lane

Botley's Farm

G H J K L M

Wiltshire County
Hampshire County

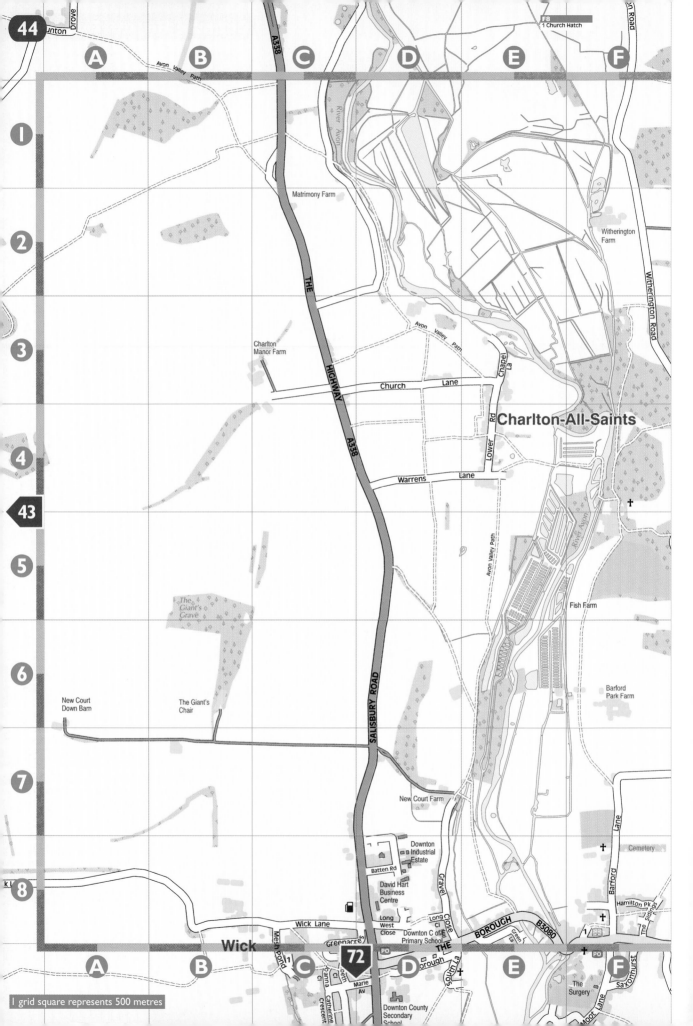

44

A B C D E F

F8
1 Church Hatch

I

2

Matrimony Farm

Witherington
Farm

River Avon

3

Charlton
Manor Farm

Avon Valley Path

Church   Lane

Chapel La

Lower Rd

Witherington Road

Charlton-All-Saints

4

Warrens   Lane

43

Avon Valley Path

River Avon

5

The
Giant's
Grave

Fish Farm

6

New Court
Down Barn

The Giant's
Chair

Barford
Park Farm

7

SALISBURY ROAD

New Court Farm

8

Downton
Industrial
Estate

Cemetery

Batten Rd

Barford Lane

David Hart
Business
Centre

Gravel

Hamilton Pk

Long
Ci

Long
West
Close

THE BOROUGH

B3080

The Sidings

Wick

Wick Lane

Greenacres

Downton C of E
Primary School

South La

Green La

THE
Borough

PO

Saxonhurst

72

Joanna Cl

Joan

PO

The
Surgery

Catherine
Crescent

Marie
Av

Downton County
Secondary
School

1 grid square represents 500 metres

A B C D E F

G H J K L M

1
2
3
4
46
5
6
7
8

A36(T)

Windwhistle Lane

Witherington Down

Standlynch Farm

Privett Farm

Standlynch Down

Langford Lane

Barford Down Farm

Barford Down

Langford Lane

Muddyford Road

Templeman Farm

Down House

Low Pensworth Farm

LODE HILL B3080

Dowton

73

G H J K L M

The Business Centre

PH

Chalk's Rd

Morgans Cl

Rise Road

The Row

Bowers Hill

Princes

Grove Lane

Slab Lane

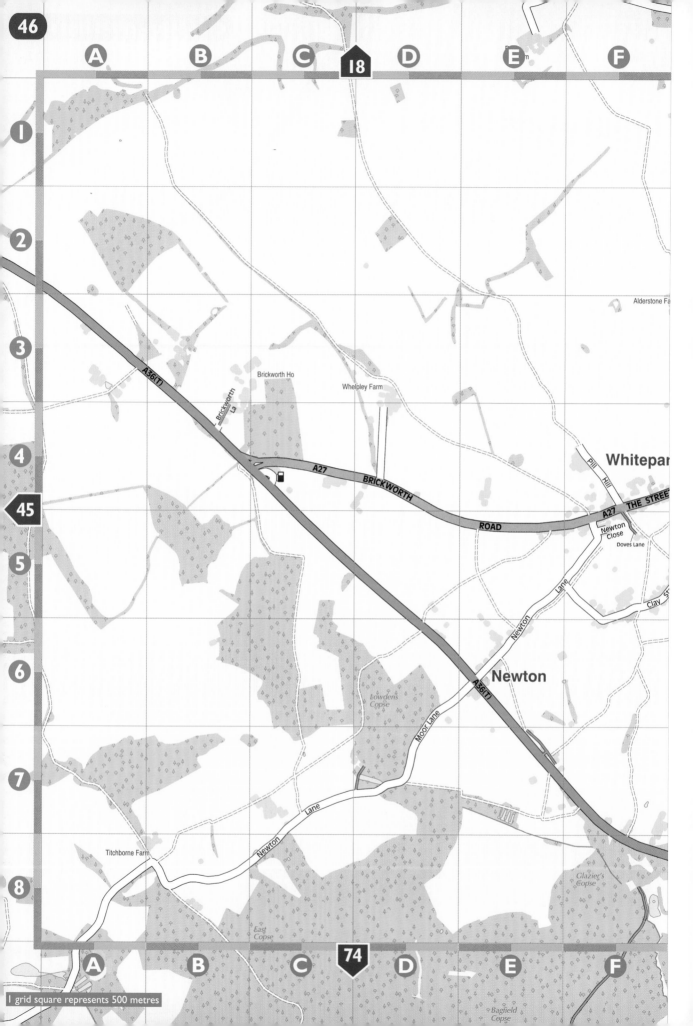

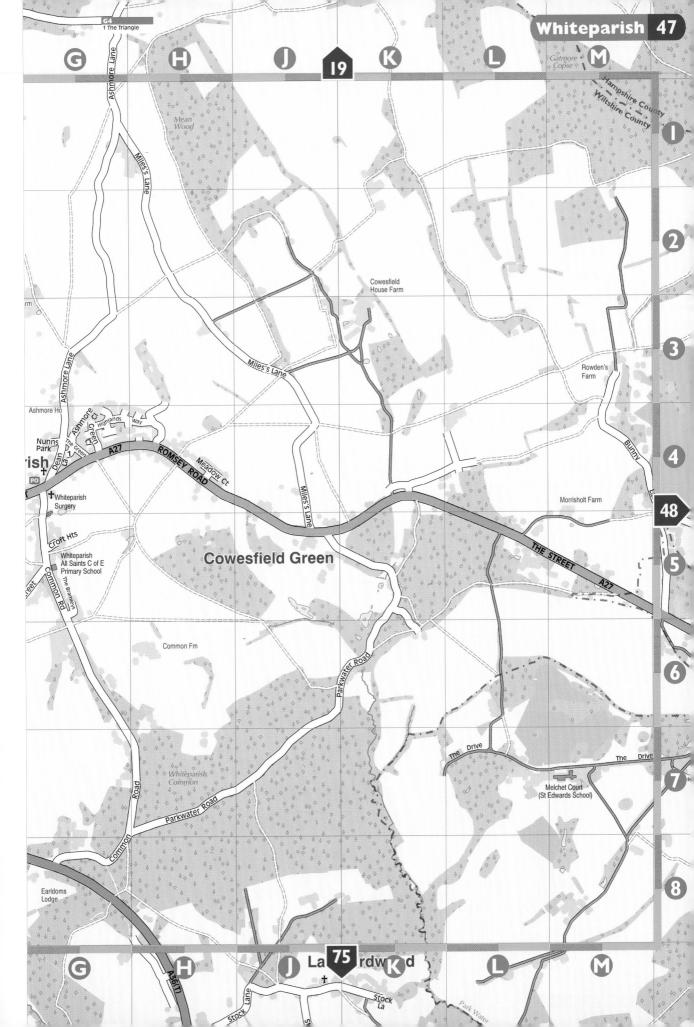

G H J **19** K L M

Gatmore
Copse

Hampshire County
Wiltshire County

I

Mean
Wood

2

Cowesfield
House Farm

3

Rowden's
Farm

Miles's Lane

Ashmore Lane

Miles's Lane

Ashmore Ho

Nunns
Park

Ashmore
Green

Highlands

Way

The Green

Dean

A27

ROMSEY ROAD

Meadow Ct

Bunny La

4

Morrisholt Farm

48

Whiteparish
Surgery

PO

Croft Hts

Miles's Lane

THE STREET
A27

5

Whiteparish
All Saints C of E
Primary School

Common Rd

The Bramleys

Cowesfield Green

6

Common Fm

Parkwater Road

The Drive

The Drive

7

Whiteparish
Common

Common Road

Parkwater Road

Melchet Court
(St Edwards School)

Earldoms
Lodge

8

A36(T)

G H **75** J La rdw K d L M

Stock Lane

Stock
La

Park Water

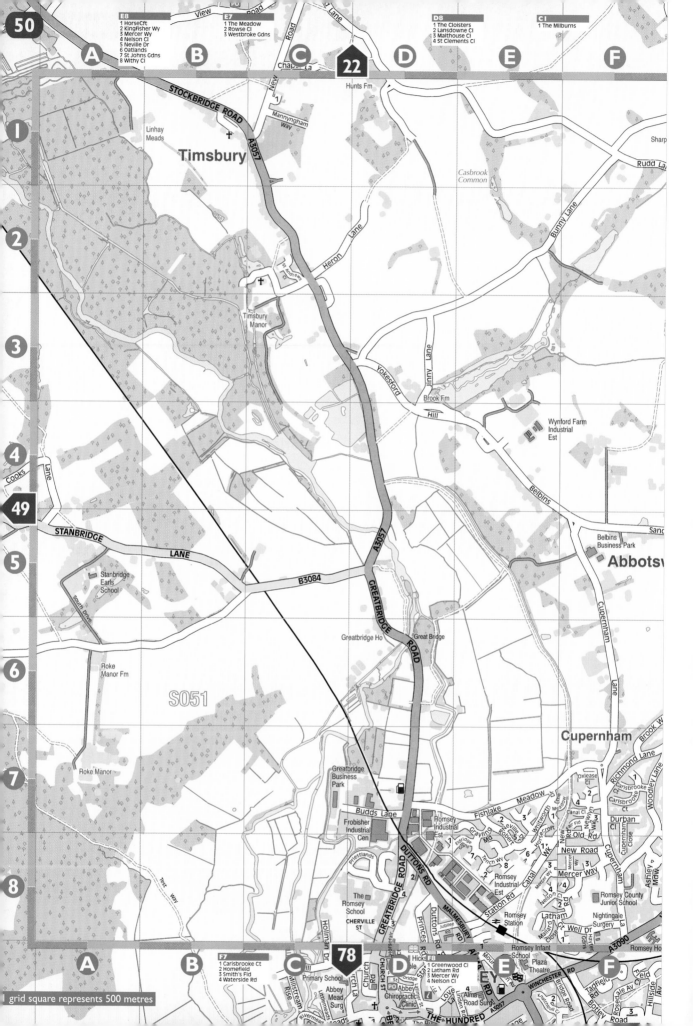

A   B   C   D   E   F

E8
1 HorseCft
2 KingFisher Wy
3 Mercer Wy
4 Nelson Cl
5 Neville Dr
6 Oatlands
7 St Johns Gdns
8 Withy Cl

E7
1 The Meadow
2 Rowse Cl
3 Westbroke Gdns

D8
1 The Cloisters
2 Lansdowne Cl
3 Malthouse Cl
4 St Clements Cl

C1
1 The Milburns

22

I
2
3
4
49
5
6
7
8

STOCKBRIDGE ROAD A3057

Linhay Meads

Timsbury

View
Chapel La
New Road
Mannyngham Way
Hunts Fm

Heron Lane
Bunny Lane
Rudd Lane
Sharp

Casbrook Common

St Andrews

Timsbury Manor

Yokesford
Jinny Lane
Lansdowne

Brook Fm
Hill
Wynford Farm Industrial Est

Belbins

Cooks Lane
STANBRIDGE LANE
Sand

Belbins Business Park
Abbotsw

Stanbridge Earls School
South Drive

B3084
A3057
GREATBRIDGE ROAD

Cupernham Lane

Roke Manor Fm

S051

Greatbridge Ho
Great Bridge

Cupernham

Roke Manor

Test Way

Greatbridge Business Park
Budds Lane
Frobisher Industrial Cen
Priestlands
The Romsey School
CHERVILLE ST

DUTTONS RD
MALMESBURY
Romsey Industrial Est
Fishlake Meadow
Whitworth
Canal
Station Rd
Romsey Industrial Est

Oxlease Cl
Richmond Lane
Woodley Lane
Carisbrooke
Carisbrooke Ct
Durban Cl
New Road
Mercer Way
Romsey County Junior School
Nightingale Surgery

Romsey Station

Ashley
Brook Wy
Cupernham Close
Cupernham

A3090 Romsey Ho

A   B   C   D   E   F

F7
1 Carisbroke Ct
2 Homefield
3 Smith's Fld
4 Waterside Rd

F8
1 Greenwood Cl
2 Latham Rd
3 Mercer Wy
4 Nelson Cl

Primary School
Abbey Mead Surg
Chiropractic Clinic
Romsey Infant School
Plaza Theatre
WINCHESTER RD
THE HUNDRED A3057
Alma Road Surgery
Botley Road
Rosedale Av
Hillside
Tadfield

I grid square represents 500 metres

G6
1 Cavendish Cl

G7
1 Clarendon Cl
2 Nogarth Cl
3 Savernake Cl
4 Sutherland Cl
5 Tavistock Rd
6 Waverley Cl

G8
1 Barton Cl
2 Brickwoods
3 Harefield Ct
4 Nerquis Cl
5 St Blaize Rd
6 Strongs Cl
7 Windfield Dr

G **H** **J** 23 **K** **L** **M**

I

Lower Slackstead

Paynes Hay Farm

Braishfield

Dores Lane

Woolley Green Fm

Monarch's Way

Pucknall

Newport Lane

Hill Vw Rd PO

Braishfield CP School

2

Kiln Lane

3

Megana Wy

Fairbornes Fm

Abbotswood Fm

Jermyns Ho

4

Braishfield Road

Jermyns Lane

52

...wood

Lane

Cemetery

5

A3090

South Holmes Copse

Woodley Close

Woodley Lane

THE STRAIGHT MILE

Ganger Fm

6

Gosp

Woodley Lane

Horseshoe Dr

Hunters

North Crs

Woodley

Peel

Grove Wy

Lane

7

Kinver Cl

Anstey Road

Braishfield Road

School Road

Cedar Lawn

WINCHESTER RD

Crampmoor Lane

Crampmoor

Junior & Infant School

Winterbourne

Winchester Rd

LC

Crampmoor

Fairview Dr

HILL

Viney Av

Halterworth Lane

Stroud School

Green Lane

8

WINCHESTER

The Crs

Selsdon Av

Viney Av

Highwood La

Hospital

Eight Acres

79 **K** **L** **M**

H7
1 Abbotswood Cl
2 Beverley Gdns
3 Bramble Dr
4 Coltsfoot Wk
5 Primrose Wy
6 South Cl
7 Westering
8 Winterbourne Rd

H6
1 Anderson Cl
2 Ganger Rd
3 The Green
4 Norris Cl
5 Woodley Wy

H8
1 Seward Rl
2 Westering

G **H** **J** **Halterworth**

Halterworth CP School

Warren Fm

Baddesley Common

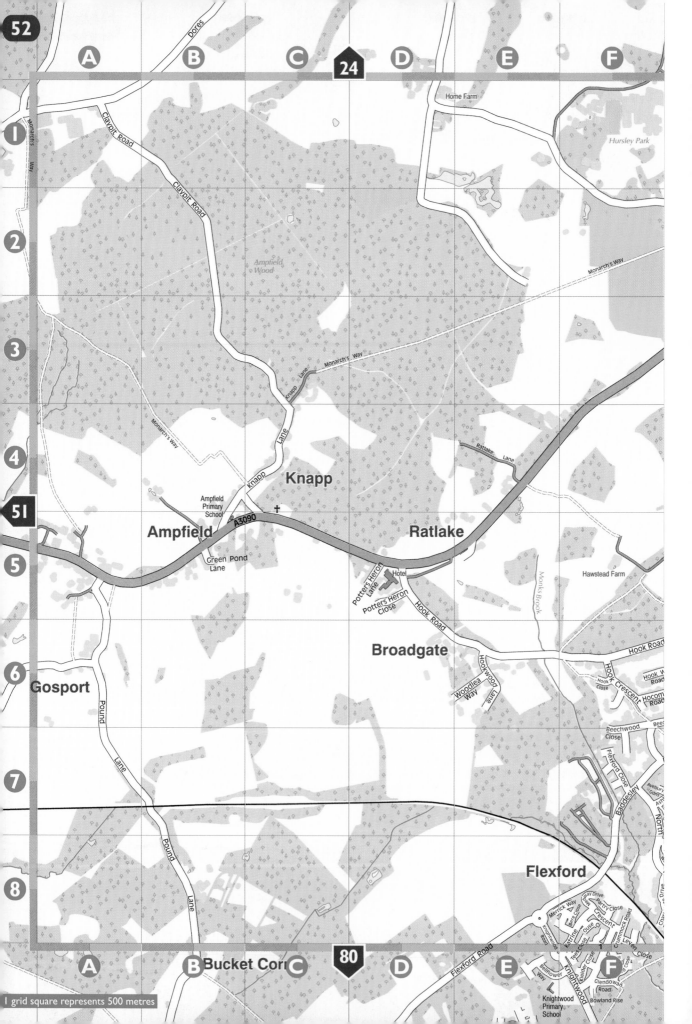

G6
1 Clevelands Cl
2 Rothville Pl
3 Tithewood Cl

G7
1 Albury Pl
2 Apsley Pl
3 Chillington Gdns
4 Lauriston Dr
5 Stratfield Dr
6 The Tanyards
7 Vanburgh Wy

G8
1 Balmoral Cl
2 Barford Cl
3 Drummond Wy
4 Polesden Cl

H6
1 Charnwood Gdns

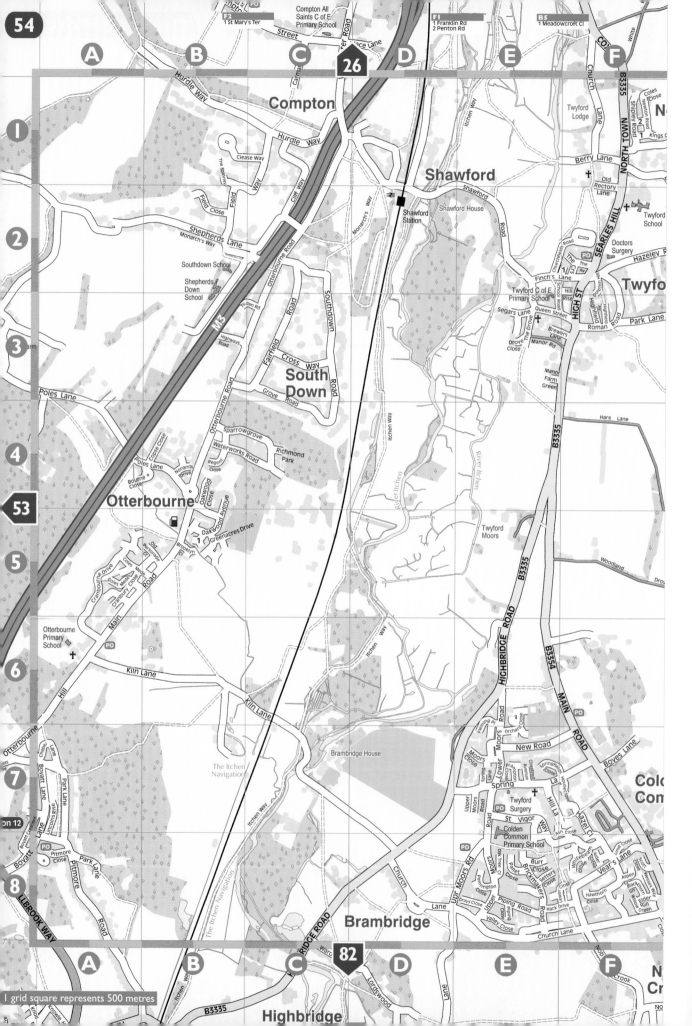

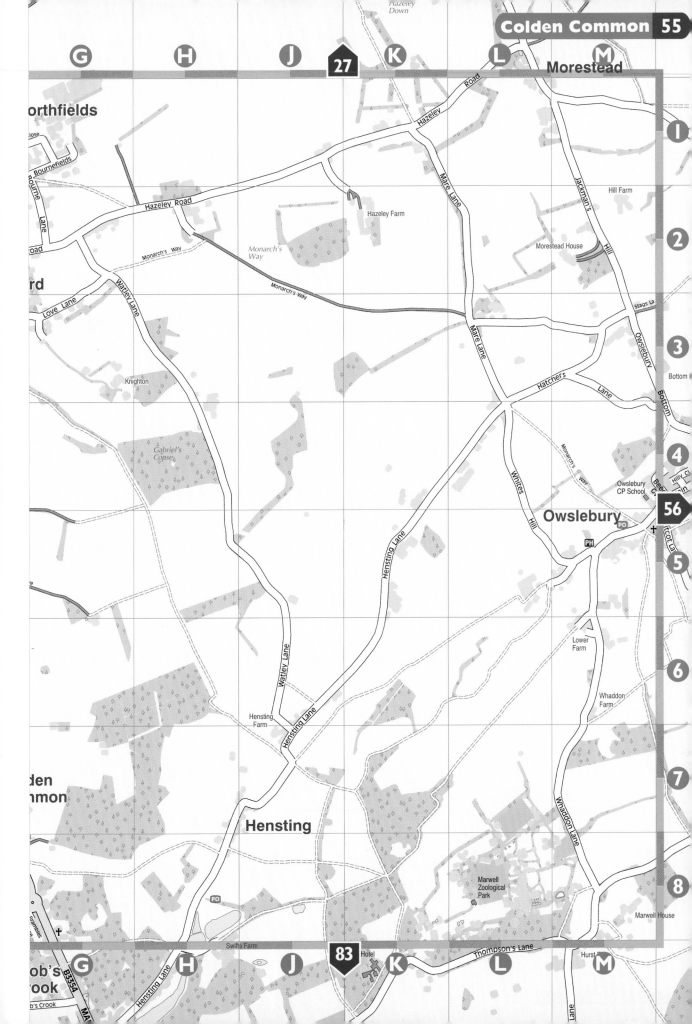

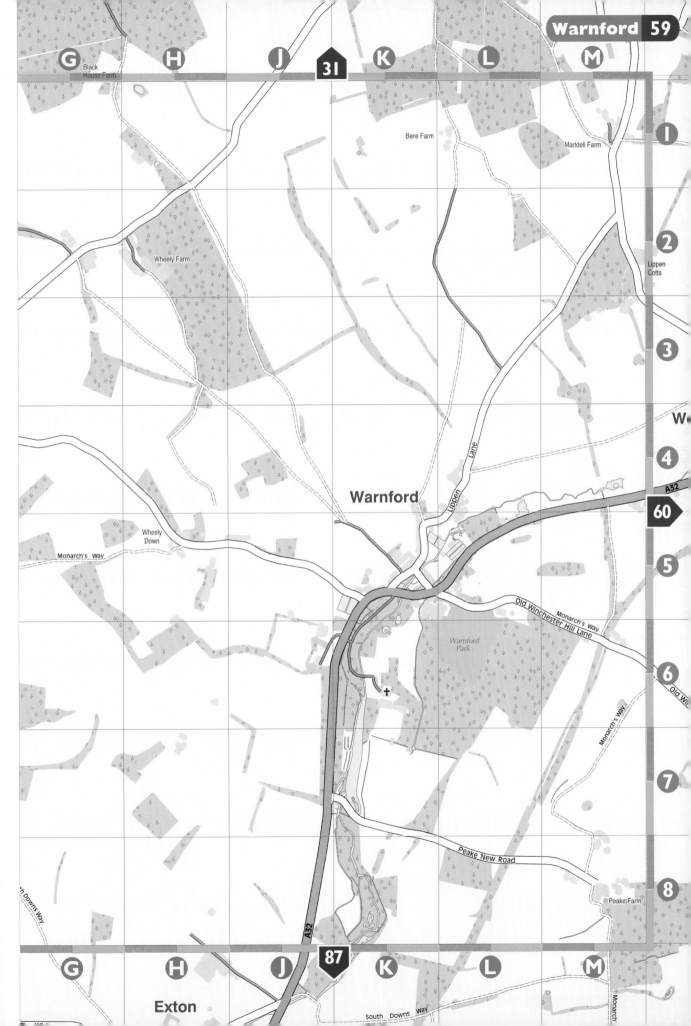

G H J 31 K L M

I

2

3

4

A32

60

5

6

7

8

G H J 87 K L M

Black House Farm

Bere Farm

Marldell Farm

Lippen Cotts

Wheely Farm

W

Warnford

Lippen Lane

Wheely Down

Monarch's Way

Old Winchester Hill Lane

Monarch's Way

Warnford Park

Monarch's Way

Old Wi

Peake New Road

Peake Farm

A32

Exton

South Downs Way

Monarch'

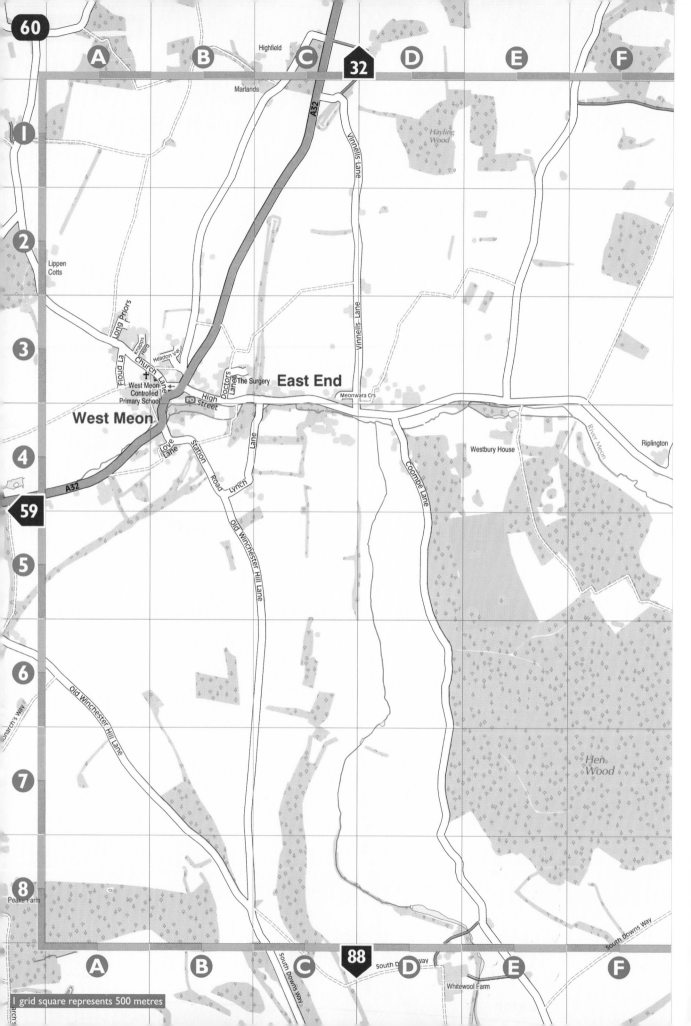

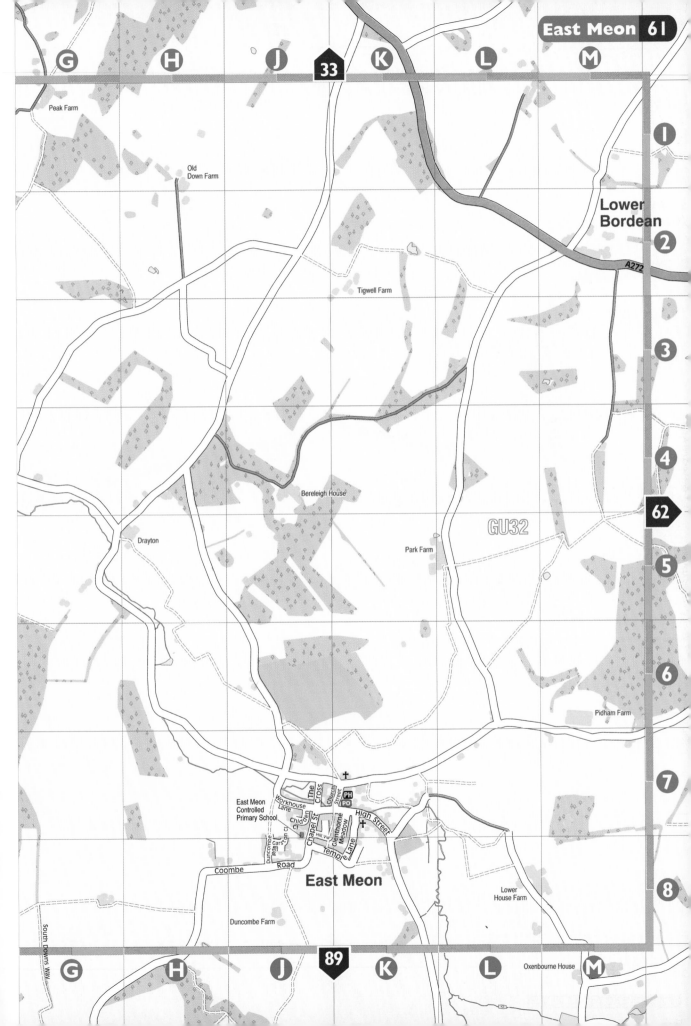

G H J **33** K L M

I

Lower
Bordean

2

A272

Peak Farm

Old
Down Farm

Tigwell Farm

3

4

62

Bereleigh House

GU32

5

Drayton

Park Farm

6

Pidham Farm

7

†

The Cross

Workhouse Lane

Church Street

PH
PO

High Street

East Meon
Controlled
Primary School

Chidden Ct

Chapel St

Glenthorne Meadow

Hill Vw

Garston Cl

Temple Lane

†

Duncombe Road

8

Coombe Road

East Meon

Lower
House Farm

South Downs Way

Duncombe Farm

G H J **89** K L Oxenbourne House M

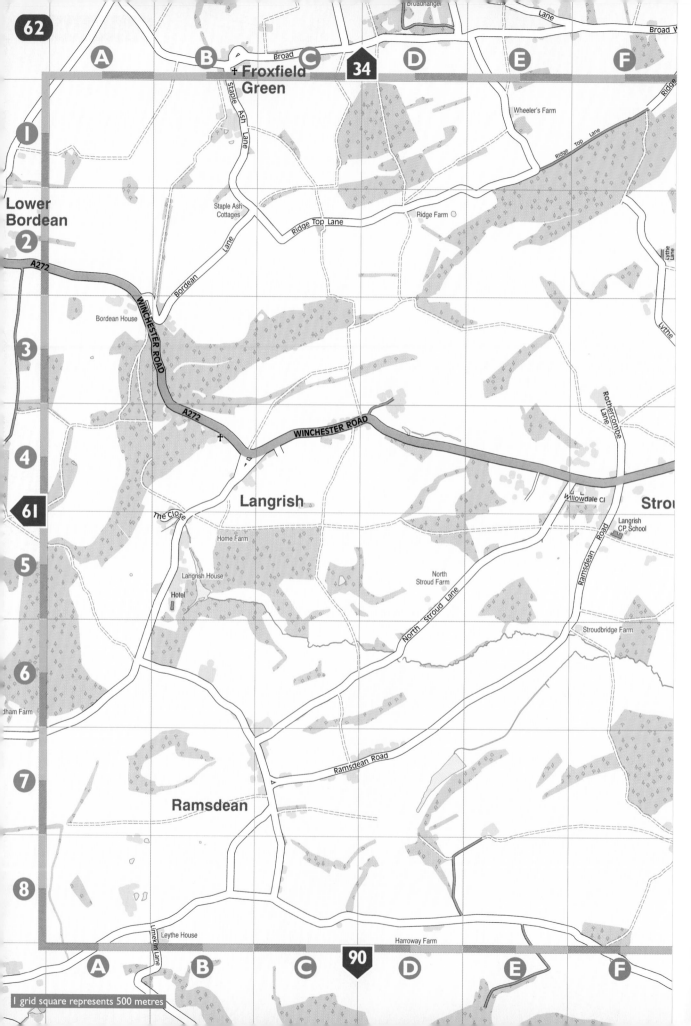

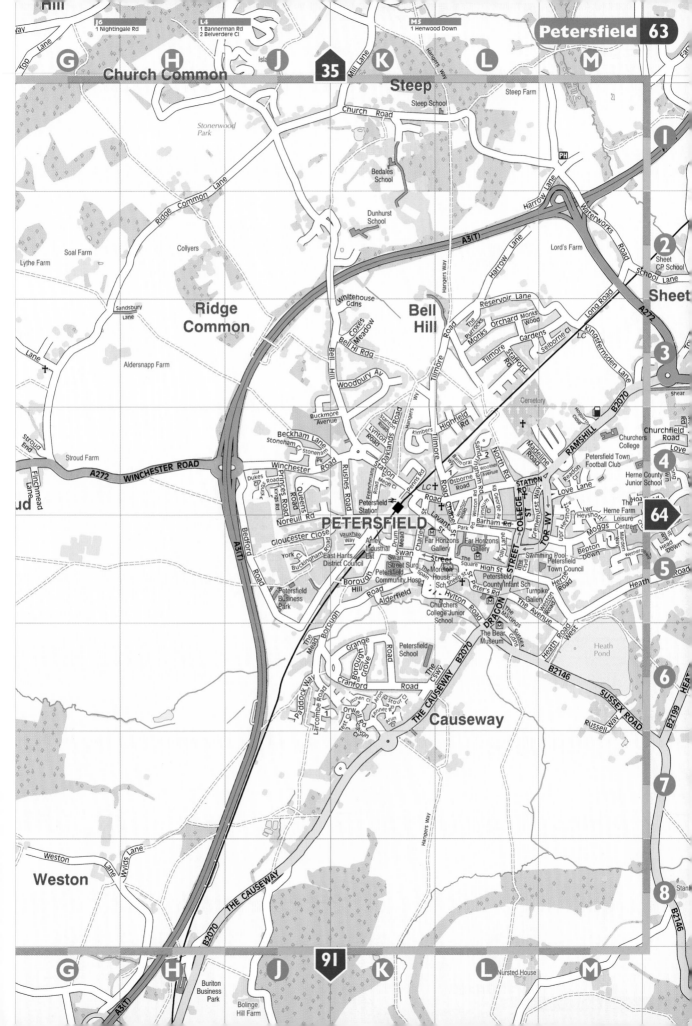

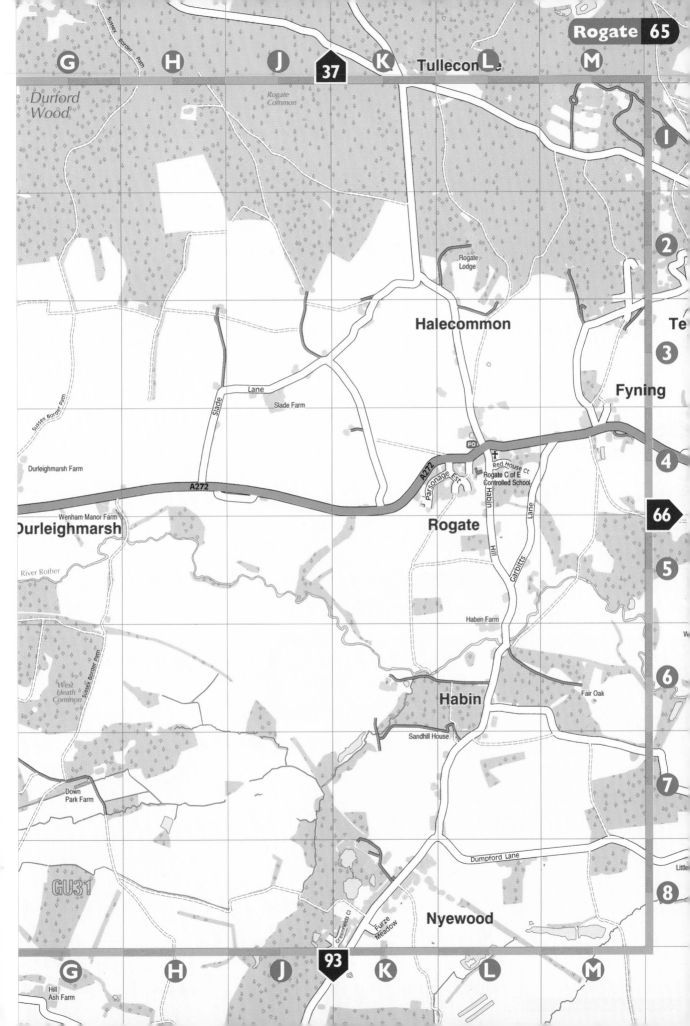

G H J 37 K Tullecom L M

I

Durford Wood

Rogate Common

Rogate Lodge

2

Halecommon

Te

3

Fyning

Slade Lane

Slade Farm

Durleighmarsh Farm

PO

Red House Ct

Rogate C of E
Controlled School

A272

Parsonage Est

Habin

4

66

Durleighmarsh

Wenham Manor Farm

River Rother

Rogate

Hill

Carbitts Lane

5

Haben Farm

West Heath Common

Sussex Border Path

Habin

Sandhill House

Fair Oak

6

Down Park Farm

7

Dumpford Lane

Littl

GU31

8

Greenfields Cl

Furze Meadow

Nyewood

Hill Ash Farm

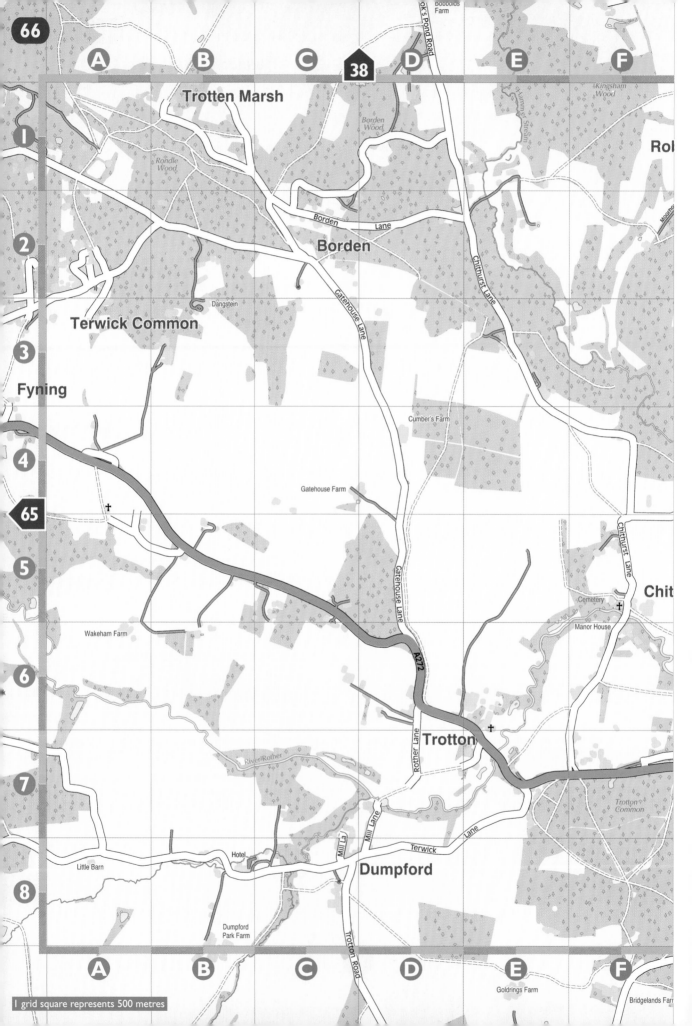

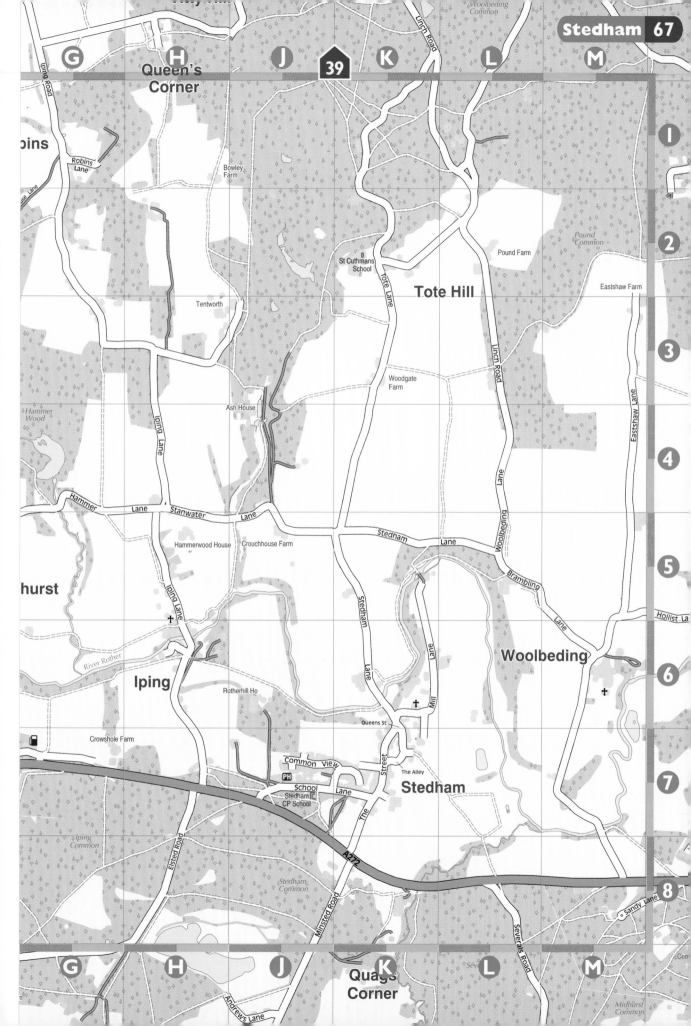

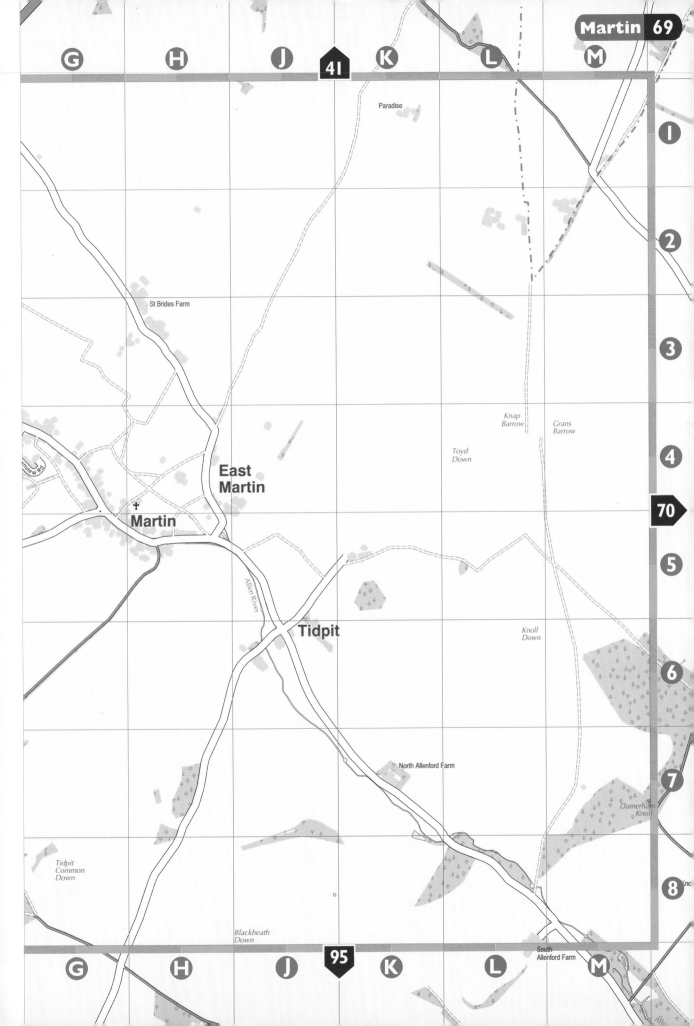

G H J **41** K L M

I

2

3

Paradise

St Brides Farm

Knap
Barrow

Grans
Barrow

Toyd
Down

4

70

**East
Martin**

5

† **Martin**

Allen River

Tidpit

Knoll
Down

6

North Allenford Farm

Damerham
Knoll

7

Tidpit
Common
Down

8

Blackheath
Down

South
Allenford Farm

G H J **95** K L M

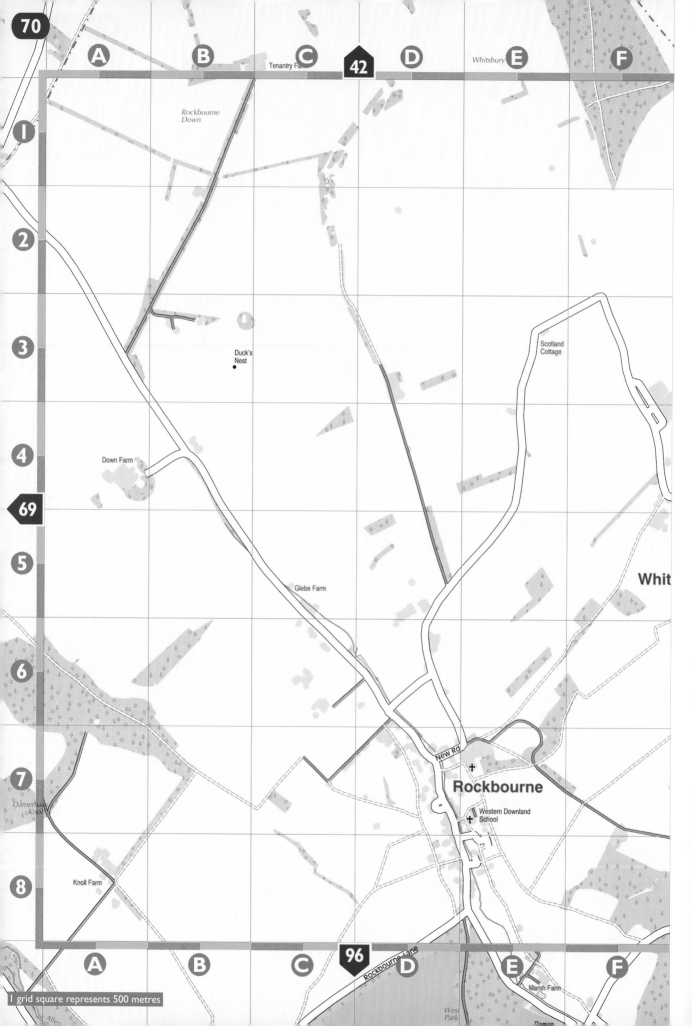

A **B** **C** **42** **D** Whitsbury **E** **F**

Tenantry Farm

Rockbourne
Down

1

2

3
Duck's
Nest

Scotland
Cottage

4
Down Farm

69

5
Glebe Farm

Whit

6

7
Damerham
Knoll

New Rd

Rockbourne

Western Downland
School

8
Knoll Farm

A **B** **C** **96** **D** **E** **F**

Rockbourne Lane

Marsh Farm

West
Park

G   H   J   **43**   K   L   M

I

2

Wick
Down

Botley's Farm

Wiltshire County
Hampshire County

North Charford Drove

South

Charford

Drove

North

3

North Charford
Down Farm

Breamore
Down

Giant's Grave

Manor Farm

Castle
Ditches

Manor House

South   Cha   rov

4

Down Farm

72

Breamore
Wood

5

Well
House
Cl

Breamore
House

sbury

Lower Farm

Lower LN

6

Upper Street

Long Steeple Lane

Rookery La

7

Whitsbury
Common

Roundhill Farm

Bream

8

Outwick

Rockstead Farm

Green Lane

Radnall Wood

G   H   J   **97**   K   L   M   Flood Street

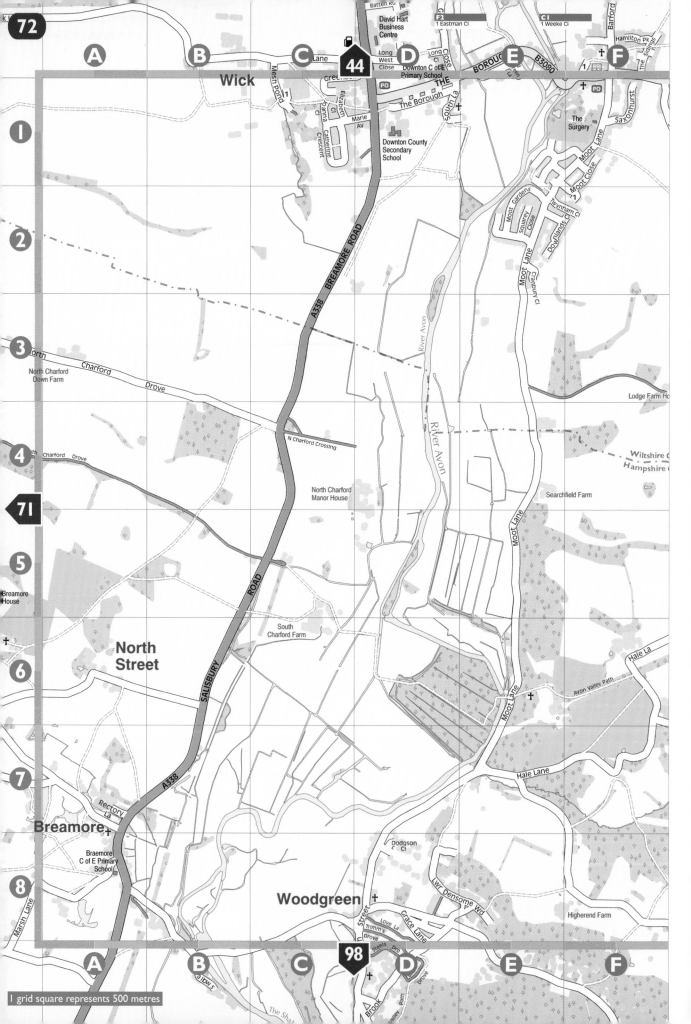

A B C 44 D E F

Wick

David Hart Business Centre
1 Eastman Ci
1 Weeke Ci
Barford
Hamilton Pk

Long West Close
Long Close Ci
Downton C of E Primary School

BOROUGH
B3080

Batten Rd
F2
C1

THE

The Surgery
PO
Saxonhurst

1

Elizabeth Ci
Joanna Ci
Catherine Crescent
Marie Av

Greenhill

The Borough
South La

Downton County Secondary School

Moot Gardens
Squarey Close
Trevnham Ci
Dowlands
Moot Close

Moot Lane
Cranbury Ci

BREAMORE ROAD

A338

River Avon

River Avon

North Charford Down Farm

North Charford Drove

Lodge Farm Ho

North Charford Drove

N Charford Crossing

Wiltshire Co
Hampshire Co

North Charford Manor House

Searchfield Farm

Breamore House

Moot Lane

SALISBURY ROAD

North Street

South Charford Farm

Moot Lane

Hale La

Avon Valley Path

Avon Valley Path
Hale Lane

A338

Rectory La

Breamore

Braemore C of E Primary School

Dodgson Ci

LWR Densome Wd

Higherend Farm

Woodgreen

Street
Trimm's Drove
Steels Dro
Love La
Grace Lane

Marsh Lane

A B C 98 D E F

1 grid square represents 500 metres

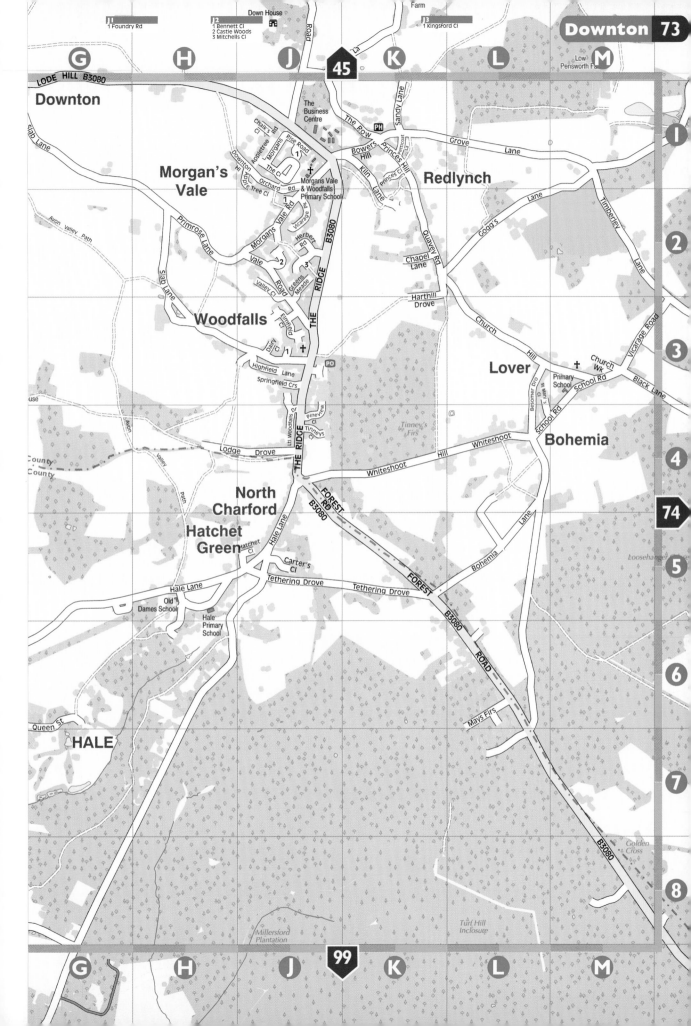

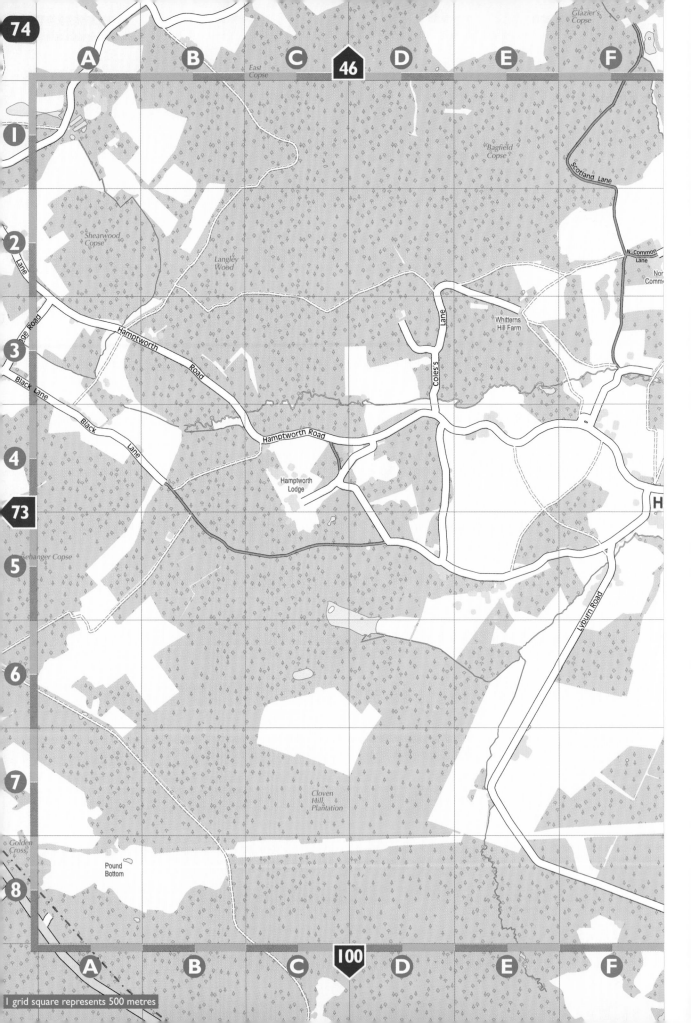

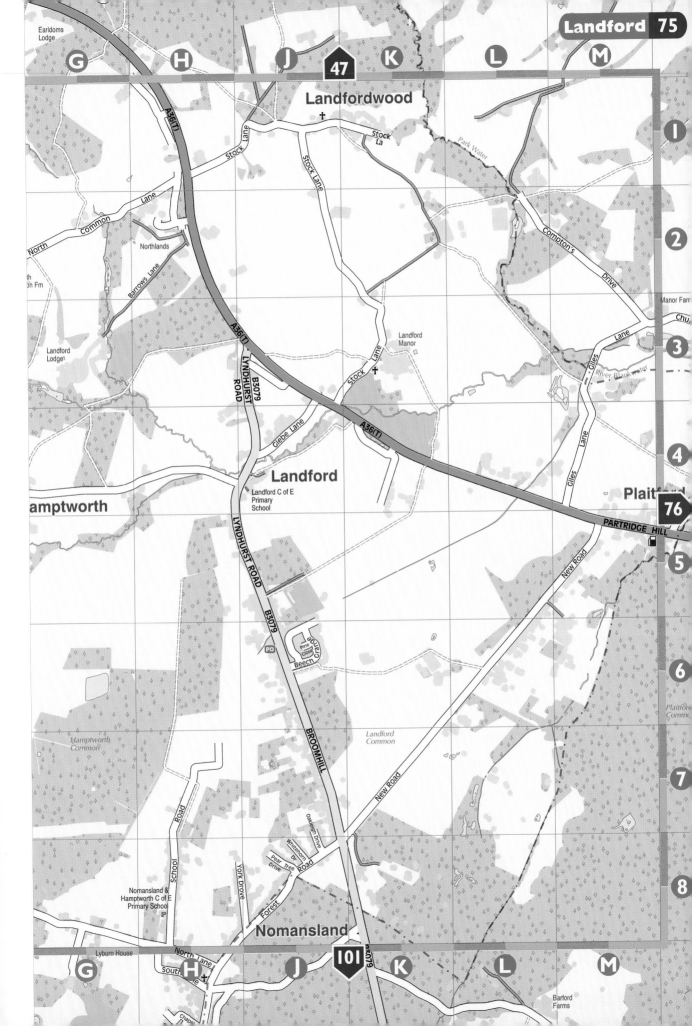

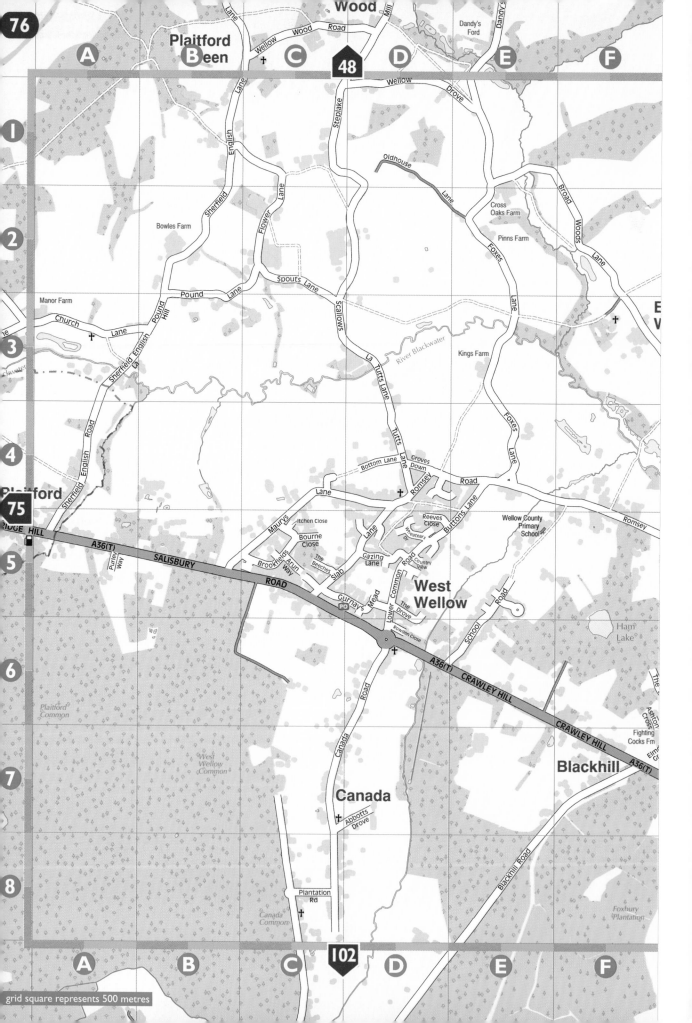

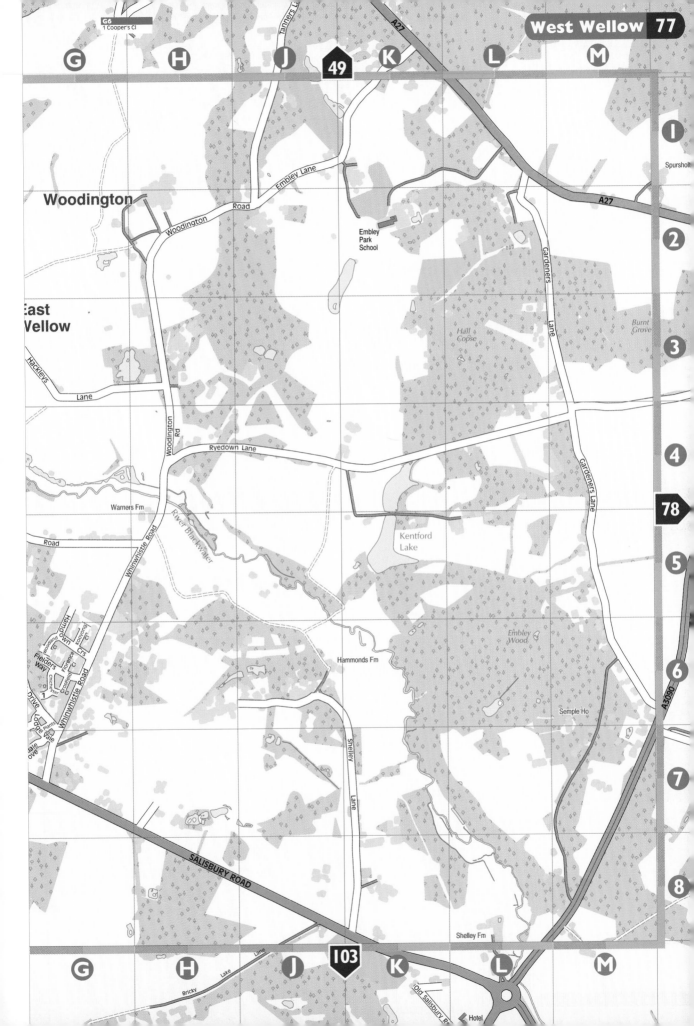

G6
1 Cooper's Cl

G   H   J   49   K   L   M

I
Spursholt

A27

Woodington

Embley Lane
Woodington   Road

Embley
Park
School

Gardeners   Lane

Hall
Copse

Burnt
Grove

**East
Wellow**

Hackleys

Lane

Woodington   Rd

Ryedown Lane

Warners Fm

River Blackwater

Road

Whinwhistle Road

Kentford
Lake

Gardeners Lane

78

Embley
Wood

Hambo
Wm
Woodland
Florence Cl
Cricket
Chichester
Cl

Fielder's
Way

1

Whinwhistle Road

Drive
Lodge Plants
Vale
dale
Grove

Hammonds Fm

Semple Ho

Shelley

Lane

SALISBURY ROAD

Shelley Fm

G   H   Lake Lane   J   103   K   L   M

Bricky

Old Salisbury R

Hotel

1   2   3   4   5   6   7   8

A3090

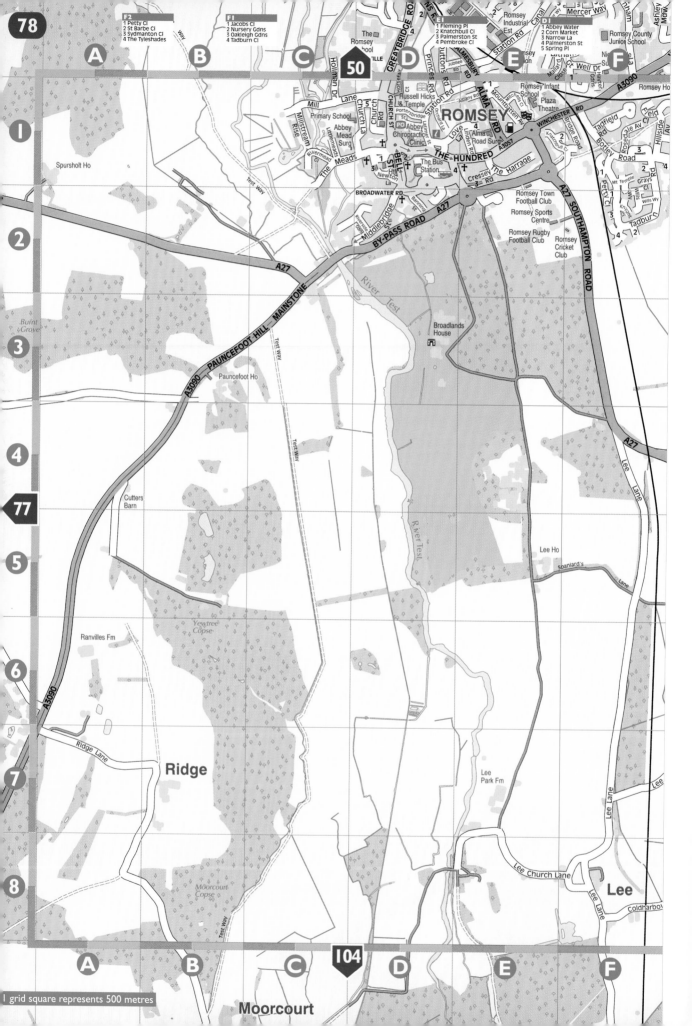

G · H · J · 51 · K · L · M

51

G1
1 Eight Acres
2 Halterworth Cl
3 Hereward Cl
4 Nightingale Cl
5 The Vikings

H1
1 Montfort Heights

H2
1 The Thicket

Halterworth

Whitenap

Halterworth
CP School

Cemetery

Botley Road

Elmtree Gdns

Sycamore
Cl

Northlands
Rd

Pine
Rd

Ash
Cl

The Thicket

Mountbatten
Secondary
School

Premier

LUZBOROUGH LANE

A27

LUZBOROUGH
LANE

Ashfield

A3057

BOTLEY ROAD A27

Warren Fm

Baddesley
Common

S05

North
Baddesley

West Lane

Ringwood

Ringwood Drive

Cerne Cl

Queen's Ride

Hoe Fm

Hoe Lane

Tanner's Brook

Telegraph
Wood

Toothill   Road

Toothill

Drove

A3057

Nightingale
Wood

Packridge

Rownhams Lane

Lane

Upton

Greenhill Lane

Toothill
Road

Rownhams Service Area

M27

Rownhams Service Area

80

PO

A27

Brown Rd

Willis Av

Church

Brownhill
Road

Fleming

BOTLEY ROAD

I · 2 · 3 · 4 · 80 · 5 · 6 · 7 · 8

105

M3
1 Emer Cl

L4
1 Heathrbr Gdns
2 Northerwood Cl
3 Tutland Rd
4 Woodside Rd

L3
1 Heatherview Cl
2 Pine Cl

L2
1 Stragwyne Cl

K3
1 Broad La
2 Highlands Cl
3 Overbrook Wy

G · H · J · 105 · K · L · M

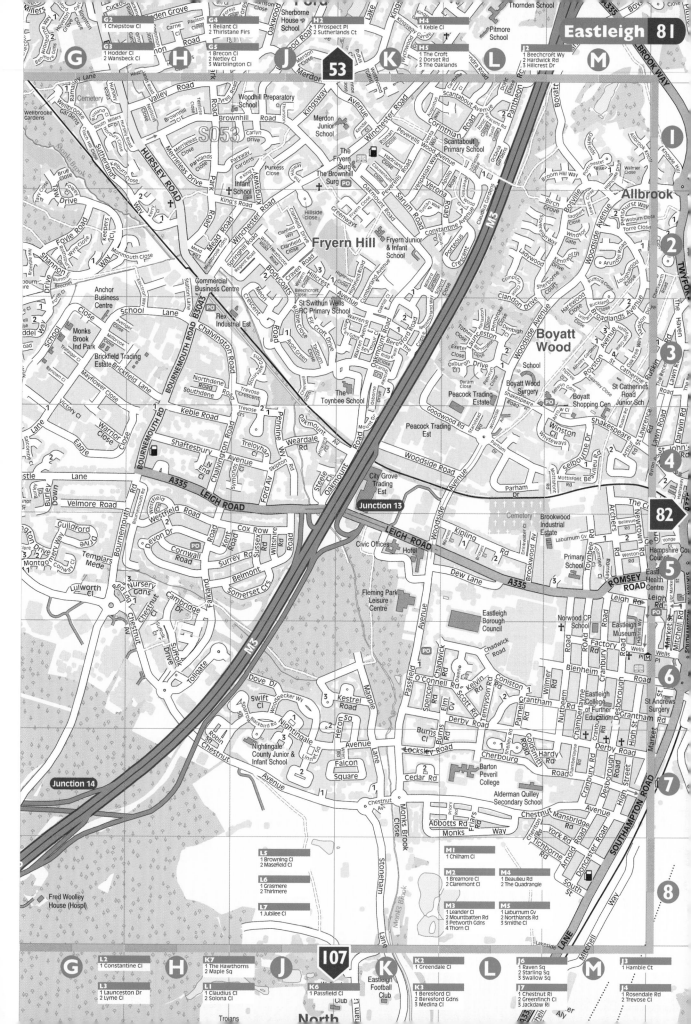

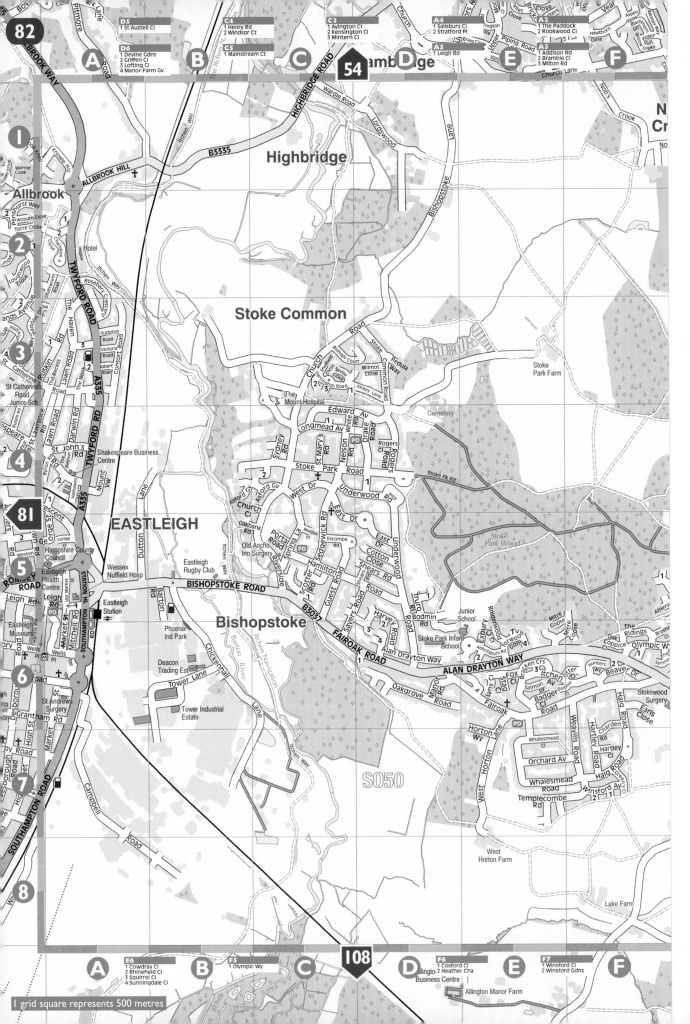

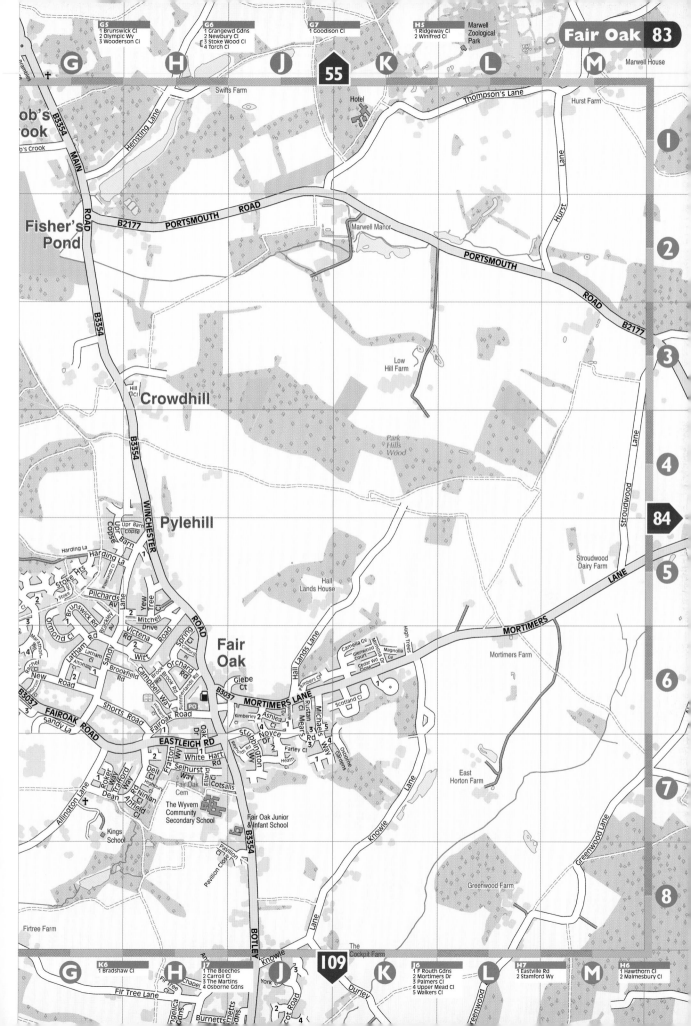

G5
1 Brunswick Cl
2 Olympic Wy
3 Wooderson Cl

G6
1 Grangewd Gdns
2 Newbury Cl
3 Stoke Wood Cl
4 Torch Cl

G7
1 Goodison Cl

H5
1 Ridgeway Cl
2 Winifred Cl

Marwell Zoological Park

Marwell House

G · H · J · 55 · K · L · M

Swifts Farm
Hotel
Thompson's Lane
Hurst Farm

Fisher's Pond

Henstung Lane
B2177 PORTSMOUTH ROAD
Marwell Manor
PORTSMOUTH ROAD B2177

ob's rook
Job's Crook
B3354 MAIN ROAD

Low Hill Farm

Hurst Lane
Stroudwood Lane

Crowdhill
Hill Cl

Pylehill
Park Hills Wood

84

Winchester Road
B3354
Upr Barn Copse
Upr Barn Copse
Harding La

Stroudwood Dairy Farm

STROUDWOOD LANE

Stoke Hts
Pilchards Av
Yew Tree Road
Mitchel Drive
Victena Rd
Witt
Spring Cl
Clifford
Orchard Road

Fair Oak

Hall Lands House

MORTIMERS

Mortimers Farm

Brunswick Rd
Brackens
Latham Ct
Alton
Latham
Sandy Road
Brookfield Rd
Campbell Way
Brook Cl
Brook Rd
Orchard Rds
Glebe Ct
B3037 MORTIMERS LANE

Camellia Gv
Glenwood Court
Cedar Wd Close
Magnolia Gv
Mimosa Gv
Magnolia Gv
High Trees
Pembers Cl
Scotland Cl

New Road
B3037
FAIROAK ROAD
Sandy La
Shorts Road
Fairoak Road
Oak Road
PO

Kimberley Cl
Ashlea
Willow
Rustan Cl
Mears
Michaels Rd
Osborne Gardens
Knowle Lane

Marathon
Rachel
Marcus
EASTLEIGH RD
White Hart Rd
Noyce Dr
Stubbington Wy
Reynolds Rd
Farley Cl
Heath Cl
Michaels Way

Roker Wy
Trafford Way
Selhurst
Highbury
Dell Cl
Eiland
Cotsalls
Fratton

East Horton Farm

Dean
De Ninian Cl
Anfield Cl
Fair Oak Cem
The Wyvern Community Secondary School

Fair Oak Junior & Infant School
B3354

Kings School

Pavilion Close
Pavilion Road

Firtree Farm

BOTLEY ROAD
Knowle Lane
Durley

The Cockpit Farm

Greenwood Lane
Greenwood Farm

K6
1 Bradshaw Cl

J7
1 The Beeches
2 Carroll Cl
3 The Martins
4 Osborne Gdns

J6
1 F Routh Gdns
2 Mortimers Dr
3 Palmers Cl
4 Upper Mead Cl
5 Walkers Cl

H7
1 Eastville Rd
2 Stamford Wy

H6
1 Hawthorn Cl
2 Malmesbury Cl

Fir Tree Lane
Chapel
Fir Tree
York
Cot Road
Greenwood
Angelica
Burnetts Gdns

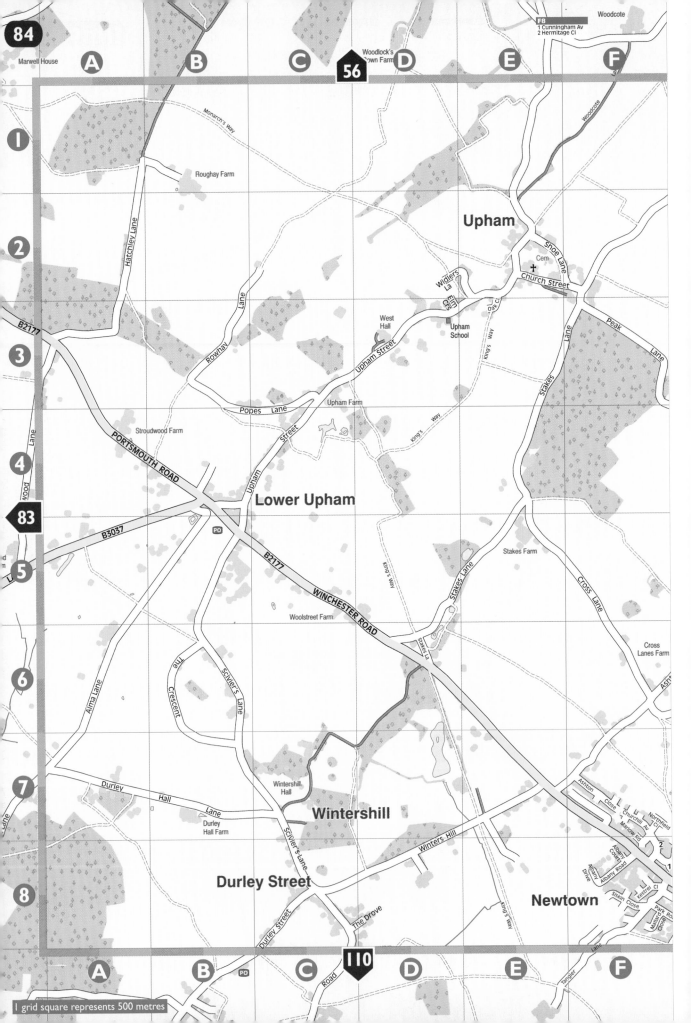

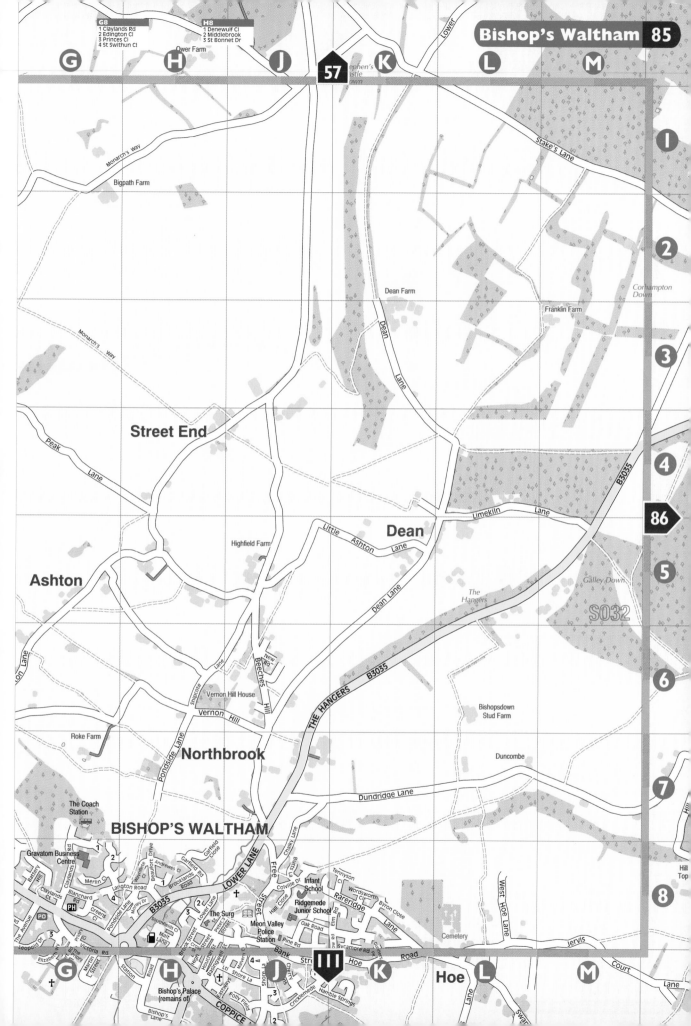

G8
1 Claylands Rd
2 Edington Cl
3 Princes Cl
4 St Swithun Cl

H8
1 Denewulf Cl
2 Middlebrook
3 St Bonnet Dr

G   H   J   57   K   L   M

I
2
3
4
86
5
6
7
8

Ower Farm

Monarch's Way

Bigpath Farm

Dean Farm

Franklin Farm

Cornhampton Down

Monarch's Way

Street End

Peak Lane

Dean Lane

Highfield Farm

Little Ashton Lane

Dean

Limekiln Lane

B3035

Ashton

Dean Lane

The Hangers

Galley Down

S032

New Rd

Beeches Hill

Shipcote Lane

Vernon Hill House

Vernon Hill

The Hangers B3035

Bishopsdown Stud Farm

Roke Farm

Pondside Lane

Northbrook

Duncombe

The Coach Station

Dundridge Lane

BISHOP'S WALTHAM

Gravatom Business Centre

Claylands Rd

Battery Hill

Blanchard Rd

Claylands Cl

Merlin

Greens Cl

PH

PO

The Avenue

Leopold Dr

Elizabeth Cl

Martin Street

Victoria Rd

Station Road

Langton Road

Morley Dr

Beaufort Drive

Andrewes Cl

Brooklands Road

LOWER LANE

Garfield Close

B3035

Lower Lane

Southfields Cl

Malt Lane

Brook Cross

High Street

Bishopsfield

Basingwell St

Houchin St

Shore La

Priory St

The Surg

Bank Street

Free Street

Chalky Lane

Colville Dr

Hill Close

Pine Rd

Oak Road

Meon Valley Police Station

Infant School

Ridgemede Junior School

Tennyson Cl

Wordsworth Cl

Byron Close

Rareridge Lane

Elm Rd

Sycamore Rd

Cricklemede

Hamble Springs

Coombes Cl

Hoe Road

West Hoe Lane

Cemetery

Jervis

Hill Top

G   H   J   K   L   **Hoe**   M

Bishop's Palace (remains of)

Bishop's Lane

COPPICE

Swan

Court Lane

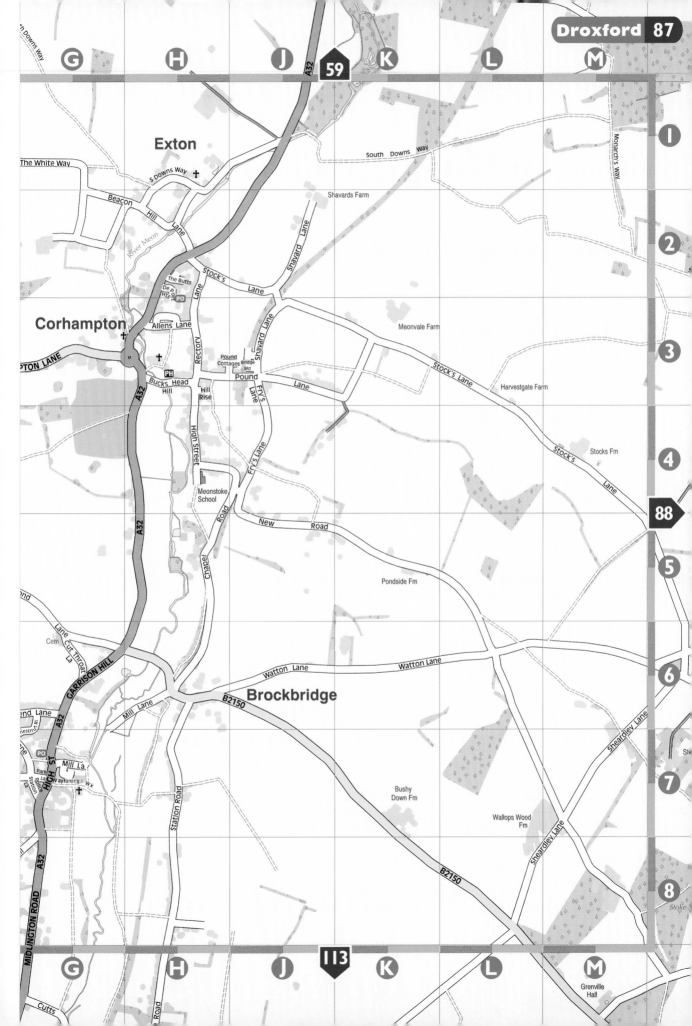

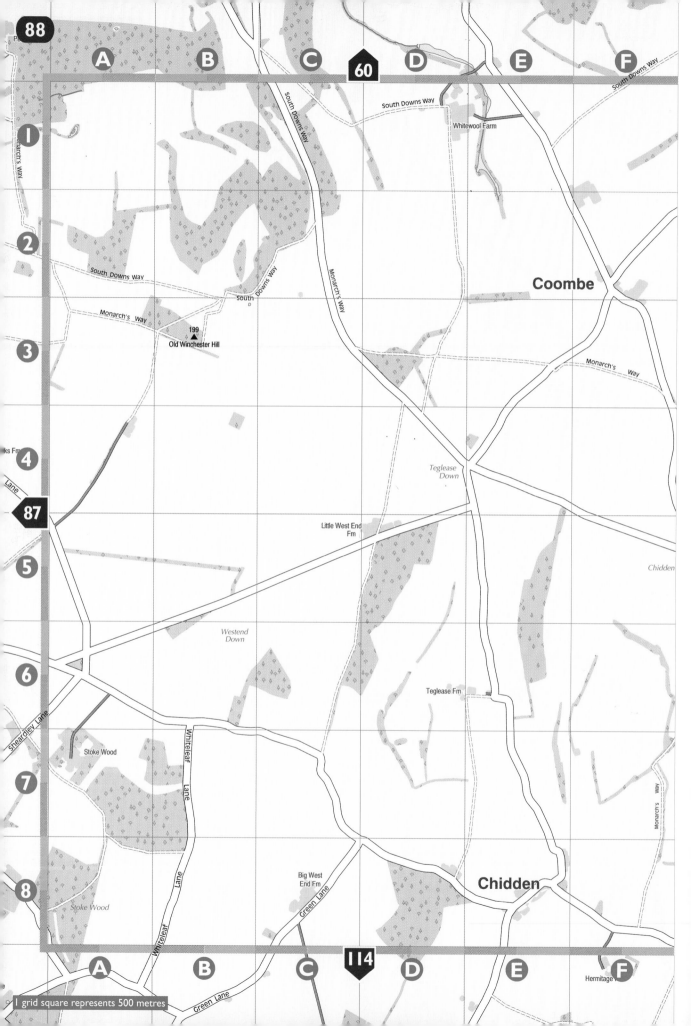

A B C 60 D E F

South Downs Way

South Downs Way
Whitewool Farm

1
Monarch's Way

2
South Downs Way

Monarch's Way
South Downs Way

South

Coombe

3
Monarch's Way
199
▲
Old Winchester Hill

Monarch's Way

4
Teglease
Down

87
Little West End
Fm

5
Chidden

Westend
Down

6
Teglease Fm

Sheardley Lane

Stoke Wood
Whiteleaf Lane

7

8
Stoke Wood

Big West
End Fm
Green Lane

Chidden

Monarch's Way

Whiteleaf Lane

Green Lane

A B C 114 D E Hermitage F

East Meon

Coombe

Duncombe Farm

Lower
House Farm

Oxenbourne House

Coombe
Cross

South Farm

Stonylands Farm

233
▲
Salt Hill

Down

South Downs Way

Old
Hambledonians
Cricket Club

South Downs Way

Hyden
Wood

Coombe
Wood

Hyden Farm Lane

Hyden Farm

North Fm

Monarch's W

Harvesting La

Little Hyden Lane

South Downs Way

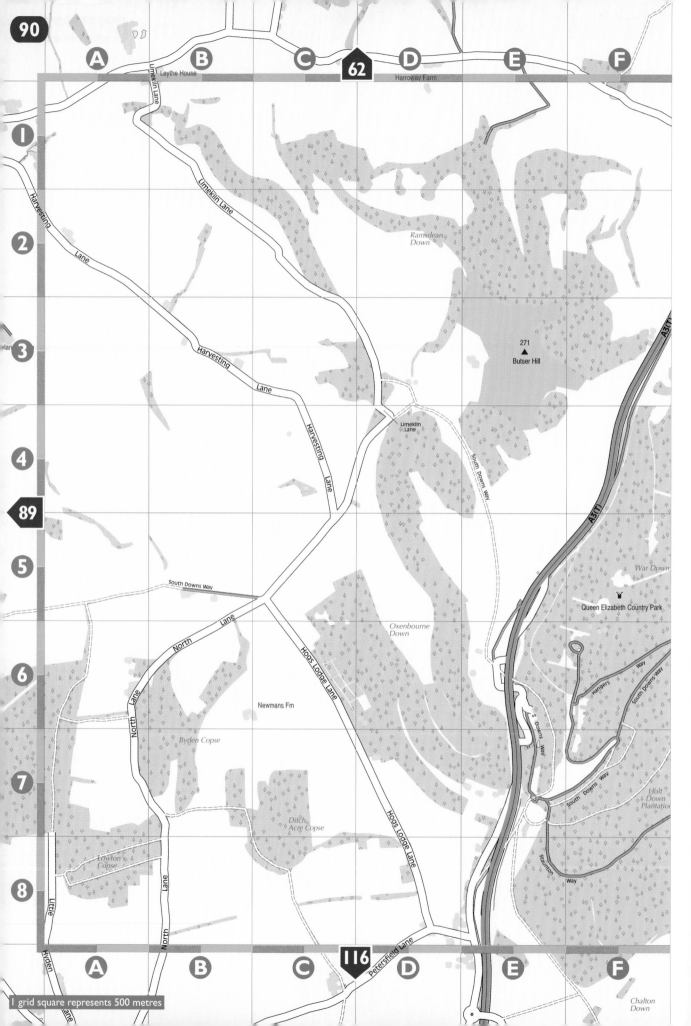

A B C **62** D E F

Leythe House
Harroway Farm

I

Harvesting

2

Lane

Limekiln Lane

Ramsdean
Down

3

Harvesting

Lane

271
▲
Butser Hill

4

Limekiln
Lane

South Downs Way

89

5

South Downs Way

War Down

Queen Elizabeth Country Park

North

Lane

Oxenbourne
Down

6

Hogs Lodge Lane

Newmans Fm

Hangers

Way

South Downs Way

7

Byden Copse

Ditch
Acre Copse

S. Downs Way

Holt
Down
Plantation

Lowton's
Copse

Staunton

Way

8

Little

North

Lane

Hogs Lodge Lane

Petersfield Lane

A3(T)

A B C **116** D E F

Hyden

Chalton
Down

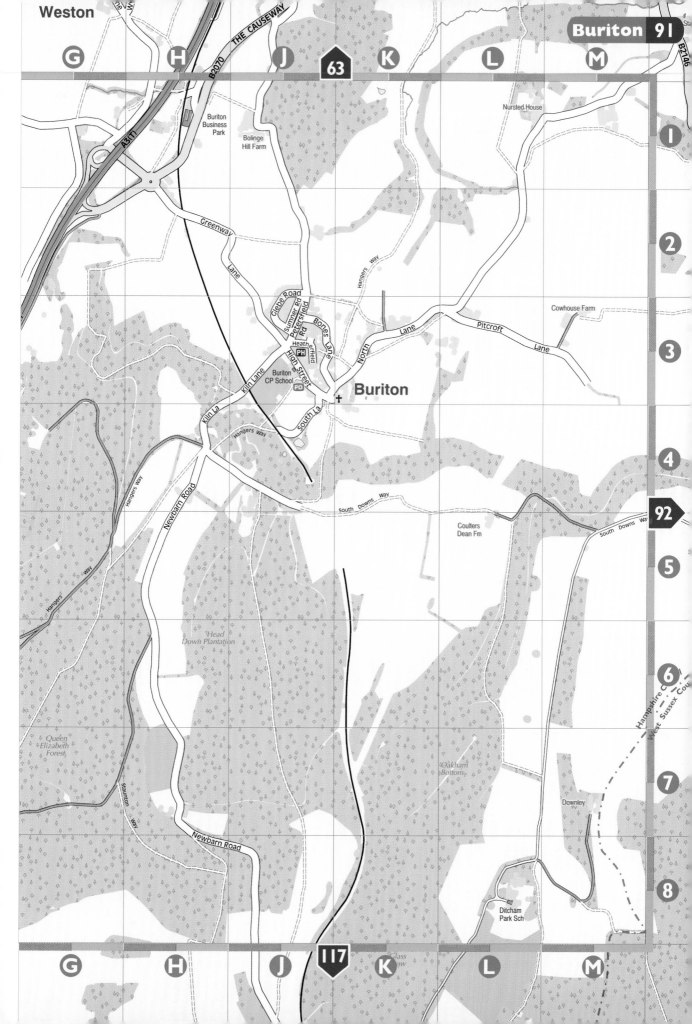

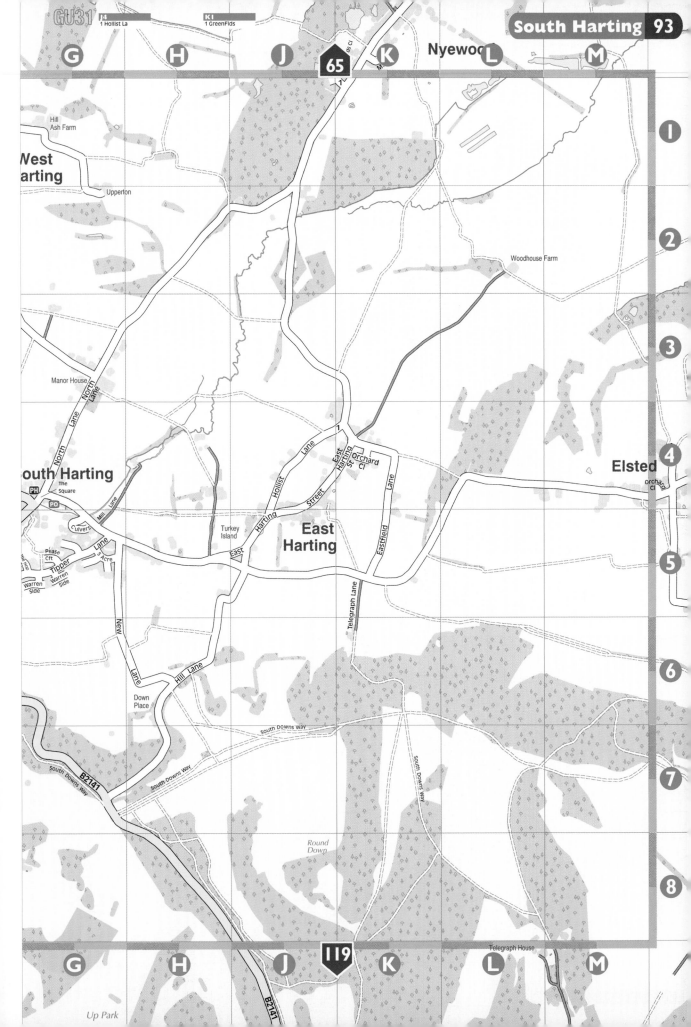

GU31
J4
1 Hollist La
K1
1 GreenFlds

G H J 65 K Nyewood L M

Hill
Ash Farm

West
Harting

Upperton

Woodhouse Farm

Manor House

North Lane

South Harting

PH
The
Square

PO

Culvers

Mill Lane

Pease
Cft

Tipper

Acre

Warren
Side

Warren
Side

Turkey
Island

East

Harting Lane

Hollist Lane

Street

East Harting

East
Harting
St

Orchard
Cl

Lane

Eastfield
Lane

Elsted

Orchard
Cl

Telegraph Lane

New Lane

Hill Lane

Down
Place

South Downs Way

South Downs Way

South Downs Way

B2141

South Downs Way

Round
Down

Telegraph House

G H J 119 K L M

B2141

Up Park

1
2
3
4
5
6
7
8

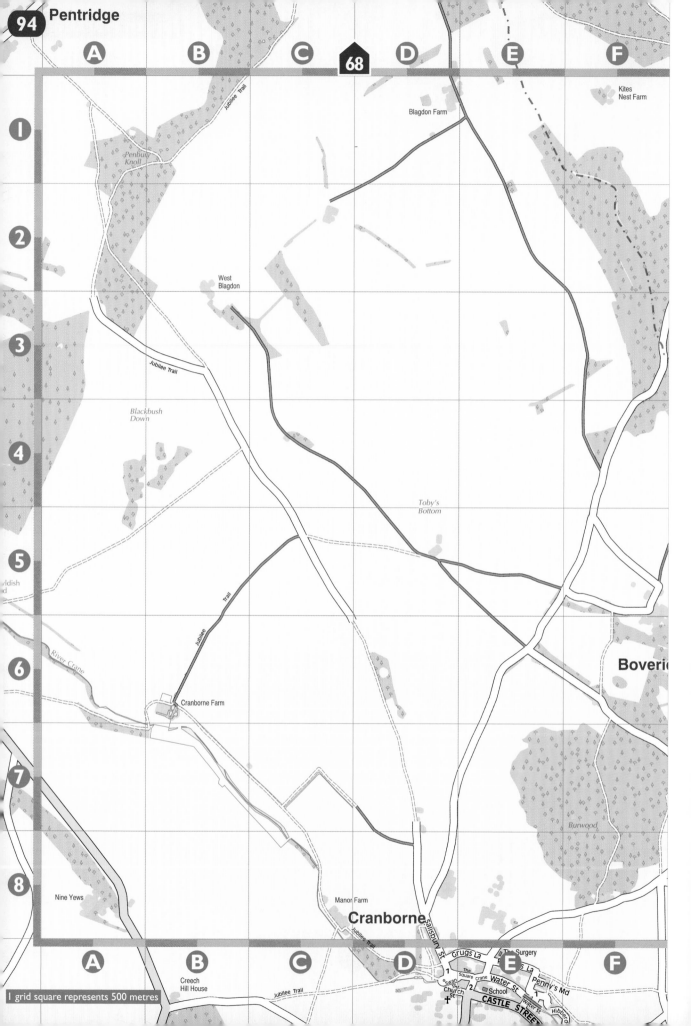

A B C **68** D E F

I

Kites
Nest Farm

Blagdon Farm

Penbury
Knoll

2

West
Blagdon

3

Jubilee Trail

Jubilee Trail

*Blackbush
Down*

4

*Toby's
Bottom*

5

/ldish
/d

Jubilee Trail

6

River Crane

Boveri

Cranborne Farm

7

Burwood

8

Nine Yews

Manor Farm

Cranborne

The Surgery

Salisbury St

Grugs La

s La

The
Square crane

Penny's Md

Swan

Water St

St

School

Church †
St †

CASTLE STREET

Water St

Hibberd

A B
Creech
Hill House

C
Jubilee Trail

D

E

F

G H J **69** K L M

Blackheath Down

South Allenford Farm

Allen River

I

2

Martin Wood

3

Boulsbury Farm

Hampshire County
Dorset County

4

Stony

96

Stapleton Farm

Ashley Park Farm

5

Boulsbury Wood

Boveridge
House
School

6

idge

Common Down

Biddlesgate
Farm

Hyde Farm

7

Bratch Copse

Bellows
Cross

Lopshill

8

Ashes Farm

Lower Daggons

G H J **120** K L M

Crendell

Holwell Farm

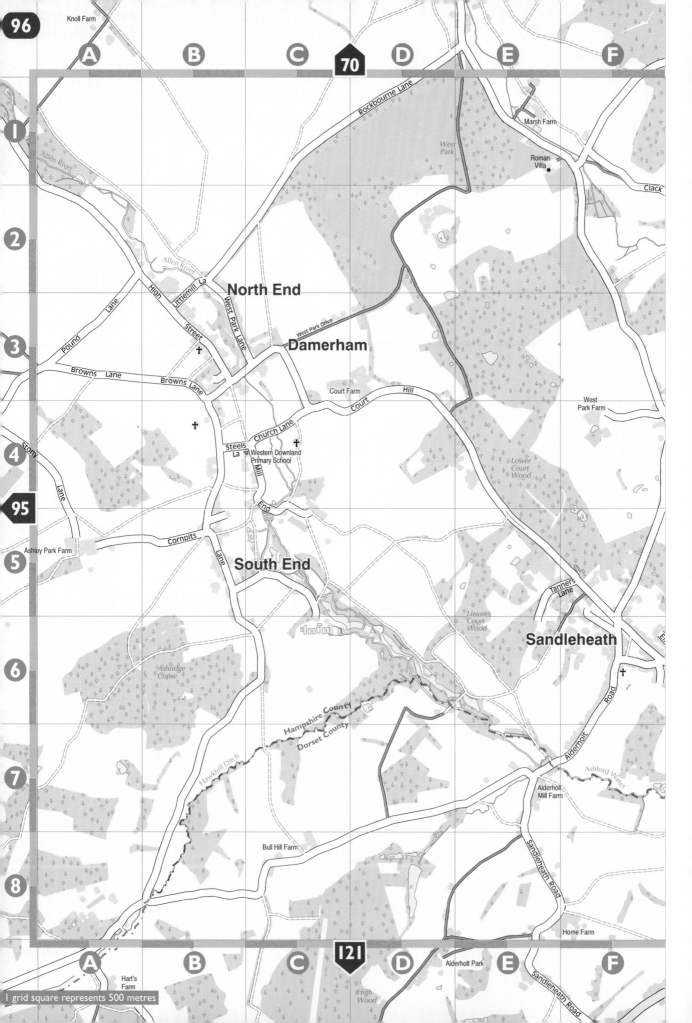

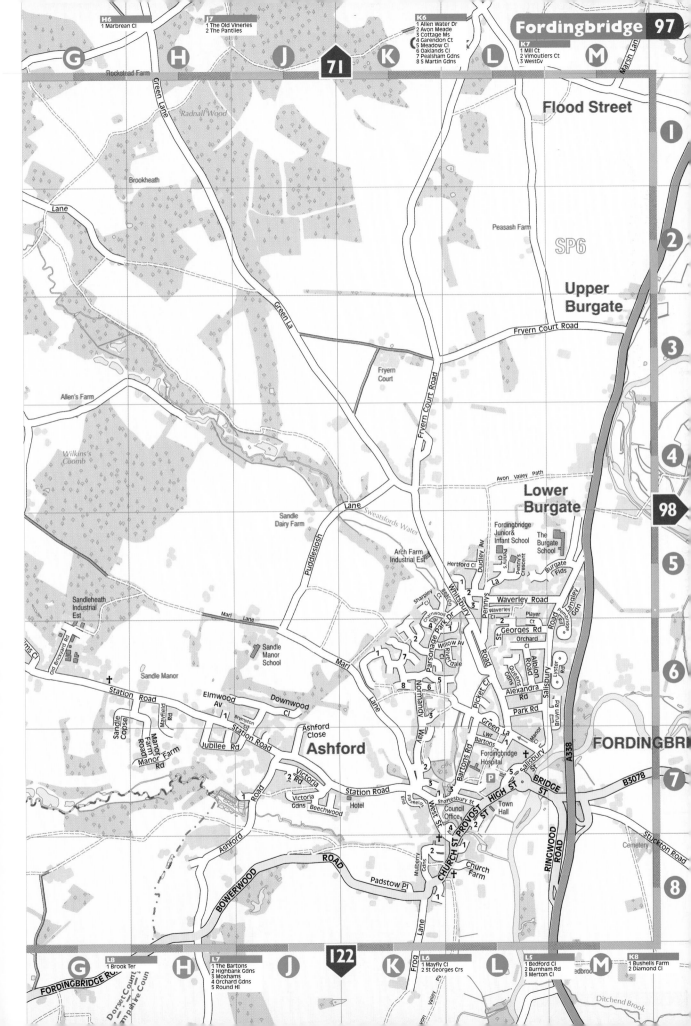

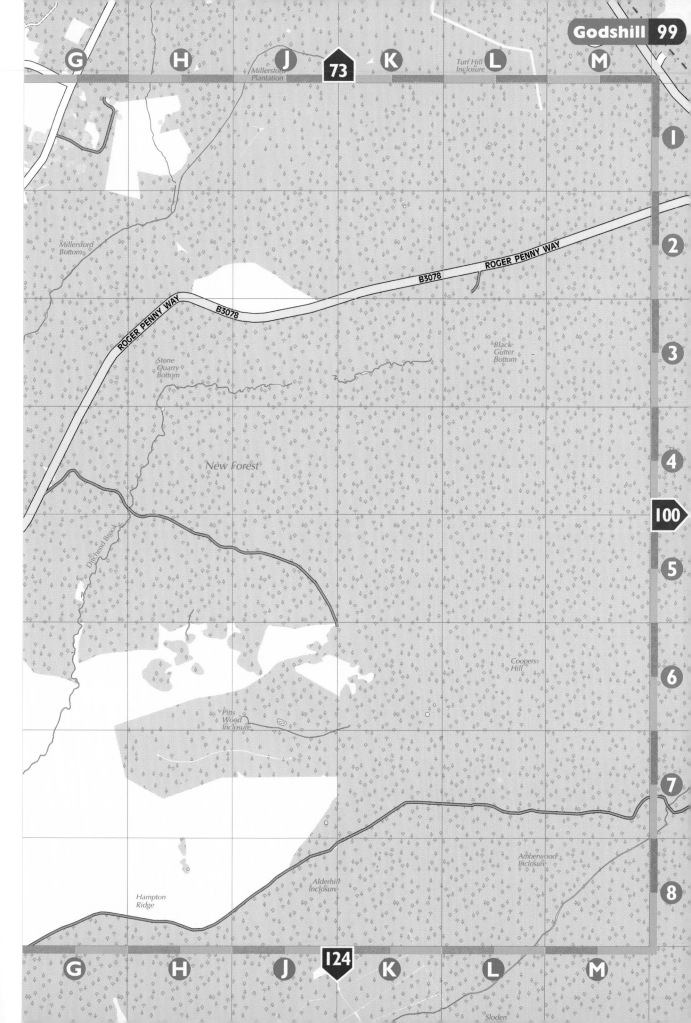

G   H   J   ◆ 73   K   L   M

I

2

3

4

100

5

6

7

8

*Millersford
Plantation*

*Turf Hill
Inclosure*

*Millersford
Bottom*

ROGER PENNY WAY

B3078   ROGER PENNY WAY

ROGER PENNY WAY

B3078

*Stone
Quarry
Bottom*

*Black
Gutter
Bottom*

New Forest

Ditchend Brook

*Coopers
Hill*

*Pitts
Wood
Inclosure*

*Amberwood
Inclosure*

*Hampton
Ridge*

*Alderhill
Inclosure*

G   H   J   ◆ 124   K   L   M

Sloden

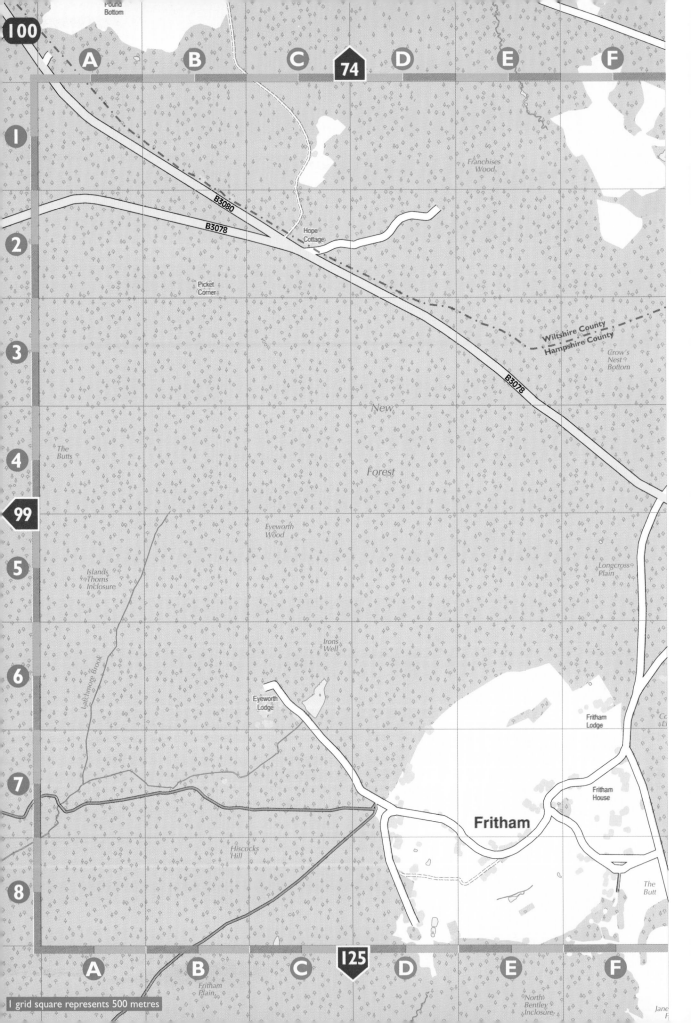

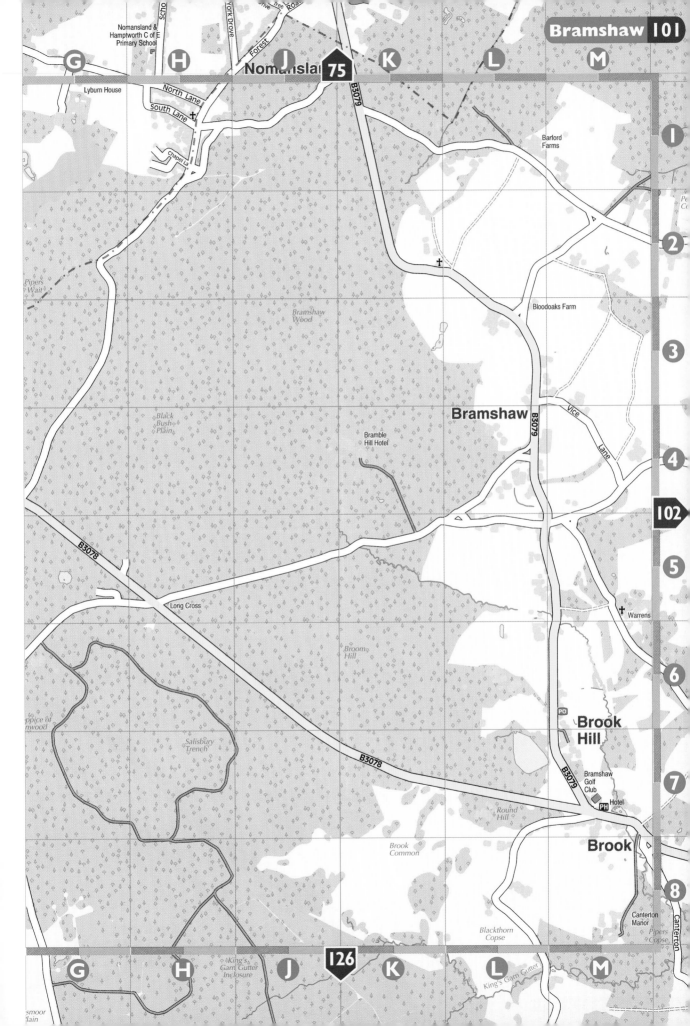

Nomansland & Hamptworth C of E Primary School

Scho

York Drove

Forest

Tree Roa

Nomanslan 75

B3079

G

H

J

K

L

M

Lyburn House

North Lane

south Lane

Chapel La

Pipers Wait

Bramshaw Wood

Black Bush Plain

Bramble Hill Hotel

Barford Farms

I

2

Bloodoaks Farm

3

Bramshaw

B3079

Vice Lane

4

102

B3078

Long Cross

Broom Hill

Warrens

5

6

Coppice of nwood

Salisbury Trench

B3078

PO

Brook Hill

Brook Common

Round Hill

B3079

Bramshaw Golf Club

Hotel

PH

7

Brook

smoor lain

Blackthorn Copse

King's Garn Gutter Inclosure

King's Garn Gutter

Canterton Manor

Pipers Copse

Canterton

8

G

H

J

126

K

L

M

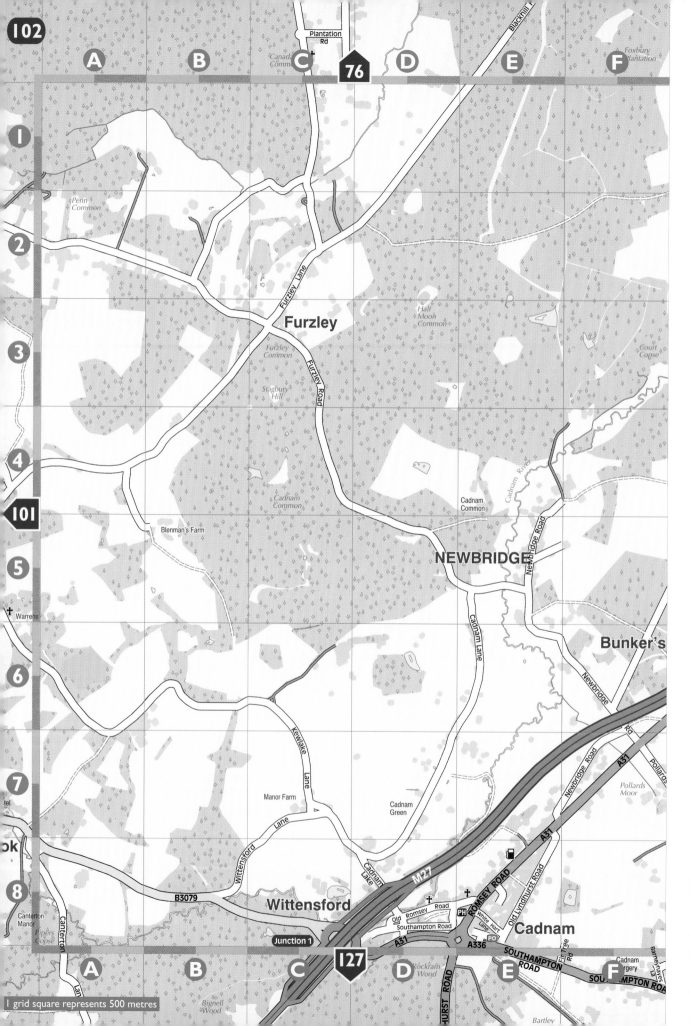

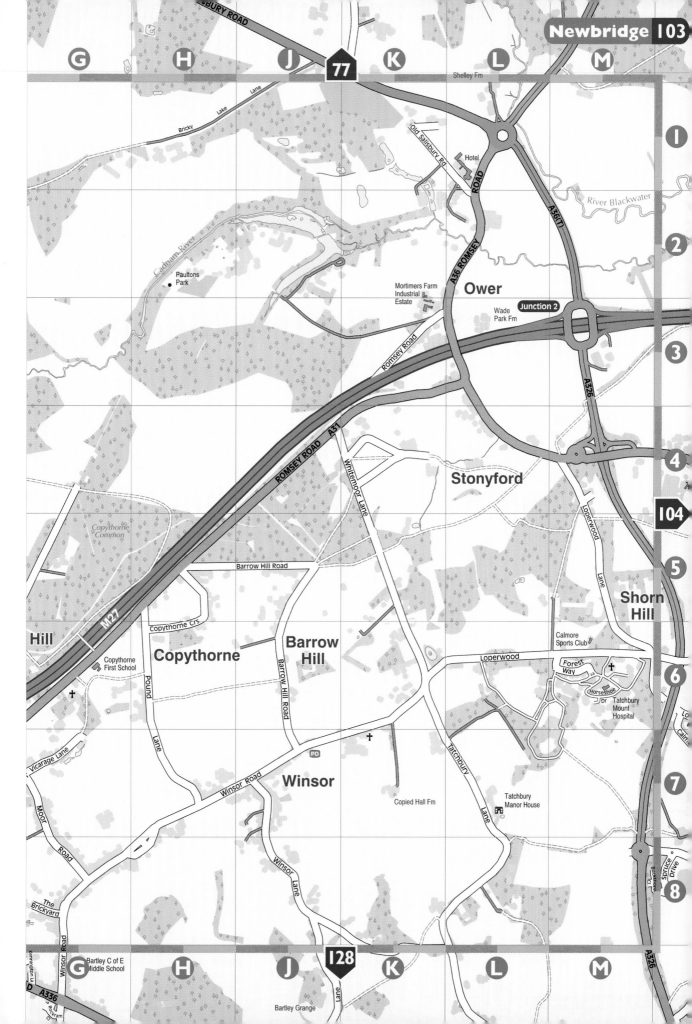

G H J K L M

77

I
2
3
4
104
5
6
7
8

Shelley Fm

River Blackwater

Old Salisbury Rd

Hotel

ROAD

A36 ROMSEY

Mortimers Farm
Industrial
Estate

Paultons
Park

Cadnam River

Ower

Wade
Park Fm

Junction 2

A36(T)

A326

Romsey Road

Stonyford

Whitemoor Lane

A31

ROMSEY ROAD

Copythorne
Common

Loperwood
Lane

Shorn
Hill

Barrow Hill Road

Hill

M27

Copythorne Crs

Copythorne
First School

Copythorne

Barrow
Hill

Barrow Hill Road

Loperwood

Calmore
Sports Club

Forest
Way

Horseshoe
Dr

Tatchbury
Mount
Hospital

Pound
Lane

Winsor Road

Winsor

PO

†

Tatchbury
Lane

Copied Hall Fm

Tatchbury
Manor House

Spruce
Drive

Vicarage Lane

Moor
Road

Winsor
Lane

The
Brickyard

Winsor Road

Kennington La

A356

Bartley C of E
Middle School

G H J K L M

128

A326

Bartley Grange

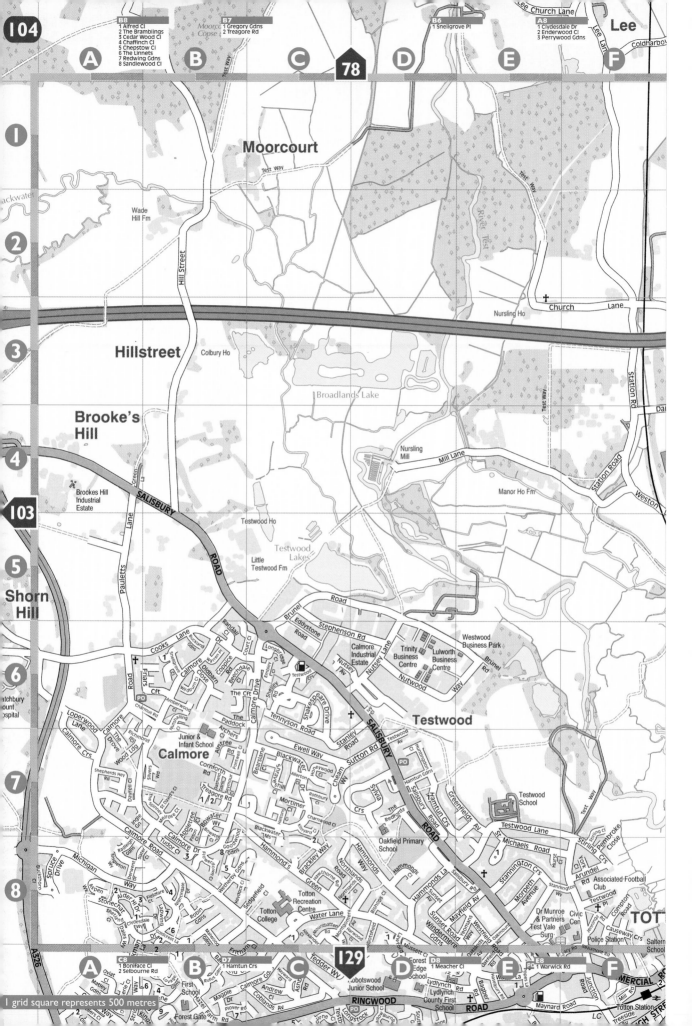

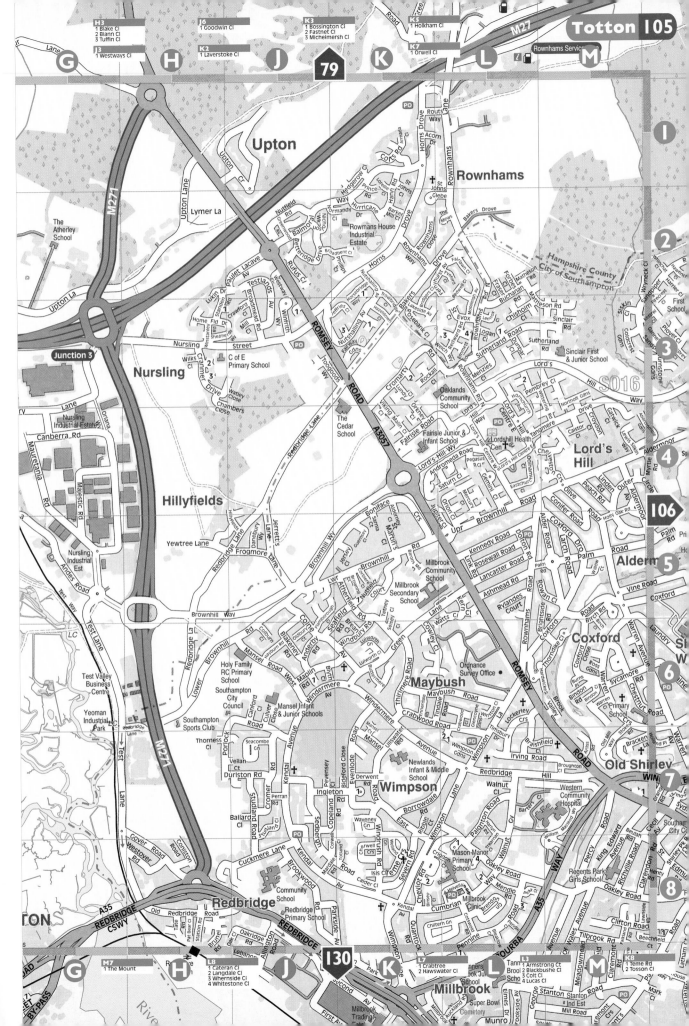

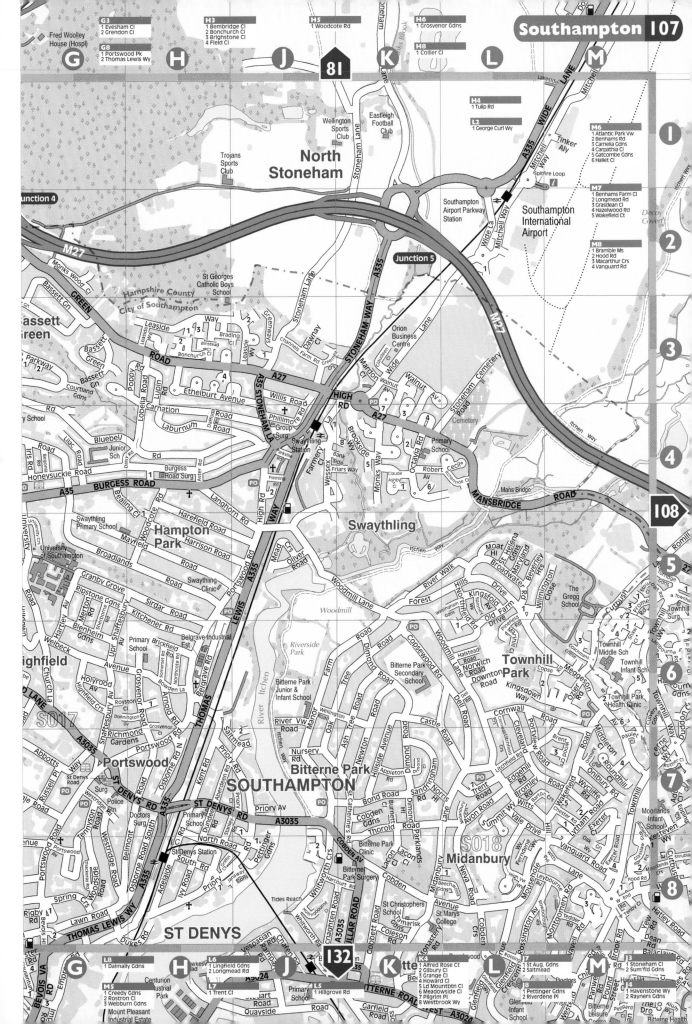

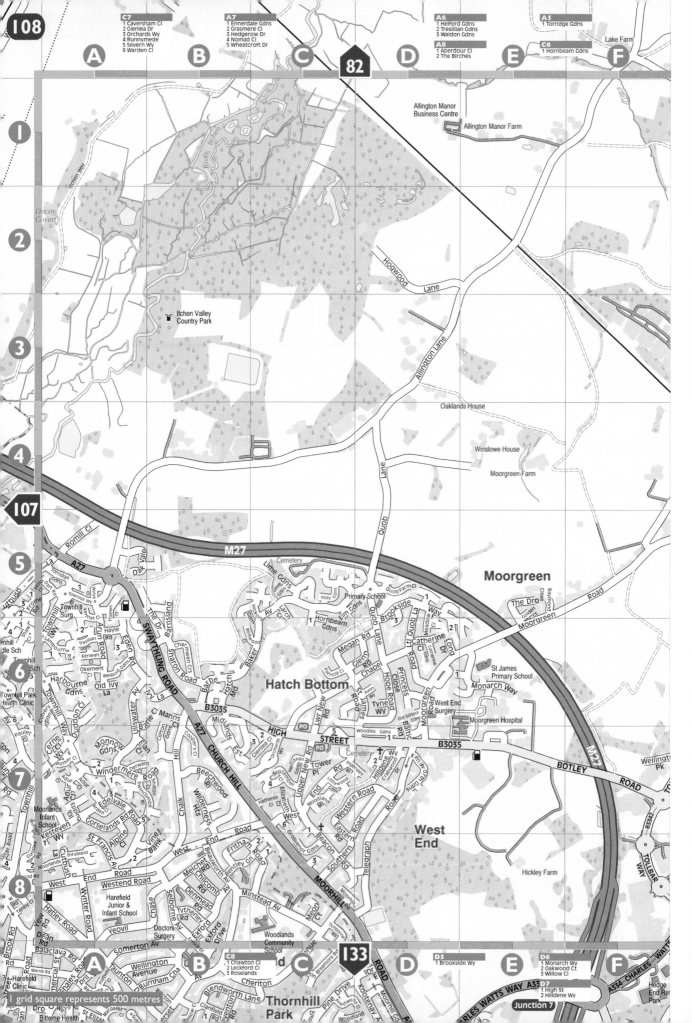

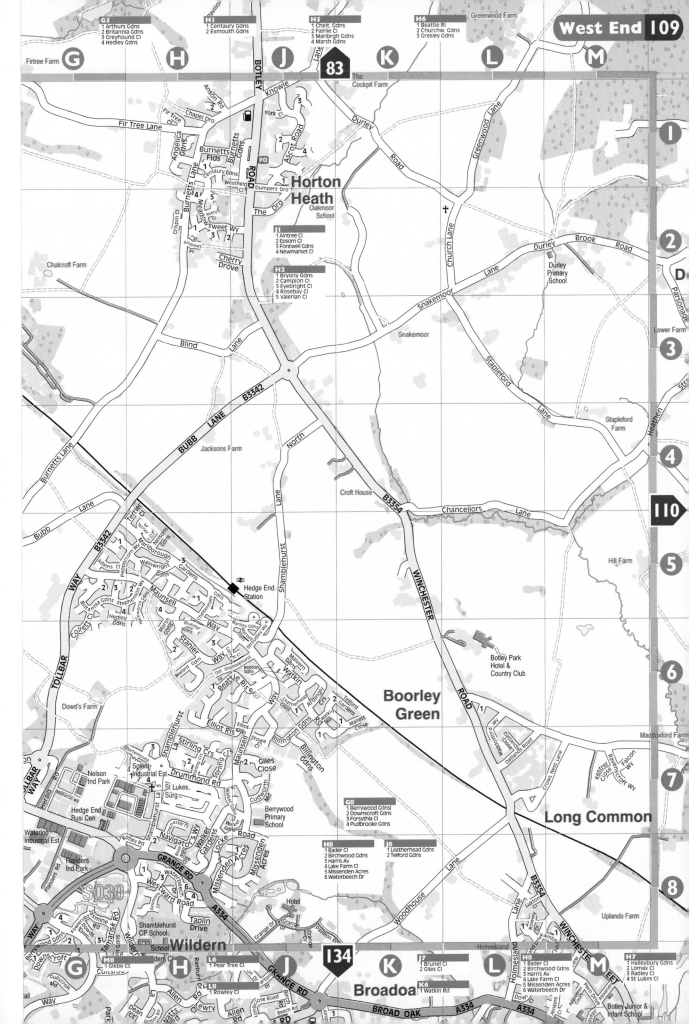

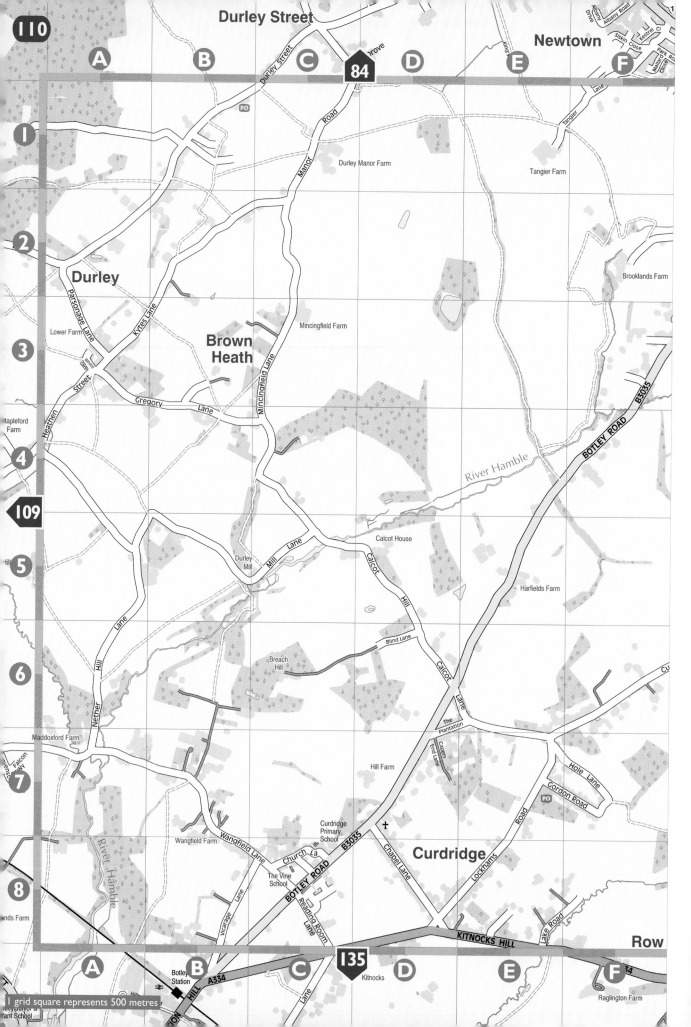

Durley Street

Newtown

A B C D E F

84

Durley Street

Durley Manor Farm

Tangier Farm

Brooklands Farm

1

Manor Road

2

Durley

Parsonage Lane

Lower Farm

Kytes Lane

Mincingfield Farm

Brown Heath

Mincingfield Lane

River Hamble

Botley Road

B3035

3

Heathen Street

White Gate

Gregory Lane

Stapleford Farm

4

109

Calcot House

Mill Lane

Durley Mill

Calcot Hill

Harfields Farm

5

Nether Hill Lane

Breach Hill

Blind Lane

Calcot Lane

6

Maddoxford Farm

The Plantation

Falcon Way

Hill Farm

Capers End Lane

Hole Lane

7

Gordon Road

PO

Wangfield Farm

Wangfield Lane

Curdridge Primary School

B3035

Curdridge

Lockhams Road

Lake Road

Church La

Chapel Lane

The Vine School

Botley Road

Vicarage Lane

8

River Hamble

Reading Room Lane

Kitnocks Hill

Row

ands Farm

A B C D E F

135

Botley Station

A334

Kitnocks

Raglington Farm

1 grid square represents 500 metres

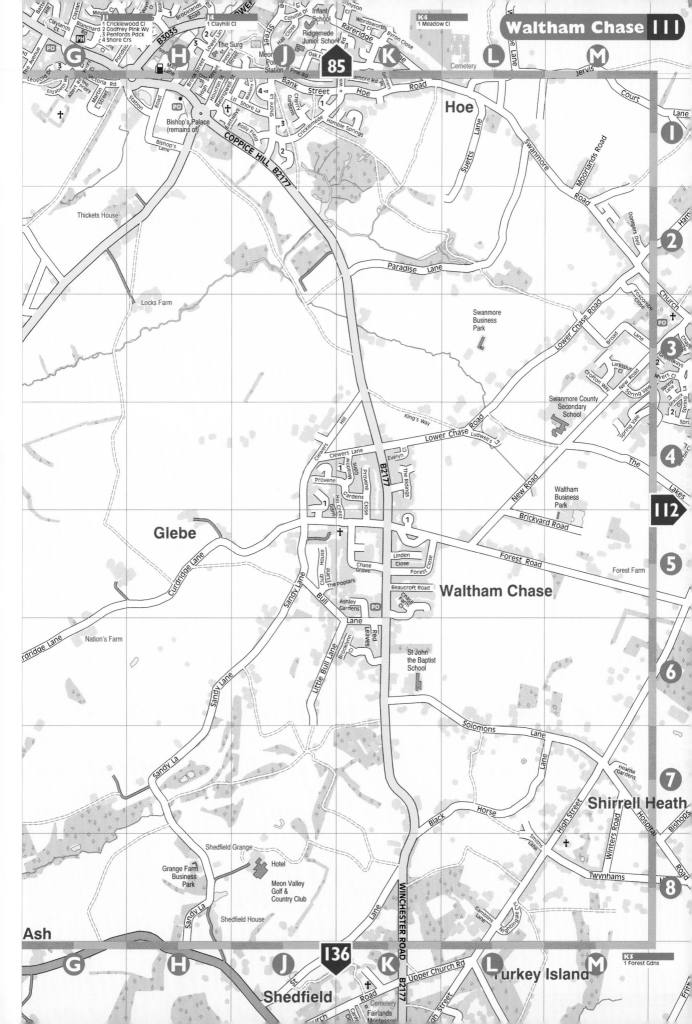

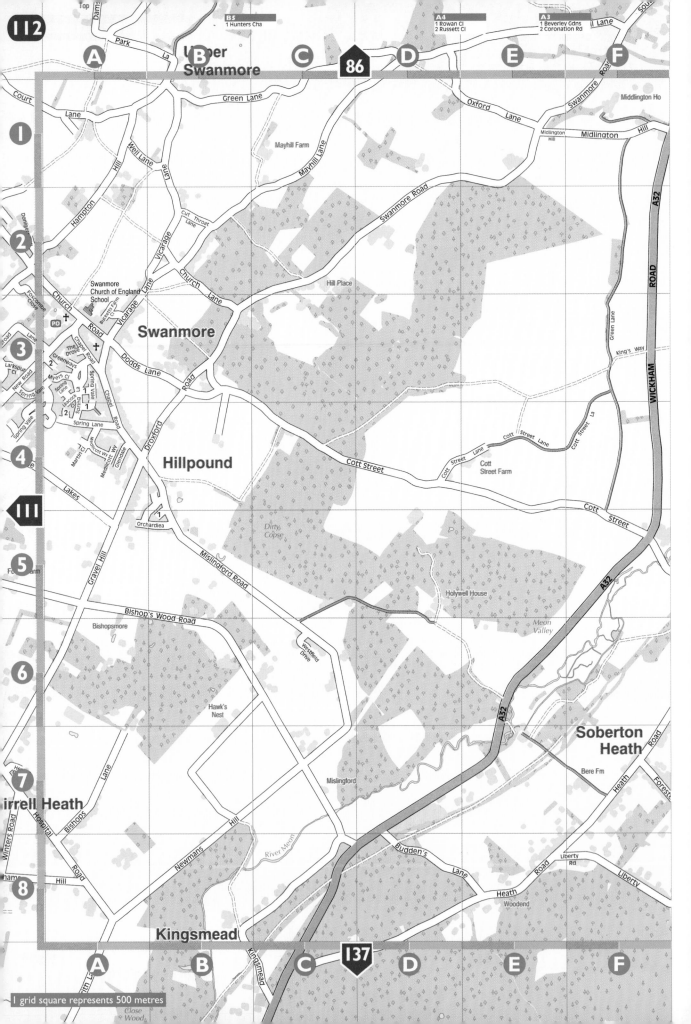

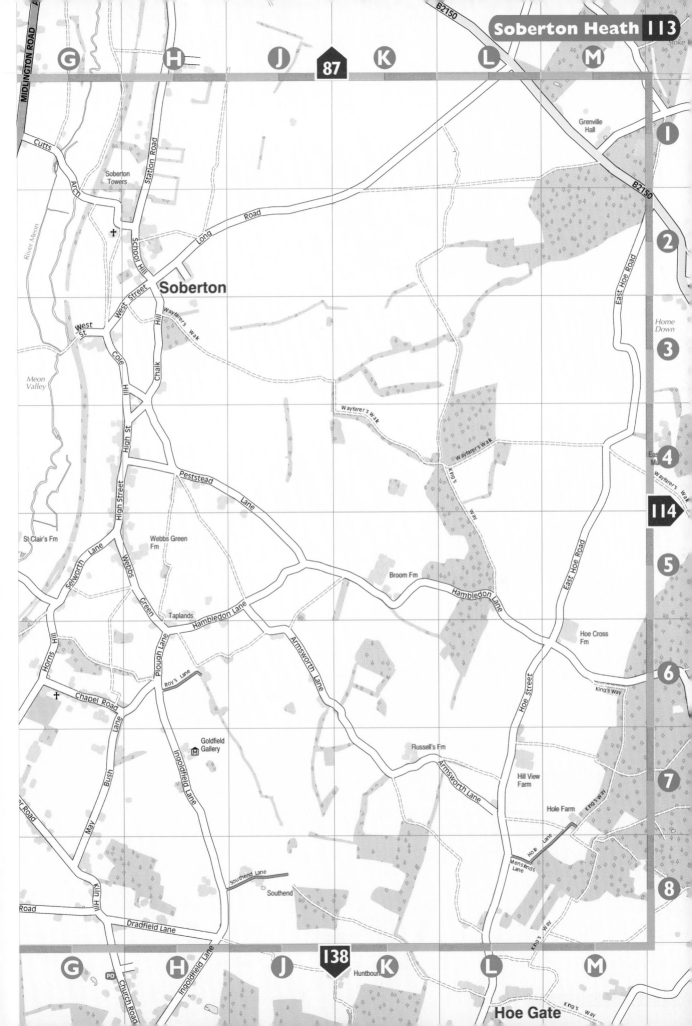

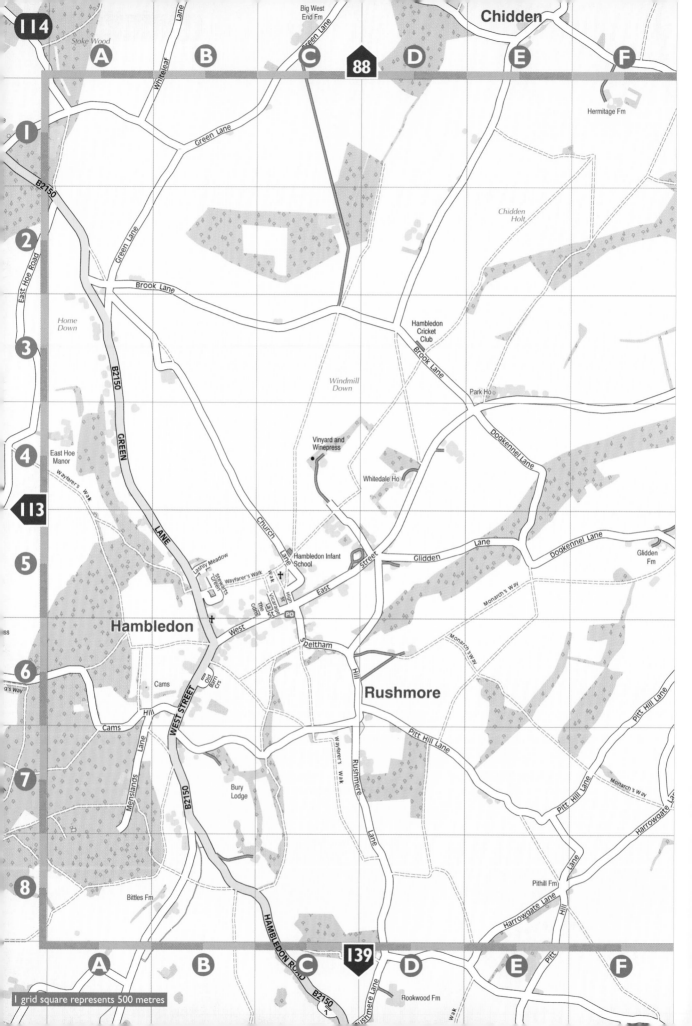

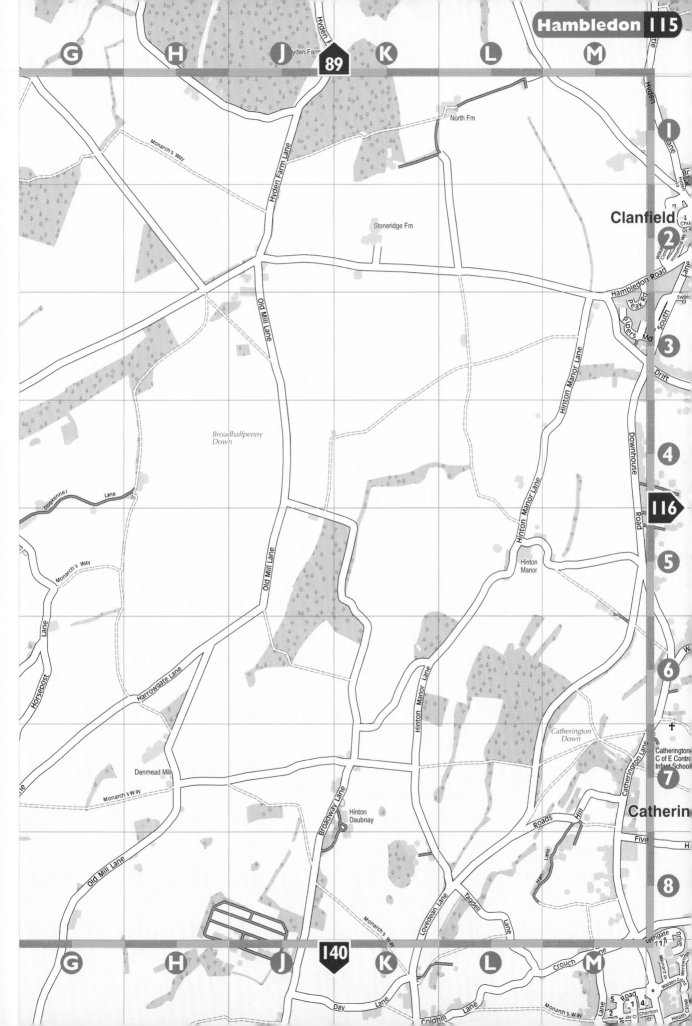

G   H   J   89   K   L   M

I

Clanfield

2

3

4

116

5

6

7

Catherin

8

G   H   J   140   K   L   M

Monarch's Way

Hyden Farm Lane

North Fm

Stoneridge Fm

Old Mill Lane

Broadhalfpenny
Down

Dogkennel   Lane

Monarch's Way

Horsepost   Lane

Harrowgate Lane

Old Mill Lane

Denmead Mill

Monarch's Way

Hinton Manor Lane

Hinton Manor Lane

Hinton
Manor

Hinton Manor Lane

Broadway Lane

Hinton
Daubnay

Monarch's Way

Lovedean Lane

Taggell Lane

Day   Lane

Coldhill   Lane

Monarch's Way

Hambledon Road

Peak Rd

Pipers

South   Lane

Drift

Downhouse   Road

Catherington Lane

Catherington
Down

Catherington
C of E Controlled
Infant School

Roads   Hill

Ham   Lane

Five

Crouch

Lychgate   Drive

Hyden   Lane

Monarch's Way

Old Mill Lane

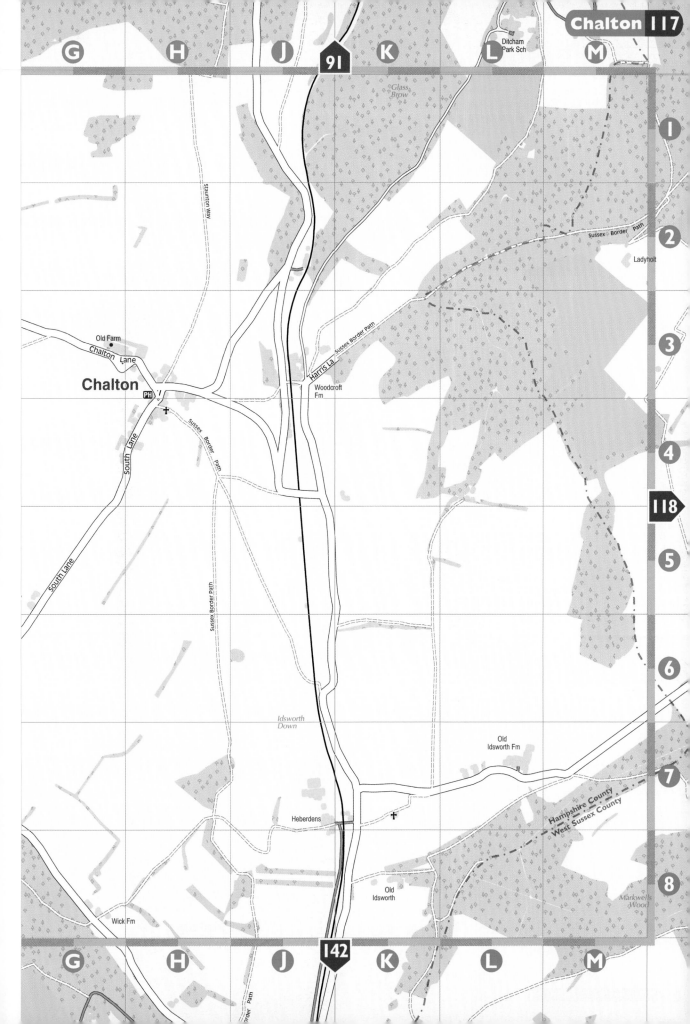

G H J K L M

91

I
2
3
4
118
5
6
7
8

Glass Brow

Ditcham Park Sch

Sussex Border Path

Ladyholt

Old Farm

Chalton Lane

Chalton PH

Harris La

Sussex Border Path

Woodcroft Fm

Staunton Way

South Lane

Sussex Border Path

Sussex Border Path

Idsworth Down

Old Idsworth Fm

Hampshire County
West Sussex County

Heberdens

Old Idsworth

Wick Fm

Markwells Wood

G H J K L M

142

Border Path

118

A B C 92 D E F

NT Uppark

I

2 Ladyholt

Hale Wood

Eckensfield

3 Hucksholt Fm

B2146

4 Little Green School

Cowdown Lane

117 Cowdown Fm

5

B2146

6 Compton

PO

PH School Lane

Compton & Upmarden C of E Primary School

7

8 Markwells Wood

Horsley Farm

Locksash Lane

Locksash Fm

A B C 143 D E F

West Marden

B2146

1 grid square represents 500 metres

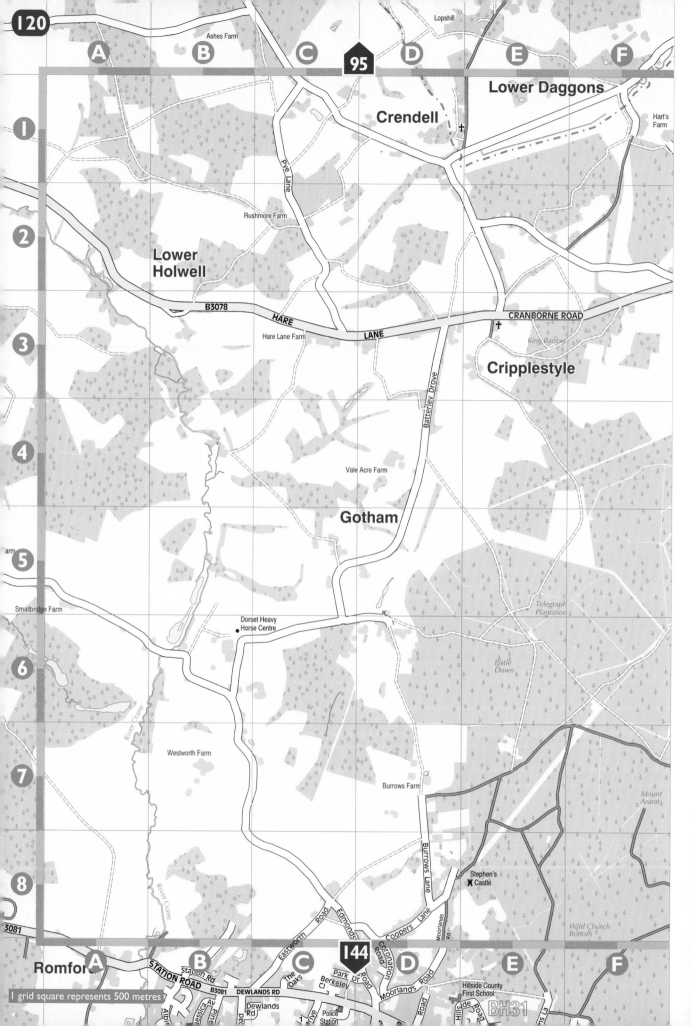

120

A   B   C   95   D   E   F

Lopshill

Lower Daggons

Crendell

Hart's Farm

1

Ashes Farm

Pye Lane

Rushmore Farm

2

Lower
Holwell

B3078   HARE   LANE   CRANBORNE ROAD

King Barrow

3

Hare Lane Farm

Cripplestyle

4

Vale Acre Farm

Battelley Drove

Gotham

arm

5

Smallbridge Farm

Telegraph
Plantation

Dorset Heavy
Horse Centre

6

River Crane

Bistle
Down

Westworth Farm

7

Burrows Farm

Mount
Ararat

River Crane

Burrows Lane

Stephen's
Castle

8

Wild Church
Bottom

3081

Romford   A   STATION ROAD   B   Station Rd   B3081   DEWLANDS RD   Eastworth Road   The Oaks   C   144   Park Dr   Berkeley Cl   Edmonds Road   Coopers Lane   Coronation Road   Moorlands Rd   D   Moorlands Road   Hillside Road   Hillside County First School   E   BH31   F

Albion Av   Jessica   Pine   Dewlands Rd   Drive   Police Station   Moorlands   Hillside   Ls La

1 grid square represents 500 metres

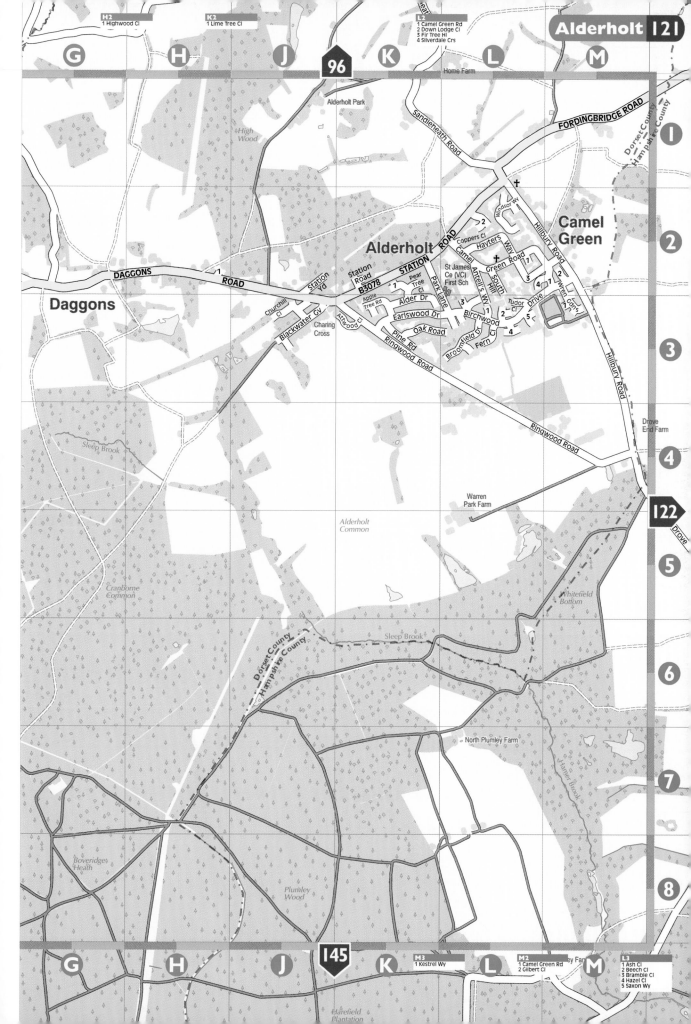

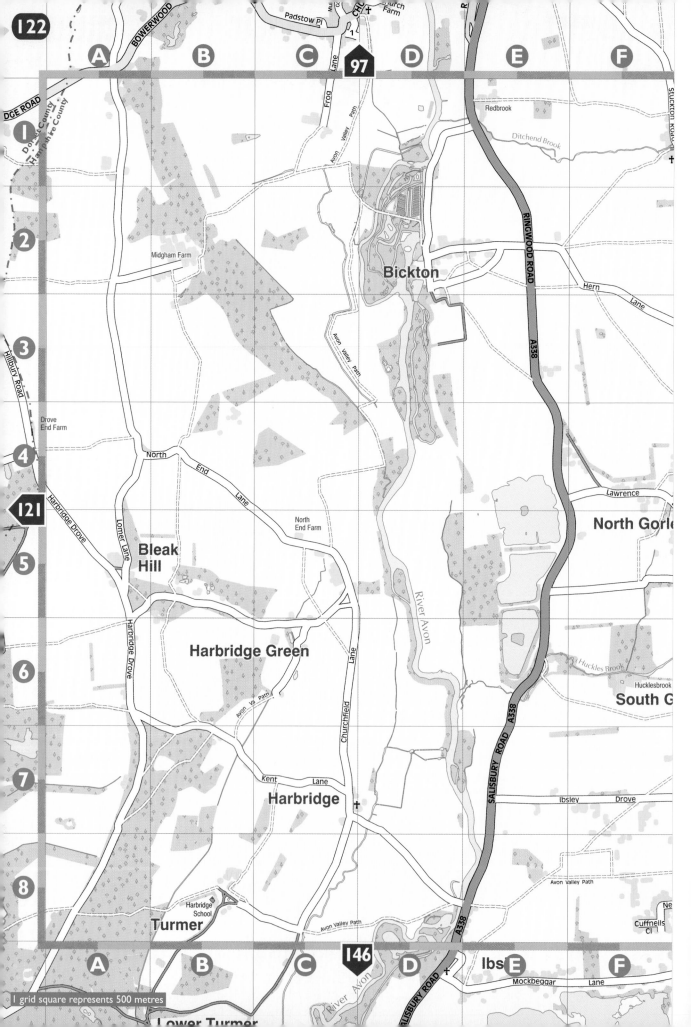

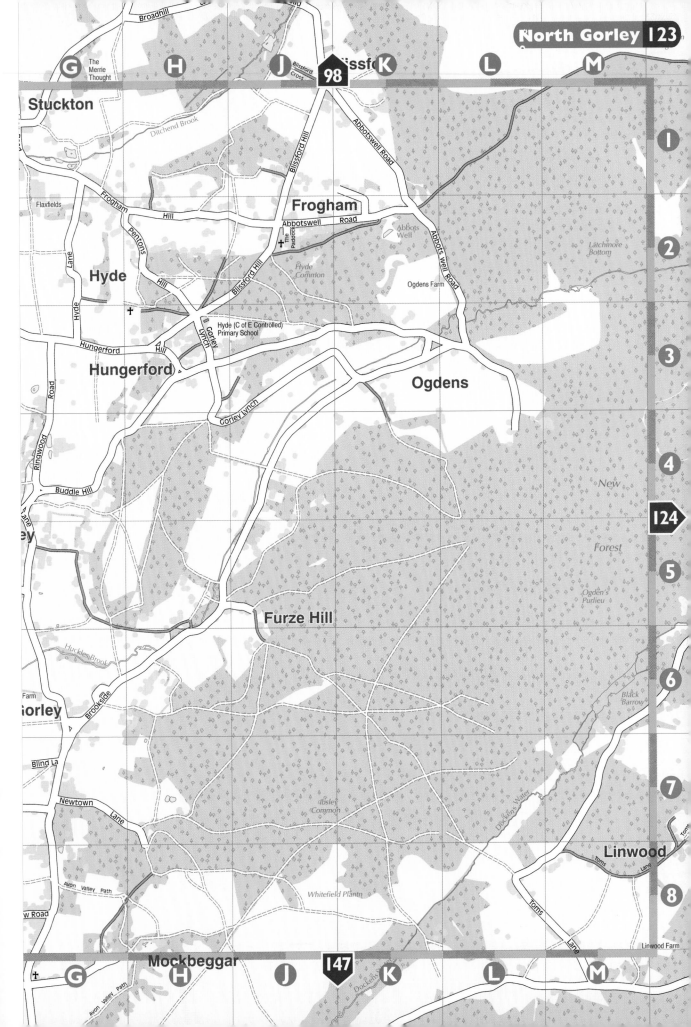

G H J **98** Bissford K L M

Broadhill

The Merrie Thought

Stuckton

Ditchend Brook

Flaxfields

Frogham Hill

Pentons Lane

Hyde

Hyde Hill

Hungerford

Hungerford Hill

Buddle Hill

Ringwood Road

Gorley

Farm

Gorley

Brookside

Huckles Brook

Blind Lane

Newtown Lane

Avon Valley Path

w Road

Blissford Hill

Blissford Cross

Frogham

Abbotswell Road

Abbotswell Road

The Paddock

Hyde Common

Bissford Hill

Gorley Lynch

Hyde (C of E Controlled) Primary School

Gorley Lynch

Furze Hill

Abbots Well

Abbots Well Road

Ogdens Farm

Ogdens

New Forest

Latchmore Bottom

Ogden's Purlieu

Black Barrow

Dockens Water

Ibsley Common

Whitefield Plantn

Linwood

Toms Lane

Toms Lane

Torre

Linwood Farm

Mockbeggar

G H J **147** K L M Dockens

I

2

3

4

124

5

6

7

8

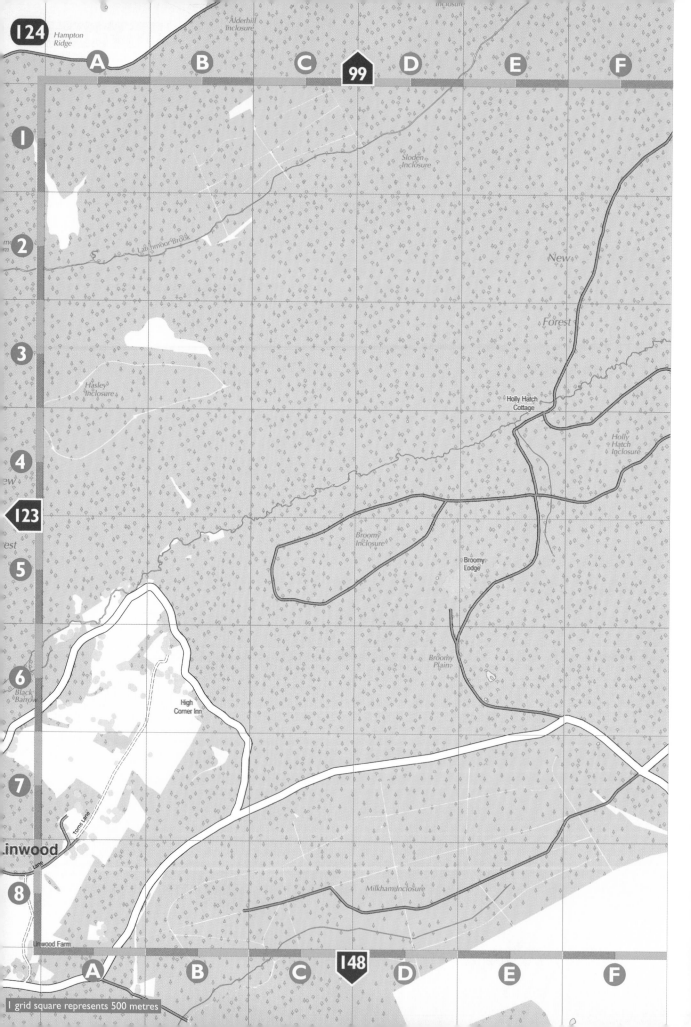

A   B   C   99   D   E   F

1

Alderhill
Inclosure

Sloden
Inclosure

New

2

Latchmoor Brook

Forest

3

Hasley
Inclosure

Holly Hatch
Cottage

Holly
Hatch
Inclosure

4

123

Broomy
Inclosure

Broomy
Lodge

5

6

Black
Barrow

High
Corner Inn

Broomy
Plain

7

Toms Lane

inwood

Lane

8

Milkham Inclosure

inwood Farm

A   B   C   148   D   E   F

1 grid square represents 500 metres

G   H   J   **100**   K   L   M

I

2

3

4

126

5

6

7

8

Fritham
Plain

North
Bentley
Inclosure

Janesmoor
Plain

The
Butt

South
Bentley
Inclosure

Anses
Wood

Cadman's
Pool

Ocknell
Inclosure

Ocknell
Plain

A31(T)

Slufters
Inclosure

Fritham Cross

A31(T)

Highland Water

Bratley Water

Bratley A

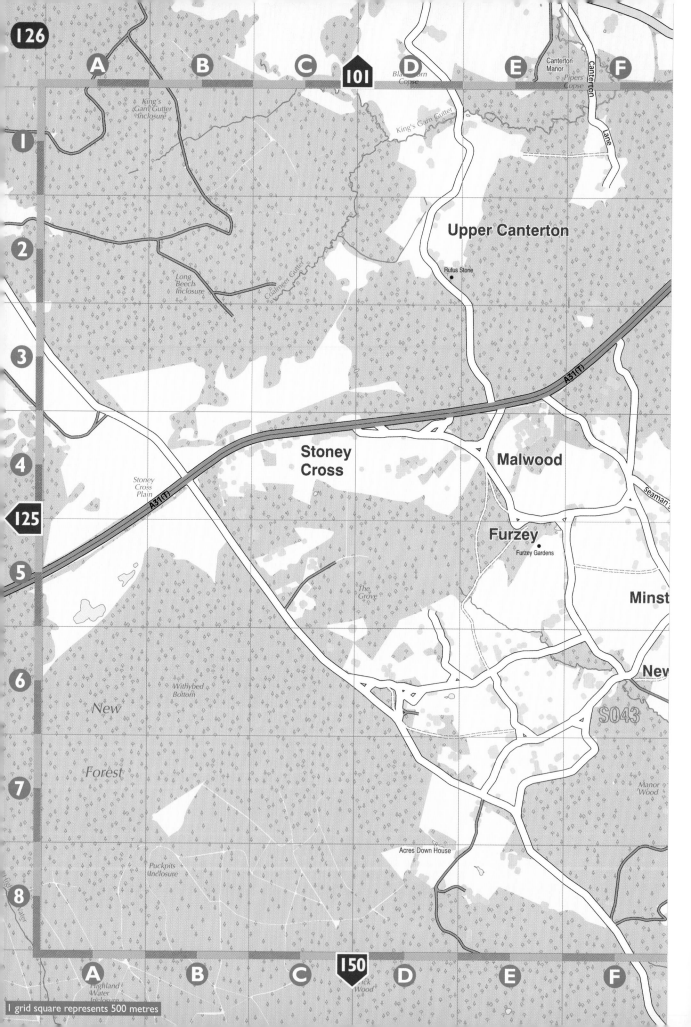

A B C **101** D E F

Canterton Manor

Pipers' Copse

Canterton Lane

Blackthorn Copse

1

King's Garn Gutter Inclosure

King's Garn Gutter

2

Long Beech Inclosure

Coalmeer Gutter

Upper Canterton

Rufus Stone

3

A31(T)

4

Stoney Cross

Malwood

Seaman

Stoney Cross Plain

A31(T)

Furzey

Furzey Gardens

Minst

5

The Grove

6

Withybed Bottom

New

Minst

New

S043

7

Forest

Manor Wood

Acres Down House

8

Puckpits Inclosure

Highland Water Inclosure

A B **150** C D E F

ck Wood

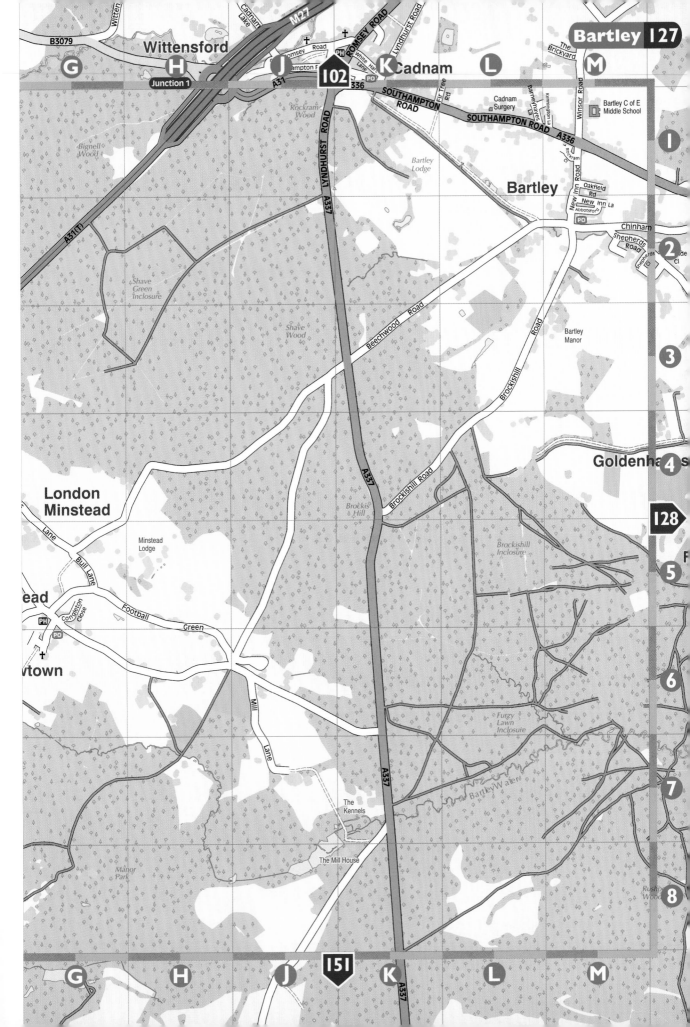

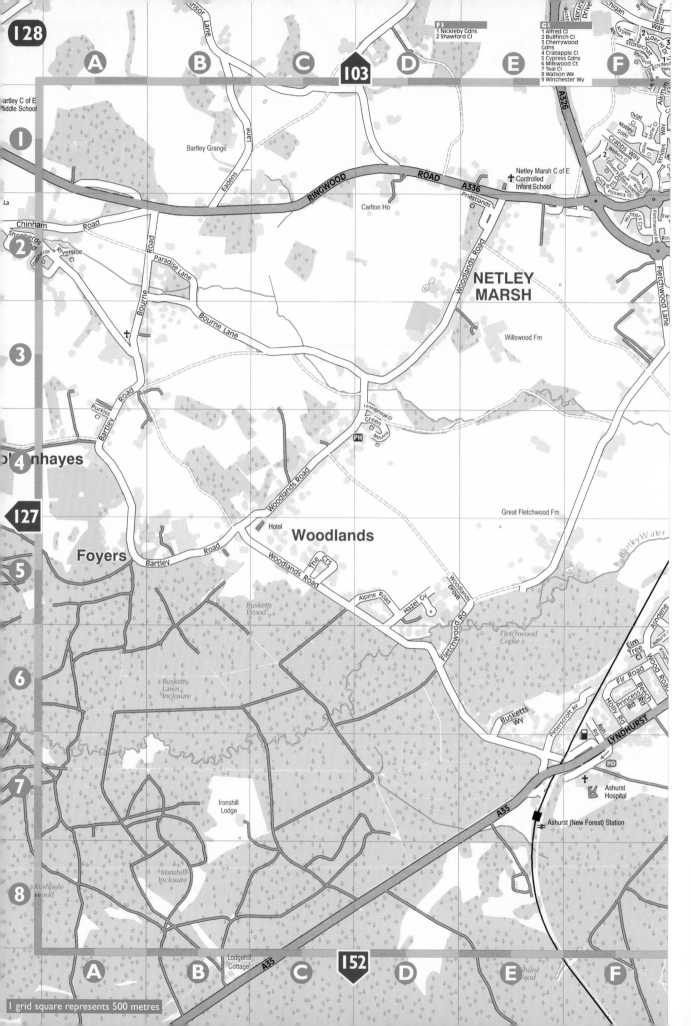

A   B   C   **103**   D   E   F

1

Bartley C of E Middle School

Bartley Grange

Eadens Lane

Windsor Lane

Netley Marsh C of E Controlled Infant School

RINGWOOD   ROAD   A336

Carlton Ho

Priestlands Cl

A326

Crabbs Way

Wellers Cl

Oviat Cl

2

La

Chinham   Road

Shepherds La

Riverside Cl

Paradise Lane

Bourne Road

NETLEY MARSH

Woodlands Road

Fletchwood Lane

3

Bourne Lane

Willswood Fm

Lanespridge Cl

Green Cl

Millview Cl

127

4

Purkiss Cl

Bartley Road

PH

Great Fletchwood Fm

olnhayes

5

Foyers

Bartley   Road

Hotel

Woodlands

Woodlands Road

The Crs

Alpine Road

Hazel Gv

Woodlands Drive

Fletchwood Rd

Fletchwood Copse

BartleyWater

Elm Tree Cl

Ashdene

6

Busketts Wood

Busketts Lawn Inclosure

Busketts Wy

Fir Road

Princess Rd

Beech Cl

Holly Rd

Wood Road

Peterscroft Av

Ash Rd

LYNDHURST

PO

7

Ironshill Lodge

Ashurst Hospital

A35

Ashurst (New Forest) Station

8

Rushpole Wood

Ironshill Inclosure

Lodgehill Cottage

A35

A   B   C   **152**   D   E   F

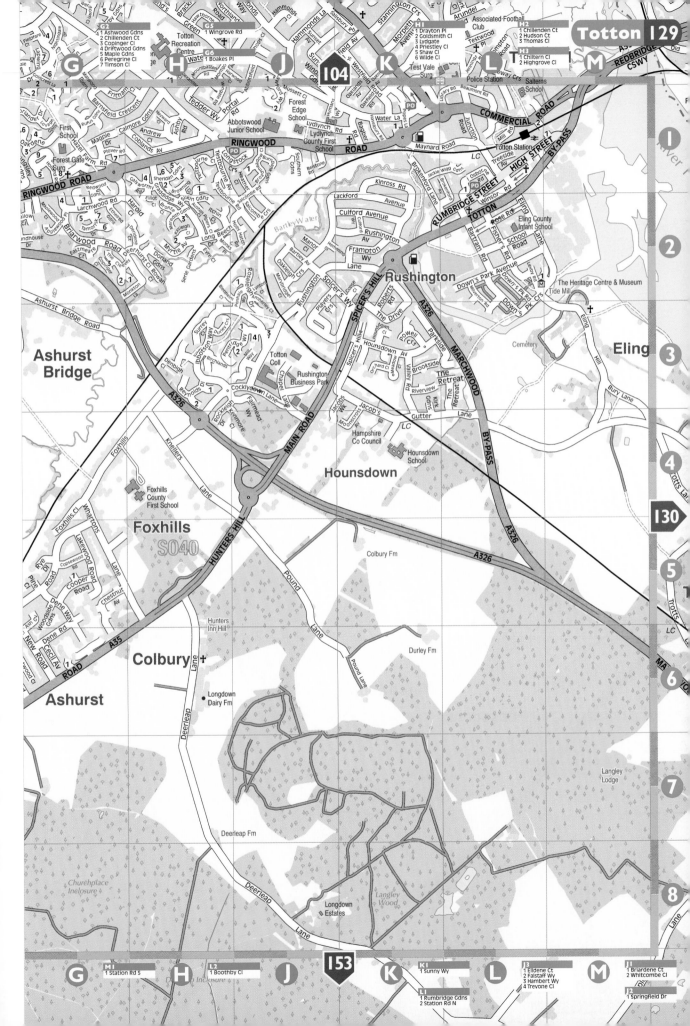

G2
1 Ashwood Gdns
2 Chillenden Ct
3 Copinger Cl
4 Driftwood Gdns
5 Maple Gdns
6 Peregrine Cl
7 Timson Cl

G5
1 Wingrove Rd

G6
1 Boakes Pl

H1
1 Drayton Pl
2 Goldsmith Cl
3 Lydgate
4 Priestley Cl
5 Shaw Cl
6 Wilde Cl

H2
1 Chillenden Ct
2 Hudson Ct
3 Thomas Cl

H3
1 Chiltern Cl
2 Highgrove Cl

G   H   J   **104**   K   L   M

Ashwood Gdns

Totton Recreation Centre

Abbotswood Junior School

Forest Edge School

RINGWOOD ROAD

Abbotswood Junior School

Lydlynch County First School

Test Vale Surg

COMMERCIAL ROAD

Police Station

Salterns School

Associated Football Club

BY-PASS

REDBRIDGE CSWY

Totton Station

HIGH STREET

Maynard Road

1

RINGWOOD ROAD

First School

Forest Gate

BartleyWater

Lackford Avenue

Culford Avenue

Rushington Avenue

Frampton Wy Lane

RUMBRIDGE STREET

TOTTON

Eling County Infant School

Rose Rd

The Heritage Centre & Museum Tide Mill

2

Rushington

A326

Manor

Down's Park Avenue

Down's Pk Crs

Cemetery

Eling

Eling

3

Ashurst Bridge Road

A326

Totton Coll

Rushington Business Park

Spicer's Wy

The Drive

Hounsdown Av

Powell Crs

Parkside

MARCHWOOD

The Retreat

Bury Lane

Ashurst Bridge

4

Foxhills

Reynolds

Cocklydown Lane

Chapel Lane

MAIN ROAD

Jacob's Wk

Jacob's Gutter Lane

Hampshire Co Council

Hounsdown School

BY-PASS

A326

130

Foxhills County First School

Foxhills

S040

HUNTERS HILL

Hounsdown

Colbury Fm

A326

5

Rye Dl

Lakewood Road

Cooper Road

Chestnut Av

Dene Way

Dene Rd

A35

Colbury

Hunters Inn Hill

POUND LANE

Durley Fm

MA

6

New Road

CECIL Av

ROAD

Ashurst

Deerleap Lane

Longdown Dairy Fm

Langley Lodge

7

Churchplace Inclosure

Deerleap Fm

Deerleap Lane

Longdown Estates

Langley Wood

Langley Lodge

8

G1
1 Station Rd S

L2
1 Boothby Cl

K1
1 Sunny Wy

L1
1 Rumbridge Gdns
2 Station Rd N

J3
1 Elldene Ct
2 Falstaff Wy
3 Hambert Wy
4 Trevone Cl

M1
1 Briardene Ct
2 Whitcombe Cl

M2
1 Springfield Dr

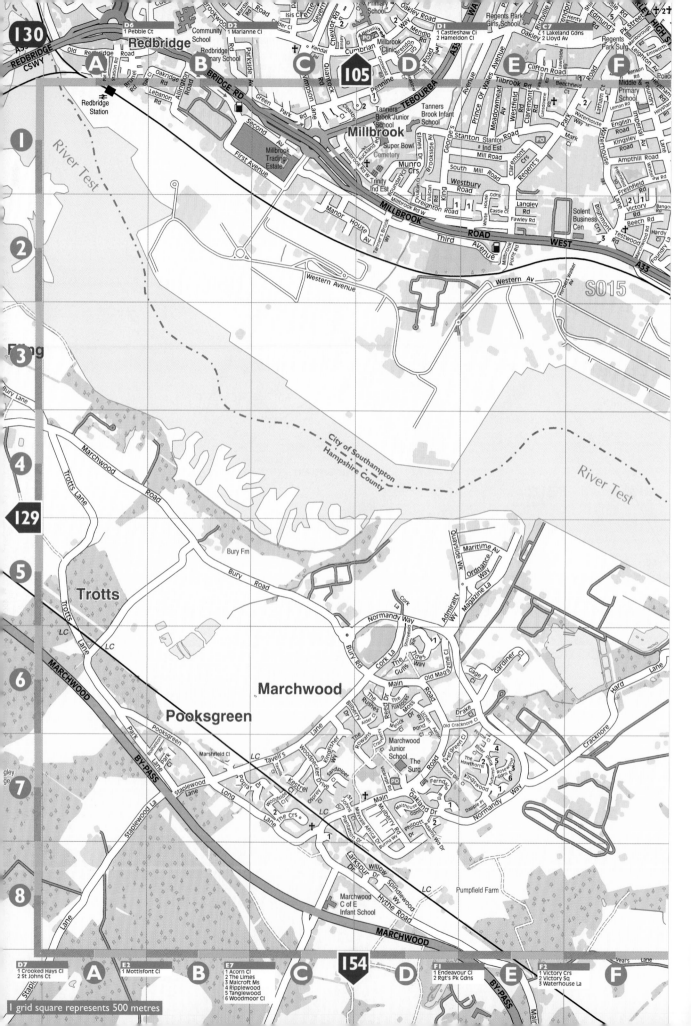

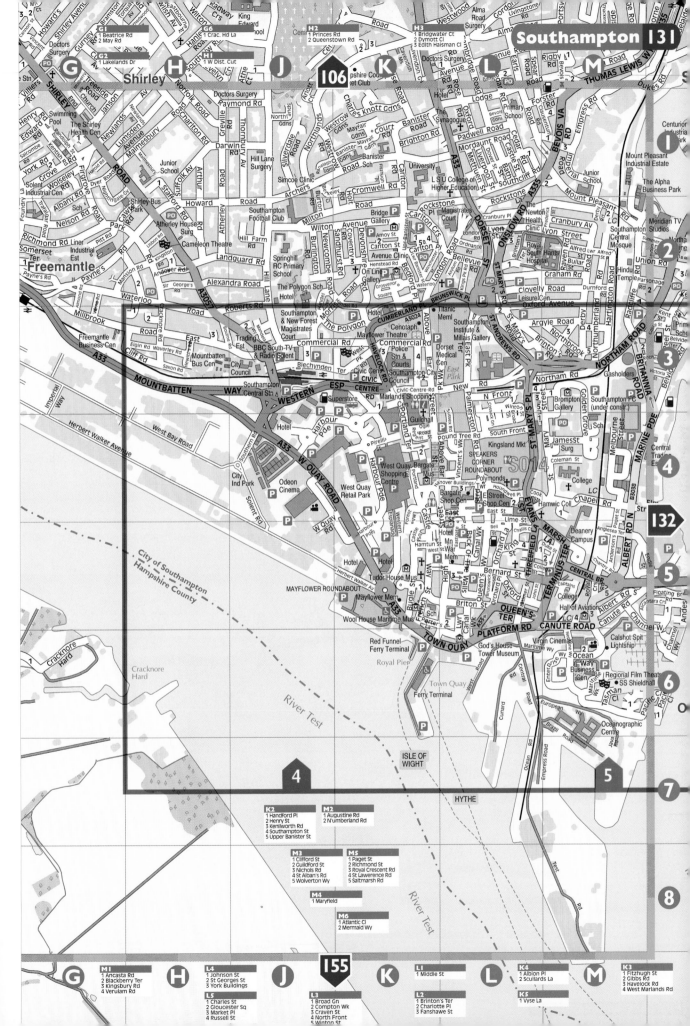

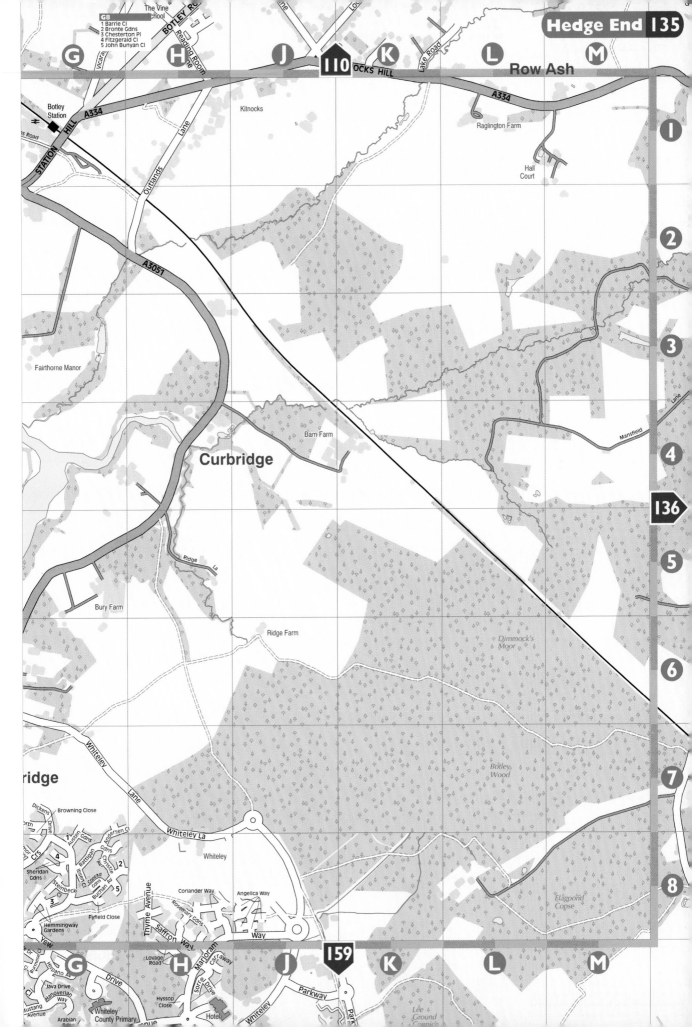

Row Ash

G8
1 Barrie Cl
2 Bronte Gdns
3 Chesterton Pl
4 Fitzgerald Cl
5 John Bunyan Cl

G **H** **J** 110 OCKS HILL **K** **L** **M**

A334

Kitnocks

Raglington Farm

Botley Station

A334

Hall Court

I

STATION HILL

Outlands Lane

Reading Room

Vicarage

A3051

2

Fairthorne Manor

3

Lane

Mansfield

Curbridge

Barn Farm

4

136

Ridge La

5

Bury Farm

Ridge Farm

Dimmock's Moor

6

Whiteley Lane

Botley Wood

7

ridge

Dickens Drive

Browning Close

Whiteley La

Whiteley

Austen Gdns

Andersen Cl

Christie Gdns

Rattigan Gdns

Ibsen Cl

Buchan Av

Conrad Gdns

Coriander Way

Angelica Way

Flagpond Copse

8

Sheridan Gdns

Steinbeck Cl

Fyfield Close

Thyme Avenue

Rosemary Gdns

Saffron Way

Way

Hemmingway Gardens

Lovage Road

Marjoram

Caraway

G **H** Sorrel Drive **J** 159 **K** **L** **M**

Java Drive

Hispano Av

Hanoverian Way

Mustang Avenue

Arabian

Drive

Whiteley County Primary

Hyssop Close

Parkway

Whiteley Parkway

Hotel

Lee Ground Copse

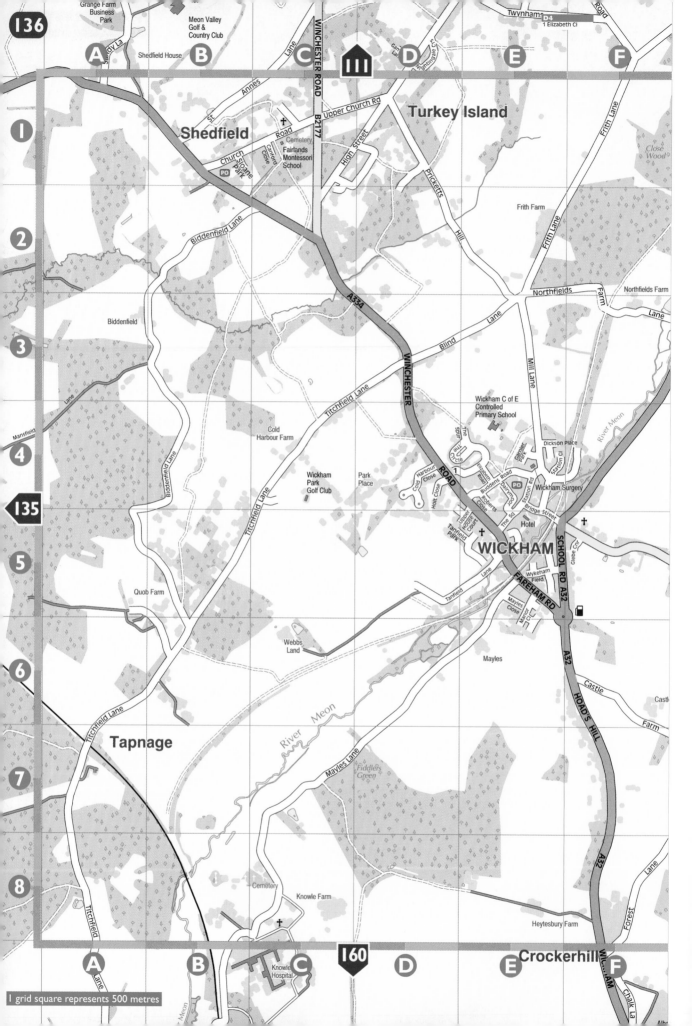

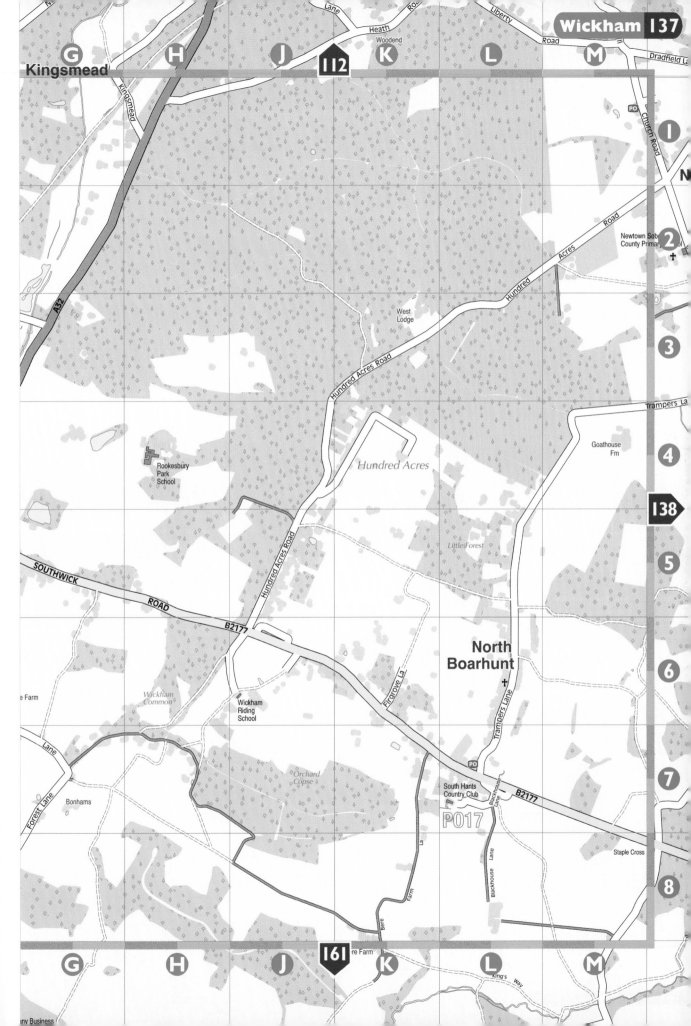

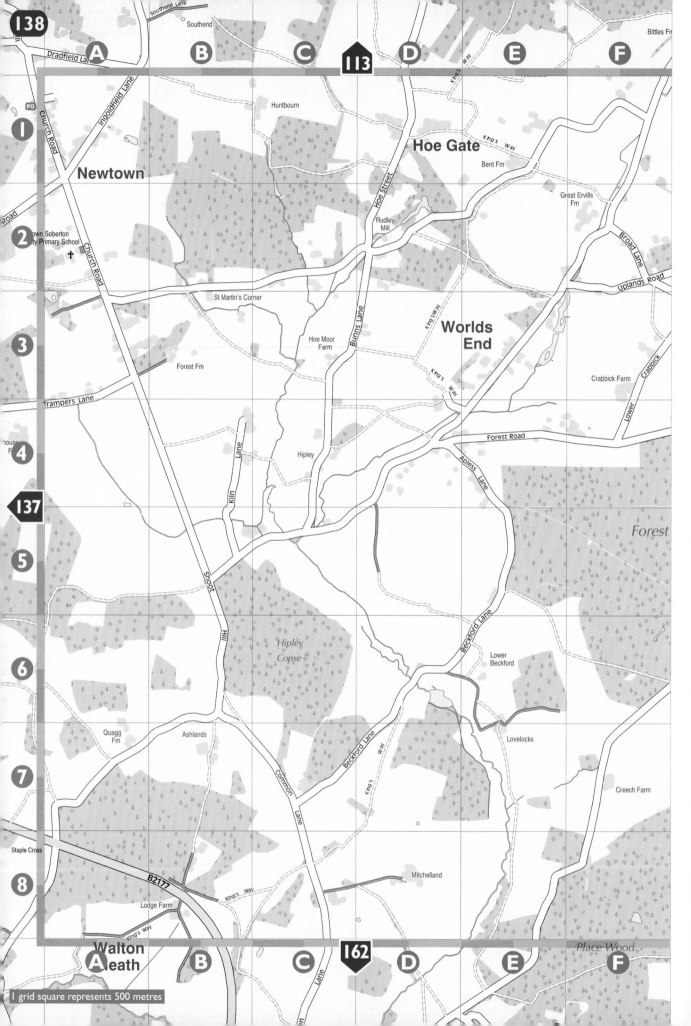

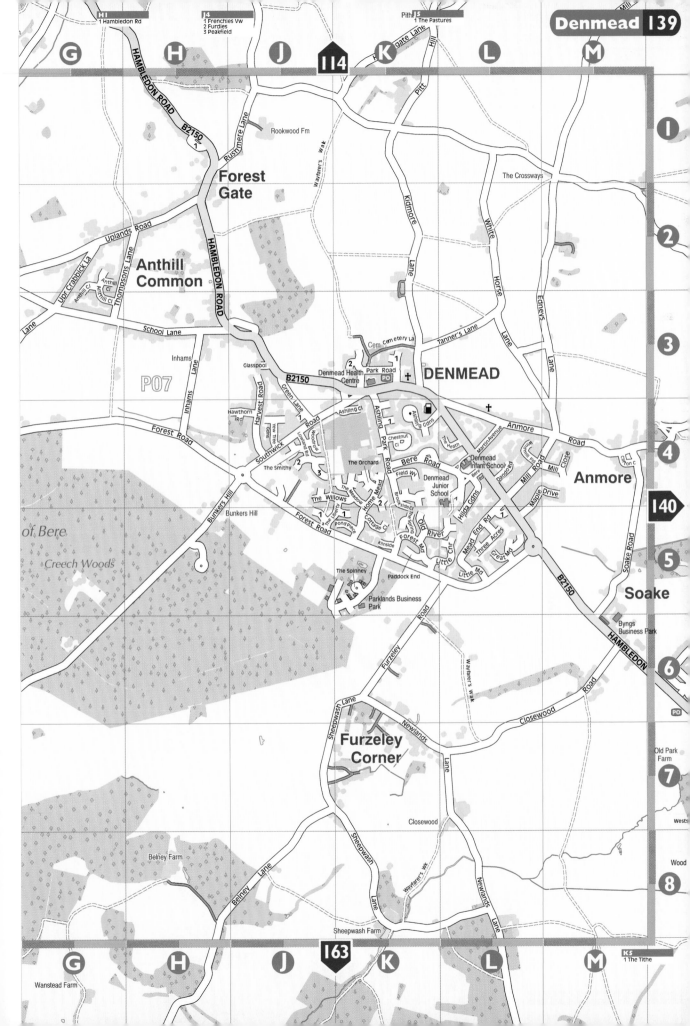

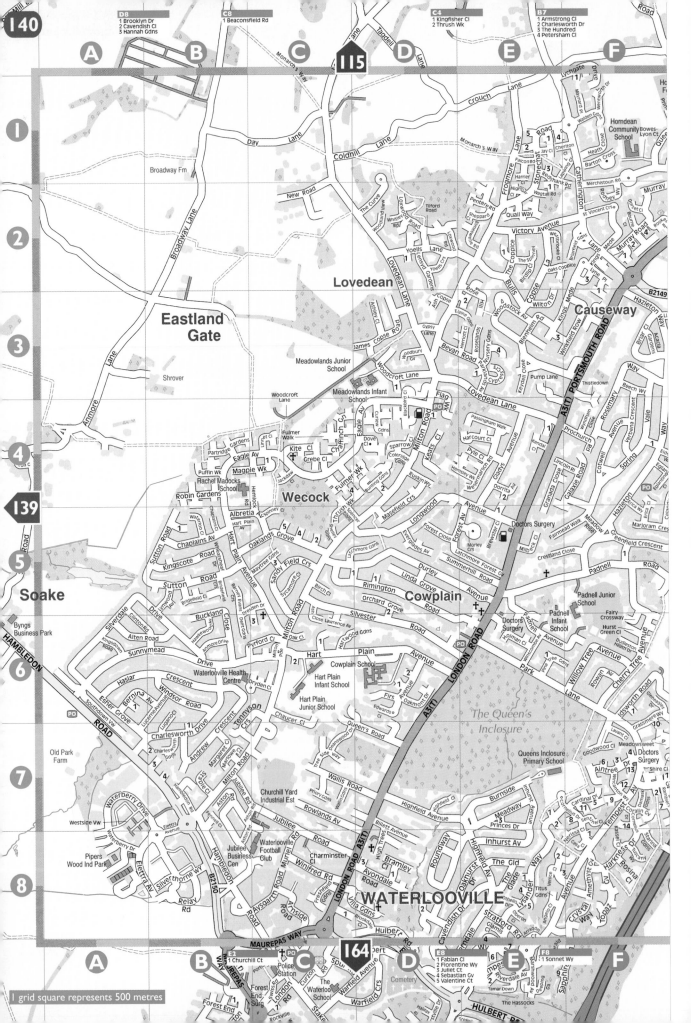

G H J K L M

Horsley Farm

Locksash Lane

We **118** arden

Nore Down Wy

B2146

Locksash Lane

I

Nore Down

Oldhouse Lane

2

Lodge Fm

3

Lodge Lane

Watergate

4

Watergate Hanger

Broadreed Fm

B2146

5

Lumley Seat

Monarch's Way

Monarch's Way

Cooks Lane

6

Monarch's Wy

Woodlands

Monarch's Wy

Wal

Woodlands Cotts

B2146

Stanstead House

7

B2146

Newbarn Lane

8

Park Lane

Sindle's Fm

Monument La

B2146

Grevitts Copse

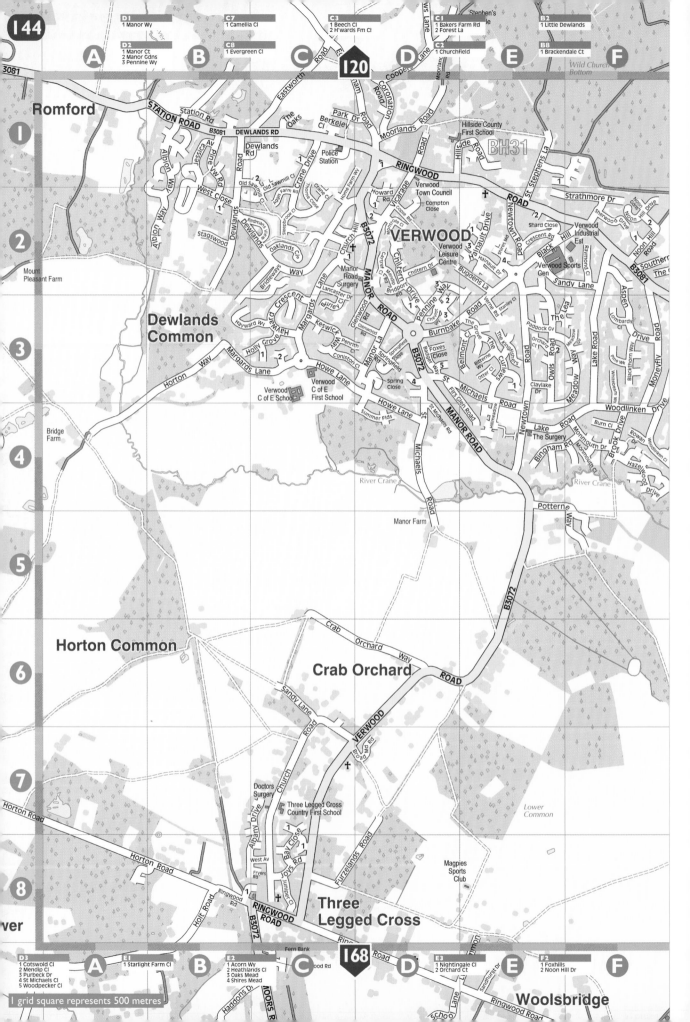

G H J 121 K L M

Heath

Plumley
Wood

Plumley Farm

Harefield
Plantation

I

1 Lavender Cl

Shepherds   Lane

Home Farm

2

Chestnut

hay Rd

Nea Drive

cha

3

The

Chase

Hunters
Cl

Nea Drive

Sor

1

Barberry

Fairwood Rd

Hunters
Cl

The Forestside

RINGWOOD

Ringwood Forest

4

Magnolia

Laburnum
Cl

Acacia Cl

Rosebery
Close

ROAD

Woodlinken
Wy

Wisteria Dr Av

Black

Moor Rd

Cemetery

Parsland
Cl

Ebblake

146

Brunel Cl

Forest Cl

Bessemer
Close

Ebblake Industrial
Est

B3081

5

6

Hampshire County

Dorset County

7

Moors Valley
Country Park

VERWOOD ROAD B3081

Baker's
Hanging

8

Moors River

Watch
Wood

Ashley Heath
Industrial Est

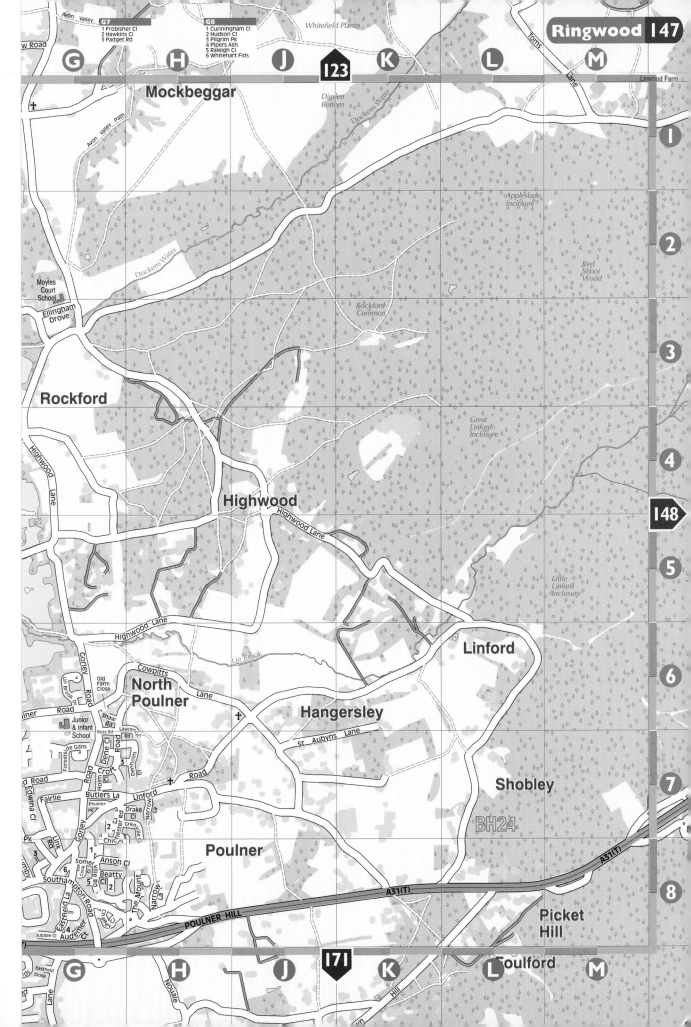

G7
1 Frobisher Cl
2 Hawkins Cl
3 Padget Rd

G8
1 Cunningham Cl
2 Hudson Cl
3 Pilgrim Pk
4 Pipers Ash
5 Raleigh Cl
6 Whitehart Flds

G H J K L M

123

Linwood Farm

Mockbeggar

Whitefield Plantn

Digden
Bottom

Dockens Water

Appleslade
Inclosure

Avon Valley Path

Dockens Water

Red
Shoot
Wood

Moyles
Court
School

Ellingham
Drove

Rockford
Common

Rockford

Great
Linford
Inclosure

148

Highwood

Highwood Lane

Little
Linford
Inclosure

Highwood Lane

Linford

Lin Brook

Cowpitts

North
Poulner

Corley Road

Old Farm
Close

Lin Brook Dr

Lane

Hangersley

Shaw Rd

Lawrence Rd

Ross Rd

St Aubyns Lane

Poulner Road

Junior
& Infant
School

Forest side Gdns

Dene Cl

Croft

Holm

Denholm

Road

Road

Shobley

BH24

Butlers La

Linford

Narrow La

Road

Edwina Cl

Fairlie

Poulner
Pk

Drake
Cl

Grenville Cl

Corley

Link Rd

Chester Rd

Chl Cl

Poulner

Pk

Someville Rd

Anson Cl

Beatty

A31(T)

Southampton Road

The Mount

Narrow La

Eastfield La

Audemer Ct

Jubilee Cl

POULNER HILL

A31(T)

Picket
Hill

Eastfield
Close

Lane

Noule

Hill

Foulford

G H J K L M

171

1
2
3
4
5
6
7
8

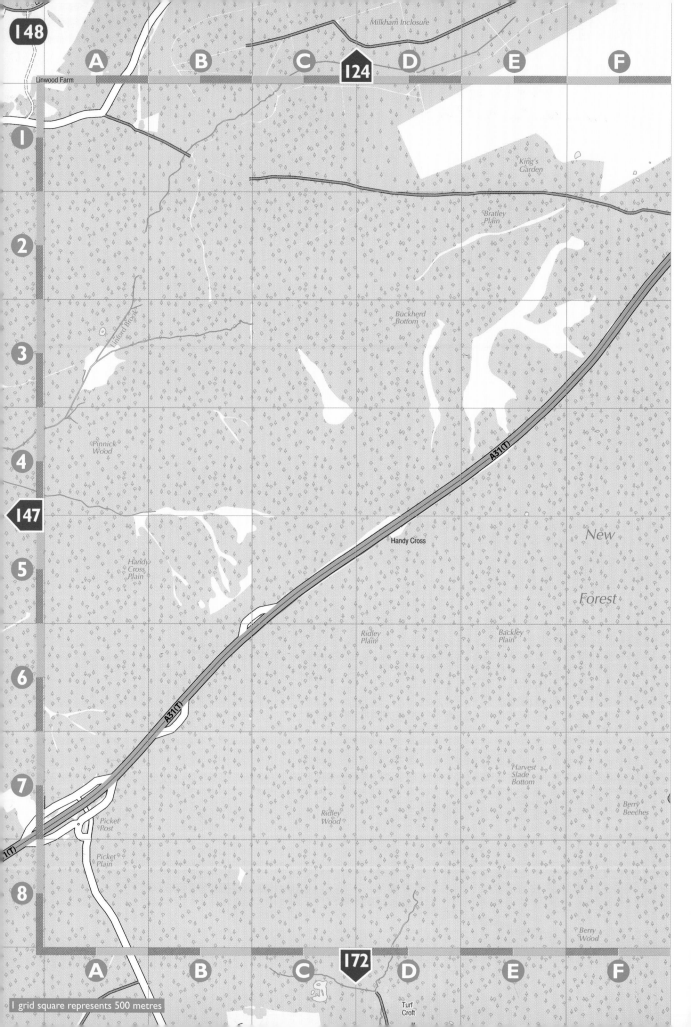

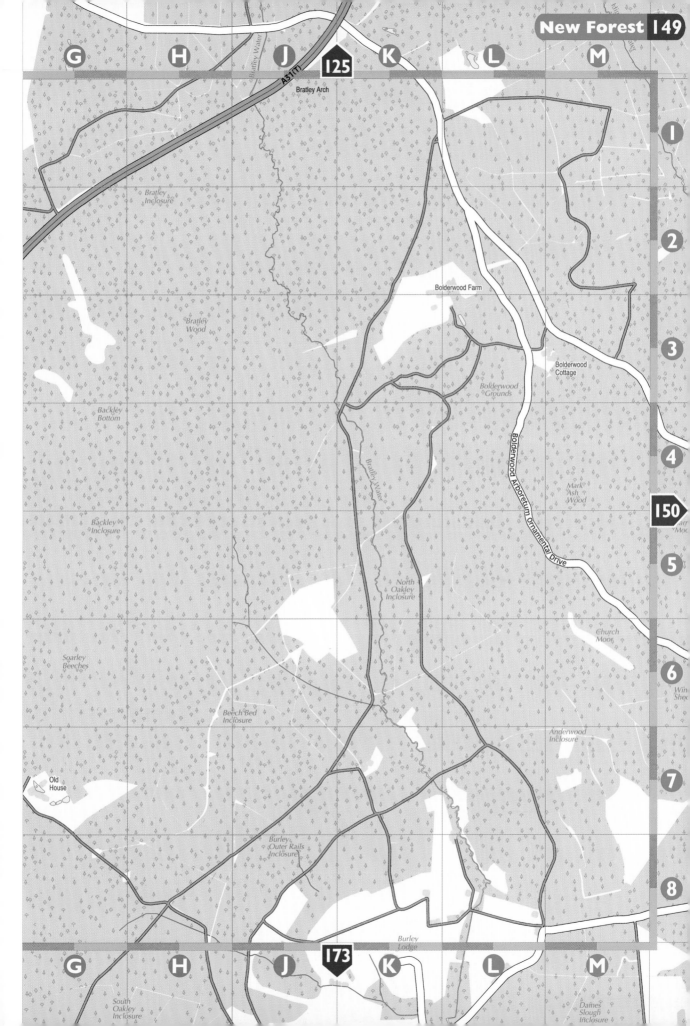

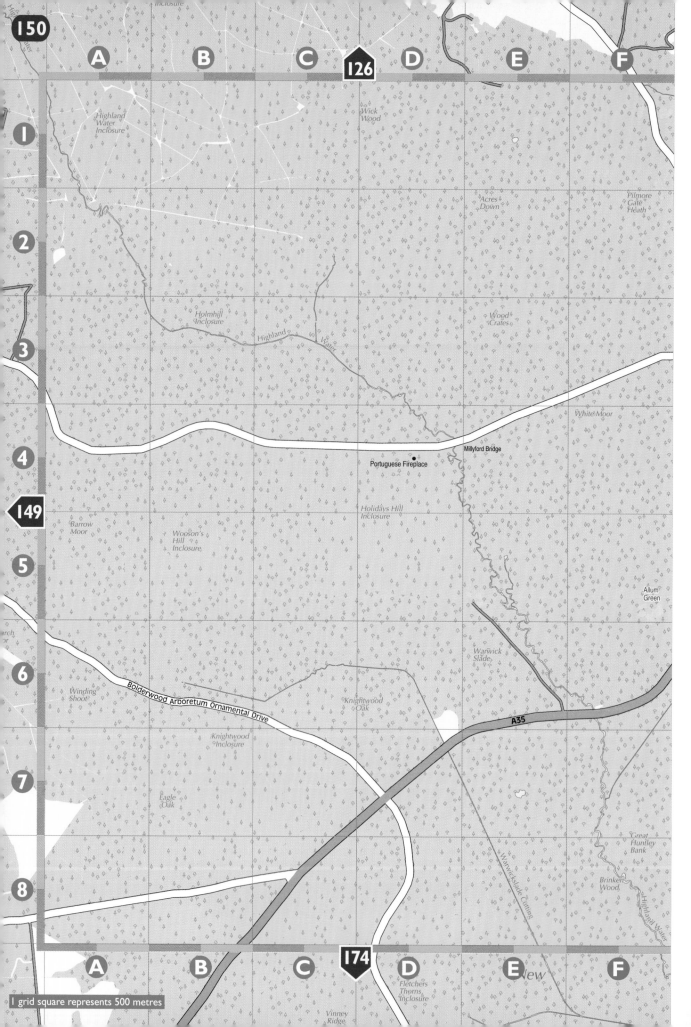

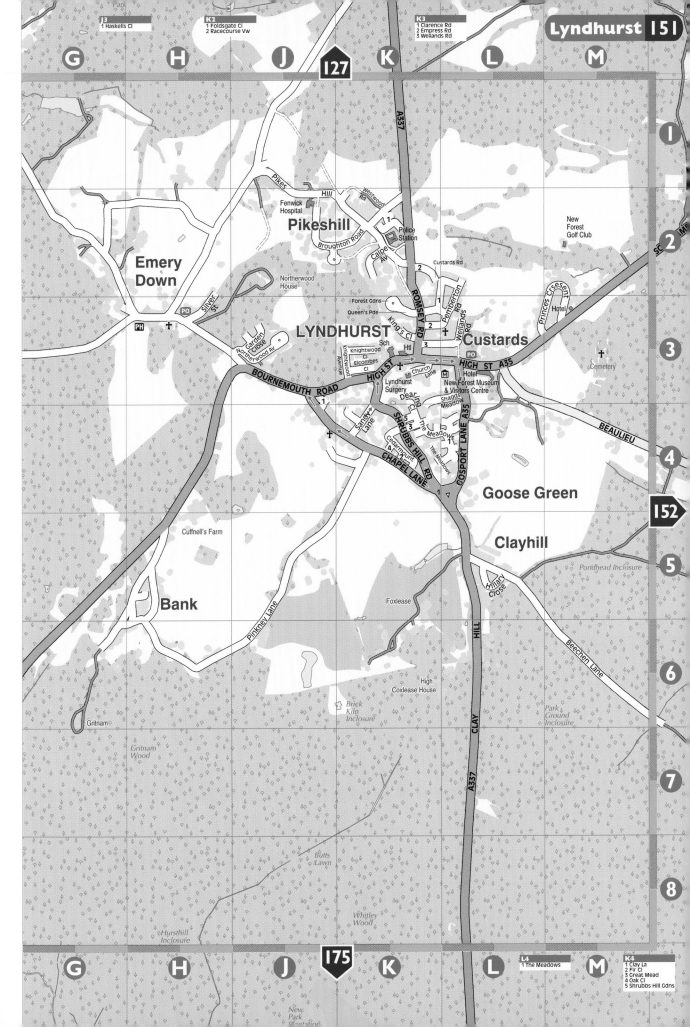

J3
1 Haskells Cl

K2
1 Foldsgate Cl
2 Racecourse Vw

K3
1 Clarence Rd
2 Empress Rd
3 Wellands Rd

G   H   J   **127**   K   L   M

I
2
3
4
152
5
6
7
8

SC IMP

Emery
Down

Pikeshill

Fenwick
Hospital

Pikes Hill

Westwood Rd

Police
Station

Calpe Av

Northerwood
House

New
Forest
Golf Club

Custards Rd

Silver St.

PO

PH

Garden
Close

Northerwood Av.

LYNDHURST

Forest Gdns

Queen's Pde

King's Cl

ROMSEY RD

Pemberton Rd

Wellands Rd

Princes Cresent

Hotel

Custards

Cemetery

Knightwood
Avenue

Knightwood
Cl
Elcombes
Cl

Sch

Htl

HIGH ST

Church
Lane

HIGH ST A35

Hotel

New Forest Museum
& Visitors Centre

BEAULIEU

BOURNEMOUTH ROAD

Lyndhurst
Surgery

Dear Cl

Cedarmount

SHRUBBS HILL RD

Sandy Lane

CHAPEL LANE

Shaggs
Meadow

The Meadows

GOSPORT LANE A35

Goose Green

Clayhill

Cuffnell's Farm

Pondhead Inclosure

Hillary
Close

Bank

Pinkney Lane

Foxlease

CLAY HILL

Beechen Lane

High
Coxlease House

Park
Ground
Inclosure

Gritnam

Brick
Kiln
Inclosure

Gritnam
Wood

A337

Butts
Lawn

Whitley
Wood

Hurshill
Inclosure

New
Park
Plantation

G   H   J   **175**   K   L   M

L4
1 The Meadows

K4
1 Clay La
2 Fir Cl
3 Great Mead
4 Oak Cl
5 Shrubbs Hill Gdns

A   B   C   128   D   E   F

I

2

3

4

151

5

6

7

8

A   B   C   176   D   E   F

Lodgehill
Cottage

A35

Ashurst
Wood

SOUTHAMPTON   ROAD

Mallard
Wood

Ashurst Lodge

Dunces Arch

White
Moor

Beaulieu River

Matley
Wood

BEAULIEU

ROAD

Matley
Heath

B3056

Matley
Passage

Hotel

Little
Holmhill
Inclosure

Denny
Inclosure

Park Hill

Denny
Wood

Denny
Lodge

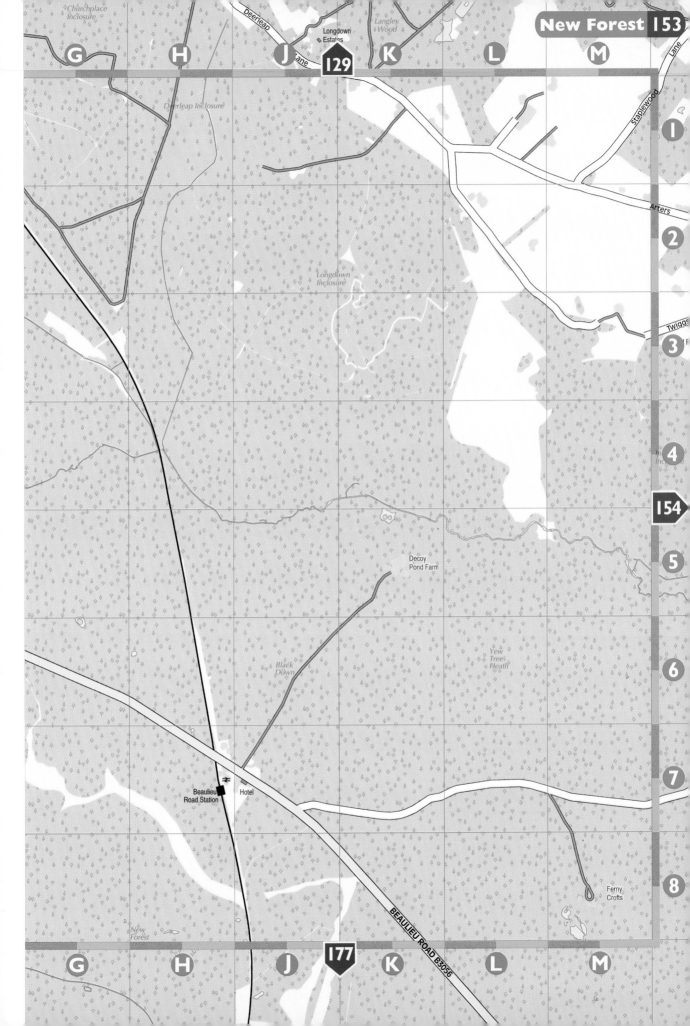

A   B   C   **130** MARCHWOOD   D   E   F

Marchwood
C of E
Infant School

Pumpfield Farm

Veal's Lane

Marchwood
Priory
Hospital

1

Taplewood Lane

Arters   Lawn

Twiggs Lane

BY-PASS

Main   Road

A326

Church Farm Close

2

City
Con

Church Farm

†

Lane   End

Twiggs   Lane

Beaulieu Road

Birchlands Farm

Carter's Lane

3

Foxhill Farm

The Old
Manor

4

Ipley
Inclosure

Marchwood
Inclosure

Applemore

Manor Road

HYTHE   BY-PASS

A326

5

Sizer Way

Ipley
Manor

6

7

8

Beaulieu River

The
Noads

ofts

King's
Hat
Inclosure

A   B   C   **178** ▼   D   E   F

Crabhat
Inclosure

1 grid square represents 500 metres

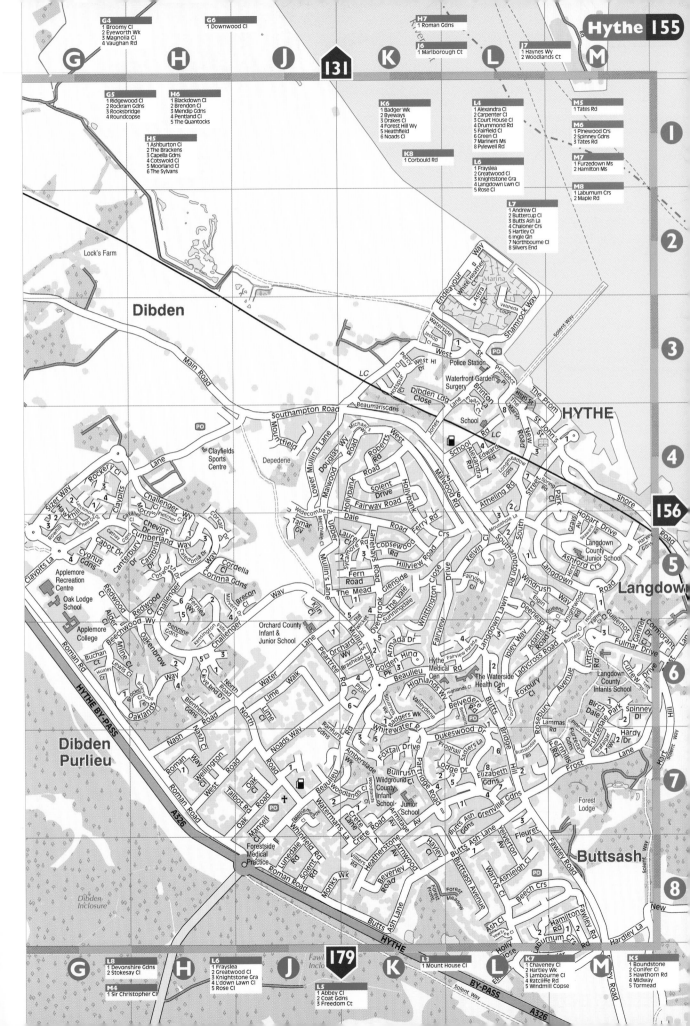

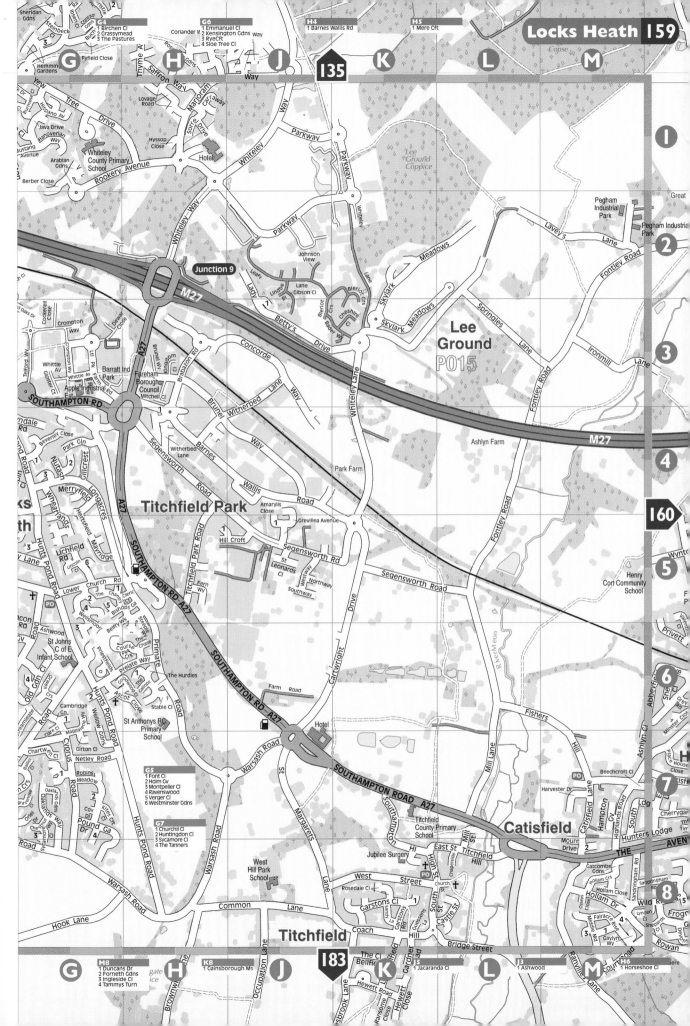

A B C D E F

B8
1 Cherry Tree Av
2 Hayling Cl
3 Sibland Cl
4 Thorney Cl
5 Tortworth Cl

B6
1 Badger Cl
2 Barfleur Cl
3 Pelican Cl
4 Shannon Cl
5 Triumph Cl

B5
1 Beaumont Cl

B3
1 Deer Leap

A7
1 Friars Pond Rd

Knowle Farm

A8
1 Cromhall Cl
2 Pilning Cl
3 Sandisplatt
4 Sharpness Cl
5 Thornbury Cl

B7
1 Appleton Rd
2 Wood Barn Rd

B4
1 Beaumont Ri

Heytesbury Farm

Crockerhill

C5
1 Craven Ct
2 Dundee Cl
3 Mary Rose Cl

Charity Farm   Albany

Knowle Hospital

Great Funtley Farm

Pegham Industrial Park

River Meon

Dean Farm

Lakeside

Funtley

Kneller Court

Dean Farm Estate

Junction 10

M27

WICKHAM ROAD

A32

Pook Lane

159

Kingston Gdns
Lechlade Gdns
Watton Ct
Marlow Gdns
Red Barn Lane

The Copse
The Old
Winnington

Orchard Lea Junior & Infant Schools

West Downs Close

Greenwood Cl

Potters Avenue

Cornfield

Hill Park

Junior School

Fareham Park Infant School

Highlands Road

Frosthole

Hill Park Clinic

Inverness

Highlands Medical Centre

Gudge Heath Surgery

Uplands County Primary School

Mallory Crs

Fareham Leisure Centre

Harrison Primary Sc

Homewood Chiropractic Health Centre

Cort Community School

Privett Road

Woodvale

Oak Road

Abbey Road

Priory Rd

Blackbrook Road

Blackbrook Business Park

Fernham Rd

Heathfield 6

Meadowbank Road

Southmead Rd

Julie Av   Blackbrook Pk Av

Brookmeadow

FAREHAM

Fareham Station

The Practice Doctors Surgery

Magistrates Court

West End

Heathfield School

Ranvilles Junior & Infant School

St Francis School

Fareham College

St Judes Catholic Primary Sch

Wallisdean County Infant School

Wallisdean County Junior School

The Avenue   A27

WESTERN WAY

The Boatyard Industrial Est

Neville Lovett Community School

184

A B C D E F

C6
1 Marigold Cl

C8
1 Whitebeam Cl

D6
1 Lawrence Rd
2 Rowland Rd

E6
1 Tennyson Gdns

E7
1 The Gillies
2 Maytree Rd

E8
1 Alexander Gv

Redlands County

E
1 Hanover Gdns
2 The Potteries
3 Swallow Wd

Elms

1 grid square represents 500 metres

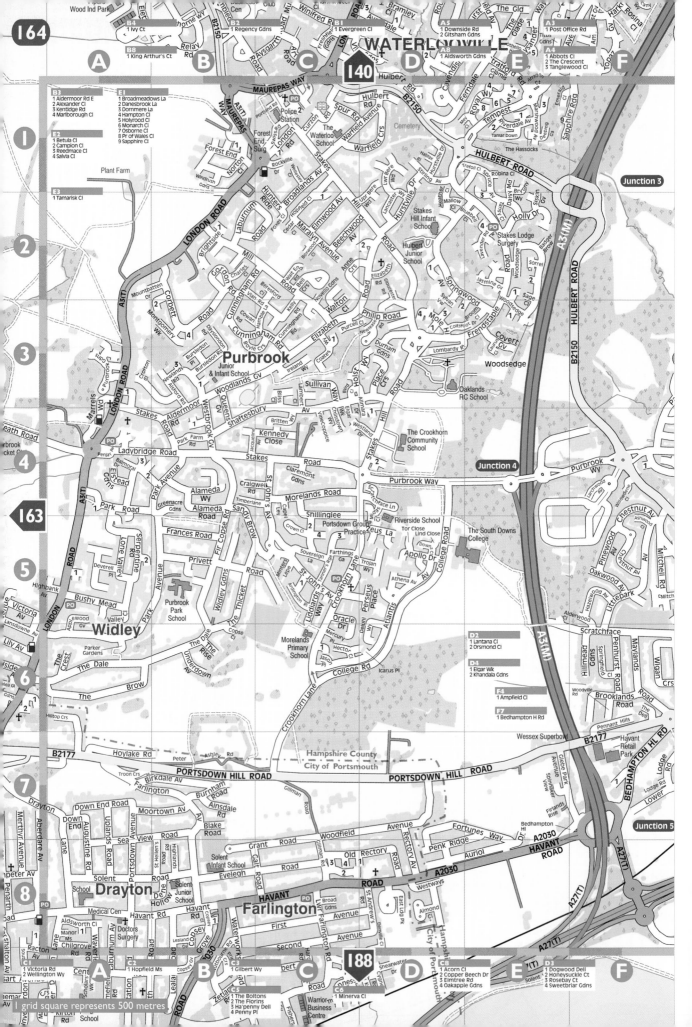

G   H   J   **143**   K   L   M

B2146

Park Lane

Sindle's Fm

Monument   La

I   The

B2146

Staines   2

B2147   Racton
Park Fm

HARES

Aldsworth

Ractonpark
Wood

Common Road   3

Common Road

B2147

Marlpit Lane

Hambrook Business
Cen   4

Primary School   **FOXBURY**   **LANE**

Woodmancote Lane

Cheesemans

Woodmancote

Marlpit Lane   W Ashling Rd   La

stbourne   Woodmancote Lane   Woodmancote Lane   Hambrook Hl (North)   5

Cemetery   Cemetery Lane   Duffield Lane   South La   Nightingale Lane

Surg   Walnut
Tree
Dr   Devils Copse

A27(T)   A27(T)

Farm   Lane   Stein Rd   Lane

A27(T)   Hambrook Hl (South)   Broad Road   6

Hither
Gn   Scant   Road   We

South   Fraser
Gdns   PO   Conifer
Dr

Lauder
Cl   Hambrook   The Avenue

Haslemere
Road   Breach Avenue   **Hambrook**

Bourne
Vw Cl   East
Fld
Cl   Yeomans Fld   7

The Bourne Community
College   Clovelly Road   Kelsey Av   Priors Leaze Lane

Mountwood
Road   Glenwood
Rd   Priors Leaze   Oak Tree
Farm

Park Road   Smallcutts Av   Funtston   Priors Leaze Lane

Breach   Hartland
Ct   PO   Priors
Cl

St John's Rd   Manor Road   Cooks   Lane   Inlands   Road   LC

LC   Manor
Gdns   Manor
Way   Hurstwood Av

Tuppenny Lane   LC   Guildford   Nutbourne
Station   LC   8

First Av   Southbourne Station

The Drive   Lodgebury
Close   Southbourne County
Junior & Infant School   Flatt
Rd

Alfrey
Cl   Garsons Road   Longlands
Road   New Rd   Goodwood
Court   Pottery
La   Flatt
Rd   Flatt
Rd

MAIN ROAD   Mosdell
Rd   **Southbourne**

A259   The
Crescent   Surgery   MAIN RD   PO   A259   A259

Ham
La   Prinsted Lane   Frarydene   Church Rd   School   Farm

G Prinsted   **H**   **J**   **191**   **K** Nutbourne   **L**   **M**

Maybush Drive

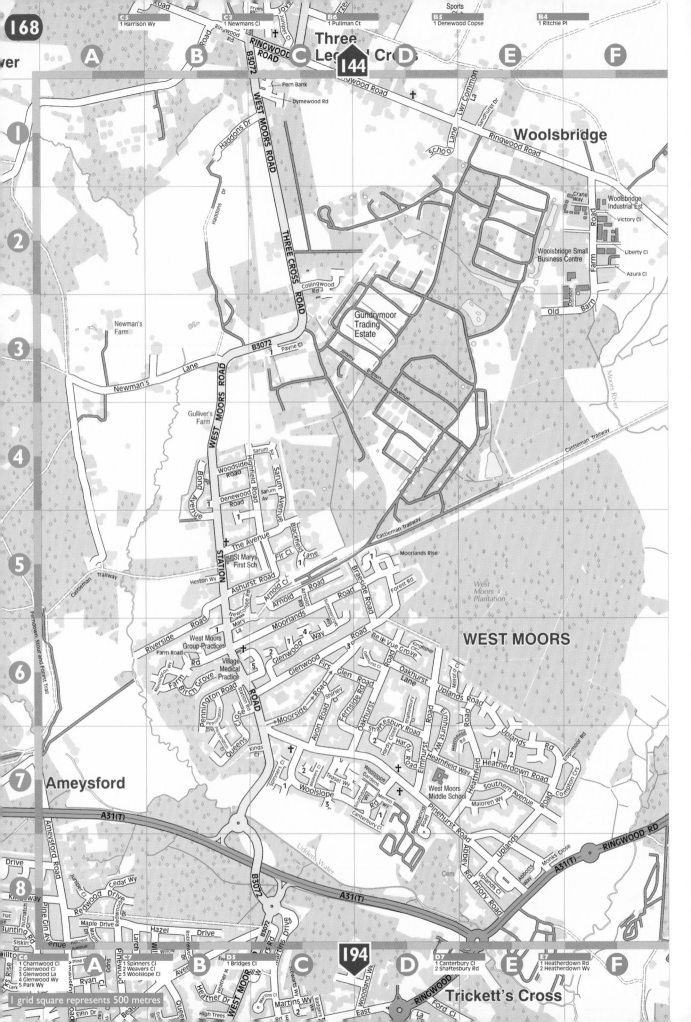

A B C D E F

Sports Club

RINGWOOD ROAD

Three Legged Cr

144

Fryers Rd
Ringwood Rd
Juniper Cl
Joys Rd
Hazel

B3072

Fern Bank
Dymewood Rd

Ringwood Road

Lwr Common La
Sandhurst Dr
School Lane

Woolsbridge

1

Haddons Dr

WEST MOORS ROAD

Ringwood Road

Crane Way

Woolsbridge Industrial Est

Victory Cl

2

Newman's Farm

THREE CROSS ROAD

Collingwood Rd

Woolsbridge Small Business Centre

Liberty Cl

Azura Cl

Old Barn

Condor

Farm Road

3

Newman's Lane

B3072

Payne Cl

Gundrymoor Trading Estate

Jimmy Brown Avenue

Moors River

Gulliver's Farm

Castleman Trailway

4

WEST MOORS ROAD

Bond Avenue

Woodside Road

Highfield Road

Sarum Av

Sarum Avenue

Sarum Av

Denewood Road

Castleman Trailway

Castleman Trailway

5

Castleman Trailway

The Avenue

St Marys First Sch

Heston Wy

Blackfield Lane

Fir Cl

Moorlands Rise

West Moors Plantation

STATION

Ashurst Road

Newcombe Rd

Arnold Cl

Arnold Road

Arnold Road

Braeside Road

Forest Rd

WEST MOORS

6

Riverside Road

West Moors Group Practices

Farm Road

Mary La

Moorlands Way

Glenwood

Glenwood

Glenwood Firs

Glen Road

Belle Vue Grove

Kingfisher Cl

Oakhurst Lane

Uplands Road

Mannington Wy

Farm Rd

Birch Grove

Village Medical Practice

Station Road

Shirley Road

Fernside Rd

Oakhurst Rd

Oakhurst Rd

Elmhurst Rd

Uplands Rd

Edgemoor Rd

Pennington Road

Pennington Cres

Moorside Road

Avon Road

Shaftesbury Road

Shaftesbury

Hardy Close

Elmhurst Wy

Heathfield Rd

Heatherdown Road

Compton Crs

7

Ameysford

Queens Close

Kings Close

Spinners Cl

Weavers Cl

Teasel Wy

Woolslope Gardens

Hardy Road

Heathfield Way

1

2

Uplands Rd

Woolslope

Merino Wy

West Moors Middle School

Southern Avenue

Maloren Wy

Canterbury Cl

Pinehurst Road

Beechwood Road

Abbey Rd

Uplands

Monks Close

RINGWOOD RD

A31(T)

A31(T)

Ameysford Road

B3072

Udden's Water

Priory Road

Uplands Cl

Abbotts Way

A31(T)

8

Drive

Redwood Drive

Cedar Wy

Juniper Cl

Kingsway

Pine Gln Avenue

Maple Drive

Hillcrest Avenue

Hazel Drive

Willow

Cem

B3072

A31(T)

Trickett's Cross

A B C D E F

C6
1 Charnwood Cl
2 Glenwood Cl
3 Glenwood La
4 Glenwood Wy
5 Park Wy
C7
1 Spinners Cl
2 Weavers Cl
3 Woolslope Cl
D5
1 Bridges Cl
D7
1 Canterbury Cl
2 Shartesbury Rd
E7
1 Heatherdown Rd
2 Heatherdown Wy

Ryan

WEST MOOR

RINGWOOD

1 grid square represents 500 metres

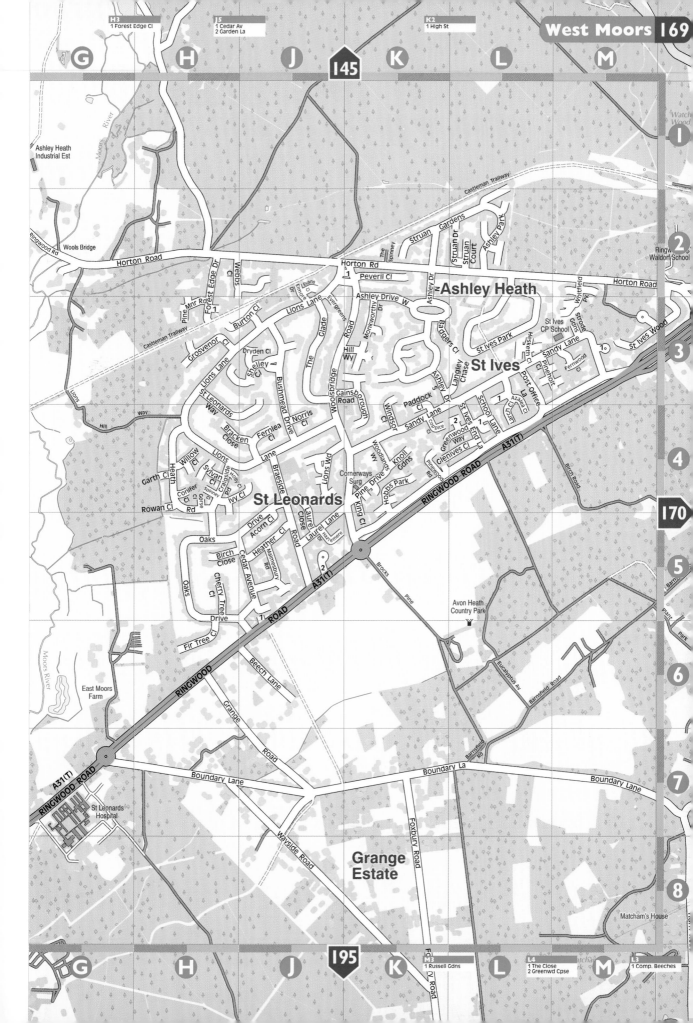

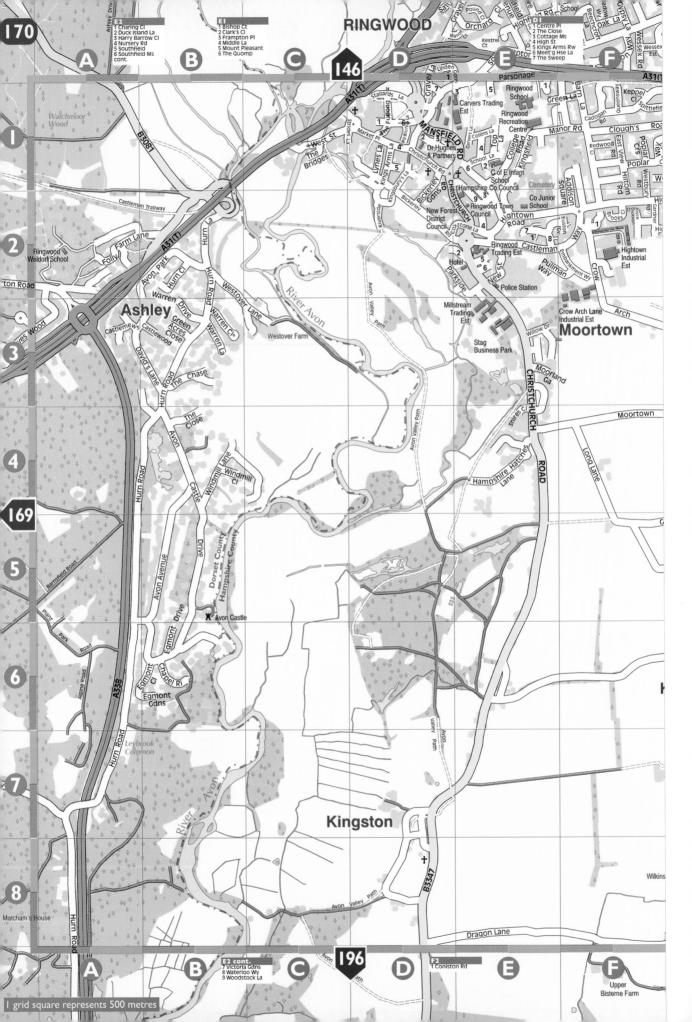

G

1 The Cloisters
2 Greenfinch Wk
3 Linnet Cl
4 Lych Gate Ct
5 Old Stacks Gdns
6 Sanderlings
7 Wren Cl

H2
1 Forest Court Hills

Beatty
Cl
G2

Southampton Road

Nelow La

HOULNER HILL

H

A31(T)

J

147

K

L

M

**Picket
Hill**

Foulford

1

Hightown Hill

Hightown

2

Eastfield
Close

Eastfield La

Jubilee Cl

Ville Rd

Eastfield
Lane

Eastfield

Ash Cl

Nouale Lane

Hightown Gdns

Hightown Rd

Hightown Road

Hightown Hill

Forest Lane

Forest Lane

Hurn Farm

3

Lakeview Dr

Crow Lane

Pelican Md

Swan Md

Lakeside

Holmwood
Garth

Ashburn
Garth

Forestlake Av

Ashley Av

Ship Dr

Merlin
Cl

Water Cl

1

1

2

3

4

6

Wood End Rd

Forest Edge Rd

✝

Knaves
Ash

Vales
Moor

Crow
Hill
Top

4

172

Crow Lane

Lane

Crow

Streets Lane

Lane

Barrack

Lane

Charles's Lane

Strodgemoor
Bottom

5

Green

Upper
Kingston Farm

6

Lakes Farm

**North
Kingston**

Charles's Lane

Charles's Lane

Bagnum Farm

Kingston
Great
Common

Brixey's Farm

7

Farm

Dragon Lane

Sandford

A31(T)

197

Bisterne
Common

8

G

H

J

K

L

M

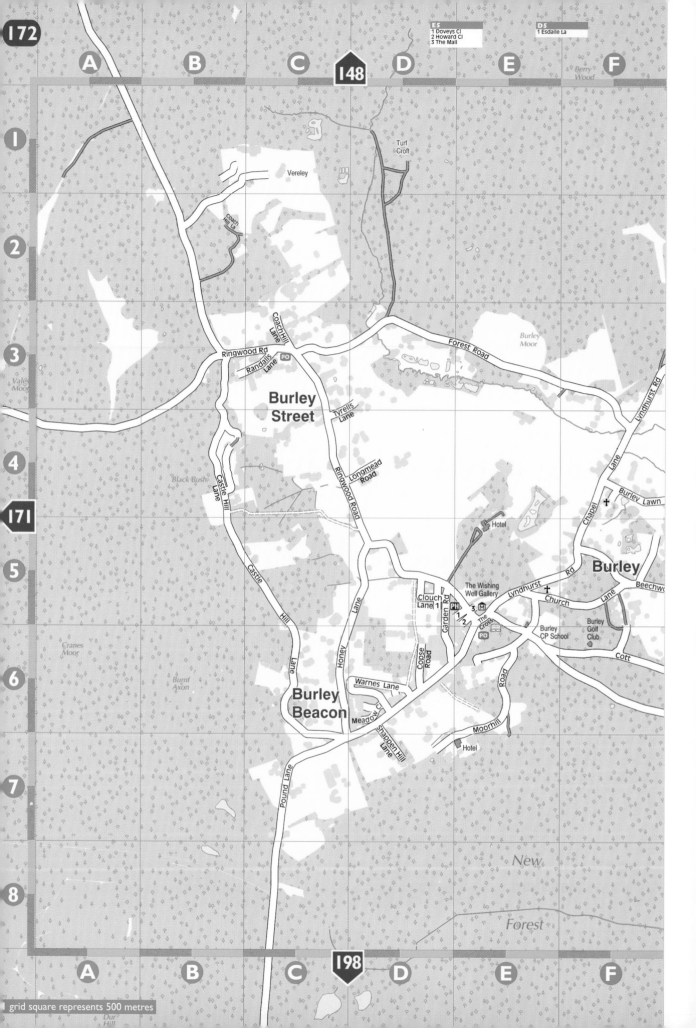

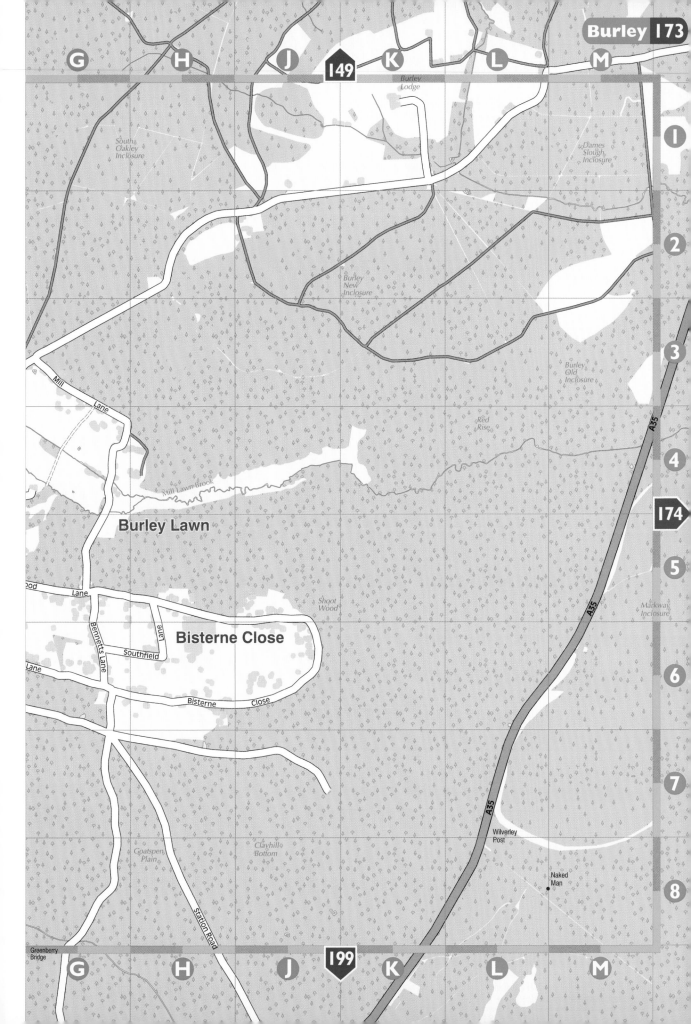

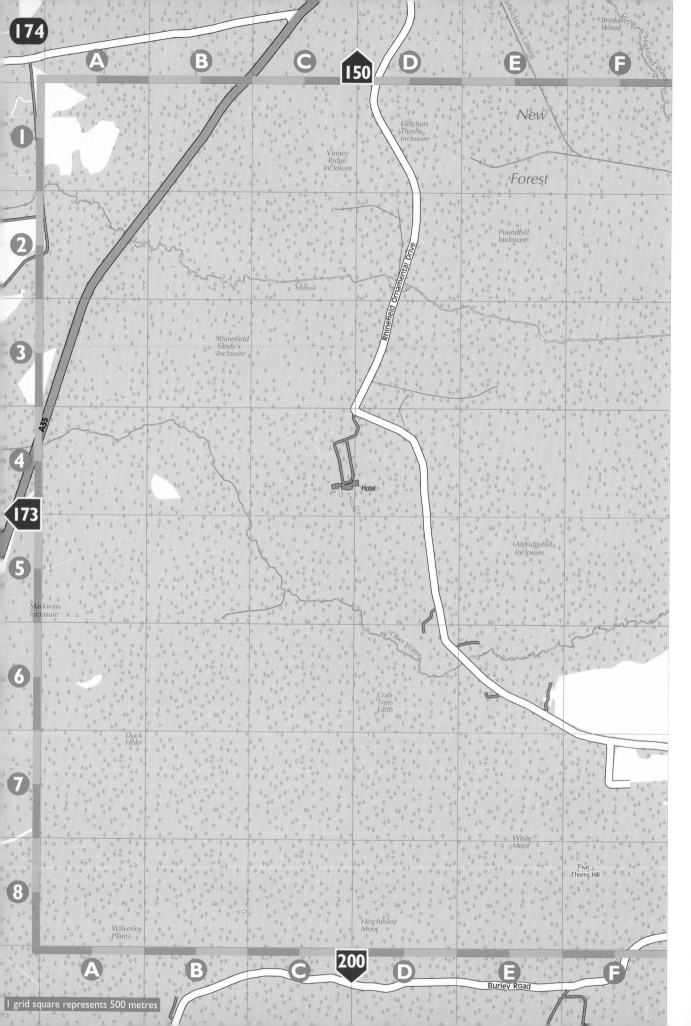

A   B   C   150   D   E   F

1

New

Fletchers
Thorns
Inclosure

Vinney
Ridge
Inclosure

Forest

2

Poundhill
Inclosure

3

Rhinefield
Sandy's
Inclosure

Rhinefield Ornamental Drive

A35

4

Hotel

Aldridgehill
Inclosure

5

Markway
Inclosure

Ober Water

6

Crab
Tree
Earth

Duck
Hole

7

White
Moor

8

Five
Thorns Hill

Wilverley
Plain

Hincheslea
Moor

A   B   C   200   D   E   Burley Road   F

A   B   C   152   D   E   F

Denny Lodge

1

Parkhill Inclosure

2

Ramnor Inclosure

3

Pignal Inclosure

Stubby Copse Inclosure

4

Perrywood Haseley Inclosure

5

merlawn

S042

New Copse Inclosure

6

Hotel

Ladycross Lodge

B3055

B3055

B3055

7

Perrywood Ironshill Inclosure

Round Hill

kenhurst

8

Lymington River

A   B   C   202   D   Dilton   E   F

1 grid square represents 500 metres

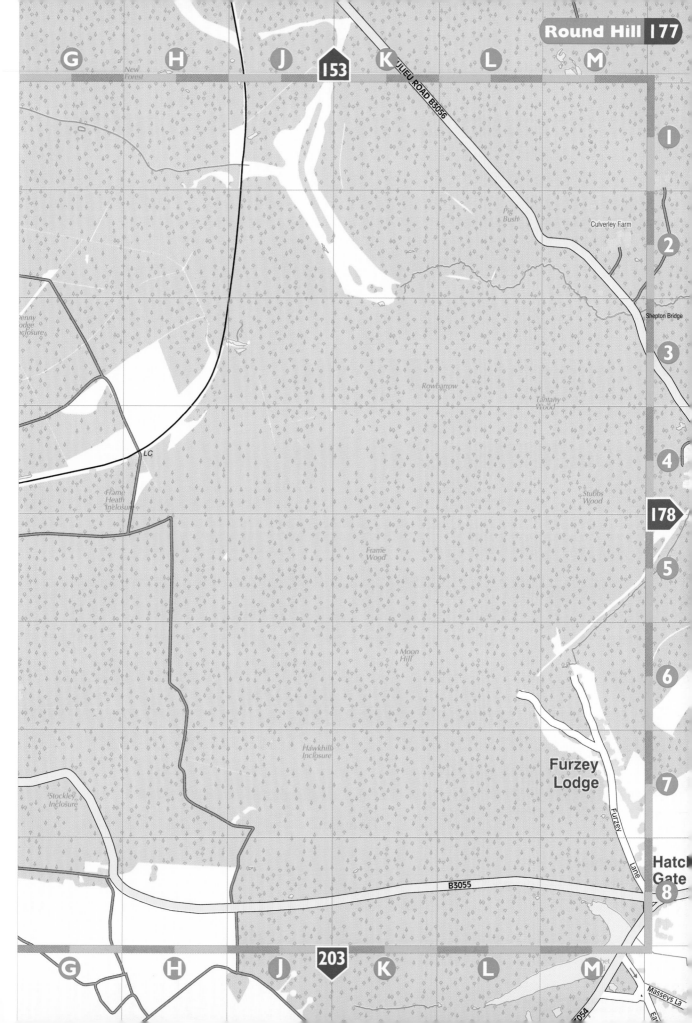

G   H   J   **153**   K   L   M

I

2

3

4

178

5

6

7

8

New
Forest

'LIEU ROAD B3056

Pig
Bush

Culverley Farm

Shepton Bridge

Denny
Lodge
Inclosure

Rowbarrow

Tantany
Wood

LC

Ffame
Heath
Inclosure

Stubbs
Wood

Frame
Wood

Moon
Hill

Hawkhill
Inclosure

Stockley
Inclosure

**Furzey
Lodge**

Furzey

**Hatc
Gate**

B3055

Lane

Masseys La

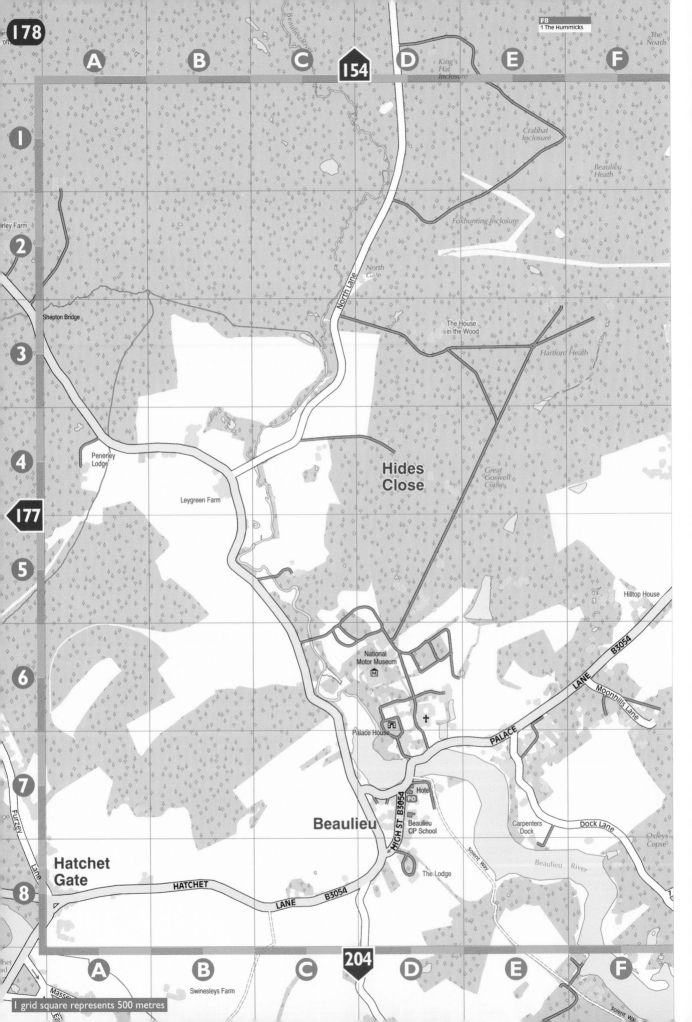

F8
1 The Hummicks

The Noads

A B C 154 D King's Hat Inclosure E F

Crabhat Inclosure

Beaulieu Heath

1

Foxhunting Inclosure

rley Farm

2

Shepton Bridge

North Lane

North Gate

The House in the Wood

Hartford Heath

3

Penerley Lodge

4

Hides Close

Great Goswell Copse

177

Leygreen Farm

5

Hilltop House

National Motor Museum

6

B3054

MOONHILLS LANE

Palace House

PALACE

7

Furzey Lane

Hotel
PO

Carpenters Dock

Dock Lane

Oxleys Copse

Beaulieu

HIGH ST B3054

Beaulieu CP School

Solent Way

Beaulieu River

Hatchet Gate

The Lodge

HATCHET LANE B3054

8

A B Swinesleys Farm C 204 D E F

Masse

Solent Way

1 grid square represents 500 metres

G H J **157** K L Hamble Spit M

Solent Way

1

2

ISLE OF WIGHT 4

182

5

Calshot Castle

6

Calshot Castle

7

North Trestle Road
Burmah Road N
South Trestle Road
...ty Road
Old Agwi Road
Aglior Road
Flume Rd
4

Copthorne Lane
Ashlett Cl
Copthorne Lane
Ashlett
Ashlett Road
...ast Clinic

...LEY BY-PASS
B3053
Stonehills
Stonehills
Northern Access Road
Norther Access Rd
Badminston Lane
Badminston Farm
Badminston Drove
B3053
Ower

Ashlett Creek

Calshot
PO
Calshot Cl

Stanswood Road

G H J **207** K L M

F5 cont.
6 Meadow Wy
7 The Paddocks
8 Rhyme Hall Ms
9 The Square
10 Whites La

Castle Lane B3053

3

G

H

J

K

L

M

1 Fitzwilliam Av

1 Hazelwood

West Street

PO

Rosedale Cl

1 Dolphin Ct
2 Forties Cl
3 Shannon Rd
4 Tawny Owl Cl

Common Lane

Hill Park School

Garstons Cl

Castle Hill

Bridge Street

Coach

The Cl
Bellfield

Cem

Lwr Bellfield

Gardner Road

Hewett Road

Hewett Close

Ransome Close

Titchfield Road

Rowan

Templemere

Ranvilles Lane

Harcourt Road

Lynden

Shepards

Gaylyn Wy

Hookgate Coppice

Brownwich Lane

Occupation Lane

Posbrook Lane

Ranvilles Lane

I

2

Cemetery

3

Lychdale Grn

Garnett Close

Singledge

Little Posbrook

Country Vw

Cuckoo Lane

Puffin Crs

The Oakes

Turtle Close

Anker Lane

4

Brownwich Lane

Triangle Lane

Finisterre Cl

Old St

Upr Old St

Kestrel

184

Cromarty Close

Old Street

Cuckoo La

5

Malin

Meon

River Meon

Shannon Road

Meon View Farm

Old Street

Fair Isle La

Plover Cl

Fury Way

Viking

Robins Close

Berry Lane

Vixen Cl

Plymouth

Plover Cl

Anne Dale County Junior & Infant School

Bells

6

Brownwich Farm

Solent Way

The Gannets

Cowans Park

Pitcher Cl

Whaden Cl

Fernie Cl

Andrew Place

Hawk Cl

The Grove

Harriet Cl

Violet Av

PO

Mancroft Avenue

Hammond Junior Infant Sc

Carisbrooke

Barrow Close

Pembroke Crescent

Corfe Close

Berkeley Close

Avenue

Denham Close

Walnut Drive

Old Farm

Midways

7

Titchfield Haven

Bank Road

Old Street

Short Road

Elsfred Rd

Sanross Cl

Bell Davies Road

Robinson Road

Caspar John Close

Farm Edge Road

Beverley Road

Springfield Way

Knights

Haven

Gt Gays

Hill Head

Cliff

Solent Road

Osborne Vw Rd

Cottesway East

Elleray Close

Bramble Cl

Cottes

Croften Lane

Valsheba Drive

Hill Head Road

Solent Way

Pilgrims Way

Seafield Park Road

Monks Way

Salterns

Solent Way

Road

8

G
M7
1 Boyd Cl

H
M6
1 Blankney Cl
2 Bramham Moor
3 Goodsell Cl
4 Sea Kings

J

K
M5
1 Biscay Cl
2 Crab. Fm La
3 Faroes Cl
4 Fastnet Wy
5 Fisher Cl
6 Forth Cl
7 Hebrides Cl
8 Humber Cl
9 The Scimitars

L

M

The Solent

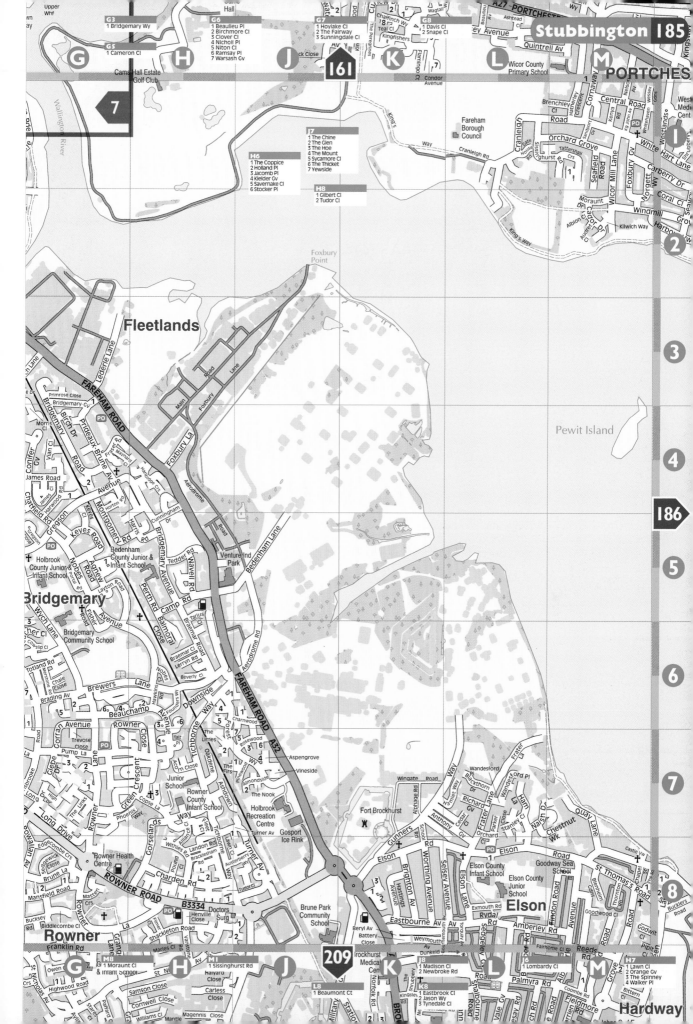

Drayton

Farlington

A B C D E F

HAVANT ROAD

A27(T)

A27

Farlington
Marshes

North Binness
Island

RSPB
Reserve

Baker's Island

Anchorage
Park

187

South Binness
Island

Broom Channel

Langstone Harbour

Russell's Lake

Admiral Lord
Nelson
School

Burrfields Road

Burrfields Retail
Park

Hotel

Baffins

Portsmouth
Sixth Form
College

A B C D E F

212

Hampshire County

Langstone Channel

I grid square represents 500 metres

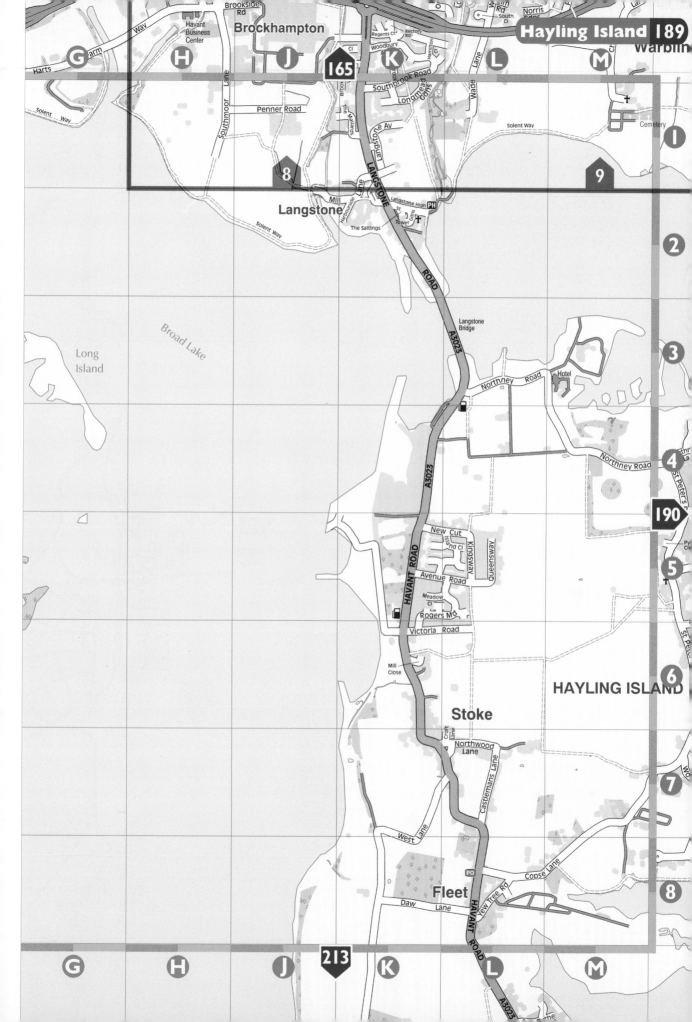

Warbling

Brockhampton

Havant Business Center

Brookside Rd

Regents Ct

Rectory Rd

Southbrook Road

Longmead Gdns

Hamilton Lane

Southmoor Lane

Penner Road

The Maylands

Langstone Av

165

Langstone Lane

Solent Way

Cemetery

8

9

Mill

Langstone

Harbourside Lane

Langstone High

St Gdns

Tower

The Saltings

Solent Way

LANGSTONE ROAD

I

2

Broad Lake

Langstone Bridge

A3023

Northney Road

Hotel

3

Long Island

A3023

Northney Road

St Peter's La

4

190

New Cut

Island Cl

Kingsway

Queensway

5

HAVANT ROAD

Avenue Road

Meadow Cl

Rogers Md

Victoria Road

St Pe

HAYLING ISLAND

Mill Close

6

Stoke

Croft Lane

Northwood Lane

Castlemans Lane

7

West Lane

PO

Copse Lane

Wo

8

Fleet

Daw Lane

Yew Tree Rd

HAVANT ROAD

A3023

G H J K L M

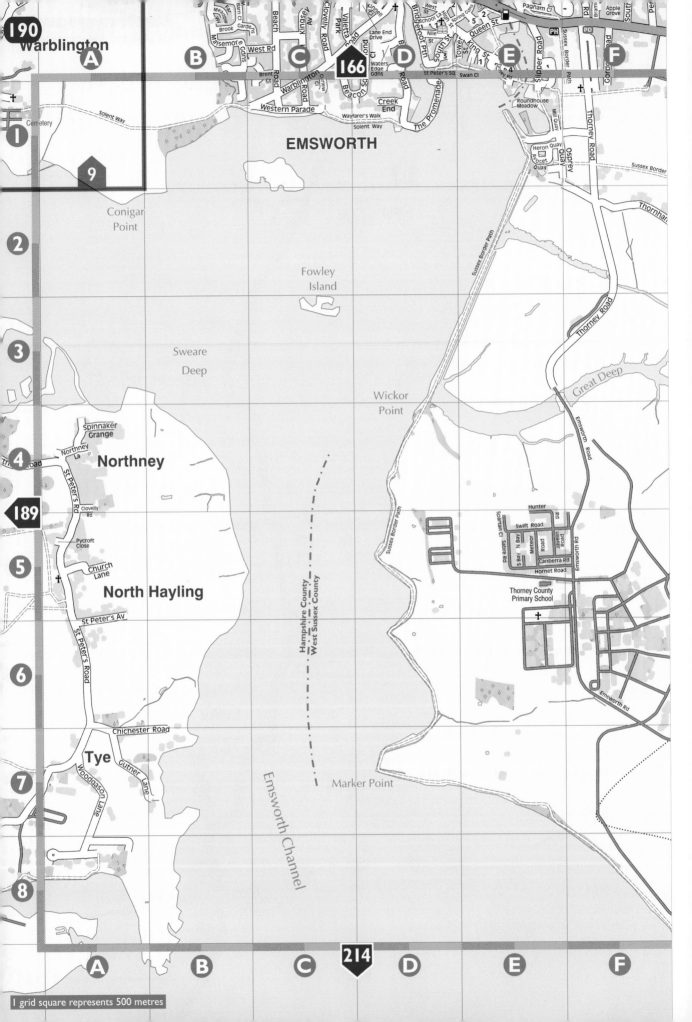

166

A · B · C · D · E · F

189

214

EMSWORTH

Cemetery

Solent Way

Western Parade

Wayfarer's Walk

Solent Way

The Promenade

Creek End

Waters Edge Gdns

Lane End Drive

St Peter's Sq

Swan Cl

Queen St

Roundhouse Meadow

Heron Quay

Osprey Quay

Avocet Quay

Mill Quay

Thorney Road

Sussex Border Path

Thornham

Sussex Border Path

Thorney Road

Conigar Point

Fowley Island

Sweare Deep

Great Deep

Wickor Point

Spinnaker Grange

Northney La

Northney

Clovelly Rd

St Peter's Rd

Pycroft Close

Church Lane

North Hayling

St Peter's Av

St Peter's Road

Hampshire County

West Sussex County

Sussex Border Path

Hunter Rd

Swift Road

Spartan Cl

Sabre Rd

Meteor Road

S Bay

N Bay

Lilliput Road

Canberra Rd

Hornet Road

Emsworth Rd

Emsworth Road

Thorney County Primary School

Chichester Road

Gutner Lane

Tye

Wooddason Lane

Marker Point

Emsworth Channel

West Rd

Beach Road

Kinser Av

Clovelly Park

Valetta Road

Beacon Sq

South St

Tower Rd

King St

Brook

Maisemore Gdns

Brent Ct

Warblington Rd

Bridgefoot Pth

Pagham Cl

Apple Grove

South

Gordon Road

Slipper Road

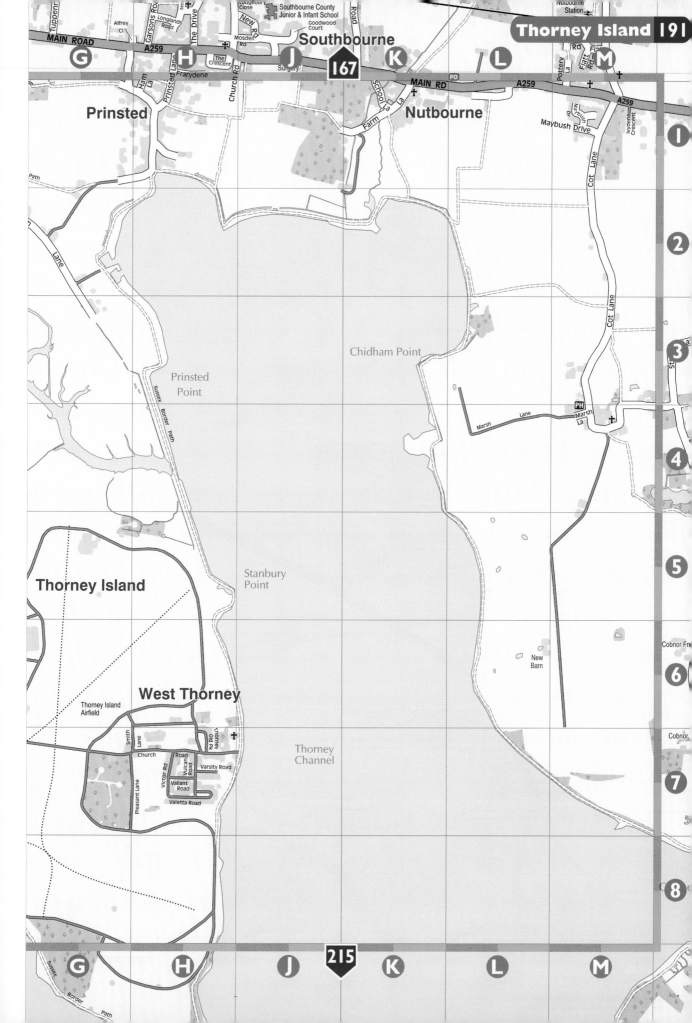

MAIN ROAD A259

G **H** **J** **167** **K** **L** **M**

Tuppenny

Alfrey Cl

Longlands Road

Carsons Rd

The Drive

New Rd

Edgebury Close

Southbourne County Junior & Infant School

Road

Goodwood Court

Southbourne

Mosdell Rd

The Crescent

Frarydene

Church Rd

Ham La

Prinsted Lane

Surgery

La

Prinsted

Farm

School La

Nutbourne

MAIN RD A259

PO

Road

Maybush Drive

Maybush Dr

Cot Lane

Pottery La

Flatt Rd

Ivydene Crescent

Nutbourne Station

A259

I

Path

Lane

2

Sussex Border Path

Prinsted Point

Chidham Point

3

Marsh Lane

Marsh La

PH

St

Cot Lane

4

Cobnor Fm

5

Thorney Island

Stanbury Point

New Barn

6

Cobnor

West Thorney

Thorney Island Airfield

Smith Lane

Church

Victor Rd

Road

Vulcan Road

Old Thorney Rd

Varsity Road

Valiant Road

Pleasant Lane

Valetta Road

Thorney Channel

7

8

Sussex Border Path

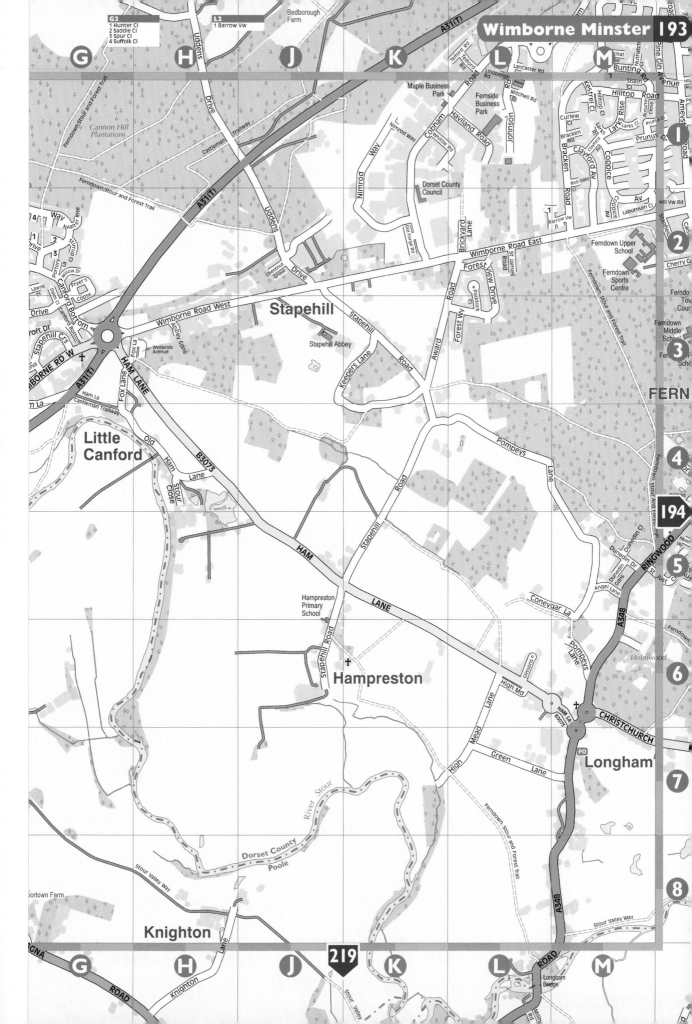

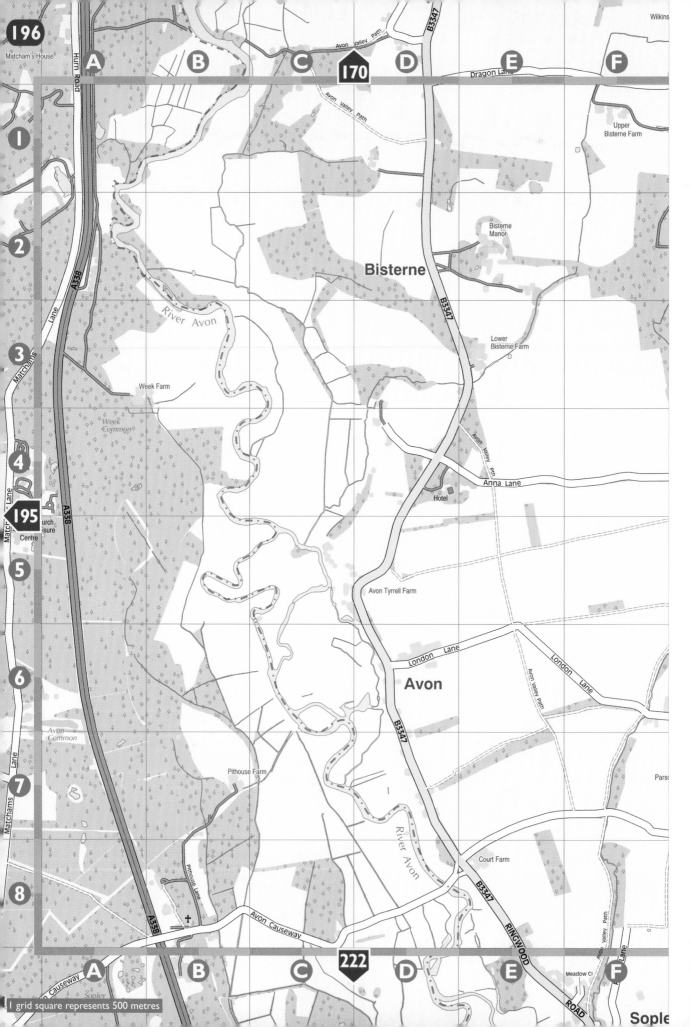

Sandford
L7 1 Brookside Cl
L8 1 Woodlands Cl

M7
1 Bramble Wy
2 Rosehill Cl
3 Shackleton Sq
4 Shears Brook Cl

G   H   J   171   K   L   M

1

2

3

Bisterne Common

Avon Tyrrell

Shirley Common

4

198

Ripley Wood

Anna Lane

North Ripley

Purlieu

5

Martin's Copse

Thatchers Lane

6

Ripley

Shirley

Lane

Stubbs

House

Thatchers Lane

Sopley CP School

Burnt

Cedar

Tyrrells Pl

Shirley Ct

Bransgore Gdns

1

7

onage Farm

Ringwood Road

Rosehill Drive

Betsy Lane

Stouts La

The New Medical Cen

Canute Drive

Whistler's

Derritt Lane

Clare Cl

Hungerford Cl

The Wishing Well Gallery.

St Georges Cl

Poplar

Merryfield Road

Peace Cl

M

Pear Tree Cl

Twin Oaks Medical Cen

PO

8

Wiltshire Gdns

West Cl

Chapel Lane

Brookside

Road

Colbourne Close

St Mary's Close

BRANSGORE

Wiltshire Rd

Westlands

Hill Lane

Hill Cl

1

M8
1 Halton Cl

G   H   J   223   K   L   M

Derritt Lane

Hampshire County
Dorset County

Westbury Cl

Meyrick Close

Burley Road

North

Brook L

A8
1 The Orchard

A7
1 Mnt P'sant Dr
2 Wedgewd Gdns

A   B   C   **172**   D   E   **Forest**   F

I

Dur
Hill
Down

Holmsley
Ridge

Whitten
Bottom

2

Thorney
Hill
Holms

3

Forest
Rd

School
Lane

School
Road

Forest Road

Shirley
Common

Brick Lane

Valley
Lane

4

Whitelands

Brick
Lane

Thorney Hill

197

Willow Lane

rlieu

Burley Road

5

Hill Farm

Plain
Heath

Dial Cl

6

Poors
Common

Forest
Lodge

Lane

Stibbs Way

Burley Road

Wy Bransgore

Gdns

A35

7

Whistler's

1   2

Heathfield

Bransgore Ho

Cuckoo Hill
Way

Poplar Lane

Blackbird
Way

St Georges Cl

Lyndhurst Road

8

St Mary's
Close

1

Poplar Cl

Ringwood Road

Beech House

North Hinton Farm

Holm   Hill

Bransgore
Primary
School

A   B   C   **224**   D   E   F

Harrow Road

Harrow

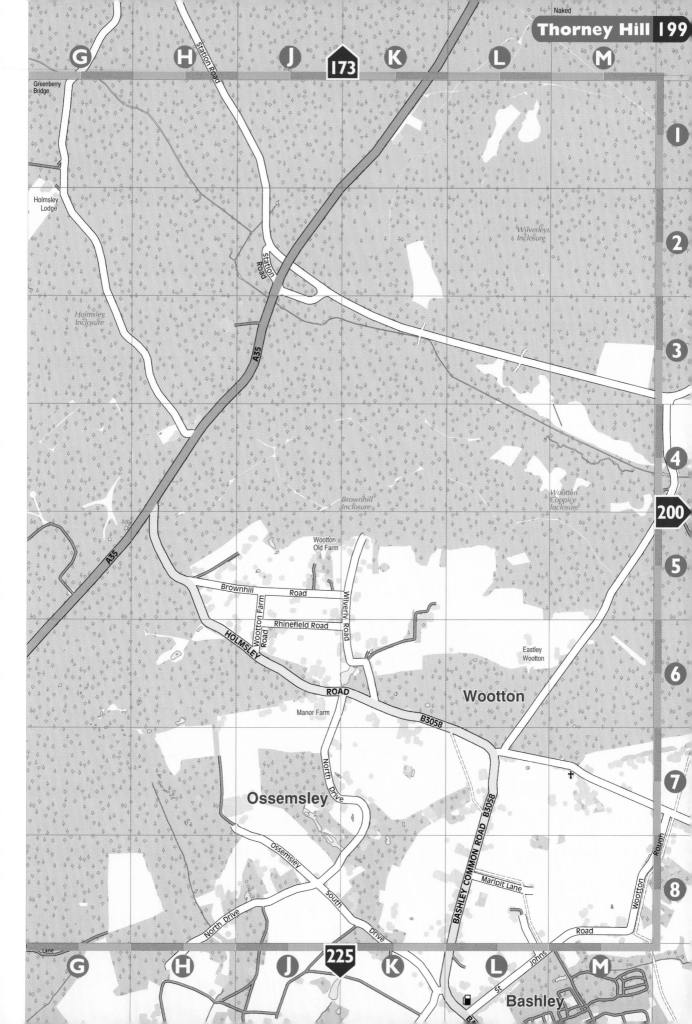

Naked

G H J 173 K L M

Greenberry
Bridge

Holmsley
Lodge

Holmsley
Inclosure

Station Road

A35

Wilverley
Inclosure

Wootton
Coppice
Inclosure

200

Brownhill
Inclosure

Wootton
Old Farm

Brownhill Road

Wootton Farm Road

Rhinefield Road

Wilverly Road

HOLMSLEY

Eastley
Wootton

ROAD

Wootton

Manor Farm

B3058

Ossemsley

North Drive

B3058

BASHLEY COMMON ROAD

Wootton Rouh

Maripit Lane

Ossemsley

North Drive

South Drive

Road

G H J 225 K L M

St Johns

Bashley

I

2

3

4

5

6

7

8

174

199

226

F6
1 Highfield Gdns

Thorns Hill

A B C D E F

Burley Road

Wilverley
Plain

Hinchslea
Moor

Hincheslea
Wood

Long
Slade
Bottom

Setthorns Cottage

AvonWater

Set
Thorns
Inclosure

Cemetery

Manchester Road

Brighton Road

Adlam's Lane

Oakenbrow

Durrant Way

Gilpin Close

Kitcher's Mill Close

Burdshine Walk

Bond Close

Broadley
Inclosure

The Close

Normanby Close

Middle Road

Station Road

Anderwood

Hyde Cl

Sway St Luke
Primary School

Cruse Cl

Mead End Road

Hotel

Heron Cl

The Gallery

Sway

Sway Station

Sway Park
Industrial Estate

Westbeams Road

The Surg

Hotel

Hollies Cl

Jubilee Court

Boundway

Mead
End

Mead End Road

Lower Mead End Road

Broadley House

Arnewood
Manor

Avon Water

Rough

Tiptoe Road

Marley Mount

Fairlight Lane

Tiptoe
CP School

Danehurst New Road

Middle Road

Crabbswood

Tiptoe

A B C D E F

Northover Lane

ARNEWOOD BRIDGE ROAD

1 grid square represents 500 metres

South Weirs

Burley Road

South Weirs

175

Blackhamsley Ho

Brockenhurst Manor Golf Club

SWAY

B3055

The Surgery

Highwood Road

Tattenham Rd

Collyers Rd

Woodlands Road

Tilebarn Lane

Tilebarn Lane

LYMINGTON

ROAD

Church Lane

Setley

PH

SOUTHAMPTON RD

Setley Plain

Setley Common

B3055

Sandy Down

A337

202

LC

Cobblers Corner

Lower

Sand

SOUTHAMPTON ROAD

Widden Bottom

Jordans Lane

Durns Town

DURNSTOWN

B3055

Badgers Cl

James Road

Thorns Rd

Centr

Critt

Back Lane

Pitmore Lane

Battramsley

Jealous Lane

Chapel Lane

Shirley Holms

B C

BIRCHY HILL B3055

Birchy Hill

Shirley Holms

7

A337

Shirley holms

St Austi

Vicarage Lane

Coombe Lane

Mount Pleasant Lane

Hotel

8

South Sway Lane

Pauls Lane

Kings Lane

Mount Pleasant

Mount Pleasant Lane

King's Farm

227

Mill Lane

North Common Lane

Mount

Pleasant

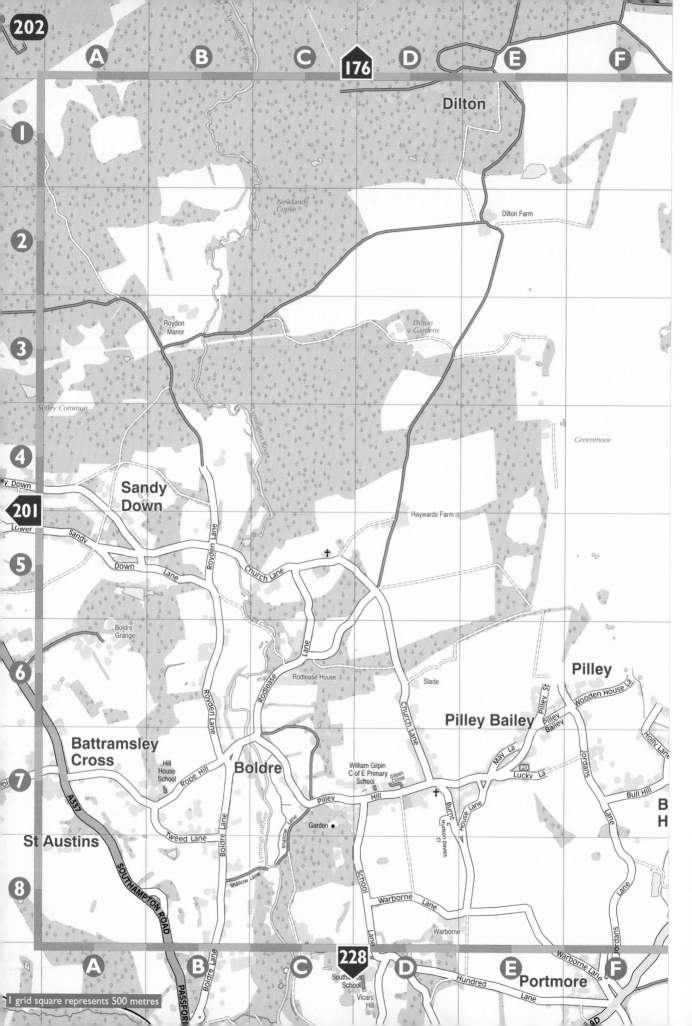

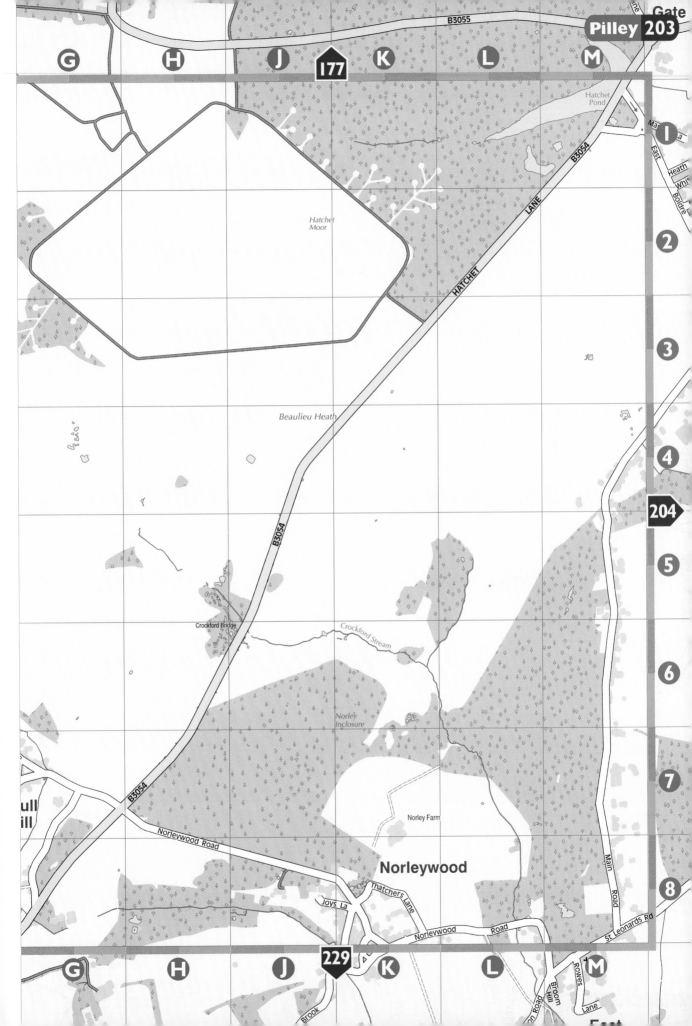

G   H   J   **177**   K   L   M

B3055

Hatchet Pond

East Heath

Boldre

Hatchet Moor

HATCHET LANE

B3054

Beaulieu Heath

B3054

204

Crockford Bridge

Crockford Stream

Norley Inclosure

Norley Farm

B3054

Norleywood Road

Norleywood

Norley Farm

Main Road

St Leonards Rd

ull ill

Norleywood Road

Joys La

Thatchers Lane

Brook

Broom Hill Lane

Rowes Lane

G   H   J   **229**   K   L   M

Gate

I   2   3   4   5   6   7   8

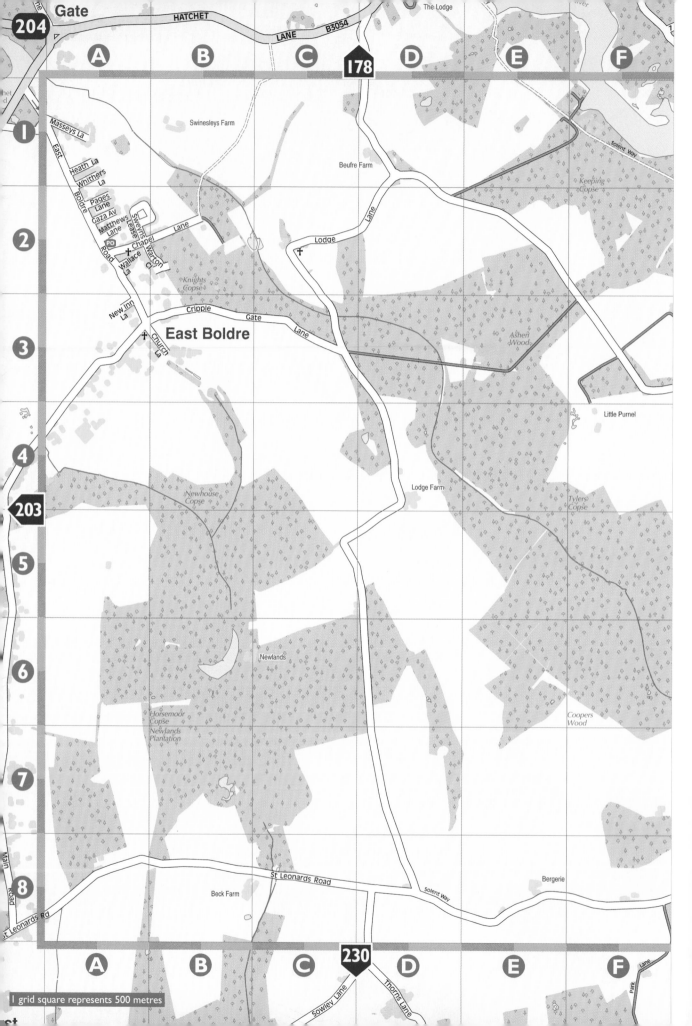

204

HATCHET LANE B3054

The Lodge

A B C 178 D E F

Masseys La

East Heath La

Whithers La

Boldre

Pages Lane

Gaza Av

Matthews Lane

PO

Swems Lease

Chapel

Wallace La

Warton Cl

Road

Lane

I

Swinesleys Farm

Beufre Farm

Keeping Copse

Solent Way

2

Lodge

Lane

Lodge

Knights Copse

3

New Inn La

† Church La

East Boldre

Cripple Gate Lane

Ashen Wood

Little Purnel

4

Newhouse Copse

Lodge Farm

Tylers Copse

203

5

6

Newlands

Coopers Wood

Horsemoor Copse

Newlands Plantation

7

8

St Leonards Road

Beck Farm

Solent Way

Bergerie

St Leonards Rd

Main Road

A B C 230 D E F

Sowley Lane

Thorns Lane

Park Lane

1 grid square represents 500 metres

G
H
J
179
K
L
M

I

2

Summer Lane

Steerley's Copse

Beaulieu River

Yard Wood

3

Keeping

Bucklers Hard

Gilbury Hard

Main Drive

Exbury House

Exbury

PH Hotel

M Maritime Museum

4

206

Clobb

Salternshill Copse

5

Salternshill

Lower Exbury

6

Drokes

Gins

7

Beaulieu River

St Leonards Grange

Gins Lane

8

Ne
Ore Point

The Log House

Gins House

Warren Lane

G
H
J
231
K
L
M

Warren Lane

Warren Farm

G   H   J   181   K   L   M

Badminston

Sprat's Down

Stanswood Road

PO
Calshot

Castle Lane

B3053

Hillhead

Eaglehurst

I

Stanswood Road

The Solent

2

Stanswood Farm

Nelson's Place

Stanswood Bay

3

Stanswood Road

4

Cadland House

5

6

Stansore Point

7

8

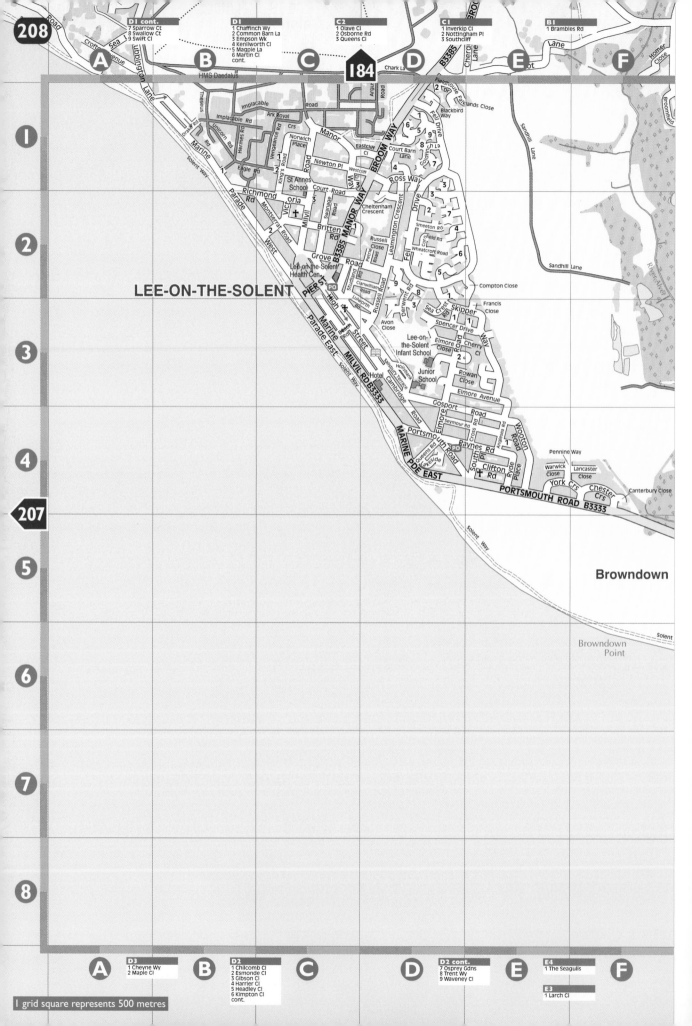

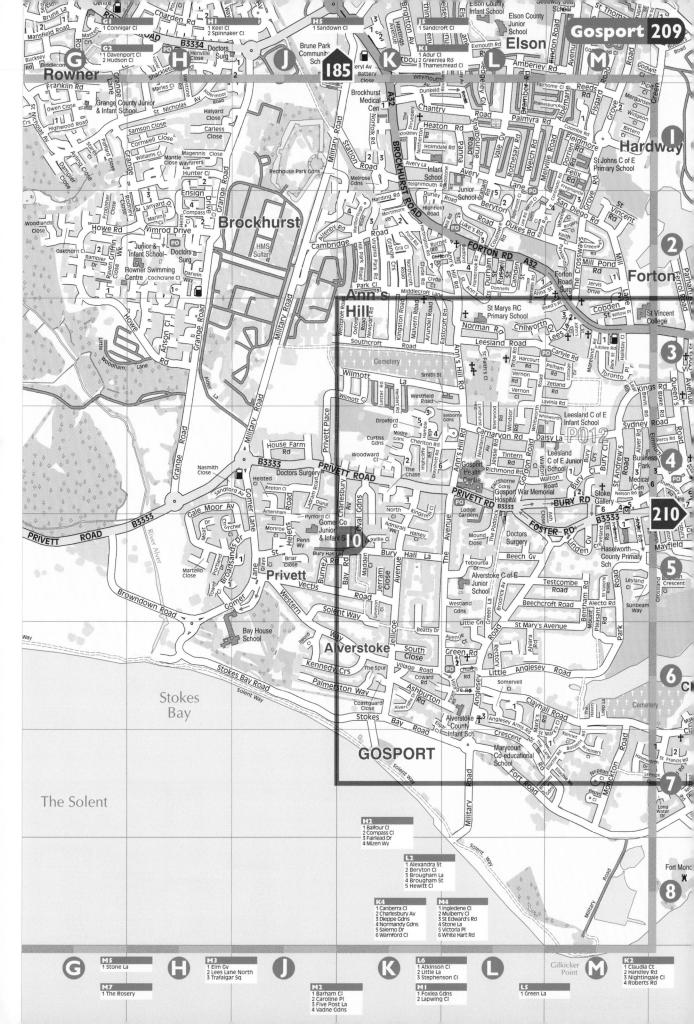

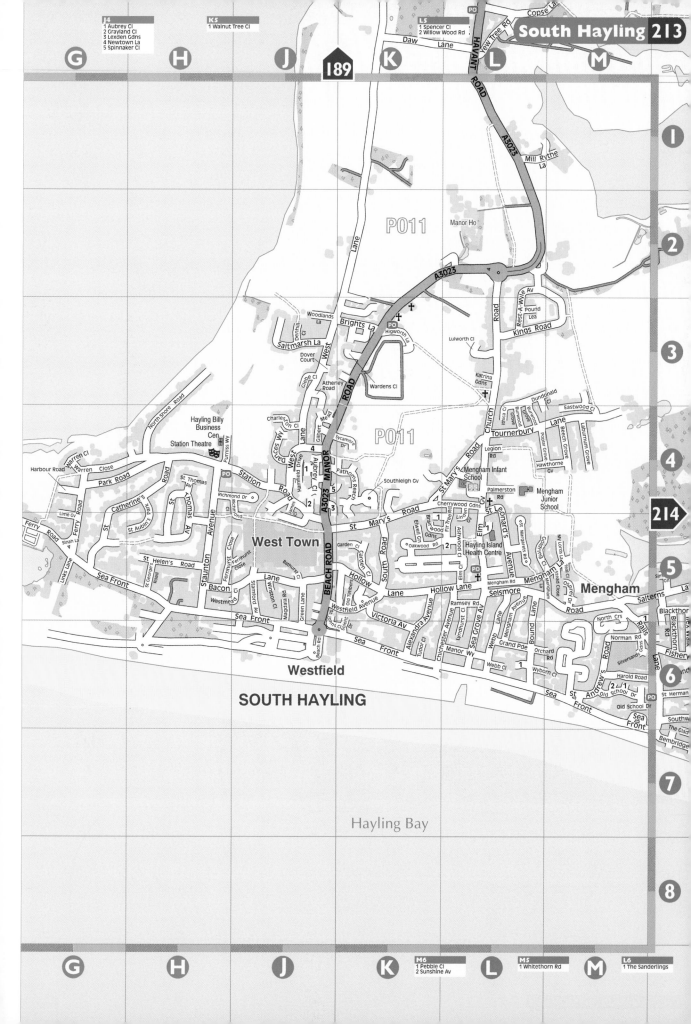

A   B   C   190   D   E   F

1

Mill Rithe

2

3

Pilsey
Sand

4

Stocker's Lake

213

5

Mengham
Salterns

gham

Simmons
Crs

Salterns Ci

Salterns
Lane

Marine

Seaview
Rd

Walk

Black Point

Salterns

Blackthorn
Rd

Blackthorn Dr

Seaview   Road

Bracklesham
Rd

th Crs

Ralls
Lane

Blackthorn

Ilex Walk

Kingfisher

Selsmore Avenue

Astone Ci

1

Norman Rd

1

Selsmore

Fishery

Lane

2

Foreland
Ct

Marshall Rd

Silversands

d School Dr

6

St Hermans Rd

Eastoke

Rowin Close

Avenue

Fishermans Wk

Eastoke

Earnley
Rd

Witering Rd

Selsey Rd

Sidlesham Ci

Pagham
Gdns

Itchenor Rd

Road

PO

Old School Dr

Sea
Front

Southwood

The Clade

Road

Eastoke

Burgess Ci

Creek

Birdham
Rd

Haven Road

Haven

Haven   Road

Road

Bosmere
Rd

Haslemere Gdns

Bracklesham
Rd

West Sussex County
Hampshire County

Bembridge Drive

Meath Ci

The Strand

West
Haye
Road

Sandy

Nutbourne Road

Point

Coronation
Rd

Treloar
Rd

Treloar
Rd

7

Winsor Ci

Wheatlands

1

Avenue

Southwood Road

Eastoke Point

8

A   B   C   D   E   F

G   H   J   **191**   K   L   M

I
2
3
4
5
6
7
8

Sussex
Border
Path

Longmere
Point

Pilsey
Island

Chichester Harbour

East Head

Rookwood
Lane

Rookwood
Lane

Sheepwash Lane

ROOKWOOD RD

Rookwood
Road

Nunnington Farm

Roman Landing

Roman Landing

Roman
Landing

Roman
Landing

Summerfield
Rd

Summerfield Road

Elmstead
Park Road

Cunliffe
Close

Elmstead Pk Rd

Meadow

Locksash

Elmstead
Gdns

Elms
Wy

Ellanore
Lane

PO

Pound Rd

B2179

Elms Lane

Elms Lane

Coastguard Lane

West Wittering
Parochial School

The Wad

Royce
Close

Royce Way

Elms
Ride

Elms
Ride

The Byeway

West Wittering

Wellsfield

Middlefield

Seaward
Dr

West

Strand

Berrybarn

Lane

East

Strand

CAKEHAM

ROAD

**East
Wittering**

B2179

Howard
Avenue

Southcote

Jolliffe
Road

Ella

Marine Dr West

Owers

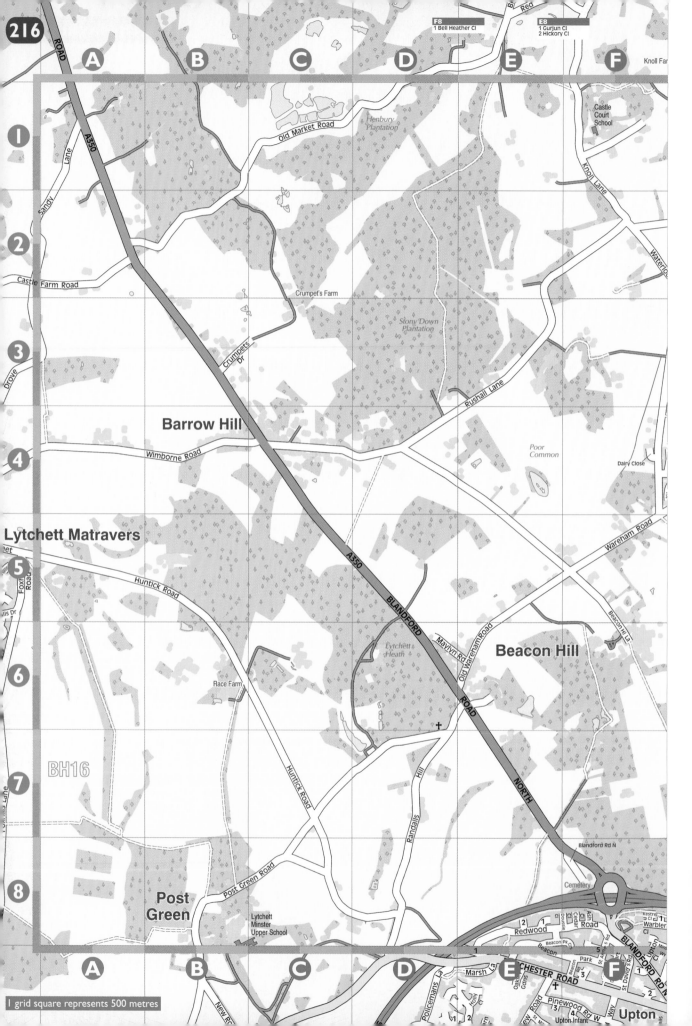

A B C D E F

F8
1 Bell Heather Cl

E8
1 Gurjun Cl
2 Hickory Cl

ROAD

A350

Sandy Lane

Castle Farm Road

Drove

Crumpers Dr

Old Market Road

Henbury Plantation

Crumpet's Farm

Stony Down Plantation

Knoll Farm

Castle Court School

Knoll Lane

Waterlo

Barrow Hill

Wimborne Road

Rushall Lane

Poor Common

Dairy Close

Wareham Road

Lytchett Matravers

Foxt Road

Huntick Road

alls Dr

A350

BLANDFORD

Mavlyn Rd

Old Wareham Road

Beacon Hill

Beacon Hill La

Race Farm

Lytchett Heath

BH16

Huntick Road

Randalls Hill

yms Lane

ROAD

NORTH

Blandford Rd N

Cemetery

Post Green

Post Green Road

Lytchett Minster Upper School

Redwood

Cedar

Ash Road

Kestrel Cl

Warbler

Upton

BLANDFORD RD

Marsh La

Policemans La

Oakley Gdns

CHESTER ROAD

St Anne's Rd

St David's Rd

Beacon Pk

Pinewood Rd W

Upton Infant

Upton

I 2 3 4 5 6 7 8

A B C D E F

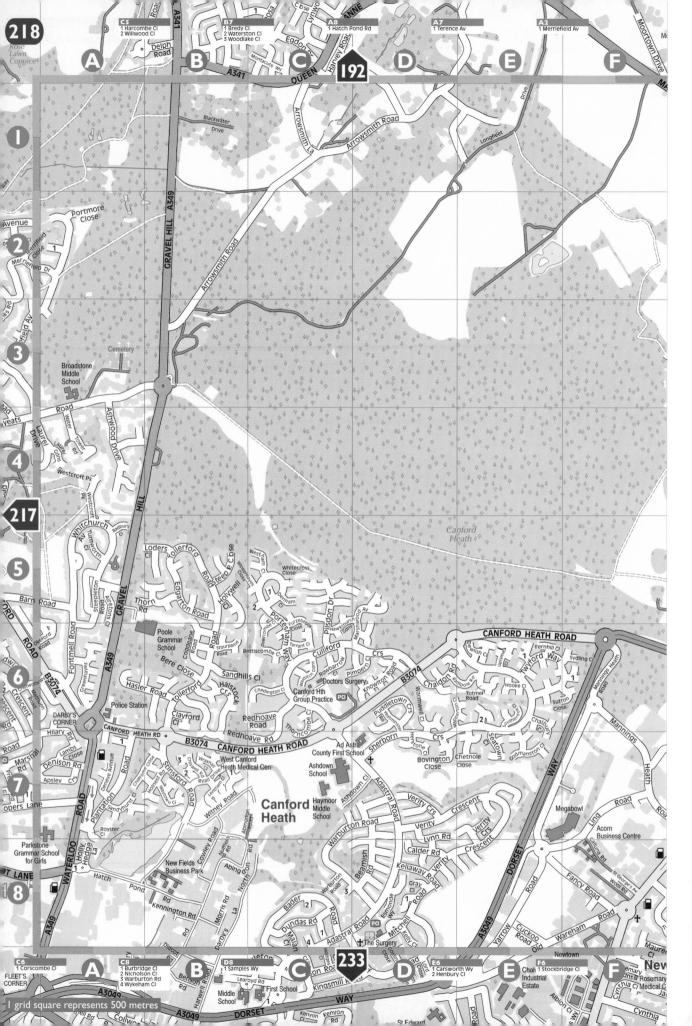

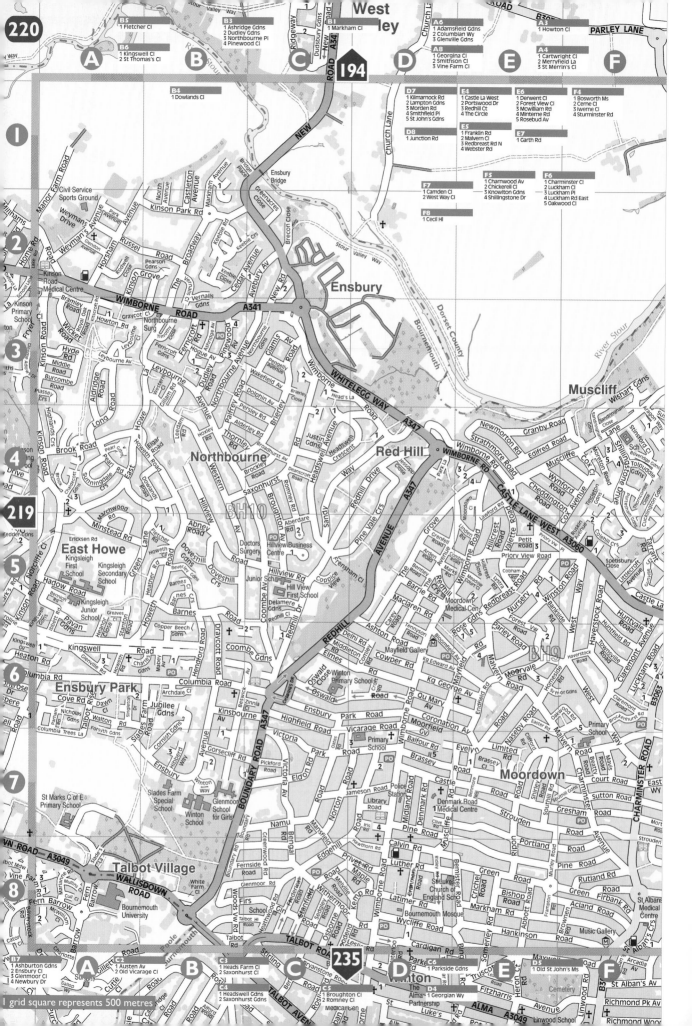

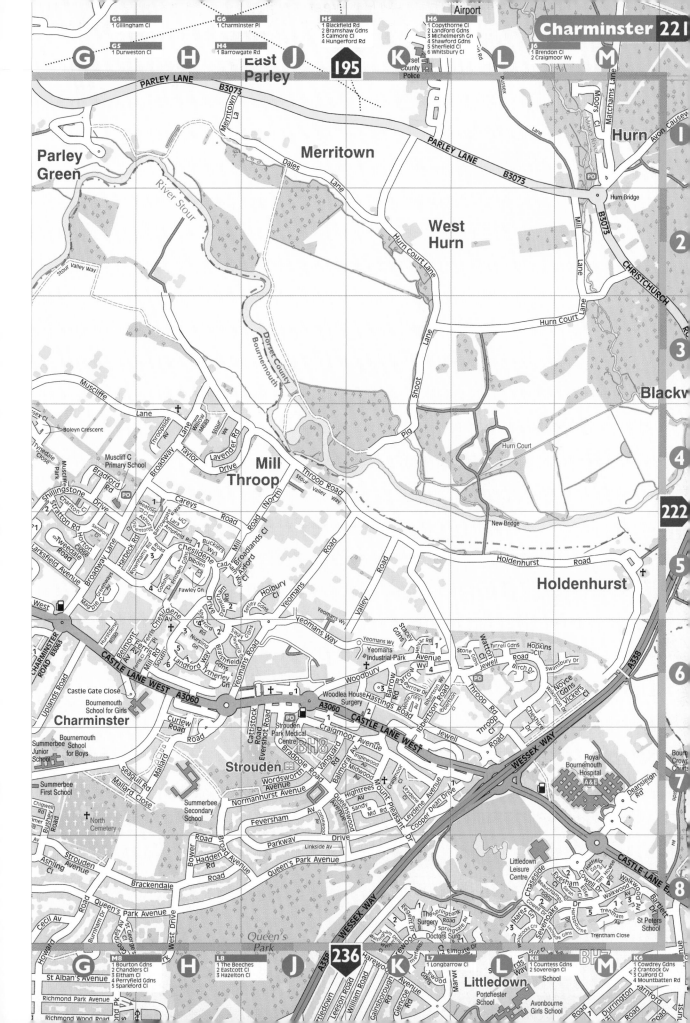

G4
1 Gillingham Cl
G6
1 Charminster Pl
H5
1 Blackfield Rd
2 Bramshaw Gdns
3 Calmore Cl
4 Hungerford Rd
H6
1 Copythorne Cl
2 Landford Gdns
3 Michelmersh Gn
4 Shawford Gdns
5 Sherfield Cl
6 Whitsbury Cl

G5
1 Durweston Cl
H4
1 Barrowgate Rd
J6
1 Brendon Cl
2 Craigmoor Wy

G H J 195 K L M

Airport

Hurn

PARLEY LANE B3073

Merritown

Parley
Green

River Stour

East
Parley

Dorset
County
Police

PARLEY LANE B3073

Hurn Bridge

West
Hurn

Hurn Court Lane

Stour Valley Way

Dorset County
Bournemouth

Muscliffe
Lane

Boleyn Crescent

Muscliff C
Primary School

Mill
Throop

Throop Road (North)

Shoot
Lane

Pig
Lane

Hurn Court

New Bridge

Holdenhurst Road

Holdenhurst

Blackw

222

Charminster
School for Girls

Bournemouth
School for Boys

Summerbee
Junior
School

Charminster

Strouden

Summerbee
First School

North Cemetery

Summerbee
Secondary
School

BH8

Stouden
Park Medical
Centre

Castle Lane West A3060

Woodlea House
Surgery

Castle Lane West

Yeomans
Industrial Park

Yeomans Way

Yeomans Wy

Holdenhurst

A338

Royal
Bournemouth
Hospital
A&E

Wessex Way

Littledown
Leisure
Centre

CASTLE LANE E

Littledown

Queen's
Park

Queen's Park Avenue

Wessex Way

A338 236

St Peters
School

Avonbourne
Girls School

G M8
1 Bourton Gdns
2 Chandlers Cl
3 Eltham Cl
4 Perryfield Gdns
5 Sparkford Cl
H L8
1 The Beeches
2 Eastcott Cl
3 Hazelton Cl
J K L7
1 Longbarrow Cl
L K8
1 Countess Gdns
2 Sovereign Cl
M K6
1 Cowdrey Gdns
2 Crantock Gv
3 Culford Cl
4 Mountbatten Rd

St Alban's Avenue
Richmond Park Avenue
Richmond Wood Road

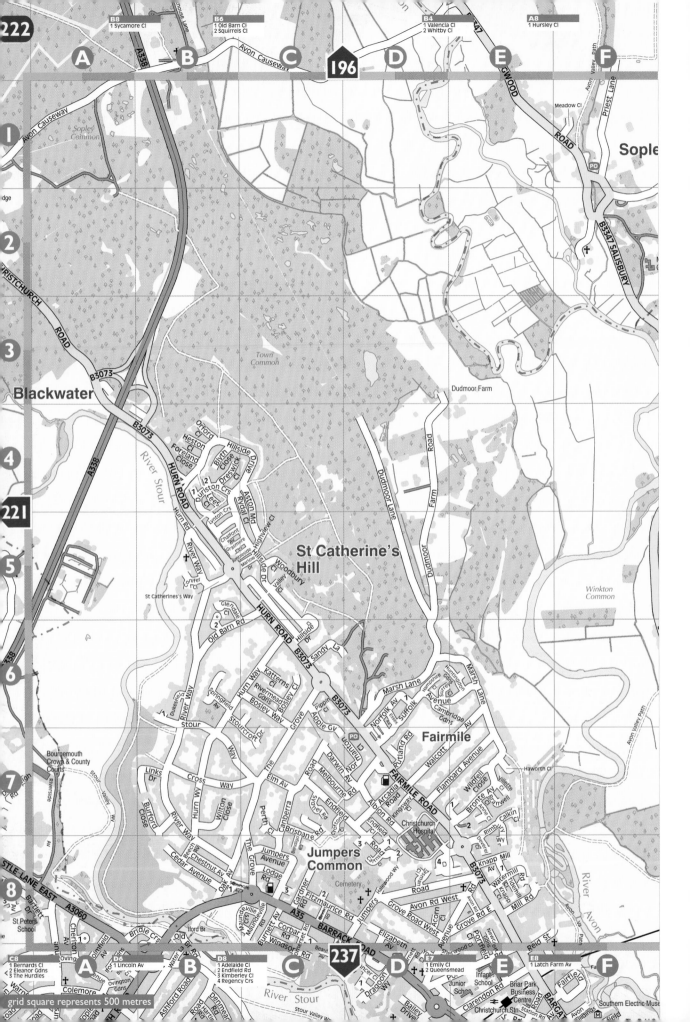

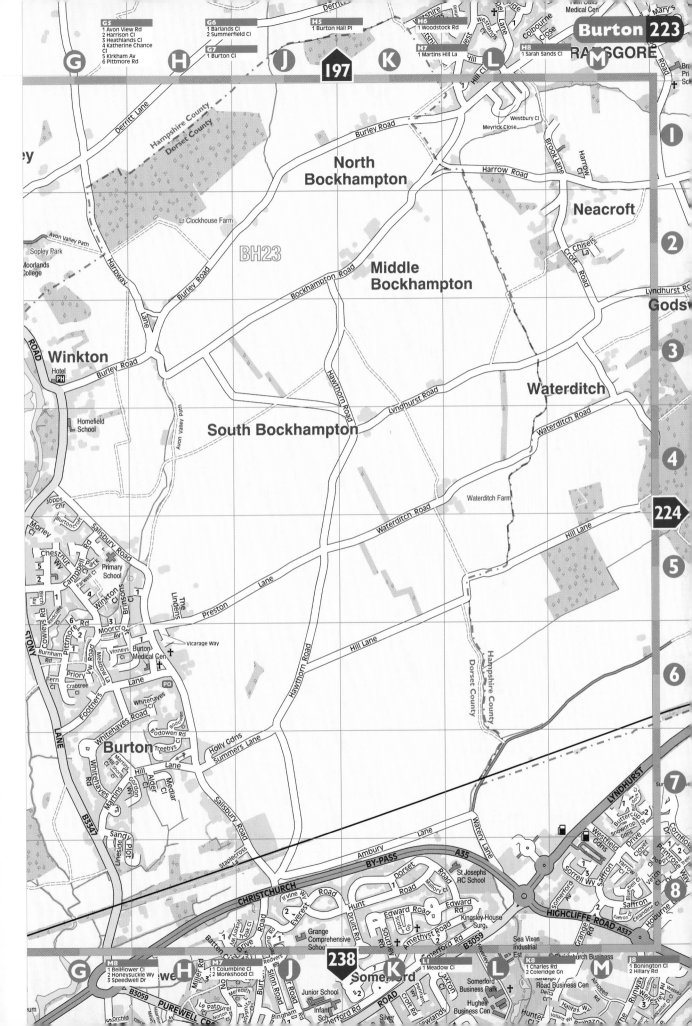

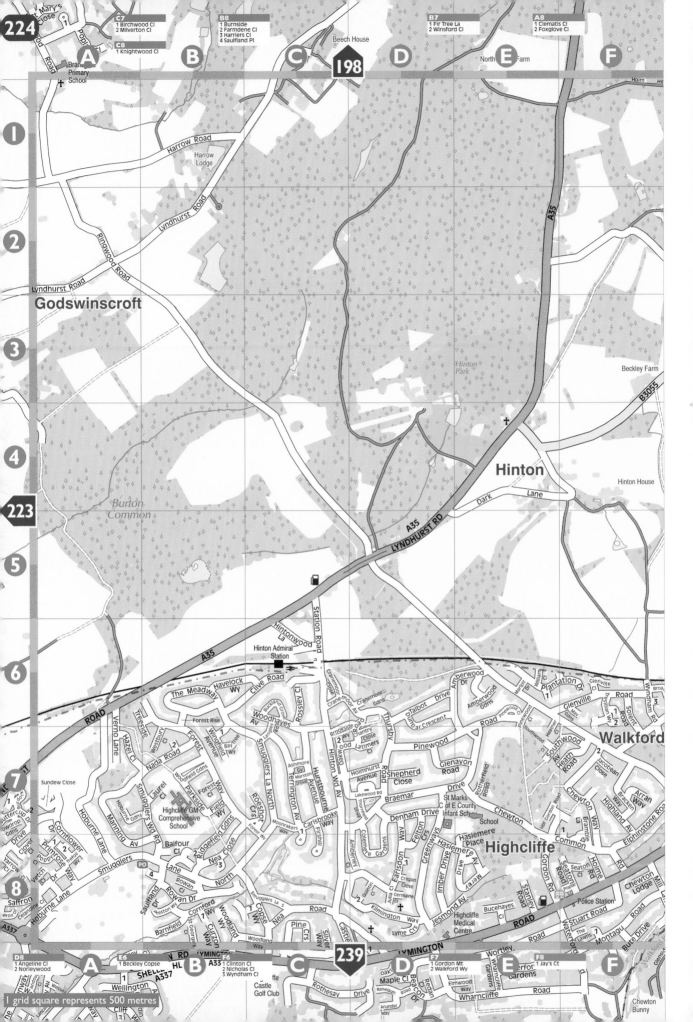

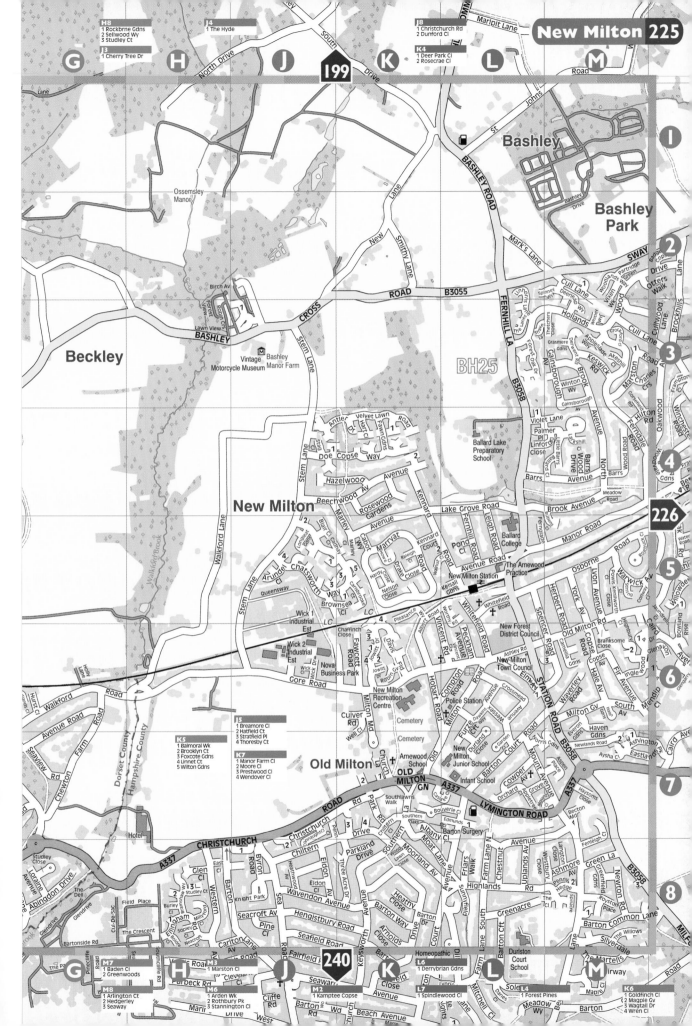

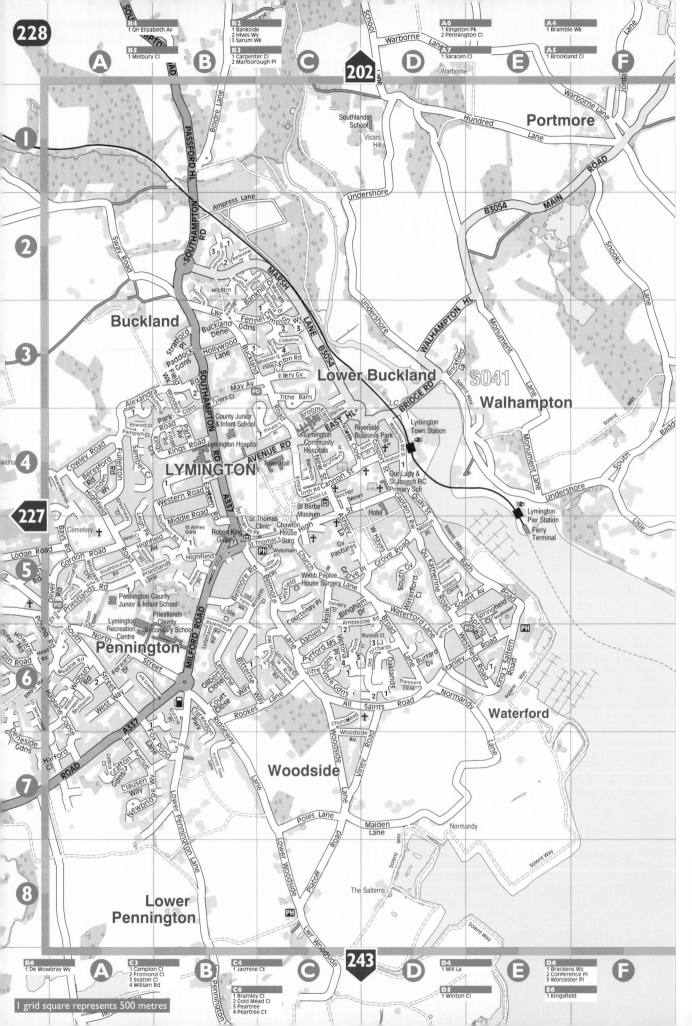

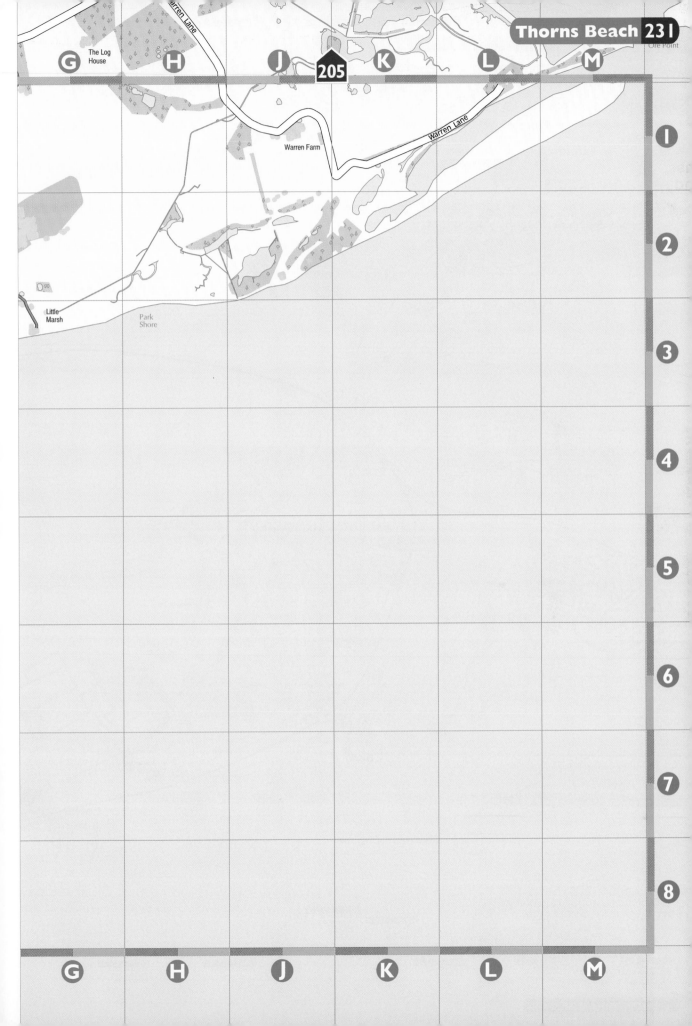

G   The Log
     House

H

J   205

K

L

M

Ore Point

Warren Farm

Warren Lane

Warren Lane

Little
Marsh

Park
Shore

1

2

3

4

5

6

7

8

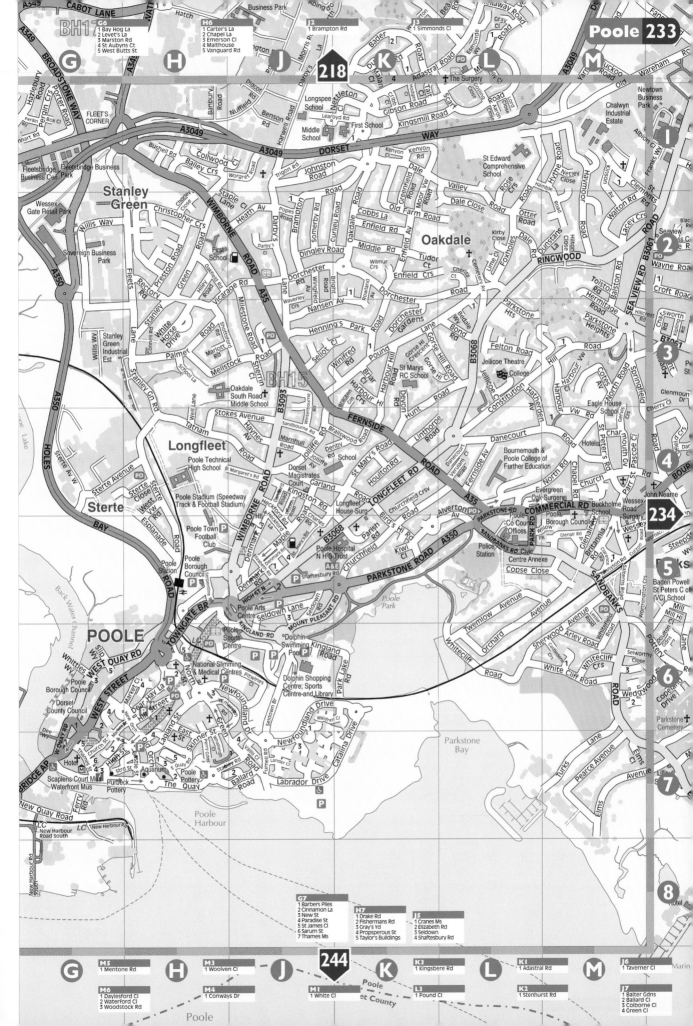

HIGHCLIFFE

G1
1 Regent Wy
2 Silver St
3 Wickfield Cl

A4
1 Roscrea Cl

J1
1 Beaufort Cl
2 Britannia Wy
3 Caledonian Cl
4 Sunderland Dr
5 Swordfish Dr

G2
1 B Homage Gdns
2 Sopwith Cl
3 The Coppice

H1
1 Auckland Rd
2 Saxonford Rd

Highcliffe Medical Centre

Christchurch Business Cen
Business Cen

Runway
Welles
Andover
Wander
Wessex
Valiant Cl
Halifax Wy
Brabazon Dr
Austen Cl
Viscount Dr
Blenheim
Stirling
Tangmere
Homage La
Bure

LYMINGTON RD
SHELLEY HL
SHELLEY CL
A337
LYMINGTON RD
A337
LYMINGTON
A337

Wellington Av
Dunedin Av
East Cliff Wy
Seaway Avenue
Seafield Road
Hynesbury Road
Southcliffe Road
Bure Lane
Bure Rd
Friars Rd
Rook Hill Rd
Glengarry
Vecta Cl
Cliff Dr

Friars Cliff

Priors Rd
Freshwater Rd
Medina Wy
Seaway Av

Barnfield
Shelley
Rowan
Gowan Dr
Copse
Nea Rd
La S
Nea
Road
Kiming
Germaine
Castle Av

Highcliffe Castle Golf Club

Rothesay
Drive
Ranelagh
Road
Regan Rd
Beacon Dr
Arundel Wy

Maple Cl
Oakley Way
Elmwood Wy

Highcliffe Medical Centre

Bucehaves
Stuart Rd
The Lawns
Wortley Rd
Waterford Gardens
Wharncliffe Gardens
Wharncliffe
Road
Waterford
Road

Mudeford

Avon Run
Bure Lane
Island View La
Avon Run
Wren Cl
Robins Wy

Capesthorne

Highcliffe Medical Centre

I 240

L1
1 Abbots Cl

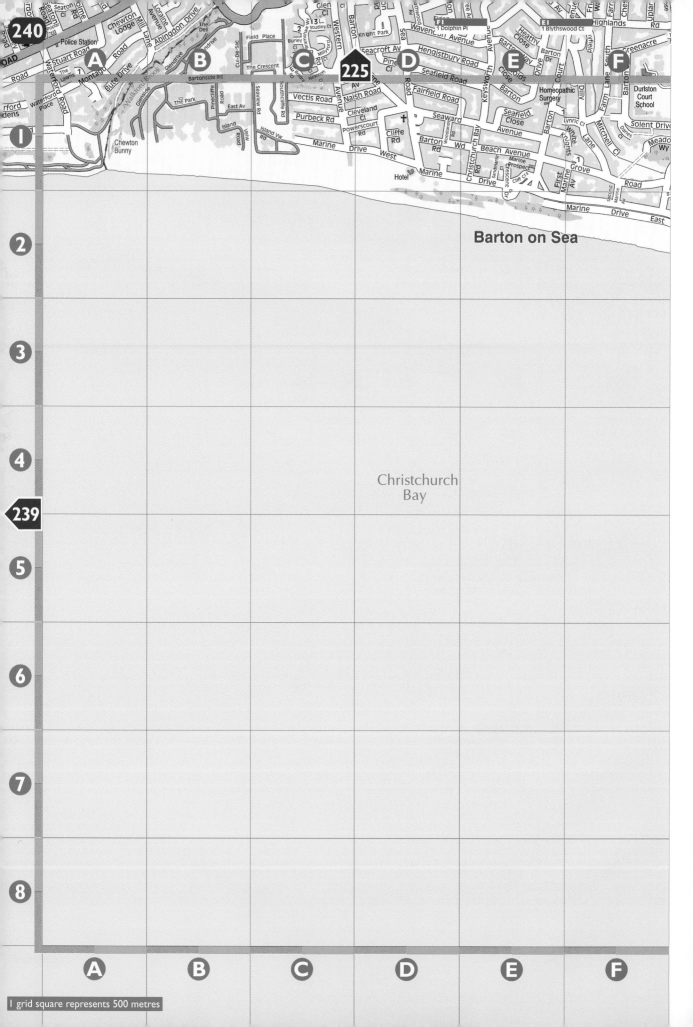

A   B   C   225   D   E   F

Police Station

Chewton Lodge

Abingdon Drive

The Dell

Field Place

The Crescent

Bartonside Rd

Glen Cl

Studley Ct

Barton

Seacroft Av

Knight Park

Dolphin Pl

Wavencliff Avenue

Hengistbury Road

1 Blythswood Ct

Heathy Close

Barton Court

Highlands Rd

Greenacre

Durlston Court School

The Lawns

Stuart Road

Waterford Place

Montagu

Elite Drive

Glendrive

Glenside

Walkford Brook

The Park

Pinecliffe Road

East Av

Island Road

Island Vw Rd

Seaview Rd

Southcliffe Rd

Vectis Road

Burley Cl

Milly Ct

Western

Naish Road

AV

Cleveland Cl

Powerscourt Rd

Pine

Seafield Road

Fairfield Road

Seaward

Seafield Close

Avenue

Homeopathic Surgery

Keysworth Av

Barton Drive

Lynric Cl

White Knights

Mill Rd

Farm Lane South

Solent Drive

Danes

Meadow Wy

Chewton Bunny

Island Vw

Marine

Drive

Cliffe Rd

Barton Rd

Wd

Beach Avenue

Christchurch Bay Rd

Marine Prospect

Cliff C'S

First Marine Av

Second Marine AV

Grove

Road

Hotel

West

Marine

Sandmartin Dr

Crescent

Marine

Drive

East

Barton on Sea

Christchurch Bay

239

A   B   C   D   E   F

I grid square represents 500 metres

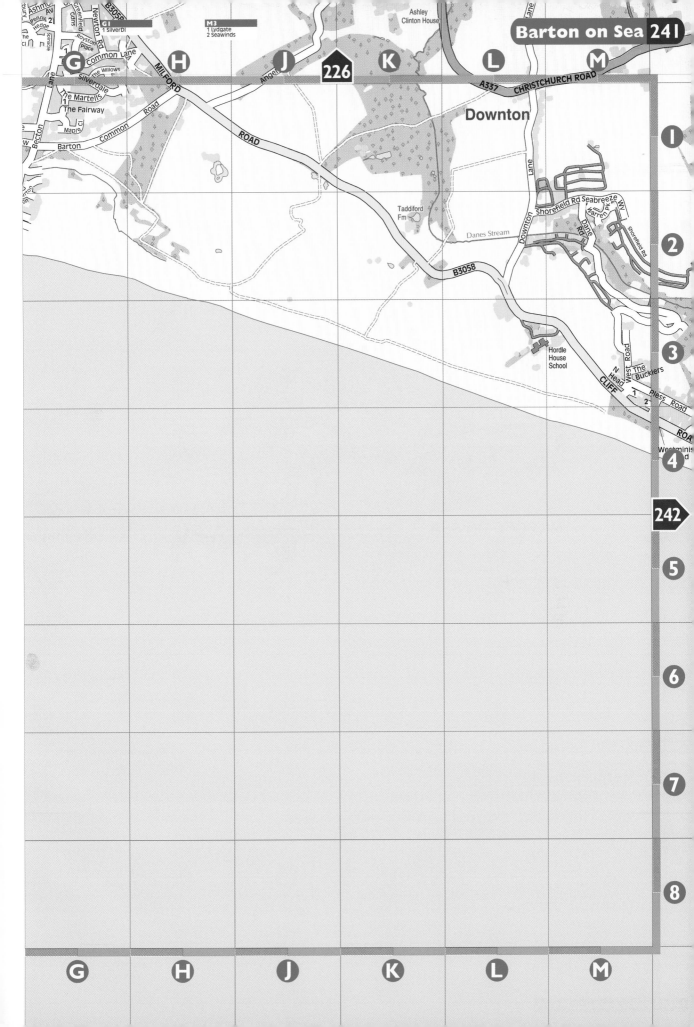

226

Downton

Ashley
Clinton House

Taddiford
Fm

Danes Stream

B3058

Hordle
House
School

CHRISTCHURCH ROAD
A337

Downton Shorefield Rd Seabreeze
Warren Pk
Dane
Rd
Shorefield Rd

Lane

N
Head
CLIFF
West Road
Pless Road
The
Bucklers
ROA

Westminis

MILFORD
ROAD
Common Road
Barton
Angel

Becton
The Martells
The Fairway
Maple Cl
Newton Rd
Royston
Place
Common Lane
The Willows
Silverdale
Greenfield
Gdns
SilverDl
G1
Ashmc
AV
penk
Hedge

M3
1 Lydgate
2 Seawinds

G H J K L M

I
2
3
242
4
5
6
7
8

Lower
Pennington

G   H   J   228   PH   K   L   M

Woodside
Platoff
The Salterns
Solent Way
Lwr Pennington Lane
Pennington House
E Woodside
Pennington
Marshes
Solent Way
Iley Lane

I

2

Avon Water

3

Van Farm

Keyhaven
Marshes

4

Harewood
Gn

Solent Way

5

Solent Way

6

7

Solent Way
Solent Way

8

G   H   J   K   L   M

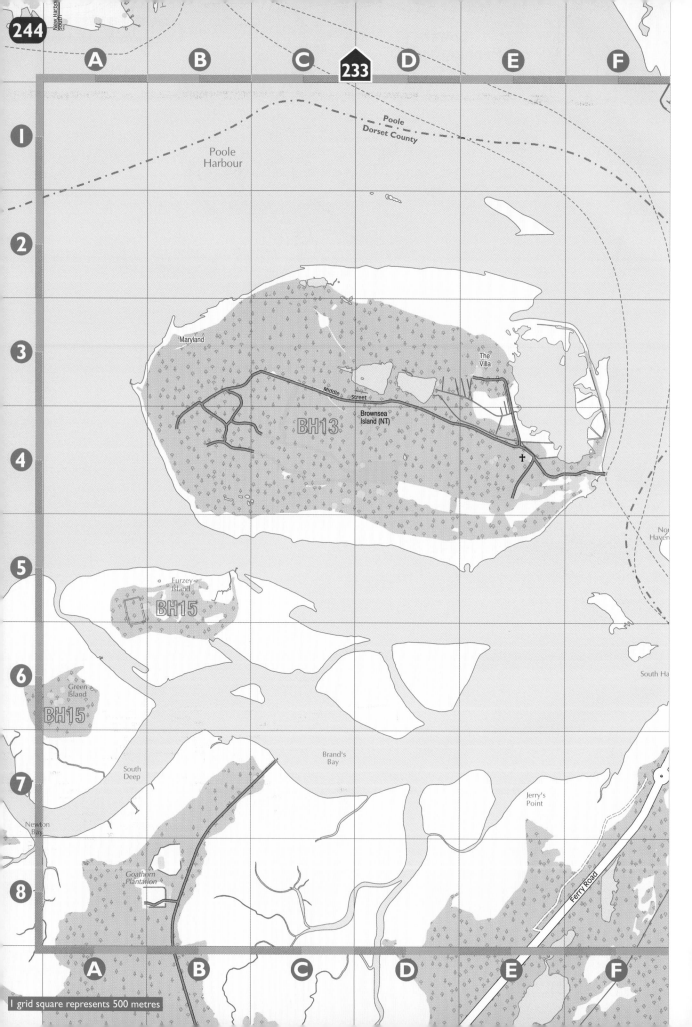

A B C D E F

I

2

3

4

5

6

7

8

A B C D E F

Poole
Dorset County

Poole
Harbour

Maryland

The Villa

Middle Street

Brownsea
Island (NT)

BH13

North
Haven

Furzey
Island

BH15

Green
Island

BH15

South Ha

South
Deep

Brand's
Bay

Jerry's
Point

Newton
Bay

Goathorn
Plantation

Ferry Road

New Harbour
South

1 grid square represents 500 metres

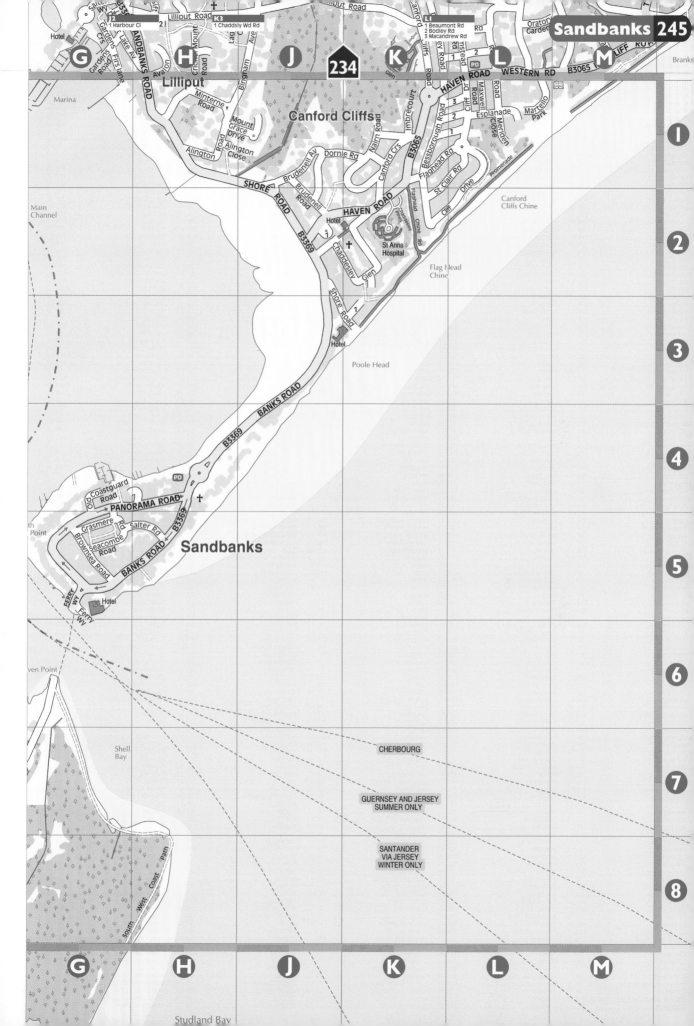

Branks

I

2

3

4

5

6

7

8

G **H** **J** **K** **L** **M**

Hotel

Marina

Lilliput

Canford Cliffs

1 Harbour Ci
1 Chaddsly Wd Rd

1 Beaumont Rd
2 Bodley Rd
3 Macandrew Rd

Lilliput Road

ANDBANKS ROAD

Minterne Road

Mount Grace Drive

Alington Road

Alington Close

Alington

SHORE ROAD

Brudenell Av

Dornie Rd

Nairn Road

Canford Crs

B3065

HAVEN ROAD

Hotel

Chaddesley Glen

St Anns Hospital

Flaghead Chine Rd

St Clair Rd

Cliff

Cliff Drive

Canford Cliffs Chine

Flag Head Chine

WESTERN RD

Esplanade

Merden Close

Martello Park

Promenade

B3065

Main Channel

Shore Road

Hotel

Poole Head

BANKS ROAD

B3369

Coastguard Road

Old Coastguard Road

PANORAMA ROAD

Grasmere Rd

Salter Rd

Seacombe Road

Brownsea Road

BANKS ROAD

B3369

Sandbanks

PO

th Point

FERRY WY

Ferry WY

Hotel

ven Point

Shell Bay

CHERBOURG

GUERNSEY AND JERSEY
SUMMER ONLY

SANTANDER
VIA JERSEY
WINTER ONLY

South West Coast Path

Studland Bay

Place	Pg	Grid
Abbotswood	50	F5
Abbots Worthy	17	J2
Abshot	158	E8
Alderholt	121	K2
Aldermoor	105	M5
Allbrook	81	M2
Alverstoke	10	B7
Ameysford	168	A7
Ampfield	52	B5
Anchorage Park	188	A5
Anmore	139	M4
Ann's Hill	10	A1
Anthill Common	139	H2
Applemore	154	E4
Ashfield	79	G4
Ashford	97	J7
Ashlett	181	L5
Ashley	170	A3
Ashley	226	A5
Ashley Heath	169	K2
Ashton	85	G5
Ashurst	129	G6
Ashurst Bridge	129	G3
Awbridge	49	K4
Baffins	211	M1
Bailey Green	33	H5
Balmerlawn	175	M5
Bank	151	H5
Bar End	27	G2
Barrow Hill	103	J6
Barrow Hill	216	B4
Bartley	127	L1
Barton on Sea	240	E2
Bashley	225	L1
Bashley Park	225	M2
Bassett	106	F3
Bassett Green	106	F3
Battramsley	201	L6
Battramsley Cross	202	A7
Baybridge	56	B5
Beacon Hill	216	E6
Beaulieu	178	C7
Beauworth	29	M8
Beckley	225	G3
Bedhampton	165	G7
Bell Hill	63	K3
Bickton	122	D2
Birchy Hill	201	G7
Bishopstoke	82	B6
Bishop's Waltham	85	G7
Bisterne	196	D2
Bisterne Close	173	H6
Bitterne	132	C1
Bitterne Park	107	J7
Blackfield	180	E8
Blackhill	76	F7
Blashford	146	D5
Bleak Hill	122	A5
Blendworth	141	H1
Blissford	98	D8
Boarhunt	161	M3
Bohemia	73	M4
Boldre	202	B7
Boorley Green	109	K6
Borden	66	C2
Botley	134	F2
Bournemouth	15	G6
Boveridge	94	F6
Bowling Green	227	K2
Boyatt Wood	81	L3
Braishfield	51	H1
Brambridge	54	C8
Bramdean	31	L4
Bramshaw	101	L4
Breach	167	H7
Breamore	71	M7
Bridgemary	184	F5
Broad Chalke	40	A1
Broadgate	52	D6
Broadoak	134	C1
Brockbridge	87	H6
Brockenhurst	175	J7
Brockhampton	8	A7
Brockhurst	209	H2
Brook	22	B2
Brook	101	M7
Brooke's Hill	104	A4
Brook Hill	101	M6
Brown Heath	110	B3
Bucket Corner	80	B1
Buckland	228	A3
Bucklers Hard	205	G3
Bull Hill	202	F7
Bunker's Hill	102	F6
Bunstead	53	H2
Burgates	36	D2
Buriton	91	K3
Burley	172	F5
Burley Beacon	172	C6
Burley Lawn	173	G5
Burley Street	172	C3
Burridge	134	F7
Bursledon	133	L8
Butlocks Heath	157	H1
Buttsash	155	M8
Butt's Green	20	F7
Cadnam	102	E8
Calmore	128	B7
Calshot	181	K8
Camel Green	121	M2
Canada	76	D7
Canford Cliffs	245	J1
Carter's Clay	48	F2
Catherington	115	M7
Catisfield	159	L7
Causeway	63	K6
Causeway	140	F3
Chalton	117	H3
Chandler's Ford	53	J8
Charlton-All-Saints	44	E4
Cheriton	30	C3
Chidden	88	E8
Chilcomb	27	L3
Chilworth	80	C7
Chilworth Old Village	80	B6
Chithurst	66	F7
Church Common	35	G8
Clanfield	115	M2
Clayhall	11	G8
Clayhill	151	L5
Colbury	129	H6
Colden Common	54	F7
Colehill	192	D1
Compton	22	B1
Compton	54	C1
Compton	118	E6
Compton End	26	B7
Coombe	88	E2
Copnor	187	L7
Copythorne	103	H6
Corfe Mullen	217	G2
Corhampton	87	G3
Cosham	163	L8
Cowesfield Green	47	H5
Cowplain	140	D5
Coxford	105	M6
Crab Orchard	144	C6
Crampmoor	51	K7
Cranborne	94	C8
Crendell	120	D1
Criddlestyle	98	A7
Cripplestyle	120	E3
Critchell's Green	20	D8
Crockerhill	160	E1
Croucheston	40	F1
Crow	171	G4
Crowdhill	83	H3
Cupernham	50	F7
Curbridge	135	H4
Curdridge	110	D8
Custards	151	L3
Daggons	120	F3
Damerham	96	C3
Dean	85	K5
Deanlane End	142	B3
Denmead	139	K3
Denvilles	9	L2
Dewlands Common	144	B3
Dibden	155	H3
Dibden Purlieu	155	G7
Dilton	202	D1
Downton	73	C1
Downton	241	L1
Drayton	164	A8
Droxford	87	G7
Dumpford	66	D8
Dunbridge	21	H7
Dundridge	86	A7
Durleighmarsh	64	F5
Durley	110	A2
Durley Street	84	B3
Durns Town	201	G6
Durrants	141	M8
East Boldre	204	B3
East Dean	19	M6
East End	60	C3
East End	229	M1
East Grimstead	18	B4
East Harting	93	J5
Eastland Gate	140	B3
Eastleigh	82	A5
East Liss	37	G5
East Marden	119	L6
East Martin	69	H4
East Meon	61	J8
Eastney	212	A5
Easton	17	M3
East Tytherley	20	D1
East Wellow	76	F3
Ebblake	145	H4
Eling	129	M3
Ellingham	146	C3
Elmers Marsh	39	K3
Elson	185	L8
Elsted	93	M4
Emery Down	151	H2
Emsworth	190	C1
Everton	227	J7
Exbury	205	M3
Exton	87	H1
Fair Oak	83	H6
Fareham	6	F5
Farlington	164	B8
Fawley	180	F6
Ferndown	193	M3
Filmore Hill	32	F4
Finchdean	142	B2
Fisher's Pond	83	G2
Fleet	189	K8
Fleetend	158	D7
Fleetlands	185	G3
Flexford	52	E8
Flood Street	97	L1
Fordingbridge	97	M7
Forest Gate	139	H1
Forestside	142	F2
Forton	209	M2
Foulford	171	L1
Foxhills	129	H5
Foyers	128	A5
Fratton	211	J2
Freemantle	131	G2
The Frenches	49	G6
Frenchmoor	19	L3
Fritham	100	E7
Frogham	123	J2
Frostlane	156	A6
Froxfield Green	34	B8
Fryern Hill	81	J2
Fulflood	2	B6
Funtley	160	C3
Furzedown	23	C1
Furze Hill	123	J5
Furzeley Corner	139	K7
Furzey	126	E5
Furzey Lodge	177	M7
Fyfield	102	C3
Fyning	65	M3
Glebe	111	H5
Godshill	98	D6
Goldenhayes	127	M4
Golden Hill	226	B5
Goose Green	151	L4
Gosport	11	H2
Gosport	51	M6
Gotham	120	C5
Grange Estate	169	K8
The Green	20	A1
Habin	65	L6
Hale	73	G7
Halecommon	65	K3
Halterworth	79	H1
Hambledon	114	B6
Hamble-le-Rice	157	K5
Hambrook	167	L6
Hampton Park	107	H5
Hamworthy	232	D5
Hangersley	147	J6
Harbridge	122	C7
Harbridge Green	122	B6
Hardley	180	A2
Hardway	209	M1
Harefield	133	G1
Harestock	16	B5
Hatch Bottom	108	C6
Hatchet Gate	177	M8
Hatchet Green	73	H5
Hatt Hill	21	J7
Havant	8	E1
Hawkley	35	K1
Hayling Island	189	L6
Headbourne Worthy	16	E3
Heathfield	160	A7
Hedge End	133	M1
Hensting	55	J7
Hermitage	166	E7
Hides Close	178	D4
Highbridge	82	C1
Highbury	187	K2
Highcliffe	224	E8
High Cross	34	E6
Highfield	106	F6
Hightown	133	J4
Hightown	171	H2
Highwood	147	H4
Hill Brow	37	H6
Hill Head	183	K7
Hill Park	6	A1
Hillpound	112	B4
Hill Side	36	F4
Hillstreet	104	A3
Hill Top	179	G4
Hill View	217	H4
Hillyfields	105	H4
Hilsea	187	K4
Hiltingbury	53	J6
Hinton	224	E4
Hinton Ampner	30	D4
Hocombe	53	H5
Hoe	111	L1
Hoe Gate	138	D1
Holbury	180	A5
Hook	182	C1
Hook Park	182	B2
Hooksway	119	M3
Hordle	226	E4
Horndean	141	G2
Horton Common	144	A6
Horton Heath	109	J1
Hound	157	J2
Hounsdown	129	J4
Hungerford	123	G3
Hursley	53	G1
Hyde	3	H5
Hyde	123	G2
Hythe	155	M4
Ibsley	146	E1
Iping	67	H6
Itchen	132	C5
Kents Oak	49	K3
Keyhaven	242	F5
Kilmeston	30	C7
Kimbridge	21	K8
Kingsmead	112	B8
Kingston	170	C7
Kingston	211	K1
Kings Worthy	17	H2
Knapp	52	C4
Ladwell	53	G4
Lake	232	C7
Landford	75	J4
Landfordwood	75	J1
Lane End	29	H8
Lane End	33	J1
Langdown	155	M5
Langley	37	L2
Langley	206	B1
Langrish	62	B4
Langstone	189	J2
Leagreen	226	E8
Lee	78	F8
Lee Ground	159	L3
Lee-on-the-Solent	208	A2
Leigh Park	165	H4
Lepe	206	E6
Lilliput	245	H1
Linford	147	L6
Linwood	123	M8
Liss	36	F5
Liss Forest	36	E1
Little Holbury	179	M3
Little Posbrook	183	J3
Littleton	16	A3
Lockerley	20	D7
Locks Heath	158	F4
London Minstead	127	G4
Long Common	109	L7
Lord's Hill	105	M4
Lordswood	106	C4
Lovedean	140	C2
Lover	73	L3
Lower Bordean	61	M2
Lower Brook	22	A4
Lower Buckland	228	C3
Lower Burgate	97	L4
Lower Daggons	120	E1
Lower Holwell	120	B2
Lower Pennington	228	A8
Lower Ratley	49	L5
Lower Slackstead	51	L1
Lower Swanwick	134	A8
Lower Turmer	146	B1
Lower Upham	84	C4
Lowford	133	L7
Lumley	166	E7
Lymington	228	B4
Lymore	242	E2
Lyndhurst	151	J3
Malwood	126	E4
Marchwood	130	C6
Martin	69	H5
Martin Drove End	68	B1
Maybush	105	K6
Mead End	139	L5
Mead End	200	C7
Meon	183	J5
Merry Oak	132	C3
Meyrick Park	14	C1
Michelmersh	22	B7
Midanbury	107	L8
Milford on Sea	242	A5
Milland	38	D6
Millbrook	130	C1
Milton	212	A4
Minstead	126	F5
The Mint	36	F3
Mockbeggar	147	H1
Moorcourt	104	B1
Moorgreen	108	E5
Moortown	170	E3
Morestead	27	L8
Morgan's Vale	73	H1
Mottisfont	21	K6
Mount Sorrel	40	A2
Netley	156	F7
Netley Hill	133	L4
Netley Marsh	128	E2
Newbridge	102	D5
New Brighton	166	E5
New Cheriton	30	C4
Newgrounds	98	F6
New Milton	225	J4
Newton	46	E6
Newton	49	G4
Newton	84	E8
Newton	126	F6
New Town	132	E7
Newtown	138	A2
Newtown	182	B1
Nob's Crook	82	F1
No Man's Land	17	L8
Nomansland	75	J8
Norleywood	203	K8
North Baddesley	79	M4
North Boarhunt	137	L6
Northbrook	85	H7
North Charford	73	H4
North End	30	B1
North End	96	B3
North End	187	K6
Northfields	54	F1
North Gorley	122	F5
North Hayling	189	M5
North Kingston	171	G6
North Marden	119	L4
Northney	190	A4
North Pouliner	147	H6
North Stoneham	107	J1
North Street	72	A6
North Weirs	175	G7
Nursling	105	H3
Nursted	92	B1
Nutbourne	191	K1
Nutburn	80	A3
Nutwood	179	J7
Nyewood	65	K8
Oakshott	35	J4
Ocean Village	5	K7
Ogdens	123	G3
Old Milton	225	J7
Old Netley	133	J7
Old Portsmouth	12	C3
Old Shirley	105	M7
Oliver's Battery	25	M5
Ossemsley	199	J7
Otterbourne	54	A4
Otterwood	179	H8
Outwick	71	K8
Ower	103	K2
Owslebury	55	M5
Park Gate	158	F3
Paulsgrove	162	E8
Peartree Green	132	B4
Peel Common	184	D6
Pennington	228	A6
Pentridge	68	A8
Petersfield	63	J5
Picket Hill	147	L8
Pikeshill	151	J2
Pilley	202	F6
Pilley Bailey	202	D6
Pitt	25	M5
Plaitford	75	M4
Plaitford Green	48	B8
Pooksgreen	130	B6
Portchester	161	M8
Portmore	228	E1
Portsea	12	E1
Portsea Island	187	M8
Portswood	107	G7
Post Green	216	D2
Pouliner	147	H6
Prince's Marsh	36	E6
Prinsted	191	G1
Privett	33	H6
Privett	209	J5
Pucknall	51	L2
Purbrook	164	B3
Pylehill	83	H5
Queen's Corner	39	H8
Rake	37	K4
Ramsdean	62	B7
Ratlake	52	D5
Redbridge	105	H8
Redford	39	K7
Red Hill	141	M7
Redlynch	73	K2
Ridge	78	B7
Ridge Common	63	H3
Ringwood	146	C3
Robins	66	F1
Rockbourne	70	D7
Rockford	147	G3
Rogate	65	K5
Romsey	78	D1
Round Hill	176	D8
Row Ash	110	F8
Rowland's Castle	142	A6
Rowner	185	G3
Rownhams	105	L1
Rushcombe Bottom	217	J1
Rushington	129	K2
Rushmore	114	D6
St Austins	201	M8
St Cross	26	E3
St Denys	107	H8
St Giles's Hill	3	K8
St Ives	169	L3
St Leonards	169	J4
Sandbanks	245	L5
Sandford	171	G8
Sandleheath	96	E6
Sandy Down	202	A4
Sarisbury	158	C3
Setley	201	L3
Shawford	54	D1
Shedfield	136	B1
Sheet	64	A3
Sherfield English	48	C7
Shirley	106	C8
Shirley Holms	201	L7
Shirley Warren	106	A6
Shirrell Heath	111	M7
Shobley	147	L7
Sholing	132	F4
Sholing Common	132	E3
Shootash	49	J7
Shorley	30	A7
Shorn Hill	103	M5
Silkstead	53	K3
Sleepers Hill	26	C2
Soake	139	M5
Soberton	113	H2
Soberton Heath	112	F7
Southampton	4	F7
South Baddesley	229	J2
Southbourne	167	J8
South Down	54	C3
South End	96	B5
South Gorley	122	F6
South Harting	92	F4
South Hayling	213	J6
South Weirs	175	H8
Southwick	162	C2
Spearywell	21	J5
Springbourne	15	M1
Stamshaw	186	F7
Standon	24	F6
Stanmore	26	C3
Stapehill	193	J3
Stedham	67	K7
Steep	63	K1
Steep Marsh	35	M7
Stockheath	165	J5
Stoke	189	L7
Stoke Common	82	B3
Stonehills	181	G6
Stoner Hill	35	G8
Stoney Cross	126	C4
Stonyford	103	L4
Stonymarsh	21	M7
Street End	85	H4
Stroud	62	F4
Stubbermere	142	E8
Stubbington	184	B5
Stuckton	123	G1
Swanmore	112	A3
Swanwick	158	E1
Sway	200	E7
Swaythling	107	K5
Tapnage	136	A7
Terwick Common	66	A3
Testwood	104	D6
Thorney Hill	198	C4
Thorney Island	191	G5
Thornhill	133	J3
Thornhill Park	133	H1
Thorns Beach	230	F2
Three Legged Cross	144	C8
Tidpit	69	J6
Timsbury	50	B1
Tipner	186	F5
Tiptoe	200	B8
Titchfield	159	J8
Titchfield Common	158	E7
Titchfield Park	159	H5
Titty Hill	39	H8
Toothill	79	K7
Tote Hill	67	K3
Totton	104	F8
Townhill Park	107	L6
Trickett's Cross	194	D1
Trotten Marsh	66	B1
Trotton	66	D7
Trotts	130	A5
Tullecombe	37	K8
Turkey Island	93	H5
Turkey Island	136	D1
Turlin Moor	232	A4
Turmer	122	B8
Twyford	54	F2
Tye	190	A2
Upham	84	E2
Up Marden	119	J8
Upper Burgate	97	M2
Upper Canterton	126	D2
Upper Pennington	227	L5
Upper Ratley	49	L4
Upper Shirley	106	C6
Upper Slackstead	23	M7
Upper Street	71	L6
Upper Swanmore	86	B8
Upper Wardley	38	F3
Upton	105	J1
Upton	232	A1
Verwood	144	D2
Walhampton	228	C3
Walkford	224	F7
Wallington	7	M4
Waltham Chase	111	K5

Walton Heath 162 A1
Warblington 9 L6
Wardley 38 F4
Warnford 59 K4
Warren Corner 34 F3
Warsash 158 B7
Waterford 228 E6
Waterlooville 140 D8
Wecock 140 C4
Weeke 2 B4
Wellow Wood 48 C8
Westbourne 166 F4

West Cliff 14 B8
West Common 206 C2
West Dean 19 J5
West End 6 E8
West End 108 D8
West Harting 92 F1
West Leigh 165 L3
West Liss 36 E3
West Marden 118 D8
West Meon 60 A4
West Meon Woodlands 32 B6
West Moors 168 E6

Weston 63 G8
Weston 132 C7
Weston Common 132 H4
West Thorney 191 H6
West Tisted 32 D1
West Wellow 76 D5
Whitenap 79 H1
Whiteparish 46 F4
Whitsbury 70 F5
Wick 72 B1
Wickham 136 E5
Widley 164 A6

Wildern 134 A1
Wimborne Minster 192 A3
Wimpson 105 K7
Winchester 3 G9
Winnall 3 L6
Winsor 103 J7
Wintershill 84 C7
Wittensford 102 D8
Woodcot 184 E5
Woodfalls 73 H3
Woodgreen 72 C8
Woodington 77 G2

Woodlands 128 C5
Woodley 51 H7
Woodmancote 167 K4
Woodmansgreen 39 K5
Woodside 228 C7
Woolbeding 67 L6
Woolsbridge 168 E1
Woolston 132 C6
Wootton 199 L6
Worlds End 138 D3
Wymering 163 J8

USING THE STREET INDEX

Street names are listed alphabetically. Each street name is followed by its postal town or area locality, the Postcode District, the page number, and the reference to the square in which the name is found.

Abbey Cl *FAWY* SO45 .... 155 L5 [box]

Some entries are followed by a number in a blue box. This number indicates the location of the street within the referenced grid square. The full street name is listed at the side of the map page.

GENERAL ABBREVIATIONS

ACC ... ACCESS
ALY ... ALLEY
AP ... APPROACH
AR ... ARCADE
ASS ... ASSOCIATION
AV ... AVENUE
BCH ... BEACH
BLDS ... BUILDINGS
BND ... BEND
BNK ... BANK
BR ... BRIDGE
BRK ... BROOK
BTM ... BOTTOM
BUS ... BUSINESS
BVD ... BOULEVARD
BY ... BYPASS
CATH ... CATHEDRAL
CEM ... CEMETERY
CEN ... CENTRE
CFT ... CROFT
CH ... CHURCH
CHA ... CHASE
CHYD ... CHURCHYARD
CIR ... CIRCLE
CIRC ... CIRCUS
CL ... CLOSE
CLFS ... CLIFFS
CMP ... CAMP
CNR ... CORNER
CO ... COUNTY
COLL ... COLLEGE
COM ... COMMON
COMM ... COMMISSION
CON ... CONVENT
COT ... COTTAGE
COTS ... COTTAGES
CP ... CAPE
CPS ... COPSE
CR ... CREEK
CREM ... CREMATORIUM
CRS ... CRESCENT
CSWY ... CAUSEWAY
CT ... COURT
CTRL ... CENTRAL
CTS ... COURTS
CTYD ... COURTYARD

CUTT ... CUTTINGS
CV ... COVE
CYN ... CANYON
DEPT ... DEPARTMENT
DL ... DALE
DM ... DAM
DR ... DRIVE
DRO ... DROVE
DRY ... DRIVEWAY
DWGS ... DWELLINGS
E ... EAST
EMB ... EMBANKMENT
EMBY ... EMBASSY
ESP ... ESPLANADE
EST ... ESTATE
EX ... EXCHANGE
EXPY ... EXPRESSWAY
EXT ... EXTENSION
F/O ... FLYOVER
FC ... FOOTBALL CLUB
FK ... FORK
FLD ... FIELD
FLDS ... FIELDS
FLS ... FALLS
FLS ... FLATS
FM ... FARM
FT ... FORT
FWY ... FREEWAY
FY ... FERRY
GA ... GATE
GAL ... GALLERY
GDN ... GARDEN
GDNS ... GARDENS
GLD ... GLADE
GLN ... GLEN
GN ... GREEN
GND ... GROUND
GRA ... GRANGE
GRG ... GARAGE
GT ... GREAT
GTWY ... GATEWAY
GV ... GROVE
HGR ... HIGHER
HL ... HILL
HLS ... HILLS
HO ... HOUSE

HOL ... HOLLOW
HOSP ... HOSPITAL
HRB ... HARBOUR
HTH ... HEATH
HTS ... HEIGHTS
HVN ... HAVEN
HWY ... HIGHWAY
IMP ... IMPERIAL
IN ... INLET
IND EST ... INDUSTRIAL ESTATE
INF ... INFIRMARY
INFO ... INFORMATION
INT ... INTERCHANGE
IS ... ISLAND
JCT ... JUNCTION
JTY ... JETTY
KG ... KING
KNL ... KNOLL
L ... LAKE
LA ... LANE
LDG ... LODGE
LGT ... LIGHT
LK ... LOCK
LKS ... LAKES
LNDG ... LANDING
LTL ... LITTLE
LWR ... LOWER
MAG ... MAGISTRATE
MAN ... MANSIONS
MD ... MEAD
MDW ... MEADOWS
MEM ... MEMORIAL
MKT ... MARKET
MKTS ... MARKETS
ML ... MALL
ML ... MILL
MNR ... MANOR
MS ... MEWS
MSN ... MISSION
MT ... MOUNT
MTN ... MOUNTAIN
MTS ... MOUNTAINS
MUS ... MUSEUM
MWY ... MOTORWAY
N ... NORTH
NE ... NORTH EAST

NW ... NORTH WEST
O/P ... OVERPASS
OFF ... OFFICE
ORCH ... ORCHARD
OV ... OVAL
PAL ... PALACE
PAS ... PASSAGE
PAV ... PAVILION
PDE ... PARADE
PH ... PUBLIC HOUSE
PK ... PARK
PKWY ... PARKWAY
PL ... PLACE
PLN ... PLAIN
PLNS ... PLAINS
PLZ ... PLAZA
POL ... POLICE STATION
PR ... PRINCE
PREC ... PRECINCT
PREP ... PREPARATORY
PRIM ... PRIMARY
PROM ... PROMENADE
PRS ... PRINCESS
PRT ... PORT
PT ... POINT
PTH ... PATH
PZ ... PIAZZA
QD ... QUADRANT
QU ... QUEEN
QY ... QUAY
R ... RIVER
RBT ... ROUNDABOUT
RD ... ROAD
RDG ... RIDGE
REP ... REPUBLIC
RES ... RESERVOIR
RFC ... RUGBY FOOTBALL CLUB
RI ... RISE
RP ... RAMP
RW ... ROW
S ... SOUTH
SCH ... SCHOOL
SE ... SOUTH EAST
SER ... SERVICE AREA
SH ... SHORE
SHOP ... SHOPPING

SKWY ... SKYWAY
SMT ... SUMMIT
SOC ... SOCIETY
SP ... SPUR
SPR ... SPRING
SQ ... SQUARE
ST ... STREET
STN ... STATION
STR ... STREAM
STRD ... STRAND
SW ... SOUTH WEST
TDG ... TRADING
TER ... TERRACE
THWY ... THROUGHWAY
TNL ... TUNNEL
TOLL ... TOLLWAY
TPK ... TURNPIKE
TR ... TRACK
TRL ... TRAIL
TWR ... TOWER
U/P ... UNDERPASS
UNI ... UNIVERSITY
UPR ... UPPER
V ... VALE
VA ... VALLEY
VIAD ... VIADUCT
VIL ... VILLA
VIS ... VISTA
VLG ... VILLAGE
VLS ... VILLAS
VW ... VIEW
W ... WEST
WD ... WOOD
WHF ... WHARF
WK ... WALK
WKS ... WALKS
WLS ... WELLS
WY ... WAY
YD ... YARD
YHA ... YOUTH HOSTEL

POSTCODE TOWNS AND AREA ABBREVIATIONS

ALTN ... Alton
BDST ... Broadstone
BKME/WDN ... Branksome/Wallisdown
BMTH ... Bournemouth
BOSC ... Boscombe
BPWT ... Bishop's Waltham
BROC ... Brockenhurst
BWD ... Bearwood
CCLF ... Canford Cliffs
CFDH ... Canford Heath
CHAM ... Cosham
CHAR ... Charminster
CHCH/BSGR ... Christchurch/Bransgore
CHFD ... Chandler's Ford
ELGH ... Eastleigh
EMRTH ... Emsworth/Southbourne

ENEY ... Eastney
EPSF ... Petersfield East
FAWY ... Fawley/Hythe
FBDG ... Fordingbridge
FERN ... Ferndown/West Moors
FHAM ... Fareham
FHAM/PORC ... Fareham/Portchester
FHAM/STUB ... Fareham/Stubbington
GPORT ... Gosport
HASM ... Haslemere
HAV ... Havant
HEND ... Hedge End
HISD ... Hayling Island
HLER ... Hamble-le-Rice
HORN ... Horndean
HSEA ... Hilsea

ITCH ... Itchen
LIPH ... Liphook
LISS ... Liss
LSOL/BMARY ... Lee-on-the-Solent/Bridgemary
LTDN ... Littledown
LYMN ... Lymington
LYND ... Lyndhurst
MIDH ... Midhurst
MOOR/WNTN ... Moordown/Winton
NALR ... New Alresford
NBAD ... North Baddesley
NBNE ... Northbourne
NEND ... North End
NMIL/BTOS ... New Milton/Barton on Sea
PLE ... Poole

PSEA ... Portsea
PSF ... Petersfield
PSTN ... Parkstone
PTSW ... Portswood
RCCH ... Rural Chichester
RGWD ... Ringwood
ROMY ... Romsey
ROWN ... Rownhams
RSAL ... Rural Salisbury
RWIN ... Rural Winchester
SBNE ... Southbourne
SELS ... Selsey
SHAM ... Southampton
SSEA ... Southsea
STOK ... Stockbridge
SWGE ... Swanage

TOTT ... Totton
TWDS ... Talbot Woods
UPTN ... Upton
VWD ... Verwood
WBNE ... Westbourne
WCLF ... West Cliff
WEND ... West End
WHAM ... Wickham
WIMB ... Wimborne Minster
WINC ... Winchester
WINW ... Winchester west
WSHM ... Southampton west
WVILLE ... Waterlooville/Denmead

Index - streets

10th - Ake

10th St *FAWY* SO45 ... 180 B4
11th St *FAWY* SO45 ... 180 B3
12th St *FAWY* SO45 ... 180 B3
13th St *FAWY* SO45 ... 180 B2
14th St *FAWY* SO45 ... 180 A3
1st St *FAWY* SO45 ... 180 E5
2nd St *FAWY* SO45 ... 180 E3
3rd St *FAWY* SO45 ... 180 D4
4th St *FAWY* SO45 ... 180 D4
5th St *FAWY* SO45 ... 180 D3
6th St *FAWY* SO45 ... 180 D2
7th St *FAWY* SO45 ... 180 C4
8th St *FAWY* SO45 ... 180 C4
9th St *FAWY* SO45 ... 180 B4

A

Aaron Cl *CFDH* BH17 ... 233 L1
Aaron Ct *TOTT* SO40 ... 130 D6
A Av *FAWY* SO45 ... 180 B3
Abbey Cl *FAWY* SO45 ... 155 L5 [box]
Abbeydore Rd *CHAM* PO6 ... 163 G7
Abbeyfield Dr *FHAM* PO15 ... 160 A6
Abbeyfields Cl *HLER* SO31 ... 157 H2
Abbey Gdns *WIMB* BH21 ... 193 H3
Abbey Hl *ITCH* SO19 ... 132 C8
Abbey Hill Cl *WINC* SO23 ... 3 G3
Abbey Hill Rd *WINC* SO23 ... 2 F3
Abbey Rd *FERN* BH22 ... 168 E8
FHAM PO15 ... 6 B4
Abbey Water *ROMY* SO51 ... 78 D1 [box]
Abbotsbury Rd *BDST* BH18 ... 217 J3
ELGH SO50 ... 82 E6
Abbots Cl *CHCH/BSGR* BH23 ... 239 L1 [box]
WVILLE PO7 ... 164 A4 [box]
Abbotsfield *TOTT* SO40 ... 129 J1
Abbotsfield Cl *ROWN* SO16 ... 106 B3
Abbotsford *TOTT* SO40 ... 127 M2
Abbotstone Av *HAV* PO9 ... 165 L4
Abbots Wy *FHAM* PO15 ... 6 A5
HLER SO31 ... 157 H2
Abbots Well Rd *FBDG* SP6 ... 123 K1
Abbotswood Cl *ROMY* SO51 ... 51 H7 [box]
Abbott Rd *MOOR/WNTN* BH9 ... 220 E8
Abbotts Cl *WINC* SO23 ... 3 H2
Abbotts Ann Rd *FUFL* SO22 ... 16 C5
Abbotts Dro *ROMY* SO51 ... 76 D7
Abbotts Rd *ELGH* SO50 ... 81 K7
WINC SO23 ... 3 G2
Abbotts Wy *FERN* BH22 ... 168 E8
PTSW SO17 ... 107 G7
Abercrombie Gdns
ROWN SO16 ... 105 M4
Aberdare Av *CHAM* PO6 ... 163 M7
Aberdare Rd *NBNE* BH10 ... 220 C5
Aberdeen Cl *FHAM* PO15 ... 6 D2
Aberdeen Rd *PTSW* SO17 ... 107 H7
Aberdour Cl *WEND* SO18 ... 108 A8 [box]
Abingdon Dr
CHCH/BSGR BH23 ... 225 G8
Abingdon Gdns *ROWN* SO16 ... 106 D5 [box]
Abingdon Rd *CFDH* BH17 ... 218 B7
Abinger Rd *LTDN* BH7 ... 236 F2
Abney Rd *NBNE* BH10 ... 220 B5
Above Bar St *SHAM* SO14 ... 4 F1
Abraham Cl *HEND* SO30 ... 134 B3
Abshot Cl *FHAM/STUB* PO14 ... 158 F7
Abshot Rd *FHAM/STUB* PO14 ... 158 F7
Acacia Av *VWD* BH31 ... 145 G4
Acacia Gdns *HORN* PO8 ... 140 F3
Acacia Rd *ITCH* SO19 ... 132 D3
LYMN SO41 ... 226 D4
Acer Wy *HAV* PO9 ... 165 M4
Ackworth Rd *HSEA* PO3 ... 187 L3
Acland Rd *MOOR/WNTN* BH9 ... 220 E8
Acorn Cl *CHAM* PO6 ... 164 C8 [box]
CHCH/BSGR BH23 ... 222 D8
FUFL SO22 ... 2 A3
LSOL/BMARY PO13 ... 185 H7
NMIL/BTOS BH25 ... 226 A4 [box]
RGWD BH24 ... 169 J5
TOTT SO40 ... 130 E7 [box]
Acorn Ct *HLER* SO31 ... 157 K5 [box]
Acorn Dr *ROWN* SO16 ... 105 K1
Acorn Gv *NBAD* SO52 ... 80 E4
The Acorns *HLER* SO31 ... 133 K8
WIMB BH21 ... 192 E4
Acorn Wy *VWD* BH31 ... 144 E2 [box]
Acre La *HORN* PO8 ... 141 G7
Acres Rd *BWD* BH11 ... 219 M6
Acton Rd *NBNE* BH10 ... 219 M7
Adair Rd *ENEY* PO4 ... 211 L6
Adames Rd *PSEA* PO1 ... 211 J2
Adams Cl *HEND* SO30 ... 109 G5
Adamsfield Gdns
NBNE BH10 ... 220 A6 [box]
Adamson Cl *CHFD* SO53 ... 53 J8
Adams Rd *FAWY* SO45 ... 155 L6
Adams Wood Dr *TOTT* SO40 ... 130 D7
Adastral Rd *CFDH* BH17 ... 233 K1 [box]
Adderbury Av *EMRTH* PO10 ... 166 D4
Addington Pl
CHCH/BSGR BH23 ... 238 C2 [box]
Addiscombe Rd
CHCH/BSGR BH23 ... 237 M1 [box]
Addison Rd *BROC* SO42 ... 175 K8
ELGH SO50 ... 82 A3 [box]
ENEY PO4 ... 13 L5
HLER SO31 ... 158 D2
Addison Sq *RGWD* BH24 ... 170 F1
Addison Cl *FUFL* SO22 ... 26 B3
Adelaide Cl
CHCH/BSGR BH23 ... 222 D8 [box]
Adelaide Rd *PTSW* SO17 ... 107 H8
Adela Verne Cl *ITCH* SO19 ... 133 J5 [box]
Adeline Rd *BMTH* BH1 ... 236 D4
Adey Cl *ITCH* SO19 ... 132 F6
Adhurst Rd *HAV* PO9 ... 165 L4
Adlam's La *LYMN* SO41 ... 200 D5
Admirals Cl *FAWY* SO45 ... 180 F5 [box]
Admirals Rd *HLER* SO31 ... 158 F4
Admirals Wk *GPORT* PO12 ... 10 A4
Admiralty Rd *PSEA* PO1 ... 12 C1
SBNE BH6 ... 237 L5 [box]
Admiralty Wy *TOTT* SO40 ... 130 D5
Adsdean Cl *HAV* PO9 ... 165 J4 [box]
Adstone La *HSEA* PO3 ... 188 A4 [box]
Adur Cl *GPORT* PO12 ... 209 K1 [box]
WEND SO18 ... 108 A7
Aerial Rd *CHAM* PO6 ... 162 F6
Aerodrome Rd
LSOL/BMARY PO13 ... 185 H4
Africa Dr *TOTT* SO40 ... 130 D7
Agars La *LYMN* SO41 ... 226 E1
LYMN SO41 ... 226 F3
Agarton La *LYMN* SO41 ... 242 E2
Aggis Farm Rd *VWD* BH31 ... 144 C2
Agincourt Rd *NEND* PO2 ... 211 H1
Agitor Rd *FAWY* SO45 ... 181 G3
Agnew Rd *LSOL/BMARY* PO13 ... 185 G5
Aikman La *TOTT* SO40 ... 128 F1
Ailsa La *ITCH* SO19 ... 132 B4
Aintree Cl *ELGH* SO50 ... 109 J1 [box]
Aintree Dr *WVILLE* PO7 ... 140 F7
Aintree Rd *TOTT* SO40 ... 104 B7
Airetons Cl *BDST* BH18 ... 218 A5
Airfield Rd *CHCH/BSGR* BH23 ... 238 E1
Airfield Wy *CHCH/BSGR* BH23 ... 238 E1
Airport Service Rd *HSEA* PO3 ... 187 M5
Ajax Cl *FHAM/STUB* PO14 ... 184 B7
Akeshill Cl *NMIL/BTOS* BH25 ... 225 M3

Alameda Rd WVILLE PO7 ...... 164 B4
Alameda Wy WVILLE PO7 ...... 164 B4
Alandale Rd ITCH SO19 ...... 133 H4
Alan Gv FHAM PO15 ...... 6 C4
Albacore Av HLER SO31 ...... 158 C7
Albany Cl NMIL/BTOS BH25 ...... 225 K7
Albany Ct BPWT SO32 ...... 84 F8
Albany Dr BPWT SO32 ...... 84 F8
  WIMB BH21 ...... 144 C8
Albany Gdns PLE BH15 ...... 232 E6
Albany Rd BPWT SO32 ...... 84 F8
  FAWY SO45 ...... 180 A4
  ROMY SO51 ...... 78 D1
  SSEA PO5 ...... 13 J6
  WSHM SO15 ...... 131 G2
Albatross Wk
  LSOL/BMARY PO13 ...... 184 F6
Albemarle Av GPORT PO12 ...... 209 M1
Albemarle Rd TWDS BH3 ...... 235 L1
Albert Cl HLER SO31 ...... 157 G3
Albert Gv SSEA PO5 ...... 13 K6
Albert Rd BKME/WDN BH12 ...... 234 C3
  BMTH BH1 ...... 14 E5
  BPWT SO32 ...... 111 G1
  CHAM PO6 ...... 187 K1
  ELGH SO50 ...... 82 A3
  FERN BH22 ...... 194 B3
  FHAM/STUB PO14 ...... 184 D6
  HEND SO30 ...... 133 M3
  NMIL/BTOS BH25 ...... 225 K6
  SSEA PO5 ...... 13 K7
  WIMB BH21 ...... 217 H3
Albert Rd North SHAM SO14 ...... 5 K5
Albert Rd South SHAM SO14 ...... 5 K6
Albert St GPORT PO12 ...... 11 G2
Albion Pl FHAM/PORC PO16 ...... 185 M2
  FBDG SP6 ...... 97 L6
Albion Wy VWD BH31 ...... 144 B2
Albretia Av HORN PO8 ...... 140 B5
Albury Rd CHFD SO53 ...... 53 G7
Alby Rd BKME/WDN BH12 ...... 234 E3
Alcantara Crs SHAM SO14 ...... 5 K6
Alcester Rd BKME/WDN BH12.. 234 C2
Alder Cl CHCH/BSGR BH23 ...... 223 H7
  FAWY SO45 ...... 155 G5
  ROMY SO51 ...... 79 J2
  RWIN SO21 ...... 54 F8
  TOTT SO40 ...... 130 F4
Alder Crs BKME/WDN BH12 ...... 234 E1
Alder Dr FBDG SP6 ...... 121 K3
Alderfield PSF GU32 ...... 63 K5
Alder Hill Dr TOTT SO40 ...... 104 A8
Alder Hills BKME/WDN BH12 ...... 234 F1
Alderholt Rd FBDG SP6 ...... 96 F7
Alder La LSOL/BMARY PO13 ...... 209 H3
Alderley Rd NBNE BH10 ...... 220 B4
Aldermoor Av ROWN SO16 ...... 105 M4
Aldermoor Cl ROWN SO16 ...... 106 B4
Aldermoor Rd
  LSOL/BMARY PO13 ...... 209 H1
  ROWN SO16 ...... 105 M4
  WVILLE PO7 ...... 164 B4
Aldermoor Rd East
  WVILLE PO7 ...... 164 B3
Alderney Av BKME/WDN BH12 .. 219 M7
Alderney Cl ROWN SO16 ...... 105 K4
Alder Rd BKME/WDN BH12 ...... 219 L8
  ROWN SO16 ...... 105 L5
Alders Rd FHAM/PORC PO16 ...... 184 F1
Alderwood Av CHFD SO53 ...... 80 F2
Alderwood Cl HAV PO9 ...... 164 E5
Aldis Gdns PLE BH15 ...... 232 D5
Aldrich Rd PSEA PO1 ...... 210 E2
Aldridge Cl HORN PO8 ...... 116 B3
Aldridge Rd FERN BH22 ...... 194 C5
  NBNE BH10 ...... 220 A3
Aldroke St CHAM PO6 ...... 187 K1
Aldsworth Cl CHAM PO6 ...... 164 A8
Aldsworth Gdns CHAM PO6 ...... 164 A8
Aldwell St SSEA PO5 ...... 13 J3
Alec Rose La PSEA PO1 ...... 13 G2
Alecto Rd GPORT PO12 ...... 10 E6
Alencon Cl GPORT PO12 ...... 186 A8
Alexander Cl
  CHCH/BSGR BH23 ...... 238 D2
  TOTT SO40 ...... 104 D8
  WVILLE PO7 ...... 164 B3
Alexander Gv
  FHAM/PORC PO16 ...... 7 H8
Alexandra Av HISD PO11 ...... 213 K6
Alexandra Cl FAWY SO45 ...... 155 L4
Alexandra Rd CHFD SO53 ...... 53 L8
  FAWY SO45 ...... 155 L4
  FBDG SP6 ...... 97 L6
  HEND SO30 ...... 133 M3
  LYMN SO41 ...... 228 A3
  PSEA PO1 ...... 211 H2
  PSTN BH14 ...... 237 G3
  SBNE BH6 ...... 237 G3
  WSHM SO15 ...... 131 H2
Alexandra St GPORT PO12 ...... 209 L2
Alexandra Ter WINC SO23 ...... 2 E9
Alexandra Wy HEND SO30 ...... 134 E1
Alford Rd TWDS BH3 ...... 235 J1
Alfred Cl TOTT SO40 ...... 104 B8
  TOTT SO40 ...... 129 G1
Alfred Rd FHAM/STUB PO14 ...... 184 B5
  PSEA PO1 ...... 12 F1
Alfred Rose Ct WEND SO18 ...... 107 K4
Alfred St SHAM SO14 ...... 131 M2
Alfrey Cl EMRTH PO10 ...... 167 G8
Alfriston Gdns ITCH SO19 ...... 132 F5
Algiers Rd HSEA PO3 ...... 187 M8
Alhambra Rd ENEY PO4 ...... 13 L9
Alington Cl PSTN BH14 ...... 245 H1
Alington Rd PSTN BH14 ...... 245 H1
  TWDS BH3 ...... 235 M2
Alipore Cl PSTN BH14 ...... 234 C1
Allan Gv ROMY SO51 ...... 79 G1
Allaway Av CHAM PO6 ...... 162 D8
Allbrook Cl HAV PO9 ...... 165 H2
Allbrook Hl ELGH SO50 ...... 82 A1
Allbrook Knoll ELGH SO50 ...... 81 M1
Allbrook Wy ELGH SO50 ...... 53 M8
Allcot Rd HSEA PO3 ...... 187 K6

Allenby Cl CFDH BH17 ...... 217 M6
Allenby Gv FHAM/PORC PO16 .. 186 A1
Allenby Rd CFDH BH17 ...... 217 M7
  GPORT PO12 ...... 209 J2
Allen Ct WIMB BH21 ...... 192 A3
Allendale Av EMRTH PO10 ...... 166 C5
Allen Rd HEND SO30 ...... 134 A1
  WIMB BH21 ...... 192 A4
Allens La BPWT SO32 ...... 87 H3
  UPTN BH16 ...... 232 C3
Allen's Rd SSEA PO5 ...... 13 L7
  UPTN BH16 ...... 232 B2
Allenview Rd WIMB BH21 ...... 192 A3
The Alley MIDH GU29 ...... 67 K7
Alliance Cl LSOL/BMARY PO13.. 185 H8
Allington La HEND SO30 ...... 108 C3
Allington Rd WSHM SO15 ...... 130 M3
Allmara Dr WVILLE PO7 ...... 164 C3
Allotment Rd HLER SO31 ...... 158 C3
All Saints Rd LYMN SO41 ...... 228 C6
  PSEA PO1 ...... 211 H1
Alma La BPWT SO32 ...... 84 A6
Alma Rd MOOR/WNTN BH9 ...... 235 M1
  ROMY SO51 ...... 78 E1
  SHAM SO14 ...... 106 F8
Alma St GPORT PO12 ...... 209 L2
Almatade Rd WEND SO18 ...... 132 E1
Alma Ter ENEY PO4 ...... 211 L5
Alner Rd PLE BH15 ...... 232 D5
Almond Cl CHAM PO6 ...... 164 D8
  HORN PO8 ...... 141 G4
Almond Gv BKME/WDN BH12 .. 234 C1
Almond Rd WSHM SO15 ...... 131 G3
Almondsbury CHAM PO6 ...... 162 D5
Almondside
  LSOL/BMARY PO13 ...... 185 J7
Alpine Cl WEND SO18 ...... 108 A3
Alpine Rd RGWD BH24 ...... 170 A6
Alresford Rd HAV PO9 ...... 165 J4
  RWIN SO21 ...... 27 L1
  WINC SO23 ...... 3 L8
Alsford Rd WVILLE PO7 ...... 164 B3
Alten Rd WVILLE PO7 ...... 140 A6
Althorpe Dr HSEA PO3 ...... 188 A4
Alton Cl ELGH SO50 ...... 83 G6
Alton Gv FHAM/PORC PO16 ...... 186 A2
Alton Rd NBNE BH10 ...... 219 M7
  PSTN BH14 ...... 234 A5
Alton Rd East PSTN BH14 ...... 234 C6
Alum Chine Rd WBNE BH4 ...... 235 K6
Alum Cl FAWY SO45 ...... 180 B5
Alumdale Rd WBNE BH4 ...... 235 K6
Alumhurst Rd WBNE BH4 ...... 235 G6
Alum Wy FHAM/PORC PO16 ...... 161 L2
  WEND SO18 ...... 132 F1
Alvara Rd GPORT PO12 ...... 10 D7
Alvercliffe Dr GPORT PO12 ...... 10 B8
Alver Rd GPORT PO12 ...... 10 F5
  PSEA PO1 ...... 211 J2
Alverstone Rd ENEY PO4 ...... 211 L4
Alverton Av PLE BH15 ...... 233 L5
Alveston Av FHAM/STUB PO14 .. 160 A3
Alyth Rd TWDS BH3 ...... 235 H2
Amarylis Cl FHAM PO15 ...... 159 J4
Ambassador Cl
  CHCH/BSGR BH23 ...... 238 F2
Amberley Cl CHCH/BSGR BH23 .. 224 C8
  HEND SO30 ...... 109 L8
  NBAD SO52 ...... 79 K3
Amberley Ct TOTT SO40 ...... 129 J2
Amberley Rd GPORT PO12 ...... 185 L3
  HORN PO8 ...... 116 C3
  NEND PO2 ...... 187 K5
Amber Rd WIMB BH21 ...... 217 G4
Amberslade Wk FAWY SO45 .. 155 K7
Amberwood FERN BH22 ...... 194 C1
Amberwood Cl TOTT SO40 ...... 104 B6
Amberwood Dr
  CHCH/BSGR BH23 ...... 224 E6
Amberwood Gdns
  CHCH/BSGR BH23 ...... 224 E6
Ambledale HLER SO31 ...... 158 C4
Ambleside CHCH/BSGR BH23 .. 222 B5
  HEND SO30 ...... 134 B3
Ambleside Gdns ITCH SO19 ...... 132 E5
Ambleside Rd LYMN SO41 ...... 228 C6
Ambury La CHCH/BSGR BH23 .. 223 K8
Amersham Cl GPORT PO12 ...... 209 J3
Amesbury Rd SBNE BH6 ...... 237 H2
Amethyst Gv WVILLE PO7 ...... 140 E8
Amethyst Rd
  CHCH/BSGR BH23 ...... 238 E1
Ameysford Rd FERN BH22 ...... 168 A7
Ameys La FERN BH22 ...... 194 D1
Amoy St WSHM SO15 ...... 131 K2
Ampfield Cl HAV PO9 ...... 164 F4
Ampfield Rd CHAR BH8 ...... 221 H5
Amport Cl FUFL SO22 ...... 16 B5
Amport Ct HAV PO9 ...... 165 H2
Ampthill Rd WSHM SO15 ...... 130 F1
Amsterdam Sq
  CHCH/BSGR BH23 ...... 238 C2
Amyas Ct ENEY PO4 ...... 212 A4
Ancasta Rd SHAM SO14 ...... 131 M1
Anchorage Rd HSEA PO3 ...... 187 M5
The Anchorage GPORT PO12... 11 H4
Anchor Cl BWD BH11 ...... 219 K3
  CHCH/BSGR BH23 ...... 238 F3
Anchor Ga PSEA PO1 ...... 210 E2
Anchor La PSEA PO1 ...... 210 E2
Anchor Ms LYMN SO41 ...... 228 C4
Anchor Rd BWD BH11 ...... 219 K3
Andalusian Gdns HLER SO31 .. 134 F8
Anderby Rd ROWN SO16 ...... 105 J4
Andersen Cl HLER SO31 ...... 135 G8
Anderson Cl HAV PO9 ...... 9 G1
  ROMY SO51 ...... 51 H6
Anderwood Dr LYMN SO41 ...... 200 F6
Andes Cl SHAM SO14 ...... 5 K5
Andes Rd ROWN SO16 ...... 105 G5
Andlers Ash Rd LISS GU33 ...... 36 D6
Andover Rd CHCH/BSGR BH23 .. 239 C1
Andover Rd ENEY PO4 ...... 211 K6
  FUFL SO22 ...... 2 E2

WSHM SO15 ...... 131 H2
Andover Rd North FUFL SO22... 16 B1
Andrew Bell St PSEA PO1 ...... 211 G2
Andrew Cl FAWY SO45 ...... 155 L7
  PSEA PO1 ...... 211 K2
  TOTT SO40 ...... 129 H1
Andrew Crs WVILLE PO7 ...... 140 B7
Andrewes Cl BPWT SO32 ...... 85 H8
Andrew La NMIL/BTOS BH25 .. 225 J5
Andrew Pl FHAM/STUB PO14 .. 183 M6
Andromeda Rd ROWN SO16 ...... 105 K4
Anfield Cl LSOL/BMARY PO13 .. 185 J8
Angel Crs ITCH SO19 ...... 132 D2
Angelica Gdns ELGH SO50 ...... 109 H1
Angelica Wy FHAM PO15 ...... 135 J8
Angeline Cl
  CHCH/BSGR BH23 ...... 224 D8
Angel La FERN BH22 ...... 193 M5
  NMIL/BTOS BH25 ...... 226 B8
Angelo Cl WVILLE PO7 ...... 140 E8
Angelus Cl FHAM/STUB PO14 .. 184 A6
Angerstein Rd NEND PO2 ...... 187 H7
Anglers Wy HLER SO31 ...... 134 B8
Anglesea Rd
  LSOL/BMARY PO13 ...... 208 E4
  PSEA PO1 ...... 12 D2
  WSHM SO15 ...... 106 A7
Anglesea Ter SHAM SO14 ...... 5 K5
Anglesey Arms Rd GPORT PO12.. 10 C8
Anglesey Rd GPORT PO12 ...... 10 C8
Angmering Rd FHAM/STUB PO14.. 184 A4
Angus Cl FHAM PO15 ...... 6 C2
Anjou Cl BWD BH11 ...... 219 H3
Anjou Crs FHAM PO15 ...... 6 B4
Anker La FHAM/STUB PO14 ...... 184 A4
Ankerwyke
  LSOL/BMARY PO13 ...... 184 F7
Anmore Cl WEND SO18 ...... 108 A8
Anmore Dr WVILLE PO7 ...... 140 A4
Anmore La WVILLE PO7 ...... 140 A4
Anmore Rd WVILLE PO7 ...... 139 L4
Anna La CHCH/BSGR BH23 ...... 196 E4
Anne Cl CHCH/BSGR BH23 ...... 222 E7
  WVILLE PO7 ...... 164 C2
Annerley Rd BMTH BH1 ...... 15 L4
Annet Cl PLE BH15 ...... 232 D6
Ann's Hill Rd GPORT PO12 ...... 10 C4
Anson Cl CHCH/BSGR BH23 ...... 238 C7
  LSOL/BMARY PO13 ...... 209 H3
  RGWD BH24 ...... 147 G3
Anson Dr ITCH SO19 ...... 133 G3
Anson Gv FHAM/PORC PO16 .. 162 B7
Anson Rd ELGH SO50 ...... 109 H1
  ENEY PO4 ...... 211 K3
Anstey Cl BWD BH11 ...... 219 L2
Anstey Rd BWD BH11 ...... 219 L3
  ROMY SO51 ...... 51 G7
Antell's Wy FBDG SP6 ...... 121 L2
Anthill Cl WVILLE PO7 ...... 139 G2
Anthony Gv GPORT PO12 ...... 185 K7
Anthony's Av PSTN BH14 ...... 234 B7
Antler Dr NMIL/BTOS BH25 ...... 225 J4
Anton Cl ROMY SO51 ...... 79 H1
Anvil Cl HORN PO8 ...... 141 G7
Anvil Crs BDST BH18 ...... 217 J3
Anzac Cl FHAM/STUB PO14 ...... 184 A4
Apless La WVILLE PO7 ...... 138 D4
Apollo Cl BKME/WDN BH12 ...... 234 C1
Apollo Dr WVILLE PO7 ...... 164 D5
Apollo Rd ELGH SO50 ...... 81 L1
Apple Cl BKME/WDN BH12 ...... 234 F4
Apple Gv CHCH/BSGR BH23 ...... 222 C6
  EMRTH PO10 ...... 166 F8
Appleshaw Cl FUFL SO22 ...... 16 C4
Appleslade Wy
  NMIL/BTOS BH25 ...... 225 M3
  WEND SO18 ...... 107 K7
Apple Tree Cl RSAL SP5 ...... 73 J1
Appletree Cl NMIL/BTOS BH25 .. 225 L7
  SBNE BH6 ...... 237 H3
  TOTT SO40 ...... 104 B8
Appletree Ct HEND SO30 ...... 134 E1
Apple Tree Gv FERN BH22 ...... 194 C3
Apple Tree Rd FBDG SP6 ...... 121 K3
Appletree Rd RSAL SP5 ...... 73 J1
Applewood Gdns ITCH SO19 .. 132 E5
Applewood Gv WVILLE PO7 ...... 164 A6
Applewood Pl TOTT SO40 ...... 129 G2
Applewood Rd HAV PO9 ...... 165 G5
Approach Rd PSTN BH14 ...... 234 A5
April Cl BWD BH11 ...... 219 L4
  WEND SO18 ...... 132 F1
April Gv HLER SO31 ...... 158 C5
April Sq PSEA PO1 ...... 211 H2
Apsley Crs CFDH BH17 ...... 218 A7
Apsley Pl CHFD SO53 ...... 53 G7
Apsley Rd ENEY PO4 ...... 211 L4
Aquila Wy HLER SO31 ...... 157 K6
Arabian Gdns FHAM PO15 ...... 159 G1
Aragon Wy MOOR/WNTN BH9 .. 220 F3
Arcadia Av CHAR BH8 ...... 236 A1
Arcadia Cl ROWN SO16 ...... 106 A5
Arcadia Rd CHCH/BSGR BH23 .. 222 D7
Archdale Cl NBNE BH10 ...... 220 B6
Archers Cl TOTT SO40 ...... 104 B6
Archers Rd ELGH SO50 ...... 81 M4
  WSHM SO15 ...... 131 J2
Archery Gdns ITCH SO19 ...... 132 D6
Archery Gv ITCH SO19 ...... 132 D6
Archery La FHAM/PORC PO16... 7 L4
  WINC SO23 ...... 2 E8
Archery Rd ITCH SO19 ...... 132 C7
Archway Rd CCLF BH13 ...... 234 D4
Arden Cl WEND SO18 ...... 108 A7
Arden Rd MOOR/WNTN BH9 .. 220 F3
Arden Wk NMIL/BTOS BH25 .. 225 M6
Ardington Ri WVILLE PO7 ...... 164 C5
Ardmore Rd PSTN BH14 ...... 234 A4
Argosy Cl HLER SO31 ...... 158 D7
Argus Rd LSOL/BMARY PO13 .. 208 D1
Argyle Crs CHAM PO6 ...... 6 D3
Argyle Rd CHCH/BSGR BH23 .. 238 D3
  SHAM SO14 ...... 5 H1
Argyll Rd BKME/WDN BH12.. 234 C2
  BOSC BH5 ...... 236 D4
Ariel Cl SBNE BH6 ...... 238 A3

Ariel Dr SBNE BH6 ...... 238 A4
Ariel Rd PSEA PO1 ...... 13 L1
Ark Royal Crs
  LSOL/BMARY PO13 ...... 208 C1
Arle Cl HORN PO8 ...... 116 A4
Arley Rd PSTN BH14 ...... 233 M6
Arlington Ct
  NMIL/BTOS BH25 ...... 225 M8
Arliss Rd ROWN SO16 ...... 105 M7
Arlott Ct WSHM SO15 ...... 131 J1
Armada Cl ROWN SO16 ...... 105 K1
Armada Dr FAWY SO45 ...... 155 K6
Arminers Cl GPORT PO12 ...... 10 E9
Armitage Av FAWY SO45 ...... 155 K7
Armory La PSEA PO1 ...... 12 D4
Armstrong Cl BROC SO42 ...... 175 J7
  WVILLE PO7 ...... 140 B7
Armstrong Ct ROWN SO16 ...... 105 L3
Armstrong La BROC SO42 ...... 175 J7
Armstrong Rd BROC SO42 ...... 175 J7
Armsworth La BPWT SO32 ...... 113 J5
Arnaud Cl NEND PO2 ...... 211 H1
Arne Av BKME/WDN BH12 ...... 234 D1
Arne Crs BKME/WDN BH12 ...... 234 D1
Arnheim Cl ROWN SO16 ...... 106 B4
Arnheim Rd ROWN SO16 ...... 106 C4
Arnhelm Rd ROWN SO16 ...... 106 C4
Arnold Cl FERN BH22 ...... 168 C5
Arnold Rd ELGH SO50 ...... 81 M8
  FERN BH22 ...... 168 C5
  PTSW SO17 ...... 107 H6
Arnolds Cl NMIL/BTOS BH25 .. 225 K6
Arnside Rd WVILLE PO7 ...... 140 C8
Arnwood Av FAWY SO45 ...... 155 K8
Aron Cl PSF GU32 ...... 63 K6
Arragon Ct WVILLE PO7 ...... 140 E8
Arran Cl CHAM PO6 ...... 163 K7
Arran Wy CHCH/BSGR BH23 .. 224 C7
Arreton HLER SO31 ...... 157 G2
Arrow Cl ELGH SO50 ...... 81 M4
  ITCH SO19 ...... 132 B7
Arrowsmith La WIMB BH21 ...... 218 C1
Arrowsmith Rd WIMB BH21 ...... 218 B2
Arters Lawn TOTT SO40 ...... 153 M2
Arthur Cl CHCH/BSGR BH23 .. 237 M1
  ELGH SO50 ...... 81 M4
  WINC SO23 ...... 3 G4
  WSHM SO15 ...... 131 H1
Arthurs Gdns HEND SO30 ...... 109 G5
Arthur St NEND PO2 ...... 211 J1
Artillery Cl CHAM PO6 ...... 163 G8
Arun Cl EPSF GU31 ...... 63 K6
Arundel Cl NMIL/BTOS BH25 .. 225 J5
Arundel Dr FHAM/PORC PO16... 7 G4
Arundel Rd ELGH SO50 ...... 81 M2
  GPORT PO12 ...... 10 B1
  TOTT SO40 ...... 104 F8
Arundel St PSEA PO1 ...... 13 K1
Arundel Wy CHCH/BSGR BH23 .. 239 L1
Arun Rd WEND SO18 ...... 108 A6
Arun Wy ROMY SO51 ...... 76 C5
Ascham Rd CHAR BH8 ...... 15 J2
Ascot Cl FHAM/STUB PO14 ...... 159 G6
  ELGH SO50 ...... 109 J1
  HSEA PO3 ...... 211 L1
Ascupart St SHAM SO14 ...... 5 J3
Asford Gv ELGH SO50 ...... 82 C4
Ashbarn Crs FUFL SO22 ...... 25 J2
Ashbourne Rd BOSC BH5 ...... 237 G3
Ashbridge Ri CHFD SO53 ...... 52 F7
Ashburn Garth RGWD BH24... 171 H2
Ashburnham Cl ITCH SO19 ...... 132 B3
Ashburton Cl FAWY SO45 ...... 155 H5
Ashburton Gdns NBNE BH10 .. 220 B7
Ashburton Rd GPORT PO12 ...... 10 B8
  SSEA PO5 ...... 13 G7
Ashby Pl SSEA PO5 ...... 13 G7
Ashby Rd ITCH SO19 ...... 132 F5
  TOTT SO40 ...... 129 H1
Ash Cl FAWY SO45 ...... 155 L8
  FBDG SP6 ...... 121 L3
  FHAM/STUB PO14 ...... 6 C7
  GPORT PO12 ...... 10 E4
  HLER SO31 ...... 133 K8
  HORN PO8 ...... 140 C5
  ITCH SO19 ...... 133 G2
  NBAD SO52 ...... 79 L3
  ROMY SO51 ...... 79 H2
  RWIN SO21 ...... 54 E8
  UPTN BH16 ...... 216 F8
Ash Copse HORN PO8 ...... 140 D3
Ashcroft La HORN PO8 ...... 142 B2
Ashdene WSHM SO15 ...... 106 A8
Ashdene Cl WIMB BH21 ...... 192 B3
Ashdene Rd TOTT SO40 ...... 128 F6
Ashdown FAWY SO45 ...... 180 D5
  LSOL/BMARY PO13 ...... 185 H7
Ashdown Cl CHFD SO53 ...... 53 H6
Ashdown Dr CHFD SO53 ...... 53 H6
Ashdown Rd CHFD SO53 ...... 53 H7
  FAWY SO45 ...... 180 D5
Ashdown Wk
  NMIL/BTOS BH25 ...... 226 A6
Ashdown Wy ROMY SO51 ...... 79 G1
Ashen Cl CHFD SO53 ...... 53 H8
Ashe Rd HAV PO9 ...... 165 M3
Ashford Cl CHAM PO6 ...... 163 J7
Ashford Crs FAWY SO45 ...... 155 M5
Ashford Rd FBDG SP6 ...... 97 H3
Ash Gv LYMN SO41 ...... 227 H8
  RGWD BH24 ...... 171 G1
  TOTT SO40 ...... 129 G6
Ashington Cl HORN PO8 ...... 140 E5
Ashington Pk
  NMIL/BTOS BH25 ...... 225 M7
Ashlea Cl ELGH SO50 ...... 83 J6
Ashleigh Cl FAWY SO45 ...... 155 J6
Ashlet Gdns NMIL/BTOS BH25.. 226 B4
Ashlett Cl FAWY SO45 ...... 181 G5
Ashlett Rd FAWY SO45 ...... 181 G5
Ashley Cl BMTH BH1 ...... 236 C2

  FUFL SO22 ...... 16 B5
  HAV PO9 ...... 165 H4
  HLER SO31 ...... 158 F1
  HORN PO8 ...... 140 D3
  RGWD BH24 ...... 171 H2
Ashley Common Rd
  NMIL/BTOS BH25 ...... 226 A4
Ashley Ct HLER SO31 ...... 133 L6
Ashley Crs ITCH SO19 ...... 133 G6
Ashleycross Cl FAWY SO45 .. 180 B5
Ashley Dr RGWD BH24 ...... 146 A8
Ashley Dr North RGWD BH24 .. 169 K3
Ashley Dr South RGWD BH24 .. 169 K3
Ashley Dr West RGWD BH24 .. 169 K3
Ashley Gdns BPWT SO32 ...... 111 K5
  CHFD SO53 ...... 81 K3
Ashley La LYMN SO41 ...... 228 C4
  NMIL/BTOS BH25 ...... 226 B4
Ashley Mdw ROMY SO51 ...... 50 F8
Ashley Meads
  NMIL/BTOS BH25 ...... 226 B4
Ashley Pk BKME/WDN BH24 .. 168 C2
Ashley Rd LTDN BH7 ...... 236 E3
  NMIL/BTOS BH25 ...... 225 L6
  PSTN BH14 ...... 234 B3
Ashling Cl CHAR BH8 ...... 221 G8
  WVILLE PO7 ...... 139 K4
Ashling Gdns WVILLE PO7 ...... 139 K4
Ashling La NEND PO2 ...... 187 H8
Ashling Park Rd WVILLE PO7 .. 139 K4
Ashlyn Cl FHAM PO15 ...... 159 M7
Ashmead Rd ROWN SO16 ...... 105 L5
Ashmeads Cl WIMB BH21 ...... 192 E2
Ashmeads Wy WIMB BH21 ...... 192 E2
Ashmore WIMB BH21 ...... 192 B4
Ashmore Av NMIL/BTOS BH25 .. 225 M8
  PLE BH15 ...... 232 E7
Ashmore Cl RSAL SP5 ...... 47 G4
Ashmore Gv CHCH/BSGR BH23 .. 224 C7
Ashmore La RSAL SP5 ...... 47 G3
Ashmore Rd FUFL SO22 ...... 16 B7
Ashridge Av NBNE BH10 ...... 220 B3
Ashridge Cl WSHM SO15 ...... 106 D3
Ashridge Gdns NBNE BH10 .. 220 B3
Ash Rd TOTT SO40 ...... 128 F6
Ashstead Cl FHAM/PORC PO16 .. 161 L4
Ashton Cl BPWT SO32 ...... 84 F7
Ashton Cross ROMY SO51 ...... 76 F6
Ashton La BPWT SO32 ...... 84 F6
Ashton Md MOOR/WNTN BH9 .. 220 D6
Ashton Wy FHAM/STUB PO14 .. 184 B8
Ashtree Cl NMIL/BTOS BH25 .. 226 B6
Ash Tree Rd WEND SO18 ...... 107 K7
Ashurst Bridge Rd TOTT SO40.. 129 G2
Ashurst Cl FUFL SO22 ...... 16 C5
  ITCH SO19 ...... 132 F7
  TOTT SO40 ...... 128 F6
Ashurst Rd CHAM PO6 ...... 163 J8
  CHAR BH8 ...... 221 H5
  FERN BH22 ...... 168 B5
Ashwood FHAM PO15 ...... 159 J3
  HLER SO31 ...... 159 G6
Ashwood Cl HAV PO9 ...... 164 F5
  HISD PO11 ...... 213 L5
Ashwood Dr BDST BH18 ...... 218 A4
Ashwood Gdns ROWN SO16 .. 106 D5
  TOTT SO40 ...... 129 G2
Aspen Av HLER SO31 ...... 158 B8
Aspen Cl HEND SO30 ...... 134 B1
  RWIN SO21 ...... 54 F8
Aspen Dr VWD BH31 ...... 144 F2
Aspen Gdns BKME/WDN BH12 .. 234 E1
Aspen Rd BKME/WDN BH12 ...... 234 E1
Aspen Wk TOTT SO40 ...... 104 A8
Aspen Wy BKME/WDN BH12 ...... 234 E1
  HORN PO8 ...... 140 E3
Asquith Cl CHCH/BSGR BH23 .. 238 C3
Astbury Av BKME/WDN BH12 .. 219 L8
Aster Rd ROWN SO16 ...... 107 H4
Astley St SSEA PO5 ...... 13 G4
Aston Md CHCH/BSGR BH23 .. 222 C4
Aston Rd WVILLE PO7 ...... 140 B7
Astra Ct FAWY SO45 ...... 155 L3
Astral Gdns HLER SO31 ...... 157 K5
Astrid Cl HISD PO11 ...... 214 A5
Asturias Wy SHAM SO14 ...... 5 L6
Athena Av WVILLE PO7 ...... 164 D5
Athena Cl ELGH SO50 ...... 82 F5
Atherfield Rd ROWN SO16 ...... 105 K5
Atherley Ct WSHM SO15 ...... 106 D3
  WSHM SO15 ...... 131 H2
Atherley Rd HISD PO11 ...... 213 J3
  WSHM SO15 ...... 131 H2
Atkinson Cl GPORT PO12 ...... 10 D8
Atkins Pl FHAM PO15 ...... 160 A5
Atlantic Cl SHAM SO14 ...... 5 K8
Atlantic Park Vw
  WEND SO18 ...... 107 M6
Atlantis Av WVILLE PO7 ...... 164 D6
Attwood Cl FBDG SP6 ...... 121 K3
Attwoods Dro RWIN SO21 ...... 26 B8
Aubrey Cl HISD PO11 ...... 213 J4
  LYMN SO41 ...... 242 E4
Auckland Rd
  CHCH/BSGR BH23 ...... 239 H1
  WSHM SO15 ...... 130 D1
Auckland Rd East SSEA PO5 .. 13 H8
Auckland Rd West SSEA PO5 .. 13 G8
Audemer Ct RGWD BH24 ...... 147 G8
Audret Cl FHAM/PORC PO16 .. 185 M2
Augustine Rd CHAM PO6 ...... 164 A7
  SHAM SO14 ...... 131 M2
Augustus Wy CHFD SO53 ...... 81 K1
Aukland Gv BROC SO42 ...... 175 L7
Auriol Dr CHAM PO6 ...... 164 E6
Austen Av FUFL SO22 ...... 26 B5
Austen Cl NBNE BH10 ...... 220 C2
Austen Cl TOTT SO40 ...... 129 H2
  WINC SO23 ...... 3 H2

Austen Gdns *HLER* SO31............ **135** G8
Austerberry Wy
  LSOL/BMARY PO13........... **185** H8
Auster Rd *CHCH/BSGR* BH23.... **239** G1
Austin Av *PSTN* BH14 .... **234** A6
Austin Cl *CHCH/BSGR* BH23.... **239** G1
Austin Ct *GPORT* PO6 .... **162** F7
Australia Cl *PSEA* PO1 .... **13** J1
Aust Rd *FHAM/STUB* PO14....... **6** A7
Autumn Cl *FERN* BH22 .... **193** M1
Autumn Rd *BWD* BH11 .... **219** H5
  TOTT SO40 .... **130** E7
Avalon *PSTN* BH14................... **234** B8
Avebury Av *NBNE* BH10 .... **220** C2
Avebury Gdns *CHFD* SO53 .... **52** F7
Avenger Cl *CHFD* SO53 .... **81** G3
Avens Cl *ELGH* SO50 .... **109** H2
Avenue C *FAWY* SO45 .... **156** C8
Avenue Ct *GPORT* PO12 .... **10** C7
Avenue D *FAWY* SO45 .... **156** C8
Avenue E *FAWY* SO45 .... **156** C8
Avenue La *WCLF* BH2 .... **14** D6
Avenue Rd *BROC* SO42 .... **175** K7
  CHCH/BSGR BH23............. **225** G2
  CHCH/BSGR BH23............. **237** L1
  FHAM/STUB PO14............... **6** F6
  FUFL SO22 .... **2** D6
  GPORT PO12 .... **11** C2
  HISD PO11 .... **189** K5
  LYMN SO41 .... **228** B4
  NMIL/BTOS BH25 .... **225** L5
  SHAM SO14 .... **106** F8
  WCLF BH2 .... **14** D6
  WIMB BH21 .... **192** B4
The Avenue *BPWT* SO32 .... **85** G8
  CCLF BH13 .... **234** F8
  EPSH GU31 .... **63** L5
  FERN BH22 .... **168** B5
  FHAM PO15 .... **6** C6
  FHAM/STUB PO14................. **6** F6
  GPORT PO12 .... **10** C7
  MOOR/WNTN BH9 .... **220** D5
  PTSW SO17 .... **106** E6
  RCCH PO18 .... **167** M7
  RWIN SO21......................... **54** F2
Avery La *GPORT* PO12 .... **209** K1
Avington Cl *ELGH* SO50 .... **82** C3
Avington Ct *ROWN* SO16 .... **106** E4
Avocet Quay *EMRTH* PO10 ...... **190** C1
Avocet Wk *LSOL/BMARY* PO13 . **184** B5
Avon Av *RGWD* BH24 .... **170** B5
Avonborne Wy *CHFD* SO53 ...... **53** G8
Avon Buildings
  CHCH/BSGR BH23............. **238** A1
Avon Castle Dr *RGWD* BH24..... **170** B4
Avon Cswy *CHCH/BSGR* BH23 . **221** M1
Avoncliffe Rd *SBNE* BH6 .... **237** K5
Avon Cl *BMTH* BH1 .... **236** C2
  LSOL/BMARY PO13............. **208** D3
  LYMN SO41 .... **228** A5
  PSF GU32 .... **63** K6
Avon Crs *ROMY* SO51 .... **79** H1
  WVILLE PO7 .... **140** D8
Avon Gdns *CHCH/BSGR* BH23 . **197** M7
Avon Gn *CHFD* SO53 .... **81** J3
Avondale Rd *PSEA* PO1 .... **211** K1
Avon Meade *FBDG* SP6 .... **97** K6
Avon Pk *RGWD* BH24 .... **170** B2
Avon Rd *CHAR* BH8 .... **236** B2
  FERN BH22 .... **168** C7
  WEND SO18 .... **107** L7
Avon Rd East
  CHCH/BSGR BH23............. **222** E8
Avon Rd West
  CHCH/BSGR BH23............. **222** D8
Avon Run Cl *CHCH/BSGR* BH23 . **239** G3
Avon Run Rd
  CHCH/BSGR BH23............. **239** G3
  RSAL SP5 .... **44** E5
Avon Vw *FBDG* SP6 .... **98** C7
Avon View Rd
  CHCH/BSGR BH23............. **223** G5
Avon Wy *HEND* SO30 .... **108** D6
Award Rd *WIMB* BH21 .... **193** K3
Awbridge Rd *HAV* PO9 .... **165** G4
Axford Cl *CHAR* BH8 .... **221** H5
Aylen Rd *HSEA* PO3 .... **187** L5
Aylesbury Rd *BMTH* BH1 .... **236** C4
  NEND PO2 .... **187** K8
Ayling Cl *LSOL/BMARY* PO13 ... **209** L3
Aylward St *PSEA* PO1 .... **12** D1
Aysgarth Rd *WVILLE* PO7 .... **140** C8
Aysha Cl *NMIL/BTOS* BH25 ..... **225** M7
Azalea Cl *HAV* PO9 .... **166** A4
  RGWD BH24....................... **169** L3

B

Back La *LYMN* SO41 .... **201** G6
  ROMY SO51 .... **21** J3
  WHAM PO17 .... **162** C2
Back of the Walls *SHAM* SO14 ...... **5** G5
Back St *WINC* SO23 .... **26** D5
Bacon Cl *ITCH* SO19 .... **132** D7
Bacon La *HISD* PO11 .... **213** J5
Badbury Cl *BDST* BH18 .... **218** A5
Badbury Vw *WIMB* BH21 .... **192** B3
Baddesley Cl *NBAD* SO52 .... **79** L3
Baddesley Rd *CHFD* SO53 .... **52** F7
Baden Cl *NMIL/BTOS* BH25 ..... **225** M7
Bader Cl *HEND* SO30 .... **109** H8
Bader Rd *CFDH* BH17 .... **218** C8
Bader Wy *FHAM* PO15 .... **159** J3
Badger Brow *WVILLE* PO7 .... **164** E2
Badger Cl *ELGH* SO50 .... **82** E6
  FHAM PO15 .... **6** A3
Badger Farm Rd *FUFL* SO22 ...... **26** A3
Badgers *LYMN* SO41 .... **201** G6
  RGWD BH24....................... **169** K3
Badgers Copse
  NMIL/BTOS BH25 .... **226** A2
Badgers Run *HLER* SO31 .... **158** C5
The Badgers *HLER* SO31 .... **157** G2
Badgers Wk *FAWY* SO45 .... **155** K6

  FERN BH22 .... **194** C1
Badger Wy *VWD* BH31 .... **144** D3
Badminston Dro *FAWY* SO45 .... **181** G8
Badminston La *FAWY* SO45 ...... **181** G7
Badshear La *NARL* SO24 .... **30** D1
Baffins Rd *HSEA* PO3 .... **211** L2
Bagber Rd *TOTT* SO40 .... **129** K1
Baigent Cl *WINC* SO23 .... **3** L7
Bailey Cl *FUFL* SO22 .... **26** C2
  HEND SO30 .... **134** D2
  NMIL/BTOS BH25 .... **226** B4
Bailey Crs *PLE* BH15 .... **233** H1
Bailey Dr *CHCH/BSGR* BH23 ... **237** L1
Bailey's Rd *SSEA* PO5 .... **13** J3
Baiter Gdns *PLE* BH15 .... **233** J7
Baker Rd *BWD* BH11 .... **219** K3
Bakers Dro *ROWN* SO16 .... **105** K3
Bakers Farm Rd *VWD* BH31 ..... **144** C1
Baker St *NEND* PO2 .... **211** H1
Balaclava Rd *WEND* SO18 .... **132** E1
Balcombe Rd *CCLF* BH13 .... **234** F5
Balderton Cl *NEND* PO2 .... **187** K4
Baldwin Cl *CHCH/BSGR* BH23 . **238** C2
Balfour Cl *CHCH/BSGR* BH23 .. **238** A1
  LSOL/BMARY PO13............. **209** H2
Balfour Dr *LISS* GU33 .... **36** D4
Balfour Rd *ITCH* SO19 .... **132** F3
  MOOR/WNTN BH9 .... **220** D7
  NEND PO2 .... **187** J7
Ballam Cl *UPTN* BH16 .... **232** B1
Ballard Cl *NMIL/BTOS* BH25 .... **225** M4
  PLE BH15 .... **233** J7
  ROWN SO16 .... **105** H7
Ballard Rd *PLE* BH15 .... **233** J7
Balliol Cl *FHAM/STUB* PO14 .... **159** G7
Balliol Rd *NEND* PO2 .... **211** J1
Balmer Lawn Rd *BROC* SO42 ... **175** M5
Balmoral Av *CHAR* BH8 .... **221** J7
Balmoral Cl *CHFD* SO53 .... **53** G8
  LSOL/BMARY PO13............. **185** H5
  ROWN SO16 .... **106** B3
Balmoral Dr *WVILLE* PO7 .... **164** A4
Balmoral Rd *FHAM* PO15 .... **6** D2
  PSTN BH14.......................... **234** B5
Balmoral Wk
  NMIL/BTOS BH25 .... **225** K5
Balmoral Wy *PSF* GU32 .... **63** L4
Balston Rd *PSTN* BH14 .... **233** M3
Baltic Rd *HEND* SO30 .... **108** D6
Banbury Av *ITCH* SO19 .... **133** G4
Bangor Rd *WSHM* SO15 .... **130** F2
Banister Gdns *WSHM* SO15 .... **131** K1
Banister Rd *WSHM* SO15 .... **131** K1
Bankhill Dr *LYMN* SO41 .... **228** B3
Bankside *LYMN* SO41 .... **228** B2
Bank Side *WEND* SO18 .... **107** J4
Bankside Rd
  MOOR/WNTN BH9 .... **220** E5
Banks Rd *CCLF* BH13 .... **245** G5
The Banks *ROMY* SO51 .... **48** F3
Bank St *BPWT* SO32 .... **111** J1
Bankview *LYMN* SO41 .... **228** B2
Bannerman Rd *PSF* GU32 .... **63** L4
Banning St *ROMY* SO51 .... **78** D2
Banstead Rd *HSEA* PO3 .... **187** K3
Bapaume Rd *HAV* PO9 .... **165** L4
Barbe Baker Av *HEND* SO30 .... **108** B6
Barberry Wy *VWD* BH31 .... **145** G3
Barbers Piles *PLE* BH15 .... **233** G7
Bardon Wy *FHAM/STUB* PO14..... **6** B8
Bar End Rd *WINC* SO23 .... **27** G2
Barfield Cl *WINC* SO23 .... **27** G2
Barfields *LYMN* SO41 .... **228** C4
Barfleur Rd *FHAM* PO15............. **6** A3
Barfleur Rd *FHAM/STUB* PO14 . **184** C3
Barford Cl *CHFD* SO53 .... **53** G8
Barford La *RSAL* SP5 .... **44** F8
Bargates *CHCH/BSGR* BH23 .... **237** M1
Bargate St *SHAM* SO14 .... **4** F4
Barham Cl *GPORT* PO12 .... **209** M2
Barham Rd *PSF* GU32 .... **63** L5
Barham Wy *NEND* PO2 .... **187** H4
Baring Rd *SBNE* BH6 .... **237** M4
  WINC SO23 .... **3** K9
Barker Mill Cl *ROWN* SO16 ...... **105** K2
Barlands Cl
  CHCH/BSGR BH23............. **223** G6
Barle Cl *WEND* SO18 .... **108** A7
Barley Down Dr *FUFL* SO22 .... **26** C4
Barlow Cl *FHAM/STUB* PO14 ... **183** M6
Barnbrook Rd *HLER* SO31 .... **158** C4
Barn Cl *EMRTH* PO10 .... **166** B8
Barncroft Wy *HAV* PO9 .... **165** H5
Barnes Cl *HLER* SO31 .... **158** B4
  ITCH SO19 .... **133** G7
  NBNE BH10 .... **220** B5
  WINC SO23 .... **26** D3
Barnes Crs *NBNE* BH10 .... **220** B5
  WIMB BH21 .... **192** C4
Barnes La *HLER* SO31 .... **158** C3
  LYMN SO41 .... **227** G8
Barnes Rd *ITCH* SO19 .... **133** G2
  NBNE BH10 .... **220** B5
  PSEA PO1 .... **211** J2
Barnes Wallis Rd
  FHAM PO15 .... **159** H4
Barnes Wy *HAV* PO9 .... **165** G5
Barnet Side La *PSF* GU32 .... **34** C3
Barney Evans Crs *HORN* PO8 ... **140** B5
Barnfield *CHCH/BSGR* BH23 ... **224** B8
Barnfield Cl *EMRTH* PO10 .... **167** J6
  ITCH SO19 .... **132** C7
Barnfield Ct *FHAM/STUB* PO14 ... **6** D8
  ITCH SO19 .... **132** C7
Barnfield Rd *EPSH* GU31 .... **64** B5
  ITCH SO19 .... **132** C7
Barnfield Wy *ITCH* SO19 .... **132** D7
Barn Fold *HORN* PO8 .... **140** F7
Barn Green Cl *WVILLE* PO7 ..... **139** K4
Barn Piece *NBAD* SO52 .... **80** B3
Barns Rd *BDST* BH18 .... **217** M5
Barnsfield Crs *TOTT* SO40 .... **129** G1
Barnsfield Rd *NBAD* SO52 .... **169** L1
Barnside Wy *LISS* GU33 .... **36** E5
Barnsland *HEND* SO30 .... **108** B6
Barns Rd *FERN* BH22 .... **194** B2

Baron Rd *HLER* SO31 .... **157** K5
Barons Md *ROWN* SO16 .... **105** K5
Barons Rd *BWD* BH11 .... **219** H2
Barrack La *RGWD* BH24 .... **171** H4
Barrack Rd *CHCH/BSGR* BH23 . **222** C8
  FERN BH22 .... **194** E6
Barrie Rd *LYMN* SO41 .... **228** A5
Barrie Rd *MOOR/WNTN* BH9 .. **220** D5
Barrington Cl *ELGH* SO50 .... **81** L3
Barrow Down Gdns *ITCH* SO19 . **133** J5
Barrow Dr *CHAR* BH8 .... **221** K6
Barrowgate Rd *CHAR* BH8 ...... **221** H4
Barrowgate Wy *CHAR* BH8 ..... **221** J4
Barrow Hill Rd *TOTT* SO40 ...... **103** J5
Barrow Rd *CHAR* BH8 .... **221** K6
Barrows La *LYMN* SO41 .... **226** F1
Barrow Vw *BH22* **193** G2
Barrow Vw *CHAR* BH8 .... **221** K6
Barrs Wood Dr
  NMIL/BTOS BH25 .... **225** M4
Barrs Wood Rd
  NMIL/BTOS BH25 .... **225** M4
Barry Gdns *BDST* BH18 .... **217** K3
Barry Rd *ITCH* SO19 .... **132** F3
Barters Cl *ROWN* SO16 .... **105** L7
Barters La *BDST* BH18 .... **217** K4
Bartlett Cl *FHAM* PO15 .... **6** C2
Bartlett Dr *LTDN* BH7 .... **221** M8
The Bartletts *HLER* SO31 .... **157** L6
Bartley Av *TOTT* SO40 .... **129** J2
Bartley Rd *TOTT* SO40 .... **128** A3
Barton Cl *ROMY* SO51 .... **51** G8
Barton Common La
  NMIL/BTOS BH25 .... **225** M8
Barton Common Rd
  NMIL/BTOS BH25 .... **241** G1
Barton Court Av
  NMIL/BTOS BH25 .... **240** E1
Barton Court Rd
  NMIL/BTOS BH25 .... **225** L7
Barton Crs *WEND* SO18 .... **107** L7
Barton Cft *NMIL/BTOS* BH25 ... **240** F1
Barton Cross *HORN* PO8 .... **140** F1
Barton Dr *HEND* SO30 .... **134** B1
  HLER SO31 .... **157** K5
  NMIL/BTOS BH25 .... **225** K8
Barton Gn *NMIL/BTOS* BH25 ... **240** F2
Barton La *NMIL/BTOS* BH25 .... **225** K8
Barton Rd *ELGH* SO50 .... **82** B5
Bartonside Rd
  NMIL/BTOS BH25 .... **225** G8
Bartons Rd *FBDG* SP6 .... **97** L7
The Bartons *FBDG* SP6 .... **97** L7
Barton Wy *NMIL/BTOS* BH25 .. **225** K8
Barton Wood Rd
  NMIL/BTOS BH25 .... **240** D1
Bartram Rd *TOTT* SO40 .... **129** L2
Barwell Gv *EMRTH* PO10 .... **166** C5
Bascott Cl *BWD* BH11 .... **219** L7
Bascott Rd *BWD* BH11 .... **219** K7
Bashley Common Rd
  NMIL/BTOS BH25 .... **199** L8
Bashley Cross Rd
  CHCH/BSGR BH23............. **224** B6
Bashley Dr *NMIL/BTOS* BH25... **225** M2
Bashley Rd *NMIL/BTOS* BH25 .. **225** L1
Basing Dean *ALTN* GU34 .... **33** K3
Basing Rd *HAV* PO9 .... **165** J3
Basingstoke Rd *WINC* SO23 ...... **17** J2
Basing Wy *CHFD* SO53 .... **80** F4
Basingwell St *BPWT* SO32 .... **111** H1
Basin St *NEND* PO2 .... **187** H8
Bassett Av *ROWN* SO16 .... **106** E3
Bassett Crs East *ROWN* SO16 .. **106** E4
Bassett Crs West *ROWN* SO16 . **106** E5
Bassett Dl *ROWN* SO16 .... **106** E5
Bassett Gdns *ROWN* SO16 ...... **106** D4
Bassett Gn *ROWN* SO16 .... **107** G3
Bassett Green Cl *ROWN* SO16 . **106** F3
Bassett Green Dr *ROWN* SO16 . **106** F2
Bassett Green Rd *ROWN* SO16 . **106** F1
Bassett Heath Av *ROWN* SO16 . **106** E1
Bassett Meadow *ROWN* SO16 . **106** E5
Bassett Ms *ROWN* SO16 .... **106** E3
Bassett Rd *BKME/WDN* BH12 .. **234** A2
Bassett Rw *ROWN* SO16 .... **106** E2
Bassett Wood Dr *ROWN* SO16 . **106** E2
Bassett Wood Rd *ROWN* SO16 . **106** E2
Batchelor Crs *BWD* BH11 .... **219** K5
Batchelor Gn *HLER* SO31 .... **133** L8
Batchelor Rd *BWD* BH11 .... **219** J5
Batcombe Cl *BWD* BH11 .... **219** J5
Bath Cl *ITCH* SO19 .... **132** F2
Bath Hill Rbt *BMTH* BH1 .... **14** F7
Bathing La *PSEA* PO1 .... **12** B4
Bath La *FHAM/PORC* PO16 .... **7** M6
Bath Lane (Lower)
  FHAM/PORC PO16 .... **7** M7
Bath Rd *BMTH* BH1 .... **14** F7
  EMRTH PO10 .... **166** D4
  ENEY PO4 .... **211** K5
  ITCH SO19 .... **132** F2
  LYMN SO41 .... **228** D5
Bath Sq *PSEA* PO1 .... **12** B4
Bath St *SHAM* SO14 .... **131** L1
Bathurst Cl *HISD* PO11 .... **213** J5
Battenburg Av *NEND* PO2 .... **187** K6
Battenburg Rd *GPORT* PO12 .... **11** C2
Batten Cl *CHCH/BSGR* BH23 ... **223** H8
Batten Rd *RSAL* SP5 .... **44** D8
Battens Wy *HAV* PO9 .... **165** K6
Batterley Dro *WIMB* BH21 .... **120** D4
Battery Cl *GPORT* PO12 .... **185** K3
Battery Hl *BPWT* SO32 .... **85** G8
Battery Rw *PSEA* PO1 .... **12** C6
  FUFL SO22 .... **26** B2
Battle Cl *HLER* SO31 .... **158** D4
B Av *FAWY* SO45 .... **180** B3
Baverstock Rd
  BKME/WDN BH12 .... **219** M8
Baxter Rd *ITCH* SO19 .... **133** J4
Baybridge La *BPWT* SO32 .... **56** D6
Baybridge Rd *HAV* PO9 .... **165** M3
Bay Cl *ITCH* SO19 .... **132** E5

  UPTN BH16 .... **232** A2
  WIMB BH21 .... **144** C8
Bay Hog La *PLE* BH15 .... **233** G6
Bay Rd *GPORT* PO12 .... **10** A6
  ITCH SO19 .... **132** E5
Bays Rd *LYMN* SO41 .... **228** A5
Baythorn Cl *NEND* PO2 .... **211** H1
Bay Trees *ITCH* SO19 .... **133** J2
Bay Tree Wy *CHCH/BSGR* BH23.. **224** B7
Beach Av *NMIL/BTOS* BH25 .... **240** E1
Beach Dr *CHAM* PO6 .... **162** D4
Beach Rd *HLER* SO31 .... **234** F8
  EMRTH PO10 .... **166** C8
  HISD PO11 .... **213** J5
  LSOL/BMARY PO13............. **208** C3
  SSEA PO5 .... **13** K9
Beachway *FHAM/PORC* PO16 .. **186** B2
Beacon Bottom *HLER* SO31 .... **158** E3
Beacon Cl *HLER* SO31 .... **158** E3
  LYMN SO41 .... **227** H7
Beacon Ct *FBDG* SP6 .... **97** K5
Beacon Dr *CHCH/BSGR* BH23 . **239** L1
Beacon Gdns *BDST* BH18 .... **217** J5
Beacon Hill La *BPWT* SO32 ...... **58** E8
  BPWT SO32 .... **87** G2
  UPTN BH16 .... **216** F5
Beacon Mt *HLER* SO31 .... **158** E2
Beacon Park Crs *UPTN* BH16 .. **216** E8
Beacon Park Rd *UPTN* BH16 ... **216** E8
Beacon Rd *BDST* BH18 .... **217** H5
  HEND SO30 .... **108** C8
  UPTN BH16 .... **232** A1
  WCLF BH2 .... **14** D7
Beaconsfield Av *CHAM* PO6 .... **187** L1
Beaconsfield Rd
  BKME/WDN BH12 .... **234** C3
  CHCH/BSGR BH23............. **238** A1
  FHAM/PORC PO16 .... **7** J8
  WVILLE PO7 .... **140** C8
Beacon Sq *EMRTH* PO10 .... **190** C1
Beacon Wy *BDST* BH18 .... **217** H5
  HLER SO31 .... **158** E2
Bealing Cl *ROWN* SO16 .... **107** G4
Beamish Rd *CFDH* BH17 .... **218** D8
Bear Cross Av *BWD* BH11 .... **219** J2
Bearslane Cl *TOTT* SO40 .... **104** C7
Beatrice Rd *ENEY* PO4 .... **13** M7
  WSHM SO15 .... **131** G1
Beattie Ri *HEND* SO30 .... **109** H6
Beatty Cl *HLER* SO31 .... **158** F4
  RGWD BH24....................... **147** G8
Beatty Dr *GPORT* PO12 .... **10** A5
Beatty Rd *MOOR/WNTN* BH9 . **220** F7
Beauchamp Av
  LSOL/BMARY PO13............. **185** G6
Beauchamps Gdns *LTDN* BH7 . **221** L8
Beaucroft La *WIMB* BH21 .... **192** C2
Beaucroft Rd *WIMB* BH21 .... **192** B2
Beaufort Av *FHAM/PORC* PO16 . **6** E2
Beaufort Cl
  CHCH/BSGR BH23............. **239** G1
Beaufort Dr *BPWT* SO32 .... **85** H8
Beaufort Rd *HAV* PO9 .... **8** A3
  SBNE BH6 .... **237** H6
  SSEA PO5 .... **13** K9
  WINC SO23 .... **26** E2
Beaufoys Av *FERN* BH22 .... **194** A1
Beaufoys Cl *FERN* BH22 .... **194** A1
Beaulieu Av *CHCH/BSGR* BH23 . **237** K1
  FHAM/PORC PO16 .... **161** L8
  HAV PO9 .... **165** H2
Beaulieu Cl *FUFL* SO22 .... **16** C4
  ROWN SO16 .... **106** A3
Beaulieu Pl
  LSOL/BMARY PO13............. **185** G6
Beaulieu Rd *BROC* SO42 .... **153** K8
  BROC SO42 .... **179** G4
  CHCH/BSGR BH23............. **237** K1
  ELGH SO50 .... **81** M4
  FAWY SO45 .... **155** J7
  LYND SO43 .... **151** M4
  NEND PO2 .... **187** J2
  TOTT SO40 .... **154** B3
  WBNE BH4 .... **235** G7
Beaumaris Gdns *FAWY* SO45 .. **155** K4
Beaumont Gn *WINC* SO23 .... **2** F8
Beaumont Cl *FHAM* PO15 .... **6** B1
  ROWN SO16 .... **106** D5
Beaumont Ct *GPORT* PO12 ..... **185** L8
Beaumont Ri *FHAM* PO15 .... **160** B4
Beaumont Rd *CCLF* BH13 .... **245** L1
  TOTT SO40 .... **129** L1
Beauworth Av *WEND* SO18 ..... **108** A4
Beaver Dr *ELGH* SO50 .... **82** F6
Beccles Cl *PLE* BH15 .... **232** E1
Becher Rd *PSTN* BH14 .... **234** D4
Beck Cl *HLER* SO31 .... **158** C5
Beckford La *WHAM* PO17 .... **138** C7
Beckham La *PSF* GU32 .... **63** J4
Beckhampton Rd *PLE* BH15 ... **232** D5
Beckley Copse
  CHCH/BSGR BH23............. **224** E6
Beck St *PSEA* PO1 .... **12** E1
Becton La *NMIL/BTOS* BH25 .... **241** G1
Becton Md *NMIL/BTOS* BH25 .. **225** M7
Bedale Wy *PLE* BH15 .... **233** L3
Bedenham La
  LSOL/BMARY PO13............. **185** J5
Bedfield La *WINC* SO23 .... **17** G3
Bedford Av *ITCH* SO19 .... **132** C5
Bedford Cl *FBDG* SP6 .... **97** L5
  HAV PO9 .... **9** J7
  HEND SO30 .... **134** B2
Bedford Crs *LTDN* BH7 .... **237** H1
Bedford Pl *WSHM* SO15 .... **131** K2
Bedford Rd *PSF* GU32 .... **63** J5
  HAV PO9 .... **9** J7
Bedford Rd North
  BKME/WDN BH12 .... **219** G3
Bedford Rd South
  BKME/WDN BH12 .... **219** G3
Bedford St *GPORT* PO12 .... **209** L2
  SSEA PO5 .... **13** G3
Bedhampton Hl *CHAM* PO6 ... **164** F7
Bedhampton Hill Rd
  HAV PO9 .... **164** F7

Bedhampton Rd *HAV* PO9 .... **165** G6
  NEND PO2 .... **187** K2
Bedhampton Wy *HAV* PO9 ...... **165** K4
Bedwell Cl *ROWN* SO16 .... **105** L3
Beecham Rd *PSEA* PO1 .... **211** J1
Beech Av *CHCH/BSGR* BH23 ... **222** B8
  SBNE BH6 .... **237** H4
  WEND SO18 .... **132** C1
Beech Cl *BDST* BH18 .... **217** H4
  CHFD SO53 .... **53** J8
  FBDG SP6 .... **121** L3
  FUFL SO22 .... **26** A5
  HLER SO31 .... **157** J6
  HORN PO8 .... **140** D6
  LYMN SO41 .... **227** H8
  ROMY SO51 .... **79** H2
  VWD BH31 .... **144** C3
Beech Copse *FUFL* SO22 .... **16** A7
Beech Ct *WIMB* BH21 .... **192** C4
Beech Crs *FAWY* SO45 .... **155** L8
  FHAM PO15 .... **159** M7
Beechcroft *CHFD* SO53 .... **81** J3
Beechcroft La *RGWD* BH24 ..... **146** F8
Beechcroft Rd *GPORT* PO12 .... **10** D6
Beechcroft Wy *CHFD* SO53 ...... **81** J2
Beechdale Cl *TOTT* SO40 .... **104** B6
Beechen La *LYND* SO43 .... **151** M6
Beeches Hl *BPWT* SO32 .... **85** J6
The Beeches *ELGH* SO50 .... **83** J7
  LTDN BH7 .... **221** L8
  ROMY SO51 .... **76** C5
Beechey Rd *BMTH* BH1 .... **15** H2
  CHAR BH8 .... **15** H1
Beechfield Ct *WSHM* SO15 ..... **105** M8
Beech Gdns *HLER* SO31 .... **157** J6
Beech Gra *RSAL* SP5 .... **75** J6
Beech Gv *GPORT* PO12 .... **10** C5
  HISD PO11 .... **213** M4
  RWIN SO21......................... **55** M4
Beech La *RGWD* BH24 .... **169** J6
Beechmount Rd *ROWN* SO16 . **106** E3
Beech Rd *CHFD* SO53 .... **53** J8
  FHAM PO15 .... **6** D4
  HEND SO30 .... **134** B1
  HORN PO8 .... **116** C3
  TOTT SO40 .... **128** F6
  WSHM SO15 .... **130** F2
Beech Wy *HORN* PO8 .... **140** F3
Beechwood *FBDG* SP6 .... **97** J7
Beechwood Av *BOSC* BH5 .... **236** E4
  NMIL/BTOS BH25 .... **225** J4
  WVILLE PO7 .... **164** C2
Beechwood Cl *BDST* BH18 ...... **217** H4
  HLER SO31 .... **158** B8
Beechwood Crs *CHFD* SO53 ..... **52** F6
Beechwood Gdns *BOSC* BH5 ... **236** F4
  WEND SO18 .... **107** K8
Beechwood La *RGWD* BH24 .... **172** F5
Beechwood Ri *WEND* SO18 ..... **108** B7
Beechwood Rd *FAWY* SO45 .... **180** A5
  FERN BH22 .... **168** B3
  NEND PO2 .... **187** J4
  TOTT SO40 .... **127** K3
Beechwood Wy *FAWY* SO45 ... **155** L6
Beechworth Rd *HAV* PO9 .... **9** C4
Beehive Wk *PSEA* PO1 .... **12** B4
Beggar's La *WINC* SO23 .... **3** J7
Begonia Rd *ROWN* SO16 .... **107** G4
Behrendt Cl *GPORT* PO12 .... **209** L2
Belben Cl *BKME/WDN* BH12 ... **219** H6
Belben Rd *BKME/WDN* BH12 .. **219** G6
Belbins *ROMY* SO51 .... **50** E4
Belfield Rd *SBNE* BH6 .... **237** M4
Belfry Wk *FHAM/STUB* PO14 .. **159** J2
Belgrave Rd *CCLF* BH13 .... **234** F6
  PTSW SO17 .... **107** H6
Belgravia Rd *NEND* PO2 .... **187** H7
Bellair Rd *HAV* PO9 .... **9** C5
Bell Crs *WVILLE* PO7 .... **164** C2
Bell Davies Rd
  FHAM/STUB PO14............. **183** H7
Beliemoor Rd *WSHM* SO15 .... **106** C7
Belle Vue Cl *SBNE* BH6 .... **237** J4
Belle Vue Crs *SBNE* BH6 .... **237** L4
Belle Vue Gv *FERN* BH22 .... **168** D6
Bellemere La *EMRTH* PO10 ..... **166** D6
Belle Vue Rd *PSTN* BH14 .... **234** B5
  SBNE BH6 .... **237** J5
Bellevue Rd *ELGH* SO50 .... **81** M5
  WSHM SO15 .... **131** L2
Bellevue Ter *SSEA* PO5 .... **12** E6
Belle Vue Wk *FERN* BH22 .... **194** C6
Bellflower Cl
  CHCH/BSGR BH23............. **223** M8
Bellflower Wy *NBAD* SO52 .... **80** E1
Bell Heather Cl *UPTN* BH16 .... **216** F8
Bell Hl *PSF* GU32 .... **63** J3
Bell Hill Rdg *PSF* GU32 .... **63** K3
Bellhanger Ct *FHAM/STUB* PO14 . **184** B5
Bell St *ROMY* SO51 .... **78** D1
  SHAM SO14 .... **5** H5
Belmont Av *CHAR* BH8 .... **221** G6
Belmont Cl *FAWY* SO45 .... **155** L6
  FHAM/STUB PO14............. **184** B5
  HORN PO8 .... **116** B6
  VWD BH31 .... **144** E3
Belmont Gv *HAV* PO9 .... **165** G6
Belmont Pl *SSEA* PO5 .... **13** H5
Belmont Rd *CHFD* SO53 .... **81** J5
  NMIL/BTOS BH25 .... **226** A4
  PSTN BH14........................ **234** A3
  PTSW SO17 .... **107** G8
Belmont St *SSEA* PO5 .... **13** H5
Belmore Cl *PSEA* PO1 .... **211** J1
Belmore La *LYMN* SO41 .... **228** C5
  RWIN SO21......................... **56** C3
Belmore Rd *LYMN* SO41 .... **228** B5
Belney La *WHAM* PO17 .... **139** J8
Belstone Rd *TOTT* SO40 .... **129** J1
Belton Rd *ITCH* SO19 .... **132** F5
Belvedere Rd
  CHCH/BSGR BH23............. **237** M1
  FAWY SO45 .... **155** L6
  TWDS BH3 .... **235** M2
Belverdere Cl *PSF* GU32 .... **63** L4

Belvidere Rd SHAM SO14 ...... 5 L2
Belvidere Ter SHAM SO14 ...... 5 L1
Belvoir Cl FHAM/PORC PO16 ...... 7 J7
Bembridge Cl HLER SO31 ...... 157 C2
Bembridge Cl ROWN SO16 ...... 107 H3
Bembridge Crs ENEY PO4 ...... 13 L9
Bembridge Dr HISD PO11 ...... 214 A7
Bemister Rd MOOR/WNTN BH9 ...... 220 E8
Benbow HORN PO8 ...... 141 C1
Benbow Crs BKME/WDN BH12 ...... 219 J7
Benbow Pl PSEA PO1 ...... 12 C1
Benbridge Av BWD BH11 ...... 219 K3
Bendigo Rd CHCH/BSGR BH23 ...... 222 C8
Benedict Cl ROMY SO51 ...... 79 H1
Benedict Wy FHAM/PORC PO16 ...... 162 C6
Beneficial St PSEA PO1 ...... 12 C2
Benellen Av WBNE BH4 ...... 235 H4
Benellen Gdns WBNE BH4 ...... 235 H4
Benellen Rd WBNE BH4 ...... 235 H3
Bengal Rd MOOR/WNTN BH9 ...... 220 C7
Benger's La ROMY SO51 ...... 21 J6
Benham Dr HSEA PO3 ...... 187 K4
Benham Gv FHAM/PORC PO16 ...... 186 B2
Benhams Farm Cl WEND SO18 ...... 107 M7
Benhams Rd WEND SO18 ...... 107 M6
Benjamin Rd PLE BH15 ...... 232 E6
Ben La RSAL SP5 ...... 18 C1
Benmoor Rd CFDH BH17 ...... 217 L8
Benmore Cl NMIL/BTOS BH25 ...... 226 A6
Benmore Gdns CHFD SO53 ...... 53 C8
Benmore Rd MOOR/WNTN BH9 ...... 220 E7
Bennett Cl RSAL SP5 ...... 73 J2
Bennett Rd CHAR BH8 ...... 236 B2
Bennetts La RGWD BH24 ...... 173 C6
Bennion Rd NBNE BH10 ...... 220 A5
Benridge Cl BDST BH18 ...... 217 L5
Benson Cl CHCH/BSGR BH23 ...... 197 M7
Benson Rd WSHM SO15 ...... 106 A3
Bentham Rd GPORT PO12 ...... 10 E6
Bentham Wy HLER SO31 ...... 134 E8
Bentley Cl HORN PO8 ...... 116 B8
Bentley Cl WINC SO23 ...... 17 C2
Bentley Ct HAV PO9 ...... 165 M3
Bentley Crs FHAM/PORC PO16 ...... 6 F7
Bentley Gn WEND SO18 ...... 108 B8
Bentley Rd MOOR/WNTN BH9 ...... 220 C7
Bepton Down EPSF GU31 ...... 63 M5
Berber Cl FHAM PO15 ...... 159 C1
Bercote Cl FUFL SO22 ...... 16 A3
Bere Cl CFDH BH17 ...... 218 B6
Bere Cl CHFD SO53 ...... 52 F8
Bere Cl FUFL SO22 ...... 2 A3
Bere Farm La WHAM PO17 ...... 137 K8
Bere Rd WVILLE PO7 ...... 139 L1
Beresford Cl BKME/WDN BH12 ...... 234 C2
Beresford Cl CHFD SO53 ...... 81 K3
Beresford Cl WVILLE PO7 ...... 164 C2
Beresford Gdns CHCH/BSGR BH23 ...... 238 D2
Beresford Gdns CHFD SO53 ...... 81 K3
Beresford Rd BKME/WDN BH12 ...... 234 C2
Beresford Rd CHFD SO53 ...... 81 K3
Beresford Rd FHAM/STUB PO14 ...... 184 B5
Beresford Rd LYMN SO41 ...... 228 A4
Beresford Rd NEND PO2 ...... 187 J6
Beresford Rd SBNE BH6 ...... 237 C4
Bereweeke Av FUFL SO22 ...... 2 C1
Bereweeke Cl FUFL SO22 ...... 2 C1
Bereweeke Rd FUFL SO22 ...... 2 C1
Bereweeke Wy FUFL SO22 ...... 2 D3
Bergen Crs HEND SO30 ...... 134 A3
Berkeley Av BKME/WDN BH12 ...... 219 C8
Berkeley Cl FHAM/STUB PO14 ...... 183 M6
Berkeley Cl VWD BH31 ...... 144 C1
Berkeley Cl WSHM SO15 ...... 131 J1
Berkeley Gdns HEND SO30 ...... 134 A3
Berkeley Rd TWDS BH3 ...... 235 K1
Berkeley Sq HAV PO9 ...... 9 J4
Berkley Av FERN BH22 ...... 194 B6
Berkshire Cl PSEA PO1 ...... 13 K2
Bernard Av CHAM PO6 ...... 163 L8
Bernards Cl CHCH/BSGR BH23 ...... 237 K1
Bernard St SHAM SO14 ...... 5 C5
Berney Rd ENEY PO4 ...... 212 A4
Bernina Av WVILLE PO7 ...... 140 A6
Bernina Cl WVILLE PO7 ...... 140 A6
Bernwood Gv FAWY SO45 ...... 206 C1
Berrans Av BWD BH11 ...... 219 M2
Berrybarn La SELS PO20 ...... 215 K8
Berry Cl HEND SO30 ...... 134 B2
Berrydown Rd HAV PO9 ...... 165 C1
Berryfield Rd LYMN SO41 ...... 226 E6
Berrylands LISS GU33 ...... 36 F1
Berry La FHAM/STUB PO14 ...... 183 L6
Berry La RWIN SO21 ...... 54 F1
Berrywood Gdns HEND SO30 ...... 109 C8
Berrywood Gdns HEND SO30 ...... 133 M1
Bertie Rd ENEY PO4 ...... 211 M4
Bertram Rd NMIL/BTOS BH25 ...... 226 A4
Berwick Rd TWDS BH3 ...... 235 K2
Beryl Av GPORT PO12 ...... 185 K8
Beryton Cl GPORT PO12 ...... 209 L2
Beryton Rd GPORT PO12 ...... 209 L2
Besomer Dro RSAL SP5 ...... 73 L4
Bessborough Rd CCLF BH13 ...... 245 K1
Beswick Av NBNE BH10 ...... 220 D6
Bethia Cl BMTH BH1 ...... 236 C2
Bethia Rd CHAR BH8 ...... 236 C2
Betsy Cl CHCH/BSGR BH23 ...... 197 M7
Betteridge Dr ROWN SO16 ...... 105 J2
Bettesworth Rd PSEA PO1 ...... 211 J1
Bettiscombe Cl CFDH BH17 ...... 218 B6
Betula Cl WVILLE PO7 ...... 164 E2
Bevan Cl ITCH SO19 ...... 132 C7
Bevan Rd HORN PO8 ...... 140 D3
Beverley Cl HLER SO31 ...... 159 C4
Beverley Gdns BPWT SO32 ...... 112 A3
HLER SO31 ...... 133 J7

NBNE BH10 ...... 220 B5
ROMY SO51 ...... 51 H7
Beverley Hts WEND SO18 ...... 107 L5
Beverley Rd FAWY SO45 ...... 155 K8
FHAM/STUB PO14 ...... 183 M6
Beverly Cl LSOL/BMARY PO13 ...... 185 H6
Beverston Rd CHAM PO6 ...... 162 E7
Bevis Cl FAWY SO45 ...... 180 D6
Bevis Rd GPORT PO12 ...... 10 F2
NEND PO2 ...... 187 H7
Bevois Gdns SHAM SO14 ...... 131 L1
Bevois Hl PTSW SO17 ...... 107 C8
Bevois Valley Rd SHAM SO14 ...... 131 M1
Bexington Cl BWD BH11 ...... 219 J3
Beyne Rd FUFL SO22 ...... 26 A5
Bickerley Gdns RGWD BH24 ...... 170 D2
Bickerley Rd RGWD BH24 ...... 170 D2
Bicton Rd BWD BH11 ...... 219 M5
Bidbury La HAV PO9 ...... 165 C7
Biddenfield La WHAM PO17 ...... 136 B4
Biddlecombe Cl LSOL/BMARY PO13 ...... 185 C8
Bideford Cl ROWN SO16 ...... 105 K7
Bilberry Cl HLER SO31 ...... 158 D6
Bilberry Dr TOTT SO40 ...... 130 C6
Billett Av WVILLE PO7 ...... 140 D7
Billing Cl ENEY PO4 ...... 211 M5
Billington Gdns HEND SO30 ...... 109 J7
Billy Lawn Av HAV PO9 ...... 165 K4
Bilton Wy HSEA PO3 ...... 188 A6
Bindon Cl BKME/WDN BH12 ...... 234 D1
ROWN SO16 ...... 105 M6
Bindon Rd ROWN SO16 ...... 105 M6
Bingham Av PSTN BH14 ...... 245 J1
Bingham Cl CHCH/BSGR BH23 ...... 238 D1
Bingham Dr LYMN SO41 ...... 228 C5
Bingham Rd CHCH/BSGR BH23 ...... 238 D1
MOOR/WNTN BH9 ...... 220 E8
VWD BH31 ...... 144 E4
Binnacle Wy CHAM PO6 ...... 162 F8
Binness Wy CHAM PO6 ...... 188 C1
Binnie Rd BKME/WDN BH12 ...... 234 D3
Binsey Cl ROWN SO16 ...... 105 L6
Binstead Rd ROWN SO16 ...... 107 H3
Binsteed Rd NEND PO2 ...... 187 J8
Birch Av CHCH/BSGR BH23 ...... 223 C5
FERN BH22 ...... 194 D7
NMIL/BTOS BH25 ...... 225 H2
Birch Cl HORN PO8 ...... 140 C5
LISS GU33 ...... 36 F4
PSTN BH14 ...... 234 D5
RGWD BH24 ...... 169 H5
ROMY SO51 ...... 79 H2
ROWN SO16 ...... 105 M6
WIMB BH21 ...... 217 H2
Birchdale Cl HLER SO31 ...... 158 B8
Birchdale Rd WIMB BH21 ...... 192 B3
Birch Dr CHAR BH8 ...... 221 L6
LSOL/BMARY PO13 ...... 185 G4
Birch Gv ELGH SO50 ...... 81 L2
FERN BH22 ...... 168 B6
Birchlands TOTT SO40 ...... 129 H3
Birchmore Cl LSOL/BMARY PO13 ...... 185 G6
Birch Rd HEND SO30 ...... 134 B1
RGWD BH24 ...... 169 M4
ROWN SO16 ...... 80 F8
ROWN SO16 ...... 105 M6
Birch Tree Cl EMRTH PO10 ...... 166 D4
Birch Tree Dr EMRTH PO10 ...... 166 D4
Birch Wd ITCH SO19 ...... 133 J3
Birchy Hl LYMN SO41 ...... 201 C7
Birdham Rd HISD PO11 ...... 214 C6
Birdlip Cl HORN PO8 ...... 140 E2
Birdlip Rd CHAM PO6 ...... 162 F7
Bird's Hill Rd PLE BH15 ...... 233 K4
Birdwood Gv FHAM/PORC PO16 ...... 161 K8
Birinus Rd WINC SO23 ...... 3 H5
Birkdale Av CHAM PO6 ...... 164 A7
Birkdale Cl WIMB BH21 ...... 217 L3
Birkdale Wy WIMB BH21 ...... 217 L3
Biscay Cl FHAM/STUB PO14 ...... 183 M5
Bishearne Gdns LISS GU33 ...... 36 D3
Bishop Cl BKME/WDN BH12 ...... 235 H1
Bishop Ct RGWD BH24 ...... 170 E1
Bishop Rd MOOR/WNTN BH9 ...... 220 E8
Bishops Cl LTDN BH7 ...... 236 E2
TOTT SO40 ...... 104 D8
Bishops Ct ELGH SO50 ...... 82 C3
Bishops Crs ITCH SO19 ...... 132 D4
Bishopsfield Rd FHAM/STUB PO14 ...... 6 D8
Bishops Ga FHAM/STUB PO14 ...... 159 C5
Bishop's La BPWT SO32 ...... 111 H1
BPWT SO32 ...... 112 A7
Bishops Rd ITCH SO19 ...... 132 C5
Bishopstoke La ELGH SO50 ...... 82 D2
Bishopstoke Rd ELGH SO50 ...... 82 B5
HAV PO9 ...... 165 J3
Bishop St PSEA PO1 ...... 12 D1
Bishop's Wood Rd BPWT SO32 ...... 112 A5
Bisterne Cl RGWD BH24 ...... 173 H6
Bitterne Cl GPORT PO12 ...... 209 M1
Bitterne Cl HAV PO9 ...... 165 K2
Bitterne Crs ITCH SO19 ...... 132 E2
Bitterne Rd East WEND SO18 ...... 132 E2
Bitterne Rd West WEND SO18 ...... 132 C1
Bitterne Wy ITCH SO19 ...... 132 C2
LYMN SO41 ...... 228 B6
WHAM PO17 ...... 144 E3
Black Berry Cl HORN PO8 ...... 116 C4
Blackberry La CHCH/BSGR BH23 ...... 238 E2
Blackberry Ter SHAM SO14 ...... 131 M1
Blackbird Cl CFDH BH17 ...... 217 J8

HORN PO8 ...... 140 D4
Blackbird Rd ELGH SO50 ...... 81 J6
Blackbird Wy CHCH/BSGR BH23 ...... 198 A8
LSOL/BMARY PO13 ...... 208 D1
Blackbrook House Dr FHAM PO15 ...... 6 D5
Blackbrook Park Av FHAM PO15 ...... 6 D5
Blackbrook Rd FHAM PO15 ...... 6 D5
Blackburn Rd BKME/WDN BH12 ...... 234 A2
Blackbushe Cl ROWN SO16 ...... 105 L3
Blackbush Rd LYMN SO41 ...... 242 A2
Blackcap Av HAV PO9 ...... 141 L7
Blackdown Cl FAWY SO45 ...... 155 H6
Blackdown Crs HAV PO9 ...... 165 J4
Blackfield La FERN BH22 ...... 168 C5
Blackfield Rd CHAR BH8 ...... 221 H5
FAWY SO45 ...... 180 C7
Blackfriars Cl SSEA PO5 ...... 13 J3
Blackfriars Rd SSEA PO5 ...... 13 J2
Black Hl VWD BH31 ...... 144 E2
Blackhill Rd ROMY SO51 ...... 76 E8
Black Horse La BPWT SO32 ...... 111 K7
Blackhouse La WHAM PO17 ...... 137 L8
Black La RSAL SP5 ...... 73 M3
Blackmore La PSF GU32 ...... 34 D4
Blacksmith Cl ITCH SO19 ...... 132 D3
HISD PO11 ...... 214 A5
Blackthorn Cl ITCH SO19 ...... 132 D3
LYMN SO41 ...... 227 M6
Blackthorn Dr GPORT PO12 ...... 185 L7
HISD PO11 ...... 214 A5
Blackthorn Gn RWIN SO21 ...... 54 F8
Blackthorn Rd HISD PO11 ...... 214 A5
ITCH SO19 ...... 132 D3
Blackthorn Wy VWD BH31 ...... 144 F3
Blackwater Cl CHAM PO6 ...... 163 H8
Blackwater Dr TOTT SO40 ...... 104 C7
WIMB BH21 ...... 218 B1
Blackwater Gv FBDG SP6 ...... 121 J3
Blackwater Ms TOTT SO40 ...... 104 C7
Bladon Cl HAV PO9 ...... 9 L1
Bladon Rd ROWN SO16 ...... 106 B6
Blair Av PSTN BH14 ...... 234 B4
Blair Cl NMIL/BTOS BH25 ...... 225 J5
Blake Cl ROWN SO16 ...... 105 H3
Blakedene Rd PSTN BH14 ...... 234 A7
Blake Hill Av PSTN BH14 ...... 234 B7
Blake Hill Crs PSTN BH14 ...... 234 B7
Blakemere Crs CHAM PO6 ...... 163 C7
Blakeney Rd ROWN SO16 ...... 105 J4
Blake Rd CHAM PO6 ...... 164 B7
GPORT PO12 ...... 11 C2
Blakesley La HSEA PO3 ...... 188 A4
Blanchard Rd BPWT SO32 ...... 85 C8
Blandford Cl PLE BH15 ...... 232 E6
Blandford La PLE BH15 ...... 232 F7
RSAL SP5 ...... 42 C1
UPTN BH16 ...... 232 B2
Blandford Rd North UPTN BH16 ...... 216 D5
Blaney Wy WIMB BH21 ...... 217 C2
Blankney Cl FHAM/STUB PO14 ...... 183 M6
Blann Cl ROWN SO16 ...... 105 H3
Bleaklow Cl ROWN SO16 ...... 105 L8
Blechynden Ter WSHM SO15 ...... 4 D7
Blencowe Dr NBAD SO52 ...... 80 D3
Blendworth Crs HAV PO9 ...... 165 J5
WEND SO18 ...... 133 C1
Blendworth La HORN PO8 ...... 141 H1
Blendworth Rd ENEY PO4 ...... 211 M3
Blenheim Av PTSW SO17 ...... 106 F7
Blenheim Cl NBAD SO52 ...... 80 E4
TOTT SO40 ...... 129 H2
Blenheim Crs LYMN SO41 ...... 226 C4
Blenheim Dr CHCH/BSGR BH23 ...... 239 C1
Blenheim Gdns FAWY SO45 ...... 155 H6
GPORT PO12 ...... 185 M8
HAV PO9 ...... 9 L2
PTSW SO17 ...... 107 C6
Blenheim Rd ELGH SO50 ...... 81 M6
HORN PO8 ...... 140 E3
Bleriot Crs FHAM PO15 ...... 159 K2
Blighmont Crs WSHM SO15 ...... 130 F2
Blind La BPWT SO32 ...... 109 H3
FBDG SP6 ...... 123 C7
WHAM PO17 ...... 136 D3
Bliss Cl WVILLE PO7 ...... 164 C3
Blissford Cl WVILLE PO7 ...... 165 M2
Blissford Cross FBDG SP6 ...... 98 D8
Blissford Hl FBDG SP6 ...... 123 J2
Blissford Rd FBDG SP6 ...... 98 C7
Bloomfield Av MOOR/WNTN BH9 ...... 220 D6
Blossom Cl HEND SO30 ...... 134 C2
Blount Rd PSEA PO1 ...... 12 E5
Bloxworth Rd BKME/WDN BH12 ...... 219 K8
Blue Ball Hl WINC SO23 ...... 3 H4
Bluebell Cl CHCH/BSGR BH23 ...... 223 M8
WVILLE PO7 ...... 164 D2
Bluebell Copse HLER SO31 ...... 158 D6
Bluebell La CFDH BH17 ...... 217 J7
Bluebell Rd ROWN SO16 ...... 107 C4
Bluestar Gdns HEND SO30 ...... 109 H6
Blundell La HLER SO31 ...... 134 A6
Blyth Cl CHCH/BSGR BH23 ...... 222 B4
ROWN SO16 ...... 105 J6
Blythe Rd WIMB BH21 ...... 217 H2
Blythswood Ct NMIL/BTOS BH25 ...... 240 E1
Boakes Pl TOTT SO40 ...... 129 C6
Boarhunt Cl PSEA PO1 ...... 13 J1
Boarhunt Rd WHAM PO17 ...... 144 D1
Bob Hann Cl BKME/WDN BH12 ...... 234 D1
Bockhampton Rd CHCH/BSGR BH23 ...... 223 J3
Bodley Rd CCLF BH13 ...... 245 L2
Bodmin Rd CHAM PO6 ...... 162 E8
ELGH SO50 ...... 82 D5
Bodorgan Rd WCLF BH2 ...... 14 E4
Bodowen Cl CHCH/BSGR BH23 ...... 223 H6
Bodowen Rd CHCH/BSGR BH23 ...... 223 H6
Bodycoats Rd CHFD SO53 ...... 81 J2

Bognor Rd BDST BH18 ...... 217 K4
Bohemia La RSAL SP5 ...... 73 L5
Boiler Rd PSEA PO1 ...... 210 D2
Bolde Cl HSEA PO3 ...... 187 M5
Boldens Rd GPORT PO12 ...... 10 E9
Bolderford Br BROC SO42 ...... 175 J3
Bolderwood Arboretum Ornamental Dr LYND SO43 ...... 149 L4
RGWD BH24 ...... 150 A6
Bolderwood Rd ROWN SO16 ...... 106 D4
Boldre Cl BKME/WDN BH12 ...... 234 D1
HAV PO9 ...... 165 G4
NMIL/BTOS BH25 ...... 225 H8
Boldre La LYMN SO41 ...... 228 B1
Boldrewood Rd ROWN SO16 ...... 106 D4
Boleyn Crs MOOR/WNTN BH9 ...... 221 G4
Bolhinton Av TOTT SO40 ...... 130 B7
Bolton Crs FERN BH22 ...... 194 A3
Bolton Rd SBNE BH6 ...... 237 K5
The Boltons WVILLE PO7 ...... 140 C5
Bonchurch Cl ROWN SO16 ...... 107 H3
Bonchurch Rd ENEY PO4 ...... 211 L3
Bond Av FERN BH22 ...... 168 B4
Bond Cl LYMN SO41 ...... 200 F5
Bondfields Crs HAV PO9 ...... 165 K2
Bond Rd PLE BH15 ...... 233 L3
WEND SO18 ...... 107 K7
Bond St SHAM SO14 ...... 132 A2
Bones La EPSF GU31 ...... 91 J3
Bonfire Cnr PSEA PO1 ...... 210 E2
Bonham Rd TWDS BH3 ...... 235 L1
Boniface Cl TOTT SO40 ...... 104 B1
Boniface Crs ROWN SO16 ...... 105 K5
Bonington Cl CHCH/BSGR BH23 ...... 223 J8
Boothby Cl TOTT SO40 ...... 129 L2
Bordean La LIPH GU30 ...... 62 A3
Borden La LIPH GU30 ...... 66 C2
Border Dr UPTN BH16 ...... 232 B3
Border Rd UPTN BH16 ...... 232 B3
Bordon Rd HAV PO9 ...... 165 K3
Boreham Rd SBNE BH6 ...... 237 J3
Borley Rd CFDH BH17 ...... 217 L8
Borough Gv PSF GU32 ...... 63 K6
Borough Hl PSF GU32 ...... 63 K5
Borough Rd PSF GU32 ...... 63 J6
The Borough RSAL SP5 ...... 72 D1
Borrowdale Rd ROWN SO16 ...... 105 K7
Borthwick Rd BMTH BH1 ...... 236 D3
Boscobel Rd FUFL SO22 ...... 2 E4
Boscombe Cliff Rd BOSC BH5 ...... 236 D5
Boscombe Grove Rd BMTH BH1 ...... 236 C4
Boscombe Overcliff Dr BOSC BH5 ...... 236 D5
Boscombe Spa Rd BOSC BH5 ...... 236 C4
Bosham Rd NEND PO2 ...... 187 K8
Bosham Wk LSOL/BMARY PO13 ...... 184 F6
Bosley Cl CHCH/BSGR BH23 ...... 222 C6
Bosley Wy CHCH/BSGR BH23 ...... 222 C6
Bosmere Gdns EMRTH PO10 ...... 166 C7
Bosmere Rd HISD PO11 ...... 214 D6
Bossington Cl ROWN SO16 ...... 105 K3
Boston Rd CHAM PO6 ...... 163 J7
Bosuns Cl FHAM/PORC PO16 ...... 184 F2
Bosville ELGH SO50 ...... 81 M2
Boswell Cl HEND SO30 ...... 134 D1
ITCH SO19 ...... 133 G2
Bosworth Ms MOOR/WNTN BH9 ...... 220 F4
Botany Bay Rd ITCH SO19 ...... 132 E6
Botley Dr HAV PO9 ...... 165 H3
Botley Rd BPWT SO32 ...... 110 C8
ELGH SO50 ...... 83 J8
HEND SO30 ...... 108 E7
HEND SO30 ...... 135 H2
HLER SO31 ...... 134 E8
ITCH SO19 ...... 133 H5
NBAD SO52 ...... 79 L3
Bottom La ROMY SO51 ...... 76 D4
Boulnois Av PSTN BH14 ...... 234 D5
Boulter La WHAM PO17 ...... 162 E1
Boulton Rd SSEA PO5 ...... 13 L6
Boundary Cl WIMB BH21 ...... 192 B2
Boundary Dr WIMB BH21 ...... 192 B3
Boundary La RGWD BH24 ...... 169 H7
Boundary Rd HLER SO31 ...... 133 K8
MOOR/WNTN BH9 ...... 220 D5
NBNE BH10 ...... 220 B7
Boundary Wy CHAM PO6 ...... 163 M6
HAV PO9 ...... 8 D4
Bound La HISD PO11 ...... 213 L6
Boundstone FAWY SO45 ...... 155 K5
Boundway LYMN SO41 ...... 200 F3
Bourne Av WCLF BH2 ...... 14 C5
WSHM SO15 ...... 106 B7
Bourne Cl HORN PO8 ...... 140 F2
ROMY SO51 ...... 76 C4
RWIN SO21 ...... 54 A4
WBNE BH4 ...... 14 A5
Bourne Ct WIMB BH21 ...... 192 B3
Bournefields RWIN SO21 ...... 55 C1
Bourne La RWIN SO21 ...... 54 F1
TOTT SO40 ...... 128 B3
Bournemouth Av GPORT PO12 ...... 209 L1
Bournemouth International Centre Rbt WCLF BH2 ...... 14 C7
Bournemouth Rd CHFD SO53 ...... 81 C5
LYND SO43 ...... 151 J3
PSTN BH14 ...... 234 B4
ROWN SO16 ...... 80 D7
Bournemouth Road Castle Hl PSTN BH14 ...... 234 A4
Bournemouth Station Rbt BMTH BH1 ...... 15 J4
Bourne Rd CHAM PO6 ...... 162 D4
TOTT SO40 ...... 128 A3
WSHM SO15 ...... 4 D1
Bourne Valley Rd BKME/WDN BH12 ...... 234 F3
Bourne View Cl EMRTH PO10 ...... 167 H6
Bournewood Dr WBNE BH4 ...... 235 H4
Bourton Gdns LTDN BH7 ...... 221 M8
Bouverie Cl NMIL/BTOS BH25 ...... 225 K7

Boveridge Gdns MOOR/WNTN BH9 ...... 220 F4
Bovington Cl CFDH BH17 ...... 218 D7
Bowater Cl TOTT SO40 ...... 104 B7
Bowater Wy TOTT SO40 ...... 104 B7
Bowcombe HLER SO31 ...... 157 H6
Bowden Rd BKME/WDN BH12 ...... 219 G6
Bower Cl FAWY SO45 ...... 180 A5
ITCH SO19 ...... 132 D7
Bower Rd CHAR BH8 ...... 221 H8
Bowers Cl HORN PO8 ...... 140 E4
Bowers Hl RSAL SP5 ...... 73 K1
Bowerwood Rd FBDG SP6 ...... 97 H8
Bowes Hl HAV PO9 ...... 142 A5
Bowland Ri CHFD SO53 ...... 80 F1
NMIL/BTOS BH25 ...... 226 A6
Bowland Wy FAWY SO45 ...... 206 C1
Bowler Av PSEA PO1 ...... 211 K2
Bowler Ct HSEA PO3 ...... 211 K2
Box Cl CFDH BH17 ...... 233 G1
Boxwood Cl FHAM/PORC PO16 ...... 161 M7
WVILLE PO7 ...... 164 C2
Boyatt Crs ELGH SO50 ...... 53 M8
Boyatt La CHFD SO53 ...... 53 M7
ELGH SO50 ...... 54 A7
Boyd Cl FHAM/STUB PO14 ...... 183 M7
Boyd Rd BKME/WDN BH12 ...... 234 E2
LSOL/BMARY PO13 ...... 184 F5
Boyes La RWIN SO21 ...... 54 F7
Boyle Crs WVILLE PO7 ...... 164 B3
Boyne Mead Rd WINC SO23 ...... 17 G1
Boynton Cl CHFD SO53 ...... 53 G8
Brabant Cl HLER SO31 ...... 158 F1
Brabazon Dr CHCH/BSGR BH23 ...... 239 G1
Brabazon Rd FHAM PO15 ...... 159 H3
WIMB BH21 ...... 192 D7
Brabourne Av FERN BH22 ...... 194 A4
Bracken Cl NBAD SO52 ...... 79 M5
RGWD BH24 ...... 169 H4
Bracken Crs ELGH SO50 ...... 82 E6
Brackendale Ct WIMB BH21 ...... 144 B8
Brackendale Rd CHAR BH8 ...... 221 G8
Bracken Gln PLE BH15 ...... 233 K4
Bracken Heath HORN PO8 ...... 140 F7
Brackenhill CCLF BH13 ...... 234 F7
Brackenhill Rd WIMB BH21 ...... 192 E1
Bracken La ROWN SO16 ...... 105 M7
Bracken Pl ELGH SO50 ...... 106 F1
Bracken Rd EPSF GU31 ...... 64 B6
FERN BH22 ...... 193 M1
NBAD SO52 ...... 79 M5
SBNE BH6 ...... 237 H4
The Brackens FAWY SO45 ...... 155 H5
HLER SO31 ...... 158 F6
Brackens Wy LYMN SO41 ...... 228 D6
Bracken Wy CHCH/BSGR BH23 ...... 224 F7
Brackenway Rd CHFD SO53 ...... 81 H1
Bracklesham Cl ITCH SO19 ...... 132 D5
Bracklesham Rd HISD PO11 ...... 214 D7
LSOL/BMARY PO13 ...... 185 H8
Brackley Av ELGH SO50 ...... 83 C6
Brackley Cl CHCH/BSGR BH23 ...... 195 L8
Brackley Wy TOTT SO40 ...... 104 C8
Bradburne Rd WCLF BH2 ...... 14 C5
Bradford Rd MOOR/WNTN BH9 ...... 221 G4
SSEA PO5 ...... 13 K3
Brading Av ENEY PO4 ...... 211 L6
LSOL/BMARY PO13 ...... 185 G6
Brading Cl ROWN SO16 ...... 107 H3
Bradley Ct HAV PO9 ...... 165 M3
Bradley Gn ROWN SO16 ...... 106 A4
Bradley Peak FUFL SO22 ...... 16 B7
Bradley Rd FUFL SO22 ...... 16 B5
Bradly Rd FHAM PO15 ...... 160 A7
Bradpole Rd CHAR BH8 ...... 221 J7
Bradshaw Cl ELGH SO50 ...... 83 K6
Bradstock Cl BKME/WDN BH12 ...... 219 H8
Bradstone FAWY SO45 ...... 155 K6
Braemar Av CHAM PO6 ...... 187 M4
SBNE BH6 ...... 237 M4
Braemar Cl FHAM PO15 ...... 6 D1
LSOL/BMARY PO13 ...... 185 H6
SBNE BH6 ...... 237 M4
Braemar Dr CHCH/BSGR BH23 ...... 224 D7
Braemar Rd LSOL/BMARY PO13 ...... 185 H5
Braeside Cl FUFL SO22 ...... 26 A4
Braeside Crs ITCH SO19 ...... 132 C5
Braeside Rd FERN BH22 ...... 168 C5
ITCH SO19 ...... 132 C3
RGWD BH24 ...... 169 J4
Braidley Rd WCLF BH2 ...... 14 D3
Brailswood Rd PLE BH15 ...... 233 J4
Braintree Rd CHAM PO6 ...... 163 H7
Brairwood Gdns HISD PO11 ...... 213 K5
Braishfield Cl ROWN SO16 ...... 105 L7
Braishfield Gdns CHAR BH8 ...... 221 H6
Braishfield Rd HAV PO9 ...... 165 L4
ROMY SO51 ...... 51 H7
Bramber Rd GPORT PO12 ...... 209 L1
Bramble Cl ELGH SO50 ...... 82 A3
FAWY SO45 ...... 180 A5
FBDG SP6 ...... 121 L3
FHAM/STUB PO14 ...... 183 L7
Bramble Dr ROMY SO51 ...... 51 H7
Bramble Hl CHFD SO53 ...... 81 G2
Bramble La CHCH/BSGR BH23 ...... 224 F7
HLER SO31 ...... 158 C3
HORN PO8 ...... 116 A1
Bramble Ms WEND SO18 ...... 107 M8
Bramble Rd ENEY PO4 ...... 13 L4
EPSF GU31 ...... 64 B5
Brambles Cl RWIN SO21 ...... 54 F8
Brambles Rd LSOL/BMARY PO13 ...... 208 B1
Bramble Wk LYMN SO41 ...... 228 A4
Bramble Wy CHCH/BSGR BH23 ...... 197 M7
LSOL/BMARY PO13 ...... 185 E6
Brambling Cl ROWN SO16 ...... 106 A2
Brambling La MIDH GU29 ...... 67 L5
Brambling Rd HAV PO9 ...... 141 M7
The Bramblings TOTT SO40 ...... 104 B8
Bramdean Dr HAV PO9 ...... 165 H3

Bramdean Rd WEND SO18........ 133 H1
Bramham Moor FHAM/STUB PO14........ 183 M6 [2]
Bramley Cl LYMN SO41 .... 228 C6 [1]
  WVILLE PO7 .... 140 C8
Bramley Crs ITCH SO19........ 132 F6
Bramley Gdns EMRTH PO10 ... 166 F8
  GPORT PO12 .... 209 L7
Bramley Rd FERN BH22 .... 194 B2 [2]
  NBNE BH10 .... 220 A3
The Bramleys RSAL SP5 .... 47 G5
Brampton La HSEA PO3 .... 188 A4
Brampton Rd PLE BH15 .... 233 J2 [1]
Bramshaw Cl FUFL SO22 .... 16 B5
Bramshaw Ct HAV PO9 .... 165 M3 [3]
Bramshaw Gdns CHAR BH8 ... 221 H5 [2]
Bramshaw Wy NMIL/BTOS BH25 .... 225 H8
Bramshott Rd ENEY PO4 .... 211 K4
  ITCH SO19 .... 132 D7 [1]
Bramston Rd WSHM SO15 .... 106 B8
Branches La ROMY SO51 .... 48 E6
Branders Cl SBNE BH6 .... 237 M4
Branders La SBNE BH6 .... 237 M3
Brandon Rd SSEA PO5 .... 13 J8
Branksea Av WSHM SO15 .... 106 B7
Branksea Cl PLE BH15 .... 232 C7
Branksome Av WSHM SO15 .... 106 B7
Branksome Cl FUFL SO22 .... 26 A2
  NMIL/BTOS BH25 .... 225 M6
Branksome Dene Rd WBNE BH4 .... 235 G6
Branksome Hill Rd WBNE BH4 .... 235 G3
Branksome Towers CCLF BH13 .. 235 G8
Branksome Wood Gdns WCLF BH2 .... 14 B3
Branksome Wood Rd WBNE BH4 .... 235 H3
Bransbury Cl ROWN SO16 .... 106 B4 [1]
Bransbury Rd ENEY PO4 .... 211 M5
Bransgore Av HAV PO9 .... 165 G4
Bransgore Gdns CHCH/BSGR BH23 .... 197 M7
Bransley Cl ROMY SO51 .... 51 G7
Branwell Cl CHCH/BSGR BH23 .. 222 E7
Branwood Cl LYMN SO41 .... 227 J7 [1]
Brasenose Cl FHAM/STUB PO14........ 159 G7
Brasher Cl ELGH SO50 .... 82 F6
Brassey Cl MOOR/WNTN BH9 .. 220 E7
Brassey Rd FUFL SO22 .... 2 E4
  MOOR/WNTN BH9 .... 220 D7
Brasted Ct ENEY PO4 .... 212 A3 [1]
Brazil Rd SHAM SO14 .... 5 J8
Breach Av EMRTH PO10 .... 167 H6
Breamore Cl ELGH SO50 .... 81 M2 [1]
  NMIL/BTOS BH25 .... 225 J5 [1]
Breamore Rd RSAL SP5 .... 72 C2
  WEND SO18 .... 133 H1
Brean Cl ROWN SO16 .... 105 K5
Brecon Av CHAM PO6 .... 163 M7
Brecon Cl CHFD SO53 .... 81 G5 [1]
  FAWY SO45 .... 155 J5
  FHAM/STUB PO14........ 6 B7
  NBNE BH10 .... 220 C2
  NMIL/BTOS BH25 .... 226 A6
Brecon Rd ITCH SO19 .... 133 G2
Bredenbury Crs CHAM PO6 .... 163 G7
Bredy Cl CFDH BH17 .... 218 B7 [3]
Breech Cl HSEA PO3 .... 187 K4 [1]
Bremble Cl BKME/WDN BH12 .. 219 L6 [1]
Brenchley Cl FHAM/PORC PO16 .... 185 L1
Brendon Cl CHAR BH8 .... 221 J6 [1]
  FAWY SO45 .... 155 H6 [2]
Brendon Gn ROWN SO16 .... 105 L8
Brendon Rd FHAM/STUB PO14 .. 6 B8
Brent Ct EMRTH PO10 .... 166 C8
Brentwood Crs WEND SO18 .... 107 M7
Breton Cl FHAM PO15 .... 158 F1
Brewells La LISS GU33 .... 37 K2
Brewer Cl HLER SO31 .... 158 F4
Brewers La LSOL/BMARY PO13 .. 185 G6
  NARL SO24 .... 33 G1
  RWIN SO21 .... 54 E3
Brewer St PSEA PO1 .... 211 G2 [2]
Brewhouse Sq GPORT PO12 .... 11 J1 [1]
Brewster Cl HORN PO8 .... 140 E5
Briar Cl GPORT PO12 .... 209 J5
  HORN PO8 .... 140 F3
  PLE BH15 .... 233 K3
Briardene Ct TOTT SO40 .... 129 J1 [1]
Briarfield Gdns HORN PO8...... 140 F2
Briarswood ROWN SO16 .... 106 A7
Briarswood Ri FAWY SO45 ...... 155 H6
Briarswood UPTN BH16 .... 232 B1 [1]
Briar Wy ROMY SO51 .... 51 H7
  WIMB BH21 .... 192 F3
Briar Wy LISS GU33 .... 36 F1
Briarwood Cl FHAM/PORC PO7 .. 7 J7
Briarwood Rd TOTT SO40 .... 129 G2
Brickfield La CHFD SO53........ 81 G3
  LYMN SO41 .... 228 D3
Brickfield Rd PTSW SO17 .... 107 H6
Brick Kiln La NARL SO24 .... 32 E1
Brick La CHCH/BSGR BH23 .... 198 C4
Brickmakers Rd RWIN SO21 .... 54 E8
Brickwoods ROMY SO51 .... 51 G8 [2]
Brickworth La RSAL SP5 .... 46 B4
Brickworth Rd RSAL SP5 .... 46 D4
Brickyard La WIMB BH21 .... 193 L2
Brickyard Rd BPWT SO32 .... 111 L6
The Brickyard TOTT SO40 .... 103 G8
Bricky Lake La ROMY SO51 .... 103 H1
Bridefield Cl HORN PO8 .... 140 B5
Bridefield Crs HORN PO8 .... 140 B5
Bridge Ap PLE BH15 .... 233 G7
Bridge Cl HLER SO31 .... 133 M7
Bridgefoot Dr FHAM/PORC PO16 .... 7 M5
Bridgefoot Pth EMRTH PO10 .. 166 D7
Bridgemary Av LSOL/BMARY PO13........ 185 H5
Bridgemary Gv LSOL/BMARY PO13........ 185 G4

Bridgemary Rd LSOL/BMARY PO13........ 185 G3
Bridgemary Wy LSOL/BMARY PO13........ 185 G3 [1]
Bridge Md BPWT SO32 .... 87 J3
Bridge Mdw LISS GU33 .... 36 E4
Bridge Pl NBNE BH10 .... 220 B1
  HLER SO31 .... 133 M7
  HLER SO31 .... 158 C2
  ITCH SO19 .... 132 B5
  LYMN SO41 .... 228 D4
  ROMY SO51 .... 78 E1
  RSAL SP5 .... 41 G1
Bridgers Cl ROWN SO16 .... 105 K3
Bridges Cl ELGH SO50 .... 81 L5
  FERN BH22........ 168 D5 [1]
Bridget Cl HORN PO8 .... 141 G1
Bridgewater Rd BKME/WDN BH12 .... 234 C2 [2]
Bridgewater Ct WSHM SO15 .... 4 A1
Bridle Cl UPTN BH16 .... 232 C1 [1]
Bridle Crs LTDN BH7........ 222 A8
Bridleways VWD BH31 .... 144 C2
Bridlington Av WSHM SO15 .... 106 C8
Bridport Rd BKME/WDN BH12 .. 219 K8
  VWD BH31 .... 144 D2
Bridport St PSEA PO1 .... 13 H1
Brierley Av FERN BH22 .... 194 C7
Brierley Cl NBNE BH10 .... 220 C3
Brierley Rd NBNE BH10 .... 220 C4
Brigantine Rd HLER SO31 ...... 158 C7
Brighstone Cl ROWN SO16 .... 107 H3 [3]
Brightlands Av SBNE BH6 ...... 237 L4
Brighton Av GPORT PO12 ...... 185 K8
Brighton Rd LYMN SO41 .... 200 E5
  WSHM SO15........ 131 K1
Bright Rd PLE BH15 .... 233 J2
Brightside Rd WVILLE PO7 ...... 164 B2
Brightside Rd ROWN SO16...... 105 L6
Brights La HISD PO11 .... 213 K3
Brightstone Cl CHAM PO6 ...... 187 J1
Brindle Cl ROWN SO16 .... 106 F3
Brinsons Cl CHCH/BSGR BH23 .. 223 G5
Brinton La FAWY SO45 .... 155 L3
Brinton's Rd SHAM SO14 .... 5 H1
Brinton's Ter SHAM SO14 ...... 131 L2 [1]
Brisbane Rd CHCH/BSGR BH23 .... 222 C7
Bristol Rd ENEY PO4 .... 211 K6
Britain St PSEA PO1 .... 12 D2
Britannia Gdns HEND SO30 .... 109 G5 [2]
  SHAM SO14 .... 5 K1
  SSEA PO5........ 13 K4 [1]
Britannia Rd North SSEA PO5 .. 13 K4
Britannia Wy CHCH/BSGR BH23 .... 239 G1 [7]
Briton St SHAM SO14 .... 4 F6
Britten Rd LSOL/BMARY PO13.. 206 C2
Britten Wy WVILLE PO7 .... 164 C1
Brixey Cl BKME/WDN BH12 .... 234 B1
Brixey Rd BKME/WDN BH12 .... 234 B1
Broad Av CHAR BH8 .... 221 H8
Broadbent Cl ROWN SO16 ...... 105 J2
Broad Cft HAV PO9 .... 142 A6
Broadcut FHAM/PORC PO16 .... 7 M3
Broadfields Cl LYMN SO41 ...... 242 C3 [1]
Broad Gdns CHAM PO6........ 164 C8
Broad Gn SHAM SO14 .... 5 H2
Broadhill La FBDG SP6 .... 98 C3
Broadhurst Av NBNE BH10 .... 220 C4
Broadlands Av ELGH SO50 ...... 81 M3
  SBNE BH6 .... 237 L4
  WVILLE PO7 .... 164 C2
Broadlands Cl CHAR BH8 ...... 221 H5
Broadlands Rd BROC SO42 .... 175 J6
  PTSW SO17 .... 107 G5
Broad La BPWT SO32 .... 111 M3
  LYMN SO41 .... 228 D5
  NBAD SO52 .... 79 K3 [1]
Broadley Cl FAWY SO45 .... 180 A4 [1]
Broadmayne Rd LYMN SO41 .... 227 M6
Broadmayne Rd BKME/WDN BH12 .... 234 E1
Broadmeadow Cl TOTT SO40 .... 129 J1 [1]
Broadmeadows La WVILLE PO7 .... 164 E1 [1]
Broadmead Rd ROWN SO16 .... 105 J2
Broad Mead Rd WIMB BH21 .... 144 C7
Broadmere Av HAV PO9 .... 165 K3
Broadmoor Rd WIMB BH21 .... 217 G2
Broad Oak HEND SO30........ 134 C1
Broadoak Cl FAWY SO45 .... 180 A5
Broadoak Rd RCCH PO18........ 167 M8
Broadsands Dr GPORT PO12 .. 209 H5
Broadshard La ROMY SO51 .... 51 G8 [2]
Broadstone Wy BDST BH18 .... 217 K7
Broad St PSEA PO1 .... 12 B5
Broad View La FUFL SO22 ...... 25 M5
Broadwater Rd ROMY SO51 .... 78 D2
  WEND SO18 .... 107 L5
Broad Wy HLER SO31 .... 157 J3
  PSF GU32 .... 34 C8
Broadway SBNE BH6 .... 237 M4
Broadway La CHAR BH8........ 221 G5
  HORN PO8 .... 140 B2
The Broadway NBNE BH10 .... 220 B2
  WINC SO23 .... 3 H1
Broad Woods La ROMY SO51 .. 76 F1
Brockenhurst Av HAV PO9 .... 165 H2
Brockenhurst Rd MOOR/WNTN BH9 .... 220 F6
Brockhampton La HAV PO9 .... 8 D5

Brockhampton Rd HAV PO9 .... 8 B5
Brockhills La NMIL/BTOS BH25 .. 226 A3
Brockhurst Rd GPORT PO12 .... 209 K1
Brockishill Rd LYND SO43 ...... 127 K4
  TOTT SO40 .... 127 L3
Brocklands HAV PO9 .... 8 B4
Brockley Rd NBNE BH10 .... 220 B4
Brocks Cl FAWY SO45 .... 155 H6
Brocks Pine RGWD BH24 ...... 169 K5
Brockwood Bottom NARL SO24 .. 31 K7
Brodrick Av GPORT PO12 .... 10 D6
Brokenford Av TOTT SO40 ...... 129 L1
Brokenford La TOTT SO40 ...... 129 K1
Bromley Rd WEND SO18 .... 107 L7
Brompton Rd ENEY PO4 .... 211 K6
Bromyard Crs CHAM PO6 ...... 163 G8
Bronte Av CHCH/BSGR BH23 .. 222 E7
Bronte Cl TOTT SO40 .... 129 H2
Bronte Gdns FHAM PO15 ...... 135 G8 [2]
Bronte Wy ITCH SO19 .... 132 C2
Brook Av HLER SO31 .... 158 A5
  NMIL/BTOS BH25 .... 225 M4
Brook Av North NMIL/BTOS BH25 .... 225 M3
Brook Cl HLER SO31 .... 158 B5 [1]
  NBAD SO52 .... 79 M5
  NBNE BH10 .... 220 A4
Brookdale Cl WIMB BH21 ...... 217 L4
  WVILLE PO7 .... 140 C8
Brook Dr VWD BH31 .... 144 F4
Brookers La LSOL/BMARY PO13........ 184 E5
Brook Farm Av FHAM PO15 .... 6 E5
Brookfield Cl HAV PO9 .... 8 E8
Brookfield Gdns HLER SO31 .. 158 D4
Brookfield Rd ELGH SO50 ...... 83 G6
  PSEA PO1 .... 211 J2
Brookfields ROMY SO51 .... 76 C5
Brook Gdns EMRTH PO10 ...... 166 B8
Brook Hl LYMN SO41 .... 229 J1
Brookland Cl LYMN SO41 ...... 228 A3 [1]
Brooklands Rd BPWT SO32 .... 85 H8
  HAV PO9 .... 164 F6
Brook La CHCH/BSGR BH23 .. 223 L1
  FBDG SP6 .... 98 D1
  HEND SO30 .... 134 D2
  HLER SO31 .... 158 A7
  WIMB BH21 .... 217 G2
  WVILLE PO7 .... 114 A2
Brookley Rd BROC SO42 .... 175 K7
Brooklyn Cl RWIN SO21 .... 54 B5
Brooklyn Ct NMIL/BTOS BH25 .... 225 K5 [3]
Brooklyn Dr WVILLE PO7 ...... 140 D8 [1]
Brooklynn Cl BPWT SO32........ 111 K6
Brookmeadow FHAM PO15 .... 6 E5
Brookmead Wy HAV PO9 .... 8 E8
Brook Rd BKME/WDN BH12 .... 234 B3
  ELGH SO50 .... 83 H6
  NBNE BH10 .... 220 A4
  WEND SO18 .... 132 E1
  WIMB BH21 .... 192 C4
Brooks Cl RGWD BH24........ 170 F2
Brookside FBDG SP6 .... 123 G6
  LSOL/BMARY PO13........ 184 F3
  TOTT SO40 .... 129 K3
Brookside Av WSHM SO15 ...... 130 D1
Brookside Cl CHCH/BSGR BH23 .... 197 L7 [8]
  WVILLE PO7 .... 139 K4
Brookside Rd BROC SO42 ...... 175 K6
  CHCH/BSGR BH23 .... 197 L8
  HAV PO9 .... 8 B6
  WIMB BH21 .... 192 D4
Brookside Wy CHCH/BSGR BH23 .... 224 C7
  HEND SO30 .... 108 D5 [1]
  WEND SO18 .... 107 K4
Brook St BPWT SO32 .... 111 K4
Brook Ter FBDG SP6 .... 97 L8 [1]
Brookvale Rd PTSW SO17 ...... 106 F7
Brook Va ROWN SO16 .... 105 M6
Brook Wy CHCH/BSGR BH23 .. 239 H1
  ROMY SO51 .... 50 F7
Brookwood Av ELGH SO50 .... 81 L5
Brookwood Rd ROWN SO16 .... 105 J8
Broom Cl ENEY PO4 .... 212 B4
  WVILLE PO7 .... 164 E3
Broomfield Crs LSOL/BMARY PO13........ 208 F1
Broomfield La FBDG SP6 .... 121 L3
Broomfield La LYMN SO41 ...... 228 A3
Broom Hl LYMN SO41 .... 229 M1
Broomhill RSAL SP5 .... 75 J7
Broom Hill Wy ELGH SO50 .... 81 L1
Broom Rd BKME/WDN BH12 .. 219 G2
  EPSF GU31........ 64 B6
Brooms Gv ITCH SO19 .... 133 H5
Broom Sq ENEY PO4 .... 212 B4
Broom Wy LSOL/BMARY PO13 .. 208 D1
Broomy Cl FAWY SO45 .... 155 G4 [1]
Brougham La GPORT PO12 .... 209 L2 [8]
Brougham Rd SSEA PO5 .... 13 G4
Brougham St GPORT PO12 .... 209 L2 [6]
Broughton Av NBNE BH10 .... 220 C4
Broughton Cl NBNE BH10 ...... 220 C5 [1]
  ROWN SO16........ 105 M7
Broughton Cl HSEA PO3 .... 188 A4 [1]
Broughton Rd LYND SO43 ...... 151 J2
Browndown Rd LSOL/BMARY PO13........ 209 G5
Browne Rd MOOR/WNTN BH9 .... 220 F8
Brownhill Cl CHFD SO53 .... 81 H1
Brownhill Ct ROWN SO16........ 105 K5
Brownhill Rd CHFD SO53 .... 81 H1
  NBAD SO52 .... 80 A4
  NMIL/BTOS BH25 .... 199 H5
Brownhill Wy ROWN SO16 ...... 105 H5
Browning Av BOSC BH5........ 236 E4
  CHAM PO6 .... 163 H8
  ITCH SO19 .... 133 H2
Browning Cl ELGH SO50........ 81 L5 [1]
  HLER SO31 .... 135 G4
  TOTT SO40 .... 129 H1
Browning Dr FUFL SO22 .... 2 B6

Browning Rd BKME/WDN BH12 .... 234 C2 [3]
Brownings Cl LYMN SO41........ 227 L4
Brownlow Av ITCH SO19 .... 132 C2
Brownlow Cl PSEA PO1 .... 211 H1 [2]
Brownlow Gdns ITCH SO19 .... 132 C2
Brownsea Cl NMIL/BTOS BH25 .. 225 J3
Brownsea Rd CCLF BH13 ...... 245 G5
Brownsea View Av PSTN BH14 .. 244 A7
Browns La FBDG SP6 .... 96 A3
  LYMN SO41 .... 230 A3
Brownwich La FHAM/STUB PO14........ 183 H3
The Brow WVILLE PO7 .... 164 A6
Broxburn Cl CHFD SO53 .... 53 K7
Broxhead Rd HAV PO9 .... 165 L2 [1]
Bruce Cl FHAM/PORC PO16 .... 7 H2
Bruce Rd ENEY PO4 .... 211 K6
Brudenell Av WIMB BH21 ...... 217 H2
Brudenell Rd CCLF BH13 ...... 245 J1
Brue Cl CHFD SO53 .... 81 G1
Brune La LSOL/BMARY PO13 .. 184 E7
Brunel Cl HEND SO30 .... 109 J7 [3]
  TOTT SO40 .... 104 C5
  WSHM SO15........ 130 A1
Brunel Rd NEND PO2 .... 187 J5
  WSHM SO15 .... 130 A1
Brunstead Pl BKME/WDN BH12 .... 235 G4
Brunstead Rd BKME/WDN BH12 .... 234 F4
Brunswick Cl ELGH SO50 ...... 83 G5 [1]
Brunswick Gdns HAV PO9 ...... 8 A3
Brunswick Pl LYMN SO41 ...... 228 C4
  WSHM SO15........ 131 K2
Brunswick Rd ELGH SO50 ...... 83 G5
Brunswick Sq SHAM SO14 .... 5 G4 [1]
Brunswick St SSEA PO5 .... 13 G4 [1]
Bruyn Rd FBDG SP6 .... 97 M7
Bryanston Rd TWDS BH3 ...... 235 K1
Bryanston Rd ITCH SO19 ...... 132 B4
Bryant Rd BKME/WDN BH12 .. 219 L8
Bryher Island CHAM PO6 ...... 186 F1
Brympton Cl FBDG SP6 .... 97 H6
Bryon Rd WIMB BH21 .... 192 A2
Bryony Cl BDST BH18 .... 217 K5
  HLER SO31 .... 158 D6 [1]
Bryony Gdns ELGH SO50 ...... 109 H2 [1]
Bryony Wy WVILLE PO7 .... 164 E2
Bryson Rd CHAM PO6 .... 163 H8 [2]
Bubb La BPWT SO32 .... 109 H3
Bub La CHCH/BSGR BH23 .... 238 D2
Buccaneers Cl CHCH/BSGR BH23 .... 238 D2 [3]
Buccleuch Rd CCLF BH13 ...... 234 F7
Bucehayes Cl CHCH/BSGR BH23 .... 224 E8
Buchanan Av LTDN BH7 .... 236 D2
Buchanan Rd ROWN SO16 .... 105 L3
Buchan Av FHAM PO15 .... 135 G8
Buchan Ct FAWY SO45 .... 155 G6
Buckby La PSEA PO1 .... 188 A4
Buckingham Rd BKME/WDN BH12 .... 234 C1
  PSF GU32 .... 63 J5
  WVILLE PO7 .... 140 B6
Buckland Cl ELGH SO50 .... 81 M3
Buckland Gdns TOTT SO40 .... 104 B6
Buckland Gv CHCH/BSGR BH23 .. 224 C6
Buckland Rd BKME/WDN BH12 .. 234 B3
Buckland St NEND PO2 .... 211 J1 [3]
Buckland Ter BKME/WDN BH12 .... 234 B3
Bucklers Ct HAV PO9 .... 165 H1
  NEND PO2 .... 187 H7 [2]
The Bucklers LYMN SO41 ...... 241 M3
Bucklers Wy CHAR BH8 .... 221 H5
Buckmore Av PSF GU32 .... 63 J4
Bucksey Rd LSOL/BMARY PO13........ 185 G8
Bucks Head Hl BPWT SO32 .... 87 H3
Buckstone Cl LYMN SO41 ...... 227 J7 [1]
Buckthorn Cl TOTT SO40 ...... 103 M8
  WIMB BH21 .... 217 K6 [1]
Budden's La WHAM PO17 ...... 112 C8
Buddens Rd WHAM PO17 ...... 136 E4
Buddle Hl FBDG SP6 .... 123 G4
Budds La ROMY SO51 .... 50 D7
Bude Cl CHAM PO6 .... 162 D7
Bugdens La VWD BH31 .... 144 D2
Bugle St SHAM SO14 .... 4 F6
Bulbeck Rd HAV PO9 .... 8 E5
Buldowne Wk LYMN SO41 .... 200 F5
Bullar Rd WEND SO18 .... 132 C1
Bullar St SHAM SO14 .... 131 M2
Bull Dro WINC SO23 .... 27 G3
Bullfinch Cl CFDH BH17........ 217 K7
  TOTT SO40 .... 129 G1 [8]
Bull Hl LISS GU33 .... 37 K4
  LYMN SO41 .... 202 T1 [1]
Bull La BPWT SO32 .... 111 J5
  LYND SO43 .... 127 G5
Bullrush Cl FAWY SO45 .... 155 K7
Bulls Copse La HORN PO8 ...... 140 E2
Bulls Dro RSAL SP5 .... 19 M2
Bulls La RSAL SP5 .... 40 A1
Bunkers Hl WVILLE PO7 .... 139 H5
Bunns La WVILLE PO7 .... 138 C3
Bunny La ROMY SO51 .... 50 E2
  RSAL SP5 .... 47 M4
Bunstead La RWIN SO21 .... 53 J2
Bunting Gdns HORN PO8 ...... 140 F4
Burbidge Gv ENEY PO4 .... 211 L6
Burbridge Cl CFDH BH17 ...... 218 C3 [3]
Burbush Cl FAWY SO45 .... 180 A5
Burcombe Rd NBNE BH10 .... 220 A3
Burcote Dr HSEA PO3 .... 187 M4
Burdale Dr HISD PO11 .... 214 B5
Burdock Cl CHCH/BSGR BH23 .. 223 M4
Bure Cl CHCH/BSGR BH23 .... 239 G2

Bure Haven Dr CHCH/BSGR BH23 .... 238 F2
Bure Homage Gdns CHCH/BSGR BH23 .... 239 G2 [2]
Bure Homage La CHCH/BSGR BH23 .... 238 F2
Bure La CHCH/BSGR BH23 .... 239 G3
Bure Pk CHCH/BSGR BH23 .... 239 G2
Bure Rd CHCH/BSGR BH23 .... 239 G2
Burford Cl CHCH/BSGR BH23 .. 222 B7
Burford La BROC SO42 .... 175 L4
Burgate Cl HAV PO9 .... 165 H5
Burgate Flds FBDG SP6 .... 97 M5
Burgess Cl BWD BH11 .... 219 K4
  HISD PO11 .... 214 B7
Burgess Gdns ROWN SO16 .... 106 D5 [3]
Burgess Rd PTSW SO17 .... 107 G4
  WSHM SO15 .... 106 C6
Burghclere Rd HAV PO9 .... 165 M2
  ITCH SO19 .... 132 D8 [3]
Burgoyne Rd ITCH SO19........ 133 J4
  SSEA PO5 .... 211 H7
Burgundy Cl HLER SO31 ...... 158 D6 [3]
Buriton Cl FHAM/PORC PO16 .. 162 B7
Buriton St PSEA PO1 .... 211 H2
Buriton Rd FUFL SO22 .... 16 C4
Burke Dr ITCH SO19 .... 133 G2
Burleigh Rd NEND PO2 .... 187 J7
  SBNE BH6 .... 237 J2
Burley Cl CHFD SO53 .... 81 G4
  HAV PO9 .... 165 M2 [3]
  NMIL/BTOS BH25 .... 225 H5
  VWD BH31 .... 144 C3
Burley Down CHFD SO53 ...... 81 G4
Burley Lawn RGWD BH24 ...... 172 F4
Burley Rd BKME/WDN BH12 .. 234 B2
  BROC SO42 .... 200 E1
  CHCH/BSGR BH23 .... 198 B3
  FUFL SO22 .... 16 C4
Burlington Rd NEND PO2 ...... 187 J7
  WSHM SO15 .... 131 J2
Burmah Rd North FAWY SO45 .. 181 G2
Burmah Rd South FAWY SO45 .. 180 F3
Burma Wy TOTT SO40 .... 130 D8
Burmese Cl FHAM PO15 .... 159 G1
Burnaby Rd PSEA PO1 .... 12 E2
  WBNE BH4 .... 235 H7
Burnbake Rd VWD BH31 .... 144 D3
Burnbank Gdns TOTT SO40 .... 129 J1
Burnbrae Rd FERN BH22 ...... 194 B7
Burn Cl VWD BH31 .... 144 F4
Burnett Av CHCH/BSGR BH23 .. 237 K1
Burnett Cl FAWY SO45 .... 155 M6
  FUFL SO22 .... 16 B6
  WEND SO18 .... 107 K7
Burnett Rd CHCH/BSGR BH23 .... 237 L1
  GPORT PO12 .... 209 K4
Burnetts Flds ELGH SO50 ...... 109 H1
Burnetts Gdns ELGH SO50 .... 109 J1
Burnetts La HEND SO30 .... 109 G4
Burney Rd GPORT PO12 .... 209 J5
Burngate Rd PLE BH15........ 232 D6
Burnham Beeches CHFD SO53 .. 81 K7 [2]
Burnham Cha WEND SO18 .... 132 F1
Burnham Dr CHAR BH8 .... 236 B1
Burnham Rd CHAM PO6 .... 164 B7
  CHCH/BSGR BH23 .... 223 G6
  FBDG SP6 .... 97 L5 [2]
Burnham Wd FHAM/PORC PO16 .... 7 G1
Burnleigh Gdns NMIL/BTOS BH25 .... 226 A4 [2]
Burns Cl ELGH SO50 .... 81 K7
Burnside CHCH/BSGR BH23 .. 224 B8 [8]
  LSOL/BMARY PO13........ 184 F5
  WVILLE PO7 .... 140 E7
Burns Pl ROWN SO16 .... 105 M6
Burns Rd ELGH SO50 .... 81 L7
  ITCH SO19 .... 133 H3
  SBNE BH6 .... 237 J1
Burnt House La CHCH/BSGR BH23 .... 197 M7
  FHAM/STUB PO14........ 184 B5
  WVILLE PO7 .... 202 D7
Burrard Gv LYMN SO41 .... 228 D6
Burr Cl RWIN SO21 .... 54 E8
Burrfields Rd HSEA PO3 .... 187 M7
Burridge Rd HLER SO31 .... 134 E6
Burrill Av CHAM PO6 .... 163 L8
Burrows Cl HAV PO9 .... 9 H1
Burrows La VWD BH31 .... 120 D8
Bursledon Hts HLER SO31 .... 133 M7
Bursledon Pl WVILLE PO7 ...... 164 B3
Bursledon Rd HEND SO30 .... 133 M3
  ITCH SO19 .... 132 E2
  WVILLE PO7 .... 164 B3
Burtley Rd SBNE BH6 .... 237 K5
Burton Cl CHCH/BSGR BH23 .. 223 G2
  RGWD BH24........ 169 L5
Burtoncroft CHCH/BSGR BH23 .... 223 G5
Burton Hall Pl CHCH/BSGR BH23 .... 223 H5 [1]
Burton Rd CCLF BH13 .... 234 F5
  CHCH/BSGR BH23 .... 238 D1
  WSHM SO15 .... 131 J1
Burt's Hl WIMB BH21 .... 192 A2
Burwood Gv HISD PO11 .... 213 L4
Bury Cl GPORT PO12 .... 10 D3
Bury Crs GPORT PO12 .... 10 A5
Bury Hall La GPORT PO12...... 10 A5
Bury La TOTT SO40 .... 130 C6
Bury Rd CCLF BH13 .... 234 E6 [1]
  GPORT PO12 .... 10 C4
  TOTT SO40 .... 130 C6
Bushell Rd PLE BH15 .... 233 H1
Bushells Farm FBDG SP6 ...... 97 K8 [1]
Bushey Rd CHAR BH8 .... 221 J3
Bushmead Dr RGWD BH24 .... 169 J3
Bush Saint West SSEA PO5 .... 13 G5 [1]
Bush St East SSEA PO5 .... 13 H5
Bushy Md WVILLE PO7 .... 164 A5 [1]
Busket La WINC SO23 .... 3 H8
Busketts Wy TOTT SO40 .... 128 C6
Butcher St PSEA PO1 .... 12 C2
Bute Dr CHCH/BSGR BH23 .... 240 A1

Butlers Cl ROMY SO51 ... 20 F7 1
Butlers La RGWD BH24 ... 147 G7
Buttercup Cl FAWY SO45 ... 155 L7 2
HEND SO30 ... 133 L2 1
Buttercup Dr
CHCH/BSGR BH23 ... 223 M7
Buttercup Wy HLER SO31 ... 158 C5
Butterfield Rd ROWN SO16 ... 106 D4
Butterfly Dr CHAM PO6 ... 162 E6
Buttermere Cl ROWN SO16 ... 105 K6
The Buttery CHCH/BSGR BH23 .. 238 C1
Buttons La ROMY SO51 ... 76 D5
Buttsash Av FAWY SO45 ... 155 L8
Butts Ash Gdns FAWY SO45 ... 155 L7
Butts Ash La FAWY SO45 ... 155 L7 3
Butts Bridge Hl FAWY SO45 ... 155 L6
Buttsbridge Rd FAWY SO45 ... 155 L7
Butts Cl FUFL SO22 ... 2 B4
ITCH SO19 ... 133 H4 1
Butt's Crs ITCH SO19 ... 133 G4 1
Butts La BPWT SO32 ... 85 J8
Butts Lawn BROC SO42 ... 175 K6
Butts Paddock BROC SO42 ... 175 K6
Butt's Rd ITCH SO19 ... 132 F5
ITCH SO19 ... 133 H4 2
Butt's Sq ITCH SO19 ... 133 G4
The Butts BPWT SO32 ... 87 H2
Byerley Cl EMRTH PO10 ... 166 F3 1
Byerley Rd PSEA PO1 ... 211 K2
Byeways FAWY SO45 ... 155 K6 2
The Byeway SELS PO20 ... 215 L7
By-pass Rd ROMY SO51 ... 78 D2
Byrd Cl WVILLE PO7 ... 164 C3
Byron Av FUFL SO22 ... 2 A7
Byron Cl BPWT SO32 ... 85 K8
FHAM/PORC PO16 ... 7 G3
Byron Rd BOSC BH5 ... 236 E4
ELGH SO50 ... 82 A4
ITCH SO19 ... 133 H2
NEND PO2 ... 187 K8
NMIL/BTOS BH25 ... 225 J8

C

Cable St SHAM SO14 ... 5 L1
Cabot Dr FAWY SO45 ... 155 G5
Cabot La CFDH BH17 ... 217 L8
Cabot Wy NMIL/BTOS BH25 ... 225 K5
Cadgwith Pl CHAM PO6 ... 186 F1
Cadhay Cl NMIL/BTOS BH25 ... 225 J5
Cadland Rd FAWY SO45 ... 180 B1
Cadlands Park Est FAWY SO45 .. 180 A2
Cadnam La TOTT SO40 ... 102 E5
Cadnam Rd ENEY PO4 ... 211 M5
Cadnam Wy CHAR BH8 ... 221 H5
Cadogan Rd RGWD BH24 ... 170 F1
Cador Dr FHAM/PORC PO16 ... 185 M2
Caerleon Av ITCH SO19 ... 133 G2
Caerleon Dr ITCH SO19 ... 132 F2
Caernarvon Gdns CHFD SO53 ... 80 F4 1
Caesar's Wy WIMB BH21 ... 217 J4
Cains Cl FHAM/STUB PO14 ... 184 A5
Caird Av NMIL/BTOS BH25 ... 225 M5
Cairns Cl CHCH/BSGR BH23 ... 222 D8
Cairo Ter NEND PO2 ... 211 H1
Caister Cl FERN BH22 ... 194 A2
Caistor Cl ROWN SO16 ... 105 M4
Cakeham Rd SELS PO20 ... 215 L8
Calabrese HLER SO31 ... 158 F1
Calbourne HLER SO31 ... 157 G1 1
Calcot Hl BPWT SO32 ... 110 D5
Calcot La BPWT SO32 ... 110 D5
Calder Cl ROWN SO16 ... 105 K8
Calder Rd CFDH BH17 ... 218 D8
Calderwood Dr ITCH SO19 ... 132 E4
Caledonia Dr FAWY SO45 ... 155 H5
Caledonian Cl
CHCH/BSGR BH23 ... 239 G1 5
Caledon Rd PSTN BH14 ... 234 C5
Calkin Cl CHCH/BSGR BH23 ... 222 E7
Calluna Rd BKME/WDN BH12 ... 218 F7
Calmore Cl CHAR BH8 ... 221 H5 3
Calmore Crs TOTT SO40 ... 104 A7
Calmore Dr TOTT SO40 ... 104 B6
Calmore Gdns TOTT SO40 ... 129 G1
Calmore Rd TOTT SO40 ... 104 A7
Calpe Av LYND SO43 ... 151 K2
Calshot Cl FAWY SO45 ... 181 K8
Calshot Dr CHFD SO53 ... 80 F4
Calshot Rd FAWY SO45 ... 180 F5
HAV PO9 ... 165 G1
Calshot Wy
LSOL/BMARY PO13 ... 184 F7 2
Calvin Rd MOOR/WNTN BH9 ... 220 D8
Camargue Cl HLER SO31 ... 134 F8
Camber Pl PSEA PO1 ... 12 B5
Cambria Dr FAWY SO45 ... 155 H5
Cambrian Cl HLER SO31 ... 133 L6 2
Cambridge Dr CHFD SO53 ... 81 H5
Cambridge Gdns
CHCH/BSGR BH23 ... 222 D6
Cambridge Gn
FHAM/STUB PO14 ... 159 G6
Cambridge Rd GPORT PO12 ... 209 J2
LSOL/BMARY PO13 ... 208 D4
PSEA PO1 ... 12 E4
SHAM SO14 ... 106 F8
WCLF BH2 ... 14 B5
Camcross Cl CHAM PO6 ... 162 F7 1
Camden Cl
MOOR/WNTN BH9 ... 220 F7 1
Camden St GPORT PO12 ... 209 L2
FBDG SP6 ... 121 L2 1
Camel Green Rd FBDG SP6 ... 121 M2 1
Camelia Cl HAV PO9 ... 165 M5
NBAD SO52 ... 79 M3
Camelia Gdns WEND SO18 ... 107 M6 3
Camelia Gv ELGH SO50 ... 83 K6
Camellia Cl WIMB BH21 ... 144 C7 1
Camellia Gdns
NMIL/BTOS BH25 ... 225 M6
Camelot Crs FHAM/PORC PO16 .. 161 M7
Cameron Cl
LSOL/BMARY PO13 ... 185 G5 1
Cameron Rd
CHCH/BSGR BH23 ... 238 C1 2
Camley Cl ITCH SO19 ... 132 C7
Cammel Rd FERN BH22 ... 194 B6
Campbell Rd BMTH BH1 ... 236 D3
CHCH/BSGR BH23 ... 223 G5
ELGH SO50 ... 82 A7
SSEA PO5 ... 13 K5
Campbell St SHAM SO14 ... 132 A2 1
Campbell Wy ELGH SO50 ... 83 H6
Campion Cl ELGH SO50 ... 109 H2 2
HLER SO31 ... 158 C7
LYMN SO41 ... 228 C3 1
WVILLE PO7 ... 164 E2 1
Campion Dr ROMY SO51 ... 51 H7
Campion Gv CHCH/BSGR BH23 .. 238 E2
Campion Rd ITCH SO19 ... 133 H3
Campion Wy LYMN SO41 ... 228 C3
WINC SO23 ... 17 H2
Camp Rd LSOL/BMARY PO13 ... 185 H5
Cams Bay Cl
FHAM/PORC PO16 ... 161 K7 1
Cams Hl FHAM/PORC PO16 ... 161 J7
WVILLE PO7 ... 114 A7
Canada Rd ITCH SO19 ... 132 C6
ROMY SO51 ... 76 C7
Canal Cl ROMY SO51 ... 50 F7
Canal Wk ROMY SO51 ... 50 E8
SHAM SO14 ... 5 G5
SSEA PO5 ... 13 J2
Canberra Cl GPORT PO12 ... 10 B4
Canberra Rd CHCH/BSGR BH23 .. 222 C7
EMRTH PO10 ... 190 E5
ROWN SO16 ... 105 G4
Candy La WEND SO18 ... 133 J1
Canford Av BWD BH11 ... 219 K7
Canford Bottom WIMB BH21 ... 193 G2
Canford Cliffs Av PSTN BH14 ... 234 C6
Canford Cliffs Rd CCLF BH13 ... 234 D6
Canford Cl BPWT SO32 ... 136 C1
ROWN SO16 ... 105 J6
Canford Crs CCLF BH13 ... 245 K1
Canford Heath Rd CFDH BH17 .. 218 B7
Canford Rd BWD BH11 ... 219 L7
PLE BH15 ... 233 J4
Canford View Dr
WIMB BH21 ... 192 F2 1
Canford Wy BKME/WDN BH12 .. 219 G6
Canhouse La LISS GU33 ... 37 L5
Cannon Cl BDST BH18 ... 217 K7
Cannon Hill Gdns WIMB BH21 . 192 F1 1
Cannon Hill Rd WIMB BH21 ... 192 E1
Cannon St LYMN SO41 ... 228 C4
WSHM SO15 ... 106 B8
Canoe Cl HLER SO31 ... 158 D7
Canon's Barn Cl
FHAM/PORC PO16 ... 162 A7 1
Canon St WINC SO23 ... 2 F9
Canterbury Av ITCH SO19 ... 133 G5
Canterbury Cl FERN BH22 ... 168 D7 1
LSOL/BMARY PO13 ... 208 F4
Canterbury Dr FAWY SO45 ... 155 G5
Canterbury Rd ENEY PO4 ... 211 K5
FHAM/STUB PO14 ... 184 A5
Canterton La LYND SO43 ... 102 A8
Canton St WSHM SO15 ... 131 K2
Canute Dr CHCH/BSGR BH23 ... 197 M7
Canute Rd SHAM SO14 ... 5 K6
WINC SO23 ... 27 G2
Capella Gdns FAWY SO45 ... 155 H5 3
Capel Ley WVILLE PO7 ... 164 C4
Capers End La BPWT SO32 ... 110 D7
Capesthorne
CHCH/BSGR BH23 ... 239 G3
Capstone Pl CHAR BH8 ... 236 C2
Capstone Rd CHAR BH8 ... 236 B2
Captains Pl SHAM SO14 ... 5 J6
Captain's Rw LYMN SO41 ... 228 D4
PSEA PO1 ... 12 B5
Carberry Dr FHAM/PORC PO16 .. 185 M1
Carbery Av SBNE BH6 ... 237 J4
Carbery Ct HAV PO9 ... 165 H1
Carbery Gdns SBNE BH6 ... 237 K3
Carbis Cl CHAM PO6 ... 186 E1
Cardew Rd LISS GU33 ... 36 F5
Cardiff Rd NEND PO2 ... 187 H6
Cardigan Rd CCLF BH13 ... 234 E4 1
MOOR/WNTN BH9 ... 220 D8
Cardinal Dr WVILLE PO7 ... 140 F7
Cardinal Wy HLER SO31 ... 158 F5
Carey Rd ITCH SO19 ... 133 G3
MOOR/WNTN BH9 ... 220 D6
Careys Cottages BROC SO42 ... 175 K6
Careys Rd CHAR BH8 ... 221 H4
Carisbrooke HLER SO31 ... 157 G1 2
Carisbrooke Av
FHAM/STUB PO14 ... 183 L6
Carisbrooke Cl HAV PO9 ... 9 J3
Carisbrooke Ct
NMIL/BTOS BH25 ... 225 K5
ROMY SO51 ... 50 F7 1
Carisbrooke Crs CHFD SO53 ... 81 K3
PLE BH15 ... 232 D5 3
Carisbrooke Dr ITCH SO19 ... 132 D2
Carisbrooke Rd ENEY PO4 ... 211 L4 1
LSOL/BMARY PO13 ... 184 F5
Carisbrooke Wy
CHCH/BSGR BH23 ... 224 C7
Carless Cl LSOL/BMARY PO13 ... 209 H1
Carlisle Rd ROWN SO16 ... 106 A8
SSEA PO5 ... 13 K2
Carlton Av NMIL/BTOS BH25 ... 240 C1
Carlton Crs WSHM SO15 ... 131 K2
Carlton Gv PSTN BH14 ... 234 C3
Carlton Pl WSHM SO15 ... 131 K2
Carlton Rd BMTH BH1 ... 15 M3
FHAM/PORC PO16 ... 162 B7
GPORT PO12 ... 11 H3
WSHM SO15 ... 131 K1
Carlton Wy GPORT PO12 ... 11 H2
Carlyle Rd GPORT PO12 ... 10 E1
SBNE BH6 ... 237 J2
Carlyn Dr CHFD SO53 ... 81 J1
Carmans La RWIN SO21 ... 54 C1
Carmarthen Av CHAM PO6 ... 163 M7
Carnarvon Rd BOSC BH5 ... 236 D4 1
GPORT PO12 ... 10 C3
NEND PO2 ... 187 K8
Carnation Rd ROWN SO16 ... 107 H4
Carne Cl CHFD SO53 ... 53 H8
Carnegie Cl BKME/WDN BH12 ... 234 C3 1
Caroline Av CHCH/BSGR BH23 ... 238 D3
Caroline Rd BWD BH11 ... 219 M5
Carolyn Cl ITCH SO19 ... 132 C6
Carpathia Cl WEND SO18 ... 107 M6 3
Carpenter Cl ENEY PO4 ... 211 L5 2
FAWY SO45 ... 155 L4 2
LYMN SO41 ... 228 B3 1
Carraway FHAM PO15 ... 159 H1
Carrbridge Cl TWDS BH3 ... 235 J1
Carrbridge Rd TWDS BH3 ... 235 J1
Carrick Wy NMIL/BTOS BH25 ... 226 A6
Carrington Cl LYMN SO41 ... 242 D4
Carrington La LYMN SO41 ... 242 D3
Carroll Av FERN BH22 ... 194 B3
Carroll Cl BKME/WDN BH12 ... 234 F2
ELGH SO50 ... 83 J7 2
Carronade Wk HSEA PO3 ... 187 K3
Carshalton Av CHAM PO6 ... 163 M8
Carsworth Wy CFDH BH17 ... 218 E6 1
Carters Av PLE BH15 ... 232 C4
Carter's Clay Rd ROMY SO51 ... 49 G3
Carter's Cl FBDG SP6 ... 73 J5
Cartersland LIPH GU30 ... 38 E5
Carter's La PLE BH15 ... 233 H6 1
TOTT SO40 ... 154 C3
Carthage Cl CHFD SO53 ... 81 L1
Cartref Cl VWD BH31 ... 144 D2
Cartwright Cl NBNE BH10 ... 220 A4 1
Cartwright Dr FHAM PO15 ... 159 K6
Carvers La RGWD BH24 ... 170 E1
Carysfort Rd BMTH BH1 ... 236 C4
Cashmoor Cl
BKME/WDN BH12 ... 234 E1 1
Cask St PSEA PO1 ... 211 G2
Caslake Cl NMIL/BTOS BH25 ... 225 K7
Caspar John Cl
FHAM/STUB PO14 ... 183 M7
Caspian Cl HLER SO31 ... 158 F1
Cassel Av WBNE BH4 ... 235 G7
Castle Av CHCH/BSGR BH23 ... 224 C8
HAV PO9 ... 9 K5
Castle Cl LYMN SO41 ... 242 D5
SSEA PO5 ... 13 G5
Castle Ct WSHM SO15 ... 130 E2
Castledene Crs PSTN BH14 ... 233 M6
Castle Farm La WHAM PO17 ... 136 F6
Castle Gate Cl CHAR BH8 ... 221 G6
Castle Gv FHAM/PORC PO16 ... 186 B1
Castle Hill La RGWD BH24 ... 172 B4
Castle La CHFD SO53 ... 80 F4
FAWY SO45 ... 207 K1
NBAD SO52 ... 80 A4
SHAM SO14 ... 4 F4
Castle La East LTDN BH7 ... 221 M8
Castle La West CHAR BH8 ... 221 K6
MOOR/WNTN BH10 ... 220 E4 1
Castlemain Av SBNE BH6 ... 237 H3
Castlemans La HISD PO11 ... 189 L7
Castleman Trailway
CFDH BH17 ... 217 J8
FERN BH22 ... 168 A5
RGWD BH24 ... 169 H3
WIMB BH21 ... 192 E5
Castleman Wy RGWD BH24 ... 170 E2
Castlemews RGWD BH24 ... 170 A3
Castle Rd HAV PO9 ... 141 L6
HLER SO31 ... 156 F2
MOOR/WNTN BH9 ... 220 D7
SSEA PO5 ... 13 G6
WEND SO18 ... 107 K6
WHAM PO17 ... 162 D2
Castleshaw Cl ROWN SO16 ... 130 D1 1
Castle Sq SHAM SO14 ... 4 F5
Castle St CHCH/BSGR BH23 ... 238 A2
FHAM/PORC PO16 ... 186 B1
FHAM/STUB PO14 ... 159 K8
PLE BH15 ... 233 H7
SHAM SO14 ... 131 L1
Castleton Av NBNE BH10 ... 220 B2
Castle Vw GPORT PO12 ... 185 M8
Castle View Rd
FHAM/PORC PO16 ... 186 B2
Castleway HAV PO9 ... 9 K5
Castle Wy SHAM SO14 ... 4 F4
Castlewood RGWD BH24 ... 170 B3
Castle Woods RSAL SP5 ... 73 J2 2
Catalina Cl CHCH/BSGR BH23 ... 238 F2
Catalina Dr PLE BH15 ... 233 K7
Catamaran Cl HLER SO31 ... 158 D7
Cateran Cl ROWN SO16 ... 105 L8 1
Cathay Gdns FAWY SO45 ... 155 G5
Cathedral Vw WINC SO23 ... 27 G2
Catherine Cl HEND SO30 ... 108 D6
Catherine Crs RSAL SP5 ... 72 C1
Catherine Gdns HEND SO30 ... 108 D6
Catherington La HORN PO8 ... 140 F1
Catherington Wy HAV PO9 ... 165 K4
Catisfield La FHAM PO15 ... 159 M7
Catisfield Rd ENEY PO4 ... 211 M3
FHAM PO15 ... 160 A7
Caton Cl BKME/WDN BH12 ... 219 M8
Cattistock Rd CHAR BH8 ... 221 J7
Causeway Crs TOTT SO40 ... 104 F8
Causeway Farm HORN PO8 ... 140 F3
The Causeway EPSF GU31 ... 63 K6
FHAM/PORC PO16 ... 161 J7
Cavalier Cl FAWY SO45 ... 155 G5
Cavan Crs CFDH BH17 ... 217 M7
Cavanna Cl LSOL/BMARY PO13 .. 184 F5
Cavell Dr CHAM PO6 ... 163 J7
Cavendish Cl ROMY SO51 ... 51 G6 1
WVILLE PO7 ... 140 D8 2
Cavendish Dr WVILLE PO7 ... 164 D1
Cavendish Gv WINC SO23 ... 3 J1
WSHM SO15 ... 106 E8
Cavendish Ms WSHM SO15 ... 106 E8
Cavendish Pl BMTH BH1 ... 15 G2
Cavendish Rd BMTH BH1 ... 15 G2
SSEA PO5 ... 13 J6
WCLF BH2 ... 14 F2
C Av FAWY SO45 ... 180 B3
Caversham Cl HEND SO30 ... 108 C7 1
ITCH SO19 ... 132 E4
PLE BH15 ... 232 D5
Cawdor Rd TWDS BH3 ... 235 J1
Cawte Rd WSHM SO15 ... 131 G2
Caxton Av ITCH SO19 ... 132 F2
Caxton Cl CHCH/BSGR BH23 ... 238 E1
Cecil Av CHAR BH8 ... 221 G8
ROWN SO16 ... 106 A7
TOTT SO40 ... 129 G6
Cecil Cl WIMB BH21 ... 217 J2
Cecil Gv SSEA PO5 ... 12 F6
Cecil Hl MOOR/WNTN BH9 ... 220 F8 1
Cecil Pl SSEA PO5 ... 12 F6 1
Cecil Rd BKME/WDN BH12 ... 234 C2
BOSC BH5 ... 236 D4
ITCH SO19 ... 132 D5
Cedar Av CHCH/BSGR BH23 ... 222 B8
NBNE BH10 ... 220 B2
RGWD BH24 ... 169 J5 1
WSHM SO15 ... 106 C8
Cedar Cl GPORT PO12 ... 185 L7
HEND SO30 ... 134 A1
HLER SO31 ... 133 K8
UPTN BH16 ... 216 F8
WVILLE PO7 ... 164 C2
Cedar Crs HORN PO8 ... 141 G3
NBAD SO52 ... 79 L3
Cedar Dr LYMN SO41 ... 227 H8 2
WIMB BH21 ... 192 F3
Cedar Gdns HAV PO9 ... 9 G2
Cedar Gv HSEA PO3 ... 211 M1
Cedar Lawn ROMY SO51 ... 51 H7
Cedarmount LYND SO43 ... 151 K4
Cedar Pl CHCH/BSGR BH23 ... 197 M7
Cedar Rd ELGH SO50 ... 81 K7
FAWY SO45 ... 179 L1
SHAM SO14 ... 106 F8
Cedars Vw RSAL SP5 ... 20 D1
Cedar Wy FERN BH22 ... 168 A8
Cedarwood WINC SO23 ... 17 H1
Cedar Wood Cl ELGH SO50 ... 83 K6
TOTT SO40 ... 104 B8 3
Cedric Cl FAWY SO45 ... 180 D8
Celandine Av HLER SO31 ... 158 D6
HORN PO8 ... 141 G5
Celandine Cl CHCH/BSGR BH23 .. 223 M8
NBAD SO52 ... 80 E3 1
Celia Cl WVILLE PO7 ... 140 F8
Cellars Farm Rd SBNE BH6 ... 237 M5
Cement Ter SHAM SO14 ... 4 F5 1
Cemetery Av PLE BH15 ... 233 L2
Cemetery La EMRTH PO10 ... 167 G5
WVILLE PO7 ... 139 K3
Cemetery Rd WSHM SO15 ... 106 D8
Centaur St NEND PO2 ... 187 H8
Centaury Gdns ELGH SO50 ... 109 H1 1
Centenary Cl LYMN SO41 ... 201 G6
Centenary Wy BMTH BH1 ... 236 D3
Central Av BKME/WDN BH12 .. 234 D2 1
WIMB BH21 ... 217 H1 1
Central Br SHAM SO14 ... 5 J5
Central Dr WCLF BH2 ... 14 D1
Central Rd CHAM PO6 ... 188 A1
FHAM/PORC PO16 ... 185 M1
SHAM SO14 ... 5 H7
Central Station Br WSHM SO15 ... 4 C2
Central St PSEA PO1 ... 211 H2
Centre La LYMN SO41 ... 227 J7
Centre Pl RGWD BH24 ... 170 D1 1
Centre Wy HLER SO31 ... 158 E5
Cerdic Ms HLER SO31 ... 157 L4
Cerne Cl MOOR/WNTN BH9 ... 220 F4 2
NBAD SO52 ... 79 K4
WEND SO18 ... 108 A7
Chadderton Gdns PSEA PO1 ... 12 E5
Chaddesley Gln CCLF BH13 ... 245 J2
Chaddesley Wood Rd
CCLF BH13 ... 245 K3 1
Chadwell Av ITCH SO19 ... 132 F4
Chadwick Rd ELGH SO50 ... 81 K6
Chafen Rd WEND SO18 ... 107 J8
Chaffey Cl RGWD BH24 ... 147 G8
Chaffinch Cl CFDH BH17 ... 217 K6 2
NMIL/BTOS BH25 ... 225 K6
TOTT SO40 ... 104 B8 4
Chaffinch Grn HORN PO8 ... 140 C4
Chaffinch Wy
FHAM/PORC PO16 ... 161 K8
LSOL/BMARY PO13 ... 208 D1 1
Chalbury Cl CFDH BH17 ... 218 E6
Chaldecott Gdns NBNE BH10 ... 220 A4
Chaldon Rd CFDH BH17 ... 218 D6
Chale Cl LSOL/BMARY PO13 ... 185 G6
Chalewood Rd FAWY SO45 ... 206 C1
Chalfont Av CHCH/BSGR BH23 .. 222 B5
Chalice Ct HEND SO30 ... 133 M2 1
Chalk Hl BPWT SO32 ... 113 H3
WEND SO18 ... 108 B7
Chalk La WHAM PO17 ... 160 F1
Chalkpit Rd CHAM PO6 ... 162 F6
Chalk Rdg HORN PO8 ... 116 C5
WINC SO23 ... 3 M9
Chalkridge Rd CHAM PO6 ... 163 L7
Chalk's Cl RSAL SP5 ... 73 J1
Chalky La BPWT SO32 ... 85 J8
Challenger Wy FAWY SO45 ... 155 H4
Challis Ct SHAM SO14 ... 5 H5
Chalmers Wy HLER SO31 ... 157 J5
Chaloner Crs FAWY SO45 ... 155 L7 4
Chalton Crs HAV PO9 ... 165 H3
Chalton La HORN PO8 ... 116 E2
Chalvington Rd CHFD SO53 ... 81 H3
Chalybeate Cl ROWN SO16 ... 106 A6
Chamberlain Gv
FHAM/STUB PO14 ... 7 G8
Chamberlain Rd PTSW SO17 ... 106 F5
Chamberlayne Rd ELGH SO50 ... 81 M7
HLER SO31 ... 133 K8 2
Chambers Av ROMY SO51 ... 79 G1
Chambers Cl ROWN SO16 ... 105 H3
Champion Cl LYMN SO41 ... 242 D4
Chancellors La BPWT SO32 ... 109 K5
Chancel Rd HLER SO31 ... 158 F5
Chander Cl FERN BH22 ... 194 C4
Chandlers Cl HISD PO11 ... 214 A6 1
LTDN BH7 ... 221 M8 2
Chandlers Wy HLER SO31 ... 158 F2
Chandos Av BKME/WDN BH12 .. 219 L8
Chandos St SHAM SO14 ... 5 H5
Channels Farm Rd
ROWN SO16 ... 107 J3
Channel Wy SHAM SO14 ... 5 K6
Chant Cl CHCH/BSGR BH23 ... 238 C1 3
Chantry Cl CHCH/BSGR BH23 ... 224 D7
Chantry Rd GPORT PO12 ... 209 L1
HORN PO8 ... 140 F1
SHAM SO14 ... 5 K5
The Chantry FHAM/STUB PO14 .. 159 G5
Chapel Cl WIMB BH21 ... 217 G2
Chapel Crs ITCH SO19 ... 132 E4
Chapel Dro ELGH SO50 ... 109 H1
HEND SO30 ... 133 M2
Chapel La BPWT SO32 ... 110 D8
BROC SO42 ... 204 A2
CHCH/BSGR BH23 ... 195 G5
CHCH/BSGR BH23 ... 197 L8
ELGH SO50 ... 54 A7
FAWY SO45 ... 180 C8
FAWY SO45 ... 180 E5
LYMN SO41 ... 201 H7
LYND SO43 ... 151 K4
PLE BH15 ... 233 H6 2
RGWD BH24 ... 172 F5
ROMY SO51 ... 22 C8
ROMY SO51 ... 48 D2
RSAL SP5 ... 41 G1
RSAL SP5 ... 44 E3
RSAL SP5 ... 73 K2
RSAL SP5 ... 101 H1
RWIN SO21 ... 17 M6
TOTT SO40 ... 129 J3
WIMB BH21 ... 217 G3
Chapel Ri RGWD BH24 ... 170 B6
Chapel Rd BPWT SO32 ... 87 H5
BPWT SO32 ... 112 A3
BPWT SO32 ... 113 G6
HEND SO30 ... 108 D6
HLER SO31 ... 158 C2
PSTN BH14 ... 233 M4
SHAM SO14 ... 5 J4
Chapelside FHAM/STUB PO14 ... 159 L8
Chapel St GPORT PO12 ... 185 M8
NEND PO2 ... 187 H8 1
PSF GU32 ... 61 J8
PSF GU32 ... 63 L4
SSEA PO5 ... 12 F5 1
Chaplains Av HORN PO8 ... 140 B5
Chaplains Cl HORN PO8 ... 140 B4
Charborough Rd BDST BH18 ... 217 M5
Charden Rd ELGH SO50 ... 82 F7
LSOL/BMARY PO13 ... 185 H8
Charfield Cl FHAM/STUB PO14 ... 6 A7
FUFL SO22 ... 26 D3
Charing Cl RGWD BH24 ... 170 E2 1
Chark La LSOL/BMARY PO13 ... 184 D8
Charlecote Dr CHFD SO53 ... 52 F8
Charlesbury Av GPORT PO12 ... 10 A4
Charles Cl WINC SO23 ... 3 H2
WVILLE PO7 ... 164 B2
Charles Crs NMIL/BTOS BH25 ... 225 M3
Charles Dickens St PSEA PO1 ... 13 G2 1
Charles Gdns NBNE BH10 ... 220 A6
Charles Knott Gdns
WSHM SO15 ... 131 K1
Charles Rd CHCH/BSGR BH23 .. 223 K8 1
PLE BH15 ... 233 J5
Charles's La RGWD BH24 ... 171 H6
Charles St PSEA PO1 ... 211 H2
PSF GU32 ... 63 K5
SHAM SO14 ... 5 H5 1
Charleston Cl HISD PO11 ... 213 J4
Charleston Rd FAWY SO45 ... 156 B8
Charles Watts Wy HEND SO30 .. 133 J1
Charlesworth Dr
WVILLE PO7 ... 140 B7 2
Charlesworth Gdns
WVILLE PO7 ... 140 B7
Charliejoy Gdns SHAM SO14 ... 132 A2 2
Charlotte Cl BKME/WDN BH12 .. 235 H1
CHCH/BSGR BH23 ... 238 F2
Charlotte Pl SHAM SO14 ... 131 L2 2
Charlotte St PSEA PO1 ... 211 G2 3
Charlton Cl LYMN SO41 ... 226 D5 1
MOOR/WNTN BH9 ... 221 G4
Charlton Rd WSHM SO15 ... 131 H1
Charminster Av
MOOR/WNTN BH9 ... 220 F7
Charminster Cl
MOOR/WNTN BH9 ... 220 F6 1
WVILLE PO7 ... 140 C8
Charminster Pl CHAR BH8 ... 221 G6 1
Charminster Rd CHAR BH8 ... 220 F7
Charmouth Gv PSTN BH14 ... 233 M4
Charmus Rd TOTT SO40 ... 104 A6
Charmwen Crs HEND SO30 ... 108 B6
Charnock Cl LYMN SO41 ... 226 D5
Charnwood
LSOL/BMARY PO13 ... 185 H6
Charnwood Av
MOOR/WNTN BH9 ... 220 F5 1
Charnwood Cl CHFD SO53 ... 53 H6
FERN BH22 ... 168 C6 1
TOTT SO40 ... 104 C7
Charnwood Crs CHFD SO53 ... 53 H6
Charnwood Dr FBDG SP6 ... 97 K6
Charnwood Gdns CHFD SO53 ... 53 H6 1
Charnwood Wy FAWY SO45 ... 206 B1
Charterhouse Wy HEND SO30 ... 109 G7
Charter Rd BWD BH11 ... 219 H2
Chartwell Cl ELGH SO50 ... 82 A2
FHAM/STUB PO14 ... 159 G7
Chartwell Dr HAV PO9 ... 9 L1
Chase Cl LISS GU33 ... 36 F4
Chase Farm Cl BPWT SO32 ... 111 K5
Chase Gv BPWT SO32 ... 111 K5
Chase Rd LISS GU33 ... 36 F4
Chaseside LTDN BH7 ... 221 L8
The Chase FHAM/STUB PO14 ... 159 H6
GPORT PO12 ... 10 A4
RGWD BH24 ... 170 B3
VWD BH31 ... 144 F2
Chasewater Av HSEA PO3 ... 211 L1
Chatburn Av HORN PO8 ... 140 C5
Chatfield Av NEND PO2 ... 186 E7
Chatfield Rd
LSOL/BMARY PO13 ... 185 G4
Chatham Dr PSEA PO1 ... 12 E5
Chatham Rd FUFL SO22 ... 26 B3
Chatsworth Av CHAM PO6 ... 187 L2
Chatsworth Cl FHAM PO15 ... 160 A7
Chatsworth Rd CHAR BH8 ... 236 A2

ELGH SO50 82 A2
ITCH SO19 132 E3
PSTN BH14 234 A3
Chatsworth Wy
NMIL/BTOS BH25 225 J5
Chaucer Av CHAM PO6 162 C7
Chaucer Cl FHAM/PORC PO16 6 F4
WIMB BH21 192 A2 1
WVILLE PO7 140 C6
Chaucer Dr LYMN SO41 242 C3
Chaucer Rd CCLF BH13 234 E8 1
ITCH SO19 133 H2
Chaundler Rd WINC SO23 3 H3
Chaveney Cl FAWY SO45 155 K7 1
Chawton Cl FUFL SO22 16 C4
WEND SO18 108 C8 1
Cheam Rd BDST BH18 217 K4
Cheam Wy TOTT SO40 104 C7
Cheddar Cl ITCH SO19 132 C5 1
Cheddington Rd
MOOR/WNTN BH9 220 E4
Chedington Cl CFDH BH17 218 C6
Chedworth Crs CHAM PO6 162 E7
Cheesecombe Farm La
LISS GU33 35 L2
Chelmsford Rd NEND PO2 187 K6
UPTN BH16 232 A1
Chelsea Rd SSEA PO5 13 K6
Cheltenham Crs
LSOL/BMARY PO13 208 D2
Cheltenham Gdns
HEND SO30 109 H5 1
Cheltenham Rd
BKME/WDN BH12 234 B3
CHAM PO6 163 G8
Chelveston Crs ROWN SO16 105 L4
Chene Rd WIMB BH21 192 B4
Cheping Gdns HEND SO30 134 E2
Chepstow Cl CHFD SO53 81 G2 1
TOTT SO40 104 B8 5
Chepstow Ct WVILLE PO7 140 F7
Cherbourg Rd ELGH SO50 81 L7
Cherford Rd BWD BH11 219 M6
Cherita Ct PLE BH15 233 L2
Cheriton Av LTDN BH7 222 A8
WEND SO18 133 G1
Cheriton Cl FUFL SO22 2 B5
HAV PO9 165 H4 1
HORN PO8 140 E1
Cheriton Rd ELGH SO50 81 L8
FUFL SO22 2 C5
GPORT PO12 10 B3
Cheriton Wy WIMB BH21 192 A2
Cherque La LSOL/BMARY PO13 184 E8
Cherrett Cl BWD BH11 219 K4 1
Cherries Dr MOOR/WNTN BH9 220 C6
Cherry Cl LSOL/BMARY PO13 208 D3
PSTN BH14 234 A4
Cherry Dro ELGH SO50 109 H2
Cherry Gdns BPWT SO32 111 J1
Cherrygarth Rd FHAM PO15 160 A7
Cherry Gv FERN BH22 194 A2
Cherry Hill Gv UPTN BH16 232 A2
Cherryton Gdns FAWY SO45 179 M5 1
Cherry Tree Av
FHAM/STUB PO14 6 B8
HORN PO8 140 F6
Cherry Tree Cl
LYMN SO41 227 H8 5
RGWD BH24 169 H5
Cherry Tree Dr
NMIL/BTOS BH25 225 J3 1
Cherry Wk WSHM SO15 106 B8
Cherrywood HEND SO30 133 M2
Cherrywood Gdns
TOTT SO40 129 G1 3
HISD PO11 213 K4
Chervil Cl HORN PO8 116 B7
Cherville St ROMY SO51 50 C8
Cherwell Crs ROWN SO16 105 K8
Cherwell Gdns CHFD SO53 81 J3
Cheshire Cl FHAM PO15 159 K3
Cheshire Dr CHAR BH8 221 L6
Cheshire Wy EMRTH PO10 167 J6
Chesildene Av CHAR BH8 221 H6
Chesildene Dr CHAR BH8 221 H5
Chesil St WINC SO23 3 J9
Cheslyn Rd HSEA PO3 211 M2
Chessel Av BOSC BH5 236 E4
ITCH SO19 132 C1
Chessel Crs ITCH SO19 132 C1
Chester Crs LSOL/BMARY PO13 208 F4
Chesterfield Cl CCLF BH13 234 E8
Chesterfield Rd HSEA PO3 211 L1
Chester Pl SSEA PO5 13 J7
Chester Rd CCLF BH13 234 F6
WEND SO18 107 M7
WINC SO23 3 J8
Chesterton Gdns HORN PO8 140 C5
Chesterton Pl FHAM PO15 135 G8 3
Chestnut Av CHCH/BSGR BH23 222 B8
CHFD SO53 81 H5
ELGH SO50 81 K7
ENEY PO4 211 K4 1
FUFL SO22 16 A4
HAV PO9 164 F5
HORN PO8 141 G3
NMIL/BTOS BH25 225 L8
RGWD BH24 145 M2
RWIN SO21 54 E7
SBNE BH6 237 H4
TOTT SO40 129 G5
Chestnut Cl CHFD SO53 81 H6
ROMY SO51 79 J2
WVILLE PO7 139 K4
Chestnut Gv WIMB BH21 193 J2
Chestnut Ri BPWT SO32 86 F7
ELGH SO50 81 J7 1
Chestnut Rd BROC SO42 175 L7
ROWN SO16 105 M6
The Chestnuts HLER SO31 158 E6
Chestnut Wk GPORT PO12 185 M7
Chestnut Wy
CHCH/BSGR BH23 223 G5
FHAM/STUB PO14 159 G7
Chetnole Cl CFDH BH17 218 D7
Chettle Rd ITCH SO19 133 J3
Chetwode Wy CFDH BH17 217 M6
Chetwynd Dr ROWN SO16 106 E4
Chetwynd Rd ENEY PO4 13 L5
ROWN SO16 106 E4
Chevening Ct ENEY PO4 211 M3 2
Cheviot Dr FAWY SO45 155 H5
Cheviot Gn HLER SO31 158 B8 5
Cheviot Rd ROWN SO16 105 K8
Cheviot Wy VWD BH31 144 D3
Chewter Cl SSEA PO5 13 L9
Chewton Common Rd
CHCH/BSGR BH23 224 E7
Chewton Farm Rd
CHCH/BSGR BH23 225 G7
Chewton Ldg
CHCH/BSGR BH23 224 F8
Chewton Wy
CHCH/BSGR BH23 224 F7
Cheyne Gdns WBNE BH4 235 H6
Cheyne Wy
LSOL/BMARY PO13 208 D3 1
Chichester Av HISD PO11 213 K6
Chichester Cl HEND SO30 109 H7
HLER SO31 158 C5
LSOL/BMARY PO13 184 F6
ROMY SO51 77 G6
Chichester Rd HISD PO11 190 A7
NEND PO2 187 J8
RGWD BH24 147 G8
WEND SO18 132 E1
Chichester Wk WIMB BH21 192 C7
Chickenhall La ELGH SO50 82 B6
Chickerell Cl
MOOR/WNTN BH9 220 F5 2
Chidden Cl PSF GU32 61 J7
Chidden Holt CHFD SO53 80 F3
Chideock Cl
BKME/WDN BH12 234 D2 2
Chidham Cl HAV PO9 8 D2
Chidham Dr HAV PO9 8 C2
Chidham Rd CHAM PO6 163 L7
Chidham Sq HAV PO9 8 C3
Chigwell Rd CHAR BH8 221 G7
Chilbolton Av FUFL SO22 2 A6
Chilbolton Ct HAV PO9 165 M2 5
Chilcomb Cl
LSOL/BMARY PO13 208 D2 1
Chilcombe Cl HAV PO9 165 J5
Chilcombe Rd SBNE BH6 237 G3 2
Chilcomb La RWIN SO21 27 K3
WINC SO23 27 G3
Chilcomb Rd WEND SO18 108 B8
Chilcote Rd HSEA PO3 211 L1
Childe Sq NEND PO2 187 G6
Chilfrome Cl CFDH BH17 218 A7
Chilgrove Rd CHAM PO6 164 A8
Chilham Cl ELGH SO50 81 M1 1
Chillenden Ct TOTT SO40 129 H2 2
Chillerton HLER SO31 157 G2
Chilling La HLER SO31 182 C3
Chillington Gdns CHFD SO53 53 G7 3
Chilsdown Wy WVILLE PO7 164 C3
Chiltern Cl NMIL/BTOS BH25 225 K7
TOTT SO40 129 H3 1
WBNE BH4 235 G3
Chiltern Dr NMIL/BTOS BH25 225 J8
VWD BH31 144 D2
Chiltern Gn ROWN SO16 105 K8
Chilworth Cl ROWN SO16 80 C7
Chilworth Dro ROWN SO16 80 B8
Chilworth Gdns HORN PO8 116 C4 1
Chilworth Gv GPORT PO12 10 D1
Chilworth Rd ROWN SO16 80 D7
Chine Av ITCH SO19 132 C2
Chine Cl HLER SO31 158 E4
Chine Crs WCLF BH2 14 B7
Chine Crescent Rd WBNE BH4 14 B7
The Chine LSOL/BMARY PO13 185 J7 1
Chine Wk FERN BH22 194 C7
Chinham Rd TOTT SO40 127 M2
Chipstead Rd CHAM PO6 163 K8
Chisels La CHCH/BSGR BH23 223 M2
Chisholm Cl ROWN SO16 105 L3
Chiswell Rd CFDH BH17 218 B7
Chithurst La LIPH GU30 66 E2
Chitty Rd ENEY PO4 211 L6
Chivers Cl SSEA PO5 13 H5 1
Chorley Cl PLE BH15 233 H2
Christchurch Bay Rd
NMIL/BTOS BH25 240 E1
Christchurch By-pass
CHCH/BSGR BH23 223 J8
Christchurch Gdns
CHAM PO6 163 M6 1
WINC SO23 26 D3
Christchurch Rd BMTH BH1 15 M5
BOSC BH5 236 F3
CHCH/BSGR BH23 221 M2
FERN BH22 193 M6
LYMN SO41 241 L1
NMIL/BTOS BH25 225 J8 1
RGWD BH24 170 D1
WINC SO23 26 D3
Christie Av HLER SO31 135 G8
Christopher Crs PLE BH15 233 H2
Christopher Wy EMRTH PO10 166 D6
Church Cl ELGH SO50 82 B4
HLER SO31 158 F5
HORN PO8 116 A2
NBAD SO52 79 M4
Churcher Cl GPORT PO12 209 H5
Churcher Rd EMRTH PO10 166 F4
Church Farm FBDG SP6 97 L8
Church Farm Cl FAWY SO45 154 F2
Churchfield VWD BH31 144 C2 1
Churchfield Crs PLE BH15 233 K4
Churchfield La RGWD BH24 122 C6
Churchfield Rd EPSF GU31 64 A4
PLE BH15 233 K5
Churchfields FAWY SO45 180 F5 2
Churchfields Rd RWIN SO21 54 E2
Church Hatch RSAL SP5 44 F8 1
Church Hl HEND SO30 108 B7
LYMN SO41 242 D3
RSAL SP5 73 L3
VWD BH31 144 C2
Churchill Av BPWT SO32 84 F7
Churchill Cl FBDG SP6 121 J3
FHAM/STUB PO14 159 G7 1
Churchill Ct HORN PO8 140 E2 1
Churchill Crs BKME/WDN BH12 234 B2
Churchill Dr EMRTH PO10 166 D4
Churchill Gdns
BKME/WDN BH12 234 B3 1
Churchill Rd BKME/WDN BH12 234 B3
BMTH BH1 236 C3
WIMB BH21 192 B5
Church La ALTN GU34 33 H5
BPWT SO32 109 L2
BPWT SO32 110 C8
BPWT SO32 112 B2
BROC SO42 175 L8
BROC SO42 204 B3
CHCH/BSGR BH23 238 A2
ELGH SO50 54 D8
FAWY SO45 180 E5
FBDG SP6 96 C4
FERN BH22 220 D1
HAV PO9 9 K7
HEND SO30 133 M3
HEND SO30 134 E3
HISD PO11 190 A5
HLER SO31 133 M8
LYMN SO41 200 F7
LYMN SO41 202 B5
LYMN SO41 228 C5
LYND SO43 151 K3
NARL SO24 31 H4
NMIL/BTOS BH25 225 K7
PSF GU32 60 A3
PTSW SO17 107 G6
RGWD BH24 172 E5
ROMY SO51 21 L6
ROMY SO51 48 C5
ROMY SO51 49 K4
ROMY SO51 51 H1
ROMY SO51 76 A3
ROMY SO51 78 D1
ROWN SO16 104 E3
RSAL SP5 44 D3
RWIN SO21 17 L3
RWIN SO21 26 F8
RWIN SO21 54 E8
WINC SO23 17 H2
WVILLE PO7 114 C5
Church Md LYMN SO41 228 C6
Churchmoor Rd WIMB BH21 192 E5
Church Pth EMRTH PO10 166 D8
FHAM/PORC PO16 7 L5
GPORT PO12 11 K4
HORN PO8 141 H2
Church Pth North PSEA PO1 211 G2 4
Church Rd BPWT SO32 112 A2
BPWT SO32 136 B1
ELGH SO50 82 C3
EMRTH PO10 166 F5
EMRTH PO10 191 H1
EMRTH PO10 191 H7
FERN BH22 194 A2
FHAM/PORC PO16 186 C2
GPORT PO12 10 C7
HISD PO11 213 L3
HLER SO31 158 B8
HLER SO31 158 F5
ITCH SO19 132 B7
PSF GU32 63 K1
PSTN BH14 233 M4
ROMY SO51 22 C6
ROMY SO51 78 D1
RSAL SP5 18 B1
SBNE BH6 237 L5
WHAM PO17 137 M1
WIMB BH21 144 C7
Church St BPWT SO32 84 E2
CHCH/BSGR BH23 238 A2
FBDG SP6 97 K8
FHAM/STUB PO14 159 K8
LISS GU33 36 D2
PLE BH15 233 G7
PSEA PO1 211 G1 1
PSF GU32 61 J7
ROMY SO51 78 D1
WSHM SO15 106 A8 2
Church Street Rbt PSEA PO1 211 G1
Church Vw EMRTH PO10 166 F5 1
ENEY PO4 211 L4
Church View Cl ITCH SO19 132 E5
Church Wk RSAL SP5 73 M3
Churchward Gdns HEND SO30 109 H6 2
Cinderford Cl CHAM PO6 163 G7 1
Cinnamon La PLE BH15 233 G7 2
The Circle MOOR/WNTN BH9 220 E4 1
SSEA PO5 13 J8
WHAM PO17 136 D4
Circular Rd PSEA PO1 210 F2
The Circus WVILLE PO7 162 E6
Cirrus Gdns HLER SO31 157 K6
PSEA PO1 211 J2
City Rd WINC SO23 2 F6
Civic Centre Rd HAV PO9 8 E2
SHAM SO14 4 F2
Civic Wy FHAM/PORC PO16 7 L5
Clack La FBDG SP6 96 F2
Clacton Rd CHAM PO6 163 G8
Claire Gdns HORN PO8 116 B6
Clandon Dr ELGH SO50 81 L2
Clanfield Cl CHFD SO53 81 J2
Clanfield Dr CHFD SO53 81 G1
Clanfield Rd WEND SO18 133 G1
Clanfield Wy CHFD SO53 81 J2
Clanwilliam Rd
LSOL/BMARY PO13 208 C2
Clare Cl FHAM/STUB PO14 159 G7
Clare Gdns EPSF GU31 64 B5
FAWY SO45 206 D1
Clare Lodge Cl
CHCH/BSGR BH23 197 L8
Claremont Av
MOOR/WNTN BH9 220 F6
Claremont Cl ELGH SO50 81 M2 2
Claremont Crs WSHM SO15 130 E1
Claremont Gdns WVILLE PO7 164 C4
Claremont Rd
MOOR/WNTN BH9 220 F6
PSEA PO1 13 L2
WSHM SO15 130 E1
Clarence Esp SSEA PO5 12 E7
Clarence Pde SSEA PO5 12 F7
Clarence Park Rd LTDN BH7 236 F2
Clarence Rd GPORT PO12 11 K2
LYND SO43 151 K3 1
PSTN BH14 233 M5
SSEA PO5 13 J9
Clarence St PSEA PO1 211 G2
Clarendon Cl BDST BH18 217 L4
ROMY SO51 51 G7 1
Clarendon Crs
FHAM/STUB PO14 158 F7
Clarendon Pk LYMN SO41 228 B6
Clarendon Pl PSEA PO1 13 H1 1
PSEA PO1 211 H2 3
Clarendon Rd BDST BH18 217 J5
CHCH/BSGR BH23 237 M1
HAV PO9 8 D5
ROWN SO16 105 M8
SSEA PO5 13 H7
WBNE BH4 14 A7
Clarendon St PSEA PO1 211 H2
Clarendon Wy STOK SO20 24 B1
Clarkes Rd PSEA PO1 211 K2
Clark's Cl RGWD BH24 170 E1 2
Claude Ashby Cl WEND SO18 107 K4
Claudeen Cl WEND SO18 107 K3
Claudia Ct GPORT PO12 209 K2 1
Claudius Cl CHFD SO53 81 L1 1
Claudius Gdns CHFD SO53 81 L2
Clausentum Cl CHFD SO53 81 K1
Clausentum Rd SHAM SO14 131 L1
WINC SO23 26 E3
Clausen Wy LYMN SO41 228 A7
Claxton St PSEA PO1 13 J1
Claybank Sp HSEA PO3 187 L7
Claydon Av ENEY PO4 211 L4
Clayford Av FERN BH22 193 M1
Clayford Cl CFDH BH17 218 B6
Clayhall Rd GPORT PO12 10 D8
Clay Hl BROC SO42 151 L7
Clayhill Cl BPWT SO32 111 J4 1
Claylake Dr VWD BH31 144 E3
Claylands Ct BPWT SO32 85 G8
Claylands Rd BPWT SO32 85 G8 1
Clay La LYND SO43 151 K4 1
Claypit Rd ROMY SO51 52 A1
Claypits La FAWY SO45 155 G4
Claypitt La ALTN GU34 34 B2
Clay St RSAL SP5 46 F5
Cleasby Cl ROWN SO16 130 C1
Clease Wy RWIN SO21 54 B1
Clee Av FHAM/STUB PO14 6 A7
Cleethorpes Rd ITCH SO19 132 F4
Cleeve Cl CHAM PO6 162 F7 2
Cleeves Cl BKME/WDN BH12 219 H6 1
The Cleeves TOTT SO40 129 G2
Clegg Rd ENEY PO4 211 L5
Clematis Cl
CHCH/BSGR BH23 224 A8 1
Clement Attlee Wy CHAM PO6 162 F8
Clem's Wy ROMY SO51 20 F7
Cleric Ct FHAM/STUB PO14 159 H5
Cleveland Cl NMIL/BTOS BH25 240 C1
Cleveland Dr FAWY SO45 155 H6
FHAM/STUB PO14 6 B7
Cleveland Gdns BMTH BH1 15 M1
Cleveland Rd BMTH BH1 236 C3
GPORT PO12 10 F5 1
SSEA PO5 13 L4
WEND SO18 107 L6
Clevelands Cl CHFD SO53 53 G6 1
Clewers Hl BPWT SO32 111 J4
Clewers La BPWT SO32 111 J4
Cliff Crs NMIL/BTOS BH25 240 E1
Cliff Dr CCLF BH13 245 K2
CHCH/BSGR BH23 239 H2
Cliffe Av HLER SO31 157 J5
Cliffe Rd NMIL/BTOS BH25 240 D1
Clifford Dibben Ms
SHAM SO14 106 F8 1
Clifford Pl ELGH SO50 83 H6
Clifford Rd MOOR/WNTN BH9 220 E7
Clifford St SHAM SO14 5 J2
Cliff Rd FHAM/STUB PO14 183 K7
LYMN SO41 241 M3
WSHM SO15 4 A1
Cliff Wy RWIN SO21 54 C2
Clifton Crs WVILLE PO7 139 M4
Clifton Gdns FERN BH22 194 A4
WEND SO18 108 B7
Clifton Hl FUFL SO22 2 E7
Clifton Rd FUFL SO22 2 D6
LSOL/BMARY PO13 208 E4
PSTN BH14 234 C6
SBNE BH6 237 J5
SSEA PO5 13 G8
WSHM SO15 105 M8
Clifton St GPORT PO12 209 K2
PSEA PO1 211 J2
Clifton Ter FUFL SO22 2 E7
Clingan Rd SBNE BH6 237 J2
Clinkley Rd NARL SO24 32 C1
Clinton Cl CHCH/BSGR BH23 224 F6 1
Clinton Rd LYMN SO41 228 C3
WVILLE PO7 140 A5
Clipper Cl HLER SO31 158 C7
Cliveden Cl FERN BH22 194 A1
Clive Gv FHAM/PORC PO16 186 A1
Clive Rd CHCH/BSGR BH23 224 C6
MOOR/WNTN BH9 220 D7
PSEA PO1 211 J2
Clock St PSEA PO1 12 C2
Clocktower Dr ENEY PO4 211 M6
The Cloisters FHAM PO15 160 A6
RGWD BH24 171 G2 1
ROMY SO51 50 D8 1
ROWN SO16 106 F4
The Close Bellfield
FHAM/STUB PO14 183 K1
The Close BDST BH18 217 J5
CHAM PO6 187 L1 1
FAWY SO45 180 B5
FHAM/PORC PO16 162 A8
HEND SO30 133 M2
LYMN SO41 200 E6
NMIL/BTOS BH25 225 L8
PSF GU32 62 B5
RGWD BH24 169 L4 1
RGWD BH24 170 D1 2
RSAL SP5 73 J1
WEND SO18 133 H1
Closewood Rd WVILLE PO7 139 L7
Clouch La RGWD BH24 172 D5
Clough's Rd RGWD BH24 170 F1
Clovelly Rd EMRTH PO10 166 C8
EMRTH PO10 167 H7
ENEY PO4 211 L4
HISD PO11 190 A4
SHAM SO14 131 L2
Clover Cl CHCH/BSGR BH23 223 M8
HLER SO31 158 C6
LSOL/BMARY PO13 185 G6 3
Clover Ct NMIL/BTOS BH25 226 B4
Clover Dr CFDH BH17 217 K7
The Clovers
BKME/WDN BH12 219 L8 2
Clover Wy HEND SO30 133 L2 2
ROMY SO51 51 H8
Clowes Av SBNE BH6 238 A5
Club House La BPWT SO32 111 J5
Clydebank Rd NEND PO2 187 H8
Clyde Ct GPORT PO12 209 K2
Clyde Rd CFDH BH17 217 M6 2
GPORT PO12 209 K2
Clydesdale Dr TOTT SO40 104 A8 1
Clydesdale Rd HLER SO31 158 F1
Clydesdale Wy TOTT SO40 104 A8
Coach Hl FHAM/STUB PO14 159 K8
Coach Hill Cl CHFD SO53 81 G1
Coach Hill La RGWD BH24 172 B2
Coach House Pl BMTH BH1 15 H2
Coachmans Copse
WEND SO18 107 M6
Coach Rd HLER SO31 157 J6
Coal Park La HLER SO31 134 B7
Coalville Rd ITCH SO19 132 F4
Coastguard Cl GPORT PO12 10 A8
Coastguard La SELS PO20 215 J7
Coastguard Wy
CHCH/BSGR BH23 238 E4
Coates Rd ITCH SO19 133 H4
Coates Wy WVILLE PO7 164 C3
Coat Gdns FAWY SO45 155 L5 2
Cobbett Cl FUFL SO22 26 B3
Cobbett Rd WEND SO18 132 C1
Cobbett Wy HEND SO30 134 C1
Cobblers Cnr LYMN SO41 201 L5
Cobblewood EMRTH PO10 166 D5
Cobbs La PLE BH15 233 K2
Cobb's Rd WIMB BH21 192 C2
Cobden Av HSEA PO3 187 L8
WEND SO18 107 J8
Cobden Crs WEND SO18 107 L8
Cobden Gdns WEND SO18 107 K7
Cobden St GPORT PO12 10 E1
Cobham Rd MOOR/WNTN BH9 220 E5
WIMB BH21 193 K1
Cobham Wy WIMB BH21 192 C7
Coblands Av TOTT SO40 129 H1
Coburg St PSEA PO1 13 K1
SHAM SO14 132 A2
Cochcrane Cl
LSOL/BMARY PO13 209 H2
Cockerell Cl WIMB BH21 192 D7
Cockleshell Gdns ENEY PO4 212 A5
Cocklydown La TOTT SO40 129 J3
Cockshott La PSF GU32 35 H6
Cogdeane Rd CFDH BH17 218 B6
Coghlan Cl FHAM/PORC PO16 7 J3
Coker Cl FUFL SO22 2 D6
Colborne Av WIMB BH21 192 D3
Colborne Cl LYMN SO41 228 C3
PLE BH15 233 J7 3
Colbourne Cl
CHCH/BSGR BH23 197 L8
Colburn Cl ROWN SO16 105 J6
Colbury Gv HAV PO9 165 G4
Colchester Av ELGH SO50 82 D4
Colchester Rd CHAM PO6 163 H7
Cold East Cl HLER SO31 158 C3
Coldeast Wy HLER SO31 158 D3
Cold Harbour Cl WHAM PO17 136 D4
Coldharbour Farm Rd
EMRTH PO10 166 D7
Coldharbour La ROWN SO16 78 F8
Coldhill La HORN PO8 140 C1
Colebrook Av HSEA PO3 211 M1
WSHM SO15 106 B7
Colebrook Pl WINC SO23 3 J9
Colebrook St WINC SO23 3 H9
Cole Hl BPWT SO32 113 G3
Colehill Crs MOOR/WNTN BH9 220 F5
Colehill La WIMB BH21 192 C1
Coleman Rd BWD BH11 219 L5
Coleman St SHAM SO14 5 J3
Colemere Gdns
CHCH/BSGR BH23 224 D7
Colemore Rd LTDN BH7 237 H1
Colemore Sq HAV PO9 165 K4 1
Colenso Rd FHAM/PORC PO16 7 H4
Coleridge Cl HLER SO31 158 B7
Coleridge Gdns HORN PO8 140 D4
Coleridge Gn
CHCH/BSGR BH23 223 K8 2
Coleridge Rd CHAM PO6 162 D7
Coles Av PLE BH15 232 D6
Colesbourne Rd CHAM PO6 162 F7
Coles Cl RWIN SO21 54 F1
Coles Gdns PLE BH15 232 D6
Coles Mede RWIN SO21 54 A5
Coleson Rd WEND SO18 107 K8
Coles's La RSAL SP5 74 D3
Coleville Av FAWY SO45 180 F5
Colin Cl WIMB BH21 217 H3
Colinton Av FHAM/PORC PO16 7 H2
Collard Wy LISS GU33 36 E4 1
College Cl HAV PO9 142 A7
HLER SO31 157 K6 1
College La PSEA PO1 12 C2 2
College Rd BOSC BH5 236 F4
ITCH SO19 132 C6
PSEA PO1 12 C1
RGWD BH24 170 E1
WVILLE PO7 164 C6
College St EPSF GU31 63 L5
PSEA PO1 12 C2
SHAM SO14 5 H5

WINC SO23 3 G9
College Wk WINC SO23 26 F2
Collett Cl HEND SO30 109 G6
Collier Cl PTSW SO17 107 H8 1
Collingbourne Av SBNE BH6 237 J2
Collingbourne Dr CHFD SO53 80 F2
Collington Crs CHAM PO6 162 F7
Collingwood Rd SSEA PO5 13 K7
WIMB BH21 168 C2
Collingworth Cl HLER SO31 158 F2
Collins Cl NBAD SO52 80 E2 1
Collins La EPSF GU31 92 E1
RGWD BH24 170 E1
RWIN SO21 53 H1
Collins Rd ENEY PO4 211 L6
Collis Rd HSEA PO3 187 L8
Collwood Cl PLE BH15 233 H1
Collyers Rd BROC SO42 175 K8
Colne Av ROWN SO16 105 J5
Colonnade Rd BOSC BH5 236 F3 1
Colpoy St SSEA PO5 12 F4
Colson Rd WINC SO23 3 K6
Colt Cl ROWN SO16 105 L3 3
WIMB BH21 192 F2
Coltsfoot Cl HEND SO30 133 M1
Coltsfoot Dr HLER SO31 158 C6
WVILLE PO7 164 D3
Coltsfoot Wk ROMY SO51 51 H7 4
Coltsmead CHAM PO6 162 D8
Colts Rd ROWN SO16 105 K1
Columbian Wy NBNE BH10 220 A6 2
Columbia Rd NBNE BH10 219 M6
Columbia Trees La NBNE BH10 220 A7
Columbine Cl
CHCH/BSGR BH23 223 M7 1
Colville Cl BOSC BH5 236 F3
Colville Dr BPWT SO32 85 J8
Colville Rd BOSC BH5 236 F3
CHAM PO6 163 L8
Colwell Cl ROWN SO16 105 J8
Colwell Rd CHAM PO6 187 K1
Combe Rd LISS GU33 37 G7
Comber Rd MOOR/WNTN BH9 220 D5
Comet Wy CHCH/BSGR BH23 238 F2
Comfrey Cl HORN PO8 116 B7 1
ROMY SO51 51 H7
Comines Wy HEND SO30 133 J2
Comley Hl HAV PO9 166 A1
Comley Rd MOOR/WNTN BH9 220 D6
Commercial Pl PSEA PO1 211 G2 5
Commercial Rd PLE BH15 233 L4
PSEA PO1 13 G1
PSEA PO1 211 G2 6
TOTT SO40 129 L1
WCLF BH2 14 C6
WSHM SO15 4 F1
Commercial St WEND SO18 132 F1
Common Barn La
LSOL/BMARY PO13 208 D1 2
Common Cl CHFD SO53 53 H8
Common Gdns CHFD SO53 53 H8
Common Hill Rd ROMY SO51 51 J2
Common La FHAM/STUB PO14 159 H8
WHAM PO17 138 C7
Common Rd CHFD SO53 53 H8
EMRTH PO10 167 K3
RSAL SP5 47 G5
Commonside EMRTH PO10 166 F3
Common St PSEA PO1 211 H2 1
Common Vw MIDH GU29 67 J7
Compass Cl
LSOL/BMARY PO13 209 H2 2
Compass Rd CHAM PO6 162 F8
Compton Av PSTN BH14 234 C6
Compton Beeches
RGWD BH24 169 L3 1
Compton Cl ELGH SO50 81 L2
FUFL SO22 26 A5
HAV PO9 8 E1
LSOL/BMARY PO13 208 E2
VWD BH31 144 D2
Compton Crs FERN BH22 168 E7
Compton Dr PSTN BH14 234 B6
Compton Gdns PSTN BH14 234 B6
Compton Rd NEND PO2 187 K5
NMIL/BTOS BH25 225 L6
TOTT SO40 104 F8
WINC SO23 2 E9
Compton's Dr ROMY SO51 75 L2
Compton St RWIN SO21 26 B8
Compton Wk SHAM SO14 5 G1
Compton Wy FUFL SO22 26 A5
Conan Rd NEND PO2 187 J4
Concorde Wy FHAM PO15 159 J3
Condor Av FHAM/PORC PO16 161 K8
Condor Cl ITCH SO19 132 B5 1
Coneygar La FERN BH22 193 L5
Conference Dr HLER SO31 158 F5 1
Conference Pl LYMN SO41 228 D6 2
Conford Ct HAV PO9 165 H2
Congleton Cl LYND SO43 127 G5
Conifer Av PSTN BH14 234 A6
Conifer Cl CHCH/BSGR BH23 222 B5
FAWY SO45 155 K5 2
FERN BH22 194 D7
FUFL SO22 2 D5
HORN PO8 140 E6
RGWD BH24 169 H4
Conifer Crs LYMN SO41 227 M5
Conifer Gv
LSOL/BMARY PO13 185 G4
Conifer Ms
FHAM/PORC PO16 162 B7 1
Conifer Rd ROWN SO16 105 M4
Conigar Rd EMRTH PO10 166 D5
Coniston Av BWD BH11 219 J3
HSEA PO3 187 L8
Coniston Cl VWD BH31 144 C3
Coniston Gdns HEND SO30 133 M3
Coniston Rd ELGH SO50 81 L6
RGWD BH24 170 F2 1
ROWN SO16 105 H8
Connaught Cl
NMIL/BTOS BH25 225 J8
Connaught Crs
BKME/WDN BH12 234 D2
Connaught Rd HAV PO9 9 G4
NEND PO2 187 H6 1
SBNE BH6 237 G3 3
Connell Rd PLE BH15 233 H3
Connemara Crs HLER SO31 158 F1
Connigar Cl
LSOL/BMARY PO13 209 G1 1
Conqueror Wy
FHAM/STUB PO14 184 B6
Conrad Gdns FHAM PO15 135 G8
Consort Cl BKME/WDN BH12 234 B3 2
Consort Rd ELGH SO50 82 A3
Constable Cl GPORT PO12 10 F9
ITCH SO19 133 G6
Constable's Ga WINC SO23 2 E8
Constantine Av CHFD SO53 81 K2
Constantine Cl CHFD SO53 81 L2 1
Constitution Hill Rd
PSTN BH14 233 L4
Convent La EMRTH PO10 166 D8
Conway Cl CHFD SO53 81 G5
NMIL/BTOS BH25 225 M5
Conways Dr PSTN BH14 233 M4 1
Cook Cl RGWD BH24 147 G8
Cooke Rd BKME/WDN BH12 234 E2
Cooks La EMRTH PO10 167 J7
RCCH PO18 143 M6
ROMY SO51 48 C1
ROMY SO51 49 M4
TOTT SO40 104 B6
Cook's Pond Rd LIPH GU30 38 D8
Cook St SHAM SO14 5 H4
Coombe Av NBNE BH10 220 C6
Coombedale HLER SO31 158 F6 1
Coombe Farm Av
FHAM/PORC PO16 7 H8
Coombe Gdns NBNE BH10 220 B6
Coombe La LYMN SO41 201 H7
PSF GU32 60 D4
ROMY SO51 49 L5
Coombe Rd GPORT PO12 209 M1
PSF GU32 61 H8
Coombs Cl HORN PO8 116 B7 2
Cooper Dean Dr CHAR BH8 221 K7
Cooper Gv FHAM/PORC PO16 186 B2
Cooper Rd HSEA PO3 211 M1
TOTT SO40 129 G5
Cooper's Cl ROMY SO51 77 G6 1
WEND SO18 108 B7
Cooper's La ITCH SO19 132 B5 2
VWD BH31 144 D1
Copeland Dr PSTN BH14 234 A6
Copeland Rd ROWN SO16 105 J7
Copinger Cl TOTT SO40 129 G2 3
Copnor Rd NEND PO2 187 K4
Copper Beech Cl
BKME/WDN BH12 234 F4
Copper Beech Dr CHAM PO6 164 C8 2
Copper Beech Gdns
NBNE BH10 220 B6
Copperfield Rd ROWN SO16 106 F3
Copperfields TOTT SO40 128 F1
Coppers Cl FBDG SP6 121 L2
Copper St SSEA PO5 12 F5
Coppice Av FERN BH22 193 M2
Coppice Cl FUFL SO22 16 B7
NMIL/BTOS BH25 226 B4
RGWD BH24 169 K4
Coppice Hl BPWT SO32 111 H1
Coppice Rd TOTT SO40 104 B6
The Coppice BROC SO42 175 H6
CHCH/BSGR BH23 239 G2 3
HORN PO8 140 E2
LSOL/BMARY PO13 185 H6 1
Coppice Vw NBNE BH10 220 C5
Coppice Wy FHAM PO15 6 A2
Coppins Gv FHAM/PORC PO16 186 A2
Copse Av NMIL/BTOS BH25 225 M6
Copse Cl EPSF GU31 64 B4
LISS GU33 36 F4
NBAD SO52 79 L4
PLE BH15 233 L5
RWIN SO21 54 B4
TOTT SO40 129 K2
WVILLE PO7 164 B6
Copse La HISD PO11 189 L8
HLER SO31 157 K6
LSOL/BMARY PO13 185 H7
ROWN SO16 80 E7
Copse Rd NMIL/BTOS BH25 225 M6
RGWD BH24 172 D6
VWD BH31 144 D2
WEND SO18 107 L6
The Copse CHFD SO53 81 K3
FHAM PO15 160 B4
Copse Vw ITCH SO19 133 J3
Copse Wy CHCH/BSGR BH23 224 C8
Copsewood Av CHAR BH8 221 J7
Copsewood Rd FAWY SO45 155 K5
TOTT SO40 129 G5
WEND SO18 107 K6
Copsey Cl CHAM PO6 164 B8
Copsey Gv CHAM PO6 164 B8
Copthorne La FAWY SO45 180 F5
Copythorne Cl CHAR BH8 221 H6 1
Copythorne Crs TOTT SO40 103 H6
Copythorn Rd NEND PO2 187 K7
Coracle Cl HLER SO31 158 D7
Coral Cl FHAM/PORC PO16 186 A2
Coralin Gv WVILLE PO7 140 F7
Coram Cl WINC SO23 3 H2
Corbar Rd CHCH/BSGR BH23 222 C8
Corbett Rd WVILLE PO7 164 B2
Corbiere Av
BKME/WDN BH12 219 H7
Corbiere Cl ROWN SO16 105 K5
Corbin Av FERN BH22 194 E2
Corbin Rd LYMN SO41 227 M6
Corbould Rd FAWY SO45 155 K8 1
Corby Crs HSEA PO3 187 M4
Cordelia Cl FAWY SO45 155 H5
Corfe Cl FHAM/STUB PO14 183 L6
Corfe Lodge Rd WIMB BH21 217 G4
Corfe View Rd PSTN BH14 234 A5
WIMB BH21 217 G3
Corfe Wy BDST BH18 217 J5
Corhampton Crs HAV PO9 165 H4
Corhampton La BPWT SO32 86 C3
Corhampton Rd SBNE BH6 237 H2
Coriander Dr TOTT SO40 128 F1
Coriander Wy FHAM PO15 135 H8
Corinna Gdns FAWY SO45 155 H5
Corinthian Rd CHFD SO53 81 K1
Cork La TOTT SO40 130 D5
Cormorant Cl
FHAM/PORC PO16 161 K8 1
Cormorant Dr FAWY SO45 155 M6
Cornaway La
FHAM/PORC PO16 185 M1
Cornbrook Gv HORN PO8 141 G7
Cornelia Crs BKME/WDN BH12 234 F2
Cornelius Dr WVILLE PO7 140 F7
Cornel Rd ITCH SO19 132 D3
Corner Md WVILLE PO7 139 K4
Cornes Cl FUFL SO22 2 A7
Cornfield FHAM/PORC PO16 160 F4
Cornfield Cl NBAD SO52 80 E2
Cornfield Rd
LSOL/BMARY PO13 208 D2
Cornflower Cl HLER SO31 158 C6
Cornflower Dr
CHCH/BSGR BH23 224 A7
Cornford Wy
CHCH/BSGR BH23 224 B8
Cornforth Rd TOTT SO40 104 B7
Cornish Gdns NBNE BH10 220 B7
Corn Market ROMY SO51 78 D1 2
Cornpits La FBDG SP6 96 B5
Cornwall Crs WEND SO18 107 L6
Cornwallis Crs PSEA PO1 211 G2
Cornwallis Rd LYMN SO41 242 A4
Cornwall Rd CHFD SO53 81 H5
PSEA PO1 13 L2
WEND SO18 107 L6
Cornwell Cl LSOL/BMARY PO13 209 H1
NEND PO2 186 F6
Coronado Rd GPORT PO12 209 M2
Coronation Av
MOOR/WNTN BH9 220 D6
UPTN BH16 232 A1 1
Coronation Pde HLER SO31 157 J5 1
Coronation Rd BPWT SO32 112 A3 2
HISD PO11 214 C7
VWD BH31 144 D1
Corporation Rd BMTH BH1 15 K3
Corsair Dr FAWY SO45 155 H4
Corscombe Cl CFDH BH17 218 C6 1
Cortina Wy HEND SO30 134 A3
Cort Wy FHAM PO15 160 A4
Corvette Av HLER SO31 158 D7
Cosford Cl ELGH SO50 82 F6 1
Cosham Park Av CHAM PO6 187 K1
Cossack Gn SHAM SO14 5 H3
Cossack La WINC SO23 3 H7
Cosworth Dr FAWY SO45 155 H5
Cotes Av PSTN BH14 233 M3
Cotlands Rd BMTH BH1 15 J4
Cot La RCCH PO18 191 M3
Cotsalls ELGH SO50 83 H7
Cotswold Cl FAWY SO45 155 H5 4
HAV PO9 165 J2 1
VWD BH31 144 D3 1
Cotswold Rd ROWN SO16 105 L8
Cottage Cl WVILLE PO7 139 K5
Cottage Gdns
BKME/WDN BH12 234 B3
Cottage Gv GPORT PO12 10 E2
SSEA PO5 13 H4
Cottage La LISS GU33 35 L4
Cottage Ms FBDG SP6 97 K6 3
RGWD BH24 170 D1 3
Cottagers La LYMN SO41 226 E5
Cottage Vw PSEA PO1 13 J1
Cottes Wy FHAM/STUB PO14 183 L7
Cottesway East
FHAM/STUB PO14 183 L7
Cott La RGWD BH24 172 F6
Cotton Cl BDST BH18 217 K3
ELGH SO50 82 D5
Cotton Dr EMRTH PO10 166 C5
Cott St BPWT SO32 112 F4
Cott Street La BPWT SO32 112 F4
Cotwell Av HORN PO8 140 F4
Coulmere Rd GPORT PO12 209 L2
Coulsdon Rd HEND SO30 134 A2
Coultas Rd CHFD SO53 53 K6
Countess Cl WIMB BH21 192 C7
Countess Gdns LTDN BH7 221 K8 1
Country Vw FHAM/STUB PO14 183 M4
ROMY SO51 76 D5
County Gdns
FHAM/STUB PO14 160 A8
Course Park Crs
FHAM/STUB PO14 159 G6
Court Barn La
LSOL/BMARY PO13 208 D1
Court Cl CHAM PO6 187 M1
CHCH/BSGR BH23 238 D1 2
LYMN SO41 228 B6
TOTT SO40 104 B6
Courtenay Dr WIMB BH21 192 A2 2
Courtenay Pl LYMN SO41 228 C6
Courtenay Rd PSTN BH14 234 A4
WINC SO23 3 G2
Court Hl FBDG SP6 96 D4
Courthill Rd PSTN BH14 234 B4
Court House Cl FAWY SO45 155 L4 3
Courtland Gdns ROWN SO16 107 G3
Court La CHAM PO6 187 M1
Court Md CHAM PO6 187 M1 1
Courtmount Gv CHAM PO6 163 L8
Court Rd LSOL/BMARY PO13 208 C1
MOOR/WNTN BH9 220 F7
WINC SO23 17 H3
WSHM SO15 131 K1
Court Royal Ms WSHM SO15 106 E8 2
The Courtyard EPSF GU31 63 L5
Cousins Gv ENEY PO4 211 L6
Covena Rd SBNE BH6 237 J2
Coventry Cl WIMB BH21 217 G4
Coventry Crs CFDH BH17 217 L7
Coventry Rd WSHM SO15 131 K2
Coverack Wy CHAM PO6 186 F1
Cove Rd NBNE BH10 220 A6
Covert Gv WVILLE PO7 164 E3
The Covert ROMY SO51 79 G2
Covington Rd EMRTH PO10 166 F3
Cowan Rd WVILLE PO7 164 B3
Coward Rd GPORT PO12 10 B8
Cowdown La RCCH PO18 118 B4
Cowdray Cl ELGH SO50 82 E6 1
ROWN SO16 106 A4
Cowdray Pk
FHAM/STUB PO14 183 L6
Cowdrey Gdns CHAR BH8 221 K6 1
Cowell Dr LTDN BH7 221 L8
Cowes La HLER SO31 182 B2
Cow La CHAM PO6 187 H1
EPSF GU31 92 F4
FHAM/PORC PO16 186 C1
Cowley Cl ROWN SO16 105 K6
Cowley Rd LYMN SO41 228 A4
Cowleys La BROC SO42 179 J8
Cowleys Rd CHCH/BSGR BH23 223 G6
Cowper Av NMIL/BTOS BH25 225 L7
Cowper Rd ITCH SO19 133 H2
MOOR/WNTN BH9 220 D6
PSEA PO1 211 J1 3
Cowpitts La RGWD BH24 147 H6
Cowslip Cl HLER SO31 158 C7
LSOL/BMARY PO13 185 G6
Cowslip Rd WIMB BH21 217 J6 1
Cox Av MOOR/WNTN BH9 220 F5
Cox Cl MOOR/WNTN BH9 220 F4
Cox Dl FHAM/STUB PO14 159 G7
Coxes Meadow PSF GU32 63 K3
Coxford Cl ROWN SO16 105 M6
Coxford Dro ROWN SO16 105 M5
Coxford Rd ROWN SO16 105 L6
Cox Rw CHFD SO53 81 J5
Cox's Dr ITCH SO19 132 F6
Coxs Hl RWIN SO21 26 F8
Coxstone La RGWD BH24 170 E2
Coy Pond Rd
BKME/WDN BH12 234 F3
Cozens Cl ITCH SO19 132 C7 1
Crabapple Cl TOTT SO40 129 G1 4
Crabbe Ct SSEA PO5 13 H4 1
Crabbs Wy TOTT SO40 128 F1
Crabbswood La LYMN SO41 200 C8
Crabden La HORN PO8 116 D8
Crableck La HLER SO31 158 A3
Crab Orchard Wy WIMB BH21 144 C6
Crabthorne Farm La
FHAM/STUB PO14 183 M5 2
Crabton Close Rd BOSC BH5 236 E3
Crabtree ROWN SO16 105 L7 1
Crabtree Cl CHCH/BSGR BH23 223 G6
Crabwood Cl ROWN SO16 105 L7
Crabwood Ct HAV PO9 165 H1 1
Crabwood Dr HEND SO30 108 D7
Crabwood Rd ROWN SO16 105 K6
Cracknore Hard TOTT SO40 131 G6
Cracknore Hard La TOTT SO40 130 F7
TOTT SO40 131 G6 1
Cracknore Rd WSHM SO15 4 A2
Craigmoor Av CHAR BH8 221 J7
Craigmoor Cl CHAR BH8 221 K7
Craigmoor Wy CHAR BH8 221 J6 2
Craigside Rd RGWD BH24 169 H4
Craigwell Rd WVILLE PO7 164 B4
Craigwood Dr FERN BH22 194 C4
Crampmoor La ROMY SO51 51 J7
Cranberry Cl TOTT SO40 130 D7
Cranborne Crs
BKME/WDN BH12 219 J8
Cranborne Gdns CHFD SO53 53 G7
Cranborne Rd CHAM PO6 163 L7
FBDG SP6 120 E3
WCLF BH2 14 D7
Cranbourne Cl WSHM SO15 106 C7 1
Cranbourne Dr RWIN SO21 54 A5
Cranbourne Rd GPORT PO12 11 G5
Cranbrook Rd
BKME/WDN BH12 234 A2
Cranbury Av SHAM SO14 131 M2
Cranbury Cl RSAL SP5 72 E2
RWIN SO21 54 A5
Cranbury Gdns HLER SO31 133 K7
Cranbury Pl SHAM SO14 131 L2
Cranbury Rd ELGH SO50 81 M6
ITCH SO19 132 D5
Crane Cl VWD BH31 144 C1
Crane Dr VWD BH31 144 C2
Cranemoor Av
CHCH/BSGR BH23 224 C6
Cranemoor Cl
CHCH/BSGR BH23 224 C6
Cranemoor Gdns
CHCH/BSGR BH23 224 D6
Cranes Ms PLE BH15 233 J5 1
Craneswater Av ENEY PO4 13 M8
Craneswater Ga ENEY PO4 13 M9 1
Craneswater Pk ENEY PO4 13 M9
Cranfield Av WIMB BH21 192 B3
Cranford Gdns CHFD SO53 53 G8
Cranford Rd PSF GU32 63 K6
Cranford Wy PTSW SO17 106 F6
Cranleigh Av PSEA PO1 211 J2
Cranleigh Cl SBNE BH6 237 K3
Cranleigh Gdns SBNE BH6 237 K3
Cranleigh Rd
FHAM/PORC PO16 185 L1
HEND SO30 134 A2
PSEA PO1 211 J2
SBNE BH6 237 J2
Cranmer Dr ROWN SO16 105 H3
Cranmer Rd MOOR/WNTN BH9 220 D8
Cranmore HLER SO31 157 G1
Crantock Gv CHAR BH8 221 K6 2
Cranwell Cl BWD BH11 219 J4 1
CHCH/BSGR BH23 197 M7
Cranworth Rd FUFL SO22 2 E5
Crasswell St PSEA PO1 211 G2
Craven Ct FHAM PO15 6 B2
Craven Rd CHFD SO53 81 J2
Craven St SHAM SO14 5 H2 1
Crawford Cl ROWN SO16 105 J3
Crawford Dr FHAM/PORC PO16 6 E1
Crawley Av HAV PO9 165 L2
Crawley Hl ROMY SO51 76 E6
Crawshaw Rd PSTN BH14 234 A6
Crawte Av FAWY SO45 180 B6
Creasey Rd BWD BH11 219 L3
Credenhill Rd CHAM PO6 163 G7
Creech Rd BKME/WDN BH12 234 B3
Creedy Gdns WEND SO18 107 M5 1
Creek End EMRTH PO10 190 D1
Creekmoor La CFDH BH17 217 K7
Creek Rd GPORT PO12 11 J3
HISD PO11 214 B6
Creighton Rd WSHM SO15 130 D2
Cremyll Cl FHAM/STUB PO14 184 A6
Crescent Cl FUFL SO22 26 A4
Crescent Dr NMIL/BTOS BH25 240 E1
Crescent Rd FHAM/PORC PO16 7 H6
GPORT PO12 10 C9
HLER SO31 158 D5
NBAD SO52 79 L3
PSTN BH14 234 D4
VWD BH31 144 E2
WCLF BH2 14 C5
WIMB BH21 192 A4
The Crescent BMTH BH1 236 D4
BPWT SO32 84 B6
ELGH SO50 81 M4
EMRTH PO10 167 H8
HLER SO31 156 F2
ITCH SO19 132 E6
NMIL/BTOS BH25 225 G8
ROMY SO51 51 G8
RWIN SO21 54 F2
TOTT SO40 128 C5
WVILLE PO7 164 A4 2
Crescent Wk FERN BH22 194 C6
Cressey Rd ROMY SO51 78 E1
Cressy Rd NEND PO2 211 H1
Cresta Gdns FERN BH22 194 C6
Crest Cl FHAM/PORC PO16 161 H7
Crestland Cl HORN PO8 140 E5
Crest Rd BKME/WDN BH12 234 B2
The Crest WVILLE PO7 164 A6
Crest Wy ITCH SO19 133 G4
Crete La FAWY SO45 155 K7
Crete Rd FAWY SO45 155 K8
Cribb Cl CFDH BH17 233 K1
Crichel Mount Rd PSTN BH14 234 B8
Crichel Rd MOOR/WNTN BH9 220 E8
Cricket Cl CHCH/BSGR BH23 238 E3
Cricket Dr HORN PO8 140 E3
Cricklemede BPWT SO32 111 J1
Cricklewood Cl BPWT SO32 111 J1 1
Crigdon Cl ROWN SO16 105 K8
Crimea Rd MOOR/WNTN BH9 235 L1 2
Cringle Av SBNE BH6 237 M4
Crinoline Gdns ENEY PO4 211 L6
Cripple Gate La BROC SO42 204 B3
Crispin Cl CHCH/BSGR BH23 224 D8
ELGH SO50 109 H2
HLER SO31 158 F4
Crispstead La WINC SO23 26 E3
Crisspyn Cl HORN PO8 140 F2
Crittall Cl LYMN SO41 201 G6
Crockford Br LYMN SO41 203 H6
Crockford Cl NMIL/BTOS BH25 225 M3
Crockford Rd EMRTH PO10 166 F4
Croft Cl WIMB BH21 217 H1
Croft Hts RSAL SP5 47 G5
Croftlands Av
FHAM/STUB PO14 184 A5
Croft La HISD PO11 189 L7
Crofton Av LSOL/BMARY PO13 184 A8
Crofton Cl CHCH/BSGR BH23 222 C8
PTSW SO17 106 F7 1
WVILLE PO7 164 A3
Crofton La FHAM/STUB PO14 183 M7
Crofton Rd ENEY PO4 211 M3
NEND PO2 187 J6
Crofton Wy BPWT SO32 111 M3
HLER SO31 158 A7
Croft Rd BKME/WDN BH12 234 A2
CHCH/BSGR BH23 223 M2
CHCH/BSGR BH23 238 E1
MOOR/WNTN BH9 220 D6
NEND PO2 187 H7 2
RGWD BH24 147 G7
The Croft CHFD SO53 81 H5 1
FHAM/STUB PO14 184 A4
TOTT SO40 104 B6
Cromarty Av ENEY PO4 211 M4
Cromarty Cl FHAM/STUB PO14 183 M5
Cromarty Rd ROWN SO16 105 K3
Crombie Cl HORN PO8 140 D4
Cromer Gdns
BKME/WDN BH12 234 E3 1
Cromer Rd BKME/WDN BH12 234 E3
CHAM PO6 163 H7
CHAR BH8 236 C1
ROWN SO16 105 J7
Cromhall Cl
FHAM/STUB PO14 160 A8 1
Crompton Wy FHAM PO15 159 G3
Cromwell Pl BOSC BH5 237 G3 4
Cromwell Rd
BKME/WDN BH12 234 C3
BOSC BH5 237 G3
ENEY PO4 211 M6
FUFL SO22 26 C2
WSHM SO15 131 K1
Crondall Av HAV PO9 165 J2
Crooked Hays Cl TOTT SO40 130 D7 1
Crooked Walk La WHAM PO17 162 C5
Crookham Cl HAV PO9 165 G4 2
Crookham Rd ITCH SO19 132 D8 2
Crookhorn La WVILLE PO7 164 C7
Crosby Rd WBNE BH4 235 H7 1
Crosfield Cl ROMY SO51 77 G6
Crossbill Cl HORN PO8 140 E1
Crosshouse Rd SHAM SO14 5 L6
Cross Keys Pas WINC SO23 3 H8 1
Crossland Cl GPORT PO12 11 G6
Crossland Dr HAV PO9 9 G1
Cross La BPWT SO32 84 F5
HORN PO8 140 E3
Crossmead Av
NMIL/BTOS BH25 225 L6
Cross Rd ITCH SO19 132 C1
LSOL/BMARY PO13 208 E4
Cross St BPWT SO32 85 H8
PSEA PO1 12 D1
SSEA PO5 13 J3 3
WINC SO23 2 F7
The Cross PSF GU32 61 J7
RGWD BH24 172 E5

RSAL SP5 .... 41 G1
Cross Wy *CHCH/BSGR* BH23 ... 222 B7
  HAV PO9 .... 8 C3
  RWIN SO51 .... 54 C3
Crossways *LYMN* SO41 ...... 227 H7
The Crossways *GPORT* PO12 .... 209 M2
  UPTN BH16 .... 232 B1
The Crossway
  FHAM/PORC PO16 .... 162 A8
Crosswell Cl *ITCH* SO19 .... 133 C3
Croucher's Cft *FUFL* SO22 ...... 16 A7
Croucheston Dro *RSAL* SP5 ..... 41 G1
Crouch La *HORN* PO8 .... 140 E1
Crow Arch La *RGWD* BH24 ..... 170 F2
Crow La *RGWD* BH24 .... 171 G2
Crown Cl *BKME/WDN* BH12 .... 234 A1
  WVILLE PO7 .... 140 A4
Crown Md *WIMB* BH21 .... 192 A3 ▢
Crown St *PSEA* PO1 .... 211 H2
  WSHM SO15 .... 106 A8
Crowsbury Cl *EMRTH* PO10 ..... 166 C5
Crows Nest La *BPWT* SO32 ...... 109 L7
Crowsport *HLER* SO31 .... 157 L5
Crowther Cl *ITCH* SO19 .... 133 G4
Croydon Cl *ROWN* SO16 .... 105 M4
Crummock Rd *CHFD* SO53 .... 80 F1
Crumpets Dr *UPTN* BH16 .... 216 B3
Crundles *EPSF* GU31 .... 63 M5
Crusader Rd *HEND* SO30 .... 134 B3
  WIMB BH21 .... 219 H4
Crusaders Wy *NBAD* SO52 ...... 80 E2
Cruse Cl *LYMN* SO41 .... 200 F6
Crystal Wy *WVILLE* PO7 .... 140 F1
Cucklington Gdns
  MOOR/WNTN BH9 .... 220 F5
Cuckmere La *ROWN* SO16 ...... 105 J8
Cuckoo Bushes La *CHFD* SO53 ... 53 G8
Cuckoo Hill Wy
  CHCH/BSGR BH23 .... 198 A7
Cuckoo La *FHAM/STUB* PO14 .... 183 M4
Cuckoo Rd *BKME/WDN* BH12 ... 218 G8
Cudnell Av *BWD* BH11 .... 219 L1
Cudworth Md *HEND* SO30 ...... 109 J7
Cuffnells Cl *RGWD* BH24 .... 122 F8
Cul-de-sac *NMIL/BTOS* BH25 ... 225 G8
Culford Cl *CHAR* BH8 .... 221 K6 ▢
Culford Wy *TOTT* SO40 .... 129 K2
Cull Cl *BKME/WDN* BH12 .... 220 A8
Culliford Crs *CFDH* BH17 .... 218 C6
Cull La *NMIL/BTOS* BH25 .... 225 M3
Culloden Cl *FHAM* PO15 .... 6 D3
Culloden Rd *FHAM/STUB* PO14 .. 184 D2
Cullwood La *NMIL/BTOS* BH25 ... 226 A2
Culver *HLER* SO31 .... 157 G1 ▢
Culver Cl *ROWN* SO16 .... 105 J6
Culver Dr *HISD* PO11 .... 214 D7
Culverley Cl *BROC* SO42 .... 175 K7 ▢
Culver Rd *ENEY* PO4 .... 211 L6
  NMIL/BTOS BH25 .... 225 K6
  WINC SO23 .... 26 E2
Culvers *EPSF* GU31 .... 93 G5
Culverwell Gdns *WINC* SO23 ..... 2 F1
Culvery Gdns *WEND* SO18 ...... 107 M6
Cumberland Cl *CHFD* SO53 ...... 81 K3
  EMRTH PO10 .... 166 C4
Cumberland Pl *WSHM* SO15 ...... 4 E1
Cumberland Rd *SSEA* PO5 .... 13 L2 ▢
Cumberland St *PSEA* PO1 .... 210 E2
  SHAM SO14 .... 5 J3 ▢
Cumberland Wy *FAWY* SO45 .... 155 H5
Cumber Rd *HLER* SO31 .... 158 C7
Cumbrian Wy *ROWN* SO16 ...... 105 K8
Cumnor Rd *BMTH* BH1 .... 15 C3
Cunard Av *WSHM* SO15 .... 106 B8
Cunard Rd *SHAM* SO14 .... 5 J7
Cunliffe Cl *SELS* PO20 .... 215 L6
Cunningham Cl *BPWT* SO32 ..... 84 F8 ▢
  CHCH/BSGR BH23 .... 219 L5 ▢
  RGWD BH24 .... 147 G8 ▢
Cunningham Crs *BWD* BH11 ..... 219 L5
  ITCH SO19 .... 132 F4 ▢
Cunningham Dr *HLER* SO31 ..... 158 C4
  LSOL/BMARY PO13 ...... 185 J1
Cunningham Pl *BWD* BH11 ...... 219 L5 ▢
Cunningham Rd *HORN* PO8 ...... 141 C1 ▢
  WVILLE PO7 .... 164 B3
Cupernham Cl *ROMY* SO51 ...... 50 F2
Cupernham La *ROMY* SO51 ...... 50 F5
Curdridge Cl *HAV* PO9 .... 165 L3 ▢
Curdridge La *BPWT* SO32 .... 110 F6
Curlew Cl *EMRTH* PO10 .... 166 C4
  FERN BH22 .... 193 M1
  ROWN SO16 .... 106 A3
Curlew Dr *FAWY* SO45 .... 155 M6
  FHAM/PORC PO16 .... 161 K8
Curlew Gdns *HORN* PO8 .... 140 F4
Curlew Rd *CHAR* BH8 .... 221 H6
  CHCH/BSGR BH23 .... 238 C7
The Curlews *VWD* BH31 .... 144 E3
Curlieu Rd *PLE* BH15 .... 233 K2 ▢
Curtis Md *NEND* PO2 .... 187 K4
Curtis Rd *BKME/WDN* BH12 .... 234 C4
Curtiss Gdns *GPORT* PO12 ...... 10 A3
The Curve *HORN* PO8 .... 140 D2
  LSOL/BMARY PO13 ...... 184 F6
Curzon Howe Rd *PSEA* PO1 ...... 12 D1
Curzon Pl *LYMN* SO41 .... 228 B6
Curzon Rd *CHAR* BH8 .... 236 C2
  PSTN BH14 .... 233 M5
  WVILLE PO7 .... 164 C1
Curzon Wy *CHCH/BSGR* BH23 ... 224 B8
Custards Rd *LYND* SO43 .... 151 K2
Cutbush La *WEND* SO18 .... 107 M6
  WEND SO18 .... 108 A6
Cuthbert Rd *PSEA* PO1 .... 211 K4
Cuthburga Rd *WIMB* BH21 ...... 192 A3 ▢
Cutler Cl *BKME/WDN* BH12 ..... 235 H1
  NMIL/BTOS BH25 .... 226 A5
Cutlers La *FHAM/STUB* PO14 .... 184 A5
Cutlers Pl *WIMB* BH21 .... 192 E3
Cutter Av *HLER* SO31 .... 158 C7
Cut Throat La *BPWT* SO32 .... 87 G6
  BPWT SO32 .... 112 B2
Cutts Arch *BPWT* SO32 .... 113 C1
Cygnet Ct *FHAM/PORC* PO16 ... 161 K8 ▢

Cygnet Rd *CHAM* PO6 .... 188 D1
Cygnus Gdns *FAWY* SO45 ...... 155 C5
Cynthia Cl *BKME/WDN* BH12 ... 234 A1
Cynthia Rd *BKME/WDN* BH12 ... 234 A1
Cypress Av *ITCH* SO19 .... 132 D3
Cypress Crs *HORN* PO8 .... 140 E3
Cypress Gdns *HEND* SO30 ...... 134 E1
  TOTT SO40 .... 129 C1 ▢
Cyprus Rd *FHAM/STUB* PO14 .... 159 G7
  NEND PO2 .... 187 J3
Cyril Rd *CHAR* BH8 .... 236 B2

D

Dacombe Cl *UPTN* BH16 .... 232 B1
Dacombe Dr *UPTN* BH16 .... 232 B1
Daffodil Rd *ROWN* SO16 .... 107 H4
Daggons Rd *FBDG* SP6 .... 121 G2
Dahlia Rd *ROWN* SO16 .... 106 F4 ▢
Daintree Cl *ITCH* SO19 .... 133 H5
Dairy Cl *CHCH/BSGR* BH23 ..... 238 C1
  RSAL SP5 .... 73 J3
  WIMB BH21 .... 216 F4
Dairy La *ROWN* SO16 .... 104 F4
Dairymoor *WHAM* PO17 .... 136 E4
Daisy Cl *GPORT* PO12 .... 10 D3
  HLER SO31 .... 158 F5
Daisy Md *WVILLE* PO7 .... 164 E2
Daisy Rd *ROWN* SO16 .... 107 H4
Dale Cl *WIMB* BH21 .... 193 C2
Dale Dr *LSOL/BMARY* PO13 .... 184 F3
Dale Rd *FAWY* SO45 .... 155 K5
  FHAM/STUB PO14 ...... 184 B5
  PLE BH15 .... 233 L2
  ROWN SO16 .... 106 B6
Dales Cl *WIMB* BH21 .... 193 C2
Dales Dr *WIMB* BH21 .... 192 F3
Dales Wy *TOTT* SO40 .... 104 A8
The Dale *WVILLE* PO7 .... 164 A6
Dale Valley Cl *ROWN* SO16 .... 106 B6
Dale Valley Gdns *ROWN* SO16 .. 106 B6
Dale Valley Rd *PLE* BH15 ...... 233 K1
  ROWN SO16 .... 106 B5
Dalewood Av *BWD* BH11 ...... 219 J3
Dalewood Rd *FHAM* PO15 .... 6 B3
Dalkeith Rd *BKME/WDN* BH12 .. 234 F5
  WIMB BH21 .... 217 H4 ▢
Dallington Cl
  FHAM/STUB PO14 ...... 184 A7 ▢
Dalmally Gdns *WEND* SO18 ..... 107 L8 ▢
Dalmeny Rd *SBNE* BH6 .... 237 M5
Damask Gdns *WVILLE* PO7 ..... 140 F7
Damen Cl *HEND* SO30 .... 133 M3
Damerham Rd *CHAR* BH8 .... 221 H5
Dampier Cl *LSOL/BMARY* PO13 .. 209 C1
Damson Hl *BPWT* SO32 .... 86 A8
Danbury Ct *EMRTH* PO10 .... 166 E6
Dances Wy *HISD* PO11 .... 213 J4
Dandelion Cl
  LSOL/BMARY PO13 ...... 184 F6 ▢
Dando Rd *WVILLE* PO7 .... 139 L4
Dandy's Ford La *ROMY* SO51 .... 48 E8
Danebury Cl *HAV* PO9 .... 165 J2 ▢
Danebury Gdns *CHFD* SO53 .... 80 F4 ▢
Danebury Wy *ROWN* SO16 ..... 105 J5
Dane Cl *FAWY* SO45 .... 180 D7
Danecourt Cl *PSTN* BH14 ...... 233 L4
Danecourt Rd *PSTN* BH14 ..... 233 L4
Danecrest Rd *LYMN* SO41 ..... 226 D5
Dane Dr *FERN* BH22 .... 194 C5
Danehurst New Rd
  LYMN SO41 .... 200 A8
Dane Rd *LYMN* SO41 .... 241 M2
Danesbrook La *WVILLE* PO7 .... 164 E1 ▢
Danesbury Av *SBNE* BH6 ...... 237 L4
Danes Cl *NMIL/BTOS* BH25 ... 240 F1
Danes Rd *FHAM/PORC* PO16 ... 161 M7
  ROMY SO51 .... 49 J4
  WINC SO23 .... 3 G4
Danestream Cl *LYMN* SO41 .... 242 C4 ▢
Daneswood Rd
  NMIL/BTOS BH25 ...... 226 A5 ▢
Daniell's Cl *LYMN* SO41 ...... 228 C5
Daniell's Wk *LYMN* SO41 ..... 228 C6
Dansie Cl *PSTN* BH14 .... 234 A4
Dapple Pl *TOTT* SO40 .... 130 E7
Darby's Cl *PLE* BH15 .... 233 J2
Darby's La *PLE* BH15 .... 233 J2
Dark La *CHCH/BSGR* BH23 .... 224 E4
  FAWY SO45 .... 180 D7
  NARL SO24 .... 30 C3
Darley Rd *FERN* BH22 .... 194 A5
Darlington Gdns *WSHM* SO15 .. 106 C8
Darlington Rd *ENEY* PO4 ...... 13 L5
Darracott Rd *BOSC* BH5 ...... 236 F4
Darren Cl *FHAM/STUB* PO14 ... 184 B4
Dartington Rd *ELGH* SO50 .... 82 C3
Dartmouth Rd *HSEA* PO3 ..... 187 L6
Dart Rd *WEND* SO18 .... 108 A5
Darwin Av *CHCH/BSGR* BH23 .. 222 C7
Darwin Rd *ELGH* SO50 .... 82 A4
  WSHM SO15 .... 131 H1
Darwin Wy *LSOL/BMARY* PO13 .. 209 H2
Daulston Rd *PSEA* PO1 .... 211 J1
Davenport Cl
  LSOL/BMARY PO13 .... 209 C2 ▢
  UPTN BH16 .... 232 B1 ▢
Daventry La *HSEA* PO3 ...... 188 A4
D Av *FAWY* SO45 .... 180 B2
David's La *RGWD* BH24 ...... 170 A3
David Wy *PLE* BH15 .... 232 C6
Davis Cl *LSOL/BMARY* PO13 .. 185 C8 ▢
Davis Fld *NMIL/BTOS* BH25 .. 225 K6
Davis Rd *PSTN* BH14 .... 234 A4
Davis Wy *NMIL/BTOS* BH25 .. 225 L6
Dawkins Wy *NMIL/BTOS* BH25 .. 225 L6
Dawlish Av *WSHM* SO15 ..... 106 C8
Dawnay Cl *ROWN* SO16 ...... 107 J3
Dawn Cl *NBNE* BH10 .... 220 A6
Dawn Gdns *FUFL* SO22 .... 26 B2
Daws Av *BWD* BH11 .... 219 M6
Dawson Rd *ITCH* SO19 ...... 133 G6 ▢
Day La *HORN* PO8 .... 140 D1

Daylesford Cl *PSTN* BH14 ..... 233 M6 ▢
Dayrell Cl *TOTT* SO40 .... 104 A7
Day's Ct *WIMB* BH21 .... 217 H3
Dayshes Cl *LSOL/BMARY* PO13 .. 184 F5
Dayslondon Rd *WVILLE* PO7 ... 164 B3
Deacon Cl *ITCH* SO19 .... 132 E5
Deacon Crs *ITCH* SO19 .... 132 E2
Deacon Rd *BWD* BH11 .... 219 L3
  HLER SO31 .... 158 F5
  ITCH SO19 .... 132 E5
Deal Cl *FHAM/STUB* PO14 .... 184 A4
Deal Rd *CHAM* PO6 .... 163 J7
Dean Cl *FUFL* SO22 .... 16 B6
  PLE BH15 .... 232 D5
Dean Ct *HEND* SO30 .... 133 M1
Deane Ct *HAV* PO9 .... 165 M3 ▢
Deane Down Dro *FUFL* SO22 ... 16 A4
The Deanery *CHFD* SO53 ..... 53 G8
Deane's Park Rd
  FHAM/PORC PO16 ...... 161 H7
Deanfield Cl *HLER* SO31 ...... 157 K6
Dean La *BPWT* SO32 .... 85 K5
  HORN PO8 .... 142 B3
  RSAL SP5 .... 87 G4
Dean Park Crs *BMTH* BH1 ..... 14 F4
  WCLF BH2 .... 14 F4
Dean Park Rd *BMTH* BH1 ..... 14 F4
Dean Rd *CHAM* PO6 .... 187 K1
  ELGH SO50 .... 83 G7
  RSAL SP5 .... 18 C5
  WEND SO18 .... 132 E1
Deans Ct *LYMN* SO41 ...... 242 C3
Deanscroft Rd *NBNE* BH10 ... 220 C4
Deans Dell *PSF* GU32 ...... 34 D7
Deans Ga *FHAM/STUB* PO14 .. 184 A7
Deans Gv *WIMB* BH21 ...... 192 B1
Deansleigh Rd *LTDN* BH7 .... 221 M7
Dean's Rd *BDST* BH5 .... 237 C3
The Deans *BMTH* BH1 .... 14 F3
Dean St *PSEA* PO1 .... 12 D2 ▢
Dean Swift Crs *PSTN* BH14 ... 234 B8
Deanswood Dr *WVILLE* PO7 ... 140 C7
Dear Hay La *PLE* BH15 ...... 233 H6
Dearing Cl *RGWD* BH24 ..... 151 K3
Decies Rd *PSTN* BH14 .... 234 A3 ▢
De Courtenai Cl *BWD* BH11 ... 219 J3
Dee Cl *CHFD* SO53 .... 80 F3
Deepdene La *BPWT* SO32 .... 219 J3 ▢
Deeping Cl *ITCH* SO19 ...... 132 D7 ▢
Deeping Ga *WVILLE* PO7 ..... 164 E1
Deerhurst Cl *TOTT* SO40 ..... 129 H2
Deerhurst Crs *CHAM* PO6 .... 162 E7
Deer Leap *FHAM* PO15 ...... 160 B3 ▢
Deerleap La *TOTT* SO40 ..... 129 J8
Deerleap Wy *FAWY* SO45 .... 155 L5
  NMIL/BTOS BH25 ..... 225 M2
Deer Park Cl
  NMIL/BTOS BH25 ..... 225 K4 ▢
Dee Wy *PLE* BH15 .... 233 C6
Defender Rd *ITCH* SO19 ..... 132 E5
De Grouchy La *PTSW* SO17 ... 106 F4
De Haviland Cl *WIMB* BH21 ... 192 D6
De Haviland Wy
  CHCH/BSGR BH23 ..... 238 F3
Delamere Gdns *NBNE* BH10 .. 220 C5
Delamere Rd *ENEY* PO4 ..... 13 M5
De La Warr Rd *LYMN* SO41 ... 242 B4
Delft Cl *HLER* SO31 .... 158 D5
Delft Gdns *WVILLE* PO7 ..... 140 B6
Delft Ms *CHCH/BSGR* BH23 .. 238 C2 ▢
Delhi Cl *PSTN* BH14 .... 234 C5
Delhi Rd *NBNE* BH10 ...... 220 C6
Delilah Rd *PLE* BH15 ...... 232 C6
De Lisle Cl *NEND* PO2 ...... 187 K4
De Lisle Rd *TWDS* BH3 ..... 235 L1
Delius Av *ITCH* SO19 ...... 133 H5
Dell Cl *BDST* BH18 .... 217 J4
  CHAM PO6 .... 163 M6
  ELGH SO50 .... 83 H7
Dellcrest Pth *CHAM* PO6 .... 163 M7
Dellfield *PSF* GU32 .... 34 D6
Dellfield Cl *CHAM* PO6 ..... 162 E7 ▢
Dell Piece East *HORN* PO8 ... 141 H3
Dell Piece West *HORN* PO8 .. 141 C3
Dell Quay Cl *FHAM/STUB* PO14 .. 184 E6
Dell Rd *WEND* SO18 .... 107 L6
  WINC SO23 .... 27 C2
The Dell *FHAM/PORC* PO16 ... 161 H7
  HAV PO9 .... 165 J1 ▢
  NMIL/BTOS BH25 ..... 225 C8
Delme Dr *FHAM/PORC* PO16 .. 161 H6
Delph Cl *WIMB* BH21 ...... 192 B8
Delph Rd *WIMB* BH21 ...... 192 B8
Delta Cl *CHCH/BSGR* BH23 .. 238 F1
Ditcham Crs *HAV* PO9 ...... 165 J4
De Mauley Rd *CCLF* BH13 ... 234 D8
De Montfort Rd *WIMB* BH21 .. 192 B7
De Mowbray Wy *LYMN* SO41 .. 228 B6 ▢
Dempsey Cl *ITCH* SO19 ..... 132 F4
Denbigh Cl *ELGH* SO50 ..... 81 L3
  TOTT SO40 .... 129 H3
Denbigh Dr *FHAM/PORC* PO16 .. 6 B5
Denbigh Gdns *ROWN* SO16 ... 106 E4
Denby Rd *PLE* BH15 .... 233 J4
Dene Cl *HLER* SO31 .... 158 C4
  RGWD BH24 .... 147 G3
  ROWN SO16 .... 105 J5
Dene Hollow *CHAM* PO6 .... 164 B8
Dene Rd *TOTT* SO40 .... 129 C6
Deneside Copse *LYMN* SO41 .. 227 M7
Deneside Gdns *LYMN* SO41 ... 227 M6
Deneve Av *CFDH* BH17 ..... 218 A1
Dene Wk *FERN* BH22 .... 194 C7
Dene Wy *TOTT* SO40 .... 129 C5
Denewood Copse
  FERN BH22 .... 168 B5 ▢
Denewood Rd *FERN* BH22 ... 168 B4
  WBNE BH4 .... 235 C1
Denewulf Cl *BPWT* SO32 .... 85 H8 ▢
Denham Cl *CFDH* BH17 ..... 218 C5
  FHAM/STUB PO14 ..... 183 M6
  WINC SO23 .... 2 F5
Denham Ct *WINC* SO23 ...... 3 G3
Denham Dr *CHCH/BSGR* BH23 .. 224 D7
Denham Gdns *HLER* SO31 ... 156 F3
Denhill Cl *HISD* PO11 ...... 213 J3
Denholm Cl *RGWD* BH24 .... 147 H3

Denison Rd *CFDH* BH17 ..... 218 A1
Denmark La *PLE* BH15 ...... 233 J5
Denmark Rd
  MOOR/WNTN BH9 ..... 220 D7
  PLE BH15 .... 233 J5
Denmead *NMIL/BTOS* BH25 .. 226 B4 ▢
  WEND SO18 .... 108 B8
Dennis Rd *WIMB* BH21 ..... 217 H3
Dennistoun Av
  CHCH/BSGR BH23 .... 238 E1
Dennis Wy *LISS* GU33 ..... 36 F5
Denny Cl *FAWY* SO45 ...... 180 F5 ▢
Denville Av *FHAM/PORC* PO16 .. 186 B2
Denville Cl *CHAM* PO6 ..... 164 D8
Denvilles Cl *HAV* PO9 .... 9 J2
Denzil Av *HLER* SO31 .... 157 C2
Depedene Cl *FAWY* SO45 .... 179 M4
De Port Hts *BPWT* SO32 ..... 87 H2
Derby Rd *BMTH* BH1 .... 15 M4
  ELGH SO50 .... 81 L6
  NEND PO2 .... 187 H7
  SHAM SO14 .... 5 J1
De Redvers Rd *PSTN* BH14 ... 234 B8
Dereham Wy *BKME/WDN* BH12 .. 234 C2
Deridene Ct *TOTT* SO40 .... 129 H2
Derlyn Rd *FHAM/PORC* PO16 ... 7 H5
Derritt La *CHCH/BSGR* BH23 .. 223 C1
Derrybrian Gdns
  NMIL/BTOS BH25 ..... 225 L6 ▢
Derwent Cl *FERN* BH22 ..... 194 E2
  FHAM/STUB PO14 ..... 184 B4 ▢
  HORN PO8 .... 116 B6
  MOOR/WNTN BH9 .... 220 E6 ▢
  WEND SO18 .... 108 A7
Derwent Dr *TOTT* SO40 .... 104 A8
Derwent Rd *LSOL/BMARY* PO13 .. 208 D3
  NMIL/BTOS BH25 ..... 225 M3
  ROWN SO16 .... 105 K7
Derwentwater Rd *WIMB* BH21 .. 192 B6
Desborough Cl *CHAM* PO6 ... 162 E7 ▢
Desborough Rd *ELGH* SO50 ... 81 M6
Devenish Rd *FUFL* SO22 ...... 2 B1
Deverel Cl *CHCH/BSGR* BH23 .. 222 E8
Deverell Pl *WVILLE* PO7 .... 164 B3
Devine Gdns *ELGH* SO50 ..... 82 D6 ▢
Devon Dr *CHFD* SO53 .... 81 H5
Devon Rd *CHCH/BSGR* BH23 .. 222 C8
  HSEA PO3 .... 187 L5
  PLE BH15 .... 233 K3
Devonshire Av *ENEY* PO4 ... 211 M4
Devonshire Gdns *FAWY* SO45 .. 155 L8 ▢
  HLER SO31 .... 133 K6 ▢
  HLER SO31 .... 133 L6 ▢
Devonshire Rd *WSHM* SO15 .. 131 K2
Devonshire Sq *ENEY* PO4 ... 211 K4
Devonshire Wy
  FHAM/STUB PO14 ..... 160 A8
Dewlands Rd *VWD* BH31 .... 144 B1
Dewlands Wy *VWD* BH31 ... 144 B2
Dew La *ELGH* SO50 .... 81 L5
Dewlish Cl *CFDH* BH17 ..... 218 E6
Dial Cl *CHCH/BSGR* BH23 ... 198 A6
Diamond Cl *FBDG* SP6 .... 97 K8 ▢
Diamond St *SSEA* PO5 ...... 12 F5 ▢
Diana Cl *EMRTH* PO10 ..... 166 C4
  GPORT PO12 .... 209 J4
Diana Wy *WIMB* BH21 ..... 217 J1
Dibble Dr *NBAD* SO52 ..... 79 C5
Dibden Cl *CHAR* BH8 ...... 221 H5
  HAV PO9 .... 165 G4 ▢
Dibden Lodge Cl *FAWY* SO45 .. 155 K3
Dibles Rd *HLER* SO31 ...... 158 B7
Dickens Cl *NEND* PO2 ...... 211 H1 ▢
Dickens Dell *TOTT* SO40 .... 128 F1
Dickens Dr *HLER* SO31 .... 135 C8
Dickens Rd *SBNE* BH6 ..... 237 J1
Dickson Pl *WHAM* PO17 .... 136 E1
Didcot Rd *WSHM* SO15 .... 106 B7 ▢
Dieppe Crs *NEND* PO2 ..... 187 J4
Dieppe Gdns *GPORT* PO12 ... 10 B3
Diligence Cl *HLER* SO31 .... 133 L7
Dilly La *NMIL/BTOS* BH25 .. 240 F1
Dimond Cl *WEND* SO18 .... 107 K7
Dimond Hl *WEND* SO18 .... 107 K7
Dimond Rd *WEND* SO18 .... 107 K6
Dingle Rd *BOSC* BH5 ...... 237 C4
Dingle Wy *HLER* SO31 .... 158 C4
Dingley Rd *PLE* BH15 ..... 233 K4
Dinham Rd *NMIL/BTOS* BH25 .. 226 B4 ▢
Diprose Rd *WIMB* BH21 .... 217 J1
Discovery Cl
  FHAM/STUB PO14 ..... 184 A3 ▢
Disraeli Cl *CHCH/BSGR* BH23 .. 238 C2
Ditcham Crs *HAV* PO9 ..... 165 J4
Ditchbury *LYMN* SO41 ..... 228 B3
Ditton Cl *FHAM/STUB* PO14 .. 184 A5
Dockenfield Cl *HAV* PO9 .... 165 G4 ▢
Dock La *BROC* SO42 .... 178 F7
Dock Rd *GPORT* PO12 ...... 11 H4
Doctor's Hl *ROMY* SO51 .... 48 F5
Doctors La *PSF* GU32 ...... 60 B3
Dodds La *BPWT* SO32 ...... 112 A3
Dodgson Cl *FBDG* SP6 ...... 72 D8
Dodwell La *HLER* SO31 .... 133 M5
Doe Copse Wy
  NMIL/BTOS BH25 ..... 225 J4
Dogkennel La *WVILLE* PO7 ... 114 E8
Dogwood Dell *WVILLE* PO7 ... 164 D3 ▢
Dogwood Rd *WIMB* BH21 ... 217 H1
Dolbery Rd North
  BKME/WDN BH12 .... 219 H6
Dolbery Rd South
  BKME/WDN BH12 .... 219 G7
Dolman Rd *GPORT* PO12 ... 11 H5
Dolphin Av *NBNE* BH10 ... 220 C5
Dolphin Cl *ELGH* SO50 .... 82 E6
Dolphin Ct
  FHAM/STUB PO14 ..... 183 M4 ▢
  HLER SO31 .... 158 F3
Dolphin Crs *GPORT* PO12 ... 10 F5
Dolphin Hl *RWIN* SO21 .... 54 F3
Dolphin Pl *NMIL/BTOS* BH25 .. 240 F1 ▢
Dolton Rd *ROWN* SO16 .... 105 J8
Dome Aly *WINC* SO23 ...... 3 C4 ▢
Dominion Rd *BWD* BH11 ... 219 J5
Domum Rd *NEND* PO2 ..... 187 K6
  WINC SO23 .... 27 G2

Domvilles Ap *NEND* PO2 .... 186 F7
Donaldson Rd *CHAM* PO6 ... 187 K2
Doncaster Rd *ELGH* SO50 ... 81 M8
Donigers Dell *BPWT* SO32 ... 111 M2
Donnelly Rd *SBNE* BH6 .... 237 L3
Donnelly St *GPORT* PO12 ... 209 L2
Donnington Dr
  CHCH/BSGR BH23 .... 239 C1
  CHFD SO53 .... 80 F5
Donnington Gv *PTSW* SO17 .. 107 C5
Donoughmore Rd *BMTH* BH1 .. 236 C4
Dorcas Cl *WVILLE* PO7 .... 140 E7 ▢
Dorchester Gdns *PLE* BH15 .. 233 K3
Dorchester Rd *PLE* BH15 ... 233 K2
Dore Av *FHAM/PORC* PO16 .. 161 M8
Dores La *ROMY* SO51 ...... 24 A6
Doric Cl *CHFD* SO53 .... 81 L1
Dorking Crs *CHAM* PO6 .... 187 K1
Dorland Gdns *TOTT* SO40 .. 129 H2
Dormington Rd *CHAM* PO6 .. 163 G7
Dormy Cl *HLER* SO31 ..... 158 B5
Dormy Wy *LSOL/BMARY* PO13 .. 184 F7
Dornie Rd *CCLF* BH13 ..... 245 J1
Dornmere La *WVILLE* PO7 ... 164 E1 ▢
Dorothy Dymond St
  PSEA PO1 .... 13 G2 ▢
Dorrien Rd *GPORT* PO12 ... 209 M1
Dorrita Av *HORN* PO8 ..... 140 F4
Dorrita Cl *ENEY* PO4 ...... 211 K6
The Dorrits *TOTT* SO40 .... 128 F1
Dorset Av *FERN* BH22 .... 194 B4
Dorset Cl *HORN* PO8 ...... 140 F4
Dorset Lake Av *PSTN* BH14 .. 234 A8
Dorset Rd *CHCH/BSGR* BH23 .. 223 K8
  CHFD SO53 .... 81 H5 ▢
  WBNE BH4 .... 235 H3
Dorset St *PTSW* SO17 ..... 131 L2
Dorset Wy *BKME/WDN* BH12 .. 218 E8
  PLE BH15 .... 233 J1
Dorstone Rd *CHAM* PO6 ... 163 G7 ▢
Douglas Av *CHCH/BSGR* BH23 .. 237 L2
Douglas Cl *UPTN* BH16 .... 232 B1
Douglas Crs *ITCH* SO19 ... 133 G2
Douglas Gdns
  BKME/WDN BH12 .... 234 D3
  HAV PO9 .... 165 L4 ▢
Douglas Ms *SBNE* BH6 .... 237 H3 ▢
Douglas Rd *BKME/WDN* BH12 .. 234 D3
  PSEA PO1 .... 211 K1
  SBNE BH6 .... 237 K5
Douglas Wy *FAWY* SO45 ... 155 J4
Doulton Gdns *PSTN* BH14 .. 234 A4
Doussie Cl *UPTN* BH16 .... 216 E8
Dove Cl *HORN* PO8 .... 140 D4
Dove Dl *ELGH* SO50 ...... 82 D3
Dove Gdns *HLER* SO31 .... 158 F3 ▢
Dover Cl *CCLF* BH13 ..... 234 F5
  FHAM/STUB PO14 ..... 183 M5
Dovercourt Rd *CHAM* PO6 .. 187 L2
Dover Rd *CCLF* BH13 ..... 234 F5
  HSEA PO3 .... 187 L8
Dover St *SHAM* SO14 ..... 131 L1
Doveshill Crs *NBNE* BH10 .. 220 B5
Doveshill Gdns *NBNE* BH10 .. 220 B5
Doves La *RSAL* SP5 ...... 46 D3
Doveys Cl *RGWD* BH24 ... 172 E5 ▢
Dowds Cl *HEND* SO30 .... 109 C8
Dowlands Cl *NBNE* BH10 .. 220 B4 ▢
Dowlands Rd *NBNE* BH10 .. 220 A4
Down End Cl *CHAM* PO6 .. 164 A7
Down End Rd *CHAM* PO6 .. 164 A7
Downend Rd
  FHAM/PORC PO16 ...... 161 L6
Downey Cl *BWD* BH11 .... 219 K6
Down Farm Pl *HORN* PO8 .. 116 B7 ▢
Downham Cl *HORN* PO8 ... 140 D5
Downhouse Rd *HORN* PO8 .. 115 M4
Downland Cl *HEND* SO30 .. 134 C1
  HLER SO31 .... 158 C4
Downland Pl *HEND* SO30 .. 133 M4
Downlands Cl *RSAL* SP5 ... 72 C3
Downlands Rd *FUFL* SO22 .. 26 A4
Downley Rd *HAV* PO9 .... 165 M4
Down Lodge Cl *FBDG* SP6 .. 121 L2 ▢
Downs Cl *WVILLE* PO7 .... 164 D5
Downscroft Gdns
  HEND SO30 .... 109 C8 ▢
  HEND SO30 .... 133 M1 ▢
Downside *LSOL/BMARY* PO13 .. 185 H6
Downside Av *ITCH* SO19 .. 132 C3
Downside Rd *FUFL* SO22 ... 22 A2
  WVILLE PO7 .... 164 A5 ▢
Down's Park Av *TOTT* SO40 .. 129 L2
Down's Park Crs *TOTT* SO40 .. 129 L2
Down's Park Rd *TOTT* SO40 .. 129 L2
The Downsway
  FHAM/PORC PO16 ...... 162 A8
Downton Cl *CHAR* BH8 .... 221 C5
Downton Hl *RSAL* SP5 .... 73 H1
Downton La *LYMN* SO41 .. 241 L2
Downton Rd *WEND* SO18 .. 107 L6
Downview Rd *FAWY* SO45 .. 155 G6 ▢
Downwood Cl *FAWY* SO45 .. 155 G6 ▢
  FBDG SP6 .... 97 J2
Downwood Wy *HORN* PO8 .. 116 B7
Doyle Av *NEND* PO2 ..... 187 J4
Doyle Cl *NEND* PO2 ..... 187 J4
Doyle Ct *ITCH* SO19 ..... 132 D7
Doyne Rd *PSTN* BH14 .... 234 D4
Dradfield La *BPWT* SO32 ... 113 H8
Dragon La *RGWD* BH24 ... 170 F2
Dragon St *EPSF* GU31 .... 63 L6
Dragoon Cl *ITCH* SO19 ... 133 G4
Dragoon Wy
  CHCH/BSGR BH23 .... 237 L1
Drake Cl *CHCH/BSGR* BH23 .. 238 E2 ▢
  HLER SO31 .... 158 F3
  NMIL/BTOS BH25 ..... 225 K5
  RGWD BH24 .... 147 G2
  TOTT SO40 .... 130 D6
Drakeleys Fld *LIPH* GU30 ... 38 E6
Drake Rd *ELGH* SO50 ..... 82 D4
  LSOL/BMARY PO13 .... 185 J1
  PLE BH15 .... 233 H7 ▢
Drakes Cl *FAWY* SO45 .... 155 K6 ▢
Draper Rd *BWD* BH11 .... 219 L4

CHCH/BSGR BH23 ..... 238 D1
Draycote Rd HORN PO8 ..... 116 B5
Draycott Rd NBNE BH10 ..... 220 B6
Drayton Cl ITCH SO19 ..... 132 D8
Drayton La CHAM PO6 ..... 163 M7
Drayton Pl TOTT SO40 ..... 129 H1
Drayton Rd NPO2 ..... 187 J7
Drayton St FUFL SO22 ..... 26 B2
Dreadnought Rd
FHAM/STUB PO14 ..... 184 C3
Dresden Dr HORN PO8 ..... 140 B6
Dreswick Cl CHCH/BSGR BH23 ..... 242 B4
Drift Rd FHAM/PORC PO16 ..... 7 M3
HORN PO8 ..... 116 A3
The Drift HAV PO9 ..... 141 M7
Driftwood Gdns ENEY PO4 ..... 212 A6
TOTT SO40 ..... 129 G2
Drill Shed Rd NEND PO2 ..... 186 F7
Drinkwater Cl ELGH SO50 ..... 81 L5
The Drive EMRTH PO10 ..... 167 H8
FHAM/PORC PO16 ..... 7 C5
HAV PO9 ..... 8 E1
HEND SO30 ..... 108 A5
LSOL/BMARY PO13 ..... 184 C6
PSTN BH14 ..... 234 C3 [3]
ROMY SO51 ..... 47 L7
ROMY SO51 ..... 76 F6
TOTT SO40 ..... 129 K3
Drove Cl RWIN SO21 ..... 54 E3
Drove Rd ITCH SO19 ..... 132 F4
WHAM PO17 ..... 162 E4
The Drove BPWT SO32 ..... 84 C8
BPWT SO32 ..... 112 A3
ELGH SO50 ..... 109 J2
FAWY SO45 ..... 180 C7
HEND SO30 ..... 108 C5
ROMY SO51 ..... 76 D5
RWIN SO21 ..... 54 E3
TOTT SO40 ..... 104 A7
WEND SO18 ..... 132 E1
Droxford Cl GPORT PO12 ..... 10 B3 [3]
Droxford Rd BPWT SO32 ..... 112 B4
LTDN BH7 ..... 237 G2
Druids Cl FERN BH22 ..... 194 B6
Druitt Rd CHCH/BSGR BH23 ..... 223 K8
Drum Md PSF GU32 ..... 63 K5
Drummond Cl FUFL SO22 ..... 26 D3 [3]
Drummond Rd BMTH BH1 ..... 236 C4
FAWY SO45 ..... 155 L4 [3]
HEND SO30 ..... 109 H7
PSEA PO1 ..... 211 H2 [3]
Drummond Wy CHFD SO53 ..... 53 G8 [3]
Drury Rd WBNE BH4 ..... 235 G6 [3]
Dryden Av CHAM PO6 ..... 162 C7
Dryden Cl FHAM/PORC PO16 ..... 6 F4
RGWD BH24 ..... 169 J3
WVILLE PO7 ..... 140 B6
Dryden Pl LYMN SO41 ..... 242 C3
Dryden Rd ITCH SO19 ..... 133 J3
Drysdale Ms ENEY PO4 ..... 211 M6 [3]
Ducking Stool La
CHCH/BSGR BH23 ..... 238 A2
Duck Island La RGWD BH24 ..... 170 E2 [3]
Duck La BWD BH11 ..... 219 K4
Duckmead La LISS GU33 ..... 37 L1
Duddon Cl WEND SO18 ..... 108 A7
Dudleston Heath Dr
HORN PO8 ..... 140 F6
Dudley Av FBDG SP6 ..... 97 L5
LYMN SO41 ..... 226 D6
Dudley Gdns NBNE BH10 ..... 220 B3 [3]
Dudley Rd HSEA PO3 ..... 211 L1 [3]
NBNE BH10 ..... 220 B3
Dudmoor Farm Rd
CHCH/BSGR BH23 ..... 222 D5
Dudmoor La CHCH/BSGR BH23 ..... 222 D4
Dudsbury Av FERN BH22 ..... 194 B4
Dudsbury Crs FERN BH22 ..... 194 C8
Dudsbury Gdns FERN BH22 ..... 194 C8
Dudsbury Rd FERN BH22 ..... 194 B6
Duffield La EMRTH PO10 ..... 167 H5
Dugald Drummond St
PSEA PO1 ..... 13 G2 [3]
Dugdell Cl FERN BH22 ..... 194 D2 [3]
Duisburg Wy SSEA PO5 ..... 12 C6
Duke Av PSEA PO1 ..... 211 H1
Duke Rd HEND SO30 ..... 134 B3
Dukes Cl PSF GU32 ..... 63 J4
Dukes Dr BWD BH11 ..... 219 J3
Dukesfield CHCH/BSGR BH23 ..... 223 L2
Dukes Rd GPORT PO12 ..... 209 L2
SHAM SO14 ..... 107 C8
Duke St SHAM SO14 ..... 5 J5
Dukeswood Dr FAWY SO45 ..... 155 K7
Dulsie Rd TWDS BH3 ..... 235 H1
Dumbarton Cl NEND PO2 ..... 187 H8 [3]
Dumbleton Cl ITCH SO19 ..... 133 K4
Dummer Ct HAV PO9 ..... 165 H2
Dummers Rd ROMY SO51 ..... 51 J1
Dumpers Dro ELGH SO50 ..... 109 J2
Dumpford La EPSF GU31 ..... 65 L8
Dunbar Cl ROWN SO16 ..... 105 L3
Dunbar Crs CHCH/BSGR BH23 ..... 224 D6
Dunbar Rd ENEY PO4 ..... 211 M4
TWDS BH3 ..... 235 K2
Dunbridge La ROMY SO51 ..... 21 L3
Duncan Cl ITCH SO19 ..... 132 C9
Duncan Rd HLER SO31 ..... 158 F3
NMIL/BTOS BH25 ..... 226 B4
SSEA PO5 ..... 13 K7
Duncans Dr
FHAM/STUB PO14 ..... 159 M8 [3]
Duncliff Rd SBNE BH6 ..... 237 M4
Duncombe Dr RGWD BH24 ..... 145 M6
Duncombe Rd PSF GU32 ..... 61 J8
Duncton Rd HORN PO8 ..... 116 C3
Dundas Cl HSEA PO3 ..... 187 M6
Dundas La HSEA PO3 ..... 187 M7
Dundas Rd CFDH BH17 ..... 218 C8
Dundas Sp HSEA PO3 ..... 187 M6
Dundee Cl FHAM PO15 ..... 6 D2
Dundee Rd PTSW SO17 ..... 107 H7
Dundonald Cl HISD PO11 ..... 213 L3
Dundridge La BPWT SO32 ..... 85 K7
Dundry Wy HEND SO30 ..... 134 A1
Dunedin Cl FERN BH22 ..... 193 M5

Dunedin Dr FERN BH22 ..... 193 M5
Dunedin Gdns FERN BH22 ..... 193 M5
Dunedin Gv CHCH/BSGR BH23 ..... 239 H1
Dunford Cl NMIL/BTOS BH25 ..... 225 J8 [2]
Dunford Rd BKME/WDN BH12 ..... 234 C3
Dunhurst Cl HAV PO9 ..... 165 L5
Dunkeld Rd GPORT PO12 ..... 209 L1
TWDS BH3 ..... 235 J2
Dunkirk Cl ROWN SO16 ..... 106 C4
Dunkirk Rd ROWN SO16 ..... 106 C4
Dunlin Cl CHCH/BSGR BH23 ..... 239 G3
ENEY PO4 ..... 212 B3
Dunn Cl ENEY PO4 ..... 211 M5
Dunnings La NBAD SO52 ..... 79 K3
Dunnock Cl HAV PO9 ..... 141 M7
Dunsbury Wy HAV PO9 ..... 165 J3
Dunsmore Cl SSEA PO5 ..... 13 H4 [2]
Dunstans La PSTN BH14 ..... 233 L2
Dunster Cl ROWN SO16 ..... 106 B3
Dunvegan Dr ROWN SO16 ..... 106 B3
Durban Cl ROMY SO51 ..... 50 F7
Durban Rd PSEA PO1 ..... 211 K1
Durdells Av BWD BH11 ..... 219 L3
Durdells Gdns BWD BH11 ..... 219 L3
Durford Ct HAV PO9 ..... 165 H2 [2]
Durford Rd EPSF GU31 ..... 64 B5
Durham Gdns WVILLE PO7 ..... 164 D3
Durham St GPORT PO12 ..... 209 L2
PSEA PO1 ..... 13 H1
Durland Cl NMIL/BTOS BH25 ..... 225 L7
Durlands Rd HORN PO8 ..... 116 B8 [2]
Durley Av HORN PO8 ..... 140 D5
Durley Brook Rd BPWT SO32 ..... 109 L2
Durley Chine Rd WCLF BH2 ..... 14 B6
Durley Chine Rd South
WCLF BH2 ..... 14 B8
Durley Crs TOTT SO40 ..... 129 H3
Durley Gdns WCLF BH2 ..... 14 B8
Durley Hall La WCLF BH2 ..... 14 A7
Durley Rbt WCLF BH2 ..... 14 B7
Durley Rd ELGH SO50 ..... 109 K1
GPORT PO12 ..... 209 L2
WCLF BH2 ..... 14 C7
Durley Rd South WCLF BH2 ..... 14 C7
Durley St BPWT SO32 ..... 110 C1
ROWN SO16 ..... 105 H7
Durnford Rd SHAM SO14 ..... 131 M2
Durngate Pl WINC SO23 ..... 3 J7
Durngate Ter WINC SO23 ..... 3 J7
Durnstown LYMN SO41 ..... 201 G6
Durrant Rd PSTN BH14 ..... 234 B5
WCLF BH2 ..... 14 D4
Durrants Gdns HAV PO9 ..... 141 M8
Durrants Rd HAV PO9 ..... 165 M1
Durrant Wy LYMN SO41 ..... 200 F6
Durrington Pl LTDN BH7 ..... 237 G2 [2]
Durrington Rd LTDN BH7 ..... 237 G1
Dursley Crs CHAM PO6 ..... 163 G8
Durweston Cl CHAR BH8 ..... 221 G5 [3]
Dutton La ELGH SO50 ..... 82 A5
Duttons Rd ROMY SO51 ..... 50 D8
Dyer Rd WSHM SO15 ..... 131 G1
Dymewood Rd WIMB BH21 ..... 168 C1
Dymoke St EMRTH PO10 ..... 166 C4
Dymott Cl WSHM SO15 ..... 4 A1
Dyram Cl ELGH SO50 ..... 81 L3
Dysart Av CHAM PO6 ..... 187 M1
Dyserth Cl ITCH SO19 ..... 132 F7
Dyson Dr WINC SO23 ..... 3 H2

E

Eadens La TOTT SO40 ..... 128 B1
Eagle Av HORN PO8 ..... 140 B4
Eagle Cl CHFD SO53 ..... 81 G4
FHAM/PORC PO16 ..... 161 K8 [3]
Eagle Rd BKME/WDN BH12 ..... 234 F4
LSOL/BMARY PO13 ..... 208 B1
Earle Rd WBNE BH4 ..... 235 H7
Earlham Dr PSTN BH14 ..... 234 B4
Earls Cl ELGH SO50 ..... 82 F6
Earlsdon St SSEA PO5 ..... 13 G4 [2]
Earlsdon Wy
CHCH/BSGR BH23 ..... 224 D8
Earls Rd FHAM/PORC PO16 ..... 7 J9
SHAM SO14 ..... 106 F8
Earlswood Dr FBDG SP6 ..... 121 K3
Earnley Rd HISD PO11 ..... 214 D6
Earthpits La RSAL SP5 ..... 68 A6
East Av NMIL/BTOS BH25 ..... 240 B1
TWDS BH3 ..... 235 H2
East Bank Rd BROC SO42 ..... 175 L8
East Boldre Rd BROC SO42 ..... 204 A1
Eastbourne Av GPORT PO12 ..... 185 L8
WSHM SO15 ..... 106 C8
Eastbourne Rd HSEA PO3 ..... 187 L8 [3]
Eastbrook Cl GPORT PO12 ..... 185 K8 [3]
HLER SO31 ..... 158 E3
East Cams Cl
FHAM/PORC PO16 ..... 161 K7 [3]
Eastchurch Cl ROWN SO16 ..... 105 L4
Eastcliff Cl LSOL/BMARY PO13 ..... 208 C1
East Cliff Wy
CHCH/BSGR BH23 ..... 239 H1
East Cl NMIL/BTOS BH25 ..... 225 H8
East Cosham Rd CHAM PO6 ..... 163 M8
Eastcot Cl FAWY SO45 ..... 179 M5
Eastcott Cl LTDN BH7 ..... 236 F1 [2]
East Ct CHAM PO6 ..... 163 M8
Eastcroft Rd GPORT PO12 ..... 10 C1
East Dean Rd ROMY SO51 ..... 20 C6
Eastdene Cl FAWY SO45 ..... 82 C4
Eastern Av HSEA PO3 ..... 211 M2
Eastern Pde ENEY PO4 ..... 211 K7
FHAM/PORC PO16 ..... 7 K9
Eastern Rd CHAM PO6 ..... 188 B2
ENEY PO4 ..... 211 M3
HAV PO9 ..... 9 G3
HEND SO30 ..... 108 C7
HSEA PO3 ..... 188 A4
LYMN SO41 ..... 228 B4
NEND PO2 ..... 186 F6
Eastern Villas Rd ENEY PO4 ..... 211 H7 [2]

Eastern Wy FHAM/PORC PO16 ..... 7 L6
LYMN SO41 ..... 242 E4
Easter Rd MOOR/WNTN BH9 ..... 220 L6
Eastfield Av FHAM/STUB PO14 ..... 184 D2
East Field Cl EMRTH PO10 ..... 167 A6
Eastfield Cl RGWD BH24 ..... 171 G1
Eastfield La EPSF GU31 ..... 93 K5
RGWD BH24 ..... 147 G8
Eastfield Rd CHAM PO6 ..... 162 F6
ENEY PO4 ..... 211 L5
Eastgate St SHAM SO14 ..... 5 C5
WINC SO23 ..... 3 J8
East Harting St EPSF GU31 ..... 93 J5
East HI LYMN SO41 ..... 228 C4
East Hill Cl FHAM/PORC PO16 ..... 161 H6
East Hill Dr LISS GU33 ..... 36 F5
East Hoe Rd WVILLE PO7 ..... 113 M5
East House Av
FHAM/STUB PO14 ..... 184 B6
East Howe La NBNE BH10 ..... 220 A4
Eastlake Av BKME/WDN BH12 ..... 234 A2
Eastlake Cl EPSF GU31 ..... 64 B5
Eastlands NMIL/BTOS BH25 ..... 225 M7
East La LYMN SO41 ..... 227 J7
Eastleigh Rd ELGH SO50 ..... 83 H7
East Leigh Rd HAV PO9 ..... 166 A5
East Ldg FHAM PO15 ..... 160 A7
East Lodge Pk CHAM PO6 ..... 164 D8
Eastman Cl RSAL SP5 ..... 72 F2 [3]
Eastmeare Ct TOTT SO40 ..... 128 E5
Eastney Farm Rd ENEY PO4 ..... 212 A5 [3]
Eastney Rd ENEY PO4 ..... 211 M5
Eastney St ENEY PO4 ..... 211 M6 [3]
Eastoke Av HISD PO11 ..... 214 B7
Easton La RWIN SO21 ..... 17 J6
WINC SO23 ..... 3 L6
East Overcliff Dr BMTH BH1 ..... 15 H7
Eastover Ct HAV PO9 ..... 165 H2
East Park Ter SHAM SO14 ..... 5 G1
East Quay Rd PLE BH15 ..... 233 H7
East Rd FAWY SO45 ..... 156 B8
WHAM PO17 ..... 162 E2
Eastshaw La MIDH GU29 ..... 67 M4
East Strd SELS PO20 ..... 215 K8
East St EMRTH PO10 ..... 166 F5
FHAM/PORC PO16 ..... 7 M6
FHAM/STUB PO14 ..... 159 K8
HAV PO9 ..... 8 F5
PLE BH15 ..... 233 H6
PSEA PO1 ..... 12 B4
SHAM SO14 ..... 5 G6
WVILLE PO7 ..... 114 C5
East Surrey St PSEA PO1 ..... 13 H1 [2]
East View Rd RGWD BH24 ..... 170 F1
Eastville Rd ELGH SO50 ..... 83 H7
East Wy CHAR BH8 ..... 220 F7
WIMB BH21 ..... 217 H3
Eastways BPWT SO32 ..... 111 H1
Eastwood Av FERN BH22 ..... 194 C2
Eastwood Cl HISD PO11 ..... 213 M4
East Woodhay Rd FUFL SO22 ..... 16 C4 [3]
Eastwood Rd NEND PO2 ..... 187 J4 [2]
Eastworth Rd VWD BH31 ..... 144 C1
Eaton Rd CCLF BH13 ..... 234 F6
E Av FAWY SO45 ..... 180 C3
Ebden Rd WINC SO23 ..... 3 K6
Ebery Gv HSEA PO3 ..... 211 M2
Ebor Cl FERN BH22 ..... 194 C6
Ebor Rd BKME/WDN BH12 ..... 234 C2
Eccles Rd PLE BH15 ..... 232 F6
Ecton La HSEA PO3 ..... 188 A5
Edelvale Rd WEND SO18 ..... 108 A7
Edenbridge Rd ENEY PO4 ..... 211 M3
Eden Gv WIMB BH21 ..... 192 B5
Eden Ri FHAM/PORC PO16 ..... 7 J8
Eden Rd WEND SO18 ..... 108 A6
Eden St PSEA PO1 ..... 211 G2 [2]
Edgar Crs FHAM/PORC PO16 ..... 186 B2
Edgar Rd WINC SO23 ..... 26 E2
Edgarton Rd CFDH BH17 ..... 218 B5
Edgecombe Crs
LSOL/BMARY PO13 ..... 185 G3
Edgefield Gv HORN PO8 ..... 141 G7
Edgehill Rd MOOR/WNTN BH9 ..... 220 C8
WEND SO18 ..... 107 L7
Edgell Rd EMRTH PO10 ..... 166 F4
Edgemoor Rd FERN BH22 ..... 168 F7
Edgerly Gdns CHAM PO6 ..... 187 K2
Edgeware Rd ENEY PO4 ..... 211 L3
Edifred Rd MOOR/WNTN BH9 ..... 220 E4
Edinburgh Rd PSEA PO1 ..... 12 F1
PSEA PO1 ..... 13 G1 [2]
Edington Cl BPWT SO32 ..... 85 C8 [2]
Edington Rd WINC SO23 ..... 3 C3
Edith Haisman Cl WSHM SO15 ..... 4 B1
Edmondsham Rd VWD BH31 ..... 120 C8
Edmund Rd ENEY PO4 ..... 211 M5
Edmunds Cl HEND SO30 ..... 134 B3
NMIL/BTOS BH25 ..... 225 J5
Edneys La WVILLE PO7 ..... 139 L3
Edward Av ELGH SO50 ..... 82 C4
Edward Gdns HAV PO9 ..... 165 G7
Edward Gv FHAM/PORC PO16 ..... 162 C7
Edward Rd BWD BH11 ..... 219 M5
CHCH/BSGR BH23 ..... 223 K8
FAWY SO45 ..... 155 L4
PSTN BH14 ..... 234 B3
WINC SO23 ..... 26 D4
WSHM SO15 ..... 130 F1
Edwards Cl CHAM PO6 ..... 162 F7 [2]
WVILLE PO7 ..... 140 D2
Edwina Cl ITCH SO19 ..... 132 D2
NBAD SO52 ..... 79 M4
RGWD BH24 ..... 147 G3
Edwina Dr CFDH BH17 ..... 217 M6
Effingham Gdns ITCH SO19 ..... 133 C4
Efford Wy LYMN SO41 ..... 201 M5
Egan Cl NEND PO2 ..... 187 K5
Egbert Rd WINC SO23 ..... 3 G1
Egdon Ct UPTN BH16 ..... 232 A1 [2]
Egdon Dr WIMB BH21 ..... 192 C8
Egerton Gdns BMTH BH1 ..... 236 C2 [2]
Egerton Rd CHAR BH8 ..... 236 C2
Eglantine Cl HORN PO8 ..... 140 F4
Eglantine Wk HORN PO8 ..... 140 F4

Eglantine Wk HORN PO8 ..... 140 F4
Egmont Cl RGWD BH24 ..... 170 A6
Egmont Dr RGWD BH24 ..... 170 B6
Egmont Gdns RGWD BH24 ..... 170 B6
Egmont Rd UPTN BH16 ..... 232 A4
Eight Acres ROMY SO51 ..... 79 G1 [3]
Elaine Gdns HORN PO8 ..... 140 D3
Elan Cl WEND SO18 ..... 108 A7
Elcombes Cl LYND SO43 ..... 151 K3
Elderberry La
CHCH/BSGR BH23 ..... 238 C2
Elderberry Wy HORN PO8 ..... 140 F4
Elder Cl FUFL SO22 ..... 26 B4
HLER SO31 ..... 158 D6 [3]
TOTT SO40 ..... 130 E7
Elderfield Cl EMRTH PO10 ..... 166 E5
Elderfield Rd HAV PO9 ..... 165 H1
Elder Gn RWIN SO21 ..... 54 F8
Elder Rd HAV PO9 ..... 9 K1
Eldon Av NMIL/BTOS BH25 ..... 225 J8
Eldon Cl NMIL/BTOS BH25 ..... 225 J8
Eldon Pl WBNE BH4 ..... 235 G5 [3]
Eldon Rd MOOR/WNTN BH9 ..... 220 C7
STOK SO20 ..... 22 F1
Eldon St SSEA PO5 ..... 13 G4
Eldridge Gdns ROMY SO51 ..... 50 E8
Eleanor Dr BWD BH11 ..... 219 H3
Eleanor Gdns
CHCH/BSGR BH23 ..... 222 C8 [2]
Electron Wy CHFD SO53 ..... 81 H2
Eletta Av WVILLE PO7 ..... 140 B8
Elfin Dr FERN BH22 ..... 194 A1
Elgar Cl CHAM PO6 ..... 162 C8 [2]
GPORT PO12 ..... 10 B8
Elgar Rd ITCH SO19 ..... 133 G5
NBNE BH10 ..... 220 B4
Elgar Wk WVILLE PO7 ..... 164 D4 [3]
Elgin Cl FAWY SO45 ..... 155 L5
FHAM PO15 ..... 6 E3
Elgin Rd CHAM PO6 ..... 187 K2
PSTN BH14 ..... 234 A6
WBNE BH4 ..... 14 A1
WSHM SO15 ..... 4 A1
Eling Cl FUFL SO22 ..... 16 C5
Eling Ct HAV PO9 ..... 165 H2
Eling HI TOTT SO40 ..... 129 M3
Eling La TOTT SO40 ..... 129 L2
Elise Cl LTDN BH7 ..... 221 M8
Elizabeth Av CHCH/BSGR BH23 ..... 222 D8
Elizabeth Cl HEND SO30 ..... 108 C7
RSAL SP5 ..... 72 C1
WHAM PO17 ..... 136 D4 [3]
Elizabeth Ct
FHAM/STUB PO14 ..... 184 D1 [3]
Elizabeth Crs LYMN SO41 ..... 226 E6
Elizabeth Gdns ENEY PO4 ..... 211 K6
FAWY SO45 ..... 155 L7
Elizabeth Rd
FHAM/STUB PO14 ..... 184 B6
PLE BH15 ..... 233 J5 [2]
WHAM PO17 ..... 136 C4
WIMB BH21 ..... 192 A3
WVILLE PO7 ..... 164 D2
Elizabeth Wy FHAM/STUB PO32 ..... 111 G1
Elkhams Cl LYMN SO41 ..... 227 H7
Elkstone Rd CHAM PO6 ..... 162 F7
Ellachie Gdns GPORT PO12 ..... 10 E9
Ellachie Ms GPORT PO12 ..... 10 E9
Ellachie Rd GPORT PO12 ..... 10 E9
Elland Cl ELGH SO50 ..... 83 H7
Ellanore La SELS PO20 ..... 215 J7
Elldene Ct TOTT SO40 ..... 129 J3 [3]
Ellen Gdns CHFD SO53 ..... 80 F3
Ellerslie Cl FHAM/STUB PO14 ..... 183 L1
Ellery Gv LYMN SO41 ..... 228 C3
Ellesfield Dr FERN BH22 ..... 194 B5
Ellesmere Orch EMRTH PO10 ..... 166 F4
Ellingham Dr RGWD BH24 ..... 146 C3
Ellingham Dro RGWD BH24 ..... 146 D3
Ellingham Rd
NMIL/BTOS BH25 ..... 225 H8
Elliot Cl TOTT SO40 ..... 129 K3
Elliot Ri HEND SO30 ..... 109 H6
Elliott Rd BWD BH11 ..... 219 J5
Ellisfield Rd HAV PO9 ..... 165 H4
Ellis Rd ITCH SO19 ..... 133 J3
Ellwood Av ITCH SO19 ..... 133 J2
Ellwood Cl ITCH SO19 ..... 133 J2
Elm Av CHCH/BSGR BH23 ..... 222 C6
LYMN SO41 ..... 228 A4
NMIL/BTOS BH25 ..... 225 L6
Elm Cl HISD PO11 ..... 213 L5
Elm Crs BPWT SO32 ..... 84 D2
FAWY SO45 ..... 179 L1
Elmdale Cl HLER SO31 ..... 158 A8
Elmdale Gv ROMY SO51 ..... 76 F7
Elmers Wy CHCH/BSGR BH23 ..... 197 M7
Elmes Dr WSHM SO15 ..... 130 D1
Elmes Rd MOOR/WNTN BH9 ..... 220 C6
Elmeswelle Rd HORN PO8 ..... 140 E2
Elmfield Cl RSAL SP5 ..... 73 J3
Elm Gdns HEND SO30 ..... 108 C6
WBNE BH4 ..... 235 H3
Elmgate Dr LTDN BH7 ..... 236 E1
Elm Gv ELGH SO50 ..... 81 L6
GPORT PO12 ..... 10 F1
HISD PO11 ..... 213 L5
SSEA PO5 ..... 13 H5
Elmhurst Rd BWD BH11 ..... 219 L3 [2]
FERN BH22 ..... 168 D7
FHAM/PORC PO16 ..... 7 J7
GPORT PO12 ..... 11 G3
Elmhurst Wy FERN BH22 ..... 168 D6
Elm La HAV PO9 ..... 8 E4
Elmleigh Rd HAV PO9 ..... 8 E4
Elmore Av LSOL/BMARY PO13 ..... 208 D3
Elmore Cl LSOL/BMARY PO13 ..... 208 D3
Elmore Dr RGWD BH24 ..... 169 J2
Elmore Rd LSOL/BMARY PO13 ..... 208 D3
Elm Park Rd HAV PO9 ..... 8 F3
Elm Rd BPWT SO32 ..... 85 G8
FUFL SO22 ..... 25 M5
HAV PO9 ..... 9 G5
Elms Av PSTN BH14 ..... 233 M7
Elms Cl FBDG SP6 ..... 96 F5
Elms La SELS PO20 ..... 215 L6

Elmsleigh Gdns ROWN SO16 ..... 106 F4
Elmslie Gdns HLER SO31 ..... 133 K7
Elms Ride SELS PO20 ..... 215 L7
Elms Rd FHAM/PORC PO16 ..... 7 J9
Elmstead Gdns SELS PO20 ..... 215 L6
Elmstead Park Rd SELS PO20 ..... 215 L6
Elm St SHAM SO14 ..... 5 K4
SSEA PO5 ..... 12 F5 [2]
Elms Wy SBNE BH6 ..... 237 K4
SELS PO20 ..... 215 L6
Elm Ter SHAM SO14 ..... 5 K5
Elmtree Cl TOTT SO40 ..... 128 F6
Elmtree Gdns ROMY SO51 ..... 79 H2
Elm Tree Wk FERN BH22 ..... 194 C8 [3]
Elmtree Rd CHAM PO6 ..... 164 C8 [2]
Elmwood Av FBDG SP6 ..... 97 H6
WVILLE PO7 ..... 164 C2
Elmwood Rd NEND PO2 ..... 187 J4
Elmwood Wy
CHCH/BSGR BH23 ..... 239 L1
Elphinstone Rd
CHCH/BSGR BH23 ..... 224 F8
SSEA PO5 ..... 13 G7
Elsfred Rd FHAM/STUB PO14 ..... 183 L7
Elson La GPORT PO12 ..... 185 L8
Elson Rd GPORT PO12 ..... 185 L8
Elstead Gdns WVILLE PO7 ..... 164 A4
Elstree Rd ITCH SO19 ..... 132 C4
Eltham Cl LTDN BH7 ..... 221 M8 [3]
Elvin Cl FAWY SO45 ..... 180 C4
Elwell Gn HISD PO11 ..... 213 K5
Elwyn Rd BMTH BH1 ..... 15 L2
Emanuel St NEND PO2 ..... 211 H1
Embankment Wy
RGWD BH24 ..... 170 F2
Emberley Cl FERN BH22 ..... 194 E1 [3]
Embley Cl TOTT SO40 ..... 104 C6
Embley La ROMY SO51 ..... 77 J2
Embsay Rd HLER SO31 ..... 134 B8
Emerald Cl ITCH SO19 ..... 132 E2
WVILLE PO7 ..... 164 E1
Emer Cl NBAD SO52 ..... 79 M3 [3]
Emerson Cl PLE BH15 ..... 233 H6 [2]
Emerson Rd PLE BH15 ..... 233 H6
Emily Cl CHCH/BSGR BH23 ..... 222 E7 [2]
Emmanuel Cl
FHAM/STUB PO14 ..... 159 G6 [2]
Emmett Rd ROWN SO16 ..... 105 L3
Emmons Cl HLER SO31 ..... 157 K7
Empress Rd LYND SO43 ..... 151 K3 [2]
SHAM SO14 ..... 5 J9
SHAM SO14 ..... 131 M1
Empshott Rd ENEY PO4 ..... 211 K4
Empson Wk
LSOL/BMARY PO13 ..... 208 D1 [3]
Emsbrook Dr EMRTH PO10 ..... 166 D6 [3]
Emsworth Common Rd
EMRTH PO10 ..... 166 B3
Emsworth House Cl
EMRTH PO10 ..... 166 C7
Emsworth Rd HAV PO9 ..... 9 K5
EMRTH PO10 ..... 166 D4
HAV PO9 ..... 9 G5
LYMN SO41 ..... 228 C4
NEND PO2 ..... 187 J7
WSHM SO15 ..... 106 A8
Encombe Cl BKME/WDN BH12 ..... 219 K8
Endeavour Cl GPORT PO12 ..... 11 J4
WSHM SO15 ..... 130 F1 [3]
Endeavour Wy FAWY SO45 ..... 155 K3
Enderwood Cl TOTT SO40 ..... 104 A8 [2]
Endfield Cl CHCH/BSGR BH23 ..... 222 D7
Endfield Rd
CHCH/BSGR BH23 ..... 222 D8 [2]
MOOR/WNTN BH9 ..... 220 E6
Endle St SHAM SO14 ..... 5 K5
Endofield Cl FHAM/STUB PO14 ..... 184 D2
Enfield Av PLE BH15 ..... 233 K2
Enfield Crs PLE BH15 ..... 233 K2
Enfield Gv ITCH SO19 ..... 132 C6
Enfield Rd PLE BH15 ..... 233 K2
Englands Wy BWD BH11 ..... 219 H4
Englefield Rd WEND SO18 ..... 132 B1
English Rd WSHM SO15 ..... 130 F1
Enmill La FUFL SO22 ..... 25 L3
Ennel Copse NBAD SO52 ..... 79 M4
Ennerdale Cl HORN PO8 ..... 116 B6 [3]
Ennerdale Gdns WEND SO18 ..... 108 A7 [3]
Ennerdale Rd
FHAM/STUB PO14 ..... 184 B4
ROWN SO16 ..... 105 K6
Ensbury Av NBNE BH10 ..... 220 B7
Ensbury Cl NBNE BH10 ..... 220 B7 [3]
Ensbury Park Rd
MOOR/WNTN BH9 ..... 220 C6
Ensign Dr LSOL/BMARY PO13 ..... 209 H2
Ensign Wy HLER SO31 ..... 157 J6
Enterprise Cl HLER SO31 ..... 158 C7 [3]
Enterprise Rd ROWN SO16 ..... 80 B7
Enterprise Wy SHAM SO14 ..... 5 J7
Epping Cl WEND SO18 ..... 108 A7
Epsom Cl ELGH SO50 ..... 109 J1 [3]
Epworth Rd NEND PO2 ..... 187 K7
Erica Cl HLER SO31 ..... 158 D5
HORN PO8 ..... 140 F5
Erica Dr WIMB BH21 ..... 217 H2
Erica Wy HORN PO8 ..... 140 F4
Ericksen Rd BWD BH11 ..... 219 H4
Eric Rd FHAM/STUB PO14 ..... 184 A6
Ernest Cl EMRTH PO10 ..... 166 D7
Ernest Rd HAV PO9 ..... 165 G4
PSEA PO1 ..... 211 J1
Erpingham Rd
BKME/WDN BH12 ..... 234 F3
Erskine Rd FUFL SO22 ..... 2 D9
Escombe Rd ELGH SO50 ..... 82 C5
Escur Cl NEND PO2 ..... 187 K4 [3]
Esdaile La RGWD BH24 ..... 172 D5 [3]
Esher Gv WVILLE PO7 ..... 140 A6
Eskdale Cl HORN PO8 ..... 116 B6
Esmond Cl EMRTH PO10 ..... 166 D8
Esmonde Cl
LSOL/BMARY PO13 ..... 208 D2 [3]
Esmonde Wy CFDH BH17 ..... 218 D8
Esplanade CCLF BH13 ..... 245 L1
ENEY PO4 ..... 211 J7
PLE BH15 ..... 233 H5

Esplanade Gdns ENEY PO4 212 A6
The Esplanade GPORT PO12 11 M4
Essex Av CHCH/BSGR BH23 222 D6
Essex Rd ENEY PO4 211 L4
Estella Rd NEND PO2 187 H8
Estridge Cl HLER SO31 133 L7 1
Ethelbert Rd WIMB BH21 192 B4
Ethelburt Av ROWN SO16 107 H3
Ethelred Gdns TOTT SO40 129 G2
Ethel Rd PSEA PO1 211 J2
Eton Gdns WBNE BH4 235 G4
Eton Rd SSEA PO5 13 L3
Ettrick Rd CCLF BH13 234 F7
Eucalyptus Av RGWD BH24 169 L6
European Wy SHAM SO14 5 J8
Euryalus Rd FHAM/STUB PO14 184 D2
Euston Gv RGWD BH24 170 F2
Euston Rd ENEY PO4 211 M3
Evans Cl BWD BH11 219 K7
NEND PO2 186 F6
RGWD BH24 169 J2
Evans Rd ENEY PO4 211 L4
Evans St SHAM SO14 5 H4
Evelegh Rd CHAM PO6 164 B8
Evelyn Cl BPWT SO32 111 K4
Evelyn Crs WSHM SO15 106 C8
Evelyn Rd MOOR/WNTN BH9 220 E7
Evening Gld FERN BH22 194 C5
Evenlode Rd ROWN SO16 105 K7
Everdon La HSEA PO3 188 A4 3
Everest Rd CHCH/BSGR BH23 223 J8
Everglades Av HORN PO8 140 D5
Everglades Cl FERN BH22 194 B1
Evergreen Cl TOTT SO40 130 D7
WIMB BH21 144 C8 1
WVILLE PO7 164 B1 1
Evergreens RGWD BH24 169 J3
Evering Av BKME/WDN BH12 219 H7
Evering Gdns
BKME/WDN BH12 219 G7
Everlea Cl LYMN SO41 227 H7
Everon Gdns NMIL/BTOS BH25 225 M7
Evershot Rd CHAR BH8 221 J7
Eversley Crs HAV PO9 165 H4
Eversley Pl FUFL SO22 26 C3
Everton Rd LYMN SO41 226 D4
Evesham Cl LTDN BH7 221 L8
ROWN SO16 107 G3 1
Ewart Ct FAWY SO45 155 L3
Ewart Rd PSEA PO1 211 J1 4
Ewell Wy TOTT SO40 104 C7
Ewhurst Cl HAV PO9 165 H4
Exbury Cl ELGH SO50 82 E6
Exbury Dr BWD BH11 219 K3
Exbury Rd FAWY SO45 180 C8
HAV PO9 165 L3
Excellent Rd
FHAM/STUB PO14 184 D3
Excelsior Rd PSTN BH14 234 B6
Exchange Rd PSEA PO1 12 F2 1
Exeter Cl ELGH SO50 81 L3
EMRTH PO10 166 D5
HLER SO31 158 D5
WEND SO18 107 M7
Exeter Crs WCLF BH2 14 E7
Exeter Park Rd WCLF BH2 14 E7
Exeter Rd ENEY PO4 211 K6
WCLF BH2 14 E6
WEND SO18 107 M8
Exford Av WEND SO18 108 B8
Exford Dr WEND SO18 108 B8
Exleigh Cl ITCH SO19 132 F2
Exmouth Gdns ELGH SO50 109 H1 2
Exmouth Rd GPORT PO12 185 L8
SSEA PO5 13 K7
Exton Gdns FHAM/PORC PO16 162 A7
Exton Rd HAV PO9 165 M3
SBNE BH6 237 J1
Eyebright Cl ELGH SO50 109 H2 3
Eyeworth Wk FAWY SO45 155 G4 2
Eynham Av ITCH SO19 133 G2
Eynham Cl ITCH SO19 132 F2
Eyre Cl TOTT SO40 129 H2

F

Faber Cl HAV PO9 165 L4
Fabian Cl WVILLE PO7 140 E8 1
Factory Rd ELGH SO50 81 M6
UPTN BH16 232 B2
Fairacre Ri FHAM/STUB PO14 159 M8
Fairbairn Wk NBAD SO52 80 E2
Fairbourne Cl HORN PO8 140 C6
Fairclose Dr FUFL SO22 16 A3
Faircross Cl FAWY SO45 180 A5
Fairdown Cl WINC SO23 3 M8
Fairfax Cl FUFL SO22 26 A3
Fairfax Ct ITCH SO19 133 J3 1
Fairfax Ms ITCH SO19 133 J2
Fairfield CHCH/BSGR BH23 238 A1
Fair Fld ROMY SO51 50 F7
Fairfield Av FHAM/STUB PO14 6 D9
Fairfield Cl EMRTH PO10 166 D6
FAWY SO45 155 L4 5
LYMN SO41 228 C5
WIMB BH21 192 C3
Fairfield Rd FUFL SO22 2 D5
HAV PO9 8 F4
NMIL/BTOS BH25 240 D1
RWIN SO21 54 C3
WIMB BH21 192 B4
Fairfield Sq CHAM PO6 163 J8
Fair Gn ITCH SO19 132 F3
Fairhome Cl GPORT PO12 209 L1
Fair Isle Cl FHAM/STUB PO14 183 M5
Fairisle Rd ROWN SO16 105 K4
Fair La RWIN SO21 17 M7
Fairlawn Cl ROWN SO16 105 L2
Fairlead Dr
LSOL/BMARY PO13 209 H2 3
Fairlea Rd EMRTH PO10 166 D5
LYMN SO41 228 C4
Fairlie RGWD BH24 147 G7
Fairlie Cl HEND SO30 109 H5 2
Fairlie Pk RGWD BH24 146 F7
Fairlight La LYMN SO41 200 B7
Fairmead Wk HORN PO8 140 F5
Fairmead Wy TOTT SO40 129 J3
Fairmile Rd CHCH/BSGR BH23 222 E8
Fair Oak HAV PO9 8 E1
Fairoak Rd ELGH SO50 82 C6
Fairthorne Gdns GPORT PO12 10 D4
Fairview Cl FAWY SO45 155 L5
ROMY SO51 51 G7
Fairview Crs WIMB BH21 217 L3
Fairview Dr FAWY SO45 155 K6
ROMY SO51 51 G8
WIMB BH21 217 L3
Fairview Pde FAWY SO45 155 L6
Fairview Rd WIMB BH21 217 L3
Fairwater Cl
LSOL/BMARY PO13 184 F7
Fairway Dr CHCH/BSGR BH23 237 L2
Fairway Gdns ROWN SO16 105 K3
Fairway Rd FAWY SO45 155 K4
PSTN BH14 234 B8
Fairways FERN BH22 194 D2
The Fairway
FHAM/PORC PO16 162 A8
HAV PO9 142 A6
LSOL/BMARY PO13 185 G7 2
NMIL/BTOS BH25 241 G1
Fairwood Rd VWD BH31 145 G3
Fairy Crossway HORN PO8 140 F6
Falaise Cl ROWN SO16 106 B4
Falcon Cl FHAM/PORC PO16 161 K8 4
Falcon Dr CHCH/BSGR BH23 239 G3
Falconer Ct FAWY SO45 179 M2
Falconer Dr PLE BH15 232 D4
Falcon Flds FAWY SO45 180 F5
Falcon Rd HORN PO8 140 E1
Falcon Sq ELGH SO50 81 J7
Falcon Vw FUFL SO22 26 B4
Falcon Wy BPWT SO32 109 M7
Falkland Rd CHFD SO53 81 H5
WSHM SO15 130 E1
Falklands Cl
LSOL/BMARY PO13 208 D1
Falklands Rd NEND PO2 187 J4 2
Fallow Fld FUFL SO22 26 B4
Falmouth Rd CHAM PO6 162 D7
Falstaff Wy TOTT SO40 129 J3 2
Fancy Rd BKME/WDN BH12 218 F8
Fanshawe St SHAM SO14 131 L2 3
Farcroft Rd PSTN BH14 234 A3
Fareham Park Rd FHAM PO15 160 A4
Fareham Rd
LSOL/BMARY PO13 185 G3
WHAM PO17 136 E5
WHAM PO17 162 C3
Faringdon Rd WEND SO18 133 H1
Farleigh Cl HAV PO9 165 H3 1
Farley Cl ELGH SO50 83 J7
FUFL SO22 26 A4
Farley La ROMY SO51 23 J7
Farley Mount Rd RWIN SO21 24 F2
Farlington Av CHAM PO6 164 A7
Farlington Rd NEND PO2 187 J7
Farm Cl RGWD BH24 146 E8
Farmdene Cl
CHCH/BSGR BH23 224 B8 2
Far Meadow Wy EMRTH PO10 166 B8
Farm Edge Rd
FHAM/STUB PO14 184 A7
Farmers Wk LYMN SO41 227 H8
Farmery Cl ELGH SO50 107 J4
Farm Gdns HSEA PO3 187 K4
Farmhouse Wy HORN PO8 140 E3
Farm La CHCH/BSGR BH23 238 F3
RCCH PO18 191 K1
Farm La North
NMIL/BTOS BH25 225 L8
Farm La South
NMIL/BTOS BH25 240 F1
Farmlea Rd CHAM PO6 162 D8
Farm Rd FERN BH22 168 B6
FHAM/STUB PO14 159 J6
Farmside Gdns HSEA PO3 187 K4
Farm Vw EMRTH PO10 166 D5
Farm View Av HORN PO8 116 A3
Farnham Rd BKME/WDN BH12 234 F1
LISS GU33 36 D3
PSF GU32 36 A8
Farnleys Md LYMN SO41 228 C6
Faroes Cl FHAM/STUB PO14 183 M5 3
Farriers Cl WIMB BH21 192 F2
Farriers Wy HORN PO8 141 G7
Farrier Wy
FHAM/PORC PO16 184 F2 1
Farringdon Rd HAV PO9 165 L4
Farringford Rd ITCH SO19 133 H2
Farthings Ga WVILLE PO7 164 C5
Farwell Cl CHCH/BSGR BH23 223 G5
Farwell Rd BKME/WDN BH12 219 G6
Fastnet Cl ROWN SO16 105 K3 2
Fastnet Wy
FHAM/STUB PO14 183 M5 4
Fathersfield BROC SO42 175 K7
Fathoms Reach HISD PO11 213 J4
F Av FAWY SO45 180 D2
Fawcett Rd ENEY PO4 13 L3
NMIL/BTOS BH25 225 K6
Fawley By-pass FAWY SO45 180 F5
Fawley Ct HAV PO9 165 M3 5
Fawley Gn CHAR BH8 221 H5
Fawley La ALTN GU34 33 G4
RWIN SO21 27 L8
Fawley Rd FAWY SO45 155 M8
FAWY SO45 180 C5
NEND PO2 187 J3
WSHM SO15 130 E2
Fawn Gdns NMIL/BTOS BH25 225 K4
Fay Cl FHAM/STUB PO14 184 A6
Fayre Rd FHAM/PORC PO16 7 H9
Fearon Rd NEND PO2 187 J6
Felix Rd GPORT PO12 209 M1
Fell Cl HLER SO31 158 E4
Fell Dr LSOL/BMARY PO13 208 D1
Felmer Dr WINC SO23 17 H1
Feltham Cl ROMY SO51 51 H8
Felton Crs CHCH/BSGR BH23 224 D8
Felton Rd PSTN BH14 233 L3
Feltons Pl HSEA PO3 187 K3
Fen Av FHAM/PORC PO16 184 F1
Fenleigh Cl NMIL/BTOS BH25 225 M8
Fennel Gdns LYMN SO41 228 B3
Fennell Cl WVILLE PO7 140 B7
Fenton Rd SBNE BH6 237 H2
Fern Bank WIMB BH21 168 C1
Fern Barrow
BKME/WDN BH12 219 M8
Fern Cl CHCH/BSGR BH23 223 G6
EPSF GU31 64 B5
FBDG SP6 121 L3
Ferncroft Cl
FHAM/STUB PO14 184 A7 2
Ferncroft Gdns NBNE BH10 220 B3
Ferncroft Rd NBNE BH10 220 B3
Ferndale HEND SO30 134 B3 1
WVILLE PO7 164 D1
Ferndale Ms
LSOL/BMARY PO13 184 F4
Ferndale Rd NMIL/BTOS BH25 225 M4
TOTT SO40 130 D7
Ferndene Wy WEND SO18 107 L8
Ferndown, Stour & Forest Trail
FERN BH22 193 M2
WIMB BH21 193 G1
Fern Dr HAV PO9 9 G2
Ferneham Rd FHAM PO15 160 A6
Fernglade NMIL/BTOS BH25 225 L5
Fernheath Cl BWD BH11 219 L6
Fernheath Rd BWD BH11 219 L5
Fernhill Cl CFDH BH17 218 E6
Fernhill La NMIL/BTOS BH25 225 L2
Fern Hill La ROMY SO51 23 J8
Fernhill Rd NMIL/BTOS BH25 225 L4
Fernhills Rd FAWY SO45 155 M7
Fernhurst Cl HISD PO11 213 J5
Fernhurst Rd ENEY PO4 211 K4
LIPH GU30 38 E5
Fernie Cl FHAM/STUB PO14 183 M6
Fernlea Av FERN BH22 194 B4
Fernlea Cl FERN BH22 194 B4
RGWD BH24 169 J4
Fernlea Gdns FERN BH22 194 B4
ROWN SO16 106 D5 5
Fernlea Wy FAWY SO45 155 H5
Fern Rd FAWY SO45 155 K5
ITCH SO19 132 D6 1
Fernside Av PSTN BH14 233 L4
Fernside Rd FERN BH22 168 C6
MOOR/WNTN BH9 220 B8
PLE BH15 233 K4
Fern Wy FHAM PO15 159 H5
Fernway Cl WIMB BH21 192 F4
Fernwood Cl RGWD BH24 169 M3
Fernyhurst Av ROWN SO16 105 L2
Ferris Av CHAR BH8 221 G6
Ferris Cl CHAR BH8 221 G6
Ferris Pl CHAR BH8 221 H6
Ferrol Rd GPORT PO12 210 A2
Ferry Rd ENEY PO4 212 B5
FAWY SO45 155 K5
HISD PO11 212 E4
PLE BH15 233 G7
SBNE BH6 237 L5
Ferry Wy CCLF BH13 245 G5
Festing Gv ENEY PO4 211 K6
Festing Rd ENEY PO4 211 K6
Feversham Av CHAR BH8 221 J7
Fey Rd GPORT PO12 11 G2
Fibbards Rd BROC SO42 175 K7
Field Cl HLER SO31 158 F6
LSOL/BMARY PO13 184 F3
ROMY SO51 78 F1
ROWN SO16 107 H3 4
RWIN SO21 54 B2
Fielden Cl NBAD SO52 79 L4
Field End WINC SO23 17 H1
Fielders Wy ROMY SO51 77 G6
Fieldfare Cl HORN PO8 116 B4
Fieldfare Ct TOTT SO40 104 B8
Fieldhouse Dr
LSOL/BMARY PO13 184 D8
Fieldmore Rd GPORT PO12 209 M1
Field Pl NMIL/BTOS BH25 225 G8
Fields Cl FAWY SO45 180 C7 2
Field Vw NBAD SO52 80 E2
Field Wk LYMN SO41 228 B3
Field Wy CHCH/BSGR BH23 224 B7
FBDG SP6 98 D6
RWIN SO21 54 B2
WVILLE PO7 139 K4
Fieldway RGWD BH24 146 F8
Fifth Av CHAM PO6 163 J8
HAV PO9 9 K2
Fifth St PSEA PO1 211 K1
Filmer Cl LSOL/BMARY PO13 185 H8
Filmorehill La ALTN GU34 32 E5
Filton Cl TOTT SO40 104 B8
Filton Rd LYMN SO41 228 B4
Finchdean Rd HAV PO9 142 A6
HAV PO9 165 H4
Finchfield Av BWD BH11 219 K2
Finchmead La PSF GU32 63 G4
Finch Rd ENEY PO4 212 B5
Finch's La RWIN SO21 54 E2
Findon Rd GPORT PO12 185 M8
Finisterre St
FHAM/STUB PO14 183 M4
Finzi Cl ITCH SO19 133 G5
Fiona Cl WINC SO23 3 L6
Fir Av NMIL/BTOS BH25 225 M6
Firbank Rd MOOR/WNTN BH9 220 F8
Fir Cl FERN BH22 168 C5
LYND SO43 151 K4 2
Fir Copse Rd WVILLE PO7 164 B5
Fir Croft Dr CHFD SO53 81 J3
Firecrest Cl ROWN SO16 106 A3
Firgrove Cl NBAD SO52 79 L4
Firgrove Crs HSEA PO3 187 K3
Firgrove La WHAM PO17 137 K6
Firgrove Rd NBAD SO52 79 M3
WSHM SO15 131 G1
Firlands Ri CHAM PO6 164 E7
Firmain Rd
BKME/WDN BH12 219 H7 1
Firmount Cl LYMN SO41 227 J7
Firmstone Rd WINC SO23 3 L7
Fir Rd TOTT SO40 128 F6
Firs Av WVILLE PO7 140 D6
Firs Dr HEND SO30 133 L2
Firs Glen Rd FERN BH22 168 C6
MOOR/WNTN BH9 220 B8
VWD BH31 144 D3
Firshill CHCH/BSGR BH23 224 C7
Firside Rd WIMB BH21 217 G4
Firs La PSTN BH14 234 A8
First Av CHAM PO6 163 K8
CHAM PO6 164 C8
EMRTH PO10 167 H8
HAV PO9 9 J3
HORN PO8 116 B5
WSHM SO15 130 B1
The Firs BMTH BH1 15 H4
LSOL/BMARY PO13 185 H7
ROWN SO16 106 E4
First Marine Av
NMIL/BTOS BH25 240 E1
First St FAWY SO45 156 C8
Fir Tree Cl ELGH SO50 109 H1
RGWD BH24 169 H6
Firtree Crs LYMN SO41 226 D5
Firtree Gdns HORN PO8 141 G3
Fir Tree Hl FBDG SP6 121 L2 3
Fir Tree La CHCH/BSGR BH23 224 B7 1
ELGH SO50 109 G1
Fir Tree Rd HISD PO11 213 L5
TOTT SO40 127 L1
Firtree Wy ITCH SO19 132 F3 1
Fir Vale Rd BMTH BH1 14 F5
Firwood Cl CHFD SO53 53 H8
Fisgard Rd GPORT PO12 209 M1
Fisher Cl FHAM/STUB PO14 183 M5 5
Fisherman's Av SBNE BH6 237 G4
Fishermans Rd PLE BH15 233 H7 2
The Fishermans
EMRTH PO10 166 E8 1
Fishermans Wk HISD PO11 214 C6
Fisher Rd LSOL/BMARY PO13 185 G5
Fishers Gv CHAM PO6 188 C1
Fishers Hl FHAM PO15 159 L6
Fisher's Rd TOTT SO40 129 L2
Fishery La HISD PO11 214 A6
Fishlake Mdw ROMY SO51 50 E7
Fitzgerald Cl HLER SO31 135 G8 4
Fitzharris Av
MOOR/WNTN BH9 235 M1
Fitzherbert Rd CHAM PO6 188 B1
Fitzherbert Sp CHAM PO6 188 C1
Fitzherbert St PSEA PO1 211 G1 2
Fitzhugh Pl WSHM SO15 131 K1
Fitzhugh St SHAM SO14 4 E2 1
Fitzmaurice Rd
CHCH/BSGR BH23 222 C8
Fitzpain Cl FERN BH22 194 B6
Fitzpain Rd FERN BH22 194 B6
Fitzpatrick Ct CHAM PO6 163 H7 1
Fitzroy Cl ROWN SO16 106 E1
Fitzwilliam Av
FHAM/STUB PO14 183 L6 1
Fitzwilliam Cl BWD BH11 219 J3
Fitzworth Av UPTN BH16 232 B4
Fitzwygram Crs HAV PO9 8 E1
Five Bridges Rd WINC SO23 26 D5
Five Elms Dr ROMY SO51 79 G2
Fivefields Cl WINC SO23 3 L9
Fivefields Rd WINC SO23 3 M9
Five Heads Rd HORN PO8 115 M8
Five Post La GPORT PO12 209 M2
Flaghead Chine Rd CCLF BH13 245 K2
Flaghead Rd CCLF BH13 245 K1
Flag Staff Gn GPORT PO12 210 B2
Flag Wk HORN PO8 140 D3
Flambard Av
CHCH/BSGR BH23 222 D7
Flambard Rd PSTN BH14 234 B6
Flamborough Cl ROWN SO16 105 J6
Flamingo Ct
FHAM/PORC PO16 161 K8
Flanders Rd HEND SO30 109 G8
Flathouse Rd PSEA PO1 211 G1
Flatt Rd RCCH PO18 167 M8
Flaxfields End FBDG SP6 97 K7
Flazen Cl BWD BH11 219 H5
Fleet Cl LSOL/BMARY PO13 185 H7
Fleet End Bottom HLER SO31 158 D8
Fleetend Cl HAV PO9 165 J2 3
Fleet End Rd HLER SO31 158 D8
Fleets La PLE BH15 233 H2
Fleming Av NBAD SO52 79 M4
Fleming Pl ROMY SO51 78 E1 1
RWIN SO21 54 E7
Fleming Rd FUFL SO22 16 B5
ROWN SO16 107 J4
Fletcher Cl FAWY SO45 155 H5
NBNE BH10 220 B5 1
Fletcher Rd NBNE BH10 220 B5
Fletchwood La TOTT SO40 128 F2
Fletchwood Rd TOTT SO40 128 F2
Fleuret Cl FAWY SO45 155 L8
Flexford Cl CHFD SO53 52 F7
Flexford La LYMN SO41 227 G2
Flexford Rd NBAD SO52 80 B2
Flint Cl ITCH SO19 133 J4
Flint St SSEA PO5 12 F5
Floating Bridge Rd SHAM SO14 5 L6
Floral Farm WIMB BH21 192 E6
Florence Cl ROMY SO51 77 G6
Florence Rd BOSC BH5 236 D4
ITCH SO19 132 C6 1
PSTN BH14 234 B4
SSEA PO5 13 K9
Florentine Wy WVILLE PO7 140 E8 2
The Florins HLER SO31 158 E7
WVILLE PO7 164 C5 2
Floriston Gdns
NMIL/BTOS BH25 226 B5
Floud La PSF GU32 60 A3
Flowerdown Cl TOTT SO40 104 B8
Flower La ROMY SO51 76 C2
Flowers Cl HLER SO31 157 J5
Flume Rd FAWY SO45 181 G4
Flushards LYMN SO41 228 D5
Foldsgate Cl LYND SO43 151 K2 1
Folkestone Rd HSEA PO3 211 L1
Folly Farm La RGWD BH24 170 A2
Folly Fld BPWT SO32 111 J1
Folly La EPSF GU31 63 L5
Font Cl FHAM/STUB PO14 159 G5 1
Fontley Rd FHAM PO15 159 L5
Fontmell Rd BDST BH18 218 A6
Fontwell Cl TOTT SO40 104 B7
Fontwell Gdns ELGH SO50 109 J1 3
Fontwell Ms HORN PO8 140 F7
Fontwell Rd SSEA PO5 13 J7 1
SSEA PO5 13 J7 1
Foord Rd HEND SO30 133 M4 1
Football Gn LYND SO43 127 G5
Footner Cl ROMY SO51 51 H6
Footners La CHCH/BSGR BH23 223 G6
Forbes Cl ROWN SO16 105 L2
Forbury Rd SSEA PO5 13 J3 4
Ford Av CHFD SO53 81 J4
Ford Cl FERN BH22 194 D1
Fordingbridge Rd ENEY PO4 211 M5
FBDG SP6 121 M1
Fordington Av FUFL SO22 2 B6
Fordington Rd FUFL SO22 2 C6
Ford La FERN BH22 194 E1
Ford Rd GPORT PO12 209 K2
Foreland Cl CHCH/BSGR BH23 222 B4
Foreland Ct HISD PO11 214 A6
Foreland Rd UPTN BH16 232 A4
Foreshore North FAWY SO45 180 F2
Foreshore South FAWY SO45 180 F2
Forest Av HORN PO8 140 D5
Forest Cl BPWT SO32 111 K5
CHCH/BSGR BH23 224 B7
CHFD SO53 53 H8
HORN PO8 140 D5
NBAD SO52 79 K3
VWD BH31 145 H4
Forest Cnr LISS GU33 36 F1
Forest Court Hills
RGWD BH24 171 H2 1
Forest Edge FAWY SO45 180 E5
Forest Edge Cl RGWD BH24 169 H3 1
Forest Edge Dr RGWD BH24 169 H3
Forest Edge Rd RGWD BH24 171 J3
Forest End WVILLE PO7 164 B1
Forester Rd BPWT SO32 112 F7
Foresters Ga FAWY SO45 206 C1
Foresters Rd FAWY SO45 180 D6
Forest Front FAWY SO45 155 K8
Forest Gdns BPWT SO32 111 K5 1
LYND SO43 151 K3
Forest Ga FAWY SO45 206 D1
Forest Gate Gdns LYMN SO41 228 B7
Forest Glade Cl BROC SO42 175 H7
Forest Hall BROC SO42 175 L7 2
Forest Hills Dr WEND SO18 107 K5
Forest Hill Wy FAWY SO45 155 K6 4
Forestlake Av RGWD BH24 171 H2
Forest La FAWY SO45 179 M2 1
RGWD BH24 171 J2
VWD BH31 144 C1 2
WHAM PO17 136 F8
Forest Md WVILLE PO7 139 K5
Forest Meadow FAWY SO45 155 L8
Forest Oak Dr
NMIL/BTOS BH25 225 L3
Forest Park Rd BROC SO42 175 J6
Forest Pines
NMIL/BTOS BH25 225 L4 1
Forest Ri CHCH/BSGR BH23 224 B6
LISS GU33 36 F2
Forest Rd BPWT SO32 111 L5
CCLF BH13 234 F6
CHCH/BSGR BH23 198 C3
CHFD SO53 53 J8
FBDG SP6 73 J4
FERN BH22 168 D5
LISS GU33 36 E1
RGWD BH24 172 D3
RSAL SP5 75 J8
WVILLE PO7 138 E4
Forestside Av HAV PO9 165 L3
Forestside Gdns RGWD BH24 147 G7
The Forestside VWD BH31 145 H3
Forest Vw BROC SO42 175 H7
NMIL/BTOS BH25 225 H3
SHAM SO14 4 F5
Forest View Cl
MOOR/WNTN BH9 220 E6 2
Forest View Dr WIMB BH21 193 L2
Forest View Rd
MOOR/WNTN BH9 220 E5
Forest Wy CHCH/BSGR BH23 224 B7
LSOL/BMARY PO13 185 H6
LYMN SO41 227 H7
TOTT SO40 103 M6
WIMB BH21 193 L3
Forge Cl HLER SO31 133 L7
Forge Rd FAWY SO45 206 D1
Forneth Gdns FHAM PO15 159 M8 2
Forster Rd SHAM SO14 131 L1
Forsyth Gdns NBNE BH10 220 A7
Forsythia Cl HAV PO9 165 M4
HEND SO30 109 G8 3
Fort Cumberland Rd
ENEY PO4 212 B5
Fortescue Rd
BKME/WDN BH12 234 C1
TWDS BH3 235 M2
Fort Fareham Rd
FHAM/STUB PO14 184 D2
Forth Cl CHFD SO53 81 G3
FHAM/STUB PO14 183 M5 6
Forties Cl FHAM/STUB PO14 183 M4 2
Forton Rd GPORT PO12 10 E1
PSEA PO1 211 J2 1
Fort Rd GPORT PO12 10 C9
ITCH SO19 132 C5
Fortunes Wy CHAM PO6 164 D7
Forty Acre La EPSF GU31 92 A5
Forward Dr LYMN SO41 228 A6
Foster Cl FHAM/STUB PO14 184 A4
Foster Rd GPORT PO12 10 D5
PSEA PO1 211 H2
Founders Wy
LSOL/BMARY PO13 185 H6
Foundry La WSHM SO15 106 A8
Foundry Rd RSAL SP5 73 J1 1
Fountain St PSEA PO1 13 G1 2
Fountain Wy
CHCH/BSGR BH23 238 A2

Four Acre HEND SO30...... 134 E2
Four Posts HI WSHM SO15...... 4 C1
Fourshells CI FAWY SO45...... 180 D6 [1]
Fourth Av CHAM PO6...... 163 J8
    HAV PO9...... 9 J3
Fourth St PSEA PO1...... 211 K2
Four Wells Rd WIMB BH21...... 192 E1
Fowey CI CHFD SO53...... 81 G1
The Fowey FAWY SO45...... 180 C6
Fowlers Rd HEND SO30...... 109 G8
Fowler's Wk NBAD SO52...... 80 C5
Foxbury CI FAWY SO45...... 155 L6
Foxbury Gv FHAM/PORC PO16...... 185 M1
Foxbury La EMRTH PO10...... 167 G4
    LSOL/BMARY PO13...... 185 H4
Foxbury Rd RGWD BH24...... 169 K7
Fox CI ELGH SO50...... 82 E6
Foxcombe La BPWT SO32...... 111 M2
Foxcote Gdns
    NMIL/BTOS BH25...... 225 K5 [1]
Foxcott CI ITCH SO19...... 132 D8 [1]
Foxcott Gv HAV PO9...... 165 K3
Foxcott Dr FAWY SO45...... 179 M5
    WIMB BH21...... 192 F3
Foxes CI VWD BH31...... 144 D3
    WVILLE PO7...... 164 C2
Foxes La ROMY SO51...... 76 E4
Foxglade FAWY SO45...... 206 D1 [1]
Foxglove CI
    CHCH/BSGR BH23...... 224 A8 [2]
Foxglove PI
    NMIL/BTOS BH25...... 226 B4 [1]
Foxgloves FHAM/PORC PO16...... 7 L1
    UPTN BH16...... 232 A1 [1]
The Foxgloves HEND SO30...... 134 B3 [2]
Foxhayes La FAWY SO45...... 206 D1
Foxhills TOTT SO40...... 129 G4
    VWD BH31...... 144 F2 [1]
Foxhills CI TOTT SO40...... 129 G5
Foxholes Rd PLE BH15...... 233 L2
    SBNE BH6...... 237 L4
Foxlands FAWY SO45...... 206 D1 [1]
Fox La FUFL SO22...... 26 B3
    WIMB BH21...... 193 G3
Foxlea Gdns GPORT PO12...... 209 M1 [1]
Foxley Dr HSEA PO3...... 187 M4
Fox Pond La LYMN SO41...... 228 A6
Foxtail Dr FAWY SO45...... 155 K7
Foxwood Av
    CHCH/BSGR BH23...... 238 E3
Foxy Paddock FAWY SO45...... 206 D1 [1]
Foy Gdns HLER SO31...... 158 A7
Foyle Rd CHFD SO53...... 81 G2
Frampton CI NMIL/BTOS BH25...... 226 A3
    RWIN SO21...... 54 E7
Frampton PI RGWD BH24...... 170 E1 [1]
Frampton Rd
    MOOR/WNTN BH9...... 220 E8
Frampton Wy TOTT SO40...... 129 K2
    WINC SO23...... 17 H1
Frances Av BMTH BH1...... 15 K4
    WVILLE PO7...... 164 B5
Francis Av BWD BH11...... 219 H5
    ENEY PO4...... 211 K5
Francis CI LSOL/BMARY PO13...... 208 E3
Francis Gdns WINC SO23...... 3 J2
Francis PI FHAM/STUB PO14...... 184 B6
    HORN PO8...... 116 B5
Frankland Crs PSTN BH14...... 234 D5
Frankland Ter EMRTH PO10...... 166 E8 [2]
Franklin Rd LSOL/BMARY PO13...... 209 L1
    MOOR/WNTN BH9...... 220 E5 [1]
    NMIL/BTOS BH25...... 226 A4
    RWIN SO21...... 54 F1 [1]
Franklyn Av ITCH SO19...... 132 E4
Franklyn CI UPTN BH16...... 232 A1
Frankston Rd SBNE BH6...... 237 H4
Frarydene EMRTH PO10...... 167 H8
Fraser CI ROWN SO16...... 105 L2
Fraser Gdns EMRTH PO10...... 167 J6
Fraser Rd BKME/WDN BH12...... 219 K7
    HAV PO9...... 8 B2
    LSOL/BMARY PO13...... 185 G4
    NEND PO2...... 186 F6 [1]
    SSEA PO5...... 13 J3
Frater La GPORT PO12...... 185 L7
Fratton Rd PSEA PO1...... 211 J2
Fratton Wy ELGH SO50...... 83 H7
Frayslea FAWY SO45...... 155 L6 [1]
Freda Rd CHCH/BSGR BH23...... 237 L2
Freda Routh Gdns ELGH SO50...... 83 J6 [1]
Frederica Rd
    MOOR/WNTN BH9...... 220 C8
Frederick St SHAM SO14...... 131 M2
Freedom Ct FAWY SO45...... 155 L5 [1]
Freegrounds Av HEND SO30...... 134 A2 [1]
Freegrounds CI HEND SO30...... 134 A2
Freegrounds Rd HEND SO30...... 134 A2
Freemans CI WIMB BH21...... 192 F2
Freemans La WIMB BH21...... 192 F3
Freemantle CI ITCH SO19...... 132 D3 [2]
Freemantle Common Rd
    ITCH SO19...... 132 D3
Freemantle Rd GPORT PO12...... 209 M1
Freestone Rd SSEA PO5...... 13 J8 [1]
Free St BPWT SO32...... 85 J8
Frenches La ROMY SO51...... 49 G7
Frenches Vw WVILLE PO7...... 139 J4 [1]
Frenchmans Rd PSF GU32...... 63 K4
Frenchmoor La RSAL SP5...... 19 L5
French Rd CFDH BH17...... 217 M7
French St PSEA PO1...... 12 C5 [1]
    SHAM SO14...... 4 F6 [1]
Frensham CI WVILLE PO7...... 164 A2 [1]
Frensham CI HEND SO30...... 134 A2 [1]
    NBNE BH10...... 220 C5
Frensham Rd ENEY PO4...... 211 K4
Freshfield Gdns WVILLE PO7...... 140 C8
Freshfield Rd WSHM SO15...... 130 F1
Freshfield Sq WSHM SO15...... 130 F1 [1]
Freshwater Dr PLE BH15...... 232 C5 [1]
Freshwater Rd CHAM PO6...... 187 J1 [1]
    CHCH/BSGR BH23...... 239 H2
Friarscroft HLER SO31...... 156 F1
Friars Cft TOTT SO40...... 104 A6

Friarsgate WINC SO23...... 3 H7
Friars Pond Rd FHAM PO15...... 160 A7 [1]
Friars CI CHCH/BSGR BH23...... 239 G2
    ELGH SO50...... 81 L7
Friars Wk NMIL/BTOS BH25...... 225 L8
Friars Wy WEND SO18...... 107 J4
Fritham CI TOTT SO40...... 129 G1
Fritham Gdns CHAR BH8...... 221 H5
Fritham Rd WEND SO18...... 108 B8
Frith La WHAM PO17...... 136 E2
Frobisher Av
    BKME/WDN BH12...... 219 K7
Frobisher CI
    CHCH/BSGR BH23...... 238 E2 [2]
    LSOL/BMARY PO13...... 209 G2
    RGWD BH24...... 147 G7 [2]
Frobisher Gdns
    EMRTH PO10...... 166 D8 [2]
    ITCH SO19...... 133 G4
Frobisher Gv
    FHAM/PORC PO16...... 186 A1
Froddington Rd SSEA PO5...... 13 K5 [1]
Froghall FAWY SO45...... 155 K7
Frogham HI FBDG SP6...... 123 G1
Frog La FBDG SP6...... 122 C1
Frogmore FHAM/STUB PO14...... 160 A8
Frogmore La HORN PO8...... 140 E2
    ROWN SO16...... 105 J5
Frogmore Rd ENEY PO4...... 211 K4
Frome CI TOTT SO40...... 130 E6
Frome Rd WEND SO18...... 107 M5
Fromond CI LYMN SO41...... 228 C3 [2]
Fromond Rd FUFL SO22...... 16 B5
Frosthole CI FHAM PO15...... 6 D1
Frosthole Crs FHAM PO15...... 6 D1
Frost La FAWY SO45...... 156 A6
Frost Rd BWD BH11...... 219 K4
Froud Wy WIMB BH21...... 217 G4 [1]
Froxfield Gdns
    FHAM/PORC PO16...... 162 A7 [1]
Froxfield Rd HAV PO9...... 165 M3
Froyle Ct HAV PO9...... 165 M3
    HLER SO31...... 157 L4
Fryer CI BWD BH11...... 219 M3
Fryern CI CHFD SO53...... 81 G2
Fryern Court Rd FBDG SP6...... 97 K4
Fryer's Copse WIMB BH21...... 193 G2
Fryers Rd WIMB BH21...... 144 C8
Fry's La FAWY SO45...... 180 C6
    LYMN SO41...... 227 H7
Fulflood Rd HAV PO9...... 165 J3
Fullerton CI HAV PO9...... 165 M5 [1]
    ITCH SO19...... 132 D8
Fullerton Rd LYMN SO41...... 228 A4
Fulmar CI ROWN SO16...... 106 A3
Fulmar Dr FAWY SO45...... 155 M6
Fulmar Rd CHCH/BSGR BH23...... 238 F3
Fulmer Wk HORN PO8...... 140 C4
    HORN PO8...... 140 C4
Fulwood Av BWD BH11...... 219 J3
Funtington Rd NEND PO2...... 187 K8
Funtley HI FHAM/PORC PO16...... 160 C3
Funtley Rd FHAM PO15...... 160 B3
Furdies WVILLE PO7...... 139 J4 [2]
Furley CI WINC SO23...... 3 K7
The Furlong RGWD BH24...... 170 D1
Furneaux Gdns
    FHAM/PORC PO16...... 7 J1
Furnell Rd PLE BH15...... 233 J7 [2]
Furness Rd SSEA PO5...... 211 H7 [1]
Furness Wy HISD PO11...... 213 H4
Furniss Gv EMRTH PO10...... 167 J7
Furry Wy FHAM/STUB PO14...... 183 M5
Furzebrook CI CFDH BH17...... 218 C6
Furzedale Gdns FAWY SO45...... 155 M7
Furzedale Pk FAWY SO45...... 155 M7
Furzedown Crs HAV PO9...... 165 L3
Furzedown Ms FAWY SO45...... 155 M7 [1]
Furzedown Rd PTSW SO17...... 106 F6
Furzehall Av FHAM/PORC PO16...... 7 L1
Furze Hill Dr PSTN BH14...... 234 B7
Furzelands Rd WIMB BH21...... 144 C8
Furze La ENEY PO4...... 212 B3
Furzeley Rd WVILLE PO7...... 139 K6
Furze Meadow EPSF GU31...... 65 K8
Furze Rd ITCH SO19...... 132 E3
Furze Wy HORN PO8...... 140 F4
Furzey CI FAWY SO45...... 180 D7
Furzey La BROC SO42...... 177 M7
Furzley Ct HAV PO9...... 165 G2
Furzley La ROMY SO51...... 102 C3
Furzley Rd ROMY SO51...... 102 C3
Fushia CI HAV PO9...... 166 A4
Fushsia Gdns ROWN SO16...... 106 C6 [1]
Fyeford CI ROWN SO16...... 105 L2
Fyfield CI FHAM PO15...... 135 C8
Fyfield Wy FUFL SO22...... 16 A3
Fyning St PSEA PO1...... 211 H2

G

Gables Ct ROWN SO16...... 106 E3 [1]
Gage CI TOTT SO40...... 130 E6
Gainsborough Av
    NMIL/BTOS BH25...... 225 M3
Gainsborough Ms
    FHAM/STUB PO14...... 159 K8 [1]
    RGWD BH24...... 169 J3
Gainsford Rd ITCH SO19...... 132 C3
Gain's Rd ENEY PO4...... 13 L7
Galaxie Rd HORN PO8...... 140 F4
Gale Moor Av GPORT PO12...... 209 H5
Galleon CI HLER SO31...... 158 D7 [1]
The Gallops FHAM/STUB PO14...... 159 H6
Gallop Wy BKME/WDN BH12...... 235 H1
Gallows Dr FERN BH22...... 194 B7
Galsworthy Rd TOTT SO40...... 129 H1
Galton Av CHCH/BSGR BH23...... 237 L2 [1]
Galt Rd CHAM PO6...... 164 B8
Gamble CI ITCH SO19...... 132 D4

Gambledown La ROMY SO51...... 48 D3
Gamblins La BPWT SO32...... 111 L8
Ganger Farm La ROMY SO51...... 51 H6 [1]
Ganger Rd ROMY SO51...... 51 H6 [2]
Gannet CI CHAM PO6...... 164 C8
    ROWN SO16...... 106 A3
The Gannets
    FHAM PO14...... 183 M6
Garbett Rd WINC SO23...... 3 L7
Garbitts La EPSF GU31...... 65 L5
Garden City FAWY SO45...... 154 C2
Garden CI HISD PO11...... 213 K5
    LYND SO43...... 151 J3
    NMIL/BTOS BH25...... 225 L7
Gardeners La ROMY SO51...... 77 L2
Garden-lane RGWD BH24...... 169 J5 [2]
Garden La SSEA PO5...... 13 G6
    WINC SO23...... 3 H7
Garden Ms HLER SO31...... 158 A7
Garden Rd RGWD BH24...... 172 D6
Gardens Crs PSTN BH14...... 234 A8
Garden Rd PSTN BH14...... 234 A8
The Gardens HAV PO9...... 9 K6
    WVILLE PO7...... 114 C5
Garden Wk FERN BH22...... 194 C1 [2]
Gardiner CI WINC SO23...... 130 E6
Gardner Rd CHCH/BSGR BH23...... 222 C8
    FHAM/STUB PO14...... 183 K1
    RGWD BH24...... 170 F2
Garendon Ct FBDG SP6...... 97 K6 [1]
Garfield Av BMTH BH1...... 236 C3
Garfield Av BPWT SO32...... 85 H8
Garfield Rd BPWT SO32...... 85 H8
    HLER SO31...... 156 E2
    ITCH SO19...... 132 C1
    NEND PO2...... 187 H8
Garland Av EMRTH PO10...... 166 D5
Garland Rd PLE BH15...... 233 J4
Garnett CI FHAM/STUB PO14...... 184 A4
Garnier Pk WHAM PO17...... 136 E4
Garnier Rd WINC SO23...... 26 F3
Garnier St PSEA PO1...... 13 K1
Garnock Rd ITCH SO19...... 132 B6
Garratt CI HEND SO30...... 109 H6
Garrett CI ITCH SO19...... 132 E7
Garrick Gdns ITCH SO19...... 132 E6
Garrison HI BPWT SO32...... 87 G6
Garrow Dr LYMN SO41...... 228 C3
Garsdale CI BWD BH11...... 219 J3
Garsons Rd EMRTH PO10...... 167 H8
Garston CI PSF GU32...... 61 J8
Garstons CI FHAM/STUB PO14...... 159 K8
Garstons Rd FHAM/STUB PO14...... 159 K8
Gar St WINC SO23...... 2 F8
Garth CI RGWD BH24...... 169 H4
Garth Rd MOOR/WNTN BH9...... 220 E7 [1]
Garton Rd ITCH SO19...... 132 B5
Gatcombe HLER SO31...... 157 G1
Gatcombe Av HSEA PO3...... 187 K6
Gatcombe Dr NEND PO2...... 187 K5
Gatcombe Gdns
    FHAM/STUB PO14...... 159 M8
    WEND SO18...... 107 M6 [2]
Gatehouse La EPSF GU31...... 66 C2
Gate House Rd
    FHAM/PORC PO16...... 185 L1
Gate Hyde WINC SO23...... 3 G5 [1]
Gatekeeper CI WINC SO23...... 3 M7
Gatwick CI ROWN SO16...... 105 M4
Gaulter CI HAV PO9...... 133 H3
Gavan St ITCH SO19...... 133 H3
G Av FAWY SO45...... 180 D2
Gaydon Ri BWD BH11...... 219 J4 [2]
Gayle Rd BKME/WDN BH12...... 219 K7
Gaza Av BROC SO42...... 204 A2
Gazing La ROMY SO51...... 76 D5
Geddes Wy EPSF GU31...... 64 B4
Gemini CI ROWN SO16...... 105 L4
Geneva Av SBNE BH6...... 237 L4
Genoa CI ITCH SO19...... 228 A7
Gento CI HEND SO30...... 134 C2
Geoffrey Av WVILLE PO7...... 163 M6
Geoffrey Crs
    FHAM/PORC PO16...... 184 F2
George Byng Wy NEND PO2...... 187 H4
George Curl Wy ELGH SO50...... 107 L2 [1]
George Eyston Dr FUFL SO22...... 26 C2
George Rd LYMN SO41...... 242 B3
George St ELGH SO50...... 81 M5
    GPORT PO12...... 11 H2
    PSEA PO1...... 211 J1
Georgian CI RGWD BH24...... 146 E8
Georgian Wy NBNE BH10...... 220 D4 [1]
Georgina CI
    BKME/WDN BH12...... 220 A8 [1]
Gerald Rd TWDS BH3...... 235 M2
Gerard Crs ITCH SO19...... 133 H2
Germaine CI CHCH/BSGR BH23...... 224 D8
Gervis Crs PSTN BH14...... 233 M4
Gervis PI BMTH BH1...... 14 E6
Gervis Rd BMTH BH1...... 15 H6
Gibbs Rd SHAM SO14...... 4 F2
Gibraltar CI FHAM PO15...... 6 A3
Gibraltar Rd ENEY PO4...... 212 B5
    FHAM/STUB PO14...... 184 D2
Gibson CI FHAM PO15...... 159 J2
    LSOL/BMARY PO13...... 208 D2 [3]
Gibson Rd CFDH BH17...... 233 K1
Giddylake WIMB BH21...... 192 A2
Gifford CI FHAM PO15...... 6 C1
Gilkicker Rd GPORT PO12...... 11 C9
Gillam Rd NBNE BH10...... 220 A1
Gillcrest FHAM PO15...... 159 G4
Gillett Rd BKME/WDN BH12...... 235 H1

Gillingham CI
    MOOR/WNTN BH9...... 221 G4 [1]
    WINC SO23...... 17 H1
Gillingham Rd LYMN SO41...... 242 C4
Gillman Rd CHAM PO6...... 164 C8
Gilpin CI ITCH SO19...... 133 H3
    LYMN SO41...... 202 D7
Gilpin HI LYMN SO41...... 200 F6
Gins La BROC SO42...... 205 H7
Girton CI FHAM/STUB PO14...... 159 J2
Gitsham Gdns WVILLE PO7...... 164 A5 [3]
Gladdis Rd BWD BH11...... 219 K4
Gladelands CI BDST BH18...... 217 J4 [1]
Gladelands Wy BDST BH18...... 217 J4 [2]
The Glades HLER SO31...... 158 E4
The Glade CHFD SO53...... 53 L7
    FAWY SO45...... 206 C1
    FHAM PO15...... 160 B4
    HISD PO11...... 214 A6
    RGWD BH24...... 169 J3
    WVILLE PO7...... 140 E8
Gladstone Gdns
    FHAM/PORC PO16...... 186 A1 [1]
Gladstone Rd
    BKME/WDN BH12...... 234 B3
    GPORT PO12...... 209 L1
    ITCH SO19...... 132 F3
    LTDN BH7...... 236 E3
Gladstone Rd East LTDN BH7...... 236 E3
Gladstone Rd West BMTH BH1...... 236 D3
Gladstone St WINC SO23...... 2 F6
Gladys Av HORN PO8...... 140 E4
    NEND PO2...... 187 H6
Glamis Av NBNE BH10...... 220 C3
Glamis CI WVILLE PO7...... 140 E8
Glamorgan Rd HORN PO8...... 116 A6
Glasgow Rd ENEY PO4...... 211 H6
Glasslaw Rd WEND SO18...... 107 M8
Glasspool WVILLE PO7...... 139 J3
Gleadowe Av
    CHCH/BSGR BH23...... 237 L2
Glebe CI HISD PO11...... 213 J5
Glebe Cnr WHAM PO17...... 136 F5
Glebe CI ELGH SO50...... 83 J6
    HEND SO30...... 109 H8 [1]
    PTSW SO17...... 106 F6
Glebe Ct LSOL/BMARY PO13...... 185 J8
Glebefield Gdns CHAM PO6...... 163 J8 [1]
Glebefields LYMN SO41...... 242 C3 [1]
Glebe La RSAL SP5...... 75 J4
Glebe Meadow RSAL SP5...... 19 M6
Glebe Park Av CHAM PO6...... 164 E4
Glebe Rd EPSF GU31...... 91 J3
The Glebe FHAM/STUB PO14...... 184 A7
Glenair Av PSTN BH14...... 233 M5
Glenair Rd PSTN BH14...... 233 M5
Glenavon NMIL/BTOS BH25...... 225 M6
Glenavon Rd
    CHCH/BSGR BH23...... 224 D7
Glenbrook Wk
    FHAM/STUB PO14...... 160 A8
Glencarron Wy ROWN SO16...... 106 D5
Glen CI NMIL/BTOS BH25...... 225 M6
Glencoe BKME/WDN BH12...... 234 C3
    LTDN BH7...... 236 E1
    PSEA PO1...... 211 K1
Glencoyne Gdns ROWN SO16...... 105 L6
Glenda CI HLER SO31...... 158 B8 [1]
Glendale BPWT SO32...... 112 A4
Glen DI HAV PO9...... 142 B7
Glendale HLER SO31...... 158 F6 [1]
Glendale Av FERN BH22...... 194 B2
Glendale CI CHCH/BSGR BH23...... 222 B5
    WIMB BH21...... 192 A3
Glendale Rd SBNE BH6...... 237 M4
Glendon Av NBNE BH10...... 220 A4
Glendowan Rd CHFD SO53...... 80 F1
Glendrive NMIL/BTOS BH25...... 225 M6
Gleneagles Av PSTN BH14...... 233 M6
Gleneagles CI FERN BH22...... 194 C3
Gleneagles Dr HORN PO8...... 140 F6
Glenelg FHAM PO15...... 6 E3
Glenesha Gdns FHAM PO15...... 6 E3
Glen Eyre Dr ROWN SO16...... 106 C3
Glen Eyre Rd ROWN SO16...... 106 C3
Glen Eyre Wy ROWN SO16...... 106 C3
Glenferness Av TWDS BH3...... 235 J2
Glen Fern Rd BMTH BH1...... 15 G5
Glenfield Av WEND SO18...... 132 D1
Glenfield Crs WEND SO18...... 132 D1
Glenfield Wy WEND SO18...... 132 D1
Glengariff Rd PSTN BH14...... 234 B6
Glengarry NMIL/BTOS BH25...... 226 A6
Glengarry Wy
    CHCH/BSGR BH23...... 239 H3
Glenives CI RGWD BH24...... 169 K4
Glenlea CI HEND SO30...... 108 C7
Glenlea Dr HEND SO30...... 108 C7
Glenleigh Av CHAM PO6...... 187 K1 [2]
Glenleigh Pk HAV PO9...... 9 K3
Glenme Adows Dr BWD BH11...... 219 M3
Glenmoor CI NBNE BH10...... 220 B7 [3]
Glenmoor Rd FERN BH22...... 194 B5 [2]
    MOOR/WNTN BH9...... 220 B8
Glenmount Dr PSTN BH14...... 234 A3
Glenn Rd HEND SO30...... 108 C6
    HLER SO31...... 158 C2
Glen Rd BOSC BH5...... 236 D4
    HLER SO31...... 158 C1
    ITCH SO19...... 132 B7
    PSTN BH14...... 234 A4
Glenroyd Gdns SBNE BH6...... 237 J4
Glenside FAWY SO45...... 155 K5
    NMIL/BTOS BH25...... 240 A1
Glenside Av ITCH SO19...... 133 H4
Glen Spey NMIL/BTOS BH25...... 226 A6
The Glen PSTN BH13...... 234 D8
    LSOL/BMARY PO13...... 185 J7 [2]
Glenthorne CI
    FHAM/STUB PO14...... 184 A7
Glenthorne Meadow PSF GU32...... 61 K8
Glenville Rd HSEA PO3...... 187 L7
Glenville CI CHCH/BSGR BH23...... 224 F6
Glenville Gdns NBNE BH10...... 220 A6 [3]
Glenville Rd CHCH/BSGR BH23...... 224 F6
    NBNE BH10...... 220 A6
Glenwood Av ROWN SO16...... 106 C5

Glenwood CI FERN BH22...... 168 C6 [1]
Glenwood Ct ELGH SO50...... 83 K6
Glenwood Gdns HORN PO8...... 140 F6
Glenwood La FERN BH22...... 168 C6 [2]
Glenwood Rd EMRTH PO10...... 167 H7
    FERN BH22...... 168 C6
    VWD BH31...... 144 C3
Glenwood Wy FERN BH22...... 168 C6 [3]
Glidden CI PSEA PO1...... 13 J1
Glidden La WVILLE PO7...... 114 C5
Glissons FERN BH22...... 193 L6
Gloucester CI PSF GU32...... 63 J5
Gloucester Rd
    BKME/WDN BH12...... 234 D3
    LTDN BH7...... 236 E3
    PSEA PO1...... 210 E2
    WVILLE PO7...... 164 D2
Gloucester Sq SHAM SO14...... 5 G5
Gloucester Ter SSEA PO5...... 13 G5 [3]
Gloucester Vw SSEA PO5...... 13 G5 [5]
Glyn Dr FHAM/STUB PO14...... 184 A6
Glyn Jones CI FAWY SO45...... 180 C6
Glynville CI WIMB BH21...... 192 E1
Glynville Rd WIMB BH21...... 192 E1
Glyn Wy FHAM/STUB PO14...... 184 A6
Goathorn CI UPTN BH16...... 232 C4
Godfrey Pink Wy BPWT SO32...... 111 J1 [2]
Godmanston CI CFDH BH17...... 218 E7
Godshill CI CHAR BH8...... 221 H5
Godwin CI EMRTH PO10...... 166 C5
    FUFL SO22...... 16 B5
Godwin Crs HORN PO8...... 116 B4
Godwit CI GPORT PO12...... 185 M8
Godwit Rd ENEY PO4...... 212 A2 [1]
Gofton Av CHAM PO6...... 187 M1
Gogg's La RSAL SP5...... 73 L2
Goldcrest CI
    FHAM/PORC PO16...... 161 J8 [1]
    HORN PO8...... 140 C1
Goldcrest Gdns ROWN SO16...... 105 M3
Goldcrest La TOTT SO40...... 104 B8
Golden Ct HEND SO30...... 108 E6
Golden Crs LYMN SO41...... 227 H7
Golden Gv SHAM SO14...... 5 J2
Golden Hind Pk FAWY SO45...... 155 K6
Goldenleas Dr BWD BH11...... 219 H5
Goldfinch CI
    NMIL/BTOS BH25...... 225 K6 [1]
Goldfinch La
    LSOL/BMARY PO13...... 208 D1
Goldfinch Rd CFDH BH17...... 217 J8
Gold Mead CI LYMN SO41...... 228 C3 [2]
Goldring CI HISD PO11...... 213 L5
Goldsmith Av ENEY PO4...... 13 M2
Goldsmith CI TOTT SO40...... 129 H1 [2]
Goldsmith Rd ELGH SO50...... 81 L7
Gold St SSEA PO5...... 13 L6
Golf Course Rd ROWN SO16...... 106 D2
Golf Links Rd BDST BH18...... 217 M3
    FERN BH22...... 194 C3
Goliath Rd PLE BH15...... 232 C6
Gomer La GPORT PO12...... 209 J4
Goodacre Dr NBAD SO52...... 80 E3
Goodison CI ELGH SO50...... 83 G7 [1]
Goodlands V HEND SO30...... 133 L1 [1]
Good Rd BKME/WDN BH12...... 234 B1
Goodsell Ct
    NMIL/BTOS BH25...... 183 M6 [3]
Goodwin CI ROWN SO16...... 105 J6 [3]
Goodwood CI
    FHAM/STUB PO14...... 159 G6
    GPORT PO12...... 185 M8
    WVILLE PO7...... 140 F7
Goodwood Ct EMRTH PO10...... 167 J8
Goodwood Gdns TOTT SO40...... 104 D8
Goodwood Rd ELGH SO50...... 81 K3
    PSEA PO1...... 13 L6
Gordon Av SHAM SO14...... 106 F8
    WINC SO23...... 27 H2
Gordon CI
    FHAM/STUB PO14...... 159 G6
    GPORT PO12...... 185 M8
    WVILLE PO7...... 140 F7
Gordon Mt CHCH/BSGR BH23...... 224 F7 [1]
Gordon Rd BKME/WDN BH12...... 234 F3
    BMTH BH1...... 236 C4
    BPWT SO32...... 110 E7
    CHCH/BSGR BH23...... 224 E8
    CHFD SO53...... 53 J7
    EMRTH PO10...... 190 F1
    FHAM/PORC PO16...... 7 G5
    GPORT PO12...... 10 D4
    LYMN SO41...... 228 A5
    PSEA PO1...... 12 E6
    WIMB BH21...... 192 C4
    WINC SO23...... 3 H5
    WVILLE PO7...... 164 B2
Gordon Rd South
    BKME/WDN BH12...... 234 F4
Gordon Ter ITCH SO19...... 132 E6 [1]
Gordon Wy CHCH/BSGR BH23...... 223 M7
Gore Rd NMIL/BTOS BH25...... 225 J6
Gorey Rd BKME/WDN BH12...... 219 H7 [1]
Goring Av HORN PO8...... 116 B4
Goring Fld FUFL SO22...... 16 B7
Gorleston Rd
    BKME/WDN BH12...... 234 E3
Gorley Ct HAV PO9...... 165 G2
Gorley Lynch FBDG SP6...... 123 H4
Gorley Rd RGWD BH24...... 147 G8
Gorran Av LSOL/BMARY PO13...... 185 H4
Gorsecliff Rd NBNE BH10...... 220 B7
Gorse CI HLER SO31...... 158 C5
    NMIL/BTOS BH25...... 226 B4
    RGWD BH24...... 169 H4
Gorse Hill CI PLE BH15...... 233 K3
Gorse Hill Crs PLE BH15...... 233 K3
Gorse Hill Rd PLE BH15...... 233 K3
Gorselands Rd WEND SO18...... 108 A7
Gorselands Wy
    LSOL/BMARY PO13...... 185 H8
Gorse La UPTN BH16...... 232 B1
Gorse Rd EPSF GU31...... 64 B5
    WIMB BH21...... 217 G3
Gort Crs ITCH SO19...... 132 F4 [2]
Gort Rd BWD BH11...... 219 M5
    CFDH BH17...... 217 L7
Gosling CI CFDH BH17...... 233 L1

Gosport La LYND SO43 151 L4
Gosport Rd FHAM/PORC PO16 7 K7
FHAM/STUB PO14 184 B6
LSOL/BMARY PO13 208 D3
Gosport St LYMN SO41 228 D4
Gough Crs CFDH BH17 217 M6
Gover Rd ROWN SO16 105 H7
Grace Dieu Gdns HLER SO31 133 K7 1
Grace La FBDG SP6 72 D8
Graddidge Wy TOTT SO40 129 H1
Graemar La ROMY SO51 48 B7
Grafton Cl CHCH/BSGR BH23 238 C2 3
TWDS BH3 235 M1
Grafton Gdns LYMN SO41 228 A7
ROWN SO16 106 B3
Grafton Rd TWDS BH3 235 M2
WINC SO23 26 E2
Grafton St NEND PO2 211 G1
Graham Rd ENEY PO4 13 M6
GPORT PO12 209 L2
SHAM SO14 131 M2
Graham St SHAM SO14 132 A2
Grainger Gdns ITCH SO19 133 G5 1
Granada Cl HORN PO8 140 E5
Granada Rd ENEY PO4 13 L9
HEND SO30 133 L3
Granby Gv PTSW SO17 107 G5
Granby Rd MOOR/WNTN BH9 220 E4
Grand Av SBNE BH6 237 H4
Grand Pde FUFL SO22 16 B3
HISD PO11 213 L6
PSEA PO1 12 C6
Grange Cl GPORT PO12 209 K2
HAV PO9 9 J3
LYMN SO41 227 J8
WEND SO18 107 K4 3
Grange Crs GPORT PO12 209 K2
Grange Dr HEND SO30 109 J8
Grange Gdns
BKME/WDN BH12 234 D1 1
Grange La LSOL/BMARY PO13 185 G8
Grange Ms ROMY SO51 51 H7
Grange Rd BDST BH18 217 L4
CHCH/BSGR BH23 239 G1
HEND SO30 109 H8
HLER SO31 156 E2
LSOL/BMARY PO13 209 H4
NEND PO2 187 H7
PSF GU32 63 K6
RGWD BH24 169 H6
ROWN SO16 106 A7
SBNE BH6 237 J5
WINC SO23 26 D5
The Grange LYMN SO41 227 J8
Grangewood Gdns
ELGH SO50 83 G6 1
Grantham Av HLER SO31 157 J5
Grantham Rd BMTH BH1 236 D3
ELGH SO50 81 L6
ITCH SO19 132 D2
Grantley Rd BOSC BH5 236 E4 1
Grant Rd CHAM PO6 164 B8
Grant's Av BMTH BH1 236 C2
Grants Cl BMTH BH1 236 C2
Granville Cl HAV PO9 9 H5
Granville Rd BOSC BH5 236 F3
PSTN BH14 234 A3
Granville St SHAM SO14 5 K4
Grasdean Cl WEND SO18 107 M7 3
Grasmere ELGH SO50 81 L6 1
Grasmere Cl
CHCH/BSGR BH23 222 B5
WEND SO18 108 A7 2
Grasmere Gdns
NMIL/BTOS BH25 225 M3
Grasmere Rd BOSC BH5 236 F4
CCLF BH13 245 G5
Grasmere Wy
FHAM/STUB PO14 184 B4
Grassmere Wy HORN PO8 140 F7
Grassymead FHAM PO15 159 G4 2
Grateley Crs HAV PO9 165 G4
Gravel Cl RSAL SP5 44 D8
Gravel Hl BPWT SO32 112 A5
WIMB BH21 192 B7
Gravel La RGWD BH24 146 E8
Gray Cl CFDH BH17 218 D8
HLER SO31 158 D6
Graycot Cl NBNE BH10 220 A3
Grayland Cl HISD PO11 213 J4 2
Grayling Md ROMY SO51 50 E7
Grays Av FAWY SO45 155 M5
Grays Cl ELGH SO50 54 E8
GPORT PO12 209 J5
ROMY SO51 78 F1
Grays Ct PSEA PO1 12 D4
Grayshott Cl FUFL SO22 16 C4
Grayshott Rd ENEY PO4 211 K4
GPORT PO12 10 B4
Gray's Yd PLE BH15 233 H7 3
Great Br ROMY SO51 50 D6
Greatbridge Rd ROMY SO51 50 D5
Great Copse Dr HAV PO9 165 K3
Great Elms Cl FAWY SO45 179 M5
Great Field Rd FUFL SO22 2 A1
Greatfield Wy HAV PO9 141 M6
Great Gays FHAM/STUB PO14 183 L7
Great Hanger EPSF GU31 64 A5
Great Md LYND SO43 151 K4 3
WVILLE PO7 139 L5
Great Minster St WINC SO23 3 G8
Great Southsea St SSEA PO5 13 G5
Great Well Dr ROMY SO51 50 E8
Greatwood Cl FAWY SO45 155 L6 2
Greaves Cl NBNE BH10 220 A5
Grebe Cl CFDH BH17 217 J8
CHCH/BSGR BH23 238 F2 3
FHAM/PORC PO16 161 K8 5
HORN PO8 140 C4
LYMN SO41 242 D4
Greenacre NMIL/BTOS BH25 225 L8
Greenacre Cl UPTN BH16 232 B2
Greenacre Gdns WVILLE PO7 164 B4
Greenacres RSAL SP5 72 C1
Greenacres Cl NBNE BH10 220 C1
Green Acres Cl RGWD BH24 170 B3
Greenacres Dr RWIN SO21 54 B5
Greenaway La HLER SO31 158 B6
Greenbank Crs ROWN SO16 106 E3
Greenbanks Cl LYMN SO41 242 C3
Greenbanks Gdns
FHAM/PORC PO16 161 H6
Green Bottom WIMB BH21 192 E1
Green Cl FAWY SO45 155 L4 6
RSAL SP5 47 G4
TOTT SO40 128 D4
PLE BH15 233 J7 4
Greenclose La WIMB BH21 192 B4
Green Crs LSOL/BMARY PO13 185 G7
Greendale Cl CHFD SO53 81 K2 1
The Greendale FHAM PO15 160 B4
Greenfield Crs HORN PO8 140 F5
Greenfield Gdns
NMIL/BTOS BH25 225 M8
Greenfield Ri HORN PO8 140 F5
Greenfield Rd PLE BH15 233 K2
Greenfields EPSF GU31 93 K1 1
LISS GU33 36 F4
Greenfields Av TOTT SO40 104 D7
Greenfields Cl EPSF GU31 65 K8
Greenfinch Cl CFDH BH17 217 K7
ELGH SO50 81 J7 2
Greenfinch Wk RGWD BH24 171 G2 2
Greenhayes BDST BH18 218 A6
Greenhays Ri WIMB BH21 192 A3
Greenhill Av FUFL SO22 2 C7
Greenhill Cl FUFL SO22 2 B7
WIMB BH21 192 B2
Greenhill La ROWN SO16 79 K8
WIMB BH21 192 B2
Greenhill Rd FUFL SO22 2 B7
WIMB BH21 192 B1
Greenhill Ter FUFL SO22 2 C7
Green Hollow Cl
FHAM/PORC PO16 6 D1
Green Jacket Cl FUFL SO22 26 D3
Green La BPWT SO32 112 B1
FAWY SO45 180 D8
FBDG SP6 71 H8
FERN BH22 193 L7
GPORT PO12 10 C7
HISD PO11 213 J6
HLER SO31 133 J7
HLER SO31 134 B8
HLER SO31 134 E7
HLER SO31 157 L6
HLER SO31 158 D7
HORN PO8 116 C3
HSEA PO3 187 L5
NARL SO24 32 C2
NBNE BH10 220 A5
NMIL/BTOS BH25 225 M8
PSF GU32 34 E3
RGWD BH24 170 E1
RGWD BH24 170 F5
ROMY SO51 51 K8
ROWN SO16 80 E7
ROWN SO16 105 K6
RSAL SP5 44 E8
TOTT SO40 104 A4
WVILLE PO7 113 L8
WVILLE PO7 139 J3
Greenlea Cl CHAM PO6 163 M6
Greenlea Crs ROWN SO16 107 J3
Greenlea Rd GPORT PO12 209 K1 2
Greenmead Av LYMN SO41 227 H7
Green Park Cl WINC SO23 3 J2
Green Park Rd ROWN SO16 130 C1
Green Pond Cnr HAV PO9 9 J5
Green Pond La ROMY SO51 52 B5
Green Rd FHAM/STUB PO14 184 A4
GPORT PO12 10 C7
MOOR/WNTN BH9 220 E8
PLE BH15 233 H6
SSEA PO5 13 G5
Greens Cl BPWT SO32 85 G8
ELGH SO50 82 F7
Greensleeves Av BDST BH18 217 M2
Greens Meade RSAL SP5 73 J2
Greensome Dr FERN BH22 194 D2
The Green HLER SO31 158 B2
LISS GU33 36 D3 2
ROMY SO51 51 H6 3
RSAL SP5 47 G4
Greenway Cl LYMN SO41 228 A4
Greenway La EPSF GU31 91 H2
Greenway Rd GPORT PO12 209 M2
Greenways BPWT SO32 112 A3
CHCH/BSGR BH23 224 D8
CHFD SO53 81 J2
LYMN SO41 242 B3
ROWN SO16 107 J3
Greenways Av CHAR BH8 221 G5
Greenways Rd BROC SO42 175 L7 3
The Greenwich FAWY SO45 180 C6 1
Greenwood Av CHAM PO6 163 H8
FERN BH22 194 B2
PSTN BH14 234 B8 1
ROWN SO16 105 J2
Greenwood Cl
FHAM/PORC PO16 160 E4
ROMY SO51 50 F8 1
Greenwood Copse
RGWD BH24 169 L4 2
Greenwood La BPWT SO32 83 M8
Greenwood Rd
MOOR/WNTN BH9 220 E7
Greenwoods
NMIL/BTOS BH25 225 M7 2
Greenwood Wy RGWD BH24 169 K4
Greetham St SSEA PO5 13 H2
Gregory Gdns TOTT SO40 104 B7 1
Gregory La BPWT SO32 110 A3
Gregson Cl LSOL/BMARY PO13 185 G5
Grenadier Cl HLER SO31 158 F6
Grendon Cl ROWN SO16 107 G3 2
Grenehurst Wy EPSF GU31 63 L5
Grenfell Rd MOOR/WNTN BH9 220 D5
Grenville Cl RGWD BH24 147 G7
Grenville Gdns FAWY SO45 155 L7
Grenville Rd ENEY PO4 13 L5 1
WIMB BH21 192 B4
Gresham Rd MOOR/WNTN BH9 220 E7
Gresley Gdns HEND SO30 109 H6 3
Grevillea Av FHAM PO15 159 J5
Greville Gn EMRTH PO10 166 C5
Greville Rd WSHM SO15 131 H1
Greyfriars Rd FHAM PO15 160 A6
Greyhound Cl HEND SO30 109 G5 3
Greys Farm Cl NARL SO24 30 C4
Greyshott Av
FHAM/STUB PO14 160 A8
Greystoke Av BWD BH11 219 K2
Greywell Av ROWN SO16 106 A4
Griffen Cl ELGH SO50 82 D6 2
Griffin Ct PTSW SO17 107 H8
Griffin Wk LSOL/BMARY PO13 209 G2
Griffiths Gdns BWD BH11 219 M3
Griffon Cl HLER SO31 133 L7
Grigg La BROC SO42 175 L7
Grimstead Rd RSAL SP5 18 B2
Gritanwood Rd ENEY PO4 211 M5
Grosvenor Cl PTSW SO17 107 H6
RGWD BH24 169 H3
Grosvenor Dr WINC SO23 3 J2
Grosvenor Gdns BMTH BH1 236 D4
HEND SO30 108 C7
PTSW SO17 107 H6 1
Grosvenor Rd CHFD SO53 53 K7
PTSW SO17 107 H6
WBNE BH4 235 H5
Grosvenor Sq WSHM SO15 131 K2
Grosvenor St SSEA PO5 13 H3
Grove Av FHAM/PORC PO16 186 A2
GPORT PO12 11 G2
Grove Gdns ITCH SO19 132 F7
Grovelands Rd FUFL SO22 16 A7
Grove La RSAL SP5 73 L1
Groveley Rd
CHCH/BSGR BH23 238 D2 3
WBNE BH4 235 G6 2
Grovely Av BOSC BH5 236 E4
Grovely Wy ROMY SO51 51 K7
Grove Pastures LYMN SO41 228 C5
Grove Pl ITCH SO19 132 F6
LYMN SO41 228 C5
Grove Rd BKME/WDN BH12 234 A2
BMTH BH1 15 H6
CHAM PO6 188 A1
FHAM/PORC PO16 7 G6
GPORT PO12 209 M1
HAV PO9 8 F5
LSOL/BMARY PO13 208 C2
LYMN SO41 228 D5
NMIL/BTOS BH25 240 F1
RWIN SO21 54 C3
WIMB BH21 192 A4
WSHM SO15 131 G1
Grove Rd East
CHCH/BSGR BH23 222 E8
Grove Rd North SSEA PO5 13 H5
Grove Rd South SSEA PO5 13 H6
Grove Rd West
CHCH/BSGR BH23 222 D8
Groves Down ROMY SO51 76 D4
The Grove CHCH/BSGR BH23 222 C7
EMRTH PO10 166 F5
FERN BH22 194 A4
FHAM/STUB PO14 183 M6
HLER SO31 133 L7
HLER SO31 157 H1
ITCH SO19 132 F7
MOOR/WNTN BH9 220 D5
VWD BH31 144 E3
Grower Gdns BWD BH11 219 L4
Gruneisen Rd NEND PO2 187 G6
Guardhouse Rd PSEA PO1 210 F1
Guardroom Rd NEND PO2 186 F7
Gudge Heath La FHAM PO15 6 B2
Guernsey Cl ROWN SO16 105 K5
Guernsey Rd
BKME/WDN BH12 219 H7
Guessens La FHAM/STUB PO14 159 K8
Guest Av BKME/WDN BH12 234 E2
Guest Cl BKME/WDN BH12 234 F2 1
Guest Rd ELGH SO50 82 C5
UPTN BH16 232 A1
Guildford Cl EMRTH PO10 167 H7
Guildford Dr CHFD SO53 81 G5
Guildford Rd PSEA PO1 13 M1
Guildford St SHAM SO14 5 K1 1
Guildhall Wk PSEA PO1 12 F3
Guildhill Rd SBNE BH6 237 K4
Guillemot Cl FAWY SO45 155 M5
Guillemot Gdns
LSOL/BMARY PO13 184 F5
Gull Cl LSOL/BMARY PO13 184 F6
Gulliver Cl PSTN BH14 234 B8 2
The Gulls TOTT SO40 130 D6
Gullycroft Md HEND SO30 133 M1
Gunners Pk BPWT SO32 85 K8
Gunners Rw ENEY PO4 211 M6
Gunners Wy GPORT PO12 185 K8
LSOL/BMARY PO13 185 L7
Gunville Crs MOOR/WNTN BH9 220 F5
Gunwharf Rd PSEA PO1 12 C4
Gurjun Cl UPTN BH16 216 E8 1
Gurnard Rd CHAM PO6 187 J1
Gurnays Md ROMY SO51 76 C5
Gurney Rd ENEY PO4 211 M4
WIMB BH21 217 J2
WSHM SO15 106 B8
Gussage Rd BKME/WDN BH12 219 J8
Gutner La HISD PO11 190 A7
Gwatkin Cl HAV PO9 165 G5 1
Gwenlyn Rd UPTN BH16 232 B2
Gwynne Rd BKME/WDN BH12 234 D3
Gypsy La HORN PO8 140 D3
RGWD BH24 146 F8

H

Haarlem Ms CHCH/BSGR BH23 238 C1
Habin Hl EPSF GU31 65 L4
Hack Dr RWIN SO21 54 E8
Hacketts La BPWT SO32 86 F6
Hackleys La ROMY SO51 77 G3
Hackupps La ROMY SO51 22 B7
Hackworth Gdns HEND SO30 109 H6
Hadden Rd CHAR BH8 221 H8
Haddon Cl FHAM PO15 6 D6
Haddon Dr ELGH SO50 81 M3
Haddons Dr WIMB BH21 168 B1
Hadleigh Gdns ELGH SO50 81 M3
Hadleigh Rd CHAM PO6 163 H8 3
Hadley Fld FAWY SO45 179 M3 1
Hadley Wy BDST BH18 217 J5
Hadow Rd BWD BH11 220 A5
Hadrian Cl FERN BH22 194 B6
Hadrians Cl CHFD SO53 81 K1
Hadrian Wy ROWN SO16 106 D1
Haflinger Dr HLER SO31 134 F8
Haglane Copse LYMN SO41 227 M6
Hahnemann Rd WCLF BH2 14 C7
Haig Av PSTN BH14 234 D7
Haig Rd ELGH SO50 82 F6
Haileybury Gdns HEND SO30 109 H7 1
Hainault Dr VWD BH31 144 E2
Haking Rd CHCH/BSGR BH23 238 C1 3
Halden Cl ROMY SO51 51 G7
Hale Av NMIL/BTOS BH25 225 M6
Hale Gdns NMIL/BTOS BH25 225 M6
Hale La FBDG SP6 72 E7
Hales Dr HEND SO30 133 L3
Hale St North PSEA PO1 211 H2
Hale St South PSEA PO1 211 H2
Halewood Wy
CHCH/BSGR BH23 222 D8
Halfpenny La PSEA PO1 12 D5 1
Halifax Ri WVILLE PO7 164 D1
Halifax Wy CHCH/BSGR BH23 239 G1
Hall Cl BPWT SO32 85 J8
Hallet Cl WEND SO18 107 M6 3
Hallett Rd HAV PO9 9 K3
Halletts Cl FHAM/STUB PO14 184 A5
The Halliards
FHAM/PORC PO16 184 F1
Halliday Cl GPORT PO12 10 F2
Halliday Crs ENEY PO4 212 A5
Hall Lands La ELGH SO50 83 J6
Hall Rd BWD BH11 219 K5
Halls Farm Cl FUFL SO22 16 D5
The Hall Wy FUFL SO22 16 A3
Halsey Cl GPORT PO12 10 B5
Halstead Rd CHAM PO6 163 H8
WEND SO18 107 L6
Halstock Crs CFDH BH17 218 B6
Halter Pth PLE BH15 232 D5
Halter Ri WIMB BH21 193 G2
Halterworth Cl ROMY SO51 79 G1 2
Halterworth La ROMY SO51 51 H8
Halton Cl CHCH/BSGR BH23 197 M8 1
Haltons Cl TOTT SO40 104 C7
Halyard Cl LSOL/BMARY PO13 209 H1
Hambert Wy TOTT SO40 129 J3 3
Hamble Cl HLER SO31 158 A7
Hamble Ct CHFD SO53 81 J3 1
Hambledon Cl FUFL SO22 16 C4
Hambledon Gdns SBNE BH6 237 H2
Hambledon La BPWT SO32 113 H6
Hambledon Rd HORN PO8 115 M3
LTDN BH7 237 G1
SBNE BH6 237 H2
WVILLE PO7 114 C8
WVILLE PO7 139 H1 1
Hamble House Gdns
HLER SO31 157 L6 1
Hamble La HLER SO31 133 K6
WVILLE PO7 164 C3
Hamble Rd GPORT PO12 10 B3
PLE BH15 233 L1
Hamble Springs BPWT SO32 111 J1
Hamblewood HEND SO30 134 E2
Hambrook Hl (North)
RCCH PO18 167 M5
Hambrook Hl (South)
RCCH PO18 167 M6
Hambrook Rd GPORT PO12 209 L2
Hambrook St SSEA PO5 12 F6
Hamdown Crs ROMY SO51 77 G5
Hameldon Cl ROWN SO16 130 D1 2
Hamfield Dr HISD PO11 213 J4
Hamilton Cl BMTH BH1 236 C3
CHCH/BSGR BH23 238 E4 1
HAV PO9 8 F7
PLE BH15 232 D6 1
Hamilton Ct LYMN SO41 242 B4
Hamilton Crs PLE BH15 232 D6
Hamilton Gv
LSOL/BMARY PO13 184 F7
Hamilton Ms FAWY SO45 155 M7 2
Hamilton Pk RSAL SP5 44 F8
Hamilton Rd BMTH BH1 236 C4
CHAM PO6 162 C8
ELGH SO50 82 C5
FAWY SO45 155 M8
PLE BH15 232 D6
SSEA PO5 13 J7
WIMB BH21 217 J3
Ham La EMRTH PO10 191 H1
GPORT PO12 185 L7
HORN PO8 115 L8
WIMB BH21 192 F4
Hamlet Wy GPORT PO12 185 L7
LSOL/BMARY PO13 185 K7
Hammer La MIDH GU29 67 G4
Hammond Cl FHAM PO15 6 B3
Hammond Rd FHAM PO15 6 C3
Hammonds Cl TOTT SO40 104 D8
Hammond's Gn TOTT SO40 104 C8
Hammonds La TOTT SO40 104 D8
Hammonds Wy TOTT SO40 104 D8
Hampden La SBNE BH6 237 G3 3
Hampshire Cl
CHCH/BSGR BH23 222 D6
Hampshire Hatches La
RGWD BH24 170 E4
Hampshire St PSEA PO1 211 J1
Hampshire Ter PSEA PO1 12 F4
Hampton Cl FAWY SO45 180 C8
WVILLE PO7 164 E1 4
Hampton Dr RGWD BH24 146 F7
Hampton Gdns FAWY SO45 180 C8
Hampton Gv FHAM PO15 159 M7
Hampton Hl BPWT SO32 112 A2
Hampton La FAWY SO45 180 C6
FUFL SO22 16 C5
Hamptworth Rd RSAL SP5 74 C4
Hamtun Crs TOTT SO40 104 D7 1
Hamtun Gdns TOTT SO40 104 D7
Hamtun Rd ITCH SO19 133 G6
Hamtun St SHAM SO14 4 F5
Hanbidge Crs
LSOL/BMARY PO13 185 H4
Handel Rd WSHM SO15 4 E1
Handel Ter WSHM SO15 4 D1
Handford Pl WSHM SO15 131 K2 1
Handley Rd GPORT PO12 209 K2 2
The Hangers BPWT SO32 85 M4
Hangers Wy EPSF GU31 91 H4
HORN PO8 90 F6
Hanger Wy EPSF GU31 64 A5
Hanham Rd WIMB BH21 192 A3 2
WIMB BH21 217 H3
Hankinson Rd
MOOR/WNTN BH9 220 E8
Hanley Rd WSHM SO15 106 C8
Hanlon Cl BWD BH11 219 L4
Hannah Gdns WVILLE PO7 140 D8 3
Hannay Ri ITCH SO19 133 H3
Hannington Rd HAV PO9 165 H1 2
LTDN BH7 236 F3
Hann Rd ROWN SO16 105 K2
Hanns Wy ELGH SO50 81 M6
Hanover Buildings SHAM SO14 5 G4
Hanover Gdns FHAM/PORC PO16 7 J1
Hanoverian Wy FHAM PO15 159 G1
Hanover St PSEA PO1 12 C1
Hanway Rd NEND PO2 187 H8
Ha'penny Dell WVILLE PO7 164 C5 3
Harbeck Rd CHAR BH8 221 G5
Harbour Cl CCLF BH13 245 J2 1
Harbour Crs
CHCH/BSGR BH23 238 D3 1
Harbour Hill Crs PLE BH15 233 K3
Harbour Hill Rd PLE BH15 233 K3
Harbourne Gdns WEND SO18 108 A6
Harbour Pde SHAM SO14 4 E3
WSHM SO15 4 D3
Harbour Rd GPORT PO12 11 K2
HISD PO11 213 G4
SBNE BH6 237 M5
Harbourside HAV PO9 189 K2
Harbour Vw
FHAM/PORC PO16 186 A2
Harbour View Cl PSTN BH14 233 M3
Harbour View Rd PSTN BH14 233 M3
Harbour Wy EMRTH PO10 166 E8 3
NEND PO2 187 G6
Harbridge Ct HAV PO9 165 H1
Harbridge Dro FBDG SP6 122 A4
Harcombe Cl CFDH BH17 218 C5 1
Harcourt Cl HORN PO8 140 E4
Harcourt Rd BOSC BH5 236 F3
FHAM/STUB PO14 183 M1
GPORT PO12 10 D2
PSEA PO1 211 J1
WEND SO18 107 J8
Harding La ELGH SO50 83 G5
Harding Rd GPORT PO12 209 K2
Hardley La FAWY SO45 179 M1
The Hard PSEA PO1 12 C1
Hardwicke Cl ROWN SO16 105 L6
Hardwicke Wy HLER SO31 157 J5 2
Hardwick Rd CHFD SO53 81 J2 2
Hardy Cl FERN BH22 168 D7
HLER SO31 158 F4
NMIL/BTOS BH25 225 K5
WSHM SO15 130 F2
Hardy Crs WIMB BH21 192 B4
Hardy Dr FAWY SO45 155 M7
Hardy Rd CHAM PO6 188 C1
ELGH SO50 81 L7
FERN BH22 168 D7
PSTN BH14 234 C4
Harebell Cl FHAM/PORC PO16 7 L1
Harefield Ct ROMY SO51 51 G8 3
Harefield Rd PTSW SO17 107 H5
Hare La NMIL/BTOS BH25 226 B5
RWIN SO21 54 F4
WIMB BH21 120 C3
Hares Gn LTDN BH7 221 L8
Hares La RCCH PO18 167 M1
Harestock Cl FUFL SO22 16 C3
Harestock Rd FUFL SO22 16 C4
HAV PO9 8 B1
Harewood Av LTDN BH7 236 E1
Harewood Cl ELGH SO50 81 M3
Harewood Crs LTDN BH7 236 E1
Harewood Gdns LTDN BH7 236 E1
Harewood Gn LYMN SO41 243 G4
Harewood Pl LTDN BH7 237 G2 2
Harford Cl LYMN SO41 227 M7
Harford Rd BKME/WDN BH12 219 G8
Harkness Dr WVILLE PO7 140 F8
Harkwood Dr PLE BH15 232 D4
Harland Crs WSHM SO15 106 C7
Harland Rd SBNE BH6 237 M4
Harlaxton Cl ELGH SO50 81 L3
Harlech Dr CHFD SO53 80 F4
Harlequin Gv FHAM PO15 6 D5
Harleston Rd CHAM PO6 163 H7
Harlyn Rd ROWN SO16 105 L7
Harness Cl WIMB BH21 192 F2
Harold Cl TOTT SO40 129 H2
Harold Rd EMRTH PO10 166 F4
ENEY PO4 13 M6
FHAM/STUB PO14 184 B5
HISD PO11 213 M6
WSHM SO15 131 G1
Harpway La CHCH/BSGR BH23 223 G2
The Harrage ROMY SO51 78 E1
Harrier Cl HORN PO8 140 E1
LSOL/BMARY PO13 208 D2 4
ROWN SO16 106 A2
Harrier Dr WIMB BH21 192 B6
Harriers Cl CHCH/BSGR BH23 224 B8 3
Harrier Wy EPSF GU31 64 B6
FAWY SO45 179 M2
Harriet Cl FHAM/STUB PO14 183 M6
Harris Av HEND SO30 109 H8 3
Harris La HORN PO8 117 J3
Harrison Av BMTH BH1 236 C2
Harrison Cl
CHCH/BSGR BH23 223 G5 2
Harrison Rd FHAM/PORC PO16 7 J3
PTSW SO17 107 H5
Harrison Wy FERN BH22 168 C5 1

Harris Rd *LSOL/BMARY* PO13........ 185 G5
Harrow Cl *CHCH/BSGR* BH23...... 223 M1
Harrow Down *FUFL* SO22............ 26 C4
Harrowgate La *WVILLE* PO7........ 114 E8
Harrow La *PSF* GU32.................... 63 L2
Harrow Rd *CHCH/BSGR* BH23...... 223 L1
  SSEA PO5............................ 13 L3
Harry Barrow Cl *RGWD* BH24.... 170 E2 🟦
Hart Cl *NMIL/BTOS* BH25............ 225 K4
Hart Hl *FAWY* SO45...................... 156 A7
Harthill Dro *RSAL* SP5.................. 73 K3
Harting Cl *HORN* PO8.................... 116 C4
Harting Down *EPSF* GU31............ 64 A5
Harting Gdns
  FHAM/PORC PO16................ 162 A7
Harting Rd *SBNE* BH6.................. 237 J1
Hartington Rd *GPORT* PO12........ 209 K2
  SHAM SO14................................ 5 K1
Hartland Ct *EMRTH* PO10.......... 167 H7
Hartland's Rd
  FHAM/PORC PO16.................... 7 K6
Hartley Av *PTSW* SO17.............. 107 G6
Hartley Cl *ELGH* SO50................ 82 F7
  FAWY SO45.............................. 155 L7 🟦
Hartley Ct *ROWN* SO16.............. 106 F4
Hartley Rd *ELGH* SO50................ 82 F6
  NEND PO2................................ 187 H5
Hartley Wk *FAWY* SO45............ 155 K7 🟦
Hart Plain Av *HORN* PO8............ 140 C6
Hartsbourne Dr *LTDN* BH7........ 221 M8
Harts Farm Wy *HAV* PO9............ 165 G8
Hartsgrove Cl *FAWY* SO45........ 180 C8
Harts Wy *LYMN* SO41................ 227 H7
Hartwell Rd *HSEA* PO3.............. 187 M5 🟦
Hartwood Gdns *HORN* PO8........ 140 C6
Harvest Cl *FUFL* SO22................ 26 C4
Harvester Dr *FHAM* PO15.......... 159 M7
Harvester Wy *LYMN* SO41........ 228 B2
Harvesting La *PSF* GU32............ 89 M2
Harvest Rd *NBAD* SO52.............. 80 E2
  WVILLE PO7............................ 139 J4
Harvey Ct *FAWY* SO45.............. 180 C6 🟦
Harvey Crs *HLER* SO31.............. 158 D6
Harvey Gdns *FAWY* SO45.......... 155 M5
Harvey Rd *BOSC* BH5................ 236 F3
  ELGH SO50.............................. 82 D5
  WIMB BH21.............................. 192 C8
Harwich Rd *CHAM* PO6.............. 163 H7
Harwood Cl
  LSOL/BMARY PO13................ 185 G4 🟦
  TOTT SO40.............................. 104 C8
Harwood Rd
  LSOL/BMARY PO13................ 185 G5
Haselbury Rd *TOTT* SO40.......... 129 K1
Haselfoot Gdns *HISD* SO11........ 138 J1 🟦
Haselworth Dr *GPORT* PO12...... 10 F9
Haskells Cl *LYND* SO43.............. 151 J3 🟦
Haskells Rd *BKME/WDN* BH12... 234 A1
Haslar Crs *WVILLE* PO7.............. 140 A6
Haslar Rd *GPORT* PO12.............. 11 J7
Haslemere Av
  CHCH/BSGR BH23.................. 224 D8
Haslemere Gdns *HISD* PO11...... 214 D6
Haslemere Pl
  CHCH/BSGR BH23.................. 224 E8
Haslemere Rd *EMRTH* PO10...... 167 H6
  ENEY PO4................................ 211 K6
Hasler Rd *CFDH* BH17................ 218 A6
Haslop Rd *WIMB* BH21.............. 192 D1
The Hassocks *WVILLE* PO7........ 164 E1
Hastings Av *GPORT* PO12.......... 185 K8
Hastings Rd *CFDH* BH17............ 217 M6 🟦
  CHAR BH8................................ 221 L6
Hatch Ct *HAV* PO9...................... 165 C1
Hatchers La *RWIN* SO21............ 55 L3
Hatchet Cl *FBDG* SP6.................. 73 J5
Hatchet La *BROC* SO42.............. 178 B8
Hatch La *LISS* GU33.................... 37 H4
Hatchley La *RWIN* SO21.............. 84 A2
Hatch Md *HEND* SO30................ 108 B6
Hatch Pond Rd *CFDH* BH17........ 218 A8 🟦
Hatfield Ct *NMIL/BTOS* BH25.... 225 J5 🟦
Hatfield Gdns *LTDN* BH7............ 221 M8
Hatfield Rd *ENEY* PO4................ 211 L5
Hathaway Cl *ELGH* SO50............ 82 A4
Hathaway Rd *SBNE* BH6............ 237 J4
Hatherden Av *PSTN* BH14........ 233 L3
Hatherell Cl *HEND* SO30............ 108 C7
Hatherley Crs
  FHAM/PORC PO16................ 185 M1
Hatherley Dr
  FHAM/PORC PO16................ 161 M8 🟦
  FUFL SO22................................ 2 D5
Hatherley Rd *CHAM* PO6............ 162 E7
Hatley Rd *WEND* SO18.............. 108 A8
Hatt La *ROMY* SO51.................. 21 K6
Havant Farm Cl *HAV* PO9.......... 8 F1
Havant Rd *CHAM* PO6................ 163 K8
  EMRTH PO10.......................... 9 M5
  HAV PO9.................................. 9 J6
  HISD PO11.............................. 189 K5
  HORN PO8.............................. 141 H2
  NEND PO2.............................. 187 H7
Havant St *PSEA* PO1.................. 12 C2 🟦
Havelock Rd
  BKME/WDN BH12.................. 234 F3
  HLER SO31.............................. 158 A7
  SHAM SO14................................ 4 E1
  SSEA PO5................................ 13 K4
  WSHM SO15.............................. 4 E1
Havelock Wy
  CHCH/BSGR BH23.................. 224 B6
Haven Crs *FHAM/STUB* PO14.... 183 K7
Havendale *HEND* SO30.............. 134 B3 🟦
Haven Gdns *NMIL/BTOS* BH25.. 225 M6
Haven Rd *CCLF* BH13.................. 245 K2
  HISD PO11.............................. 214 C7
  WIMB BH21.............................. 217 G2
Havenstone Wy *WEND* SO18.... 107 J4 🟦
The Haven *ELGH* SO50................ 82 A3
  ENEY PO4................................ 211 M3
Haverstock Rd
  MOOR/WNTN BH9.................. 220 F6
Haviland Rd *BMTH* BH1.............. 236 E3
  WIMB BH21.............................. 193 L1

Haviland Rd East *LTDN* BH7...... 236 E3
Haviland Rd West *LTDN* BH7.... 236 E3 🟦
Havisham Rd *NEND* PO2............ 211 H1 🟦
Hawden Rd *BWD* BH11.............. 219 J1
Hawfinch Cl *ROWN* SO16.......... 106 A2
Hawkchurch Gdns *CFDH* BH17.. 218 C6
Hawk Cl *FHAM/STUB* PO14........ 183 M6
  WIMB BH21.............................. 192 E1
Hawker Cl *WIMB* BH21.............. 192 D7
Hawke St *PSEA* PO1.................. 12 E1
Hawkeswood Rd *WEND* SO18... 132 A1
Hawkewood Av *WVILLE* PO7.... 140 B8
Hawkhill *FAWY* SO45.................. 155 G4
Hawkhurst Cl *ITCH* SO19.......... 132 E7
Hawkins Cl *RGWD* BH24............ 147 G7 🟦
Hawkins Rd *BKME/WDN* BH12... 219 K7
  LSOL/BMARY PO13................ 185 H6
Hawkley Cl *HAV* PO9.................. 165 J2 🟦
Hawkley Gn *ITCH* SO19.............. 132 D8
Hawkley Rd *LISS* GU33.............. 35 L1
Hawkwell *FHAM/PORC* PO16.... 161 K8
Hawkwood Rd *BOSC* BH5.......... 236 D4
Haworth Cl *CHCH/BSGR* BH23... 222 E7
Hawswater Rd *ROWN* SO16...... 105 L7 🟦
Hawthorn Cl *ELGH* SO50............ 83 H6 🟦
  FHAM/PORC PO16................ 161 M7
  HEND SO30............................ 134 B2 🟦
  NMIL/BTOS BH25.................. 226 A4 🟦
  RWIN SO21.............................. 54 F8
Hawthorn Crs *CHAM* PO6.......... 187 L2
Hawthorn Dr *CFDH* BH17.......... 217 K7
  LYMN SO41.............................. 200 F6
Hawthorne Gv *HISD* PO11........ 213 L4
Hawthorne Rd *TOTT* SO40........ 104 C8
Hawthorn La *HLER* SO31............ 158 C3
Hawthorn Rd
  CHCH/BSGR BH23.................. 223 J6
  FAWY SO45............................ 155 K5 🟦
  HORN PO8.............................. 116 B6
  MOOR/WNTN BH9.................. 220 D8
  PTSW SO17............................ 106 F6
  WVILLE PO7............................ 139 H4
The Hawthorns
  CHCH/BSGR BH23.................. 238 E2 🟦
  ELGH SO50.............................. 81 K7 🟦
  TOTT SO40.............................. 130 E7
Hayburn Rd *ROWN* SO16.......... 105 J6
Haydock Cl *TOTT* SO40.............. 104 B8
Haydock Ms *WVILLE* PO7.......... 140 F7
Haydon Rd *CCLF* BH13.............. 235 G7
Hayes Av *LTDN* BH7.................. 236 D2
Hayes Cl *WIMB* BH21................ 192 E4
Hayes La *WIMB* BH21................ 192 E4
Hayes Md *FAWY* SO45................ 179 M3
Hayeswood Rd *WIMB* BH21...... 192 E2
Hayle Rd *WEND* SO18................ 108 A6
Hayley Cl *FAWY* SO45................ 155 K8
Hayling Av *HSEA* PO3................ 211 M1
Hayling Cl *FHAM/STUB* PO14.... 6 A8
Haymoor Rd *PLE* BH15.............. 233 M1
Haynes Av *PLE* BH15................ 233 J4
Haynes Wy *FAWY* SO45............ 155 J7 🟦
Haysoms Cl *NMIL/BTOS* BH25.. 225 M7
Hay St *PSEA* PO1...................... 12 C1
Hayter Gdns *ROMY* SO51.......... 50 F8
Hayters Wy *FBDG* SP6.............. 121 L2
Hayward Cl *TOTT* SO40.............. 129 H1
Hayward Ct *FAWY* SO45............ 180 A4 🟦
Hayward Crs *VWD* BH31............ 144 C3
Haywards Farm Cl
  VWD BH31.............................. 144 C3 🟦
Hayward Wy *VWD* BH31............ 144 B3
Hazelbank Cl *EPSF* GU31............ 64 A4
Hazel Cl *CHCH/BSGR* BH23........ 224 A7
  CHFD SO53.............................. 53 H6
  FBDG SP6................................ 121 L3 🟦
  RWIN SO21.............................. 54 F7
Hazeldean Dr *HAV* PO9.............. 141 M7
Hazeldown Cl *ROWN* SO16........ 105 K3
Hazel Dr *FERN* BH22.................. 168 B8
Hazeleigh Av *ITCH* SO19.......... 132 C6
Hazeley Rd *RWIN* SO21.............. 54 F2
Hazel Farm Rd *TOTT* SO40........ 129 G1
Hazel Gv *FUFL* SO22.................. 26 C3
  HLER SO31.............................. 158 F6
  TOTT SO40.............................. 128 D5
Hazelgrove *HORN* PO8.............. 116 B3
Hazelholt Dr *HAV* PO9................ 8 A1
Hazell Av *NBNE* BH10................ 219 M6
Hazel Rd *HORN* PO8.................. 116 B3
  ITCH SO19.............................. 132 B5
  LYMN SO41.............................. 227 L4
Hazelton Cl *LTDN* BH7.............. 221 L8 🟦
Hazelwood
  FHAM/STUB PO14................ 183 M3 🟦
Hazelwood Av *HAV* PO9............ 164 F5
  NMIL/BTOS BH25.................. 225 J4
Hazelwood Dr *VWD* BH31.......... 144 F4
Hazelwood Rd *WEND* SO18...... 107 M7 🟦
Hazlebury Rd *CFDH* BH17.......... 233 C1
Hazlemere Dr *RGWD* BH24........ 169 J3
Hazleton Wy *HORN* PO8............ 140 F5
Head Down *EPSF* GU31.............. 64 A5
Headland Dr *HLER* SO31............ 158 E4
Headley Cl
  LSOL/BMARY PO13................ 208 D2 🟦
Headon Vw *PSF* GU32................ 60 B3
Heads Farm Cl *NBNE* BH10........ 220 C3 🟦
Head's La *NBNE* BH10................ 220 C3
Headswell Av *NBNE* BH10.......... 220 C4
Headswell Crs *NBNE* BH10........ 220 C4
Headswell Gdns *NBNE* BH10.... 220 C4 🟦
Heanor Cl *NBNE* BH10.............. 220 A6
Hearne Gdns *BPWT* SO32.......... 111 M7
Heath Av *PLE* BH15.................... 233 J2
Heath Cl *ELGH* SO50.................. 83 J7
  HORN PO8.............................. 140 F1
  WIMB BH21.............................. 192 F1
Heathcote Pl *RWIN* SO21.......... 53 G1
Heathcote Rd *BMTH* BH1.......... 236 E4
  BOSC BH5................................ 236 E4
  CHFD SO53.............................. 81 J2
  NEND PO2................................ 187 H7
Heathen St *BPWT* SO32............ 110 A4
Heatherbank Rd *CCLF*
  BH13...................................... 235 H5 🟦
Heatherbrae Gdns
  NBAD SO52.............................. 79 L4 🟦

Heatherbrae La *UPTN* BH16...... 232 A2
Heather Cha *ELGH* SO50............ 82 F6 🟦
Heather Cl *CHAR* BH8................ 221 H4
  CHCH/BSGR BH23.................. 224 E7
  LSOL/BMARY PO13................ 184 F6
  LYMN SO41.............................. 226 E5
  RGWD BH24............................ 169 J5
  TOTT SO40.............................. 129 J1
  WIMB BH21.............................. 217 J2 🟦
  WVILLE PO7............................ 164 D2
Heather Ct *WEND* SO18............ 133 G1
Heatherdeane Rd *PTSW* SO17... 106 F6
Heatherdell *UPTN* BH16............ 232 A2 🟦
Heatherdene Rd *CHFD* SO53...... 53 K7
Heatherdown Rd
  FERN BH22.............................. 168 E7 🟦
Heatherdown Wy
  FERN BH22.............................. 168 E7 🟦
Heather Dr *FERN* BH22.............. 194 B1
Heatherfield *EPSF* GU31............ 91 J3
Heather Gdns *FHAM* PO15........ 6 B2
Heatherlands Ri
  BKME/WDN BH12.................. 234 C3 🟦
Heatherlands Rd *ROWN* SO16... 80 C5
Heatherlea Rd *SBNE* BH6.......... 237 J4
Heather Rd *EPSF* GU31.............. 64 B5 🟦
  FAWY SO45............................ 180 D6
  NBNE BH10............................ 220 B5
Heatherstone Av *FAWY* SO45... 155 K8
Heatherton Ms *EMRTH* PO10.... 166 D5
Heatherview Rd *NBAD* SO52...... 79 L3 🟦
Heather View Rd
  BKME/WDN BH12.................. 234 E1
Heather Wy *FERN* BH22............ 194 B1
Heath Farm Cl *FERN* BH22........ 194 A5 🟦
Heath Farm Rd *FERN* BH22........ 194 A5
Heath Farm Wy *FERN* BH22...... 194 A5
Heathfield *FAWY* SO45.............. 155 K6 🟦
Heathfield Av
  BKME/WDN BH12.................. 219 L8
  FHAM PO15.............................. 6 A6
Heathfield Cl *ITCH* SO19............ 133 C5 🟦
Heathfield Rd *CHFD* SO53.......... 53 H6
  EPSF GU31.............................. 64 B5
  FERN BH22.............................. 168 A7
  ITCH SO19.............................. 132 F5
  NEND PO2.............................. 187 H8
Heathfield Wy *FERN* BH22........ 168 D7
Heath Gdns *HLER* SO31............ 157 H1
Heath House Cl *HEND* SO30...... 133 M4
Heath House Gdns *HEND* SO30. 133 M4
Heathhouse La *HEND* SO30...... 133 M4
Heathlands Av *FERN* BH22........ 194 B6
Heathlands Cl
  CHCH/BSGR BH23.................. 223 G6 🟦
  CHFD SO53.............................. 53 H8
  VWD BH31.............................. 144 F2 🟦
Heathlands Rd *CHFD* SO53........ 53 H8
Heath La *BROC* SO42................ 204 A1
Heath Lawns *FHAM* PO15.......... 6 A6
Heath Rd *BPWT* SO32................ 112 F7
  CHCH/BSGR BH23.................. 224 F7
  EPSF GU31.............................. 63 M5
  HLER SO31.............................. 158 D5
  ITCH SO19.............................. 132 E3
  LYMN SO41.............................. 226 D5
  RGWD BH24............................ 169 H4
  WHAM PO17............................ 112 A4
Heath Rd East *EPSF* GU31........ 64 A6
Heath Rd North *HLER* SO31...... 158 D5
Heath Rd South *HLER* SO31...... 158 D5
Heath Rd West
  CHCH/BSGR BH23.................. 195 J2
  EPSF GU31.............................. 63 M6
The Heath *WVILLE* PO7.............. 139 L4
Heathwood Av
  NMIL/BTOS BH25.................. 225 J8
Heathwood Rd
  MOOR/WNTN BH9.................. 220 C8
Heathy Cl *NMIL/BTOS* BH25...... 225 K8
Heaton Rd *GPORT* PO12............ 209 L1
  NBNE BH10............................ 220 B5
Heavytree Rd *PSTN* BH14.......... 234 A4 🟦
Hebrides Cl
  FHAM/STUB PO14................ 183 M5 🟦
Heckfield Cl *HAV* PO9................ 165 M3 🟦
Heckford La *PLE* BH15................ 233 J4
Heckford Rd *PLE* BH15.............. 233 J4
  WIMB BH21.............................. 217 G3
Hector Cl *WVILLE* PO7................ 164 C6
Hector Rd *FHAM/STUB* PO14.... 184 E3
Hedera Rd *HLER* SO31................ 157 M1
Hedgerley *NMIL/BTOS* BH25.... 225 M8 🟦
Hedgerow Cl *ROWN* SO16........ 105 K2
Hedgerow Dr *WEND* SO18........ 108 A7 🟦
Hedgerow Gdns
  EMRTH PO10.......................... 166 D5
Hedley Cl *FAWY* SO45................ 180 D7
Hedley Gdns *HEND* SO30.......... 109 G5 🟦
Heidelberg Rd *ENEY* PO4.......... 211 K4
Heights Ap *UPTN* BH16.............. 232 B1
Heights Rd *UPTN* BH16.............. 217 G8
The Heights *FHAM/PORC* PO16. 161 H6
  HEND SO30............................ 133 L2
Helena Rd *ENEY* PO4................ 211 K6
Helford Gdns *WEND* SO18........ 108 A6 🟦
Hellyer Rd *ENEY* PO4................ 211 L5
Helm Cl *LSOL/BMARY* PO13...... 209 H2
Helsted Cl *GPORT* PO12............ 209 J4
Helston Dr *EMRTH* PO10............ 166 C5
Helston Rd *CHAM* PO6................ 162 D7
Helvellyn Rd *ROWN* SO16.......... 105 L8
Helyar Rd *CHAR* BH8................ 221 K6
Hemdean Gdns *HEND* SO30...... 108 C7
Hemlock Cl *HORN* PO8.............. 140 C4
Hemlock Wy *HORN* PO8............ 80 E3
Hemming Cl *TOTT* SO40............ 129 L2
Hemmingway Gdns
  FHAM PO15............................ 135 G8
Hempland La *ALTN* GU34.......... 33 H4
Hempsted Rd *CHAM* PO6.......... 162 F7
Hemsley Wk *HORN* PO8............ 140 E4
Henbury Cl *CFDH* BH17.............. 218 E6 🟦
  WIMB BH21.............................. 217 H1
Henbury Ri *WIMB* BH21............ 217 H1
Henbury View Rd
  WIMB BH21.............................. 217 H2 🟦

Henderson Rd *ENEY* PO4.......... 211 M5
Hendford Rd *NBNE* BH10.......... 220 B6
Hendy Cl *SSEA* PO5.................... 13 J5 🟦
Henery St *GPORT* PO12.............. 11 J1 🟦
Hengistbury Rd
  NMIL/BTOS BH25.................. 225 J8
  SBNE BH6.............................. 237 L5
Hengist Rd *BMTH* BH1.............. 236 C4 🟦
Henley Gdns *FHAM* PO15.......... 160 B4
Henley Gdns *LTDN* BH7............ 236 F1 🟦
Henley Rd *ENEY* PO4................ 211 K5
Henning's Park Rd *PLE* BH15.... 233 J3
Henry Cl *FAWY* SO45................ 179 M2 🟦
Henry Rd *ELGH* SO50.................. 82 C4 🟦
  WSHM SO15............................ 130 F1
Henry St *WSHM* SO15................ 131 K2 🟦
Henstead Rd *WSHM* SO15........ 131 K2
Hensting La *RWIN* SO21............ 55 K5
Henty Rd *ROWN* SO16.............. 105 M8
Henville Cl *LSOL/BMARY* PO13. 185 H8
Henville Rd *CHAR* BH8.............. 15 L1
Henwood Down *EPSF* GU31...... 63 M5 🟦
Hepworth Cl *ITCH* SO19............ 133 G6
Herbert Av *BKME/WDN* BH12... 219 G6
Herberton Rd *SBNE* BH6............ 237 H3
Herbert Rd *ENEY* PO4................ 13 L8
  GPORT PO12.......................... 10 B2
  NMIL/BTOS BH25.................. 225 M5
  RSAL SP5................................ 73 J2
  WBNE BH4................................ 235 G6
Herbert St *PSEA* PO1................ 211 J1
Herbert Walker Av *WSHM* SO15. 4 E5
Hercules Pl *PLE* BH15................ 232 C5 🟦
Hercules St *NEND* PO2.............. 187 H8 🟦
Hereford Rd *SSEA* PO5.............. 13 J6
Hereward Cl *ROMY* SO51.......... 79 G1 🟦
Hermes Rd *LSOL/BMARY* PO13. 208 B1
Hermitage Rd *PSTN* BH14........ 233 M2 🟦
  HAV PO9.................................. 165 J4
Herm Rd *BKME/WDN* BH12...... 219 G7
Herne Rd *CHAM* PO6.................. 163 J8
  EPSF GU31.............................. 63 M5
Hern La *FBDG* SP6.................... 122 F2
Heron Cl *ENEY* PO4.................... 211 M3
  LYMN SO41.............................. 200 F6
Heron Court Rd
  MOOR/WNTN BH9.................. 235 M1
  TWDS BH3.............................. 235 M2
Heron Dr *WIMB* BH21................ 192 E1
Heron La *ROMY* SO51................ 50 C2
Heron Quay *EMRTH* PO10.......... 190 E1
Herons Cl *FHAM/STUB* PO14.... 184 A4
Heron Sq *ELGH* SO50................ 81 K7
Heron Wy *LSOL/BMARY* PO13.. 184 E5
Herrick Cl *ITCH* SO19................ 133 H4
Herriott Cl *HORN* PO8.............. 140 E3
Herstone Cl *CFDH* BH17............ 218 D7
Hertford Cl *FBDG* SP6................ 97 L5
Hertford Pl *PSEA* PO1................ 211 H1
Hertsfield *FHAM/STUB* PO14.... 159 G4
Hesketh Cl *RGWD* BH24............ 169 L3
Hester Rd *ENEY* PO4................ 211 M4 🟦
Hestia Cl *ROMY* SO51................ 51 H8
Heston Cl *CHCH/BSGR* BH23.... 222 B4
Heston Wy *FERN* BH22.............. 168 B5
Hewett Cl *FHAM/STUB* PO14.... 183 K1
Hewett Rd *FHAM/STUB* PO14... 183 K1
  NEND PO2.............................. 187 J6
Hewetts Ri *HLER* SO31.............. 158 A8
Hewitt Cl *GPORT* PO12.............. 209 L2 🟦
Hewitt Rd *PLE* BH15.................. 232 D4
Hewitt's Rd *WSHM* SO15............ 4 B2
Heyes Dr *ITCH* SO19.................. 133 C5
Heysham Rd *BDST* BH18.......... 217 L5
Heyshott Rd *ENEY* PO4.............. 211 K4
Heytesbury Rd *SBNE* BH6........ 237 J3 🟦
Heyward Rd *ENEY* PO4.............. 13 L4
Heywood Gn *ITCH* SO19............ 133 J3
Hibberd Wy *NBNE* BH10............ 220 B7
Hibbs Cl *UPTN* BH16.................. 232 B1
Hickes Cl *BWD* BH11.................. 219 K4
Hickory Cl *UPTN* BH16.............. 216 E8 🟦
Hickory Dr *FUFL* SO22................ 16 B4
Hickory Gdns *HEND* SO30.......... 108 C5
Hickory Rd *WVILLE* PO7............ 163 M5
Highbank Gdns *FBDG* SP6........ 97 L7 🟦
Highbridge Rd *ELGH* SO50........ 82 C1
  PSTN BH14.............................. 234 B5 🟦
Highbury Cl *ELGH* SO50............ 83 H7
  NMIL/BTOS BH25.................. 225 M5
Highbury Gv *CHAM* PO6............ 187 L2
Highbury St *PSEA* PO1.............. 12 D4
Highbury Wy *CHAM* PO6............ 187 K2
Highclere Rd *ROWN* SO16........ 105 C5
Highclere Wy *CHFD* SO53.......... 80 F5
Highcliff Av *SHAM* SO14............ 106 F8 🟦
Highcliffe Dr *ELGH* SO50............ 81 M1
Highcliffe Rd
  CHCH/BSGR BH23.................. 223 L8
  GPORT PO12.......................... 10 B4
  WINC SO23.............................. 27 G2
Highcroft La *HORN* PO8............ 116 B8
High Cross *PSF* GU32................ 34 D6
High Cross La *PSF* GU32............ 34 D6
Highcrown St *PTSW* SO17........ 106 F6
High Dr *LSOL/BMARY* PO13...... 185 G7
Higher Blandford Rd
  BDST BH18.............................. 217 L3
  WIMB BH21.............................. 217 K2
Highfield Av *FHAM/STUB* PO14. 6 E8
  LYMN SO41.............................. 228 A5
  PTSW SO17............................ 106 E5
  RGWD BH24............................ 146 E8
  RWIN SO21.............................. 54 F1
  WVILLE PO7............................ 140 B5
Highfield Cl *CHFD* SO53............ 81 J2
  LYMN SO41.............................. 200 F6
  PTSW SO17............................ 106 F6 🟦
  WIMB BH21.............................. 217 J3
Highfield Crs *PTSW* SO17.......... 107 G5
Highfield Dr *RGWD* BH24.......... 146 E7
Highfield Gdns *LISS* GU33........ 37 G4

Highfield La *PTSW* SO17............ 106 F6
  RSAL SP5................................ 73 J3
Highfield Rd *CHFD* SO53............ 81 K2
  FERN BH22.............................. 168 B4
  GPORT PO12.......................... 209 K2
  LYMN SO41.............................. 228 A4
  MOOR/WNTN BH9.................. 220 C6
  PSEA PO1................................ 13 K1
  PSF GU32................................ 60 D7
  PTSW SO17............................ 106 E7
  RGWD BH24............................ 146 E8
  WIMB BH21.............................. 217 J3
High Firs Gdns *ROMY* SO51...... 79 H1
High Firs Rd *ITCH* SO19............ 132 F3
  ROMY SO51............................ 51 H8
Highgate Rd *HSEA* PO3............ 187 L7
Highgrove Cl *TOTT* SO40.......... 129 H3 🟦
Highgrove Rd *HSEA* PO3.......... 187 M8
High Howe Cl *BWD* BH11.......... 219 J4
High Howe Gdns *BWD* BH11.... 219 J4 🟦
High Howe La *BWD* BH11.......... 219 J4
Highland Av *CHCH/BSGR* BH23. 224 F7
Highland Cl *EMRTH* PO10.......... 166 C5
Highland Rd *EMRTH* PO10........ 166 C5
  ENEY PO4................................ 211 K5
  PSTN BH14.............................. 234 A3
  WIMB BH21.............................. 192 B3
Highlands Cl *FAWY* SO45.......... 155 L6
  NBAD SO52............................ 79 K3 🟦
Highlands Crs *NBNE* BH10........ 220 A4
Highlands Rd *CHAM* PO6............ 164 B8
  FHAM PO15.............................. 6 A2
  NMIL/BTOS BH25.................. 225 L8
Highland St *ENEY* PO4.............. 211 L6
Highlands Wy *FAWY* SO45........ 155 K6
  RSAL SP5................................ 47 G4
Highland View Cl *WIMB* BH21... 192 B3
High Lawn Wy *HAV* PO9............ 165 J3
High Md FERN BH22...................... 193 L6
High Mead La *FERN* BH22........ 193 L7
High Meadow *ITCH* SO19.......... 133 G2
Highmoor Cl *WIMB* BH21.......... 217 H3 🟦
Highmoor Rd *BWD* BH11.......... 219 L7 🟦
  PSTN BH14.............................. 234 B5
  WIMB BH21.............................. 217 H3
Highmount Cl *WINC* SO23.......... 3 K9
Hignham Gdns *HLER* SO31........ 158 F5
High Oaks Cl *HLER* SO31.......... 158 E5
High Oaks Gdns *BWD* BH11...... 219 J4 🟦
High Park Rd *BDST* BH18.......... 217 J4
High Ridge Crs
  NMIL/BTOS BH25.................. 226 A5
High Rd *ELGH* SO50.................. 107 J3
  ROWN SO16............................ 107 J5
High St *BPWT* SO32.................. 111 H1
  BPWT SO32............................ 113 G5
  BPWT SO32............................ 136 C1
  BROC SO42............................ 203 J7
  CHAM PO6.............................. 187 K1
  CHCH/BSGR BH23.................. 238 A2
  ELGH SO50.............................. 81 M7
  EMRTH PO10.......................... 166 D8
  EPSF GU31.............................. 63 L3
  EPSF GU31.............................. 91 J3
  FAWY SO45............................ 155 J7
  FBDG SP6................................ 96 B2
  FBDG SP6................................ 96 C4
  FBDG SP6................................ 98 D1
  FHAM/PORC PO16.................... 7 L4
  FHAM/STUB PO14................ 159 K8
  GPORT PO12.......................... 11 K3
  HEND SO30............................ 108 D7 🟦
  HEND SO30............................ 134 B1
  HLER SO31.............................. 157 M1
  LSOL/BMARY PO13................ 208 C2
  LYMN SO41.............................. 228 C5
  LYMN SO41.............................. 226 A3
  LYND SO43.............................. 151 K3
  PLE BH15................................ 233 G7
  PSEA PO1................................ 12 C5
  PSF GU32................................ 60 B3
  PSF GU32................................ 61 K7
  RGWD BH24............................ 169 J2 🟦
  RGWD BH24............................ 170 D1 🟦
  RWIN SO21.............................. 54 F3
  SHAM SO14............................ 5 G6
  TOTT SO40.............................. 129 L1
  WHAM PO17............................ 112 A3
  WINC SO23.............................. 2 F7
  WVILLE PO7............................ 114 C5
High St North *PLE* BH15............ 233 J5
Hightown Gdns *RCWD* BH24.... 170 F2
Hightown Hl *RGWD* BH24.......... 171 K1
Hightown Rd *RGWD* BH24........ 170 E2
Hightrees Av *CHAR* BH8............ 221 J7
High Trees Dr *FUFL* SO22.......... 2 C3
High Trees *ELGH* SO50.............. 83 K6
  WVILLE PO7............................ 140 D8
High Trees Wk *FERN* BH22........ 194 B1
High Vw *FHAM/PORC* PO16...... 162 A7
Highview Cl *CHCH/BSGR* BH23. 222 C5
Highview Gdns
  BKME/WDN BH12.................. 234 B1
High View Wy *WEND* SO18........ 107 J3
High Wy *BDST* BH18.................. 217 K5
Highways Rd *RWIN* SO21.......... 54 E3
The Highway *RSAL* SP5.............. 44 C2
Highwood Cl *FBDG* SP6............ 121 H2 🟦
Highwood La *RCWD* BH24........ 147 G6
  ROMY SO51............................ 51 J8
Highwood Rd *BROC* SO42........ 175 K8
  LSOL/BMARY PO13................ 209 G1
  PSTN BH14.............................. 234 D4 🟦
Higworth La *HISD* PO11............ 213 K3 🟦
Hilary Av *CHAM* PO6.................. 187 L1
Hilary Rd *CFDH* BH17................ 218 A7
Hilda Gdns *WVILLE* PO7............ 139 L4
Hilda Rd *BKME/WDN* BH12...... 234 D2
Hiley Rd *PLE* BH15.................... 233 H2
Hillary Ct *FHAM/PORC* PO16.... 6 E3
  LYND SO43.............................. 151 J3
Hillary Rd *CHCH/BSGR* BH23... 223 J8 🟦
Hillborough Crs *SSEA* PO5........ 13 J6 🟦
Hillbourne Rd *CFDH* BH17........ 217 L6
Hillbrow Cl *FHAM* PO15............ 6 B1

Hill Brow Cl *HAV* PO9 .... 141 M7
Hill Brow Rd *LISS* GU33 .... 36 E5
Hillbrow Rd *SBNE* BH6 .... 237 G2
Hillbury Rd *FBDG* SP6 .... 121 L2
Hill Cl *CHCH/BSGR* BH23 .... 223 L1
ELGH *SO50* 83 H3
Hillcrest Av *CHFD* SO53 .... 81 J2
FERN BH22 .... 194 A1
Hillcrest Dr *CHFD* SO53 .... 81 J2 2
NBAD SO52 .... 79 L3
Hill Crest Gdns *BPWT* SO32 .... 111 J4
Hillcrest Rd *BKME/WDN* BH12 .. 233 M3
MOOR/WNTN BH9 .... 220 B5
WIMB BH21 .... 217 G3
Hill Cft *FHAM* PO15 .... 159 H5
Hilldene Wy *HEND* SO30 .... 108 D7 2
Hilldown Rd *PTSW* SO17 .... 106 F5
Hilldowns Rd *NEND* PO2 .... 187 G6
Hill Farm Rd *WSHM* SO15 .... 131 J2
Hillgrove Rd *WEND* SO18 .... 107 L5 5
Hill Head Rd *FHAM/STUB* PO14 .. 183 L7
Hill Houses La *NARL* SO24 ...... 30 A3
Hillier Wy *WINC* SO23 .... 3 H3
Hill La *CHCH/BSGR* BH23 .... 197 L8
CHCH/BSGR BH23 .... 223 K6
EPSF GU31 .... 93 H6
ROWN SO16 .... 106 C5
RWIN SO21 .... 54 E7
WSHM SO15 .... 106 D7
Hillman Rd *PSTN* BH14 .... 234 C3
Hillmead Gdns *HAV* PO9 .... 164 F6
Hillmeadow *VWD* BH31 .... 144 E4
Hill Park Rd *FHAM* PO15 .... 160 B4
GPORT PO12 .... 209 K2
Hill Pl *HLER* SO31 .... 133 M8
Hill Ri *BPWT* SO32 .... 87 H3
RWIN SO21 .... 54 F2
Hill Rd *FHAM/PORC* PO16 .... 162 B7
RGWD BH24 .... 195 L2
Hillside Av *ROMY* SO51 .... 78 F1
WEND SO18 .... 107 K7
WVILLE PO7 .... 163 M6
Hillside Cl *CHFD* SO53 .... 81 J2
FUFL SO22 .... 16 B6
RSAL SP5 .... 19 J6
Hillside Crs *CHAM* PO6 .... 162 D7
Hillside Dr *CHCH/BSGR* BH23 .. 222 B4
Hillside Gdns *WIMB* BH21 .... 217 G4
Hillside Rd *BKME/WDN* BH12 .. 219 K7
FUFL SO22 .... 16 B7
LYMN SO41 .... 228 A5
VWD BH31 .... 144 E1
WIMB BH21 .... 217 G3
Hillsley Rd *CHAM* PO6 .... 162 D6
Hillson Dr *FHAM* PO15 .... 160 A5
Hill St *PLE* BH15 .... 233 H6
ROMY SO51 .... 104 B2
Hilltop *FUFL* SO22 .... 16 B3
Hilltop Cl *FERN* BH22 .... 193 M1
Hilltop Crs *CHAM* PO6 .... 163 M6
Hilltop Dr *ITCH* SO19 .... 133 G4
Hilltop Gdns *HORN* PO8 .... 116 C5
Hilltop Rd *FERN* BH22 .... 193 M1
WIMB BH21 .... 217 J3
WVILLE PO7 .... 162 E6
Hillview *HORN* PO8 .... 141 G3
Hill Vw *PSF* GU32 .... 61 J7
Hill View Rd *FERN* BH22 .... 194 A2
FHAM/PORC PO16 .... 162 A7
ROMY SO51 .... 22 B8
ROMY SO51 .... 51 J7
Hillview Rd *FAWY* SO45 .... 155 K5
NBNE BH10 .... 220 C6
Hill Wy *RGWD* BH24 .... 169 J3
The Hillway *CHFD* SO53 .... 81 J1
FHAM/PORC PO16 .... 162 A8
Hilly Cl *RWIN* SO21 .... 56 A4
Hillyfields *ROWN* SO16 .... 105 H4
Hilsea Crs *NEND* PO2 .... 187 J3
Hiltingbury Av *HAV* PO9 .... 165 L3 4
Hiltingbury Cl *CHFD* SO53 .... 53 J7
Hiltingbury Rd *CHFD* SO53 ...... 53 G7
Hiltom Rd *BWD* BH24 .... 170 F1
Hilton Cl *PLE* BH15 .... 233 M2
Hilton Rd *GPORT* PO12 .... 11 H6
NMIL/BTOS BH25 .... 225 M4
Hinchliffe Cl *PLE* BH15 .... 232 E6 4
Hinchliffe Rd *PLE* BH15 .... 232 E6
Hinkler Rd *ITCH* SO19 .... 133 G3
Hinton Cl *HAV* PO9 .... 165 G4
Hinton Crs *ITCH* SO19 .... 133 J3
Hinton Flds *WINC* SO23 .... 17 H2
Hinton HI *NARL* SO24 .... 30 E4
Hinton Manor La *HORN* PO8 .... 115 K7
Hinton Rd *BMTH* BH1 .... 14 F6
Hinton Wood Av
CHCH/BSGR BH23 .... 224 C7
Hintonwood La
CHCH/BSGR BH23 .... 224 C6
Hipley Rd *HAV* PO9 .... 165 L5
Hirst Rd *FAWY* SO45 .... 155 M5
Hispano Av *FHAM* PO15 .... 159 G1
Hither Gn *EMRTH* PO10 .... 167 J6
Hitherwood Cl *HORN* PO8 .... 140 F7
Hives Wy *LYMN* SO41 .... 228 B2 5
Hoadlands *EPSF* GU31 .... 63 M4
Hoad's HI *WHAM* PO17 .... 136 F6
Hoads HI *WHAM* PO17 .... 136 F6
Hobart Dr *FAWY* SO45 .... 155 M5
Hobart Rd *NMIL/BTOS* BH25 ... 225 K6
Hobb La *HEND* SO30 .... 134 B2
Hobbs Pk *RGWD* BH24 .... 169 K4
Hobbs Rd *BKME/WDN* BH12 ... 219 G8
Hobby Cl *HSEA* PO3 .... 187 L4
Hobson Wy *FAWY* SO45 .... 180 B5 2
Hoburne Gdns
CHCH/BSGR BH23 .... 224 A7
Hoburne La *CHCH/BSGR* BH23 .. 223 M8
Hockham Ct *HAV* PO9 .... 165 G1
Hockley Cl *CHAM* PO6 .... 163 H8 2
Hockley Link *RWIN* SO21 .... 26 D6
Hocombe Cl *CHFD* SO53 .... 53 G6
Hocombe Park Cl *CHFD* SO53 .. 53 G6
Hocombe Rd *CHFD* SO53 .... 53 G6
Hocombe Wood Rd *CHFD* SO53 .. 52 F6
Hodder Cl *CHFD* SO53 .... 81 J1 1

Hodges Cl *CFDH* BH17 .... 233 K1
HAV PO9 .... 9 G1
Hoeford Cl *FHAM/PORC* PO16 .. 184 F2
Hoe La *ROMY* SO51 .... 79 H6
Hoe Rd *BPWT* SO32 .... 111 K1
Hoe St *WVILLE* PO7 .... 138 D2
The Hoe *LSOL/BMARY* PO13 ... 185 J7 3
Hogarth Cl *ROMY* SO51 .... 51 J7
Hoggarth Cl *EPSF* GU31 .... 63 M4
Hogs Lodge La *HORN* PO8 .... 90 C7
Hogue Av *NBNE* BH10 .... 220 B3
Hogwood La *HEND* SO30 .... 108 D2
Holbrook Rd *FHAM/PORC* PO16 .. 7 J7
PSEA PO1 .... 13 K1
Holbury Cl *CHAR* BH8 .... 221 J5
Holbury Ct *HAV* PO9 .... 165 M3 3
Holbury Dro *FAWY* SO45 .... 179 M4
Holbury La *RSAL* SP5 .... 20 C5
Holcombe Rd *UPTN* BH16 .... 232 A2
Holcot La *HSEA* PO3 .... 188 A4
Holcroft Rd *ITCH* SO19 .... 133 J3
Holdaway Cl *ROWN* SO16 .... 17 H1
Holdenbury Ct *HSEA* PO3 .... 188 A3
Holdenhurst Av *LTDN* BH7 .... 237 H1
Holdenhurst Rd *HORN* PO8 ...... 116 B7 2
BMTH BH1 .... 15 J5
CHAR BH8 .... 221 L5
CHAR BH8 .... 236 C2
Holden La *RWIN* SO21 .... 57 L1
Holding La *NARL* SO24 .... 29 K6
Hole La *BPWT* SO32 .... 110 F7
WVILLE PO7 .... 113 L8
Holes Bay Rd *PLE* BH15 .... 233 G4
Holes Cl *LYMN* SO41 .... 226 D4
Hollam Cl *NBAD* SO52 .... 105 K5 1
Hollam Crs *FHAM/STUB* PO14 .. 159 M8
Hollam Crs *FHAM/STUB* PO14 .. 159 M8
Hollam Dr *FHAM/STUB* PO14 ... 159 M8
Holland Cl *ENEY* PO4 .... 211 M3
Holland Pk *HLER* SO31 .... 158 D5
Holland Pl
LSOL/BMARY PO13 .... 185 H6 2
ROWN SO16 .... 106 A7
Holland Rd *ENEY* PO4 .... 13 L4
ITCH SO19 .... 132 B6
TOTT SO40 .... 129 C1
Hollands Wood Dr
NMIL/BTOS BH25 .... 225 M3
Holland Wy *BDST* BH18 .... 217 K3
Hollies Cl *LYMN* SO41 .... 200 F7
Hollingbourne Cl *WEND* SO18 .. 107 J8
Hollist La *EPSF* GU31 .... 93 J4 1
Hollman Dr *ROMY* SO51 .... 50 C8
Holloway Av *BWD* BH11 .... 219 K3
Hollow La *HISD* PO11 .... 213 K5
Hollybank *LSOL/BMARY* PO13 .. 208 D3
Holly Bank Cl *HORN* PO8 .... 141 G3
Hollybank Crs *FAWY* SO45 ...... 155 K4
Hollybank La *EMRTH* PO10 ...... 166 D4
Hollybank Rd *FAWY* SO45 .... 155 K5
Holly Cl *FAWY* SO45 .... 179 L1
HLER SO31 .... 158 C5
RGWD BH24 .... 169 H4
Holly Dell *ROWN* SO16 .... 106 D3
Holly Dr *WVILLE* PO7 .... 164 E2
Holly Gdns *CHCH/BSGR* BH23 .. 223 H7
HEND SO30 .... 108 C5
LYMN SO41 .... 242 B3
Holly Green Ri *BWD* BH11 .... 219 J4 8
Holly Gv *FHAM/PORC* PO16 .... 160 C4
VWD BH31 .... 144 B3
Holly Hatch Rd *TOTT* SO40 ...... 129 J2
Holly Hedge La *CFDH* BH17 ..... 218 A8
Holly HI *ROWN* SO16 .... 106 D3
Holly Hill Cl *ROWN* SO16 .... 106 D3
Holly Hill La *HLER* SO31 .... 158 A4
Holly La *CHCH/BSGR* BH23 .... 225 G6
LYMN SO41 .... 202 F7
NMIL/BTOS BH25 .... 226 A4
Holly Oak Rd *ROWN* SO16 .... 105 M5
Holly Rd *FAWY* SO45 .... 180 C8
TOTT SO40 .... 128 F6
Holly St *GPORT* PO12 .... 11 H3
Hollywell Dr *CHAM* PO6 .... 186 F1
Hollywood Cl *NBAD* SO52 .... 79 L4
Hollywood La *LYMN* SO41 .... 228 B3
Holman Cl *HORN* PO8 .... 140 E6
Holm Cl *RGWD* BH24 .... 147 G2
Holmdale Rd *GPORT* PO12 ...... 209 K1
Holmefield Av
FHAM/STUB PO14 .... 184 D2
Holme Rd *CHCH/BSGR* BH23 .. 224 F8
Holmesland Dr *HEND* SO30 ..... 134 D1
Holmesland La *HEND* SO30 ..... 134 D1
Holmfield Av *LTDN* BH7 .... 237 H1
Holmgrove
FHAM/STUB PO14 .... 159 G5 2
Holm Hill La
CHCH/BSGR BH23 .... 224 F1
Holmhurst Av
CHCH/BSGR BH23 .... 224 D7
Holmsley Cl *LYMN* SO41 .... 227 M6
WEND SO18 .... 133 G1 1
Holmsley Rd
NMIL/BTOS BH25 .... 199 H6
Holmwood Garth *RGWD* BH24 .. 171 H2
Holne Ct *ENEY* PO4 .... 212 A5
Holnest Rd *CFDH* BH17 .... 218 B7
Holst Wy *WVILLE* PO7 .... 164 D3
Holt Cl *WHAM* PO17 .... 136 D4
Holt Ct *ITCH* SO19 .... 132 C4
Holt Down *EPSF* GU31 .... 64 A5
Holt Gdns *HAV* PO9 .... 141 M5
Holt Rd *BKME/WDN* BH12 .... 234 A1
WIMB BH21 .... 144 B8
Holworth Cl *BWD* BH11 .... 219 J5 3
Holybone Rd *ROMY* SO51 .... 79 G1
Holybourne Rd *HAV* PO9 .... 8 E1
Holyrood Av *PTSW* SO17 .... 107 G6
Holyrood Cl *WVILLE* PO7 .... 164 E1 9
Holywell Cl *CFDH* BH17 .... 218 B5
Home Farm Cl *FAWY* SO45 ...... 155 M6
Home Farm Wy *VWD* BH31 ...... 144 C2

Homefield *ROMY* SO51 .... 50 F7 2
Home Field Dr *ROWN* SO16 ..... 105 H3
Homefield Rd *CHAM* PO6 .... 188 A1
EMRTH PO10 .... 166 F4
Homefield Wy *HORN* PO8 .... 116 A2
Homer Cl *HORN* PO8 .... 140 C6
LSOL/BMARY PO13 .... 184 F8
Homer Farm La *FAWY* SO45 .... 206 C2
Home Rd *BWD* BH11 .... 219 M2
Home Rule Rd *HLER* SO31 ...... 158 E4
Homeside Rd
MOOR/WNTN BH9 .... 220 C6
Home Wy *EPSF* GU31 .... 64 B5
Homewell *HAV* PO9 .... 8 E5
Homewood Cl
NMIL/BTOS BH25 .... 226 A5 2
Honeybourne Crs *SBNE* BH6 ... 237 M4
Honeycritch La *PSF* GU32 .... 35 G5
Honey La *FHAM* PO15 .... 160 B3
RGWD BH24 .... 172 C6
Honeysuckle Cl *FUFL* SO22 ..... 26 C4
HLER SO31 .... 158 E3
LSOL/BMARY PO13 .... 184 F5 8
Honeysuckle Ct *WVILLE* PO7 ... 164 D3 2
Honeysuckle La *CFDH* BH17 .... 217 K7
Honeysuckle Rd *ROWN* SO16 .. 107 G6
Honeysuckle Wy
CHCH/BSGR BH23 .... 223 M8 5
NBAD SO52 .... 80 F2
Honeywood Cl *HSEA* PO3 .... 187 K4
TOTT SO40 .... 104 C7
Hood Cl *HLER* SO31 .... 158 F4
NBNE BH10 .... 219 M7
Hood Crs *NBNE* BH10 .... 219 M7
Hood Rd *WEND* SO18 .... 107 M8 2
Hook Cl *CHFD* SO53 .... 52 F6
Hook Crs *CHFD* SO53 .... 52 F6
Hooke Cl *CFDH* BH17 .... 218 E6
Hook La *HLER* SO31 .... 182 E1
Hook Park Rd *HLER* SO31 .... 182 A1
Hook Rd *ROMY* SO51 .... 52 D5
Hook's Farm Wy *HAV* PO9 .... 8 A1
Hook's La *HAV* PO9 .... 8 B2
Hook Water Rd *CHFD* SO53 ..... 52 F6
Hookwood La *ROMY* SO51 .... 52 E6
Hope Rd *HEND* SO30 .... 108 D6
Hope St *PSEA* PO1 .... 211 G2
Hopfield Cl *WVILLE* PO7 .... 164 C2
Hopfield Ms *WVILLE* PO7 .... 164 C2 1
The Hop Gdn *EPSF* GU31 .... 92 F5
Hopkins Cl *CHAM* PO6 .... 162 C8 2
CHAR BH8 .... 221 L6
Horace Rd *BOSC* BH5 .... 236 D4
Hordle La *HLER* SO31 .... 226 D8
Hordle Rd *HAV* PO9 .... 165 G4
Horlock Rd *BROC* SO42 .... 175 L6 1
Hornbeam Cl *HEND* SO30 .... 134 D2 1
Hornbeam Gdns *HEND* SO30 ... 108 C6 1
Hornbeam Rd *HAV* PO9 .... 9 K1
NBAD SO52 .... 80 D3
Hornbeam Wy *WIMB* BH21 .... 192 B3
Hornby Cl *HLER* SO31 .... 158 B8
Hornchurch Rd *ROWN* SO16 .... 105 L3
Horndean Rd *EMRTH* PO10 ...... 166 B4
HORN PO8 .... 116 D8
Hornet Cl *FHAM* PO15 .... 6 A3
GPORT PO12 .... 11 H6
Hornet Rd *EMRTH* PO10 .... 190 E5
FHAM/STUB PO14 .... 184 D3
Horning Rd *BKME/WDN* BH12 .. 234 E3
Horns Dro *ROWN* SO16 .... 105 K2
Horns HI *BPWT* SO32 .... 113 G6
Horsa Cl *SBNE* BH6 .... 237 H4
Horsa Ct *SBNE* BH6 .... 237 K4
Horsa Rd *SBNE* BH6 .... 237 H4
Horsea La *NEND* PO2 .... 187 H4
Horsea Rd *NEND* PO2 .... 187 J3
Horsebridge Rd *HAV* PO9 .... 165 J4
Horsebridge Wy *ROWN* SO16 .. 105 K3
Horsecroft *ROMY* SO51 .... 50 E8 3
Horsefair Ct *ROMY* SO51 .... 78 D1
Horsepost La *WVILLE* PO7 .... 115 C6
Horse Sands Cl *ENEY* PO4 ...... 212 B5
Horseshoe Cl
FHAM/STUB PO14 .... 159 H6 4
WIMB BH21 .... 192 F2
Horseshoe Dr *ROMY* SO51 ...... 51 H6
Horsham Av *NBNE* BH10 .... 220 A2
Horseshoe Ldg *HLER* SO31 ..... 158 C7
Horton Cl *MOOR/WNTN* BH9 ... 221 D5
Horton Rd *LSOL/BMARY* PO13 .. 185 G4
RGWD BH24 .... 169 G2
Horton Wy *ELGH* SO50 .... 82 E7
VWD BH31 .... 144 B3
Hosker Rd *BOSC* BH5 .... 237 G3
Hospital La *FHAM/PORC* PO16 .. 186 C2
Hospital Rd *BPWT* SO32 .... 111 M1
Hotspur Cl *HAV* PO9 .... 141 M5
Houchin St *BPWT* SO32 .... 111 K1
Houghton Cl *HAV* PO9 .... 165 M2 4
Houlton Rd *PLE* BH15 .... 233 K4
Hound Cl *HLER* SO31 .... 157 H3
Hound Rd *HLER* SO31 .... 157 H3
Hound Road Gdns *HLER* SO31 .. 157 H3
Hounds Wy *WIMB* BH21 .... 192 F3
Hound Wy *HLER* SO31 .... 157 H2
Houndwell Pl *SHAM* SO14 .... 5 H4
Hounsdown Av *TOTT* SO40 ...... 129 K3
Hounsdown Cl *TOTT* SO40 .... 129 K3
Hounslow Cl *PLE* BH15 .... 232 D6
House Cl *HAVN* SO21 .... 54 F7
House Farm Rd *GPORT* PO12 .. 209 J4
Hoveton Gv *CHFD* SO53 .... 53 G8
Howard Cl *CHCH/BSGR* BH23 .. 238 E2
CHFD SO53 .... 81 J4
ELGH SO50 .... 83 H6
RGWD BH24 .... 172 C5
WEND SO18 .... 107 K4 4
Howard Rd *CHAR* BH8 .... 236 B1
NEND PO2 .... 187 H1
VWD BH31 .... 144 A2
WSHM SO15 .... 131 H2
Howard's Gv *WSHM* SO15 .... 106 B8
Howards Md *LYMN* SO41 .... 227 M6
Howe Cl *CHCH/BSGR* BH23 .... 238 E3
NMIL/BTOS BH25 .... 225 K5
Howe La *VWD* BH31 .... 144 C3

Howe Rd *LSOL/BMARY* PO13 .. 209 G2
Howerts Cl *HLER* SO31 .... 182 B1
Howeth Cl *NBNE* BH10 .... 220 B5
Howeth Rd *NBNE* BH10 .... 220 A4
Howgare Rd *RSAL* SP5 .... 40 A6
Howlett Cl *LYMN* SO41 .... 228 A4
Howton Cl *NBNE* BH10 .... 220 A3
Howton Rd *NBNE* BH10 .... 220 A3
Hoxley Rd *NBNE* BH10 .... 220 B4
Hoyal Rd *PLE* BH15 .... 232 C5
Hoylake
LSOL/BMARY PO13 .... 185 G7 1
Hoylake Rd *CHAM* PO6 .... 164 A7
Hoylecroft Cl *FHAM* PO15 .... 6 C1
Hubert Rd *WINC* SO23 .... 26 D4
Hudson Cl *BKME/WDN* BH12 .. 219 C6
LSOL/BMARY PO13 .... 209 G2 2
RGWD BH24 .... 147 G2 8
Hudson Ct *TOTT* SO40 .... 129 H2 2
Hudson Davies Cl *LYMN* SO41 .. 202 D7
Hudson Rd *SSEA* PO5 .... 13 J4
Hugh's Cl *FAWY* SO45 .... 180 C7
Hulbert Rd *HAV* PO9 .... 164 F3
WVILLE PO7 .... 164 F1
Hull Crs *BWD* BH11 .... 219 H4
Hulles Wy *NBAD* SO52 .... 79 L4
Hull Rd *BWD* BH11 .... 219 H4
Hull Wy *BWD* BH11 .... 219 H4
Hulse Rd *WSHM* SO15 .... 106 E8
Hulton Cl *ITCH* SO19 .... 132 B7
Humber Cl
FHAM/STUB PO14 .... 183 M5 3
Humber Gdns *HLER* SO31 .... 133 L7 2
Humber Rd *FERN* BH22 .... 194 E2
The Hummicks *BROC* SO42 ..... 178 F8 3
Hundred Acres Rd
WHAM PO17 .... 137 L3
Hundred La *LYMN* SO41 .... 228 D1
The Hundred *ROMY* SO51 .... 50 E8 1
WVILLE PO7 .... 140 B7 3
Hungerford Cl
CHCH/BSGR BH23 .... 197 L3
Hungerford Rd *CHAR* BH8 .... 221 H5 1
Hunt Av *HLER* SO31 .... 157 G2
Hunter Cl *CHCH/BSGR* BH23 .. 238 F1
FAWY SO45 .... 179 M2 3
LSOL/BMARY PO13 .... 209 H1
Hunter Rd *EMRTH* PO10 .... 190 E4
ENEY PO4 .... 211 K5
Hunters Cha *BPWT* SO32 .... 112 B5 1
Hunters Cl *VWD* BH31 .... 145 G3
Hunters Crs *ROMY* SO51 .... 51 H6
TOTT SO40 .... 128 F2
Hunters HI *TOTT* SO40 .... 129 H5
Hunters Ldg *FHAM* PO15 .... 159 M8
Hunters Ride *WVILLE* PO7 .... 164 C1
Hunters Wy *ELGH* SO50 .... 82 F6
Huntfield Rd
MOOR/WNTN BH9 .... 220 F5
Huntick Rd *UPTN* BH16 .... 216 A3
Huntingdon Cl
FHAM/STUB PO14 .... 159 G7 2
TOTT SO40 .... 104 D7
Huntingdon Dr *WIMB* BH21 ..... 192 C7
Huntingdon Gdns
CHCH/BSGR BH23 .... 222 D6
Huntley Cl *CHAM* PO6 .... 162 F7 2
Huntly Rd *TWDS* BH3 .... 235 J2
Huntly Wy *WEND* SO18 .... 132 D1
Hunton Cl *ROWN* SO16 .... 106 C5
Hunt Rd *CHCH/BSGR* BH23 .... 223 K8
PLE BH15 .... 233 K4
Huntsbottom La *LISS* GU33 ..... 37 G5
Hunts Pond Rd *HLER* SO31 ..... 158 F4
Huntvale Rd
MOOR/WNTN BH9 .... 220 F5
The Hurdles
CHCH/BSGR BH23 .... 222 C8 3
FHAM/STUB PO14 .... 159 H6
Hurdle Wy *RWIN* SO21 .... 26 B8
Hurlingham Gdns
ROWN SO16 .... 106 F3 3
Hurn Cl *RGWD* BH24 .... 170 B2
Hurn Ct *HAV* PO9 .... 165 M2
Hurn Court La
CHCH/BSGR BH23 .... 221 K2
Hurn La *RGWD* BH24 .... 170 B2
Hurn Rd *CHCH/BSGR* BH23 .... 222 C5
RGWD BH24 .... 170 A8
Hurn Wy *CHCH/BSGR* BH23 ... 222 B7
Hurricane Dr *ROWN* SO16 .... 105 K2
Hursley Cl *LTDN* BH7 .... 222 A8 1
Hursley Dr *FAWY* SO45 .... 206 C1
Hursley Rd *CHFD* SO53 .... 81 G1
HAV PO9 .... 165 H5
RWIN SO21 .... 53 C4
Hurst Rd *LYMN* SO41 .... 242 D5
RGWD BH24 .... 146 E2
Hurstville Dr *WVILLE* PO7 .... 164 D1
Hurstwood Av *EMRTH* PO10 .... 167 J4
Hussar Cl *CHCH/BSGR* BH23 .. 237 L1 8
Hussey Cl *WINC* SO23 .... 3 H1
Hutwood Rd *ROWN* SO16 .... 80 F8
Huxley Cl *HLER* SO31 .... 158 F6
Huxley Ct *FAWY* SO45 .... 155 G6
Hyacinth Cl *ITCH* SO19 .... 217 K7
Hyde Abbey Rd *WINC* SO23 ..... 3 G3
Hyde Church La *WINC* SO23 .... 3 G3
Hyde Cl *LYMN* SO41 .... 200 D1
TOTT SO40 .... 128 F1
WINC SO23 .... 2 E1

WSHM SO15 .... 106 B7
Hyde La *FBDG* SP6 .... 123 G3
Hyden Farm La *HORN* PO8 ...... 115 J2 2
Hyde Park Rd *SSEA* PO5 .... 13 H3
Hyde Rd *NBNE* BH10 .... 220 A3
Hyde St *SSEA* PO5 .... 13 G5 4
WINC SO23 .... 2 E3
The Hyde *NMIL/BTOS* BH25 .... 225 J4 1
Hylton Rd *PSF* GU32 .... 63 L3
Hymans Wy *TOTT* SO40 .... 129 J1
Hynesbury Rd
CHCH/BSGR BH23 .... 239 H2
Hyssop Cl *FHAM* PO15 .... 159 H1
Hythe By-pass *FAWY* SO45 ...... 154 F4
Hythe Rd *CHAM* PO6 .... 163 J8
PLE BH15 .... 233 M1
TOTT SO40 .... 130 D8

I

Ibberston Cl *CHAR* BH8 .... 221 K6
Ibberston Rd *CHAR* BH8 .... 221 K7
Ibberston Wy *CHAR* BH8 .... 221 K6
Ibbett Rd *NBNE* BH10 .... 220 A6
Ibbotson Wy *TOTT* SO40 .... 129 H3
Ibsen Cl *HLER* SO31 .... 135 G8
Ibsley Cl *CHAR* BH8 .... 236 B2
Ibsley Dro *RGWD* BH24 .... 122 E7
Ibsley Gv *HAV* PO9 .... 8 A1
Icarus Pl *WVILLE* PO7 .... 164 D6
Iddesleigh Rd *TWDS* BH3 .... 235 L2
Idsworth Cl *HORN* PO8 .... 141 H2
Idsworth Rd *HORN* PO8 .... 140 F6
HSEA PO3 .... 187 L8
Iford Cl *HAV* PO9 .... 165 M2 2
Iford Gdns *LTDN* BH7 .... 237 H1
Iford La *SBNE* BH6 .... 237 K1
Ilex Crs *HLER* SO31 .... 158 D5
Ilex Wk *HISD* PO11 .... 214 A5
Iley La *LYMN* SO41 .... 243 H1
Ilford Cl *SBNE* BH6 .... 237 L2
Ilford Rd *ITCH* SO19 .... 133 G4 2
Imber Dr *CHCH/BSGR* BH23 .... 224 D8
Imber Rd *WINC* SO23 .... 3 L6
Imber Wy *ITCH* SO19 .... 133 G4
Imbrecourt *CCLF* BH13 .... 245 K1 1
Imperial Av *WSHM* SO15 .... 130 F1
Imperial Rd *SHAM* SO14 .... 131 K3 2
Implacable Rd
LSOL/BMARY PO13 .... 208 B7
Ingersley Ri *HEND* SO30 .... 108 C6 1
Ingledene Cl *GPORT* PO12 .... 10 E4
HAV PO9 .... 8 A3
Ingle Gln *FAWY* SO45 .... 155 L7 2
Ingle Gn *TOTT* SO40 .... 104 A7
PLE BH15 .... 232 D4 4
Inglesham Wy *PLE* BH15 .... 232 D5 2
Ingleside *HLER* SO31 .... 157 G1
Ingleside Cl
FHAM/STUB PO14 .... 159 M8 5
Ingleton Rd *ROWN* SO16 .... 105 J7
Inglewood Av *CHAR* BH8 .... 221 K7
Inglewood Dr
NMIL/BTOS BH25 .... 225 M6
Inglis Rd *SSEA* PO5 .... 13 L5
Ingoldfield La *WHAM* PO17 ...... 138 A1
Ingworth Rd
BKME/WDN BH12 .... 234 F3
Inhams La *WVILLE* PO7 .... 139 H4
Inhurst Av *WVILLE* PO7 .... 140 E8
Inhurst Rd *NEND* PO2 .... 187 J6
Inkerman Rd *ITCH* SO19 .... 132 B5
Inlands Rd *RCCH* PO18 .... 167 K7
Inmans La *PSF* GU32 .... 64 A3
Insley Crs *WIMB* BH21 .... 217 J3
International Wy *ITCH* SO19 ..... 132 C8
Inveravon *CHCH/BSGR* BH23 .. 238 E4
Inverclyde Rd *PSTN* BH14 .... 234 B4
Invergordon Av *CHAM* PO6 ...... 187 M1
Inverkip Cl
LSOL/BMARY PO13 .... 208 C1 1
Inverleigh Rd *SBNE* BH6 .... 237 H2
Inverness Av *FHAM* PO15 .... 6 C2
Inverness Rd *PSTN* BH14 .... 211 J3
Inwood Cl *CHFD* SO53 .... 81 L1
Ionic Cl *CHFD* SO53 .... 81 L1
Iping Av *HAV* PO9 .... 165 H5
Iping La *MIDH* GU29 .... 67 H5
Iping Rd *LIPH* GU30 .... 38 L6
Ipley Wy *FAWY* SO45 .... 155 L6
Ipswich Rd *WBNE* BH4 .... 235 G4
Ireland Wy *WVILLE* PO7 .... 164 C3
Iris Rd *MOOR/WNTN* BH9 .... 220 D7
ROWN SO16 .... 107 G3
Ironbridge Crs *HLER* SO31 ...... 158 E2
Ironbridge La *ENEY* PO4 .... 212 A4
Iron Mill Cl *FHAM* PO15 .... 6 A1
Ironmill La *FHAM* PO15 .... 159 M3
Irvine Cl *FHAM/PORC* PO16 .... 7 C2
Irvine Wy *CHCH/BSGR* BH23 .. 223 J8
Irving Rd *ROWN* SO16 .... 105 L7
SBNE BH6 .... 237 J3
Irwell Cl *CHFD* SO53 .... 80 F3
Isaacs Cl *BKME/WDN* BH12 .... 234 B1
Isambard Brunel Rd *PSEA* PO1 .. 13 G2
Isis Cl *ROWN* SO16 .... 105 K8
Island Cl *HISD* PO11 .... 189 L5
Island View Av
CHCH/BSGR BH23 .... 239 G2
Island View Cl *LYMN* SO41 ...... 242 D5 1
Island View Rd
NMIL/BTOS BH25 .... 240 C1
Island View Ter *NEND* PO2 .... 187 G2 1
Islay Gdns *CHAM* PO6 .... 163 K7
Itchen Av *ELGH* SO50 .... 82 C4
ROMY SO51 .... 76 C5
Itchenor Rd *HISD* PO11 .... 214 D7
Itchen Rd *HAV* PO9 .... 165 M2 2
Itchenside Cl *WEND* SO18 .... 107 L4
Itchen Vw *ELGH* SO50 .... 82 A2
ITCH SO19 .... 132 B5
RWIN SO21 .... 17 J3
WINC SO23 .... 3 M1
Itchin Cl *TOTT* SO40 .... 129 H2
Ithica Cl *HISD* PO11 .... 213 L4

Ivamy Pl *BWD* BH11 219 K6
Ivanhoe Rd *WSHM* SO15 106 C7
Ivor Cl *FAWY* SO45 180 A4
Ivor Rd *PLE* BH15 232 F7
WIMB BH21 217 H4
Ivy Cl *FUFL* SO22 26 D3
RGWD BH24 169 H4
TOTT SO40 104 D6
Ivy Ct *WVILLE* PO7 164 B4 1
Ivy Dene *ITCH* SO19 133 H4
Ivydene Crs *RCCH* PO18 191 M1
Ivydene Gdns *HORN* PO8 140 E4
Ivyhouse La *PSF* GU32 34 D5
Ivy La *HEND* SO30 108 A6
RGWD BH24 146 E5
Ivy Rd *PTSW* SO17 107 H8
WIMB BH21 192 B8
Iwerne Cl *MOOR/WNTN* BH9 220 F4 3

J

Jacaranda Cl *FHAM* PO15 159 J5 1
Jack Cockerill Wy *SSEA* PO5 211 H7 4
Jackdaw Cl *HORN* PO8 140 C4
Jackdaw Ri *ELGH* SO50 81 J7 3
Jackie Wigg Gdns *TOTT* SO40 129 K1
Jackmans Cl *ITCH* SO19 132 B5 3
Jackman's Hl *RWIN* SO21 55 M1
Jackson Cl *CHAM* PO6 188 A2
Jackson Rd *BKME/WDN* BH12 234 B2
Jacobean Cl *CHCH/BSGR* BH23 224 F7
Jacobs Cl *HORN* PO8 116 B3
ROMY SO51 78 F1 1
Jacob's Gutter La *TOTT* SO40 129 K3
Jacobs Rd *PLE* BH15 232 D6
Jacob's St *PSEA* PO1 211 G2
Jacobs Wk *TOTT* SO40 129 J4
Jacomb Pl
LSOL/BMARY PO13 185 H6 3
Jacqueline Av *WVILLE* PO7 164 B4
Jacqueline Rd
BKME/WDN BH12 234 A1
Jago Rd *PSEA* PO1 210 D2
Jamacia Pl *GPORT* PO12 11 G4
Jamaica Pl *GPORT* PO12 11 G4
Jamaica Rd *GPORT* PO12 11 K1
James Callaghan Dr 185 K8 2
Jaundrells Cl *NMIL/BTOS* BH25 226 A5
Java Dr *FHAM* PO15 159 G1
Java Rd *SHAM* SO14 5 K9
Javelin Rd *EMRTH* PO10 190 E5
J Av *FAWY* SO45 180 D2
Jay Cl *FHAM/STUB* PO14 183 M4
HORN PO8 140 E1
Jay's Ct *CHCH/BSGR* BH23 224 F8 1
Jealous La *LYMN* SO41 201 L6
Jefferson Av *CHAR* BH8 236 C2
Jeffries Cl *ROWN* SO16 105 K3
Jellicoe Av *GPORT* PO12 10 B7
Jellicoe Cl *PSTN* BH14 233 L3
Jellicoe Dr *CHCH/BSGR* BH23 238 E2
Jenkins Cl *HEND* SO30 134 E1
Jenkins Gv *HSEA* PO3 211 M1
Jenner Wy *ROMY* SO51 51 H8
Jennings Rd *PSTN* BH14 234 B6
TOTT SO40 104 F8
Jephcote Rd *BWD* BH11 219 K4
Jermyns La *ROMY* SO51 51 H5
Jerome Ct *ITCH* SO19 133 H2
Jerram Cl *GPORT* PO12 10 A6
Jerrett's La *ROWN* SO16 105 J5
Jersey Cl *BKME/WDN* BH12 219 G7
FHAM/STUB PO14 184 B7
ROWN SO16 105 K5
Jersey Rd *BKME/WDN* BH12 219 H7
NEND PO2 187 J8
Jervis Court La *BPWT* SO32 85 M8
Jervis Dr *GPORT* PO12 209 M2
Jervis Rd *NEND* PO2 187 G6
Jesmond Av *CHCH/BSGR* BH23 224 D8
Jesmond Gv *HLER* SO31 158 E7
Jessamine Rd *ROWN* SO16 106 A6
Jessica Av *VWD* BH31 144 B1
Jessica Cl *WVILLE* PO7 140 F7
Jessie Rd *ENEY* PO4 13 M4
GPORT PO12 10 D4
HAV PO9 165 G5
Jessop Cl *FAWY* SO45 155 K3
Jessopp Cl *NBNE* BH10 220 D4
Jessopp Rd *WIMB* BH21 192 F2
Jetty Rd *FAWY* SO45 180 F3
Jewell Rd *CHAR* BH8 221 K7
Jewry St *WINC* SO23 3 G7
Jex Blake Cl *ROWN* SO16 106 A4
Jimmy Brown Av *WIMB* BH21 168 C3
Jinny La *ROMY* SO51 50 D3
Joanna Cl *RSAL* SP5 72 C1
Jockey La *ELGH* SO50 82 D3
Jodrell Cl *HORN* PO8 141 G1
John Bunyan Cl *FHAM* PO15 135 G8 5
Johnson Rd *WIMB* BH21 193 L1
Johnson St *SHAM* SO14 5 H3 1
Johnson Vw *FHAM* PO15 159 J2
Johns Rd *FHAM/PORC* PO16 7 J9
ITCH SO19 132 B5
Johnstone Rd
CHCH/BSGR BH23 238 D2 4
Johnston Rd *PLE* BH15 233 J1
John St *SHAM* SO14 5 H6
Jolliffe Av *PLE* BH15 233 J4
Jolliffe Rd *PLE* BH15 233 J4
Jonathan Cl *LYMN* SO41 228 C3
Jonathan Rd *FHAM* PO15 6 C5
Jones La *FAWY* SO45 155 K4
Jopps Cnr *CHCH/BSGR* BH23 223 G4
Jordans La *LYMN* SO41 201 G5
Joseph St *GPORT* PO12 11 H3 2
Joshua Cl *PLE* BH15 232 D6 2
Jowitt Dr *NMIL/BTOS* BH25 225 K6
Joyce Dickson Cl *RGWD* BH24 170 F2
Joys La *LYMN* SO41 203 J8
Joys Rd *WIMB* BH21 144 C8
Jubilee Av *CHAM* PO6 162 C8
Jubilee Cl *ELGH* SO50 81 L7 1
RGWD BH24 147 G8
WIMB BH21 217 J1
Jubilee Ct *FHAM/STUB* PO14 184 E1
LYMN SO41 200 F7
Jubilee Crs *PSTN* BH14 234 C3 3
Jubilee Gdns *NBNE* BH10 220 B6
WEND SO18 132 E1
Jubilee Pth *HAV* PO9 165 G7
Jubilee Rd *ENEY* PO4 211 K5
FBDG SP6 97 H7
FHAM/PORC PO16 162 B8
GPORT PO12 10 E2
PSTN BH14 234 C3
ROMY SO51 50 D8
WIMB BH21 217 J2
WVILLE PO7 140 C8
Jubilee Ter *SSEA* PO5 12 F5 5
Jubilee Trail *WIMB* BH21 94 B6
Julia Cl *CHCH/BSGR* BH23 224 D8
Julian Cl *ROWN* SO16 106 E2
Julian Rd *ITCH* SO19 132 F5
Julie Av *FHAM* PO15 6 C5
Juliet Ct *WVILLE* PO7 140 E8 3
Julius Cl *CHFD* SO53 81 K2
Julyan Av *BKME/WDN* BH12 219 L8
Jumar Cl *HLER* SO31 182 B1
Jumpers Av *CHCH/BSGR* BH23 222 C8
Jumpers Rd *CHCH/BSGR* BH23 222 D8
Junction Rd
MOOR/WNTN BH9 220 D8 1
TOTT SO40 129 L1
UPTN BH16 232 C4
Juniper Cl *FERN* BH22 168 A8
FUFL SO22 26 C3
LYMN SO41 227 M6
NBAD SO52 79 L3
WIMB BH21 144 C8
Juniper Rd *HORN* PO8 116 B7 5
WEND SO18 132 D1
Juniper Sq *HAV* PO9 8 F5
Jupiter Cl *ROWN* SO16 105 K4
Jura Cl *CHAM* PO6 163 K7
Jurds Lake Wy *ITCH* SO19 132 B7
Jurd Wy *HLER* SO31 133 K7
Justin Cl *FHAM/STUB* PO14 6 C6
Justin Gdns *NBNE* BH10 220 C4
Justinian Cl *CHFD* SO53 81 L1
Jute Cl *FHAM/PORC* PO16 161 M7
Jutland Cl *FHAM* PO15 158 F1

K

Kamptee Copse
NMIL/BTOS BH25 225 M2 1
Kanes Hl *ITCH* SO19 133 K2
Kangaw Pl *PLE* BH15 232 C6 1
Karen Av *CHAM* PO6 188 A2
Kassassin St *ENEY* PO4 211 L6
Kassel Cl *WVILLE* PO7 140 F7
Katherine Chance Cl
CHCH/BSGR BH23 223 G5 4
Kathleen Rd *ITCH* SO19 132 F5
Katrina Gdns *HISD* PO11 213 L3
Katrine Crs *CHFD* SO53 80 F1
Katterns Cl *CHCH/BSGR* BH23 222 C6
Kayak Cl *HLER* SO31 158 C7
Kayleigh Cl *TOTT* SO40 129 H2
Kealy Rd *GPORT* PO12 209 L2
Kearsney Av *NEND* PO2 187 J5 1
Keats Av *CHAM* PO6 162 C7
LYMN SO41 242 C3
Keats Cl *FUFL* SO22 26 B4
HORN PO8 140 D4
Keats Rd *WEND* SO18 133 G2
Keble Cl *CHFD* SO53 81 H4 1
Keble Rd *CHFD* SO53 81 H4
Keble St *FUFL* SO22 26 B2
Keeble Cl *NBNE* BH10 220 B2
Keeble Crs *NBNE* BH10 220 B2
Keeble Rd *NBNE* BH10 220 B2
Keel Cl *HSEA* PO3 188 A5
LSOL/BMARY PO13 209 H1 1
Keepers Cl *CHFD* SO53 81 G2
Keepers La *ROMY* SO51 21 H6
WIMB BH21 193 J3
The Keep *FHAM/PORC* PO16 162 C8
FHAM/PORC PO16 186 B1
Kefford Cl *HORN* PO8 140 F2
Keighley Av *BDST* BH18 217 K6
Keith Cl *GPORT* PO12 209 M2
Keith Rd *TWDS* BH3 235 H2
Kelburn Cl *CHFD* SO53 81 G1
Kellaway Rd *CFDH* BH17 218 D8
Kellett Rd *WSHM* SO15 106 C8
Kelly Cl *CFDH* BH17 218 D8
Kelly Rd *WVILLE* PO7 164 C3
Kelmscott Gdns *CHFD* SO53 52 F7
Kelsall Gdns *NMIL/BTOS* BH25 225 L5
Kelsey Av *EMRTH* PO10 167 J7
Kelsey Cl *FHAM/STUB* PO14 158 F7
LISS GU33 36 F3
Kelvin Cl *FAWY* SO45 155 L5
Kelvin Gv *FHAM/PORC* PO16 162 B8
HLER SO31 157 G2
Kelvin Rd *ELGH* SO50 81 L6
Kemp Rd *MOOR/WNTN* BH9 220 D8
Kempton Pk *WVILLE* PO7 140 F7
Kemshott Ct *HAV* PO9 165 H2
Ken Berry Ct *HAV* PO9 165 M2
Kendal Av *HSEA* PO3 187 L7
ROWN SO16 105 J7
Kendal Cl *CHFD* SO53 81 K1
HORN PO8 140 E4
Kenilworth Cl
LSOL/BMARY PO13 208 D1 4
NMIL/BTOS BH25 225 M5
Kenilworth Dr *ELGH* SO50 81 M2
Kenilworth Gdns *HEND* SO30 108 D7
Kenilworth Rd *SSEA* PO5 13 K9
WSHM SO15 131 K2 3
Kenmore Cl *TOTT* SO40 129 H3
Kennard Ct *NMIL/BTOS* BH25 225 K5
Kennard Rd *NMIL/BTOS* BH25 225 K4
Kennart Rd *CFDH* BH17 232 F1
Kennedy Av *FHAM* PO15 160 C4
Kennedy Cl *WVILLE* PO7 164 C4
Kennedy Crs *GPORT* PO12 209 J6
Kennedy Rd *ROWN* SO16 105 L5
Kennel Rd *FUFL* SO22 16 A4
Kennet Cl *GPORT* PO12 10 E9
WEND SO18 108 A5
Kennet Rd *PSF* GU32 63 K6
Kennett Rd *ROMY* SO51 51 H8
Kennington La *TOTT* SO40 127 M1
Ken Rd *SBNE* BH6 237 K4
Kensington Cl *ELGH* SO50 82 C3 2
Kensington Dr *WCLF* BH2 14 B4
Kensington Flds *FAWY* SO45 155 H6
Kensington Gdns
FHAM/STUB PO14 159 G6 2
Kensington Pk *LYMN* SO41 242 B4
Kensington Rd *GPORT* PO12 11 G5
NEND PO2 187 K6
Kenson Gdns *ITCH* SO19 132 E4
Kent Gv *FHAM/PORC* PO16 186 A2
Kentidge Rd *WVILLE* PO7 164 B3 3
Kentish Rd *WSHM* SO15 131 G1
Kent La *RGWD* BH24 122 C7
Kent Rd *BKME/WDN* BH12 234 D2
CHFD SO53 81 H5
LSOL/BMARY PO13 184 F4
PTSW SO17 107 H7
SSEA PO5 13 G6
Kent St *PSEA* PO1 12 D2
SHAM SO14 5 L1
Kenwood Rd
FHAM/PORC PO16 186 B3
Kenwyn Cl *WEND* SO18 108 A6
Kenya Rd *FHAM/PORC* PO16 185 M1
Kenyon Cl *PLE* BH15 233 K1
Kenyon Rd *NEND* PO2 187 K6
PLE BH15 233 K1
Keppel Cl *RGWD* BH24 170 F1
Kerley Rd *WCLF* BH2 14 D7
Kern Cl *ROWN* SO16 105 L5
Kerrfield *FUFL* SO22 2 A9
Kerrfield Ms *FUFL* SO22 2 B8
Kerry Cl *CHFD* SO53 81 H2
LYMN SO41 228 A5
Kesteven Wy *WEND* SO18 107 M8
Kestrel Cl *BPWT* SO32 84 F8
BPWT SO32 109 M7
FERN BH22 193 M1
FHAM/STUB PO14 183 M4
FUFL SO22 26 C4
HORN PO8 116 B4
ROWN SO16 106 A3
TOTT SO40 130 C7
UPTN BH16 216 F8
Kestrel Ct *RGWD* BH24 146 E8
Kestrel Dr *CHCH/BSGR* BH23 238 F2
Kestrel Pl *CHAM* PO6 188 D1
Kestrel Rd *ELGH* SO50 81 K6
Kestrel Wy *FBDG* SP6 121 M3 1
Keswick Av *HSEA* PO3 187 L8
Keswick Rd *BOSC* BH5 236 E4
ITCH SO19 132 B5
NMIL/BTOS BH25 225 M3
Keswick Wy *VWD* BH31 144 C3
Kettering Ter *NEND* PO2 187 G8
Kevlyn Crs *HLER* SO31 133 K7 2
Kewlake La *ROMY* SO51 102 C6
Kew La *HLER* SO31 157 L1
Keydell Cl *HORN* PO8 140 E3
Keyes Cl *BKME/WDN* BH12 219 K7
CHCH/BSGR BH23 238 E2
LSOL/BMARY PO13 185 G4
Keyes Rd *LSOL/BMARY* PO13 185 G5
Keyhaven Cl
LSOL/BMARY PO13 184 E6 1
Keyhaven Dr *HAV* PO9 165 G3
Keyhaven Rd *LYMN* SO41 242 D4
Keynsham Rd *ITCH* SO19 132 F2
Keysworth Av
NMIL/BTOS BH25 240 E1
Keysworth Rd *UPTN* BH16 232 B4
Khandala Gdns *WVILLE* PO7 164 D4 2
Khartoum Rd *PTSW* SO17 106 F6
Khyber Rd *BKME/WDN* BH12 234 C3
Kidmore La *WVILLE* PO7 139 K2
Kielder Cl *CHFD* SO53 80 F1
Kielder Gv
LSOL/BMARY PO13 185 H6 4
Kilford Ct *HEND* SO30 134 E2
Kilham La *FUFL* SO22 26 A2
Killarney Cl *ITCH* SO19 133 J5 3
Kilmarnock Rd
MOOR/WNTN BH9 220 D7 1
Kilmeston Rd *NARL* SO24 30 C4
Kilmington Wy
CHCH/BSGR BH23 224 D8
Kilmiston Cl *PSEA* PO1 211 J1
Kilmiston Dr
FHAM/PORC PO16 162 A7
Kiln Cl *FAWY* SO45 155 J5
WIMB BH21 217 G4
Kiln Fld *LISS* GU33 36 D3
Kiln Hl *BPWT* SO32 113 G8
Kiln La *EPSF* GU31 91 H4
ROMY SO51 51 G2
RSAL SP5 73 K1
RWIN SO21 54 A6
WVILLE PO7 138 B4
Kiln Rd *FHAM/PORC* PO16 160 D4
Kilnside *WVILLE* PO7 139 K5
Kilnyard Cl *TOTT* SO40 104 C7
Kilpatrick Cl *NEND* PO2 187 H8 4
Kilwich Wy *FHAM/PORC* PO16 185 M2
Kimberley Cl
CHCH/BSGR BH23 222 D8 3
ELGH SO50 83 J6
Kimberley Rd *ENEY* PO4 211 L6
PSTN BH14 234 A5
SBNE BH6 237 H2
Kimber Rd *BWD* BH11 219 K5 1
Kimbers *PSF* GU32 63 K4
Kimbolton Rd *HSEA* PO3 211 L2
Kimbridge Crs *HAV* PO9 165 L2
Kimbridge La *ROMY* SO51 49 L1
Kimmeridge Av
BKME/WDN BH12 219 G8
Kimpton Cl
LSOL/BMARY PO13 208 D2 6
Kimpton Ct *HAV* PO9 165 M2 6
Kineton Rd *WSHM* SO15 106 D7
King Albert St *PSEA* PO1 211 H2 4
King Alfred Pl *WINC* SO23 3 G5
King Alfred Ter *WINC* SO23 3 G5
King Arthur's Ct *CHAM* PO6 164 B8 1
King Charles St *PSEA* PO1 12 C4
King Cl *RGWD* BH24 169 K4
King Cup Av *HLER* SO31 158 D6
Kingcup Cl *BDST* BH18 217 J6
King Edward Av
MOOR/WNTN BH9 220 D6
ROWN SO16 105 M8
King Edward's Crs
NEND PO2 187 H6 2
Kingfisher Cl *FERN* BH22 168 D6
HAV PO9 141 M7
HISD PO11 214 A6
HLER SO31 157 L4 1
HORN PO8 140 C4 1
SBNE BH6 237 K2 1
Kingfisher Copse *HLER* SO31 158 F5
Kingfishers *FHAM/PORC* PO16 161 K8
The Kingfishers *VWD* BH31 144 E3
Kingfisher Wy
CHCH/BSGR BH23 238 F3
RGWD BH24 146 F7
ROMY SO51 50 E8 2
TOTT SO40 130 C7
King George Av *EPSF* GU31 63 L4
MOOR/WNTN BH9 220 D6
King George Rd
FHAM/PORC PO16 186 A1
King George's Av *WSHM* SO15 130 D2
King Henry I St *PSEA* PO1 12 F2
King John Av *BWD* BH11 219 H3
FHAM/PORC PO16 185 M1
Kingland Rd *PLE* BH15 233 J6
King La *PSF* GU32 34 E8
King Richard 1 Rd *PSEA* PO1 12 F3 1
King Richard Dr *BWD* BH11 219 H3
Kings Arms La *RGWD* BH24 170 D1
Kings Arms Rw *RGWD* BH24 170 D1 5
King's Av *CHCH/BSGR* BH23 237 L2
FUFL SO22 26 D3
HLER SO31 157 J5
PSTN BH14 234 C6
Kingsbere Av *NBNE* BH10 219 M6
Kingsbere Rd *PLE* BH15 233 K3 1
Kingsbridge Rd *PSTN* BH14 234 B5
Kingsbury Rd *SHAM* SO14 131 M1 3
Kingsbury's La *RGWD* BH24 170 D2
Kingsclere Av *HAV* PO9 165 H3
ITCH SO19 132 D7
Kingsclere Cl *ITCH* SO19 132 D7 3
King's Cl *CHFD* SO53 81 J1
FERN BH22 168 B7
HAV PO9 141 L6
LYND SO43 151 K3
RWIN SO21 54 F1
Kings Copse Av *HEND* SO30 134 B1
King's Copse Rd *FAWY* SO45 180 A8
HEND SO30 134 A3
Kingscote Rd *CHAM* PO6 162 D6
HORN PO8 140 B5
Kings Crs *LYMN* SO41 228 B4
PSTN BH14 234 D6
Kingscroft Ct *HAV* PO9 8 B5
King's Croft La *HAV* PO9 165 G7
Kingsdown Pl *PSEA* PO1 13 L2 2
Kingsdown Rd *WVILLE* PO7 140 A6
Kingsdown Wy *WEND* SO18 107 L6
Kingsey Av *EMRTH* PO10 166 C8
Kingsfernsden La *PSF* GU32 63 M3
Kings Fld *HLER* SO31 133 L7
Kingsfield *LYMN* SO41 228 E6 1
RGWD BH24 170 E1
Kings Field Gdns *HLER* SO31 133 L7
Kingsfold Av *WEND* SO18 107 L5
Kingsford Cl *RSAL* SP5 73 J3 1
Kingsgate Rd *WINC* SO23 26 E3
Kingsland Cl *CHAM* PO6 163 G7
Kings La *LYMN* SO41 201 J8
PSF GU32 34 B6
RWIN SO21 27 L2
Kingsley Av *SBNE* BH6 237 M4 1
Kingsley Cl *SBNE* BH6 237 M4
Kingsley Gdns *TOTT* SO40 128 F1
Kingsley Pl *FUFL* SO22 26 D3
Kingsley Rd *ENEY* PO4 211 M5
GPORT PO12 209 K1
WSHM SO15 130 F1
Kingsmead *WHAM* PO17 137 G1
Kingsmead Av
FHAM/STUB PO14 184 B7
Kings Mede *HORN* PO8 140 F2
Kingsmill Cl *GPORT* PO12 10 B4
Kingsmill Rd *CFDH* BH17 233 K1
King's Park Dr *LTDN* BH7 236 D2
King's Park Rd *BMTH* BH1 236 D2
WSHM SO15 131 L2
Kings Ride *FAWY* SO45 206 C1
King's Rd *CHFD* SO53 81 H2
EMRTH PO10 166 C8
FHAM/PORC PO16 7 J6
FUFL SO22 26 B2 1
GPORT PO12 10 F3
HISD PO11 213 L3
LSOL/BMARY PO13 208 C1
LYMN SO41 228 B4
NMIL/BTOS BH25 226 A4
PSEA PO1 210 D2
PSF GU32 63 J4
SSEA PO5 12 F5
TWDS BH3 235 M1
King's Saltern Rd *LYMN* SO41 228 E6
Kings Somborne Rd
ROMY SO51 23 J7
King's Ter *EMRTH* PO10 166 D8 2
PSEA PO1 12 F5
Kingston *HLER* SO31 157 G1 4
Kingston Crs *NEND* PO2 187 H8
Kingston Gdns *FHAM* PO15 160 B4
Kingston Pk *LYMN* SO41 228 A6 1
Kingston Rd *GPORT* PO12 10 B1
NEND PO2 187 J8
PLE BH15 233 J4
WSHM SO15 131 H2
King St *EMRTH* PO10 166 F5
GPORT PO12 11 K2
SHAM SO14 5 H5
SSEA PO5 12 F4
King's Wy *BPWT* SO32 56 D5
BPWT SO32 84 D5
BPWT SO32 112 F3
FHAM/PORC PO16 161 K8
RWIN SO21 28 C4
WHAM PO17 138 D7
WINC SO23 3 H4
WVILLE PO7 138 D3
Kingsway *CHFD* SO53 81 J1
HISD PO11 189 L5
Kingsway Cl *CHCH/BSGR* BH23 222 D7
Kingsway Gdns *CHFD* SO53 53 K8
The Kingsway
FHAM/PORC PO16 162 A8
Kingswell Cl *NBNE* BH10 220 B6 1
Kingswell Gdns *NBNE* BH10 219 M6
Kingswell Gv *NBNE* BH10 219 M6
Kingswell Rd *NBNE* BH10 220 A6
Kingswell St *PSEA* PO1 13 G1 3
Kingswood *TOTT* SO40 130 E7
Kingsworthy Rd *HAV* PO9 165 K5
King William St *PSEA* PO1 210 E2
Kinnell Cl *EMRTH* PO10 166 D8
Kinross Crs *CHAM* PO6 187 M1
Kinross Rd *TOTT* SO40 129 K1
TWDS BH3 235 K2
Kinsbourne Av *NBNE* BH10 220 B6
Kinsbourne Cl *ITCH* SO19 133 K2 1
Kinsbourne Ri *ITCH* SO19 133 K3
Kinsbourne Wy *ITCH* SO19 133 J2 2
Kinson Av *PLE* BH15 233 M2
Kinson Gv *NBNE* BH10 220 A2
Kinson Park Rd *NBNE* BH10 220 B2
Kinson Rd *NBNE* BH10 219 L7
Kintyre Rd *CHAM* PO6 163 K7
Kinver Cl *ROMY* SO51 51 G7
Kipling Ct *ITCH* SO19 132 D7 4
Kipling Rd *ELGH* SO50 81 L5
NEND PO2 187 J5
PSTN BH14 234 A3
Kirby Cl *PLE* BH15 233 L2
Kirby Rd *NEND* PO2 187 J6
Kirby Wy *SBNE* BH6 237 J4
Kirk Gdns *TOTT* SO40 129 K3
Kirkham Av
CHCH/BSGR BH23 223 G5 5
Kirkstall Rd *ENEY* PO4 211 J7 1
Kirkway *BDST* BH18 217 M4
Kirtley Cl *CHAM* PO6 188 A2
Kirton Rd *CHAM* PO6 188 A1
Kitchener Crs *CFDH* BH17 217 M6
Kitchener Rd *PTSW* SO17 107 H5
Kitchers Cl *LYMN* SO41 200 F5
Kite Cl *HORN* PO8 140 C4
Kites Croft Cl
FHAM/STUB PO14 159 G7
Kitnocks Hl *BPWT* SO32 110 D8
Kitscroft Rd *NBNE* BH10 220 A3
Kittiwake Cl
LSOL/BMARY PO13 184 F6
Kittiwake Cl *SBNE* BH6 237 J2 1
Kitt's La *NARL* SO24 32 B6
Kitwalls La *LYMN* SO41 242 C3
Kivernell Rd *LYMN* SO41 242 B4
Kiwi Cl *PLE* BH15 233 K5
Knapp Cl *CHCH/BSGR* BH23 222 E8
Knapp La *ROMY* SO51 52 C4
Knapp Mill Av
CHCH/BSGR BH23 222 E8
Knapps Hard *PSF* GU32 60 A3
Knatchbull Cl *ROMY* SO51 78 E1 2
Knellers La *TOTT* SO40 129 H4
Knight Cl *WINC* SO23 3 G3
Knighton Heath Cl
BWD BH11 219 J4 6
Knighton Heath Rd
BWD BH11 219 J4
Knighton La *BWD* BH11 219 H1
Knighton Pk *NMIL/BTOS* BH25 225 J8
Knighton Rd *ITCH* SO19 132 D5
RSAL SP5 40 C1
Knights Bank Rd
FHAM/STUB PO14 183 K7
Knights Cl *HLER* SO31 158 C7 3
Knights Rd *BWD* BH11 219 H3
Knightstone Gra *FAWY* SO45 155 L6 3
Knightwood Av *HAV* PO9 165 L3
LYND SO43 151 K3
Knightwood Cl
CHCH/BSGR BH23 224 C8 1
LYND SO43 151 K3
TOTT SO40 128 F6
Knightwood Rd *FAWY* SO45 155 M6
NBAD SO52 52 E8
Knole Gdns *BMTH* BH1 236 C4
Knole Rd *BMTH* BH1 236 C3
Knoll Gdns *RGWD* BH24 169 K4
Knoll La *WIMB* BH21 216 F1
Knottgrass Rd *HLER* SO31 158 C6
Knowland Dr *LYMN* SO41 242 C3
Knowle Hl *ELGH* SO50 82 A1
Knowle La *ELGH* SO50 83 K8
Knowle Rd *BROC* SO42 175 J6
Knowles Cl *CHCH/BSGR* BH23 238 D1
Knowles Meadow *LISS* GU33 37 G7
Knowlton Gdns
MOOR/WNTN BH9 220 F5 3
Knowlton Rd *CFDH* BH17 218 D6
Knowsley Crs *CHAM* PO6 187 L1
Knowsley Rd *CHAM* PO6 187 K1
Knox Rd *HAV* PO9 8 B4
NEND PO2 187 G7
Knyght Cl *ROMY* SO51 78 F2
Knyveton Rd *BMTH* BH1 15 M4
Kootenay Av *WEND* SO18 133 J1
Kooyong Cl *ROMY* SO51 77 G6
Kynegils Rd *FUFL* SO22 2 B3
Kynon Cl *GPORT* PO12 186 A8 2
Kyrchil La *WIMB* BH21 192 C2
Kyrchil Wy *WIMB* BH21 192 D1
Kytes La *BPWT* SO32 110 A3

L

Labrador Dr *PLE* BH15 233 J7

Laburnum Av CHAM P06 ..... 188 A1
Laburnum Cl FERN BH22 ..... 193 M2
  NBAD SO52 ..... 79 M3
  VWD BH31 ..... 145 G2
Laburnum Crs FAWY SO45 ..... 155 M8 2
Laburnum Dr LYMN SO41 ..... 227 J8 2
Laburnum Rd ELGH SO50 ..... 81 M5 2
  HISD PO11 ..... 213 M4
  NEND PO2 ..... 187 J7
Laburnum Rd
  FHAM/PORC PO16 ..... 184 F2
  HEND SO30 ..... 134 B2
  ROWN SO16 ..... 107 H4
  WVILLE PO7 ..... 164 C2
Lacey Crs PSTN BH14 ..... 233 M8
Lackford Av TOTT SO40 ..... 129 J2
Lacon Cl WEND 107 K8
Lacy Cl WIMB BH21 ..... 192 B2
Lacy Dr WIMB BH21 ..... 192 A2
Ladram Rd GPORT PO12 ..... 209 J4
Ladybridge Rd WVILLE PO7 ..... 164 A4
Ladycross Rd FAWY SO45 ..... 155 L6
Ladysmith Cl
  CHCH/BSGR BH23 ..... 238 D1
Lagado Cl PSTN BH14 ..... 234 B8
Lagland St PLE BH15 ..... 233 H4
Lagoon Rd PSTN BH14 ..... 234 A7
Laidlaw Cl BKME/WDN BH12 ..... 219 M8
Lainston Cl FUFL SO22 ..... 16 B4
Lake Av PLE BH15 ..... 232 D5
Lake Crs PLE BH15 ..... 232 D5
Lake Dr PLE BH15 ..... 232 C6
Lake Farm Cl HEND SO30 ..... 109 H8 2
Lake Grove Rd
  NMIL/BTOS BH25 ..... 225 L4
Lakeland Gdns TOTT SO40 ..... 130 C7 2
Lakelands Dr WSHM SO15 ..... 131 G2 2
Lake Rd BPWT SO32 ..... 110 E8
  BWD BH11 ..... 219 M2
  CHFD SO53 ..... 53 K8
  ITCH SO19 ..... 132 B6
  PLE BH15 ..... 232 D6
  PSEA PO1 ..... 211 G2 2
  VWD BH31 ..... 144 E4
Lakeside ELGH SO50 ..... 81 L8
  LSOL/BMARY PO13 ..... 208 D4
  RGWD BH24 ..... 171 G2
  WHAM PO17 ..... 160 C3
Lakeside Av HSEA PO3 ..... 211 M2
  ROWN SO16 ..... 105 K3
Lakeside Gdns HAV PO9 ..... 9 G2
Lakeside Rd CCLF BH13 ..... 234 F7
Lakesmere Rd HORN PO8 ..... 141 G2
The Lakes BPWT SO32 ..... 111 M4
Lakeview Dr RGWD BH24 ..... 171 G2
Lakewood Cl CHFD SO53 ..... 53 J8
Lakewood Rd
  CHCH/BSGR BH23 ..... 224 D7
  CHFD SO53 ..... 53 J8
  TOTT SO40 ..... 129 G5
Lamberhurst Cl ITCH SO19 ..... 132 E8
Lambert Cl WVILLE PO7 ..... 164 C3
Lambourn Cl FHAM/STUB PO14 ..... 14 B7 2
Lambourne Cl FAWY SO45 ..... 155 K7 2
Lambourne Dr HLER SO31 ..... 158 C5
Lambourne La LIPH GU30 ..... 39 C5
Lambourne Rd WEND SO18 ..... 108 A6
Lambourn Sq CHFD SO53 ..... 80 F2
Lambs Cl CFDH BH17 ..... 218 A7
Lammas Rd FAWY SO45 ..... 155 L6
Lampeter Av CHAM P06 ..... 163 M4
Lampton Gdns
  MOOR/WNTN BH9 ..... 220 D7 2
Lancaster Cl BDST BH18 ..... 217 K3
  CHCH/BSGR BH23 ..... 239 G1
  FHAM/PORC PO16 ..... 161 M7
  HLER SO31 ..... 133 L7 2
  LSOL/BMARY PO13 ..... 208 F4
Lancaster Dr BDST BH18 ..... 217 J3
  VWD BH31 ..... 144 C2
Lancaster Rd ROWN SO16 ..... 105 L5
Lancaster Wy WVILLE PO7 ..... 164 C2
Lancer Cl CHCH/BSGR BH23 ..... 237 L1
Lance's HI ITCH SO19 ..... 132 D1
Lander Cl PLE BH15 ..... 233 J7
Landford Gdns CHAR BH8 ..... 221 H6 2
Landford Wy CHAR BH8 ..... 221 H6
Landguard Rd WSHM SO15 ..... 131 H5
Landon Rd LSOL/BMARY PO13 ..... 185 M8
Landport St PSEA PO1 ..... 211 H2
  SSEA PO5 ..... 12 F4 2
Landport Ter PSEA PO1 ..... 12 F4
Landport Vw PSEA PO1 ..... 211 G2 2
Landsdowne St SSEA PO5 ..... 12 F4
The Landsdown Rbt BMTH BH1 ..... 15 H5
Landseer Rd CCLF BH13 ..... 235 H5 2
  ITCH SO19 ..... 133 G5
Lands End Rd HLER SO31 ..... 157 M1
Lane End Dr EMRTH PO10 ..... 166 D8
Lanehays Rd FAWY SO45 ..... 155 K5
Lanesbridge Cl TOTT SO40 ..... 128 D3
Lanes End FHAM/STUB PO14 ..... 184 A6
The Lanes NMIL/BTOS BH25 ..... 225 J1
The Lane ENEY PO4 ..... 211 K6
  FAWY SO45 ..... 180 F5 2
  GPORT PO12 ..... 10 D9
Langbar Cl ITCH SO19 ..... 132 C2
Langbrook Cl HAV PO9 ..... 8 E7
Langdale Av CHAM P06 ..... 187 M1
Langdale Cl ROWN SO16 ..... 105 L8 2
Langdon Rd PSTN BH14 ..... 234 E4
Langdown Lawn FAWY SO45 ..... 155 L6
Langdown Lawn Cl
  FAWY SO45 ..... 155 L6 2
Langford La RSAL SP5 ..... 45 L7
Langford Rd NEND PO2 ..... 211 K1
Langham Cl NBAD SO52 ..... 79 M3
Langhorn Rd ROWN SO16 ..... 107 H4
Langley Cha RGWD BH24 ..... 169 L3
Langley Gdn FERN BH22 ..... 97 M5

WSHM SO15 ..... 130 E2
Langrish Cl HAV PO9 ..... 165 L2 2
Langrish Rd ROWN SO16 ..... 106 A4
Langstone Av HAV PO9 ..... 8 E7
Langstone High St HAV PO9 ..... 189 K2
Langstone Rd HAV PO9 ..... 8 E7
  HSEA PO3 ..... 211 L2
Langstone Wk
  FHAM/STUB PO14 ..... 160 A8
  LSOL/BMARY PO13 ..... 184 F6
Langton Cl FUFL SO22 ..... 2 C5
  NMIL/BTOS BH25 ..... 225 M8
Langton Rd BPWT SO32 ..... 85 G8
  LTDN BH7 ..... 236 E3
Lankhills Rd WINC SO23 ..... 2 F3
Lansdowne Av
  FHAM/PORC PO16 ..... 186 B2
  WVILLE PO7 ..... 163 M5
Lansdowne Cl ROMY SO51 ..... 50 D8 2
Lansdowne Gdns BMTH BH1 ..... 15 H3
Lansdowne HI SHAM SO14 ..... 4 F5 2
Lansdowne Rd BMTH BH1 ..... 15 G1
  WSHM SO15 ..... 130 E1
Lantana Cl WVILLE PO7 ..... 164 D2 2
Lanyard Dr LSOL/BMARY PO13 ..... 209 H2
Lapthorn Cl
  LSOL/BMARY PO13 ..... 184 F4
  HORN PO8 ..... 140 L1
Lapwing Cl GPORT PO12 ..... 209 M1 2
  HORN PO8 ..... 140 E1
Lapwing Dr TOTT SO40 ..... 104 B8
Lapwing Gv
  FHAM/PORC PO16 ..... 161 K8 2
Lapwing Rd WIMB BH21 ..... 192 E1
Lara Cl CHAR BH8 ..... 221 H5
Larch Av FAWY SO45 ..... 180 A3
Larch Cl CFDH BH17 ..... 217 J7
  HEND SO30 ..... 108 C5
  LSOL/BMARY PO13 ..... 208 E3 2
  LYMN SO41 ..... 226 D5 2
  ROWN SO16 ..... 169 L4
Larchdale Cl HLER SO31 ..... 158 B8 2
Larches Gdns FHAM SO15 ..... 160 A7
Larchfield Wy HORN PO8 ..... 141 G3
Larch Rd ROWN SO16 ..... 105 M5
  HLER SO31 ..... 133 K8
Larchwood Av HAV PO9 ..... 164 F4
Larchwood Rd TOTT SO40 ..... 129 G2
Larcombe Rd PSF GU32 ..... 63 J7
Larg Dr FUFL SO22 ..... 16 B4
Lark Hill Ri FUFL SO22 ..... 26 C4
Larkhill Rd HSEA PO3 ..... 187 K4
Lark Rd CHCH/BSGR BH23 ..... 238 F2 2
Larksfield Av
  MOOR/WNTN BH9 ..... 220 F5
Larkshill Cl NMIL/BTOS BH25 ..... 225 M4
Larkspur Cha ITCH SO19 ..... 133 J3
Larkspur Cl BPWT SO32 ..... 111 M5
  HLER SO31 ..... 158 D6 2
Larkspur Dr TOTT SO40 ..... 130 C8
Larkspur Drive NBAD SO52 ..... 80 E2
Larkspur Gdns FAWY SO45 ..... 179 M4
  HEND SO30 ..... 134 A2 2
Larks Ri FERN BH22 ..... 193 M1
Lascelles Rd LTDN BH7 ..... 237 G2
Laser Cl HLER SO31 ..... 158 C7
Lashly Meadow WVILLE PO7 ..... 114 B5
Latch Farm Av
  CHCH/BSGR BH23 ..... 222 E8 2
Latchmore Dr FAWY SO45 ..... 155 G4
Latchmore Forest Gv
  HORN PO8 ..... 140 D5
Latchmore Gdns HORN PO8 ..... 140 C5
Latelie Cl HLER SO31 ..... 157 G3 2
Latham Cl ELGH SO50 ..... 83 G6
Latham Ct WSHM SO15 ..... 130 F1
Latham Rd ELGH SO50 ..... 83 G6
  ROMY SO51 ..... 50 F8 2
Latimer Ct HSEA PO3 ..... 187 M4 2
Latimer Rd MOOR/WNTN BH9 ..... 220 D8
Latimers Cl CHCH/BSGR BH23 ..... 224 D7
Latimer St ROMY SO51 ..... 78 D1
  SHAM SO14 ..... 5 H6
Lauder Cl EMRTH PO10 ..... 167 H6
Launcelyn Cl NBAD SO52 ..... 79 L5
Launceston Dr ELGH SO50 ..... 81 L3 2
Laundry La LYMN SO41 ..... 242 D4
Laundry Rd ROWN SO16 ..... 106 A6
Laurel Cl CHCH/BSGR BH23 ..... 224 B7
  FAWY SO45 ..... 155 J5
  HLER SO31 ..... 158 F4 2
  LYMN SO41 ..... 226 C4
  RGWD BH24 ..... 169 J4
  WIMB BH21 ..... 217 H2
Laurel Gdns BDST BH18 ..... 218 A4
  HLER SO31 ..... 158 F4
Laurel La RGWD BH24 ..... 169 J5
Laurel Rd HLER SO31 ..... 158 F4
  HORN PO8 ..... 141 G4
The Laurels FERN BH22 ..... 194 A1
Lauriston Dr CHFD SO53 ..... 53 G7 2
Laurus Cl WVILLE PO7 ..... 164 C5
Lavant Cl HORN PO8 ..... 140 F7
Lavant Dr HAV PO9 ..... 9 G1
Lavant St PSF GU32 ..... 63 K4
Lavender Cl ITCH SO19 ..... 132 D5 2
  VWD BH31 ..... 145 G3
Lavender Rd CHAR BH8 ..... 221 H4
  LYMN SO41 ..... 226 C5
  WVILLE PO7 ..... 164 C2
Lavender Wy BDST BH18 ..... 217 H5
Laverock Lea
  FHAM/PORC PO16 ..... 162 A7
Laverstoke Cl ROWN SO16 ..... 105 K2 2
Lavey's La FHAM PO15 ..... 159 M2
Lavington Gdns NBAD SO52 ..... 79 L5
Lavinia Rd BKME/WDN BH12 ..... 234 B1
Lawford Rd MOOR/WNTN BH9 ..... 220 E5
Lawford Wy TOTT SO40 ..... 104 D8
Lawn Cl LSOL/BMARY PO13 ..... 185 H7 2
  LYMN SO41 ..... 242 D4
Lawn Dr HLER SO31 ..... 158 E6

Lawn Rd ELGH SO50 ..... 82 A3
  FUFL SO22 ..... 16 B3
  LYMN SO41 ..... 227 M5
  LYMN SO41 ..... 242 D4
  PTSW SO17 ..... 107 G3
Lawns Cl WIMB BH21 ..... 193 G2
Lawnside Rd WSHM SO15 ..... 105 M8
Lawns Rd WIMB BH21 ..... 192 F2
Lawn St WINC SO23 ..... 3 H7
Lawnswood Cl HORN PO8 ..... 140 D6
Lawn Vw CHCH/BSGR BH23 ..... 225 H3
Lawrence Av HORN PO8 ..... 140 C6
Lawrence Ct CHAR BH8 ..... 236 B2 2
Lawrence Dr PSTN BH14 ..... 234 D7
Lawrence Gv ITCH SO19 ..... 132 C6
Lawrence La FBDG SP6 ..... 122 F4
Lawrence Rd FHAM PO15 ..... 6 A4
  RGWD BH24 ..... 147 G6
  SSEA PO5 ..... 13 L6
Lawson Cl HLER SO31 ..... 134 B8 2
Lawson Rd BKME/WDN BH12 ..... 234 A2
  SSEA PO5 ..... 13 L6
Laxton Cl HLER SO31 ..... 158 F5
  ITCH SO19 ..... 132 C6
Layard Dr WIMB BH21 ..... 192 B7
Layton Rd BKME/WDN BH12 ..... 225 H3
  LSOL/BMARY PO13 ..... 185 G5
Lazy Acre EMRTH PO10 ..... 167 H8
Leacock Cl BPWT SO32 ..... 112 A4
Leafy La FHAM PO15 ..... 159 J2
Lealand Gv CHAM P06 ..... 164 B8
Lealand Rd CHAM P06 ..... 188 B1
Leamington Crs
  LSOL/BMARY PO13 ..... 208 C2
Leamington Rd
  MOOR/WNTN BH9 ..... 235 M1
Leander Cl ELGH SO50 ..... 81 M3 2
Lea-oak Gdns FHAM PO15 ..... 6 A2
Leaphill Rd LTDN BH7 ..... 236 F2
Lea Rd FAWY SO45 ..... 206 C1
Learoyd Rd CFDH BH17 ..... 233 J1
Lear Rd GPORT PO12 ..... 10 F2
The Lea VWD BH31 ..... 144 B3
Leatherhead Gdns
  HEND SO30 ..... 109 J6 2
Lea Wy BWD BH11 ..... 219 J2
The Leaway FHAM/PORC PO16 ..... 162 B8
Lebanon Rd WSHM SO15 ..... 130 B1
Lechlade Gdns FHAM PO15 ..... 160 B4
  LTDN BH7 ..... 221 L8
Leckford Cl FHAM/PORC PO16 ..... 162 A7
  WEND SO18 ..... 108 C3 2
Leckford Rd HAV PO9 ..... 165 M2
Ledbury Rd CHAM P06 ..... 163 G7
  CHCH/BSGR BH23 ..... 238 E3
Lederle La LSOL/BMARY PO13 ..... 185 G3
Ledgard Cl PSTN BH14 ..... 234 A4
Lee Church La ROMY SO51 ..... 78 E8
Leedam Rd NBNE BH10 ..... 220 B4
Lee Dro ROMY SO51 ..... 78 F7
Lee Lands LYMN SO41 ..... 228 C2
Lee La ROMY SO51 ..... 78 E7
Leep La GPORT PO12 ..... 209 L2
Lee Rd GPORT PO12 ..... 209 J2
Lees Cl CHCH/BSGR BH23 ..... 222 B4
Leesland Rd GPORT PO12 ..... 10 C1
Lees La GPORT PO12 ..... 10 E1
Leeson Rd LTDN BH7 ..... 236 D1
Legg La WIMB BH21 ..... 192 B4
Legion Cl PLE BH15 ..... 232 D6
Legion Cl WINC SO23 ..... 17 H1
Legion Rd HISD PO11 ..... 213 L4
  PLE BH15 ..... 232 D6
Leicester Rd CCLF BH13 ..... 234 F6 2
  WSHM SO15 ..... 106 C6
Leicester Wy WINC SO23 ..... 3 M4
Leigham Vale Rd SBNE BH6 ..... 237 J4
Leigh Common WIMB BH21 ..... 192 B4
Leigh Gdns WIMB BH21 ..... 192 B4
Leigh La WIMB BH21 ..... 192 D3
Leigh Pk LYMN SO41 ..... 228 A4
Leigh Rd CHFD SO53 ..... 81 H4
  ELGH SO50 ..... 81 K5
  ELGH SO50 ..... 82 A5 2
  FHAM/PORC PO16 ..... 7 G4
  HAV PO9 ..... 8 F2
  NMIL/BTOS BH25 ..... 225 L4
  PTSW SO17 ..... 106 F7
  WIMB BH21 ..... 192 A4
Leighton Av WSHM SO15 ..... 106 A8
Leighton Rd ITCH SO19 ..... 132 C5
Leith Av FHAM/PORC PO16 ..... 162 B7
Lemon Rd WSHM SO15 ..... 130 F1
Lendorber Av CHAM P06 ..... 187 L1
Lennox Cl CHFD SO53 ..... 53 K8
  GPORT PO12 ..... 10 F9
  ROWN SO16 ..... 105 L3
Lennox Rd South SSEA PO5 ..... 13 J8
Lensyd Gdns HORN PO8 ..... 140 D2
Lentham Cl CFDH BH17 ..... 218 B7
Lentune Wy LYMN SO41 ..... 228 B6
Leofric Ct ENEY PO4 ..... 212 A5
Leominster Rd CHAM P06 ..... 162 F7
Leonard Rd GPORT PO12 ..... 11 H2
Leopold Dr BPWT SO32 ..... 111 J1
Leopold St ENEY PO4 ..... 13 M7
Le Patourel Cl
  CHCH/BSGR BH23 ..... 238 C1
Lepe Rd FAWY SO45 ..... 206 D1
Lerryn Rd LSOL/BMARY PO13 ..... 185 H6
Leslie Rd MOOR/WNTN BH9 ..... 220 C8
  PSTN BH14 ..... 233 M5
Lester Av HAV PO9 ..... 165 G6
Lester Rd GPORT PO12 ..... 10 A2
Leven Av WBNE BH4 ..... 14 A2
Leven Cl CHFD SO53 ..... 52 F8
  WBNE BH4 ..... 14 A2
Leventhorpe Ct GPORT PO12 ..... 11 G4 2
Leveson Cl GPORT PO12 ..... 10 A6
Levet's La PLE BH15 ..... 233 G6 2
Leviathan Cl FHAM/STUB PO14 ..... 184 B6
Lewens Cl WIMB BH21 ..... 192 A4
Lewes Cl ELGH SO50 ..... 81 M2
Lewesdon Dr BDST BH18 ..... 217 K4
Lewin Cl RWIN SO21 ..... 54 F8
Lewis Cl FAWY SO45 ..... 155 G6

Lewis Rd EMRTH PO10 ..... 166 E5
Lewis Silkin Wy ROWN SO16 ..... 105 M4
Lewry Cl HEND SO30 ..... 134 A1
Lexby Rd TOTT SO40 ..... 129 L2
Lexden Gdns HISD PO11 ..... 213 J4 2
Leybourne Av NBNE BH10 ..... 220 A3
  WEND SO18 ..... 107 L8
Leybourne Cl NBNE BH10 ..... 220 A3
Leydene Av CHAR BH8 ..... 221 K7
Leydene Cl CHAR BH8 ..... 221 K7
Leyland Cl GPORT PO12 ..... 10 F6
Leyland Rd BKME/WDN BH12 ..... 219 J6
Leyside CHCH/BSGR BH23 ..... 238 E2
Leyton Rd SHAM SO14 ..... 132 A2
Liam Cl HAV PO9 ..... 165 L4
Liberty Rd BPWT SO32 ..... 112 F8
The Liberty WVILLE PO7 ..... 139 J5
Library Rd BKME/WDN BH12 ..... 234 D3
  FERN BH22 ..... 194 B3
  MOOR/WNTN BH9 ..... 220 D7
  TOTT SO40 ..... 129 L1
Lichen Wy WEND SO18 ..... 130 D6
Lichfield Rd FHAM/STUB PO14 ..... 159 C5
  HSEA PO3 ..... 211 L2
Liddel Wy CHFD SO53 ..... 80 F3
Liddiards Wy WVILLE PO7 ..... 164 C5
Lidiard Gdns ENEY PO4 ..... 211 M6
Lilac Cl HAV PO9 ..... 166 A5
  RGWD BH24 ..... 146 F8
Lilac Rd ROWN SO16 ..... 107 G4
Liliput Rd PSTN BH14 ..... 234 B8
Lily Av WVILLE PO7 ..... 163 M6
Lime Av ITCH SO19 ..... 132 E3
Lime Cl FAWY SO45 ..... 155 J6
  ITCH SO19 ..... 132 E3
  PLE BH15 ..... 232 D6
Lime Gdns HEND SO30 ..... 108 C5
Lime Gv CHAM P06 ..... 162 F7
  HISD PO11 ..... 213 G5
  LYMN SO41 ..... 227 H8
Lime Kiln La FAWY SO45 ..... 179 M4
Limekiln La BPWT SO32 ..... 85 L5
  PSF GU32 ..... 62 A8
  PSF GU32 ..... 90 B7
Limes Cl LISS GU33 ..... 36 E4
The Limes LSOL/BMARY PO13 ..... 185 J4
  TOTT SO40 ..... 130 E7 2
Lime St SHAM SO14 ..... 5 H5
Lime Tree Cl FBDG SP6 ..... 121 K2 2
Limetree Wk WINC SO23 ..... 3 M7
  WINC SO23 ..... 17 J8 2
Lime Wk FAWY SO45 ..... 155 J6
Limited Rd MOOR/WNTN BH9 ..... 220 E7
Linacre Rd ITCH SO19 ..... 133 H4
Lin Brook Dr RGWD BH24 ..... 147 G6
Linch Rd HASM GU27 ..... 39 K5
  MIDH GU29 ..... 67 L3
Lincoln Av BMTH BH1 ..... 236 C2
  CHCH/BSGR BH23 ..... 222 D6 2
Lincoln Cl FHAM/STUB PO14 ..... 159 C5
Lincoln Ct WSHM SO15 ..... 106 C6 2
Lincoln Ri HORN PO8 ..... 140 E4
Lincoln Rd BKME/WDN BH12 ..... 234 C1
  PSEA PO1 ..... 13 M1
Lincolns Ri ELGH SO50 ..... 54 A8
Linda Gv HORN PO8 ..... 140 D5
Linda Rd FAWY SO45 ..... 180 F5 2
Lindberg Ri FHAM PO15 ..... 159 J2
Lind Cl WVILLE PO7 ..... 164 D5
Linden Cl BPWT SO32 ..... 111 K5
  FERN BH22 ..... 194 B7
Linden Dr LISS GU33 ..... 36 E4
Linden Gdns HEND SO30 ..... 134 B3
  RGWD BH24 ..... 146 D8
Linden Gv CHFD SO53 ..... 53 H8
  GPORT PO12 ..... 10 E5
  HISD PO11 ..... 213 L5
Linden Lea FHAM/PORC PO16 ..... 162 A7
Linden Rd BKME/WDN BH12 ..... 234 B2
  FERN BH22 ..... 194 B7
  MOOR/WNTN BH9 ..... 220 E5
  ROMY SO51 ..... 78 C2
  ROWN SO16 ..... 105 M4
Lindens Cl EMRTH PO10 ..... 166 D5
The Lindens CHCH/BSGR BH23 ..... 223 H5
Linden Wk NBAD SO52 ..... 79 L3
Linden Wy HAV PO9 ..... 165 K5 2
  HORN PO8 ..... 140 F3
  LYMN SO41 ..... 228 A4
Lindisfarne Cl CHAM P06 ..... 187 L1
Lindley Av ENEY PO4 ..... 211 L6
Lind Rd GPORT PO12 ..... 11 G9
Lindsay Rd CCLF BH13 ..... 234 F4
  ITCH SO19 ..... 133 J2
Lindway HLER SO31 ..... 158 E2
Lineside CHCH/BSGR BH23 ..... 223 G8
Linford Cl NMIL/BTOS BH25 ..... 225 L4
Linford Ct HAV PO9 ..... 165 H1
Linford Crs ROWN SO16 ..... 106 C5
Linford Rd RGWD BH24 ..... 147 H7
Ling Dl ROWN SO16 ..... 106 C5
Lingdale Rd SBNE BH6 ..... 237 J5
Lingfield Gdns WEND SO18 ..... 107 L6 2
Ling Rd BKME/WDN BH12 ..... 218 F7
Lingwood Av
  CHCH/BSGR BH23 ..... 238 E2
Lingwood Cl ROWN SO16 ..... 106 E1 2
Lingwood Wk ROWN SO16 ..... 106 E1 2
Linhorns La NMIL/BTOS BH25 ..... 225 L2
Linkenholt Wy HAV PO9 ..... 165 G3
Link Ri WIMB BH21 ..... 217 J2
Link Rd CHAM P06 ..... 162 F6
  RGWD BH24 ..... 147 G2
  ROWN SO16 ..... 105 L4
Links Cl CHCH/BSGR BH23 ..... 222 B7
Linkside Av CHAR BH8 ..... 221 H5
Links La HAV PO9 ..... 141 M5
Links Rd FUFL SO22 ..... 2 A5
  PSTN BH14 ..... 234 C6
The Links LSOL/BMARY PO13 ..... 185 G4
Links View Av CHCH/BSGR BH14 ..... 234 D7
Links View Wy ROWN SO16 ..... 106 C5
The Link WVILLE PO7 ..... 140 F7 2
Linkway FHAM/STUB PO14 ..... 184 A7
Linmead Dr BWD BH11 ..... 219 L2 2
Linnet Cl CHCH/BSGR BH23 ..... 238 F2 2
Linnet Gdns EPSF GU31 ..... 64 B6

HORN PO8 ..... 140 C4
  RGWD BH24 ..... 171 G2 2
Linnet Ct NMIL/BTOS BH25 ..... 225 K5 2
Linnet Rd CFDH BH17 ..... 217 J8
Linnets La ELGH SO50 ..... 81 J7
The Linnets
  FHAM/PORC PO16 ..... 161 K8 2
  TOTT SO40 ..... 104 B8 2
Linnies La LYMN SO41 ..... 226 E1
Linthorpe Rd PLE BH15 ..... 233 K4
Linwood Cl FAWY SO45 ..... 155 L6
Linwood Rd MOOR/WNTN BH9 ..... 236 A1
Lionheart Cl BWD BH11 ..... 219 H3
Lionheart Wy HLER SO31 ..... 133 K7
Lions Hill Wy RGWD BH24 ..... 169 G3
Lions La RGWD BH24 ..... 169 H4
Lion St PSEA PO1 ..... 12 E1
Lions Wd RGWD BH24 ..... 169 J4
Lipizzaner Flds HLER SO31 ..... 134 E2
Lippen La BPWT SO32 ..... 59 L5
Lisbon Rd WSHM SO15 ..... 131 H2
Lisle Cl FUFL SO22 ..... 25 M5
  LYMN SO41 ..... 228 F5
Lisle Court Rd LYMN SO41 ..... 228 F5
Lisle Wy EMRTH PO10 ..... 166 C5
Liss Rd ENEY PO4 ..... 211 K4
Litchfield Crs WEND SO18 ..... 107 L7
Litchfield Rd FUFL SO22 ..... 16 C4
  WEND SO18 ..... 107 L7
Litchford Rd NMIL/BTOS BH25 ..... 226 A4
  Lith Av HORN PO8 ..... 116 B8
  Lith La HORN PO8 ..... 116 B7
Lit Hyden La HORN PO8 ..... 90 A8
Little Abshot Rd
  FHAM/STUB PO14 ..... 158 F8
Little Anglesey Rd GPORT PO12 ..... 10 C7
Little Arthur St NEND PO2 ..... 211 J1 2
Little Ashton La BPWT SO32 ..... 85 J5
Little Barn Pl LISS GU33 ..... 37 G4
Little Barrs Dr
  NMIL/BTOS BH25 ..... 225 M4
Little Bull La BPWT SO32 ..... 111 J8
Little Cnr WVILLE PO7 ..... 139 K5
Littlecroft Av
  MOOR/WNTN BH9 ..... 220 F5
Little Croft Rd
  BKME/WDN BH12 ..... 234 A2 2
Little Dene Copse LYMN SO41 ..... 227 M6
Little Dewlands VWD BH31 ..... 144 B2 2
Littledown Av LTDN BH7 ..... 236 D1
Littledown Dr LTDN BH7 ..... 236 D1
Little Dro FBDG SP6 ..... 98 C1
Littlefield Crs NBAD SO52 ..... 80 C2
Littlemeads ROMY SO51 ..... 78 C1
Littlemill La FBDG SP6 ..... 96 B3
Little Minster St WINC SO23 ..... 3 G8
Little Gays FHAM/STUB PO14 ..... 183 M6
Littlemoor Av BWD BH11 ..... 219 H4
Little Oak Rd ROWN SO16 ..... 106 E4
Littlepark Av HAV PO9 ..... 164 F5
Little Park Cl HEND SO30 ..... 133 M2 2
Little Park Farm Rd
  FHAM PO15 ..... 159 G3
Little Quob La HEND SO30 ..... 108 D6
Little Shore La BPWT SO32 ..... 111 H4
Little Southsea St SSEA PO5 ..... 12 F5
Littleton Gv HAV PO9 ..... 165 K4
Little Woodfalls Dr RSAL SP5 ..... 73 J4
Littlewood Gdns HEND SO30 ..... 108 C7
  HLER SO31 ..... 158 C5 2
Little Woodham La
  LSOL/BMARY PO13 ..... 209 G2
Liverpool Rd
  FHAM/STUB PO14 ..... 184 D2
  PSEA PO1 ..... 13 M1
Liverpool St SHAM SO14 ..... 131 L1
Livery Rd RSAL SP5 ..... 18 E2
Livingstone Rd
  BKME/WDN BH12 ..... 234 B2
  BOSC BH5 ..... 237 G4
  CHCH/BSGR BH23 ..... 238 C1 2
  SHAM SO14 ..... 106 F8
  SSEA PO5 ..... 13 K5
  WIMB BH21 ..... 192 C4
Llewellin Cl UPTN BH16 ..... 217 H8
Lloyd Av TOTT SO40 ..... 130 C7 2
Loader Cl WINC SO23 ..... 17 H1
Loane Rd ITCH SO19 ..... 132 C5
Lobelia Rd ROWN SO16 ..... 107 H4
Locarno Rd HSEA PO3 ..... 187 K4
Loch Rd PSTN BH14 ..... 234 D3
Lock Appoach CHAM P06 ..... 186 E1
Lockerley Cl LYMN SO41 ..... 228 C6
Lockerley Crs ROWN SO16 ..... 105 L6
Lockerley Rd HAV PO9 ..... 165 L5
  ROMY SO51 ..... 20 F7
  ROMY SO51 ..... 49 J3
Locke Rd HEND SO30 ..... 109 H8
Lockhams Rd BPWT SO32 ..... 110 E8
Locksash Cl SELS PO20 ..... 215 K6
Locksash La RCCH PO18 ..... 118 D3
Locksheath Cl HAV PO9 ..... 165 H2 2
Locksheath Park Rd
  HLER SO31 ..... 158 F7
Locksley Dr FERN BH22 ..... 194 A5
Locksley Rd ELGH SO50 ..... 81 K7
Locks Rd HLER SO31 ..... 158 L4
Locksway Rd ENEY PO4 ..... 211 M4
Lockswood Rd HLER SO31 ..... 158 D5
Lock Vw CHAM P06 ..... 186 E1
Lockyers Dr FERN BH22 ..... 194 D2
Lode HI RSAL SP5 ..... 73 G1
Loders Cl CFDH BH17 ..... 218 A5
Lodge Av CHAM P06 ..... 163 L8
Lodgebury Cl EMRTH PO10 ..... 167 J8
Lodge Cl PSTN BH14 ..... 234 D4
Lodge Ct PSTN BH14 ..... 234 D4
Lodge Dr FAWY SO45 ..... 155 K7

Lodge Dro *RSAL* SP5 .... 73 H4
Lodge Gdns *GPORT* PO12 ...... 10 C5
Lodge La *BROC* SO42........... 204 C2
   HAV PO9............................ 143 H1
Lodge Rd *CHCH/BSGR* BH23.. 222 C8
   HAV PO9............................ 164 F7
   HLER SO31 .... 158 F5
   LYMN SO41 .... 227 M5
   SHAM SO14 .... 131 L1
Lodge V *ROMY* SO51 .... 77 G6
Lodsworth Cl *HORN* PO8 ...... 116 C4
Loewy Crs *BKME/WDN* BH12... 219 H6
Lofting Cl *ELGH* SO50 .... 82 D6
Logan Cl *ROWN* SO16 .... 105 L3
Lomax Cl *HEND* SO30 .... 109 H7
Lombard Av *SBNE* BH6 .... 237 J3
Lombard St *PSEA* PO1 .... 12 C5
Lombardy Cl
   LSOL/BMARY PO13 .... 185 J6
   VWD BH31 .... 144 F3
Lombardy Ri *WVILLE* PO7 ...... 164 D3
Lomer La *RGWD* BH24 .... 122 A5
Lomond Cl *NEND* PO2 .... 187 H8
Londesborough Rd *ENEY* PO4 ... 13 M5
London Av *NEND* PO2 .... 187 H6
London La *CHCH/BSGR* BH23.. 196 B6
London Rd *CHAM* PO6 .... 163 K8
   EPSF GU31 .... 64 A3
   HORN PO8 .... 116 B7
   NEND PO2 .... 187 J6
   WINC SO23 .... 17 G3
   WSHM SO15 .... 131 K4
   WVILLE PO7 .... 140 C8
   WVILLE PO7 .... 164 B8
Lone Barn La *BPWT* SO32 .... 86 D1
Lone Pine Dr *FERN* BH22 .... 194 D6
Lone Pine Wy *FERN* BH22 ...... 194 D6
Lone Va *WVILLE* PO7 .... 164 A5
Longacre Cl *LISS* GU33 .... 36 F4
Longbarrow Cl *CHAR* BH8 ..... 221 L7
Long Beech Dr *TOTT* SO40 ... 129 H2
Longbridge La *TOTT* SO40 .... 104 C6
Long Cl *RSAL* SP5 .... 44 D8
Longclose Rd *HEND* SO30 .... 134 B1
Long Close West *RSAL* SP5 ..... 44 D8
Long Copse *RSAL* SP5 .... 180 C5
Long Copse La *EMRTH* PO10 ... 166 D4
Long Curtain Rd *PSEA* PO1 ...... 12 D6
Longdean Cl *CHAM* PO6 ...... 162 E7
Long Down *EPSF* GU31 .... 64 A4
Long Dr *HEND* SO30 .... 108 D6
   LSOL/BMARY PO13 .... 185 G7
Long Dro *RSAL* SP5 .... 58 C3
Longespee Rd *WIMB* BH22 .... 192 C8
Longfield Av *FHAM/STUB* PO14 ... 6 B9
Longfield Cl *ENEY* PO4 .... 212 A3
Longfield Dr *BWD* BH11 .... 219 L2
   FERN BH22 .... 194 C8
Longfield Rd *EMRTH* PO10 .... 166 C5
   LYMN SO41 .... 226 F6
   WINC SO23 .... 17 J8
Longfleet Cl *WIMB* BH21 ...... 218 E1
Longfleet Rd *PLE* BH15 .... 233 K4
Longhouse Gn *WINC* SO23 ...... 3 M7
Longlands Rd *EMRTH* PO10 .... 167 H8
Long La *FAWY* SO45 .... 180 A3
   HLER SO31 .... 133 L7
   RCCH PO18 .... 119 J3
   RGWD BH24 .... 170 F4
   TOTT SO40 .... 130 B7
   WIMB BH21 .... 192 B1
Long Lane Cl *FAWY* SO45 ..... 180 B5
Longleat Gdns
   NMIL/BTOS BH25 .... 225 J5
   ROWN SO16 .... 106 A3
Longmead *LISS* GU33 .... 36 F4
Longmead Av *ELGH* SO50 ...... 82 C4
Longmead Gdns *HAV* PO9 .... 8 F8
Longmeadow Gdns
   FAWY SO45 .... 155 L6
Longmeadow La *CFDH* BH17 ... 217 J7
Longmead Rd *RGWD* BH24 ... 172 C4
   WEND SO18 .... 107 L6
Longmore Av *ITCH* SO19 ...... 132 B6
Longmore Crs *ITCH* SO19 ...... 132 B6
Longmynd Dr
   FHAM/STUB PO14 .... 6 B8
Long Priors *PSF* GU32 .... 60 A3
Longridge Rd *HEND* SO30 .... 134 A2
Long Rd *BPWT* SO32 .... 113 H2
   NBNE BH10 .... 220 B4
   PSF GU32 .... 63 M3
Longshore Wy *ENEY* PO4....... 212 B3
Longs La *FHAM/STUB* PO14 ... 184 A5
Longstaff Gdns
   FHAM/PORC PO16 .... 6 F2
Long Steeple La *FBDG* SP6 .... 71 K6
Longstock Cl *ITCH* SO19 .... 132 E8
Longstock Crs *TOTT* SO40 .... 129 H1
Longstock Rd *HAV* PO9 .... 165 M2
Long Wk *RWIN* SO21 .... 17 J4
Long Water Dr *GPORT* PO12 ... 11 G9
Longwood Av *HORN* PO8....... 140 D5
Longwood Dean La *RWIN* SO21 ... 57 H2
Longwood Rd *RWIN* SO21 ...... 56 B4
Lonsdale Av *CHAM* PO6 .... 187 L1
   FHAM/PORC PO16 .... 186 B2
Lonsdale Rd *TWDS* BH3 .... 235 L1
Loperwood *TOTT* SO40 .... 103 L6
Loperwood La *TOTT* SO40 .... 103 M4
Loraine Av *CHCH/BSGR* BH23 ... 225 G8
Lord Cl *CFDH* BH17 .... 233 L1
Lordington Cl *CHAM* PO6 ..... 163 M8
Lord Montgomery Wy
   SSEA PO5 .... 12 F3
Lord Mountbatten Cl
   WEND SO18 .... 107 K4
Lord's Hill Centre East
   ROWN SO16 .... 105 L3
Lord's Hill Centre West
   ROWN SO16 .... 105 L4
Lord's Hill Wy *ROWN* SO16 ... 105 L3
Lords St *PSEA* PO1 .... 211 H2
Lordswood *ELGH* SO50 .... 82 D1
Lordswood Cl *ROWN* SO16 .... 106 C5
Lordswood Gdns *ROWN* SO16... 106 C4
Lordswood Rd *ROWN* SO16 ... 106 B4

Loreille Cl *ROWN* SO16 .... 105 K1
Lorne Park Rd *BMTH* BH1 ...... 15 G5
Lorne Rd *SSEA* PO5 .... 13 L4
Loughwood Cl *ELGH* SO50 ..... 81 M2
Lovage Gdns *TOTT* SO40 ...... 129 C1
Lovage Rd *FHAM* PO15 .... 159 H1
Love La *WVILLE* PO7 .... 140 D2
Lovedean La *HORN* PO8 .... 140 D2
Lovett Rd *BPWT* SO32 .... 58 A5
   EPSF GU31 .... 63 M4
   FBDG SP6 .... 72 D8
   PSF GU32 .... 60 B4
   ROMY SO51 .... 78 D1
   RWIN SO21 .... 55 G3
Lovett Rd *HSEA* PO3 .... 187 K5
Lowcay Rd *SSEA* PO5 .... 13 L7
Lowden Cl *FUFL* SO22 .... 26 C4
Lower Alfred St *SHAM* SO14 ... 131 M2
Lower Ashley Rd
   NMIL/BTOS BH25 .... 226 B5
Lower Banister St *WSHM* SO15.. 131 K2
Lower Bartons *FBDG* SP6 .... 97 L7
Lower Baybridge La *RWIN* 56 A7
Lower Bellfield
   FHAM/STUB PO14.............. 183 K1
Lower Bere Wd *WVILLE* PO7 ... 164 D1
Lower Blandford Rd
   BDST BH18 .... 217 L4
Lower Brook St *WINC* SO23 ..... 3 H7
Lower Brownhill Rd
   ROWN SO16 .... 105 H6
Lower Buckland Rd
   LYMN SO41 .... 228 B3
Lower Canal Wk *SHAM* SO14 ..... 5 G7
Lower Chase Rd *BPWT* SO32 ... 111 M3
Lower Church Pth *PSEA* PO1 ... 13 H1
Lower Church Rd
   FHAM/STUB PO14.............. 159 G5
Lower Common La
   WIMB BH21 .... 168 L1
Lower Common Rd *ROMY* SO51... 76 D6
Lower Crabbick La
   WVILLE PO7 .... 138 F4
Lower Densome Wd *FBDG* SP6 ... 72 D8
Lower Derby Rd *NEND* PO2..... 187 G2
Lower Drayton La *CHAM* PO6... 188 A1
Lower Duncan Rd *HLER* SO31 ... 158 F3
Lower Farlington Rd
   CHAM PO6 .... 164 C8
Lower Forbury Rd *SSEA* PO5 ... 13 J5
Lower Golf Links Rd
   BDST BH18 .... 217 M3
Lower Gv *FBDG* SP6 .... 71 G6
Lower Grove Rd *HAV* PO9 .... 9 G6
Lower Heyshott *EPSF* GU31 ...... 63 M4
Lower Lamborough La
   NARL SO24 .... 30 C3
Lower La *BPWT* SO32 .... 85 J8
Lower Md *EPSF* GU31 .... 64 A5
Lower Mead End Rd
   LYMN SO41 .... 200 D8
Lower Moors Rd *RWIN* SO21 ... 54 E7
Lower Mortimer Rd *ITCH* SO19 ... 132 B5
Lower Mullin's La *FAWY* SO45 ... 155 J4
Lower New Rd *HEND* SO30 .... 108 C7
Lower Northam Rd
   HEND SO30 .... 134 A1
Lower Pennington La
   LYMN SO41 .... 228 B7
Lower Preshaw La *BPWT* SO32 ... 57 L8
Lower Quay Cl
   FHAM/PORC PO16 .... 7 J8
Lower Quay Rd
   FHAM/PORC PO16 .... 7 K8
Lower Rd *HAV* PO9 .... 164 F7
   RSAL SP5 .... 44 E4
Lower St Helens Rd
   HEND SO30 .... 134 A3
Lower Sandy Down La
   LYMN SO41 .... 201 M5
Lower Spinney *HLER* SO31 .... 182 A1
Lower St *ROMY* SO51 .... 51 G1
Lower Swanwick Rd
   HLER SO31 .... 134 B8
Lower Vicarage Rd *ITCH* SO19 ... 132 B5
Lower Wardown *EPSF* GU31 .... 64 A4
Lower Woodside *LYMN* SO41 ... 228 C8
Lower York St *SHAM* SO14 .... 132 B2
Lowestoft Rd *CHAM* PO6 ...... 163 H7
Lowford Hl *HLER* SO31 .... 133 K7
Lowland Rd *WVILLE* PO7 ...... 139 J4
Lowry Gdns *ITCH* SO19 .... 133 G6
Lowther Gdns *CHAR* BH8 .... 15 L1
Lowther Rd *CHAR* BH8 .... 235 M2
Loxwood Rd *HORN* PO8 .... 140 D2
Luard Ct *HAV* PO9 .... 9 J5
Lucas Rd *ROWN* SO16 .... 105 L3
Lucas Rd *BKME/WDN* BH12 ... 234 B2
Luccombe Pl *WSHM* SO15 ..... 106 C6
Luccombe Rd *WSHM* SO15 .... 106 C6
Lucerne Av *SBNE* BH6 .... 237 J3
   WVILLE PO7 .... 140 B6
Lucerne Gdns *HEND* SO30 .... 133 L2
Lucerne Rd *LYMN* SO41 .... 242 C4
Luckham Cl
   MOOR/WNTN BH9 .... 220 F6
Luckham Pl
   MOOR/WNTN BH9 .... 220 F6
Luckham Rd
   MOOR/WNTN BH9 .... 220 F6
Luckham Rd East
   MOOR/WNTN BH9 .... 220 F6
Lucknow St *PSEA* PO1 .... 13 L2
Lucky La *LYMN* SO41 .... 202 E7
Ludcombe *WVILLE* PO7 .... 139 K3
Ludlow Rd *CHAM* PO6 .... 163 G7
   ITCH SO19 .... 132 C4
Ludwell's La *BPWT* SO32 .... 111 L4
Lugano Cl *WVILLE* PO7 .... 140 B7
Lukin Dr *ROWN* SO16 .... 105 H3
Lulworth Av *PLE* BH15 .... 232 D7
Lulworth Cl *CHFD* SO53 .... 81 G5
   HISD PO11 .... 213 J3
   PLE BH15 .... 232 D7
   ROWN SO16 .... 105 K6
Lulworth Crs *PLE* BH15 .... 232 D7
Lulworth Gn *ROWN* SO16 ..... 105 K6

Lulworth Rd
   LSOL/BMARY PO13 .... 208 C2
Lumby Dr *RGWD* BH24 .... 146 F8
Lumby Drive Pk *RGWD* BH24 .. 146 F8
Lumley Rd *EMRTH* PO10 .... 166 E7
Lumsden Av *WSHM* SO15 ...... 131 G1
Lumsden Rd *ENEY* PO4 .... 212 B5
Lundy Cl *ROWN* SO16 .... 105 K3
Lunedale Rd *FAWY* SO45 ...... 155 J8
Lupin Rd *ROWN* SO16 .... 107 H3
Luscombe Rd *PSTN* BH14 ..... 234 B6
Luther Rd *MOOR/WNTN* BH9 ... 220 D8
Lutman St *EMRTH* PO10 .... 166 C4
Luton Rd *ITCH* SO19 .... 132 F4
Luxton Cl *HEND* SO30 .... 109 L8
Luzborough La *ROMY* SO51 ..... 79 G4
Lyburn Cl *RWIN* SO16 .... 106 B4
Lyburn Rd *RSAL* SP5 .... 74 F6
Lych Gate Ct *RGWD* BH24 .... 171 G2
Lychgate Dr *HORN* PO8 .... 140 F6
Lychgate Gn *FHAM/STUB* PO14... 184 A3
Lydford Gdns *BWD* BH11 ...... 219 L6
Lydford Rd *BWD* BH11 .... 219 L6
Lydgate *LYMN* SO41 .... 241 M3
   TOTT SO40 .... 129 H1
Lydgate Cl *ITCH* SO19 .... 133 H4
Lydgate Gn *ITCH* SO19 .... 133 H4
Lydgate Rd *ITCH* SO19 .... 133 H4
Lydiard Cl *ELGH* SO50 .... 81 M3
Lydlinch Cl *FERN* BH22 .... 194 B7
Lydney Cl *CHAM* PO6 .... 163 G8
Lydney Rd *HLER* SO31 .... 158 D6
Lydwell Cl *BWD* BH11 .... 219 K3
Lyell Rd *BKME/WDN* BH12 ... 234 B2
Lymbourn Rd *HAV* PO9 .... 9 C5
Lyme Cl *ELGH* SO50 .... 81 L3
Lyme Crs *CHCH/BSGR* BH23 ... 224 D8
Lymefields *LYMN* SO41 .... 242 D2
Lymer La *ROWN* SO16 .... 105 H2
Lymington Rd *BROC* SO42 ..... 201 L2
   CHCH/BSGR BH23 .... 239 J1
   LYMN SO41 .... 229 L3
   LYMN SO41 .... 242 D1
   NMIL/BTOS BH25 .... 225 L7
Lymington Road Shelley Hl
   CHCH/BSGR BH23 .... 239 H1
Lymore La *LYMN* SO41 .... 242 D1
Lymore Va *LYMN* SO41 .... 242 D1
Lynch Cl *FUFL* SO22 .... 2 C3
Lynch La *PSF* GU32 .... 60 B4
Lyndale Cl *LYMN* SO41 .... 242 D3
Lyndale Rd *HLER* SO31 .... 158 F4
Lynden Cl *FHAM/STUB* PO14 ... 159 H8
Lynden Ga *ITCH* SO19 .... 132 E5
Lyndhurst Cl *FUFL* SO22 .... 16 C4
Lyndhurst Rd *BROC* SO42 ..... 175 L6
   CHCH/BSGR BH23 .... 198 D8
   CHCH/BSGR BH23 .... 223 M7
   GPORT PO12 .... 10 C2
   NEND PO2 .... 187 K6
   RGWD BH24 .... 146 F8
   RSAL SP5 .... 75 H5
   TOTT SO40 .... 127 J1
Lyndock Cl *ITCH* SO19 .... 132 C6
Lyndock Pl *ITCH* SO19 .... 132 C6
Lyndum Cl *EPSF* GU31 .... 63 L5
Lyne Pl *HORN* PO8 .... 140 F2
Lynes La *RGWD* BH24 .... 170 D1
Lynford Av *FUFL* SO22 .... 2 C2
Lynford Wy *FUFL* SO22 .... 2 D2
Lynn Rd *CFDH* BH17 .... 218 D8
   NEND PO2 .... 187 K8
Lynn Wy *WINC* SO23 .... 17 H2
Lyric Cl *NMIL/BTOS* BH25 ..... 240 E1
Lynton Ct *TOTT* SO40 .... 129 J2
Lynton Crs *CHCH/BSGR* BH23 ... 222 B5
Lynton Gdns *FHAM/PORC* PO16 ... 6 E1
Lynton Gv *HSEA* PO3 .... 187 L8
Lynton Rd *HEND* SO30 .... 134 A1
   PSF GU32 .... 63 K4
Lynwood Av *WVILLE* PO7 ...... 140 B5
Lynwood Cl *FERN* BH22 .... 194 B1
Lynwood Dr *WIMB* BH21 ...... 192 D7
Lynx Cl *ELGH* SO50 .... 82 E6
Lyon Av *NMIL/BTOS* BH25 .... 225 M5
Lyon Rd *BKME/WDN* BH12 ... 234 D4
Lyon St *SHAM* SO14 .... 131 L2
Lysander Cl *CHCH/BSGR* BH23 ... 239 G1
Lysander Wy *WVILLE* PO7 ..... 140 C8
Lyster Rd *FBDG* SP6 .... 97 M6
Lystra Rd *MOOR/WNTN* BH9 ... 220 E5
Lytchett Dr *BDST* BH18 .... 217 L5
Lytchett Wy *UPTN* BH16 ...... 232 A2
Lyteltane Rd *LYMN* SO41 ...... 228 B6
Lytham Rd *BDST* BH18 .... 217 L5
   WEND SO18 .... 107 M8
Lythe La *PSF* GU32 .... 62 F3
Lytton Rd *BMTH* BH1 .... 15 L2
   FAWY SO45 .... 155 M6

M

Mabey Av *NBNE* BH10 .... 220 B6
Mabey Cl *GPORT* PO12 .... 11 G8
Mablethorpe Rd *CHAM* PO6 ... 163 J7
Macandrew Rd *CCLF* BH13 .... 245 L1
Macarthur Crs *WEND* SO18 ... 107 M8
Macaulay Rd *CFDH* BH17 ..... 162 D7
Macaulay Rd *BDST* BH18 ...... 217 L4
Maclaren Rd
   MOOR/WNTN BH9 .... 220 D5
Maclean Rd *BWD* BH11 .... 219 K5
Macnaghten Rd *WEND* SO18 ... 132 B1
Madden Cl *BPWT* SO32 .... 10 A6
Maddison St *SHAM* SO14 .... 4 F5
Maddoxford Wy *BPWT* SO32 ... 109 L7
Madeira Rd *BMTH* BH1 .... 15 C4
   NEND PO2 .... 187 J5
   PSTN BH14 .... 234 C3
Madeline Crs
   BKME/WDN BH12 .... 234 A1
Madeline Rd *EPSF* GU31 .... 63 L4
Madison Av *BMTH* BH1 .... 236 C2

Madison Cl
   LSOL/BMARY PO13 .... 185 J8
Mafeking Rd *ENEY* PO4 .... 211 K5
Magazine La *TOTT* SO40 .... 130 E5
Magdala Rd *CHAM* PO6 .... 187 K1
   HISD PO11 .... 213 J5
Magdalene Wy
   FHAM/STUB PO14.............. 159 G7
Magdalen Hl *WINC* SO23 .... 3 J8
Magdalen La
   CHCH/BSGR BH23 .... 237 M2
Magdalen Rd *NEND* PO2 ...... 187 J3
Magennis Cl
   LSOL/BMARY PO13 .... 209 H1
Magna Cl *BWD* BH11 .... 219 K2
Magna Gdns *BWD* BH11 .... 219 L6
Magna Rd *WIMB* BH21 .... 192 F8
Magnolia Cl *FAWY* SO45 ...... 155 G4
   FHAM/STUB PO14................. 6 C7
   SBNE BH6 .... 237 M3
   VWD BH31 .... 145 G4
Magnolia Gv *ELGH* SO50 .... 83 K6
Magnolia Rd *ITCH* SO19 .... 132 D3
Magnolia Wy *HORN* PO8 ...... 141 G4
Magpie Cl *CHAR* BH8 .... 221 L5
Magpie Dr *TOTT* SO40 .... 129 C1
Magpie Gdns *ITCH* SO19 ...... 132 F4
Magpie Gv *NMIL/BTOS* BH25 ... 225 K6
Magpie La *ELGH* SO50 .... 81 K6
   LSOL/BMARY PO13 .... 208 D1
Magpie Rd *HORN* PO8 .... 142 A3
Magpie Wk *HORN* PO8 .... 140 B4
Mag's Barrow *FERN* BH22 ..... 194 C6
Maiden La *LYMN* SO41 .... 228 D7
Maidford Gv *HSEA* PO3 .... 188 A4
Maidment Cl *BWD* BH11 .... 219 J4
Maidstone Crs *CHAM* PO6 .... 163 J7
Main Dr *FAWY* SO45 .... 205 G2
   WHAM PO17 .... 136 E2
Main Rd *EMRTH* PO10 .... 167 G8
   FAWY SO45 .... 154 E1
   FAWY SO45 .... 180 A2
   LSOL/BMARY PO13 .... 185 H4
   LYMN SO41 .... 203 M8
   LYMN SO41 .... 228 E2
   PSEA PO1 .... 12 B1
   PSEA PO1 .... 210 D2
   RWIN SO21 .... 54 A6
   RWIN SO21 .... 54 E5
   RWIN SO21 .... 54 A4
   RWIN SO21 .... 83 G1
   TOTT SO40 .... 129 J4
   TOTT SO40 .... 130 D7
Mainsail Dr *FHAM/PORC* PO16 ... 7 J8
Mainstone *ROMY* SO51 .... 78 C2
Mainstream Ct *ELGH* SO50 .... 82 C5
Maisemore Gdns *EMRTH* PO10... 166 B8
Maitland St *PSEA* PO1 .... 211 H1
Majestic Rd *ROWN* SO16 ...... 105 K4
Malan Cl *CFDH* BH17 .... 218 C8
   HLER SO31 .... 158 F5
Malcolm Rd *CHFD* SO53 .... 53 K7
Malcomb Cl *SBNE* BH6 .... 237 M5
Malcroft Ms *TOTT* SO40 .... 130 E7
Maldon Cl *ELGH* SO50 .... 82 C5
Maldon Rd *CHAM* PO6 .... 163 H8
   ITCH SO19 .... 132 C4
Malibres Rd *CHFD* SO53 .... 53 L8
Malin Cl *FHAM/STUB* PO14 .... 183 M5
   ROWN SO16 .... 105 K4
Malins Rd *NEND* PO2 .... 211 H1
Mallard Cl *BPWT* SO32 .... 84 F8
   CHAR BH8 .... 221 L5
   CHCH/BSGR BH23 .... 238 F2
   LYMN SO41 .... 226 E5
   ROMY SO51 .... 50 E8
Mallard Gdns *HEND* SO30 .... 109 H6
Mallard Rd *CHAR* BH8 .... 221 H7
   ENEY PO4 .... 211 M3
   HAV PO9 .... 141 M7
   WIMB BH21 .... 192 E1
Mallards Rd *HLER* SO31 .... 157 K1
The Mallards *FHAM/PORC* PO16... 7 H1
   HAV PO9 .... 8 D8
Mallett Cl *HEND* SO30 .... 109 K6
Mallory Cl *CHCH/BSGR* BH23 ... 223 K8
Mallory Crs *FHAM/PORC* PO16 ... 7 G2
Mallow Cl *BDST* BH18 .... 217 J5
   CHAM PO6 .... 163 K8
   WVILLE PO7 .... 164 D2
Mallow Rd *HEND* SO30 .... 133 L2
The Mallows *NMIL/BTOS* BH25 ... 226 B4
The Mall *RGWD* BH24 .... 172 C5
Malmesbury Cl *ELGH* SO50 .... 83 H6
Malmesbury Ct *CHAR* BH8 .... 236 B2
Malmesbury Gdns *FUFL* SO22 ... 2 A3
Malmesbury Park *CHAR* BH8 ... 15 M1
Malmesbury Park Rd
   CHAR BH8 .... 236 A2
Malmesbury Pl *WSHM* SO15 ... 131 H1
Malmesbury Rd *RGWD* BH24 ... 169 J5
   ROMY SO51 .... 50 D8
   WSHM SO15 .... 131 H1
Maloren Wy *FERN* BH22 .... 168 E7
Malory Cl *ITCH* SO19 .... 133 H2
Malta Rd *NEND* PO2 .... 187 J3
Malthouse *PLE* BH15 .... 233 H6
Malthouse Cl *ROMY* SO51 ...... 50 D8
   RWIN SO21 .... 17 L3
Malthouse Gdns *TOTT* SO40 ... 130 D7
Malthouse La *FHAM/PORC* PO16... 7 H3
Malthouse Rd *HEND* SO30 .... 187 H8
The Maltings *EPSF* GU31 .... 63 L5
   FHAM/PORC PO16 .... 161 H6
Malt La *BPWT* SO32 .... 85 H8
Malus Cl *FHAM/STUB* PO14 ... 184 D1
Malvern Av *CHCH/BSGR* BH23 ... 238 C1
Malvern Cl *MOOR/WNTN* BH9 ... 220 E5
Malvern Dr *FAWY* SO45 .... 155 H5
Malvern Gdns *HEND* SO30 .... 109 H4
Malvern Ms *EMRTH* PO10 ..... 166 D7
Malvern Rd *GPORT* PO12 .... 10 B1
   LISS GU33 .... 37 G3
   MOOR/WNTN BH9 .... 220 E5
   NEND PO2 .... 187 M1

   SSEA PO5 .... 13 J9
Malwood Av *ROWN* SO16 ...... 106 C5
Malwood Cl *HAV* PO9 .... 165 L2
Malwood Gdns *TOTT* SO40 ... 104 B8
Malwood Rd *FAWY* SO45 ...... 155 K4
Malwood Rd West *FAWY* SO45 ... 155 J4
Manchester Rd *LYMN* SO41 ... 200 F5
   PSEA PO1 .... 13 M1
Mancroft Av
   FHAM/STUB PO14.............. 184 A7
Mandale Cl *BWD* BH11 .... 219 L4
Mandale Rd *BWD* BH11 .... 219 K5
Mandela Wy *WSHM* SO15 .... 4 C1
Manderley *LYMN* SO41 .... 242 D5
Manley Rd *HLER* SO31 .... 133 K7
Manners La *ENEY* PO4 .... 13 L3
Manners Rd *ENEY* PO4 .... 13 M3
Manning Av *CHCH/BSGR* BH23 ... 224 A7
Manningford Cl *WINC* SO23 ..... 3 H1
Mannings Heath Rd
   BKME/WDN BH12 .... 218 F6
Mannington Pl *WCLF* BH2 ...... 14 C6
Mannington Wy *FERN* BH22 ... 168 B6
Manns Cl *WEND* SO18 .... 108 B6
Mannyngham Wy *ROMY* SO51 ... 50 C1
Manor Av *BKME/WDN* BH12 ... 219 G7
Manor Cl *FBDG* SP6 .... 97 L7
   FERN BH22 .... 194 C3
   HLER SO31 .... 133 K7
   LYMN SO41 .... 242 C3
   TOTT SO40 .... 129 J2
   WHAM PO17 .... 136 E6
   WINC SO23 .... 3 K6
Manor Ct *RGWD* BH24 .... 146 D8
   VWD BH31 .... 144 D2
Manor Crs *CHAM* PO6 .... 187 M1
Manor Farm Cl
   NMIL/BTOS BH25 .... 225 K7
   RSAL SP5 .... 40 B1
Manor Farm Gn *RWIN* SO21 ... 54 E3
Manor Farm Gv *ELGH* SO50 ... 82 D6
Manor Farm La *ROMY* SO51 ... 22 C7
Manor Farm Rd *FBDG* SP6 ..... 97 H7
   NBNE BH10 .... 220 A2
   WEND SO18 .... 107 J7
Manor Gdns *EMRTH* PO10 .... 167 H7
   RGWD BH24 .... 146 D8
   VWD BH31 .... 144 D2
Manor House Av *WSHM* SO15 ... 130 C2
Manor La *VWD* BH31 .... 144 D3
Manor Lodge Rd *HAV* PO9 .... 141 M8
Manor Ms *CHAM* PO6 .... 164 A8
Manor Park Av *HSEA* PO3 ..... 187 L8
Manor Rd *BMTH* BH1 .... 15 L8
   BPWT SO32 .... 110 C1
   CHCH/BSGR BH23 .... 237 M2
   ELGH SO50 .... 82 D6
   EMRTH PO10 .... 167 H7
   FAWY SO45 .... 180 A4
   HISD PO11 .... 213 K3
   LYMN SO41 .... 242 C2
   NMIL/BTOS BH25 .... 225 M5
   PSEA PO1 .... 211 J1
   RGWD BH24 .... 170 E1
   ROWN SO16 .... 80 C7
   RSAL SP5 .... 20 D1
   RWIN SO21 .... 54 E3
   TOTT SO40 .... 154 E3
   VWD BH31 .... 144 D2
Manor Rd North *ITCH* SO19 ... 132 C4
Manor Rd South *ITCH* SO19 ... 132 C5
Manor Wy *EMRTH* PO10 .... 167 H7
   HISD PO11 .... 213 L6
   LSOL/BMARY PO13 .... 185 H4
   VWD BH31 .... 144 D1
Mans Br *WEND* SO18 .... 107 L4
Mansbridge Rd *ELGH* SO50 .... 81 M7
   WEND SO18 .... 107 L4
Mansel Cl *BKME/WDN* BH12 ... 235 H1
Mansel Ct *ROWN* SO16 .... 105 K6
Mansel Cl *FAWY* SO45 .... 155 J8
Mansel Rd East *ROWN* SO16 ... 105 K7
Mansel Rd West *ROWN* SO16 ... 105 K4
Mansfield La *WHAM* PO17 .... 135 M4
Mansfield Rd
   LSOL/BMARY PO13 .... 185 G8
   MOOR/WNTN BH9 .... 220 C7
   PSTN BH14 .... 234 B4
   RGWD BH24 .... 170 D1
Mansion Rd *ENEY* PO4 .... 211 J7
   WSHM SO15 .... 131 G2
Mansvid Av *CHAM* PO6 .... 187 M1
Mantle Cl *LSOL/BMARY* PO13... 209 H1
Mantle Sq *NEND* PO2 .... 186 F6
Manton Rd *PLE* BH15 .... 232 D5
Maple Cl *CHCH/BSGR* BH23 ... 239 L1
   EMRTH PO10 .... 166 D6
   FHAM PO15 .... 160 A7
   LSOL/BMARY PO13 .... 208 D3
   NMIL/BTOS BH25 .... 241 G1
   ROMY SO51 .... 79 H2
Maple Crs *HORN* PO8 .... 116 B2
Maple Dr *FERN* BH22 .... 168 A8
   WVILLE PO7 .... 139 L5
Maple Gdns *TOTT* SO40 .... 129 G2
Maple Rd *FAWY* SO45 .... 155 M8
   MOOR/WNTN BH9 .... 220 D8
   PLE BH15 .... 233 J5
   SSEA PO5 .... 13 J8
   WINC SO23 .... 3 C1
Maple Sq *ELGH* SO50 .... 81 K7
The Maples *CHFD* SO53 .... 53 H8
Mapleton Rd *HEND* SO30 ..... 134 B2
Mapletree Av *HORN* PO8 ...... 141 G3
Maplewood Cl *TOTT* SO40 .... 129 G2
Mapperton Cl *CFDH* BH17 .... 218 E6
Marabout Cl *CHCH/BSGR* BH23 ... 238 C1
Maralyn Av *WVILLE* PO7 .... 164 C3
Marathon Pl *ELGH* SO50 .... 83 G6
Marbrean Cl *FBDG* SP6 .... 97 H6
Marchwood By-pass
   TOTT SO40 .... 129 L3
Marchwood Rd *HAV* PO9 ...... 165 J2
   NBNE BH10 .... 220 A3
   TOTT SO40 .... 130 A4

WSHM SO15 130 F2
Marcus Cl ELGH SO50 83 C6
Mardale Rd ROWN SO16 105 J8
Marden Wy EPSF GU31 63 M5
Mardon Cl ELGH SO50 107 K3
Mare La RWIN SO21 55 K1
Margam Av ITCH SO19 132 D3
Margards La VWD BH31 144 C3
Margaret Cl WVILLE PO7 140 B7
Margarita Rd FHAM PO15 6 C4
Margate Rd SSEA PO5 13 J4
Margery's Ct PSEA PO1 12 D2
Marguerite Rd WSHM SO15 130 D2
Marianne Rd
  BKME/WDN BH12 220 A8
  WIMB BH21 192 E1
Marian Rd WIMB BH21 217 C4
Marie Av RSAL SP5 72 C1
Marie Cl BKME/WDN BH12 234 C1
Marie Rd ITCH SO19 133 C3
Marigold Cl FHAM PO15 6 C1
Marina Cl EMRTH PO10 166 E8
Marina Dr PSTN BH14 234 A7
Marina Gv FHAM/PORC PO16 186 A2
  HSEA PO3 211 M2
Marina Keep CHAM PO6 186 E1
The Marina BOSC BH5 236 C5
Marine Ct ENEY PO4 211 L6
Marine Dr NMIL/BTOS BH25 240 C1
Marine Dr East
  NMIL/BTOS BH25 240 F1
Marine Dr West
  NMIL/BTOS BH25 240 C1
Marine Pde SHAM SO14 5 K4
Marine Pde East
  LSOL/BMARY PO13 208 D4
Marine Pde West
  LSOL/BMARY PO13 208 B1
Marine Prospect
  NMIL/BTOS BH25 240 E1
Marine Wk SBNE BH6 237 J5
Mariner's Cl HLER SO31 157 L4
Mariners Ms FAWY SO45 155 L4
Mariners Wy GPORT PO12 11 J5
  HLER SO31 158 A5
Marine Wk HISD PO11 214 B5
Marion Rd ENEY PO4 13 M8
Maritime Av TOTT SO40 130 E5
Maritime Wk SHAM SO14 5 J4
Maritime Wy SHAM SO14 5 H7
Marjoram Crs HORN PO8 140 F5
Marjoram Wy FHAM PO15 159 H1
Markall Cl NARL SO24 30 C3
Mark Cl HSEA PO3 187 K4
  WSHM SO15 130 E1
Marken Cl HLER SO31 158 C5
Market Cl PLE BH15 233 H6
Market Pde HAV PO9 8 E4
Market Pl RGWD BH24 170 D1
  SHAM SO14 5 C6
Market St ELGH SO50 82 A7
  PLE BH15 233 C7
  WINC SO23 3 C8
Marketway PSEA PO1 211 C2
Market Wy WIMB BH21 192 B4
Markham Av NBNE BH10 220 B2
Markham Cl NBNE BH10 220 B1
Markham Rd
  MOOR/WNTN BH9 220 C8
Mark's La NMIL/BTOS BH25 225 L2
Mark's Rd FHAM/STUB PO14 184 C6
  MOOR/WNTN BH9 220 D5
Marks Tey Rd
  FHAM/STUB PO14 184 A3
Markway Cl EMRTH PO10 166 F7
Marlborough Cl WVILLE PO7 164 B3
Marlborough Ct FAWY SO45 155 J6
Marlborough Gdns
  HEND SO30 109 H5
Marlborough Gv
  FHAM/PORC PO16 186 A1
Marlborough Pk HAV PO9 9 K2
Marlborough Pl LYMN SO41 228 B3
  WIMB BH21 192 B3
Marlborough Rd CHFD SO53 53 K7
  GPORT PO12 209 K2
  PSTN BH14 234 B4
  WBNE BH4 235 H5
  WSHM SO15 106 A8
Marlborough Rw PSEA PO1 210 E2
Mardell Cl HAV PO9 165 J4
Marles Cl LSOL/BMARY PO13 209 H1
Marley Av NMIL/BTOS BH25 225 J4
Marley Cl NMIL/BTOS BH25 225 K5
Marley Mt LYMN SO41 200 C4
Marlhill Cl WEND SO18 107 L6
Marlin Cl LSOL/BMARY PO13 209 H2
Marline Rd BKME/WDN BH12 234 C1
Marl La FBDG SP6 97 J6
Marlott Rd PLE BH15 233 H5
Marlow Cl FHAM PO15 160 C4
Marlow Dr CHCH/BSGR BH23 222 C5
Marlowe Ct WVILLE PO7 140 B7
Marlow Rd BPWT SO32 84 F7
Marlpit Dr CHCH/BSGR BH23 224 E6
Marlpit La EMRTH PO10 167 L4
  NMIL/BTOS BH25 199 L8
Marls Rd HEND SO30 134 B2
Marmion Av SSEA PO5 13 J7
Marmion Gn
  CHCH/BSGR BH23 238 E1
Marmion Rd SSEA PO5 13 H7
Marne Rd WEND SO18 132 E1
Marnhull Rd PLE BH15 233 J4
Marpet Cl BWD BH11 219 K2
Marples Wy HAV PO9 8 B5
Marquis Wy BWD BH11 219 H3
Marram Cl LYMN SO41 228 C2
Marrels Wd WVILLE PO7 164 A4
Marryat Rd NMIL/BTOS BH25 225 K5
Marsden Rd CHAM PO6 162 F4
Marshall Rd HISD PO11 214 A6
Marshal Rd CFDH BH17 217 M7
Marsh Cl CHAM PO6 188 A2
Marshfield WIMB BH21 192 D1

Marshfield Cl TOTT SO40 130 B7
Marsh Gdns HEND SO30 109 H5
Marshlands Rd CHAM PO6 188 B1
Marsh La CHCH/BSGR BH23 222 D6
  FAWY SO45 180 F4
  FBDG SP6 71 M8
  LYMN SO41 228 C2
  RCCH PO18 191 L4
  SHAM SO14 5 H5
The Marsh FAWY SO45 155 L3
Marshwood Av CFDH BH17 218 D6
  WVILLE PO7 164 E1
Marston Cl NMIL/BTOS BH25 225 M3
Marston Gv CHCH/BSGR BH23 224 C7
Marston La HSEA PO3 187 M4
Marston Rd ITCH SO19 133 H3
  NMIL/BTOS BH25 225 M3
  PLE BH15 233 G6
Martello Cl GPORT PO12 209 H5
Martello Pk CCLF BH13 245 L1
Martello Rd CCLF BH13 234 E7
The Martells NMIL/BTOS BH25 241 G1
Martin Av FHAM/STUB PO14 184 B6
  WVILLE PO7 139 L4
  CFDH BH17 232 D1
  LSOL/BMARY PO13 208 D1
Martindale Av WIMB BH21 192 F3
Martin Dro End FBDG SP6 68 F3
Martingale Cl UPTN BH16 232 C1
Martin Rd FHAM/STUB PO14 184 B6
  HAV PO9 165 L4
  HSEA PO3 187 L8
Martins Cl FERN BH22 194 C1
Martins Dr FERN BH22 194 C1
Martins Flds RWIN SO21 26 B7
Martins Hill Cl
  CHCH/BSGR BH23 223 G7
Martins Hill La
  CHCH/BSGR BH23 223 H7
Martin's Rd BROC SO42 175 L6
Martin St ELGH SO50 83 J7
Martins Wy FERN BH22 194 C1
Martley Gdns HEND SO30 109 J6
Marvic Ct HAV PO9 165 J2
Marvin Wy HEND SO30 134 B1
Mary Ct WEND SO18 133 G2
Marwell Cl LTDN BH7 236 F1
Marybridge Cl TOTT SO40 129 J2
Maryfield SHAM SO14 5 J4
Maryland Cl WEND SO18 107 L5
Maryland Gdns LYMN SO41 242 A4
Maryland Rd UPTN BH16 232 B4
Mary La FERN BH22 168 B6
Mary Rose Cl FHAM PO15 6 C1
The Mary Rose St PSEA PO1 13 G2
Masefield Av CHAM PO6 162 D7
Masefield Cl ELGH SO50 81 L5
Masefield Crs HORN PO8 140 D5
Maseys La BROC SO42 204 A1
Masten Crs
  LSOL/BMARY PO13 185 G8
Matapan Rd NEND PO2 187 H4
Matchams La
  CHCH/BSGR BH23 221 M1
  RGWD BH24 195 M3
Matheson Rd ROWN SO16 105 L2
Matley Gdns TOTT SO40 128 F1
Matlock Rd FERN BH22 194 A5
Matthews Cl HAV PO9 165 G5
Matthews La BROC SO42 204 A2
Maturin Cl LYMN SO41 228 B5
Maundeville Crs
  CHCH/BSGR BH23 222 C8
Maundeville Rd
  CHCH/BSGR BH23 222 C8
Maunsell Wy HEND SO30 109 H5
Maureen Cl BKME/WDN BH12 218 F8
Maurepas Wy WVILLE PO7 164 B1
Mauretania Rd ROWN SO16 105 C4
Maurice Rd ENEY PO4 212 A4
Maurys La ROMY SO51 76 C5
Mavis Crs HAV PO9 8 E3
Mavis Rd MOOR/WNTN BH9 220 F7
Maxstoke Cl SSEA PO5 13 J2
Maxwell Rd BDST BH18 217 H5
  CCLF BH13 245 L1
  ENEY PO4 211 L5
  ITCH SO19 132 E5
  MOOR/WNTN BH9 235 M1
May Av LYMN SO41 228 B3
Maybray King Wy ITCH SO19 132 E1
Maybush Dr RCCH PO18 191 M1
May Bush La BPWT SO32 113 G2
Maybush Rd ROWN SO16 105 K6
May Cl FAWY SO45 180 B5
May Copse FAWY SO45 180 B5
May Crs FAWY SO45 180 B5
Maydman Sq HSEA PO3 211 L2
Mayfair Ct HEND SO30 134 E1
Mayfair Gdns BWD BH11 219 L4
  WSHM SO15 131 K1
Mayfield Av PSTN BH14 234 B5
  TOTT SO40 104 D8
Mayfield Cl FERN BH22 194 A2
  FHAM/STUB PO14 184 B5
Mayfield Dr FERN BH22 194 A2
Mayfield Rd FBDG SP6 97 H6
  GPORT PO12 10 C7
  MOOR/WNTN BH9 220 E6
  NEND PO2 187 J6
  PTSW SO17 107 G5
Mayfield Wy FERN BH22 194 A2
Mayflower Cl CHFD SO53 81 G3
  FHAM/STUB PO14 184 A7
  LYMN SO41 228 E5
Mayflower Rd WSHM SO15 106 B8
Mayflower Rbt WSHM SO15 4 E6
The Mayflowers ROWN SO16 106 F4
Mayfly Cl FBDG SP6 97 L6
Mayford Rd BKME/WDN BH12 235 J1
May Gdns BWD BH11 219 J5
  CHCH/BSGR BH23 224 F6
Mayhall Rd HSEA PO3 187 L7
Mayhill La BPWT SO32 86 F8
  BPWT SO32 112 C1

Maylands Av ENEY PO4 211 L4
Maylands Rd HAV PO9 164 F6
May La LYMN SO41 202 E7
Mayles Cl WHAM PO17 136 E5
Mayles La WHAM PO17 136 C7
Mayles Rd ENEY PO4 211 M3
Maylings Farm Rd
  FHAM/PORC PO16 6 F2
Maylyn Rd UPTN BH16 216 D6
Maynard Cl LSOL/BMARY PO13 185 C4
Maynard Pl HORN PO8 140 F1
Maynard Rd TOTT SO40 129 K1
Mayo Cl PSEA PO1 211 H1
Mayridge FHAM/STUB PO14 159 C5
May Rd WSHM SO15 131 G1
Mays Firs FBDG SP6 73 L6
May's La FHAM/STUB PO14 184 B4
May Tree Cl FUFL SO22 26 B8
Maytree Cl HLER SO31 158 E5
Maytree Gdns HORN PO8 140 C5
Maytree Rd CHFD SO53 53 H6
  FHAM/PORC PO16 7 C6
  HORN PO8 140 C5
Mayvale Cl TOTT SO40 130 D7
Mcintyre Rd CHCH/BSGR BH23 195 K8
Mckinley Rd WBNE BH4 235 H6
Mcwilliam Cl BKME/WDN BH12 220 A8
Mcwilliam Rd
  MOOR/WNTN BH9 220 E6
Meacher Cl TOTT SO40 104 D8
Meadbrook Gdns CHFD SO53 81 H2
Mead Cl CFDH BH17 217 L7
  ROMY SO51 79 C1
Mead Crs WEND SO18 107 J1
Meadcroft Cl HLER SO31 158 B8
Meadend Cl HAV PO9 165 M3
Mead End Rd LYMN SO41 200 D7
  WVILLE PO7 139 L5
Mead Hawks LISS GU33 36 D3
Meadow Av HLER SO31 158 E4
Meadowbank Rd FHAM PO15 6 A5
Meadow Cl BPWT SO32 111 K4
  CHCH/BSGR BH23 222 F1
  CHCH/BSGR BH23 223 L1
  FBDG SP6 97 K6
  FERN BH22 194 B7
  HEND SO30 108 D6
  HISD PO11 189 K5
  NBAD SO52 79 M5
  RGWD BH24 146 F7
  RGWD BH24 172 D6
  TOTT SO40 129 K3
Meadow Court Cl
  MOOR/WNTN BH9 220 E5
Meadowcroft Cl RWIN SO21 54 B5
Meadow Edge WVILLE PO7 163 L6
Meadow Gdns BPWT SO32 111 K4
Meadow Gv VWD BH31 144 F3
Meadowhead Rd
  ROWN SO16 106 E5
Meadowland
  CHCH/BSGR BH23 238 D2
  WINC SO23 17 C1
Meadowlands HAV PO9 9 H5
  HAV PO9 142 A5
  LYMN SO41 228 A4
Meadow La CHCH/BSGR BH23 223 C6
  HLER SO31 157 L6
  SELS PO20 215 M6
Meadowmead Av WSHM SO15 130 E1
Meadow Ri BDST BH18 217 K3
  HORN PO8 140 F5
Meadow Rd LYMN SO41 228 A6
  NMIL/BTOS BH25 225 M4
  RGWD BH24 146 F8
Meadows Cl UPTN BH16 217 C8
Meadows Dr UPTN BH16 232 B1
Meadowside Cl WEND SO18 107 K4
The Meadows
  FHAM/PORC PO16 7 L1
  LYND SO43 151 L4
Meadow St SSEA PO5 12 F5
Meadowsweet WVILLE PO7 140 F7
Meadowsweet Rd CFDH BH17 223 H7
Meadowsweet Wy CHAM PO6 163 H7
  ELGH SO50 109 H2
The Meadow ROMY SO51 50 E7
  WVILLE PO7 139 K4
Meadow View Rd BWD BH11 219 J4
Meadow Wk LISS GU33 36 E4
  LSOL/BMARY PO13 184 F3
Meadow Wy FAWY SO45 180 F5
  FUFL SO22 26 B4
  NMIL/BTOS BH25 240 F1
  RGWD BH24 146 F8
  VWD BH31 144 F4
Mead Rd CFDH BH17 81 H2
  LYMN SO41 227 M6
  WINC SO23 26 D4
The Meads CHFD SO53 80 F3
  ROMY SO51 78 C1
The Mead FAWY SO45 155 J5
  LISS GU33 36 E4
  LSOL/BMARY PO13 184 F3
  PSF GU32 63 J6
Mead Wy FHAM/PORC PO16 7 J2
Meadway WVILLE PO7 140 E7
The Meadway
  CHCH/BSGR BH23 224 B6
Mears Rd ELGH SO50 83 H4
Meath Cl HISD PO11 214 A7
Medina Cl CHFD SO53 81 K3
Medina Rd CHAM PO6 163 H8
  WSHM SO15 106 A7
Medina Wy CHCH/BSGR BH23 239 H2
Medlar Cl CHCH/BSGR BH23 223 H7
  HEND SO30 134 B2
Medlicott Wy BPWT SO32 112 A4
Medstead Rd HAV PO9 165 K5
Medwall Cl HISD PO11 133 H3
Medway Dr CHFD SO53 52 F8
Medway Rd FERN BH22 194 C2
Meerut Rd BROC SO42 175 K6
Meeting House La
  RGWD BH24 170 D1
Megana Wy ROMY SO51 51 H3
Megan Rd HEND SO30 108 C6

Meggeson Av WEND SO18 107 M6
Melbourne Pl SSEA PO5 12 F3
Melbourne Rd CHAR BH8 236 M1
  CHCH/BSGR BH23 222 C7
  HEND SO30 134 A2
Melbourne St SHAM SO14 5 K4
Melbury Av BKME/WDN BH12 234 D1
Melbury Cl FERN BH22 194 B4
  LYMN SO41 228 B5
Melchet Cl ROMY SO51 48 A7
Melchet Rd WEND SO18 108 B8
Melick Cl TOTT SO40 130 D6
Mellor Cl CHAM PO6 163 H8
Mellstock Rd PLE BH15 233 H3
Melrose Cl ENEY PO4 211 M4
Melrose Ct NMIL/BTOS BH25 226 A5
  TOTT SO40 104 B7
Melrose Gdns GPORT PO12 209 K1
Melrose Rd WSHM SO15 106 C5
Melverley Gdns WIMB BH21 192 B3
Melville Av ROWN SO16 106 B5
Melville Rd ENEY PO4 212 A6
  GPORT PO12 209 L1
  MOOR/WNTN BH9 220 D1
Mendip Cl NMIL/BTOS BH25 225 M6
  VWD BH31 144 D3
Mendip Gdns FAWY SO45 155 H6
Mendip Rd ROWN SO16 105 L8
  VWD BH31 144 D2
Mendips Rd FHAM/STUB PO14 6 B8
Mendips Wk FHAM/STUB PO14 6 B8
Mengham Av HISD PO11 213 L5
Mengham La HISD PO11 213 L5
Mengham Rd HISD PO11 213 L5
Menslands La WVILLE PO7 113 L8
Mentone Rd PSTN BH14 233 M5
Menzies Cl ROWN SO16 105 L3
Meon Cl HORN PO8 116 B4
  LSOL/BMARY PO13 184 F6
  PSF GU32 63 K4
Meon Ct WEND SO18 108 C8
Meon Crs CHFD SO53 81 J2
Meon Rd ENEY PO4 211 M4
  LTDN BH7 237 C1
  ROMY SO51 79 H1
Meonstoke Cl WEND SO18 108 A2
Meon Wy HORN PO8 116 C4
Meonwara Crs PSF GU32 60 C3
Mercer Wy ROMY SO51 50 F8
Merchants Pl WINC SO23 3 H7
Merchistoun Rd HORN PO8 140 F1
Mercury Cl ROWN SO16 105 L4
Mercury Gdns HLER SO31 157 L4
Mercury Pl WVILLE PO7 164 C6
Merdon Av CHFD SO53 53 J8
Merdon Cl CHFD SO53 53 J8
Mere Cl FHAM PO15 159 H5
Meredith Cl CHCH/BSGR BH23 238 C1
Meredith Gdns TOTT SO40 129 H2
Meredith Rd NEND PO2 187 J5
Meredun Cl RWIN SO21 53 C1
Merepond La ALTN GU34 33 K5
Merganser Cl GPORT PO12 209 M1
Meriden Cl CCLF BH13 245 L1
Meriden Rd SSEA PO5 12 F3
The Meridians
  CHCH/BSGR BH23 237 L3
Merino Wy FERN BH22 168 D7
Merlewood Cl WCLF BH2 14 E2
Merley Dr CHCH/BSGR BH23 224 E8
Merley Gdns WIMB BH21 192 B7
Merley La WIMB BH21 192 B7
Merley Park Rd WIMB BH21 192 A8
Merley Ways WIMB BH21 192 B5
Merlin Cl BPWT SO32 85 C8
  RGWD BH24 171 C2
Merlin Dr HSEA PO3 187 K4
Merlin Gdns FHAM/PORC PO16 161 M7
  HEND SO30 133 M1
Merlin Wy CHCH/BSGR BH23 238 F3
Mermaid Rd FHAM/STUB PO14 184 D3
Mermaid Wy SHAM SO14 5 J7
Merrick Wy CHFD SO53 52 E8
Merridale Rd ITCH SO19 132 C4
Merriefield Av BDST BH18 218 A2
Merriefield Dr BDST BH18 217 M2
Merrieleas Cl CHFD SO53 81 H1
Merrieleas Dr CHFD SO53 81 H1
Merriemeade Cl FAWY SO45 155 J7
Merrifield WIMB BH21 192 C1
Merrifield Cl BDST BH18 217 M2
Merryfield Cl
  CHCH/BSGR BH23 197 L8
Merryfield La NBNE BH10 220 A4
Merryfield Rd EPSF GU31 64 A4
Merry Gdns NBAD SO52 79 M3
Merryoak Gn ITCH SO19 132 D3
Merryoak Rd ITCH SO19 132 D4
Mersea Gdns ITCH SO19 132 E4
Mersham Gdns WEND SO18 132 E1
Merstone Rd
  LSOL/BMARY PO13 185 G5
Merthyr Av CHAM PO6 163 M7
Merton Av FHAM/PORC PO16 186 B2
Merton Cl FBDG SP6 97 L5
Merton Rd PTSW SO17 107 G6
  SSEA PO5 13 H7
Meryl Rd ENEY PO4 212 A4
Mesh Pond RSAL SP5 44 C8
Mesh Rd ROMY SO51 22 B6
Meteor Rd EMRTH PO10 190 F6
Methuen Cl CHAR BH8 15 L2
Methuen Rd CFDH BH17 217 M6
  CHAR BH8 15 J1
  ENEY PO4 211 L5
Methuen St SHAM SO14 131 L1
Metuchen Wy HEND SO30 134 A4
Mewsey Ct HAV PO9 165 H1
Mews La FUFL SO22 2 D8

The Mews FAWY SO45 206 D1
  HAV PO9 165 J4
  HAV PO9 165 L2
Mey Cl WVILLE PO7 164 D1
Meynell Cl ELGH SO50 81 G1
Meyrick Cl CHCH/BSGR BH23 223 L1
Meyrick Park Crs TWDS BH3 235 C2
Meyrick Rd BMTH BH1 15 J5
  HAV PO9 8 B4
  NEND PO2 187 C7
Michael Crook Cl HAV PO9 165 C5
Michaels Wy ELGH SO50 83 J6
  FAWY SO45 155 K4
Michelgrove Rd BOSC BH5 236 D5
Michelmersh Cl ROWN SO16 105 K3
Michelmersh Gn CHAR BH8 221 H6
Michigan Wy TOTT SO40 104 A8
Mickleham Cl
  BKME/WDN BH12 219 M8
Midanbury Crs WEND SO18 107 L7
Midanbury La WEND SO18 107 K8
Middlebere Crs UPTN BH16 232 B4
Middlebridge St ROMY SO51 78 D2
Middlebrook BPWT SO32 85 H8
Middle Brook St WINC SO23 3 H7
Middle Common Rd
  LYMN SO41 227 K5
Middlecroft La GPORT PO12 209 K2
Middlefield SELS PO20 215 L7
Middlehill Dr WIMB BH21 192 F2
Middlehill Rd WIMB BH21 192 E1
Middle La RGWD BH24 170 E1
Middle Md FHAM/STUB PO14 159 M8
Middle Park Wy HAV PO9 165 H2
Middle Rd FUFL SO22 2 D6
  HLER SO31 158 F5
  ITCH SO19 132 E5
  LYMN SO41 200 B8
  LYMN SO41 200 F6
  LYMN SO41 228 B5
  NBAD SO52 79 M3
  NBNE BH10 220 A3
  PLE BH15 233 K2
Middlesex Rd ENEY PO4 211 L5
Middle St CCLF BH13 244 C3
  SHAM SO14 131 L1
  SSEA PO5 13 C3
Middleton Cl FHAM/STUB PO14 6 C9
  WEND SO18 107 M6
Middleton Ri HORN PO8 116 C4
Middleton Rd NBNE BH10 220 C6
  RGWD BH24 146 E8
Midfield Cl FHAM/STUB PO14 184 C1
Midland Rd MOOR/WNTN BH9 220 D7
Midlands Est HEND SO30 108 B6
Midlington Hl BPWT SO32 112 F1
Midlington Rd BPWT SO32 113 G1
Midway FAWY SO45 155 K5
Midway Rd NEND PO2 187 J3
Midways FHAM/STUB PO14 184 A7
Midwood Av CHAR BH8 221 K7
Milbeck Cl HORN PO8 140 E5
Milborne Crs BKME/WDN BH12 234 D1
Milbourne Rd FERN BH22 194 A2
Milburn Rd WBNE BH4 235 H4
Milburn Rd WBNE BH4 235 C4
The Milburns ROMY SO51 50 C1
Milbury Crs ITCH SO19 132 E2
Mildmay St FUFL SO22 26 C3
Milebush Rd ENEY PO4 212 A3
Mile End Rd PSEA PO1 211 C1
Miles's La RSAL SP5 47 J4
Milestone Rd PLE BH15 233 J2
Milford Cl FERN BH22 168 D6
  HAV PO9 165 H5
Milford Ct LYMN SO41 242 D4
Milford Crs LYMN SO41 242 D4
Milford Dr BWD BH11 219 K3
Milford Gdns CHFD SO53 81 K2
Milford Rd LYMN SO41 227 K7
  NMIL/BTOS BH25 226 A8
  PSEA PO1 13 J1
  GPORT PO12 209 J3
  GPORT PO12 209 M8
  GPORT PO12 210 A7
  HSEA PO3 187 K3
  PSEA PO1 210 F2
Milkwood Ct TOTT SO40 129 L3
Millais Rd ITCH SO19 132 C5
Milland La LIPH GU30 38 D3
Milland Rd LIPH GU30 38 E6
  WINC SO23 27 G2
Millbank St SHAM SO14 5 L1
Millbridge Gdns ITCH SO19 132 F4
Millbrook Cl CHFD SO53 81 G3
  LISS GU33 36 F4
Millbrook Dr HAV PO9 165 J3
Millbrook Point Rd
  WSHM SO15 130 E2
Millbrook Rd East
  WSHM SO15 131 G3
Millbrook Rd West
  WSHM SO15 130 C1
Mill Cl HISD PO11 189 K6
  ROWN SO16 105 J3
  WVILLE PO7 139 M4
Mill Ct FBDG SP6 97 K7
Mill End EMRTH PO10 166 F8
  FBDG SP6 96 C4
Miller Cl NMIL/BTOS BH25 226 A4
Miller Dr FHAM/PORC PO16 6 F2
Miller Rd CHCH/BSGR BH23 238 C1
Millers La FUFL SO22 25 L5
Millfield BDST BH17 232 F1
Millham Rd NBNE BH10 219 L1
Millhams St CHCH/BSGR BH23 238 A4
Millhams St North
  CHCH/BSGR BH23 238 A4
Mill Hi HEND SO30 134 E1
Mill Hill Cl PSTN BH14 234 A5
Millikens Cl FAWY SO45 180 D6
Mill La BPWT SO32 87 H6
  BPWT SO32 110 C5
  BROC SO42 175 H4
  CHCH/BSGR BH23 221 M2
  CHCH/BSGR BH23 224 F8

266 Mil - New

EMRTH PO10 166 F6
EPSF GU31 66 C8
EPSF GU31 93 G5
FHAM PO15 159 L7
GPORT PO12 209 M2
HAV PO9 165 G7
HAV PO9 189 J2
LYMN SO41 227 J1
LYMN SO41 228 D4 1
LYMN SO41 229 K3
LYND SO43 127 J6
MIDH GU29 67 K6
PSEA PO1 211 G1
PSF GU32 35 K8
PSF GU32 64 A2
PSTN BH14 234 A5
RGWD BH24 173 G3
ROMY SO51 48 D8
ROMY SO51 78 C1
ROWN SO16 104 D4
WHAM PO17 136 E3
WVILLE PO7 163 J4
Mill Meadow LYMN SO41 242 B3
Mill Pond Rd GPORT PO12 209 M2
The Mill Pond FAWY SO45 179 M2
Mill Quay EMRTH PO10 190 E1
Mill Ri ROMY SO51 21 J8
Mill Rd CHCH/BSGR BH23 222 E8
EMRTH PO10 166 F4
FHAM/PORC PO16 7 J8
GPORT PO12 209 L2
LISS GU33 36 F3
TOTT SO40 129 L1
WSHM SO15 130 E1
WVILLE PO7 139 L4
WVILLE PO7 164 B2
Mill Rd (North) CHAR BH8 221 H5
Mill Rd (South) CHAR BH8 221 H6
Mill Rythe La HISD PO11 213 L1
Mills Rd NEND PO2 187 H8
Millstream Cl CFDH BH17 232 F1
WIMB BH21 192 A4
Millstream Ri ROMY SO51 78 C1
Mill St FHAM/STUB PO14 159 L8
Mill Vale Mdw LIPH GU30 38 E5
Millvina Cl TOTT SO40 128 D4
Mill Wy TOTT SO40 129 J3
Millyford Cl NMIL/BTOS BH25 225 H8
Milne Cl FAWY SO45 155 G6
Milner Ct WSHM SO15 106 B8
Milne Rd CFDH BH17 217 M7
Milner Pl FUFL SO22 26 D2
Milner Rd WBNE BH4 235 H6
Milnthorpe La FUFL SO22 2 C9
Milton Cl PSTN BH14 234 C5
Milton Gv HLER SO31 158 F7
NMIL/BTOS BH25 225 M6
Milton Md NMIL/BTOS BH25 225 K6
Milton Pde WVILLE PO7 140 C6
Milton Park Av ENEY PO4 211 M4 3
Milton Rd CHAR BH8 15 H1
ELGH SO50 82 A3 3
ENEY PO4 211 L4
HSEA PO3 211 L1
PSTN BH14 234 C5
WIMB BH21 192 A2
WSHM SO15 131 J2
WVILLE PO7 140 B7
Milverton Cl
CHCH/BSGR BH23 224 C7 2
Milverton Rd FUFL SO22 2 C6
TOTT SO40 129 L2
Milvil Rd LSOL/BMARY PO13 208 C3
Mimosa Av WIMB BH21 192 B8
Mimosa Dr ELGH SO50 83 K6
Mincingfield La BPWT SO32 110 C4
Minden Wy FUFL SO22 26 B3
Minerva Cl WVILLE PO7 164 C6 1
Minley Ct HAV PO9 165 M3
Minnitt Rd GPORT PO12 11 L3
Minstead Av WEND SO18 108 B8
Minstead Cl FUFL SO22 16 C4 3
Minstead Rd ENEY PO4 211 M5
NBNE BH10 220 A5
Minsted Rd MIDH GU29 67 J8
Minster Cl FHAM PO15 160 A7
Minster La WINC SO23 3 G8
Minster Vw WIMB BH21 192 A3
Minster Wy UPTN BH16 232 A1
Mintern Cl ELGH SO50 82 C3 5
Minterne Rd CHCH/BSGR BH23 238 D3
MOOR/WNTN BH9 220 E6 4
PSTN BH14 245 H1
Minters Lepe WVILLE PO7 164 C5
Mint Rd LISS GU33 37 G4
Mirror Cl HLER SO31 158 D7
Mislingford Rd BPWT SO32 112 B5
Missenden Acres
HEND SO30 109 H8 5
Mission Rd BDST BH18 217 L6
Misslebrook La NBAD SO52 80 C4
Mitchell Cl NMIL/BTOS BH25 240 F1
Mitchell Dr ELGH SO50 83 H5
Mitchell Rd CFDH BH17 218 D8
ELGH SO50 82 A6
HAV PO9 164 F5
WIMB BH21 193 L1
Mitchells Cl ROMY SO51 78 E1
RSAL SP5 73 J2 3
Mitchell Wy ELGH SO50 107 M1
HSEA PO3 187 M5
Mitre Copse ELGH SO50 82 E6
Mizen Wy
LSOL/BMARY PO13 209 H2 4
Moat Cl FAWY SO45 179 M5
Moat Dr GPORT PO12 209 H5
Moat Hl WEND SO18 107 L5
Moat La NMIL/BTOS BH25 225 K7
Mockbeggar La RGWD BH24 146 E1
Moffat Rd CHCH/BSGR BH23 238 C1
Moggs Md EPSF GU31 63 M5
Mole Hl WVILLE PO7 164 D3
Molesworth Rd GPORT PO12 11 G4 2
Molyneux Rd
NMIL/BTOS BH25 226 B5
Momford Rd FUFL SO22 26 A5
Monarch Cl HLER SO31 158 E6
WVILLE PO7 164 E1 6
Monarch's Wy BPWT SO32 84 B1
HAV PO9 142 D7
HORN PO8 141 H3
ROMY SO51 21 L8
WVILLE PO7 88 F7
Monarch Wy FUFL SO22 26 B2
HEND SO30 108 D6 1
Monastery Rd WEND SO18 132 C1
Monckton Rd GPORT PO12 209 M7
HSEA PO3 187 K6
Mon Crs WEND SO18 133 G1
Moneyfield Av HSEA PO3 187 L8
Moneyfield La HSEA PO3 187 L8 2
Moneyfly Rd VWD BH31 144 F3
Monks Brook Cl ELGH SO50 81 K7
Monks Cl FERN BH22 168 E8
Monk's Hl EMRTH PO10 166 E2
Monkshood Cl
CHCH/BSGR BH23 223 M7 2
Monks Orch PSF GU32 63 L3
Monks Pl TOTT SO40 129 H2
Monks Rd HLER SO31 156 F2
WINC SO23 3 G5
Monks Wk FAWY SO45 155 J8
Monks Wy ELGH SO50 81 L7
FHAM/STUB PO14 183 M8
WEND SO18 107 K4
WIMB BH21 219 G3
Monkswell Gn
CHCH/BSGR BH23 238 C2
Monks Wd PSF GU32 63 L3
Monks Wood Cl ELGH SO50 107 G2
Monkton Cl FERN BH22 194 B2
Monkton Crs BKME/WDN BH12 219 J8
Monkton La TOTT SO40 129 G2
Monkwood Cl HAV PO9 165 H3 2
Monkworthy Dr RGWD BH24 169 K3
Monmouth Cl CHFD SO53 81 G2
VWD BH31 144 F4
Monmouth Dr VWD BH31 144 F4
Monmouth Rd NEND PO2 187 H6
Monmouth Sq FUFL SO22 26 A2 1
Monnow Gdns WEND SO18 108 A7
Monroe Cl GPORT PO12 209 J5
Monsal Av FERN BH22 194 A5
Montacute Wy WIMB BH21 192 C8
Montague Av ITCH SO19 133 H5
Montague Cl ITCH SO19 133 H5 2
Montague Gdns EPSF GU31 64 B5
Montague Rd BOSC BH5 237 G4
NEND PO2 187 J7
Montagu Rd CHCH/BSGR BH23 240 A1
Monteray Dr LYMN SO41 226 D4
Monterey Dr HAV PO9 165 L4
HLER SO31 158 E6
Montfort Cl ROMY SO51 79 H1
Montfort Hts ROMY SO51 79 H1 1
Montfort Rd ROMY SO51 79 H2
Montgomerie Rd SSEA PO5 13 J3
Montgomery Av BWD BH11 219 M5
TOTT SO40 104 C8
Montgomery Rd HAV PO9 9 G4
LSOL/BMARY PO13 185 G4
WEND SO18 107 M8
Montgomery Wk WVILLE PO7 164 A3
Montgomery Wy CHFD SO53 81 G5
Montpelier Cl HLER SO31 159 G5 3
Montrose Av
FHAM/PORC PO16 162 C7
Montrose Cl HEND SO30 134 C2 1
VWD BH31 144 D2
Montrose Dr NBNE BH10 219 M6
Montserrat Rd
LSOL/BMARY PO13 208 C2
Monument La LYMN SO41 228 E3
RCCH PO18 167 K1
WHAM PO17 161 M4
Moody Rd FHAM/STUB PO14 183 M7
Moody's Hl RSAL SP5 19 H6
Moonhills La BROC SO42 178 F6
Moonrakers Wy
CHCH/BSGR BH23 224 C7
Moonscross Av TOTT SO40 129 K4
Moorcroft Av
CHCH/BSGR BH23 223 G6
Moordown Cl
MOOR/WNTN BH9 220 E5
Moore Av BWD BH11 219 L5
Moore Cl NMIL/BTOS BH25 225 K7 2
Moore Crs HLER SO31 156 F2
Moore Gdns GPORT PO12 10 A3
Moorfield Gv
MOOR/WNTN BH9 220 D6
Moorfields Rd CCLF BH13 234 E8 2
Moorgreen Rd HAV PO9 165 L3
HEND SO30 108 D7
Moorhill Gdns WEND SO18 133 J1
Moorhill Rd HEND SO30 108 C8
RGWD BH24 172 E6
Moorhouse La MIDH GU29 66 F2
The Moorings
FHAM/PORC PO16 184 F1 1
Moorings Wy ENEY PO4 212 A2
Moorland Av NMIL/BTOS BH25 225 K8
Moorland Cl FAWY SO45 155 H5 5
HLER SO31 158 E4
Moorland Crs UPTN BH16 232 A1
Moorland Ga RGWD BH24 170 E3
Moorland Rd BMTH BH1 236 C4
PSEA PO1 211 J2
Moorlands Cl BROC SO42 175 H7
Moorlands Crs WEND SO18 107 M8
Moorlands Ri FERN BH22 168 D5
Moorlands Rd BPWT SO32 111 M2
FERN BH22 168 C6
VWD BH31 144 D1
Moorland Wy UPTN BH16 232 A1
Moor La RSAL SP5 46 D7
Moor Pk HORN PO8 140 F7
Moor Rd BDST BH18 217 M3
Moors Cl CHCH/BSGR BH23 221 M1
RWIN SO21 54 E7
Moorside Cl BWD BH11 219 M5 2
Moorside Rd BWD BH11 219 L5
FERN BH22 168 C6
WIMB BH21 217 H3
WINC SO23 3 M3
Moortown Av CHAM PO6 164 A7
Moortown Dr WIMB BH21 192 F7
Moortown La RGWD BH24 170 F4
Moorvale Rd
MOOR/WNTN BH9 220 E6
Moor View Rd PLE BH15 233 K2
Moot Cl RSAL SP5 72 F2
Moot Gdns RSAL SP5 72 E2
Moot La FBDG SP6 72 E6
RSAL SP5 72 E2
Mopley FAWY SO45 206 D1
Mopley Cl FAWY SO45 206 D1
Morant Rd RGWD BH24 146 F7
Moraunt Cl GPORT PO12 185 M8 1
Moraunt Dr FHAM/PORC PO16 185 M2
Mordaunt Rd SHAM SO14 131 L1
Morden Av FERN BH22 194 A4
Morden Rd
MOOR/WNTN BH9 220 D7 3
Moreland Rd GPORT PO12 10 E2
Morelands Rd WVILLE PO7 164 C4
Morestead Rd RWIN SO21 27 G3
Moreton Rd MOOR/WNTN BH9 220 F4
Morgan Rd ENEY PO4 212 A4
HEND SO30 134 A3 1
Morgans Dr FHAM/STUB PO14 184 A3
Morgans Rise Rd RSAL SP5 73 J1
Morgans Vale Rd RSAL SP5 73 J2
Morland Rd WSHM SO15 106 B7
Morley Cl BOSC BH5 236 F3
CHCH/BSGR BH23 223 G5
ITCH SO19 132 D2
Morley Crs HORN PO8 140 E5
Morley Dr BPWT SO32 85 H8
Morley Rd BOSC BH5 236 F3 2
ENEY PO4 211 L6
Morningside Av
FHAM/PORC PO16 162 B7
Mornington Dr FUFL SO22 16 B6
Mornish Rd CCLF BH13 234 E6
Morpeth Av TOTT SO40 104 E8
Morris Cl FAWY SO45 155 H4
LSOL/BMARY PO13 185 G4
Morrison Av BKME/WDN BH12 234 E2
Morris Rd WSHM SO15 4 D1
Morshead Crs FHAM/PORC PO16 6 F2
Mortimer Cl CHCH/BSGR BH23 238 F2
HLER SO31 156 F2
TOTT SO40 104 C7
WINC SO23 17 G2
Mortimer Rd CHAM PO6 163 G7
CHAR BH8 220 F7
HEND SO30 134 E2
ITCH SO19 132 C4
Mortimers Dr ELGH SO50 83 J6 2
Mortimers La ELGH SO50 83 J6
Mortimer Wy NBAD SO52 79 L5
Mortimore Rd GPORT PO12 209 K2
Mosaic Cl ITCH SO19 133 K4 1
Mosdell Rd EMRTH PO10 167 H8
Moss Cl LISS GU33 36 F4
Moss Dr TOTT SO40 130 D6
Mossleigh Av ROWN SO16 105 L3
Mossley Av BKME/WDN BH12 219 K7
Moss Rd WINC SO23 3 K7
Motcombe Rd CCLF BH13 234 F7
Mottisfont Cl WSHM SO15 130 E2 1
Mottisfont Rd ELGH SO50 81 M4
Mound Cl GPORT PO12 10 C5
Mountain Ash Cl WEND SO18 133 G1 2
Mount Av NMIL/BTOS BH25 225 L7
Mountbatten Av ROMY SO51 78 E1
Mountbatten Cl
CHCH/BSGR BH23 238 F3 2
LSOL/BMARY PO13 185 G4 2
Mountbatten Ct FUFL SO22 2 C1
Mountbatten Dr FERN BH22 194 A3
WVILLE PO7 164 A2
Mountbatten Rd CCLF BH13 235 G7
CHAR BH8 221 K6 4
ELGH SO50 81 M3 2
TOTT SO40 104 C8
Mountbatten Sq ENEY PO4 211 M6 3
Mount Cl FUFL SO22 2 C1
NMIL/BTOS BH25 225 L7
Mount Dr CHFD SO53 81 K4
FHAM PO15 159 M8
Mountfield FAWY SO45 155 J4
Mount Grace Dr PSTN BH14 245 H1
Mount House Cl FAWY SO45 155 L3 1
Mountjoy Cl WIMB BH21 192 D6
Mount La ROMY SO51 48 E1
Mount Pleasant RGWD BH24 170 E1 5
WINC SO23 17 G2
Mount Pleasant Dr CHAR BH8 221 K7
CHCH/BSGR BH23 198 A7 1
Mount Pleasant La
LYMN SO41 201 K8
Mount Pleasant Rd
GPORT PO12 10 E7
PLE BH15 233 J6
SHAM SO14 131 M1
Mount Rd BWD BH11 219 L4
PSTN BH14 234 A3
Mount Temple ROMY SO51 78 F1
The Mount
LSOL/BMARY PO13 185 J7 4
RGWD BH24 147 H8
ROWN SO16 105 M7 1
ROWN SO16 106 E4 1
Mount Vw ELGH SO50 82 A4
Mountview Av
FHAM/PORC PO16 162 C7
Mountwood Rd EMRTH PO10 167 H7
Mousehole La FAWY SO45 155 L5
WEND SO18 107 L8
Mousehole Rd CHAM PO6 162 D7
Mowbray Rd ITCH SO19 132 F4
Moxhams FBDG SP6 97 L7 3
Muccleshell Cl HAV PO9 165 L4 2
Muddyford Rd RSAL SP5 45 J7
Mudeford CHCH/BSGR BH23 238 E3
Mudeford Green Cl
CHCH/BSGR BH23 238 E3 1
Mudeford La
CHCH/BSGR BH23 238 E2
Mude Gdns CHCH/BSGR BH23 238 F3
Mulberry Av CHAM PO6 187 L1
FHAM/STUB PO14 184 A7
Mulberry Cl GPORT PO12 10 E4
Mulberry Gdns FBDG SP6 97 K8
Mulberry La CHAM PO6 187 L1
Mulberry Rd TOTT SO40 130 D7
Mulberry Wk WSHM SO15 106 B8
Mullen Cl ITCH SO19 132 C4
Mullins Cl BKME/WDN BH12 220 A8
Mullin's La FAWY SO45 155 K6
Mullion Cl CHAM PO6 186 F1
Mumby Rd GPORT PO12 11 K2
Mundays Rw HORN PO8 116 B7 6
Munro Crs WSHM SO15 130 D1
Munster Rd NEND PO2 187 H6
PSTN BH14 234 C5
Murefield Rd PSEA PO1 13 K1 1
Muriel Rd WVILLE PO7 140 C8
Murley Rd MOOR/WNTN BH9 220 E8
Murray Cl FHAM PO15 6 D4
ITCH SO19 133 J2
Murray Rd HORN PO8 140 F2
Murray's La PSEA PO1 210 D2
Muscliffe Ct HAV PO9 165 M3 10
Muscliffe La
MOOR/WNTN BH9 220 E4
Muscliffe Pk
MOOR/WNTN BH9 221 G4
Muscliffe Rd
MOOR/WNTN BH9 220 D8
Museum Rd PSEA PO1 12 E4
Mussett Cl TOTT SO40 129 J1
Mustang Av FHAM PO15 158 F1
Myers Cl BPWT SO32 112 A3
My Lords La HISD PO11 213 M5
Myrtle Av FHAM/PORC PO16 186 B1
TOTT SO40 129 H2
Myrtle Cl LSOL/BMARY PO13 184 F5 3
LYMN SO41 226 D4 1
Myrtle Gv HSEA PO3 211 M2
Myrtle Rd CHAR BH8 236 B2
ROWN SO16 106 A4
Myvern Cl FAWY SO45 180 A5

N

Nada Rd CHCH/BSGR BH23 224 B7
Nailsworth Rd CHAM PO6 162 F7
Nairn Rd CCLF BH13 245 K1
TWDS BH3 235 K2
Naish Ct HAV PO9 165 G1
Naish Dr GPORT PO12 185 L7
Naish Rd NMIL/BTOS BH25 240 C1
Namu Rd MOOR/WNTN BH9 220 C7
Nansen Av PLE BH15 233 J3
Napier Crs FHAM PO15 160 A7
Napier Rd HORN PO8 141 G2
ITCH SO19 133 J3
PLE BH15 232 B5
SSEA PO5 13 K7
Narrow La RGWD BH24 147 H7
ROMY SO51 78 D1 3
Narvik Rd NEND PO2 187 H4
Naseby Rd MOOR/WNTN BH9 220 E7
Nash Cl FAWY SO45 155 H6
Nashe Cl FHAM PO15 6 A2
Nashe Wy FHAM PO15 160 A6
Nash Rd FAWY SO45 155 H7
Nasmith Cl LSOL/BMARY PO13 209 H4
Nathen Gdns PLE BH15 232 C5 3
Nations Hl WINC SO23 17 G1
Navigator's Wy HEND SO30 109 H8
Navy Rd PSEA PO1 210 E2
Nea Cl CHCH/BSGR BH23 224 B8
Neacroft Cl NMIL/BTOS BH25 225 H8
Nea Dr RGWD BH24 145 L3
Nea Rd CHCH/BSGR BH23 224 C8
Neath Wy CHFD SO53 80 F3
Needles Point LYMN SO41 242 C4
Neelands Gv CHAM PO6 162 C8
Neilson Cl CHFD SO53 81 H1
Nelson Av FHAM/PORC PO16 185 M1
NEND PO2 187 H6
Nelson Cl FAWY SO45 180 A5
NMIL/BTOS BH25 225 K5
ROMY SO51 50 E8 4
ROMY SO51 50 F8 4
Nelson Ct FHAM/STUB PO14 184 D2
Nelson Crs HORN PO8 141 G1 2
Nelson Dr CHCH/BSGR BH23 238 E2
Nelson La WHAM PO17 162 A5
Nelson Pl LYMN SO41 228 D5
Nelson Rd BKME/WDN BH12 235 G4
ELGH SO50 82 C4
GPORT PO12 10 F4 1
PSEA PO1 211 H1
SSEA PO5 13 H6
WINC SO23 3 L9
WSHM SO15 131 G2
Nelsons Gdns HEND SO30 109 H5
Nepean Cl GPORT PO12 10 E9
Neptune Rd FHAM PO15 160 A6
FHAM/STUB PO14 184 D3
Neptune Wy SHAM SO14 5 J7
Nerissa Cl WVILLE PO7 140 F8
Nerquis Cl ROMY SO51 51 G8 4
Nesbitt Cl LSOL/BMARY PO13 184 F5 1
Nessus St NEND PO2 187 H8
Netherfield Cl HAV PO9 9 H6
Netherhall Gdns WBNE BH4 235 H5
Nether Hill La BPWT SO32 110 A6
Netherton Rd GPORT PO12 209 K1
Netley Cl CHFD SO53 81 G5 2
PLE BH15 233 M1
Netley Firs Rd ITCH SO19 133 K4
Netley Hill Est ITCH SO19 133 K4
Netley Lodge Cl HLER SO31 157 G3
Netley Rd FHAM/STUB PO14 159 G7
SSEA PO5 13 G8
Netley Ter SSEA PO5 13 G8
Nettlecombe Av ENEY PO4 13 L9
Nettlestone HLER SO31 157 G1 5
Nettlestone Rd ENEY PO4 211 L6 1
Nettleton Cl CFDH BH17 233 K1
Neva Rd WEND SO18 107 L8
Neville Av FHAM/PORC PO16 186 B2
Neville Dr ROMY SO51 50 E8 5
Neville Gdns EMRTH PO10 166 C5
Neville Rd HSEA PO3 211 L1
Neville Shute Rd HSEA PO3 187 L5
Newbarn La RCCH PO18 143 K8
Newbarn Rd EPSF GU31 91 H5
HAV PO9 165 G5
Newbolt Cl HORN PO8 140 C5
Newbolt Rd CHAM PO6 162 D7
New Borough Rd WIMB BH21 192 A5
Newbridge HLER SO31 157 G2 3
Newbridge Rd TOTT SO40 102 E5
Newbridge Wy LYMN SO41 228 A7
New Brighton Rd
EMRTH PO10 166 D6
Newbroke Rd
LSOL/BMARY PO13 185 J8 2
Newburgh St WINC SO23 2 F6 1
Newbury Cl ELGH SO50 83 G6 2
Newbury Dr NBNE BH10 220 B7 4
Newbury Pl HLER SO31 158 D6
Newbury Rd WSHM SO15 106 B7 2
New Cliffe Gdns HEND SO30 133 M3 1
Newcombe Rd FERN BH22 168 B5
SBNE BH6 237 K2
WSHM SO15 131 J2
Newcomen Rd NEND PO2 187 G6
Newcome Rd PSEA PO1 211 J2
Newcroft Gdns
CHCH/BSGR BH23 222 E8
New Cut HISD PO11 189 K5
New Down La WVILLE PO7 163 L6
Newenham Rd LYMN SO41 228 C6
Newfield Rd LISS GU33 36 F2
New Forest Dr BROC SO42 175 H7
Newfoundland Dr PLE BH15 233 J7
Newgate La FHAM/STUB PO14 184 E2
New Harbour Rd South
PLE BH15 233 G7
New Inn La BROC SO42 204 A3
TOTT SO40 127 M2
New Inn Rd TOTT SO40 127 M2
Newland Av GPORT PO12 10 C3
Newlands Av WSHM SO15 131 G1
Newlands Cl FAWY SO45 180 C8
NBAD SO52 80 D3
Newlands Copse FAWY SO45 180 D7
Newlands La WVILLE PO7 139 L8
Newlands Rd
CHCH/BSGR BH23 238 E1
FAWY SO45 180 C6
LTDN BH7 236 F2
NMIL/BTOS BH25 225 M7
WVILLE PO7 164 B3
Newlands Wy BDST BH18 217 H5
New La EPSF GU31 93 G6
HAV PO9 9 G3
LYMN SO41 242 E5
NMIL/BTOS BH25 225 K2
Newlease Rd WVILLE PO7 164 D3
Newlyn Wk ROMY SO51 50 F7
Newlyn Wy BKME/WDN BH12 234 D1
CHAM PO6 186 E1
Newmans Cl WIMB BH21 168 C3 1
Newmans Hl WHAM PO17 112 B8
Newman's La FERN BH22 168 A3
Newman St ROWN SO16 106 A8 3
Newmarket Cl ELGH SO50 109 J1 4
Newmer Ct HAV PO9 165 G2
New Merrifield WIMB BH21 192 D1 1
Newmorton Rd
MOOR/WNTN BH9 220 E4
Newney Cl NEND PO2 187 K4 3
Newnham Ct HAV PO9 165 M3 11
New Orch PLE BH15 233 G6
New Park Rd SBNE BH6 237 H4
Newport Cl CHFD SO53 80 F4 3
Newport La ROMY SO51 51 G2
Newport Rd GPORT PO12 10 A1
New Quay Rd PLE BH15 232 F7
New Rd BKME/WDN BH12 234 C2
BPWT SO32 85 J6
BPWT SO32 87 J5
BPWT SO32 111 L4
ELGH SO50 83 G6
EMRTH PO10 166 F5
EMRTH PO10 167 J8
FAWY SO45 179 M2
FAWY SO45 180 C7
FBDG SP6 70 D7
FERN BH22 194 B3
FERN BH22 220 C1
FHAM/PORC PO16 7 H5
FUFL SO22 16 A2
HAV PO9 8 D2
HLER SO31 134 D8
HLER SO31 156 F2
HLER SO31 158 D8
HORN PO8 116 B3
HORN PO8 140 C2
LYMN SO41 242 F4
NBNE BH10 220 C3
NEND PO2 211 J1
RGWD BH24 122 F8
ROMY SO51 50 C1
ROMY SO51 50 F8
RSAL SP5 75 K7
RWIN SO21 54 E7
SHAM SO14 5 G2
TOTT SO40 129 G6
New Rd East NEND PO2 187 K8
Newstead Rd SBNE BH6 237 J4
New St LYMN SO41 228 C4
PLE BH15 233 G7 3
RGWD BH24 170 E2
Newton Cl FHAM/STUB PO14 184 A4
RSAL SP5 46 F5
Newton La ROMY SO51 78 D1
RSAL SP5 46 C8
Newton Morrell PSTN BH14 234 C5 1
Newton Pl LSOL/BMARY PO13 208 C1
Newton Rd CCLF BH13 234 D8
NMIL/BTOS BH25 225 M8
RWIN SO21 54 F1
WEND SO18 107 K7
New Town FHAM/PORC PO16 162 B8
Newtown La HISD PO11 213 J4 4
RGWD BH24 123 G7
Newtown Rd ELGH SO50 81 M4
HLER SO31 158 A8

ITCH SO19 ... 132 F8
ROMY SO51 ... 49 C5
VWD BH31 ... 144 E2
New Valley Rd LYMN SO41 ... 242 B4
Nicholas Cl
  CHCH/BSGR BH23 ... 224 F6
Nicholas Crs FHAM PO15 ... 6 E4
Nicholas Gdns FHAM BH10 ... 220 A6
Nicholas Rd FAWY SO45 ... 206 C5
Nicholl Pl LSOL/BMARY PO13 ... 185 G6
Nichol Rd CHFD SO53 ... 53 J7
Nicholson Cl CFDH BH17 ... 218 C8
Nicholson Wk ROWN SO16 ... 105 J2
Nicholson Wy HAV PO9 ... 8 D1
Nichols Rd SHAM SO14 ... 5 K1
Nickel St SSEA PO5 ... 12 F5
Nickleby Gdns TOTT SO40 ... 128 F1
Nickleby Rd HORN PO8 ... 116 A2
Nickson Cl CHFD SO53 ... 53 C8
Nightingale Av ELGH SO50 ... 81 J6
Nightingale Cl FUFL SO22 ... 26 A2
  GPORT PO12 ... 209 G2
  HAV PO9 ... 141 L7
  ROMY SO51 ... 79 C1
  VWD BH31 ... 144 E3
Nightingale Crs BPWT SO32 ... 111 L8
Nightingale Dr TOTT SO40 ... 104 B8
Nightingale Gv WSHM SO15 ... 131 C1
Nightingale La RCCH PO18 ... 167 L5
Nightingale Pk HAV PO9 ... 9 J5
Nightingale Rd HLER SO31 ... 133 K8
  PSF GU32 ... 63 J6
  SSEA PO5 ... 12 F7
Nightingale Wk HLER SO31 ... 157 C4
Nightjar Cl CFDH BH17 ... 217 J8
  HORN PO8 ... 140 E2
Nile Rd PTSW SO17 ... 106 F6
Nile St EMRTH PO10 ... 166 D8
Nimrod Dr LSOL/BMARY PO13 ... 209 H2
Nimrod Wy WIMB BH21 ... 193 K2
Nine Elms La WHAM PO17 ... 161 J4
Ninian Cl ELGH SO50 ... 83 H7
Ninian Park Rd HSEA PO3 ... 187 L6
Niton Cl LSOL/BMARY PO13 ... 185 C6
Noads Cl FAWY SO45 ... 155 K6
Noads Wy FAWY SO45 ... 155 J7
Nobbs La PSEA PO1 ... 12 D4
Nobes Av LSOL/BMARY PO13 ... 185 C5
Nobes Cl LSOL/BMARY PO13 ... 185 H6
Noble Cl BWD BH11 ... 219 K7
Noble Rd HEND SO30 ... 134 B2
Nob's Crook RWIN SO21 ... 82 F1
Noel Cl BROC SO42 ... 175 L7
Noel Rd NBNE BH10 ... 219 M7
Nogarth Cl ROMY SO51 ... 51 G7
Nomad Cl WEND SO18 ... 108 A7
The Nook ELGH SO50 ... 82 A3
  LSOL/BMARY PO13 ... 185 J7
Noon Gdns VWD BH31 ... 144 F2
Noon Hill Dr VWD BH31 ... 144 F2
Noon Hill Rd VWD BH31 ... 144 F2
Norbury Cl HLER SO31 ... 157 J6
Norbury Gdns HLER SO31 ... 157 J6
Norcliffe Cl BWD BH11 ... 219 M5
Norcliffe Rd PTSW SO17 ... 106 F8
Nordik Gdns HEND SO30 ... 134 A3
Nore Crs EMRTH PO10 ... 166 B7
Nore Down Wy RCCH PO18 ... 118 D8
Nore Farm Av EMRTH PO10 ... 166 B7
Noreuil Rd PSF GU32 ... 63 J5
Norfolk Av CHCH/BSGR BH23 ... 222 D7
Norfolk Rd GPORT PO12 ... 209 K1
  WSHM SO15 ... 106 C8
Norfolk St SSEA PO5 ... 13 C5
Norgett Wy FHAM/PORC PO16 ... 185 M2
Norham Av ROWN SO16 ... 106 B6
Norham Cl ROWN SO16 ... 106 B6
Norland Rd ENEY PO4 ... 13 L5
Norlands Dr RWIN SO21 ... 54 B4
Norley Cl HAV PO9 ... 165 J3
Norleywood
  CHCH/BSGR BH23 ... 224 D8
Norleywood Rd LYMN SO41 ... 203 H7
Norman Av BKME/WDN BH12 ... 234 C2
Norman Cl FHAM/PORC PO16 ... 186 B2
Normandy Cl LYMN SO41 ... 200 E6
  ROWN SO16 ... 105 J2
Normandy Dr
  CHCH/BSGR BH23 ... 238 C1
Normandy Gdns GPORT PO12 ... 10 B3
Normandy La LYMN SO41 ... 228 D6
Normandy Rd NEND PO2 ... 187 H4
Normandy Wy FBDG SP6 ... 97 K6
  PLE BH15 ... 232 C6
  TOTT SO40 ... 130 D5
Norman Gdns
  BKME/WDN BH12 ... 234 F2
  HEND SO30 ... 133 L3
Normanhurst Av CHAR BH8 ... 221 H7
Norman Rd ENEY PO4 ... 13 L6
  FAWY SO45 ... 180 C1
  GPORT PO12 ... 10 C1
  HISD PO11 ... 213 M6
  WINC SO23 ... 26 E2
Normanton Cl
  CHCH/BSGR BH23 ... 222 D7
Norman Wy HAV PO9 ... 165 G6
Norris Cl RGWD BH24 ... 51 H6
  ROMY SO51 ... 51 H6
Norris Gdns HAV PO9 ... 9 H6
  NMIL/BTOS BH25 ... 225 L7
Norris Hl WEND SO18 ... 107 K7
Norrish Rd BKME/WDN BH12 ... 234 B3
Norset Rd FHAM PO15 ... 160 A6
Northam Br SHAM SO14 ... 132 A2
Northam Ms PSEA PO1 ... 13 J1
Northampton La FAWY SO45 ... 180 C8
Northam Rd SHAM SO14 ... 5 K1
Northam St PSEA PO1 ... 13 K1
  PSEA PO1 ... 211 H2
Northarbour Rd CHAM PO6 ... 187 H1
  NEND PO2 ... 187 J3
North Av NBNE BH10 ... 220 B2
North Battery Rd NEND PO2 ... 186 F6
North Bay EMRTH PO10 ... 190 E5
Northbourne Av NBNE BH10 ... 220 B4
Northbourne Cl FAWY SO45 ... 155 L7

Northbourne Gdns
  NBNE BH10 ... 220 C3
Northbourne Pl NBNE BH10 ... 220 B3
Northbrook Av WINC SO23 ... 3 K8
Northbrook Cl PSEA PO1 ... 211 H1
  WINC SO23 ... 3 L8
Northbrook Rd BDST BH18 ... 217 L6
  SHAM SO14 ... 5 J1
North Charford Crossing
  FBDG SP6 ... 72 C4
North Charford Dro FBDC SP6 ... 71 M3
North Cl GPORT PO12 ... 10 A4
  HAV PO9 ... 9 G6
  LYMN SO41 ... 228 C4
  ROMY SO51 ... 51 H7
North Common La LYMN SO41 ... 227 K1
  RSAL SP5 ... 74 F2
Northcote Av NEND PO2 ... 187 K8
Northcote Rd BMTH BH1 ... 15 L2
  ENEY PO4 ... 13 M6
  PTSW SO17 ... 107 H6
North Crs HISD PO11 ... 213 M5
Northcroft Rd PSEA PO1 ... 209 K2
North Cross St GPORT PO12 ... 11 K3
Northdene Rd CHFD SO53 ... 81 H3
North Dr FUFL SO22 ... 16 A3
  NMIL/BTOS BH25 ... 199 J7
North East Cl ITCH SO19 ... 132 F3
North East Rd ITCH SO19 ... 132 E4
North End Av NEND PO2 ... 187 H6
North End Cl CHFD SO53 ... 81 H4
North End Gv NEND PO2 ... 187 H6
Northend La BPWT SO32 ... 86 F6
North End La FBDG SP6 ... 122 A4
  NARL SO24 ... 30 C1
Northern Access Rd
  FAWY SO45 ... 181 H6
Northern Anchorage ITCH SO19... 5 M5
Northern Pde NEND PO2 ... 187 H5
Northern Rd CHAM PO6 ... 187 K2
Northerwood Av LYND SO43 ... 151 J3
Northerwood Cl NBAD SO52 ... 79 L4
Northey Rd SBNE BH6 ... 237 K2
Northfield Av
  FHAM/STUB PO14 ... 184 D1
Northfield Cl BPWT SO32 ... 84 F7
  HORN PO8 ... 116 B6
Northfield Rd LYMN SO41 ... 242 D3
  RGWD BH24 ... 146 E2
  WEND SO18 ... 107 L5
Northfields Farm La
  WHAM PO17 ... 136 E3
North Front SHAM SO14 ... 5 H2
North Greenlands LYMN SO41 ... 228 A6
North Head LYMN SO41 ... 241 M3
North Hl CHAM PO6 ... 162 F6
  FHAM/PORC PO16 ... 7 J1
North Hill Cl FUFL SO22 ... 2 F3
Northlands Cl TOTT SO40 ... 104 C8
Northlands Dr WINC SO23 ... 3 G3
Northlands Gdns WSHM SO15 ... 131 J1
Northlands Rd ELGH SO50 ... 81 M5
  ROMY SO51 ... 79 H2
  TOTT SO40 ... 104 C8
  WSHM SO15 ... 131 J1
Northleigh La WIMB BH21 ... 192 C4
North Lodge Rd PSTN BH14 ... 234 D4
Northmead Dr CFDH BH17 ... 217 K8
Northmere Dr
  BKME/WDN BH12 ... 234 E1
Northmere Rd
  BKME/WDN BH12 ... 234 E1
North Millers Dl CHFD SO53 ... 52 F7
Northmore Cl HLER SO31 ... 158 F3
Northmore Rd HLER SO31 ... 158 F3
Northney La HISD PO11 ... 190 A4
Northney Rd HISD PO11 ... 189 M4
Northolt Gdns ROWN SO16 ... 105 M4
Northover La LYMN SO41 ... 226 C1
Northover Rd HSEA PO3 ... 187 M8
  LYMN SO41 ... 227 L4
North Poulner Rd RGWD BH24 ... 146 F7
North Rd BROC SO42 ... 175 L7
  FAWY SO45 ... 155 H6
  HORN PO8 ... 116 B6
  LTDN BH7 ... 236 D3
  PLE BH15 ... 232 F6
  PSF GU32 ... 63 L4
  PSTN BH14 ... 233 M4
  PTSW SO17 ... 107 H8
  WVILLE PO7 ... 162 E6
North Rd East WHAM PO17 ... 162 E2
North Rd West WHAM PO17 ... 162 D2
North Shore Rd HISD PO11 ... 213 H5
North St EMRTH PO10 ... 166 D7
  EMRTH PO10 ... 166 F4
  HAV PO9 ... 8 A3
  HAV PO9 ... 8 F4
  LYMN SO41 ... 228 A6
  PLE BH15 ... 233 H6
  PSEA PO1 ... 12 D1
  PSEA PO1 ... 211 H2
North Stroud La PSF GU32 ... 62 D6
North Town RWIN SO21 ... 54 F1
North Trestle Rd FAWY SO45 ... 180 F2
Northumberland Rd
  SHAM SO14 ... 5 K1
  SHAM SO14 ... 131 M2
  SSEA PO5 ... 13 L2
North Wallington
  FHAM/PORC PO16 ... 7 M3
North Walls WINC SO23 ... 3 H6
Northway FHAM PO15 ... 159 J5
North Wy HAV PO9 ... 8 D4
Northways FHAM/STUB PO14 ... 184 D4
North Weirs BROC SO42 ... 175 H7
Northwood Cl ROWN SO16 ... 106 F2
Northwood La HISD PO11 ... 189 L7
Northwood Rd NEND PO2 ... 187 J4
Nortoft Rd CHAR BH8 ... 236 B2
Norton Cl CHCH/BSGR BH23 ... 238 C1
  ITCH SO19 ... 132 C5

WHAM PO17 ... 162 D2
  WVILLE PO7 ... 164 B1
Norton Dr FHAM/PORC PO16 ... 7 H3
Norton Rd MOOR/WNTN BH9 ... 220 C7
  WHAM PO17 ... 162 D2
Norton Welch Cl NBAD SO52 ... 80 A4
Norway Rd HSEA PO3 ... 187 K4
Norwich Av WCLF BH2 ... 14 B5
Norwich Av West WBNE BH4 ... 14 A5
Norwich Cl HLER SO31 ... 158 C4
Norwich Pl LSOL/BMARY PO13 ... 208 C1
Norwich Rd CHAM PO6 ... 163 H7
  WCLF BH2 ... 14 C6
  WEND SO18 ... 107 L6
Norwood Pl BOSC BH5 ... 237 G3
Nottingham Pl
  LSOL/BMARY PO13 ... 208 C1
Nouale La RGWD BH24 ... 171 H1
Novello Gdns WVILLE PO7 ... 164 C3
Noyce Dr ELGH SO50 ... 83 J7
Noyce Gdns CHAR BH8 ... 221 M6
Nuffield Rd CFDH BH17 ... 218 A5
Nugent Rd SBNE BH6 ... 237 L4
Nunns Pk RSAL SP5 ... 47 G4
Nuns Rd WINC SO23 ... 3 H4
Nuns Wk WINC SO23 ... 3 J2
Nunton Dro RSAL SP5 ... 43 J4
Nursery Cl EMRTH PO10 ... 166 D5
  LSOL/BMARY PO13 ... 184 F5
Nursery Fld LISS GU33 ... 36 D5
Nursery Gdns CHFD SO53 ... 81 H5
  FUFL SO22 ... 2 B7
  HORN PO8 ... 140 E3
  ITCH SO19 ... 132 F2
  NMIL/BTOS BH25 ... 226 A4
  UPTN BH16 ... 232 B2
Nursery Gv HEND SO30 ... 134 A3
Nursery La FHAM/STUB PO14 ... 184 A2
  MOOR/WNTN BH9 ... 220 E5
  RGWD BH24 ... 170 E2
  WEND SO18 ... 107 J7
Nursling Crs HAV PO9 ... 165 L3
Nursling Gn CHAR BH8 ... 221 H6
Nursling St ROWN SO16 ... 103 H3
Nutash FHAM PO15 ... 159 G4
Nutbeem Rd ELGH SO50 ... 81 M6
Nutbourne Rd CHAM PO6 ... 188 B1
  HISD PO11 ... 214 C7
Nutburn Rd NBAD SO52 ... 80 A3
Nutfield Ct ROWN SO16 ... 105 K5
Nutfield Pl PSEA PO1 ... 211 H2
Nutfield Rd ROWN SO16 ... 105 J2
Nuthatch Cl CFDH BH17 ... 232 E1
  HAV PO9 ... 141 M7
Nutley Cl BWD BH11 ... 219 K4
Nutley Rd HAV PO9 ... 165 H3
Nutley Wy BWD BH11 ... 219 K5
Nutsey Av TOTT SO40 ... 104 C4
Nutsey La TOTT SO40 ... 104 C6
Nutshalling Av ROWN SO16 ... 105 K3
Nutshalling Cl TOTT SO40 ... 104 B7
Nutwick Rd HAV PO9 ... 9 L1
Nutwood Wy TOTT SO40 ... 104 D6
Nyewood Av
  FHAM/PORC PO16 ... 162 B7
Nyria Wy GPORT PO12 ... 11 J4

O

Oakapple Gdns CHAM PO6 ... 164 C8
Oak Av CHCH/BSGR BH23 ... 222 B8
Oakbank Rd ELGH SO50 ... 82 B5
  ITCH SO19 ... 132 C5
Oak Cl BPWT SO32 ... 84 E3
  FAWY SO45 ... 155 J7
  FERN BH22 ... 194 C7
  HORN PO8 ... 140 C6
  LYND SO43 ... 151 K4
  RSAL SP5 ... 18 B1
  WIMB BH21 ... 217 G3
  WSHM SO15 ... 130 A1
Oak Coppice Cl ELGH SO50 ... 82 F6
Oakcroft La FHAM/STUB PO14 ... 184 A3
Oakdale La PLE BH15 ... 233 K2
Oakdene LSOL/BMARY PO13 ... 185 H7
  TOTT SO40 ... 128 F1
Oakdene Cl WIMB BH21 ... 192 B3
Oakdown Rd
  FHAM/STUB PO14 ... 184 B5
Oak Dr ELGH SO50 ... 83 H6
Oakenbrow FAWY SO45 ... 155 H6
  LYMN SO41 ... 200 E5
The Oakes FHAM/STUB PO14 ... 183 M4
Oakfield Ct HAV PO9 ... 165 M3
Oakfield Rd PLE BH15 ... 233 H2
  TOTT SO40 ... 127 M1
  TOTT SO40 ... 104 E8
Oakfields ELGH SO50 ... 81 M1
Oak Gdns LYMN SO41 ... 227 H8
Oak Green Wy WEND SO18 ... 107 M8
Oakgrove Rd ELGH SO50 ... 82 D6
Oakhill HLER SO31 ... 133 M7
Oakhill Cl CHFD SO53 ... 81 K3
  HLER SO31 ... 133 M7
Oakhurst Cl FERN BH22 ... 168 D6
  HLER SO31 ... 157 G2
Oakhurst Dr WVILLE PO7 ... 140 E8
Oakhurst Gdns CHAM PO6 ... 163 M6
Oakhurst La FERN BH22 ... 168 D6
Oakhurst Rd FERN BH22 ... 168 D6
  PTSW SO17 ... 106 F5
Oakhurst Wy HLER SO31 ... 157 G2
Oakland Dr TOTT SO40 ... 130 D7
Oaklands LYMN SO41 ... 228 D6
Oaklands Av TOTT SO40 ... 129 K1
Oaklands Cl FBDG SP6 ... 97 K6
Oaklands Gdns
  FHAM/STUB PO14 ... 159 G7
Oaklands Gv HORN PO8 ... 140 C5
Oaklands Wy FAWY SO45 ... 9 H4
  PSF GU32 ... 63 K4
The Oaklands CHFD SO53 ... 81 H5
Oaklands Wy FAWY SO45 ... 155 G6
  FHAM/STUB PO14 ... 159 G7

ROWN SO16 ... 106 E4
Oakland Wk FERN BH22 ... 194 C7
Oak La RGWD BH24 ... 146 F8
Oakleigh Crs TOTT SO40 ... 129 J2
Oakleigh Dr RSAL SP5 ... 75 J7
Oakleigh Gdns ROMY SO51 ... 78 F1
Oakleigh Wy CHCH/BSGR BH23... 239 L1
Oakley Cl FAWY SO45 ... 180 A4
Oakley Hl WIMB BH21 ... 192 B5
Oakley La WIMB BH21 ... 192 B6
Oakley Rd HAV PO9 ... 165 H3
  ROMY SO51 ... 21 K6
  ROWN SO16 ... 105 L8
  WIMB BH21 ... 192 B6
Oakley Straight WIMB BH21 ... 192 C7
Oakmead Gdns BWD BH11 ... 219 K4
Oakmeadow Cl EMRTH PO10 ... 166 E5
Oakmead Rd CFDH BH17 ... 232 F1
Oakmont Dr WVILLE PO7 ... 140 D6
Oakmount Av CHFD SO53 ... 81 J4
  PTSW SO17 ... 106 F7
  TOTT SO40 ... 104 E8
Oakmount Rd CHFD SO53 ... 81 J4
Oak Park Dr HAV PO9 ... 9 G1
Oakridge Rd WSHM SO15 ... 105 J8
Oak Rd BPWT SO32 ... 85 J8
  CHAR BH8 ... 236 B2
  FAWY SO45 ... 155 J7
  FBDG SP6 ... 121 K3
  FHAM PO15 ... 6 A4
  HAV PO9 ... 133 J8
  HORN PO8 ... 116 B3
  ITCH SO19 ... 132 B6
  NMIL/BTOS BH25 ... 226 A4
  UPTN BH16 ... 232 B2
Oaks Coppice HORN PO8 ... 140 E2
Oaks Dr RGWD BH24 ... 169 H5
Oakshott Dr HAV PO9 ... 165 L3
Oaks Md VWD BH31 ... 144 E2
The Oaks HLER SO31 ... 133 K8
  ITCH SO19 ... 132 D3
  VWD BH31 ... 144 C1
Oak St GPORT PO12 ... 11 H3
Oakthorn Cl
  LSOL/BMARY PO13 ... 209 G2
Oak Tree Cl RWIN SO21 ... 54 E8
Oak Tree Dr EMRTH PO10 ... 166 C4
  LISS GU33 ... 36 F4
Oak Tree Farm RCCH PO18 ... 167 M7
Oak Tree Gdns HEND SO30 ... 133 M2
Oak Tree Rd WEND SO18 ... 107 J7
Oak Tree Wy ELGH SO50 ... 81 M3
Oak V HEND SO30 ... 108 A5
Oakwood Av HAV PO9 ... 164 F5
  NMIL/BTOS BH25 ... 226 A4
  RWIN SO21 ... 54 B5
Oakwood Cl HLER SO31 ... 158 B8
  MOOR/WNTN BH9 ... 220 F6
  ROMY SO51 ... 51 H7
  RWIN SO21 ... 54 B4
Oakwood Ct HEND SO30 ... 108 D6
Oakwood Dr ROWN SO16 ... 106 A3
Oakwood Rd
  CHCH/BSGR BH23 ... 224 C7
  CHFD SO53 ... 53 J8
  HISD PO11 ... 213 K5
  MOOR/WNTN BH9 ... 220 E6
  NEND PO2 ... 187 G3
Oakwood Wy HLER SO31 ... 157 L5
Oates Rd MOOR/WNTN BH9 ... 220 C7
Oatfield Gdns TOTT SO40 ... 104 B7
Oatlands ROMY SO51 ... 50 E8
Oatlands Cl BPWT SO32 ... 109 L7
Oatlands Rd BPWT SO32 ... 109 L7
Oban Rd TWDS BH3 ... 235 K1
Obelisk Rd ITCH SO19 ... 132 B6
Oberfield Rd BROC SO42 ... 175 H6
Oberon Cl WVILLE PO7 ... 140 E8
Ober Rd BROC SO42 ... 175 J6
Occupation La
  FHAM/STUB PO14 ... 183 J1
Ocean Cl FHAM PO15 ... 6 B3
Ocean Rd FHAM/STUB PO14 ... 184 D3
Ocean Wy SHAM SO14 ... 5 J8
Ockendon Cl SSEA PO5 ... 13 H4
Ocknell Gv FAWY SO45 ... 155 C5
O'connell Rd ELGH SO50 ... 81 K6
Octavia Gdns CHFD SO53 ... 81 L1
Octavia Hl FUFL SO22 ... 26 C2
Octavia Rd WEND SO18 ... 107 K4
Octavius Ct WVILLE PO7 ... 140 F7
Odell Cl FHAM/PORC PO16 ... 6 E1
Odiham Cl ROWN SO16 ... 105 L4
Odstock Rd RSAL SP5 ... 43 K1
Oglander Rd WINC SO23 ... 3 H3
Ogle Rd SHAM SO14 ... 4 F3
Okeford Rd BDST BH18 ... 217 M6
Okement Cl WEND SO18 ... 108 A5
Olave Cl LSOL/BMARY PO13 ... 208 C2
Old Agwi Rd FAWY SO45 ... 181 G3
Old Barn Cl
  CHCH/BSGR BH23 ... 222 B6
  RGWD BH24 ... 170 F2
Oldbarn Cl TOTT SO40 ... 104 B6
Old Barn Crs WVILLE PO7 ... 114 B2
Old Barn Farm Rd WIMB BH21 ... 168 C3
Old Barn Rd CHCH/BSGR BH23 ... 222 B6
Old Bound Rd UPTN BH16 ... 232 B2
Old Brickyard Rd FBDG SP6 ... 97 G5
Old Bridge House Rd
  HLER SO31 ... 133 M8
Old Bridge Rd ENEY PO4 ... 13 M8
  LTDN BH7 ... 222 B8
Oldbury Ct ROWN SO16 ... 105 J4
Oldbury Wy FHAM/STUB PO14 ... 160 A8
Old Canal ENEY PO4 ... 211 M4
Old Christchurch Rd BMTH BH1 .. 15 C5
  LYMN SO41 ... 227 H8
Old Coastguard Rd CCLF BH13 ... 245 G4
Old Commercial Rd
  PSEA PO1 ... 211 G3
Old Common HLER SO31 ... 158 C5
Old Common Gdns HLER SO31 ... 158 C5
Old Copse Rd HAV PO9 ... 8 F2
Old Cracknore Cl TOTT SO40 ... 130 D6
Old Down RWIN SO21 ... 56 A1
Oldenburg HLER SO31 ... 134 F8
Old Farm Cl RGWD BH24 ... 147 G4

Old Farm Dr WEND SO18 ... 107 L6
Old Farm La EMRTH PO10 ... 166 F5
  FHAM/STUB PO14 ... 184 A7
Old Farm Rd PLE BH15 ... 233 K2
Old Farm Wk LYMN SO41 ... 228 B3
Old Farm Wy CHAM PO6 ... 188 C1
Old Forge Rd WIMB BH21 ... 193 K2
Old Garden Cl
  FHAM/STUB PO14 ... 159 G6
Old Gdns FUFL SO22 ... 2 B7
Oldgate Gdns NEND PO2 ... 187 K4
Old Gosport Rd
  FHAM/PORC PO16 ... 7 K8
Old Ham La WIMB BH21 ... 193 H4
Old Hillside Rd FUFL SO22 ... 16 B7
Oldhouse La HAV PO9 ... 143 H2
  ROMY SO51 ... 76 D1
Old Ivy La WEND SO18 ... 108 A6
Old Kennels Cl FUFL SO22 ... 25 M5
Old Kennels La RWIN SO21 ... 25 K7
Old Kiln Rd UPTN BH16 ... 232 B1
Old Litten La PSF GU32 ... 35 H5
Old Lyndhurst Rd WEND SO18 ... 102 L8
Old Magazine Cl TOTT SO40 ... 130 D6
Old Manor Cl WIMB BH21 ... 192 C4
Old Manor Wy CHAM PO6 ... 187 M1
Old Market Rd WIMB BH21 ... 216 C1
Old Mill Cl EPSF GU31 ... 64 A3
  HORN PO8 ... 115 C8
Old Mill Wy ROWN SO16 ... 105 M7
Old Milton Gn
  NMIL/BTOS BH25 ... 225 K7
Old Milton Rd
  NMIL/BTOS BH25 ... 225 K7
Old Mulberry Cl NBNE BH10 ... 219 L7
Old Orch PLE BH15 ... 233 H7
Old Orchards LYMN SO41 ... 228 D6
Old Parsonage Ct RWIN SO21 ... 54 E8
Old Pines Cl FERN BH22 ... 194 C4
Old Priory Cl HLER SO31 ... 157 L6
Old Priory Rd SBNE BH6 ... 237 L4
Old Rectory Cl EMRTH PO10 ... 166 F5
Old Rectory Gdns WINC SO23 ... 17 J2
Old Rectory La RWIN SO21 ... 54 F1
Old Rectory Rd CHAM PO6 ... 164 C8
Old Redbridge Rd WSHM SO15... 103 H8
Old Reservoir Rd CHAM PO6 ... 188 B1
Old River WVILLE PO7 ... 139 K5
Old Rd GPORT PO12 ... 11 H5
  ROMY SO51 ... 50 F8
  SHAM SO14 ... 5 J7
The Old Rd CHAM PO6 ... 187 K2
Old Romsey Rd TOTT SO40 ... 102 D8
The Old Rope Wk PLE BH15... 232 E7
Old Salisbury La ROMY SO51 ... 49 K7
Old Salisbury Rd ROMY SO51 ... 103 K1
Old Sawmill Cl VWD BH31 ... 144 C2
Old School Cl FAWY SO45 ... 179 M2
  FERN BH22 ... 194 A3
  HLER SO31 ... 157 H1
Old School Dr HISD PO11 ... 213 M6
Old School Gdns HEND SO30 ... 108 D4
Old School Rd LISS GU33 ... 36 E4
Old Shamblehurst La
  HEND SO30 ... 109 H4
Old Stacks Gdns RGWD BH24 ... 171 G2
Old Star PSEA PO1 ... 12 C1
Old Station Ap WINC SO23 ... 3 K8
Old St John's Ms NBNE BH10 ... 220 D5
Old St FHAM/STUB PO14 ... 183 M5
Old Timbers HISD PO11 ... 213 K5
Old Tpk FHAM/PORC PO16 ... 7 J2
Old Vicarage La NBNE BH10 ... 220 C2
Old Vineries FBDG SP6 ... 97 J7
Old Wareham Rd
  BKME/WDN BH12 ... 233 M1
  UPTN BH16 ... 216 E6
The Old Well Cl ITCH SO19 ... 133 H3
Old Winchester Hill La
  BPWT SO32 ... 59 L5
  PSF GU32 ... 60 B7
Old Wymering La CHAM PO6 ... 163 J8
Oleander Cl HLER SO31 ... 158 E3
Olive Crs FHAM/PORC PO16 ... 186 B2
Olive Rd ROWN SO16 ... 105 M4
Oliver Rd ENEY PO4 ... 211 K5
  LYMN SO41 ... 228 A5
  WEND SO18 ... 107 J5
Oliver's Battery Crs FUFL SO22 ... 26 A4
Oliver's Battery Gdns
  FUFL SO22 ... 26 A3
Oliver's Battery Rd North
  FUFL SO22 ... 26 A3
Oliver's Battery Rd South
  FUFL SO22 ... 26 A5
Olivers Cl TOTT SO40 ... 128 F1
Olivers Rd WIMB BH21 ... 192 E2
Olivers Wy WIMB BH21 ... 192 E2
Olivia Cl WVILLE PO7 ... 140 E7
Olympic Wy ELGH SO50 ... 82 F5
  ELGH SO50 ... 83 G5
Omdurman Rd PTSW SO17 ... 106 F6
Omega St SSEA PO5 ... 13 J2
Onibury Cl WEND SO18 ... 107 M7
Onibury Rd WEND SO18 ... 107 M7
Onslow Gdns WIMB BH21 ... 192 B2
Onslow Rd SHAM SO14 ... 131 L2
  SSEA PO5 ... 13 K9
Ophir Gdns BMTH BH1 ... 15 K3
Ophir Rd CHAR BH8 ... 15 J1
  NEND PO2 ... 187 H6
Oracle Dr WVILLE PO7 ... 164 C5
Orange Gv
  LSOL/BMARY PO13 ... 185 H7
Orange Rw EMRTH PO10 ... 166 D8
Oratory Gdns CCLF BH13 ... 234 B8
Orchard Av ELGH SO50 ... 82 E7
  PSTN BH14 ... 233 L6
Orchard Cl CHCH/BSGR BH23 ... 237 M2
  EPSF GU31 ... 93 K4
  FAWY SO45 ... 180 F5
  FBDG SP6 ... 97 L6
  FERN BH22 ... 194 C3
  GPORT PO12 ... 185 L7
  HORN PO8 ... 141 G2
  NBAD SO52 ... 79 L3
  RGWD BH24 ... 146 E8
  RWIN SO21 ... 54 E1

TOTT SO40 .... 129 K3
WIMB BH21 .... 217 H1
Orchard Ct HEND SO30 .... 134 C1
VWD BH31 .... 144 E3 🔟
Orchard Gdns FBDG SP6 .... 97 L7 🔟
Orchard Gv FHAM/PORC PO16 .... 185 L1
HORN PO8 .... 140 D5
NMIL/BTOS BH25 .... 225 L7
Orchard La EMRTH PO10 .... 166 B6
ROMY SO51 .... 78 D1
SHAM SO14 .... 5 H5
WIMB BH21 .... 217 H1
Orchardlea BPWT SO32 .... 112 A5
Orchard Pl SHAM SO14 .... 5 C7
Orchard Rd ELGH SO50 .... 83 H6
ENEY PO4 .... 13 M3
GPORT PO12 .... 210 D2
HAV PO9 .... 8 F6
HISD PO11 .... 213 L6
HLER SO31 .... 158 C6
RSAL SP5 .... 73 J1
Orchard St WCLF BH2 .... 14 D6
Orchards Wy HEND SO30 .... 108 C7 🔟
PTSW SO17 .... 106 F6
The Orchard BWD BH11 .... 219 H2
CHAM PO6 .... 187 K1
CHCH/BSGR BH23 .... 198 A8 🔟
LYMN SO41 .... 242 C4
ROWN SO16 .... 80 D7
WVILLE PO7 .... 139 K6
Orchard Wy FAWY SO45 .... 155 J6
Orcheston Rd CHAR BH8 .... 236 B2
Ordnance Rd GPORT PO12 .... 11 J3
WSHM SO15 .... 131 L2
Ordnance Rw PSEA PO1 .... 12 C2
Ordnance Wy TOTT SO40 .... 130 E5
Oregon Cl ITCH SO19 .... 132 E4
Orford Cl CHCH/BSGR BH23 .... 222 B4
Oriel Dr FHAM/STUB PO14 .... 159 G6
Oriel Rd NEND PO2 .... 187 H6
Orient Dr FUFL SO22 .... 16 E5
Orion Cl FHAM/STUB PO14 .... 184 B6 🔟
ROWN SO16 .... 105 L4
Orkney Cl ROWN SO16 .... 105 K4
Orkney Rd CHAM PO6 .... 163 K7
Ormesby Dr CHFD SO53 .... 53 C8
Ormond Cl ELGH SO50 .... 83 C5
Ormsby Rd SSEA PO5 .... 13 H6 🔟
Orpen Rd ITCH SO19 .... 133 G5 🔟
Orsmond Cl WVILLE PO7 .... 164 C7 🔟
Orwell Cl ROWN SO16 .... 105 K7 🔟
Orwell Crs FHAM/STUB PO14 .... 159 G6
Orwell Rd PSF GU32 .... 63 K4
Osborn Crs
LSOL/BMARY PO13 .... 184 F4
Osborne Cl WVILLE PO7 .... 164 E1 🔟
Osborne Dr CHFD SO53 .... 81 K3
Osborne Gdns ELGH SO50 .... 83 J7 🔟
Osborne Rd GPORT PO12 .... 11 J1
HLER SO31 .... 158 A8
LSOL/BMARY PO13 .... 208 C2 🔟
MOOR/WNTN BH9 .... 220 C8
NMIL/BTOS BH25 .... 225 M5
PSF GU32 .... 63 L4
PSTN BH14 .... 234 A5
SSEA PO5 .... 12 F1
TOTT SO40 .... 129 L1
WIMB BH21 .... 192 B4
Osborne Rd North PTSW SO17 .... 107 H7
Osborne Rd South PTSW SO17 .... 107 H7
Osborne View Rd
FHAM/STUB PO14 .... 183 L7
Osborn Rd FHAM/PORC PO16 .... 7 K5
Osborn Rd South
FHAM/PORC PO16 .... 7 J5
Osier Cl NEND PO2 .... 187 G6
Oslands Dr HLER SO31 .... 158 B1
Osprey Cl CHCH/BSGR BH23 .... 238 F3
ROWN SO16 .... 106 A3
TOTT SO40 .... 130 C7
Osprey Dr HISD PO11 .... 213 M5
Osprey Gdns
LSOL/BMARY PO13 .... 208 D2 🔟
Osprey Quay EMRTH PO10 .... 190 F1
Ossemsley South Dr
NMIL/BTOS BH25 .... 199 J8
Osterley Cl HEND SO30 .... 134 C1
Osterly Rd ITCH SO19 .... 132 C4
Oswald Cl MOOR/WNTN BH9 .... 220 C6
Oswald Rd MOOR/WNTN BH9 .... 220 C6
Othello Dr WVILLE PO7 .... 140 E6
Otterbourne Crs HAV PO9 .... 165 H3
Otterbourne Hl CHFD SO53 .... 53 M7
Otterbourne Rd RWIN SO21 .... 54 B4
Otter Cl ELGH SO50 .... 82 F6
UPTN BH16 .... 232 C4
VWD BH31 .... 144 E3
Otter Rd PLE BH15 .... 233 L2
Otters Wk NMIL/BTOS BH25 .... 226 A2
Ouse Cl CHFD SO53 .... 52 F7
Outer Cir ROWN SO16 .... 105 M4
Outlands La HEND SO30 .... 135 H2
Outram Rd SSEA PO5 .... 13 K5
Oval Gdns GPORT PO12 .... 10 A4
Oval Rd ROMY SO51 .... 20 E8
The Oval LISS GU33 .... 36 E4
Overbrook FAWY SO45 .... 155 K6
Overbrook Wy NBAD SO52 .... 79 K3 🔟
Overbury Rd PSTN BH14 .... 234 B5
Overcliff Ri ROWN SO16 .... 106 D4
Overcombe Cl CFDH BH17 .... 218 C5
Over Links Dr PSTN BH14 .... 234 C6
Overstand Crs LYMN SO41 .... 242 C4
Overton Crs HAV PO9 .... 165 H3
Oviat Cl TOTT SO40 .... 128 F1
Ovington Av ITCH SO19 .... 237 H1
Ovington Gdns LTDN BH7 .... 237 H1
Owen Cl LSOL/BMARY PO13 .... 209 G1
Owen Rd ELGH SO50 .... 81 G6
Owen's Rd FUFL SO22 .... 2 E1
Owen St ENEY PO4 .... 211 L4
Owls Rd BOSC BH5 .... 236 D5
VWD BH31 .... 144 E3
Owslebury Bottom
RWIN SO21 .... 55 M3
Owslebury Gv HAV PO9 .... 165 K3
Oxburgh Cl ELGH SO50 .... 81 L3

Oxford Av SBNE BH6 .... 237 G3
SHAM SO14 .... 5 H1
Oxford Cl FHAM/PORC PO16 .... 6 F3
Oxford La BPWT SO32 .... 112 E1
BWD BH11 .... 219 M2
Oxford Rd BMTH BH1 .... 15 J4
GPORT PO12 .... 10 A1
SHAM SO14 .... 131 L1
SSEA PO5 .... 13 L6
Oxford St SHAM SO14 .... 5 H6
Oxlease Cl ROMY SO51 .... 50 F7
Oxleys Cl FHAM/STUB PO14 .... 159 M8
Oxted Ct ENEY PO4 .... 211 M3 🔟
Oyster Ms PSEA PO1 .... 12 C5 🔟
Oyster Quay CHAM PO6 .... 186 F2
Oyster St PSEA PO1 .... 12 C5
Ozier Rd WEND SO18 .... 107 M6

P

Pacific Cl SHAM SO14 .... 5 K8
Packridge La ROMY SO51 .... 79 L7
Padbury Cl NEND PO2 .... 187 K4 🔟
Paddington Gv BWD BH11 .... 219 H5
Paddington Rd NEND PO2 .... 187 K7
Paddock Cl
BKME/WDN BH12 .... 234 A1 🔟
RGWD BH24 .... 169 K4
WIMB BH21 .... 193 L2
Paddock End WVILLE PO7 .... 139 K5
Paddock Gdns LYMN SO41 .... 228 B3
Paddock Gv VWD BH31 .... 144 E3
The Paddocks FAWY SO45 .... 180 F5 🔟
The Paddock BROC SO42 .... 175 K7 🔟
ELGH SO50 .... 82 A2 🔟
FBDG SP6 .... 123 J2
FHAM/STUB PO14 .... 184 A4 🔟
GPORT PO12 .... 10 C5
TOTT SO40 .... 104 B6
WINC SO23 .... 17 H2
Paddock Wy PSF GU32 .... 63 J6
Padfield Cl SBNE BH6 .... 237 K2
Padget Rd RGWD BH24 .... 147 G7 🔟
Padnell Av HORN PO8 .... 140 E6
WVILLE PO7 .... 113 L8
Padnell Rd HORN PO8 .... 140 F5
Padstow Pl FBDG SP6 .... 97 K8
Padwell Rd SHAM SO14 .... 131 L1
Padwick Av CHAM PO6 .... 163 L8
Paffard Cl LSOL/BMARY PO13 .... 209 G1
Page Cl FAWY SO45 .... 180 B6
Pages La BROC SO42 .... 204 A3
Paget Cl WIMB BH21 .... 192 E1
Paget Rd BWD BH11 .... 219 L4
GPORT PO12 .... 10 C8
Paget St SHAM SO14 .... 5 K5
Pagham Cl EMRTH PO10 .... 166 E8
Pagham Gdns HISD PO11 .... 214 D6
Paignton Av HSEA PO3 .... 187 L8
Paignton Rd ROWN SO16 .... 105 L8
Pain's Rd SSEA PO5 .... 13 J4
Painswick Cl CHAM PO6 .... 163 G8
HLER SO31 .... 158 D2
Paisley Rd SBNE BH6 .... 237 H3
Palace La BROC SO42 .... 178 E7
Palfrey Rd NBNE BH10 .... 220 B4
Palk Rd HAV PO9 .... 8 B4
Pallant Gdns
FHAM/PORC PO16 .... 161 H6
The Pallant HAV PO9 .... 8 F4
Pallet Cl RWIN SO21 .... 54 E8
Pallot Cl HLER SO31 .... 133 K8
Palmer Pl NMIL/BTOS BH25 .... 225 L4
Palmer Rd PLE BH15 .... 233 H3
Palmers Cl ELGH SO50 .... 83 J6 🔟
Palmers Rd EMRTH PO10 .... 166 D7
Palmerston Av
CHCH/BSGR BH23 .... 238 C2
FHAM/PORC PO16 .... 7 K5
Palmerston Cl UPTN BH16 .... 232 C1 🔟
Palmerston Dr
FHAM/STUB PO14 .... 184 E1
Palmerston Ms BMTH BH1 .... 236 D3 🔟
Palmerston Rd BOSC BH5 .... 236 D4 🔟
HISD PO11 .... 213 L4
PSTN BH14 .... 234 C4
SSEA PO5 .... 5 G2
SSEA PO5 .... 13 H8
UPTN BH16 .... 232 B1
Palmerston St ROMY SO51 .... 78 D1 🔟
ROMY SO51 .... 78 E1
Palmerston Wy GPORT PO12 .... 209 J6
Palm Hall Cl WINC SO23 .... 3 L8
Palm Rd ROWN SO16 .... 105 L5
Palmyra Rd GPORT PO12 .... 209 L1
Pamela Av CHAM PO6 .... 162 D8
Pamplyn Cl LYMN SO41 .... 228 A4
Pangbourne Av CHAM PO6 .... 187 M1
Pangbourne Cl ITCH SO19 .... 132 E4
Pannall Rd GPORT PO12 .... 209 L1
Panorama Rd CCLF BH13 .... 245 G4
Pan St PSEA PO1 .... 211 G2
Pansy Rd ROWN SO16 .... 106 F4
Pantheon Rd CHFD SO53 .... 81 L1
The Pantiles FBDG SP6 .... 97 J7 🔟
Panton Cl EMRTH PO10 .... 166 C5 🔟
Panwell Rd WEND SO18 .... 132 E1
The Parade PSEA PO1 .... 210 E2
Paradise La BPWT SO32 .... 111 K2
EMRTH PO10 .... 166 A4
FHAM/PORC PO16 .... 161 J6
TOTT SO40 .... 128 B2
Paradise St PLE BH15 .... 233 G7 🔟
PSEA PO1 .... 13 H1
Parchment St WINC SO23 .... 3 C5
The Parchment HAV PO9 .... 8 E5
Pardoe Cl HEND SO30 .... 134 A3
Parham Dr ELGH SO50 .... 81 L4
Parham Rd GPORT PO12 .... 210 A2
NBNE BH10 .... 220 A6
Parish Rd PLE BH15 .... 233 K5
Park Av LYMN SO41 .... 228 B4
NBNE BH10 .... 220 A2
WINC SO23 .... 3 H6
WVILLE PO7 .... 164 A5
Park Cl BROC SO42 .... 175 L4
Partridge Cl
CHCH/BSGR BH23 .... 238 F3 🔟
FHAM/PORC PO16 .... 161 J8 🔟
Partridge Down FUFL SO22 .... 26 A5

CHCH/BSGR BH23 .... 223 C5
FAWY SO45 .... 155 M4
GPORT PO12 .... 209 K2
LYMN SO41 .... 242 D3
NMIL/BTOS BH25 .... 226 A3
TOTT SO40 .... 130 B7
WINC SO23 .... 3 C2
Park Crs EMRTH PO10 .... 166 B7
Park Dr VWD BH31 .... 144 C1
Parker Cl GPORT PO12 .... 185 L7
Parker Gdns WVILLE PO7 .... 164 A6
Park Farm Av FHAM PO15 .... 160 A4
Park Farm Cl FHAM PO15 .... 6 A1
Park Farm Rd WVILLE PO7 .... 164 B4
Park Gln FHAM PO15 .... 159 C4
Park Gv CHAM PO6 .... 187 K1
Park Hill Cl FAWY SO45 .... 180 A5
Park Homer Dr WIMB BH21 .... 192 D2
Park Homer Rd WIMB BH21 .... 192 D1 🔟
Park House Farm Wy HAV PO9 .... 164 F3
Park Lake Rd PLE BH15 .... 233 K6
Parkland Cl VWD BH31 .... 145 H4
Parkland Dr NMIL/BTOS BH25 .... 225 M8
Parklands HLER SO31 .... 158 E4
WEND SO18 .... 107 K7
Parklands Av HORN PO8 .... 140 E3
Parklands Cl CHFD SO53 .... 81 H1
Park La BPWT SO32 .... 86 D3
BPWT SO32 .... 87 G7
CHAM PO6 .... 187 L1
ELGH SO50 .... 54 A8
EMRTH PO10 .... 142 F8
FAWY SO45 .... 179 M4
FBDG SP6 .... 121 K2
FHAM/STUB PO14 .... 184 A5
HAV PO9 .... 141 C8
HAV PO9 .... 165 G5
HORN PO8 .... 140 E6
LYMN SO41 .... 230 F2
LYMN SO41 .... 242 D4
NBNE BH10 .... 220 D4
RWIN SO21 .... 17 J2
RWIN SO21 .... 54 F3
TOTT SO40 .... 130 A6
WIMB BH21 .... 192 A4
Park Pde HAV PO9 .... 165 J4 🔟
Park Rd BMTH BH1 .... 15 H3
BPWT SO32 .... 84 F3
CHFD SO53 .... 53 H8
EMRTH PO10 .... 167 H7
FBDG SP6 .... 97 L6
FUFL SO22 .... 2 E2
GPORT PO12 .... 10 F7
HISD PO11 .... 213 C4
LYMN SO41 .... 228 B4
LYMN SO41 .... 242 D4
NMIL/BTOS BH25 .... 225 K7
NMIL/BTOS BH25 .... 226 A3
PLE BH15 .... 233 L5
PSEA PO1 .... 12 D2
PSF GU32 .... 63 L5
WSHM SO15 .... 131 G2
WVILLE PO7 .... 139 K3
WVILLE PO7 .... 164 A4
Park Rd North HAV PO9 .... 8 D3
Park Rd South HAV PO9 .... 8 E5
Parkside CHCH/BSGR BH23 .... 224 B7
HAV PO9 .... 165 G6
RGWD BH24 .... 170 D2
TOTT SO40 .... 129 K3
Parkside Gdns NBNE BH10 .... 220 C6 🔟
Parkside Rd PSTN BH14 .... 234 B4
Parkside Rd FUFL SO22 .... 16 B6
Parkstone Av ENEY PO4 .... 13 L9
PSTN BH14 .... 234 C4
Parkstone Hts PSTN BH14 .... 233 L3
Parkstone Rd PLE BH15 .... 233 K5
Park St GPORT PO12 .... 10 F2
ROWN SO16 .... 106 A8
SSEA PO5 .... 12 F4
The Park BPWT SO32 .... 86 F7
NMIL/BTOS BH25 .... 240 B1
Park Vw HEND SO30 .... 133 M1
HEND SO30 .... 134 C1
Parkville Rd ROWN SO16 .... 107 J4
Park Wk SHAM SO14 .... 5 G2
Parkwater Rd RSAL SP5 .... 47 H7
Park Wy FERN BH22 .... 168 C6 🔟
HAV PO9 .... 8 D4
Parkway FHAM PO15 .... 159 C4
Parkway Rd CHAR BH8 .... 221 J8
Parkway Gdns CHFD SO53 .... 81 H1
The Parkway
LSOL/BMARY PO13 .... 184 F6
ROWN SO16 .... 106 F3
Parkwood Rd BOSC BH5 .... 236 F4
WIMB BH21 .... 192 A4
Parley Cl FERN BH22 .... 194 D7
Parley La CHCH/BSGR BH23 .... 194 D8
Parley Rd MOOR/WNTN BH9 .... 220 E6
Parliament Pl FUFL SO22 .... 26 A1
Parmiter Dr WIMB BH21 .... 192 C4
Parmiter Rd WIMB BH21 .... 192 C4
Parmiter Wy WIMB BH21 .... 192 C4
Parnell La ROMY SO51 .... 22 F6
Parnell Rd ELGH SO50 .... 81 L6
Parr Rd CHAM PO6 .... 163 H8 🔟
Parr St PSTN BH14 .... 233 M4
Parry Rd ITCH SO19 .... 133 H4
Parsonage Barn La
RGWD BH24 .... 146 E8
Parsonage Cl EPSF GU31 .... 64 A3
Parsonage Est EPSF GU31 .... 65 K4
Parsonage Hl RSAL SP5 .... 18 A1
Parsonage La BPWT SO32 .... 110 A2
Parsonage Park Dr FBDG SP6 .... 97 K6
Parsons Cl HSEA PO3 .... 187 K4

Partridge Dr PSTN BH14 .... 234 A7
Partridge Gdns HORN PO8 .... 140 B4
Partridge Gn
NMIL/BTOS BH25 .... 225 M2
Partridge Hl RSAL SP5 .... 75 M5
Partridge Rd BROC SO42 .... 175 K8
FAWY SO45 .... 155 K7
Partridge Wk PSTN BH14 .... 234 B7 🔟
Partry Cl CHFD SO53 .... 52 F8
Pascoe Cl PSTN BH14 .... 233 M4
Passage La HLER SO31 .... 157 M7
Passfield Av ELGH SO50 .... 81 K6
Passfield Cl ELGH SO50 .... 81 K6 🔟
Passford Hl LYMN SO41 .... 228 D1
Passingham Wk HORN PO8 .... 140 E4
The Pastures
FHAM/STUB PO14 .... 159 G4 🔟
NARL SO24 .... 30 D2
WVILLE PO7 .... 139 J5 🔟
Pat Bear Cl WSHM SO15 .... 105 H8
Patchins Rd UPTN BH16 .... 232 A4
Patchway Dr
FHAM/STUB PO14 .... 160 A8
Paternoster Rw WINC SO23 .... 3 H8
Patricia Cl HEND SO30 .... 108 C6
Patricia Dr HEND SO30 .... 134 B1
Patrick's Cl LISS GU33 .... 36 F4
Paulet Cl WEND SO18 .... 107 M7
Paulet Lacave Av ROWN SO16 .... 105 J2
Paulet Pl FUFL SO22 .... 26 D3
Pauletts La TOTT SO40 .... 104 A5
Paulsgrove Rd NEND PO2 .... 187 K8
Pauls La LYMN SO41 .... 201 H8
Paulson Cl CHFD SO53 .... 53 H8
Pauncefoot Hl ROMY SO51 .... 78 B3
Pauncefote Rd BOSC BH5 .... 236 F3 🔟
Pauntley Rd CHCH/BSGR BH23 .... 238 D3
Pavan Gdns NBNE BH10 .... 220 A5
Pavilion Cl ELGH SO50 .... 83 H8
Pavilion Rd HEND SO30 .... 109 J8
Paxton Cl HEND SO30 .... 134 B3 🔟
Paxton Rd FHAM/STUB PO14 .... 6 F6
Payne Cl WIMB BH21 .... 168 C3
Paynes Hay Rd ROMY SO51 .... 23 G8
Payne's Rd WSHM SO15 .... 130 F2
Peace Cl CHCH/BSGR BH23 .... 197 L8
Peach Rd ROWN SO16 .... 105 M4
Peacock Cl FHAM/PORC PO16 .... 161 J8
Peacock La PSEA PO1 .... 12 C5
Peacock La WINC SO23 .... 3 M7
Peak Cl ROWN SO16 .... 105 L8
Peak Dr FHAM/STUB PO14 .... 6 A7
Peake New Rd BPWT SO32 .... 59 L8
Peakfield WVILLE PO7 .... 139 J4 🔟
Peak La BPWT SO32 .... 84 F3 🔟
FHAM/STUB PO14 .... 6 A8
Peak Rd HORN PO8 .... 115 M3
The Peak HAV PO9 .... 142 A6
Pealsham Gdns FBDG SP6 .... 97 J8
Pearce Av PSTN BH14 .... 233 M7
Pearce Ct GPORT PO12 .... 11 H2
Pear Cl BKME/WDN BH12 .... 235 G1
Pearl Gdns NBNE BH10 .... 220 A4
Pearl Rd NBNE BH10 .... 220 A4
Pearson Av PSTN BH14 .... 234 A3
Pearson Gdns NBNE BH10 .... 220 B4
Peartree LYMN SO41 .... 228 C6 🔟
Peartree Av ITCH SO19 .... 132 C4
Pear Tree Cl BPWT SO32 .... 109 L6 🔟
CHCH/BSGR BH23 .... 197 L8
FBDG SP6 .... 121 K2
Peartree Cl
FHAM/STUB PO14 .... 184 B5 🔟
ITCH SO19 .... 132 B4 🔟
Peartree Ct LYMN SO41 .... 228 C6 🔟
Pear Tree Dr RSAL SP5 .... 75 J8
Peartree Rd FAWY SO45 .... 155 J6
ITCH SO19 .... 132 B4
Pease Cft EPSF GU31 .... 93 G5
Pebble Cl HISD PO11 .... 213 M6 🔟
Pebble Ct TOTT SO40 .... 130 C6
Pebmarsh Rd CHAM PO6 .... 163 H8 🔟
Peckham Av
NMIL/BTOS BH25 .... 225 L6
Pedam Cl ENEY PO4 .... 211 L5 🔟
Pedula Wy ELGH SO50 .... 82 D3
Peel Cl BKME/WDN BH12 .... 234 B3
ROMY SO51 .... 51 H7
Peel Pl SSEA PO5 .... 13 G4
Peel Rd GPORT PO12 .... 11 H2
Peel St SHAM SO14 .... 5 L1
Peewit Hl HLER SO31 .... 133 G5
Peewit Hill Cl HLER SO31 .... 133 L5
Pegasus Av LYMN SO41 .... 226 E6
Pegasus Cl HLER SO31 .... 157 K6 🔟
ROWN SO16 .... 105 L4
Pelham Cl CHCH/BSGR BH23 .... 238 C2
Pelham Rd GPORT PO12 .... 10 E2
SSEA PO5 .... 13 H6
Pelham Ter EMRTH PO10 .... 166 E8 🔟
Pelican Cl FHAM PO15 .... 6 A3
Pelican Md RGWD BH24 .... 171 C2
Pelican Rd FHAM/STUB PO14 .... 184 D3
Pembers Cl ELGH SO50 .... 83 J6
Pemberton Rd LYND SO43 .... 151 L3
Pembrey Cl ROWN SO16 .... 105 L3
Pembridge Rd FBDG SP6 .... 97 M5
Pembroke Cl ELGH SO50 .... 81 L6
PSEA PO1 .... 12 D6 🔟
ROMY SO51 .... 78 E1
TOTT SO40 .... 104 F4
Pembroke Crs
FHAM/STUB PO14 .... 183 L6
Pembroke Rd
BKME/WDN BH12 .... 234 C1
FUFL SO22 .... 16 B3
ITCH SO19 .... 132 F4
PSEA PO1 .... 12 E6
WBNE BH4 .... 235 G6
Pembury Rd
FHAM/STUB PO14 .... 184 B4
HAV PO9 .... 9 H6
Pemerton Rd FUFL SO22 .... 2 B1
Penarth Av CHAM PO6 .... 163 G4
Pendennis Rd CHAM PO6 .... 162 D8
Pendle Cl ROWN SO16 .... 105 L8
Pendle Gn ROMY SO51 .... 20 E7
Pendleton Gdns FAWY SO45 .... 180 C7 🔟

Penelope Gdns HLER SO31 .... 133 K6
Penfords Paddock
BPWT SO32 .... 111 J1 🔟
Pengelly Av NBNE BH10 .... 220 C3
Penhale Gdns
FHAM/STUB PO14 .... 158 F7
Penhale Rd PSEA PO1 .... 13 M1
Penhale Wy TOTT SO40 .... 129 J3
Penhurst Rd HAV PO9 .... 164 F6
Peninsula Rd FUFL SO22 .... 2 D9
Penistone Cl ITCH SO19 .... 132 F7
Penjar Av WVILLE PO7 .... 164 A4
Penk Rdg CHAM PO6 .... 164 D8
Pennant Hills HAV PO9 .... 164 F6
Pennant Wy CHCH/BSGR BH23 .... 238 E1
Pennard Wy CHFD SO53 .... 80 F4
Penn Cl NMIL/BTOS BH25 .... 225 J7
Pennels Cl LIPH GU30 .... 38 E6
Pennerly Ct HAV PO9 .... 165 H1
Penner Rd HAV PO9 .... 8 C8
Pennine Gdns FAWY SO45 .... 155 H6
Pennine Rd ROWN SO16 .... 130 D1
Pennine Wy CHFD SO53 .... 81 J4
LSOL/BMARY PO13 .... 208 E4
VWD BH31 .... 144 D2 🔟
Pennington Cl ELGH SO50 .... 54 E8
FERN BH22 .... 168 B7
LYMN SO41 .... 228 A2
Pennington Crs FERN BH22 .... 168 B6
Pennington Ov LYMN SO41 .... 227 M6
Pennington Rd FERN BH22 .... 168 B7
Pennington Wy FHAM PO15 .... 6 B1
Penns Pl EPSF GU31 .... 64 C5
Penns Rd PSF GU32 .... 63 K4
Penn Wy GPORT PO12 .... 209 J5
Pennycress HLER SO31 .... 158 C6
Penny Hedge
NMIL/BTOS BH25 .... 225 M8
Penny La EMRTH PO10 .... 166 F8
Penny Pl WVILLE PO7 .... 164 C5 🔟
Penny's Cl FBDG SP6 .... 97 L5
Penny's Crs FBDG SP6 .... 97 L5
Pennys La FBDG SP6 .... 97 L6
RSAL SP5 .... 18 B1
Penny St PSEA PO1 .... 12 C6
Pennywell Gdns
NMIL/BTOS BH25 .... 226 B4
Penrhyn Cl ELGH SO50 .... 81 L3
Penrith Cl VWD BH31 .... 144 C3
Penrith Rd BOSC BH5 .... 236 F4
Penrose Cl NEND PO2 .... 187 H6 🔟
Penrose Rd FERN BH22 .... 194 B2
Penshurst Wy ELGH SO50 .... 81 M2
The Pentagon FAWY SO45 .... 180 C6
Pentere Rd HORN PO8 .... 140 E2
Pentire Av WSHM SO15 .... 106 C6
Pentire Wy WSHM SO15 .... 106 C6
Pentland Cl FAWY SO45 .... 155 H6 🔟
Pentland Ri FHAM/PORC PO16 .... 162 B7
Penton Ct HAV PO9 .... 165 M2
Penton Hl RWIN SO21 .... 54 F1 🔟
Pentons Hl FBDG SP6 .... 123 H2
Pentridge Wy TOTT SO40 .... 129 H3
Peper Harow HORN PO8 .... 140 F2
Peppard Cl WEND SO18 .... 132 E1
Peppercorn Wy HEND SO30 .... 109 G5
Pepys Av ITCH SO19 .... 133 H3
Pepys Cl ENEY PO4 .... 211 K5
GPORT PO12 .... 209 M7
Percival Rd NEND PO2 .... 187 K8
Percy Chandler St PSEA PO1 .... 211 H2 🔟
Percy Rd FAWY SO45 .... 155 K3
Percy Rd BOSC BH5 .... 236 D5
ENEY PO4 .... 13 L4
GPORT PO12 .... 11 C3
ROWN SO16 .... 105 M8
Peregrine Cl TOTT SO40 .... 129 G2 🔟
Peregrine Rd
CHCH/BSGR BH23 .... 238 C2
The Peregrines
FHAM/PORC PO16 .... 161 K8
Pergin Crs CFDH BH17 .... 233 G1
Pergin Wy CFDH BH17 .... 233 G1
Pern Dr HEND SO30 .... 134 E1
Peronne Cl HSEA PO3 .... 187 K3
Peronne Rd HSEA PO3 .... 187 K3
Perran Rd ROWN SO16 .... 105 J7
Perryfield Gdns LTDN BH7 .... 221 M8 🔟
Perry Gdns PLE BH15 .... 233 H7
Perryvale Rd NBAD SO52 .... 80 E3
Perrywood Cl FAWY SO45 .... 180 A5
Perrywood Gdns TOTT SO40 .... 104 A8 🔟
Perseus Pl WVILLE PO7 .... 164 D5
Pershore Cl HLER SO31 .... 158 E5
Persley Rd NBNE BH10 .... 220 B4
Perth Cl CHCH/BSGR BH23 .... 222 C7
Perth Rd ENEY PO4 .... 211 M4
LSOL/BMARY PO13 .... 185 H5
Pervin Rd CHAM PO6 .... 187 K1
Pesthouse La BPWT SO32 .... 113 H4
Peter Ashley Rd CHAM PO6 .... 164 C1
Peterborough Rd CHAM PO6 .... 163 J7
Peter Grant Wy FERN BH22 .... 194 A3
Peters Cl HLER SO31 .... 158 C5
UPTN BH16 .... 232 B2
Peterscroft Av TOTT SO40 .... 128 E7
Petersfield La HORN PO8 .... 116 A2
Petersfield Pl LTDN BH7 .... 237 G1 🔟
Petersfield Rd EPSF GU31 .... 91 J3
HAV PO9 .... 8 F1
LTDN BH7 .... 236 F2
NARL SO24 .... 30 C4
RWIN SO21 .... 27 M2
WINC SO23 .... 3 L9
Petersham Cl WVILLE PO7 .... 140 B7 🔟
Petersham Rd CFDH BH17 .... 217 K8
Peters Rd HLER SO31 .... 158 C5
Petit Rd MOOR/WNTN BH9 .... 220 E5
Petrel Wk LSOL/BMARY PO13 .... 184 C5 🔟
Petrie Rd LSOL/BMARY PO13 .... 208 D2
Petticoat La RSAL SP5 .... 73 K1
Pettinger Gdns PTSW SO17 .... 107 J8 🔟
Petty Cl ROMY SO51 .... 78 F2 🔟
Pettycot Crs
LSOL/BMARY PO13 .... 184 F5
Petworth Gdns ELGH SO50 .... 81 M3 🔟

ROWN SO16 .... 106 A3
Petworth Rd *HSEA* PO3 ..... 211 M2
Petwyn Cl *FERN* BH22 .... 194 E2
Pevensey Cl *ROWN* SO16 ..... 105 J7
Peverell Rd *UPTN* BH16 .... 232 A4 ⬚
Peverells Cl *CHFD* SO53 .... 81 K2
Peverells Wood Av *CHFD* SO53 .. 81 K1
Peverells Wood Cl *CHFD* SO53 .. 81 L1
Peveril Cl *RGWD* BH24 .... 169 K2
Peveril Rd *ITCH* SO19 .... 132 C4
Pewsey Pl *WSHM* SO15 .... 106 C6
Phelipps Rd *WIMB* BH21 .... 217 H1
Pheonix Wy
    LSOL/BMARY PO13 .... 185 G7
Philip Rd *WVILLE* PO7 .... 164 D3
Phillimore Rd *ROWN* SO16 ...... 107 J4
Phillips Cl *ROWN* SO16 .... 105 K2
Philpott Dr *TOTT* SO40 .... 130 D7
Phoenix Cl *HLER* SO31 .... 133 L7 ⬚
Phoenix Sq *NEND* PO2 .... 187 J4
Phyldon Cl *BKME/WDN* BH12 ... 234 A3
Phyldon Rd *BKME/WDN* BH12 ... 234 A3
Pickard Rd *FERN* BH22 .... 194 D1
Pickering Ct *FBDG* SP6 .... 97 L6
Picket Cl *FBDG* SP6 .... 217 L6
Pickford Rd *MOOR/WNTN* BH9 .. 220 D7
Pickwick Cl *TOTT* SO40 .... 128 F1
Pier Head Rd *NEND* PO2 .... 186 F8
Pier Rd *PSEA* PO1 .... 12 E7
    SSEA PO5 .... 12 E7
Pier St *LSOL/BMARY* PO13 ...... 208 C2
Pigeon House La *WVILLE* PO7 ... 163 H5
Pig Shoot La *CHCH/BSGR* BH23.. 221 K4
Pikes Hl *LYND* SO43 .... 151 J3
Pilands Wood Rd *HLER* SO31 .... 133 K8 ⬚
Pilchards Av *FHAM* SO31 .... 85 G5
Pilford Heath Rd *WIMB* BH21 .... 192 B3
Pilgrim Cl *NMIL/BTOS* BH25 ..... 226 A4 ⬚
Pilgrim Pk *RGWD* BH24 .... 147 G8 ⬚
Pilgrim Pl *WEND* SO18 .... 107 K4
Pilgrims Cl *NBAD* SO52 .... 80 E3
Pilgrims Ga *FUFL* SO22 .... 2 A2
Pilgrims Wy *CFDH* BH17 .... 232 F1 ⬚
    FHAM PO14 .... 183 M7
Pilley Bailey *LYMN* SO41 .... 202 E6
Pilley Hl *LYMN* SO41 .... 202 C7
Pilley St *LYMN* SO41 .... 202 E6
Pill Hl *RSAL* SP5 .... 46 F4
Pilning Cl *FHAM/STUB* PO14 ..... 160 A8 ⬚
Pilot Hight Rd *BWD* BH11 .... 219 L5
Pilsdon Dr *CFDH* BH17 .... 218 C6
Pimpern Cl *CFDH* BH17 .... 218 C6
Pimpernel Cl *HLER* SO31 .... 158 C6
Pine Av *BKME/WDN* BH12 .... 234 E3
    SBNE BH6 .... 237 H4
Pinecliffe Av *SBNE* BH6 .... 237 H4
Pinecliffe Rd *NMIL/BTOS* BH25 .. 240 B1
Pinecliff Rd *CCLF* BH13 .... 234 F8
Pine Cl *FAWY* SO45 .... 155 K6
    FERN BH22 .... 194 A1
    FUFL SO22 .... 26 A5
    NBAD SO52 .... 79 L3 ⬚
    NMIL/BTOS BH25 .... 225 J8
    RSAL SP5 .... 75 J6
    TOTT SO40 .... 129 G5
Pine Crs *CHCH/BSGR* BH23 ..... 224 C8
    CHFD SO53 .... 53 H8
Pine Dr *CCLF* BH13 .... 234 E5
    RGWD BH24 .... 169 K4
    WEND SO18 .... 133 H1
Pine Dr East *WEND* SO18 ...... 133 J1
Pinefield Rd *WEND* SO18 .... 107 L6
Pine Gv *HAV* PO9 .... 9 H5
Pinegrove Rd *ITCH* SO19 .... 132 D5
Pineholt Cl *RGWD* BH24 .... 169 L3
Pinehurst Av
    CHCH/BSGR BH23 .... 238 E3
    HORN PO8 .... 141 L6
Pinehurst Cl *FERN* BH22 .... 168 E6
    ROWN SO16 .... 106 E1 ⬚
Pinelands Rd *ROWN* SO16 ...... 80 E8
Pine Manor Rd *RGWD* BH24 ..... 169 H3
Pine Rd *BPWT* SO32 .... 85 J8
    CHFD SO53 .... 53 H7
    FBDG SP6 .... 121 K3
    MOOR/WNTN BH9 .... 220 D7
    ROWN SO16 .... 79 H2
Pinesprings Dr *BDST* BH18 ...... 217 H4
The Pines *FBDG* SP6 .... 98 D6
    FHAM/PORC PO16 .... 161 L7
Pinetops Cl *LYMN* SO41 .... 227 L5
Pine Tree Cl *WIMB* BH21 .... 192 B3
Pine Tree Gdns *HORN* PO8 ..... 140 E6
Pine Tree Gln *WBNE* BH4 .... 235 H6
Pine Trees Cl *FHAM/STUB* PO14 .. 6 B7
Pinetree Wk *CFDH* BH17 .... 217 K8
Pine Vale Crs *NBNE* BH10 ...... 220 D5
Pineview Cl *HLER* SO31 .... 133 L7
    RSAL SP5 .... 73 J4
Pine View Cl *UPTN* BH16 .... 232 B2
Pine View Rd *VWD* BH31 .... 144 F3
Pine Wk *HLER* SO31 .... 158 C5
    LISS GU33 .... 36 F2
    ROWN SO16 .... 106 E1
    VWD BH31 .... 144 F3
Pine Wy *ROWN* SO16 .... 106 E1
Pinewood *LSOL/BMARY* PO13 ... 185 J7
    NBNE BH10 .... 220 B3 ⬚
Pinewood Av *HAV* PO9 .... 164 F5
    NBNE BH10 .... 220 B3 ⬚
    ROWN SO16 .... 51 H7
Pinewood Cl *CHCH/BSGR* BH23.. 224 E7
    FHAM/STUB PO14 .... 184 B4 ⬚
    NBNE BH10 .... 220 B3 ⬚
    ROWN SO16 .... 51 H7
Pinewood Crs *FAWY* SO45 ...... 155 M6 ⬚
Pinewood Dr *FAWY* SO45 ...... 155 M6
Pinewood Gdns *FERN* BH22 ..... 194 B1
Pinewood Pk *ITCH* SO19 .... 133 K3
Pinewood Rd *CCLF* BH13 ...... 235 K7
    CHCH/BSGR BH23 .... 224 D7
    FERN BH22 .... 194 A1
    LYMN SO41 .... 226 D5
    RGWD BH24 .... 169 K4
Pinkney La *LYND* SO43 .... 151 J6
Pink Rd *NEND* PO2 .... 187 J8 ⬚
Pinks Hl *FHAM/PORC* PO16 ..... 161 H6
Pinsley Dr *WHAM* PO17 .... 162 E2
Pinto Cl *FHAM* PO15 .... 158 F1
Pipers Ash *RGWD* BH24 .... 147 G8 ⬚

Pipers Cl *TOTT* SO40 .... 129 H2
Pipers Cl *CHCH/BSGR* BH23.... 238 F1
Pipers Md *HORN* PO8 .... 115 M3
Piping Cl *RWIN* SO21 .... 54 E8
Piping Rd *RWIN* SO21 .... 54 E8
Pipit Cl *GPORT* PO12 .... 209 M1
Pippin Cl *CHCH/BSGR* BH23 .... 222 C6
    LYMN SO41 .... 228 C6
Pirelli St *SHAM* SO14 .... 4 E3
    SHAM SO15 .... 4 E3
Pirrie Cl *WSHM* SO15 .... 106 C7
Pitcairn Ms *ENEY* PO4 .... 211 M6 ⬚
Pitchponds Rd *HLER* SO31 ...... 158 A8
Pitcot La *EPSF* GU31 .... 91 L3
Pitcott La *EPSF* GU31 .... 91 L3
Pitcroft La *NEND* PO2 .... 187 H7
Pithouse La *CHCH/BSGR* BH23 .. 196 B8
Pitmore Cl *ELGH* SO50 .... 54 E8
Pitmore La *LYMN* SO41 .... 201 H6
Pitmore Rd *ELGH* SO50 .... 54 E8
Pitreavie Rd *CHAM* PO6 .... 187 L2
Pitter Cl *FUFL* SO22 .... 16 E3
Pitt Hill La *WVILLE* PO7 .... 114 D7
Pittmore Rd
    CHCH/BSGR BH23 .... 223 G5 ⬚
Pitt Rd *WSHM* SO15 .... 131 G2
Pitts Deep La *LYMN* SO41 ...... 230 A3
Pitts Pl *LYMN* SO41 .... 230 A3
Pitwines Cl *PLE* BH15 .... 233 J6
Pitymoor La *WHAM* PO17 .... 162 F4
Place Crs *WVILLE* PO7 .... 164 D3
Place House Cl *FHAM* PO15 ..... 160 A7
Place La *RWIN* SO21 .... 26 C8
Plaitford Gv *HAV* PO9 .... 165 G4
Plantaganet Crs *BWD* BH11 .... 219 H3
Plantation Dr
    CHCH/BSGR BH23 .... 224 E6
    TOTT SO40 .... 130 C7
Plantation Rd *CFDH* BH17 ...... 218 A7
    CHCH/BSGR BH23 .... 195 M4
    LISS GU33 .... 37 G6
    ROMY SO51 .... 76 C8
The Plantation *BPWT* SO32 ..... 110 D6
Plant Park Rd *RGWD* BH24 ...... 170 A5
Plants Cl *ROMY* SO51 .... 77 G6
Plassey Crs *BWD* BH11 .... 219 M3
Platform Rd *SHAM* SO14 .... 5 G7
Platoff Rd *LYMN* SO41 .... 228 C8
Player Ct *FBDG* SP6 .... 97 L5
Players Crs *TOTT* SO40 .... 129 J3
Playfair Rd *SSEA* PO5 .... 13 J4
Playfields Dr
    BKME/WDN BH12 .... 234 D2
Pleasance Wy
    NMIL/BTOS BH25 .... 225 K5
Pleasant La *EMRTH* PO10 .... 191 H7
Pleasant Rd *ENEY* PO4 .... 211 M4
Plecy Cl *FERN* BH22 .... 194 B5
Piemont Cl *BKME/WDN* BH12 ... 219 J7
Pless Rd *LYMN* SO41 .... 241 M3
Plough La *BPWT* SO32 .... 113 H6
Plough Wy *FUFL* SO22 .... 26 C4
Plover Cl *FHAM/STUB* PO14 ..... 183 M6
Plover Dr *LYMN* SO41 .... 242 E4
Plover Reach *ENEY* PO4 .... 211 M3 ⬚
Plover Rd *TOTT* SO40 .... 129 G1
Plovers Down *FUFL* SO22 .... 26 A5
Plovers *HORN* PO8 .... 140 E2 ⬚
P.l.p.h. Rd *FAWY* SO45 .... 180 F3
Plumer Rd *CFDH* BH17 .... 217 L7
Plumpton Gdns *HSEA* PO3 ...... 187 M5 ⬚
Plumpton Gv *WVILLE* PO7 ...... 140 F7
Plymouth Dr
    FHAM/STUB PO14 .... 183 M6
Plymouth St *SSEA* PO5 .... 13 H3 ⬚
Pococks La *LISS* GU33 .... 35 L1
Poets Wy *FUFL* SO22 .... 2 B6
Pointout Cl *ROWN* SO16 .... 106 D5
Pointout Rd *ROWN* SO16 ...... 106 D5
Polesden Cl *CHFD* SO53 .... 53 G8 ⬚
Poles La *LYMN* SO41 .... 228 C7
    RWIN SO21 .... 26 D1
Police Station La *BPWT* SO32 ... 87 G7
Pollards Moor Rd *TOTT* SO40 ... 102 F7
The Polygon *WSHM* SO15 ...... 4 E1
Pomona Cl *FERN* BH22 .... 194 B2
Pompeys La *FERN* BH22 .... 193 L4
Pond Cl *NMIL/BTOS* BH25 ...... 225 L5
    TOTT SO40 .... 130 D6
Pondhead Cl *FAWY* SO45 ...... 180 A5 ⬚
Pond La *HORN* PO8 .... 116 A2
Pond Piece *WVILLE* PO7 .... 139 K5
Pond Rd *HLER* SO31 .... 158 D2
Pondside La *BPWT* SO32 .... 85 H7
Ponsonby Rd *PSTN* BH14 .... 234 C4
Pony Dr *UPTN* BH16 .... 232 C1
Pook La *HAV* PO9 .... 9 J6
    WHAM PO17 .... 160 F4
Pooksgreen *TOTT* SO40 .... 130 B6
Poole Hl *WCLF* BH2 .... 14 B6
Poole La *BWD* BH11 .... 219 K4
Poole Rd *CCLF* BH13 .... 234 E4
    ITCH SO19 .... 132 C4
    UPTN BH16 .... 232 B1
    WBNE BH4 .... 235 G5
    WCLF BH2 .... 14 B6
    WIMB BH21 .... 192 A4
Popes La *BPWT* SO32 .... 84 B4
    TOTT SO40 .... 129 K1
Popes Rd *PLE* BH15 .... 233 J2
Popham Ct *HAV* PO9 .... 165 G2
Poplar Cl *CHCH/BSGR* BH23 .... 198 A8
    CHCH/BSGR BH23 .... 224 F8
    WIMB BH21 .... 192 B3
Poplar Crs *RGWD* BH24 .... 170 F1
Poplar Dr *FHAM/STUB* PO14 .... 6 C6
    TOTT SO40 .... 130 B7
Poplar Gv *HISD* PO11 .... 213 L4
Poplar La *CHCH/BSGR* BH23 .... 198 A7
Poplar Rd *ITCH* SO19 .... 132 D2
Poplars Cl *NMIL/BTOS* BH25 .... 225 M5
The Poplars *BPWT* SO32 .... 111 J5
Poplar Wy *HEND* SO30 .... 134 B7 ⬚
    NBAD SO52 .... 79 L3
    RGWD BH24 .... 170 F1
Poppy Cl *CHCH/BSGR* BH23 .... 223 M8
    HLER SO31 .... 158 D6

Poppyfields *NBAD* SO52 .... 80 F2 ⬚
Poppy Rd *ROWN* SO16 .... 107 H3
Porchester Rd *ITCH* SO19 ...... 132 C5
Porlock Rd *ROWN* SO16 .... 105 H7
Portal Rd *ELGH* SO50 .... 82 C5
    ITCH SO19 .... 132 F4
Portarlington Cl *WBNE* BH4 .... 14 A7
Portarlington Rd *WBNE* BH4.... 235 H5
Portchester La *WHAM* PO17 .... 162 B6
Portchester Pl *BMTH* BH1 ...... 15 K2
Portchester Ri *ELGH* SO50 ..... 81 K1
Portchester Rd *CHAR* BH8 ..... 15 H1
    FHAM/PORC PO16 .... 187 J8
    NEND PO2 .... 187 J8
Portelet Cl *BKME/WDN* BH12 ... 219 H7
Portelet Pl *HEND* SO30 .... 134 A3
Porteous Crs *CHFD* SO53 ...... 81 L2
Porter Rd *CFDH* BH17 .... 233 C1
Portersbridge St *ROMY* SO51 .. 78 D3
Porter's La *SHAM* SO14 .... 4 F5
    WIMB BH21 .... 193 G2
Portesham Gdns
    MOOR/WNTN BH9 .... 220 F4
Portesham Wy *CFDH* BH17 ..... 218 C5
Portfield Cl *CHCH/BSGR* BH23 .. 222 E8
Portfield Rd *CHCH/BSGR* BH23 .. 237 L1
Portland Dr *GPORT* PO12 ...... 209 H5
Portland Rd *MOOR/WNTN* BH9.. 220 E8
    SSEA PO5 .... 13 H7
    WVILLE PO7 .... 164 C1
Portland's Cl *PSF* GU32 .... 64 A3
Portland Sq *LISS* GU33 .... 36 E4
Portland St *FHAM/PORC* PO16 .. 7 K6
    PSEA PO1 .... 12 E1
    SHAM SO14 .... 4 F3
Portland Ter *SHAM* SO14 .... 4 F3
Port La *RWIN* SO21 .... 53 C1
Portman Crs *SBNE* BH6 .... 237 G5
Portman Rd *LTDN* BH7 .... 236 F5
Portmore Cl *BDST* BH18 .... 218 A2
Portobello Gv
    FHAM/PORC PO16 .... 162 B7
Port Royal St *SSEA* PO5 .... 13 K2 ⬚
Portsdown Av *CHAM* PO6 ...... 164 A8
Portsdown Hill Rd *CHAM* PO6 ... 163 K7
    WHAM PO17 .... 161 L6
Portsdown Rd *CHAM* PO6 ...... 162 C8
Portsmouth Rd *BPWT* SO32 .... 84 A4
    CHAM PO6 .... 187 K2
    ELGH SO50 .... 83 H7
    HLER SO31 .... 133 K7
    HORN PO8 .... 140 F5
    ITCH SO19 .... 132 F6
    LSOL/BMARY PO13 .... 208 D4
    RWIN SO21 .... 83 L2
Portsview Av
    FHAM/PORC PO16 .... 162 B8
Portsview Gdns
    FHAM/PORC PO16 .... 162 B7
Portswood Av *PTSW* SO17 ..... 107 G8
Portswood Dr
    MOOR/WNTN BH9 .... 220 E4 ⬚
Portswood Pk *PTSW* SO17 ..... 107 G8 ⬚
    NEND PO2 .... 187 J3 ⬚
    PTSW SO17 .... 107 G8
Portswood Rd *HAV* PO9 .... 165 H2
Portview Rd *WEND* SO18 ...... 107 H6
Port Wy *CHAM* PO6 .... 162 F8
Portway *WEND* SO18 .... 132 F1
Posbrooke Rd *ENEY* PO4 .... 211 L4
Posbrook La
    FHAM/STUB PO14 .... 183 K1
Postern Cl *FHAM/PORC* PO16 .. 162 E8
Post Green Rd *UPTN* BH16 ..... 216 B8
Post Office La *RGWD* BH24 .... 169 L3
Post Office Rd *WCLF* BH2 ..... 14 E6
    WVILLE PO7 .... 164 A3 ⬚
The Potteries *FHAM/PORC* PO16 .. 7 J3
Potterne Wy *WIMB* BH21 ...... 144 E4
Potters Av *FHAM/PORC* PO16 .. 160 E4
Potters Fld *LISS* GU33 .... 36 F4
Potters Heron Cl *ROMY* SO51 .. 52 D5
Potters Heron La *ROMY* SO51 .. 52 D5
Potters Wy *PSTN* BH14 .... 234 B4
Pottery La *RCCH* PO18 .... 191 M1
Pottery Rd *PSTN* BH14 .... 233 M6
Poulner Cl *ITCH* SO19 .... 132 E7
Poulner Ct *HAV* PO9 .... 165 G2
Poulner Hl *RGWD* BH24 .... 147 H8
Poulner Pk *RGWD* BH24 .... 147 G7
Pound Cl *LSOL/BMARY* PO13 ... 185 H8
    PSTN BH14 .... 233 L3 ⬚
    RGWD BH24 .... 146 E8
Pound Cottages *BPWT* SO32 ... 87 H3
Pound Gate Dr
    FHAM/STUB PO14 .... 159 G7
Pound Hl *ROMY* SO51 .... 76 D3
Pound La *BPWT* SO32 .... 87 J3
    FBDG SP6 .... 96 A3
    PLE BH15 .... 233 K3
    RGWD BH24 .... 172 C2
    ROMY SO51 .... 52 A6
    ROMY SO51 .... 76 B3
    TOTT SO40 .... 103 H6
    TOTT SO40 .... 129 K3
Pound Lea *HISD* PO11 .... 213 L3
Pound Rd *CHAM* PO6 .... 162 F6
    HLER SO31 .... 133 K8
    LYMN SO41 .... 227 M5
    SELS SO20 .... 215 K7
Pound St *WEND* SO18 .... 132 E1
Pound Tree Rd *SHAM* SO14 .... 5 G3
Powell Crs *TOTT* SO40 .... 129 K3
Powell Rd *PSTN* BH14 .... 234 A5
Power Rd *PSEA* PO1 .... 211 J2 ⬚
Powerscourt Rd *NEND* PO2 .... 187 J8
    NMIL/BTOS BH25 .... 240 C1
Powis Cl *NMIL/BTOS* BH25 ..... 225 M5
Poyner Cl *FHAM/PORC* PO16 ... 7 J3
Poynings Pl *PSEA* PO1 .... 12 E5 ⬚
Precosa Rd *HEND* SO30 .... 134 C3
Prelate Wy *FHAM* PO15 .... 159 G6
Preshaw Cl *ROWN* SO16 ...... 106 A4
Preston Cl *UPTN* BH16 .... 232 B1 ⬚

Preston La *CHCH/BSGR* BH23 .. 223 H5
Preston Rd *NEND* PO2 .... 187 K7
    PLE BH15 .... 233 H2
Preston Wy *CHCH/BSGR* BH23 .. 224 B8
Prestwood Cl
    NMIL/BTOS BH25 .... 225 K7 ⬚
Prestwood Rd *HEND* SO30 ..... 134 A2
Pretoria Rd *ENEY* PO4 .... 211 K5
    HEND SO30 .... 133 M3
Pricketts Hl *FHAM/STUB* PO14 .. 136 D1
Prideaux-brune Av
    LSOL/BMARY PO13 .... 185 G4
Priest Croft Dr *FAWY* SO45 .... 180 C6
Priestfields *FHAM/STUB* PO14 .. 159 C6
Priestlands *ROMY* SO51 .... 50 D8
Priestlands Cl *TOTT* SO40 ..... 128 E2
Priestlands La *LYMN* SO41 .... 228 A5
Priestlands Rd *LYMN* SO41 .... 228 A5
Priest La *CHCH/BSGR* BH23 .... 222 E2
Priestley Cl *TOTT* SO40 .... 129 H1 ⬚
Priestley Rd *NBNE* BH10 ...... 219 M7
Priestwood Cl *WEND* SO18 .... 133 H1
Primate Rd *FHAM/STUB* PO14... 159 H6
Primrose Cl *HEND* SO30 .... 134 A3 ⬚
    LSOL/BMARY PO13 .... 185 G3
    NBAD SO52 .... 80 E4 ⬚
Primrose Gdns *CFDH* BH17 .... 217 K7
    RSAL SP5 .... 73 H2
Primrose La *LISS* GU33 .... 37 J4
Primrose Rd *ROWN* SO16 ...... 106 F4
Primrose Wy
    CHCH/BSGR BH23 .... 224 A8
    HLER SO31 .... 158 D6
    ROMY SO51 .... 51 H7 ⬚
    WIMB BH21 .... 217 J1
Prince Albert Rd *ENEY* PO4 .... 211 L5
Prince Alfred St *GPORT* PO12 .. 10 E5
Prince George's St *HAV* PO9 ... 8 F4
Prince of Wales Av
    WSHM SO15 .... 130 E1
Prince of Wales Cl
    WVILLE PO7 .... 164 E1 ⬚
Prince of Wales Rd
    GPORT PO12 .... 11 H3 ⬚
    WBNE BH4 .... 235 G4
Prince Rd *FHAM/STUB* PO14 ... 184 D2
    ROWN SO16 .... 105 K1
Princes Cl *BPWT* SO32 .... 85 G8 ⬚
    RSAL SP5 .... 73 K1
Princes Crs *SHAM* SO14 ...... 132 A2
Princes Dr *WVILLE* PO7 .... 140 E7
Princes Hl *RSAL* SP5 .... 73 K1
Princes Pl *FUFL* SO22 .... 26 A5
    NMIL/BTOS BH25 .... 226 A4 ⬚
Princes Rd *FERN* BH22 .... 194 B2
    PSF GU32 .... 63 J4
    ROMY SO51 .... 52 D8
    WSHM SO15 .... 131 H2 ⬚
Princess Av *CHCH/BSGR* BH23.. 238 A2
Princess Gdns *HORN* PO8 ..... 140 F1
Princess Rd *BKME/WDN* BH12 .. 234 F4
    TOTT SO40 .... 128 E6
    WBNE BH4 .... 235 G4
Prince's St *PSEA* PO1 .... 211 H1
    SHAM SO14 .... 5 H1
Pringle Cl *FERN* BH22 .... 194 C3 ⬚
Pringles Dr *FERN* BH22 .... 194 C3
Prinstead Cl *WINC* SO23 ...... 27 G2 ⬚
Prinsted Crs *CHAM* PO6 ...... 188 B1
Prinsted La *EMRTH* PO10 ..... 191 H7
Priors Barton *WINC* SO23 ..... 26 E3
Priors Cl *CHCH/BSGR* BH23 .... 239 H1
    HLER SO31 .... 167 J7
Priorsdean Av *HSEA* PO3 ..... 211 L2
Priorsdean Crs *HAV* PO9 ...... 165 H4
Priors Dean Rd *FUFL* SO22 .... 16 C4
Priors Leaze La *RCCH* PO18 ... 167 K7
Priors Rd *CFDH* BH17 .... 217 K8
Priors Wy *FUFL* SO22 .... 26 A5
Priory Av *PTSW* SO17 .... 107 J7
Priory Cl *BPWT* SO32 .... 85 G8
    PTSW SO17 .... 107 J7
Priory Crs *ENEY* PO4 .... 211 L4
Priory Gdns *FHAM/PORC* PO16 .. 162 A8
    WVILLE PO7 .... 140 C7
Priory Rd *ELGH* SO50 .... 81 L7
    ENEY PO4 .... 211 L6
    FERN BH22 .... 168 E8
    FHAM PO15 .... 6 A4
    HLER SO31 .... 156 F2
    PTSW SO17 .... 107 H8
    WCLF BH2 .... 14 E7
    WHAM PO17 .... 162 E2
The Priory *BPWT* SO32 .... 111 G1
Priory View Pl
    MOOR/WNTN BH9 .... 220 E5
Priory View Rd
    CHCH/BSGR BH23 .... 223 G6
    MOOR/WNTN BH9 .... 220 C8
Privet Rd *MOOR/WNTN* BH9 ... 220 C8
Privett Pl *GPORT* PO12 .... 209 J4
Privett Rd *FHAM* PO15 .... 160 A6
    GPORT PO12 .... 209 J4
    LSOL/BMARY PO13 .... 209 G5
    PSF GU32 .... 34 C6
    WVILLE PO7 .... 164 B5
Prochurch Rd *HORN* PO8 ..... 140 F1
Proctor Cl *ITCH* SO19 .... 133 H3
Proctor Dr *NBAD* SO52 .... 79 L3
Proctor La *PSEA* PO1 .... 211 K3
Promenade *CCLF* BH13 .... 235 H7
The Promenade *EMRTH* PO10 .. 190 D1
    FAWY SO45 .... 155 L3
Prosperous St *PLE* BH15 ..... 233 H7 ⬚
Prospect La *HAV* PO9 .... 165 M3
Prospect Pl *CHFD* SO53 ...... 81 K2 ⬚
    FAWY SO45 .... 155 L3
Prospect Rd *NEND* PO2 ...... 211 G1
Provene Cl *BPWT* SO32 .... 111 J4
Provene Gdns *BPWT* SO32 .... 111 J4
Providence Hl *HLER* SO31 .... 133 L6
Provost St *FBDG* SP6 .... 97 L5
Pruetts La *LISS* GU33 .... 36 E7
Prunus Cl *FERN* BH22 .... 193 M1
    ROWN SO16 .... 106 B3

Prunus Dr *FERN* BH22 .... 193 M1
Pudbrooke Gdns
    HEND SO30 .... 109 C8 ⬚
Pudding La *WINC* SO23 .... 17 C4
Puddleslosh La *FBDG* SP6 ..... 97 J5
Puddletown Crs *CFDH* BH17 ... 218 D6
Puffin Cl *ROWN* SO16 .... 106 A3
Puffin Crs *FHAM/STUB* PO14 .. 183 M6
Puffin Gdns
    LSOL/BMARY PO13 .... 184 F5 ⬚
Puffin Wk *HORN* PO8 .... 140 B4
Pug's Hole *RSAL* SP5 .... 19 M1
Pulens Crs *EPSF* GU31 .... 64 B4
Pulens Gdns *EPSF* GU31 .... 64 B4
Pullman Ct *FERN* BH22 .... 168 B6 ⬚
Pullman Wy *RGWD* BH24 ...... 170 E2
Pump La *HORN* PO8 .... 140 E3
    LSOL/BMARY PO13 .... 185 G7
Punsholt La *NARL* SO24 .... 32 D5
Purbeck Av *PLE* BH15 .... 232 D7
Purbeck Cl *UPTN* BH16 .... 232 A1 ⬚
Purbeck Dr *FHAM/STUB* PO14 .. 6 A8
    VWD BH31 .... 144 D3 ⬚
Purbeck Rd *NMIL/BTOS* BH25 .. 240 C1
    WCLF BH2 .... 14 C6
Purbeck St *PSEA* PO1 .... 12 E2 ⬚
Purbrook Cl *ROWN* SO16 ...... 106 B4 ⬚
Purbrook Gdns *WVILLE* PO7 ... 164 A3
Purbrook Heath Rd
    WVILLE PO7 .... 163 K3
Purbrook Rd *PSEA* PO1 .... 13 M2
Purbrook Wy *HAV* PO9 .... 164 F4
    WVILLE PO7 .... 164 D4
Purcell Cl *WVILLE* PO7 .... 164 C3
Purcell Rd *ITCH* SO19 .... 133 H5
Purchase Rd *BKME/WDN* BH12.. 235 H1
Purewell *CHCH/BSGR* BH23 .... 238 C2
Purewell Cl *CHCH/BSGR* BH23 .. 238 D2
Purewell Cross Rd
    CHCH/BSGR BH23 .... 238 C1
Purkess Cl *CHFD* SO53 .... 81 J1
Purkiss Cl *TOTT* SO40 .... 128 A3
Purley Wy *ROMY* SO51 .... 76 A5
The Purrocks *PSF* GU32 .... 63 L3
Purvis Gdns *ITCH* SO19 ...... 132 F6
Pussex La *CHCH/BSGR* BH23 .. 195 L8
Putmans La *EPSF* GU31 .... 92 E2
Pycroft Cl *HISD* PO11 .... 190 A5
    ITCH SO19 .... 132 D5
Pye Cl *WIMB* BH21 .... 217 H1
Pye La *WIMB* BH21 .... 120 C1
Pye St *PSEA* PO1 .... 211 G2
Pyland's La *HLER* SO31 ...... 133 M5
Pyle Cl *HORN* PO8 .... 140 E4
Pylewell Rd *FAWY* SO45 ...... 155 L4 ⬚
Pyrford Cl *GPORT* PO12 ...... 209 J5
    WVILLE PO7 .... 140 B6
Pyrford Ms *LYMN* SO41 ...... 228 C6
Pytchley Cl *FHAM/STUB* PO14 .. 183 L6

Q

The Quadrangle *ELGH* SO50 .... 81 M4 ⬚
Quail Wy *HORN* PO8 .... 140 E2
Quantock Rd *ROWN* SO16 ..... 105 K8
The Quantocks *FAWY* SO45 .... 155 H6 ⬚
Quarely Rd *HAV* PO9 .... 165 J2
Quarry Rd *WIMB* BH21 .... 192 E1
    WINC SO23 .... 3 K9
Quarterdeck Av *NEND* PO2 .... 186 F7
Quartremaine Rd *HSEA* PO3 ... 187 M5
Quavey Rd *RSAL* SP5 .... 73 K2
Quay Hvn *HLER* SO31 .... 134 B8
Quay La *GPORT* PO12 .... 185 M7
Quayle Dr *BWD* BH11 .... 219 K2 ⬚
Quay Rd *CHCH/BSGR* BH23 .... 238 A3
Quayside Rd *WEND* SO18 ..... 132 B1
Quayside Wk *TOTT* SO40 ..... 130 D5
Quay St *FHAM/PORC* PO16 .... 7 L7
    LYMN SO41 .... 228 D4
The Quay *PLE* BH15 .... 233 H7
Quebec Gdns *HLER* SO31 ..... 133 K7 ⬚
Queen Anne Dr *WIMB* BH21 ... 218 C1
Queen Anne's Dr *HAV* PO9 .... 165 G6
Queen Elizabeth Av
    LYMN SO41 .... 228 B4 ⬚
Queen Katherine Rd
    LYMN SO41 .... 228 D5
Queen Mary Av
    MOOR/WNTN BH9 .... 220 D6
Queen Mary Rd
    FHAM/PORC PO16 .... 186 B1
Queen Rd *FHAM/STUB* PO14 ... 184 D2
Queens Av *CHCH/BSGR* BH23 .. 238 A3
Queens Cl *FAWY* SO45 .... 155 L5
    FERN BH22 .... 168 B7
    LSOL/BMARY PO13 .... 208 C2 ⬚
Queens Crs *FHAM/STUB* PO14 .. 184 B5
    HORN PO8 .... 140 F1
    SSEA PO5 .... 13 H6
Queens Gdns *FBDG* SP6 ...... 97 L6
    WBNE BH4 .... 14 A4
Queens Gv *NMIL/BTOS* BH25 .. 226 A4
    WVILLE PO7 .... 164 B3
    SSEA PO5 .... 13 H7
Queensland Rd *LTDN* BH7 .... 236 F3
Queensmead
    CHCH/BSGR BH23 .... 222 E7 ⬚
Queens Md *FUFL* SO22 .... 26 B2 ⬚
Queen's Pde *LYND* SO43 ..... 151 K3
Queen's Park Av *CHAR* BH8 ... 236 B1
Queen's Park Gdns *CHAR* BH8 .. 236 B1
Queen's Park South Dr
    CHAR BH8 .... 236 B1
Queen's Park West Dr
    CHAR BH8 .... 236 B1
Queen's Pl *SSEA* PO5 .... 13 H6 ⬚
Queens Ride *NBAD* SO52 ..... 79 K4
Queen's Rd *CHCH/BSGR* BH23 .. 238 D2
    CHFD SO53 .... 53 J7
    FERN BH22 .... 194 B1
    FHAM/PORC PO16 .... 7 J6
    GPORT PO12 .... 11 G2
    HLER SO31 .... 158 A4
    LSOL/BMARY PO13 .... 208 D4

NEND PO2 ... 187 J8
PSEA PO1 ... 210 D2
PSF GU32 ... 63 J4
PSTN BH14 ... 234 C4
WBNE BH4 ... 14 A5
WIMB BH21 ... 217 H3
WSHM SO15 ... 106 B6
WVILLE PO7 ... 140 C7
Queens St MIDH GU29 ... 67 K6
Queen's Ter SHAM SO14 ... 5 H6
Queenstown Rd
WSHM SO15 ... 131 H2 2
Queen St EMRTH PO10 ... 166 E8
FBDG SP6 ... 73 G7
PSEA PO1 ... 12 C1
RWIN SO21 ... 54 E3
Queens Vw HLER SO31 ... 156 F2
Queensway HISD PO11 ... 189 L5
RGWD BH24 ... 170 F1
Queen's Wy SHAM SO14 ... 5 G6
SSEA PO5 ... 13 H6 3
The Queensway
FHAM/PORC PO16 ... 161 M8
Queenswood Av CHAR BH8 ... 221 J7
Queenswood Dr FERN BH22 ... 194 B1
Querida Cl HLER SO31 ... 134 B8 3
Quilter Cl ITCH SO19 ... 133 H4 4
Quince La WIMB BH21 ... 192 B2
Quintin Cl CHCH/BSGR BH23 ... 224 D8
Quinton Cl SSEA PO5 ... 13 J3 6
Quintrell Av FHAM/PORC PO16 ... 161 L8
Quob Farm Cl HEND SO30 ... 108 D5
Quob La HEND SO30 ... 108 E5
The Quomp RGWD BH24 ... 170 E1 6

R

Racecourse Vw LYND SO43 ... 151 K2 2
Rachel Cl ELGH SO50 ... 83 G6
Racton Av CHAM PO6 ... 187 M1
Racton Rd EMRTH PO10 ... 166 D5
Radclyffe Rd FHAM/PORC PO16 ... 7 M3
Radipole Rd CFDH BH17 ... 218 D6
Radleigh Gdns TOTT SO40 ... 104 A8
Radley Cl HEND SO30 ... 109 H7 3
Radnor St SSEA PO5 ... 13 H3
Radstock Rd ITCH SO19 ... 132 C5
Radway Crs WSHM SO15 ... 106 C8
Radway Rd WSHM SO15 ... 106 C8
Raebarn Cl NARL SO24 ... 30 C3
Raeburn Dr HEND SO30 ... 134 A1
Raglan Cl CHFD SO53 ... 80 E4
Raglan Gdns BWD BH11 ... 219 L6
Raglan St SSEA PO5 ... 13 J2
Ragmore La PSF GU32 ... 34 D3
Rails La HISD PO11 ... 213 M6
Railway Vw PSEA PO1 ... 13 J1
Rake Rd LIPH GU30 ... 38 C6
LISS GU33 ... 36 F4
Raleigh Cl CHCH/BSGR BH23 ... 238 E3
NMIL/BTOS BH25 ... 225 K5
RGWD BH24 ... 147 G8 5
Raley Rd HLER SO31 ... 158 E6
Ralph Rd WIMB BH21 ... 217 J1
Ramalley La CHFD SO53 ... 81 G1
Rambler Dr LSOL/BMARY PO13 ... 209 G2
Ramblers Wy HORN PO8 ... 140 F7
Ramley Rd LYMN SO41 ... 227 K3
Rampart Gdns HSEA PO3 ... 187 K3
Rampart Rd WEND SO18 ... 132 B1
The Rampart LYMN SO41 ... 228 B3
Ramsay Pl
LSOL/BMARY PO13 ... 185 G6 6
Ramsay Rd WINC SO23 ... 17 H1
Ramsdale Av HAV PO9 ... 165 G3
Ramsdean Rd PSF GU32 ... 62 C7
Ramsey Rd HISD PO11 ... 213 L5
Ramshill EPSF GU31 ... 63 M4
Rances Wy FUFL SO22 ... 26 D3
Randall Cl TOTT SO40 ... 104 B6
Randall Rd CHFD SO53 ... 53 J6
Randalls Hl UPTN BH16 ... 216 D8
Randalls La RGWD BH24 ... 172 B3
Randolph Rd BOSC BH5 ... 234 B3 3
NEND PO2 ... 187 J5
PSTN BH14 ... 236 D4 3
Randolph St WSHM SO15 ... 131 G1
Ranelagh Gdns WSHM SO15 ... 131 J1
Ranelagh Rd
CHCH/BSGR BH23 ... 239 L1
HAV PO9 ... 8 B4
NEND PO2 ... 187 G7
WINC SO23 ... 26 D2
Ranfurly Gdns FAWY SO45 ... 155 J6
Range Gdns ITCH SO19 ... 132 F5
Range Gn NEND PO2 ... 187 G5
Rannoch Cl FHAM PO15 ... 6 C2
Ransome Cl FHAM/STUB PO14 ... 183 K1
Ranvilles La FHAM/STUB PO14 ... 183 M1
Rapson Cl CHAM PO6 ... 163 G7
Rareridge La BPWT SO32 ... 85 K8
Ratcliffe Rd FAWY SO45 ... 155 K7 4
HEND SO30 ... 134 A1
Ratlake La ROMY SO51 ... 52 E4
Rattigan Gdns HLER SO31 ... 135 G8
Raven Cl LSOL/BMARY PO13 ... 209 G2
Raven Rd SHAM SO14 ... 131 M2
Ravens Cl FHAM/STUB PO14 ... 184 B5
Ravenscourt Rd LYMN SO41 ... 228 B5
SBNE BH6 ... 237 H3
Ravenscroft Cl HLER SO31 ... 133 K7
Ravenscroft Wy BPWT SO32 ... 109 M7
Ravensdale Cl
BKME/WDN BH12 ... 234 B2 1
Raven Sq ELGH SO50 ... 81 J6 1
Ravens Wy LYMN SO41 ... 242 C4
Ravenswood
FHAM/STUB PO14 ... 159 G5 4
Raven Wy CHCH/BSGR BH23 ... 238 F3
Ravine Rd BOSC BH5 ... 237 G4
CCLF BH13 ... 234 E8
Raymond Cl FAWY SO45 ... 180 B5
HEND SO30 ... 108 E5
VWD BH31 ... 144 F2
Raymond Rd CHAM PO6 ... 162 C7
WSHM SO15 ... 131 H1
Rayners Gdns ROWN SO16 ... 107 J4 2
Raynes Rd LSOL/BMARY PO13 ... 208 D4
Reading Room La BPWT SO32 ... 110 C8
Readon Cl EPSF GU31 ... 63 M4
Rebbeck Rd LTDN BH7 ... 236 F3
The Recess ELGH SO50 ... 82 A3
Record Rd EMRTH PO10 ... 166 C7
Recreation Rd
BKME/WDN BH12 ... 234 D2
Rectory Av CHAM PO6 ... 164 D7
Rectory Cl FHAM/STUB PO14 ... 184 A5
GPORT PO12 ... 10 D7
Rectory Ct HEND SO30 ... 134 D1
Rectory Hl RSAL SP5 ... 19 J5
Rectory La BPWT SO32 ... 87 H3
FBDG SP6 ... 72 A7
Rectory Rd HAV PO9 ... 8 E6
PLE BH15 ... 233 H2
Redan Cl CHCH/BSGR BH23 ... 239 L1
The Redan GPORT PO12 ... 11 H9
Red Barn Av
FHAM/PORC PO16 ... 162 A7
Red Barn La FHAM PO15 ... 160 C4
Redbreast Rd
MOOR/WNTN BH9 ... 220 E5
Redbreast Rd North
MOOR/WNTN BH9 ... 220 E5 3
Redbridge Cswy WSHM SO15 ... 105 G8
Redbridge Gv HAV PO9 ... 165 H5
Redbridge Hl ROWN SO16 ... 105 L7
Redbridge La ROWN SO16 ... 105 G6
Redbridge Rd WSHM SO15 ... 105 J8
Redcar Av HSEA PO3 ... 187 L7
Redcliffe Cl CHCH/BSGR BH23 ... 223 G6
Redcote Cl WEND SO18 ... 132 F1 1
Redcroft La HLER SO31 ... 133 L7
The Redfords TOTT SO40 ... 104 D7
Redhill ROWN SO16 ... 106 D4
Redhill Av NBNE BH10 ... 220 C6
Redhill Cl NBNE BH10 ... 220 C6
ROWN SO16 ... 106 D4
Redhill Ct MOOR/WNTN BH9 ... 220 E4 3
Redhill Crs MOOR/WNTN BH9 ... 220 D5
Red Hill Crs ROWN SO16 ... 106 D4
Redhill Dr NBNE BH10 ... 220 C6
Redhill Rd HAV PO9 ... 141 M7
Red Hill Wy ROWN SO16 ... 106 D5
Redhoave Rd CFDH BH17 ... 218 B6
Redhorn Cl UPTN BH16 ... 232 B4 1
Red House Ct EPSF GU31 ... 65 L4
Redhouse Park Gdns
LSOL/BMARY PO13 ... 209 J1
Redlands BKME/WDN BH12 ... 234 E3
Redlands Dr ITCH SO19 ... 132 D2
Redlands Gv ENEY PO4 ... 212 A4
Redlands La EMRTH PO10 ... 166 D4
FHAM/STUB PO14 ... 6 F6
Red La RSAL SP5 ... 19 M1
Red Leaves BPWT SO32 ... 111 K6
Red Ldg CHFD SO53 ... 81 G5
Redlynch Cl HAV PO9 ... 165 M4 3
Redmans Vw VWD BH31 ... 144 B2
Redmoor Cl ITCH SO19 ... 132 C2
Red Oaks Cl FERN BH22 ... 193 M1
Red Oaks Dr FHAM PO15 ... 158 F3
Redrise Cl FAWY SO45 ... 179 M5
Redshank Cl CFDH BH17 ... 217 K7
Redshank Rd HORN PO8 ... 140 E1
Redvers Rd CHCH/BSGR BH23 ... 238 D1
Redward Rd ROWN SO16 ... 105 L3
Redwing Ct ENEY PO4 ... 212 A3 3
Redwing Gdns TOTT SO40 ... 104 B8 2
Redwing Rd HORN PO8 ... 116 B3
Redwood Cl FAWY SO45 ... 155 H5
HEND SO30 ... 108 B6
LYMN SO41 ... 228 A3
RGWD BH24 ... 170 F1
Redwood Dr FERN BH22 ... 168 A8
FHAM/PORC PO16 ... 161 M8
Redwood Gdns TOTT SO40 ... 129 G1
Redwood Gv HAV PO9 ... 165 L4
Redwood Rd UPTN BH16 ... 216 E8
Redwood Wy ROWN SO16 ... 106 F2
Reed Dr TOTT SO40 ... 130 D6
Reedmace Cl WVILLE PO7 ... 164 E2 3
Reeds La LISS GU33 ... 37 J2
Reed's Pl GPORT PO12 ... 10 D1
Reeds Rd GPORT PO12 ... 209 M1
Reeves Cl ROMY SO51 ... 76 D5
Reeves Wy HLER SO31 ... 133 K7 5
Regal Cl CHAM PO6 ... 163 K8
Regency Crs
CHCH/BSGR BH23 ... 222 D8 4
Regency Gdns WVILLE PO7 ... 164 B2 1
Regency Pl FHAM PO15 ... 6 C5
Regent Cl RWIN SO21 ... 54 B4
Regent Dr LTDN BH7 ... 221 K8
Regent Pl SSEA PO5 ... 12 F6 2
Regent Rd CHFD SO53 ... 81 J2
Regents Ct HAV PO9 ... 8 E7
Regents Ga HLER SO31 ... 158 C3
Regent's Gv WSHM SO15 ... 106 A8 3
Regent's Park Gdns
WSHM SO15 ... 130 F1 2
Regent's Park Rd WSHM SO15 ... 130 E1
Regent St PSEA PO1 ... 211 G1
SHAM SO14 ... 4 F3
Regent Wy
CHCH/BSGR BH23 ... 238 A2 1
Reginald Rd ENEY PO4 ... 211 L5
Reid St CHCH/BSGR BH23 ... 237 M1
Relay Rd WVILLE PO7 ... 140 B8
Reliant Cl CHFD SO53 ... 81 G4 1
Rempstone Rd WIMB BH21 ... 192 B7
Renault Dr BDST BH18 ... 217 L7
Renda Rd FAWY SO45 ... 180 A4
Renny Rd PSEA PO1 ... 13 M2
Renouf Cl LYMN SO41 ... 228 A5
Renown Cl CHFD SO53 ... 81 G3
Renown Gdns HORN PO8 ... 140 D3
Repton Cl GPORT PO12 ... 209 J4
Repton Gdns HEND SO30 ... 109 J6
Reservoir La HEND SO30 ... 133 L2
PSF GU32 ... 63 L3
Rest-a-wyle Av HISD PO11 ... 213 L3
Retreat Rd WIMB BH21 ... 192 B4
The Retreat ELGH SO50 ... 82 A4
SSEA PO5 ... 13 H6
TOTT SO40 ... 129 K3
Reuben Dr PLE BH15 ... 232 C6
Revenge Cl ENEY PO4 ... 212 A2 2
Rewlands Dr FUFL SO22 ... 16 B4
Reynolds Dl TOTT SO40 ... 129 H3
Reynolds Rd ELGH SO50 ... 83 J7
WSHM SO15 ... 106 B8
Rhinefield Cl BROC SO42 ... 175 J6
ELGH SO50 ... 82 E6 2
HAV PO9 ... 165 G4 5
Rhinefield Ornamental Dr
BROC SO42 ... 174 D3
Rhinefield Rd
NMIL/BTOS BH25 ... 199 J6
Rhiners Cl LYMN SO41 ... 200 F5
Rhyme Hall Ms FAWY SO45 ... 180 F5 3
Ribble Cl BDST BH18 ... 217 L6
CHFD SO53 ... 81 J3
Ribble Ct ROWN SO16 ... 105 K7
Ricardo Crs CHCH/BSGR BH23 ... 238 F2
Rice Gdns UPTN BH16 ... 232 C4
Richard Cl UPTN BH16 ... 232 A1 2
Richard Gv GPORT PO12 ... 185 L7
Richards Cl HLER SO31 ... 158 F5
Richlans Rd HEND SO30 ... 134 A2
Richmond Cl CHFD SO53 ... 53 G7
HISD PO11 ... 213 J4
TOTT SO40 ... 104 A7
Richmond Dr HISD PO11 ... 213 H4
Richmond Gdns PTSW SO17 ... 107 G7
WCLF BH2 ... 14 E5
Richmond Hl WCLF BH2 ... 14 E5
Richmond Hill Dr WCLF BH2 ... 14 E5
Richmond Hill Rbt WCLF BH2 ... 14 E4
Richmond La ROMY SO51 ... 50 F7
Richmond Pk RWIN SO21 ... 54 C4
Richmond Park Av CHAR BH8 ... 236 A1
Richmond Park Cl
BMTH BH1 ... 236 C2 3
Richmond Park Crs
CHAR BH8 ... 236 B1
Richmond Park Rd
BMTH BH1 ... 236 C2 5
Richmond Pl PSEA PO1 ... 12 E2
SSEA PO5 ... 13 H7 1
Richmond Ri
FHAM/PORC PO16 ... 162 A7
Richmond Rd GPORT PO12 ... 10 C4
LSOL/BMARY PO13 ... 208 B2
PSTN BH14 ... 234 B4
WSHM SO15 ... 131 G2
Richmond St SHAM SO14 ... 5 H5
Richmond Wood Rd
CHAR BH8 ... 236 A1
Richville Rd ROWN SO16 ... 105 M8
Ridding Cl WSHM SO15 ... 106 A8
Riders La HAV PO9 ... 165 J4
Ridge Cl HORN PO8 ... 116 B4
Ridge Common La PSF GU32 ... 63 H2
Ridgefield Gdns
CHCH/BSGR BH23 ... 224 B8
Ridge La HEND SO30 ... 135 H5
ROMY SO51 ... 78 A7
Ridgemount Av ROWN SO16 ... 106 E3
Ridgemount Gdns PLE BH15 ... 232 D5 6
The Ridge RSAL SP5 ... 73 J4
Ridge Top La PSF GU32 ... 62 F1
Ridgeway BDST BH18 ... 217 M4
FERN BH22 ... 194 C8
FUFL SO22 ... 26 B3
Ridgeway Cl CHAM PO6 ... 162 D7 1
CHFD SO53 ... 81 K3
ELGH SO50 ... 83 H5 1
Ridgeway La LYMN SO41 ... 228 B6
The Ridgeway
FHAM/PORC PO16 ... 161 J7
Ridgewood Cl FAWY SO45 ... 155 G5 1
Ridgway HAV PO9 ... 8 A5
The Ridings BPWT SO32 ... 111 K4
ELGH SO50 ... 82 F6
LISS GU33 ... 37 G4
NEND PO2 ... 187 K5
Ridley Cl FAWY SO45 ... 180 A4 3
Ridley Rd MOOR/WNTN BH9 ... 220 D8
Ridout Cl NBNE BH10 ... 219 M7
Rigby Rd SHAM SO14 ... 107 G8
Riggs Gdns BWD BH11 ... 219 K6
Rigler Rd PLE BH15 ... 232 F7
Rimbury Wy CHCH/BSGR BH23 ... 222 E8
Rimington Rd HORN PO8 ... 140 D5
Ringbury LYMN SO41 ... 228 B2
Ringlet Wy WINC SO23 ... 3 M7
Ringsgreen La PSF GU32 ... 34 F5
The Ring ROWN SO16 ... 106 D1
Ringwood Dr NBAD SO52 ... 79 K3
Ringwood Rd
BKME/WDN BH12 ... 219 H6
BWD BH11 ... 219 L2
BWD BH11 ... 219 J4 3
CHCH/BSGR BH23 ... 196 E8
CHCH/BSGR BH23 ... 224 A2
ENEY PO4 ... 211 M5
FBDG SP6 ... 97 M8
FBDG SP6 ... 121 K3
FERN BH22 ... 168 F8
PSTN BH14 ... 233 L2
RGWD BH24 ... 169 K4
RGWD BH24 ... 172 B3
TOTT SO40 ... 128 E1
VWD BH31 ... 144 D1
WIMB BH21 ... 144 C8
WIMB BH21 ... 168 F2
Ripley Gv HSEA PO3 ... 187 L8
Ripon Gdns WVILLE PO7 ... 140 F7
Ripon Rd MOOR/WNTN BH9 ... 220 E8
Ripplewood TOTT SO40 ... 130 E7 4
Ripstone Gdns PTSW SO17 ... 107 G5
The Rise BROC SO42 ... 175 K7
WVILLE PO7 ... 164 B6
Ritchie Ct ITCH SO19 ... 132 F4
Ritchie Pl FERN BH22 ... 168 B4 1
Ritchie Rd BWD BH11 ... 219 M4
Rival Moor Rd EPSF GU31 ... 64 A6
River Cl WIMB BH21 ... 192 A2
Riverdale Av WVILLE PO7 ... 164 E1
Riverdale Cl FBDG SP6 ... 97 L6
Riverdale La CHCH/BSGR BH23 ... 237 M2
Riverdene Pl WEND SO18 ... 107 J8 2
River Gdns LYMN SO41 ... 242 D4
River Gn HLER SO31 ... 157 L6
Riverhead Cl ENEY PO4 ... 211 M3
River La FHAM PO15 ... 160 A2
Riverlea Rd CHCH/BSGR BH23 ... 237 M2
Rivermead Cl ROMY SO51 ... 78 C1
Rivermead Gdns
CHCH/BSGR BH23 ... 222 C6
Riversdale Cl ITCH SO19 ... 132 C8 2
Riversdale Rd SBNE BH6 ... 237 M4
Riverside ELGH SO50 ... 82 C5
RGWD BH24 ... 170 D2
Riverside Av
FHAM/PORC PO16 ... 161 H5
LTDN BH7 ... 222 A7
Riverside Cl LISS GU33 ... 36 E4
TOTT SO40 ... 128 A2
Riverside Gdns ROMY SO51 ... 78 D2
Riverside La SBNE BH6 ... 237 L3
Riverside Rd FERN BH22 ... 168 B6
SBNE BH6 ... 237 L3 1
River's St SSEA PO5 ... 13 J3
River St EMRTH PO10 ... 166 F4
Riverview TOTT SO40 ... 129 K3
River View Rd WEND SO18 ... 107 J6
River Wk WEND SO18 ... 107 K5
River Wy CHCH/BSGR BH23 ... 222 B6
HAV PO9 ... 9 G1
R L Stevenson Av WBNE BH4 ... 235 G5
Roads Hl HORN PO8 ... 115 L7
Road Vw NEND PO2 ... 187 G8
Robert Cecil Av WEND SO18 ... 107 K4
Roberts Cl LYMN SO41 ... 227 J7
WHAM PO17 ... 136 E4
Roberts La CFDH BH17 ... 232 F1
Roberts Rd CFDH BH17 ... 217 M7
FAWY SO45 ... 155 K4
GPORT PO12 ... 209 K2 4
LTDN BH7 ... 236 F2
TOTT SO40 ... 129 K3
WSHM SO15 ... 4 B1
Robert Whitworth Dr
ROMY SO51 ... 50 E7
Robina Cl WVILLE PO7 ... 164 E1
Robin Crs NMIL/BTOS BH25 ... 225 H3
Robin Gdns HORN PO8 ... 140 B4
TOTT SO40 ... 104 B8
Robin Gv NMIL/BTOS BH25 ... 225 K6
Robinia Gn ROWN SO16 ... 106 B3
Robins Cl FHAM/STUB PO14 ... 184 A5
Robins La MIDH GU29 ... 67 G1
Robins Meadow
FHAM/STUB PO14 ... 159 G7
Robinson Rd
FHAM/STUB PO14 ... 183 M7
Robinson Wy HSEA PO3 ... 188 A5
Robin Sq ELGH SO50 ... 81 H7
Robins Wy CHCH/BSGR BH23 ... 239 G3
Robinswood Dr FERN BH22 ... 168 D7
Rochester Rd BWD BH11 ... 219 M4
ENEY PO4 ... 211 K5
Rochester St SHAM SO14 ... 5 L2
Rochford Rd CHAM PO6 ... 163 H8
Rockall Cl ROWN SO16 ... 105 K3
Rockbourne Cl HAV PO9 ... 165 G4 6
Rockbourne Gdns
NMIL/BTOS BH25 ... 225 H8 1
Rockbourne La FBDG SP6 ... 96 D1
Rockbourne Rd FUFL SO22 ... 16 C4
Rockery Cl FAWY SO45 ... 155 G4
Rockford Cl SBNE BH6 ... 237 L5
Rockingham Wy
FHAM/PORC PO16 ... 161 M8
Rockleigh Dr TOTT SO40 ... 129 H4
Rockleigh Rd ROWN SO16 ... 106 C5
Rockley Rd PLE BH15 ... 232 D6
Rockram Cl TOTT SO40 ... 127 M1
Rockram Gdns FAWY SO45 ... 155 G5 2
Rockrose Wy CHAM PO6 ... 162 E6
Rockstone La SHAM SO14 ... 131 L2
Rockstone Pl WSHM SO15 ... 131 K2
Rockville Dr WVILLE PO7 ... 164 C1
Rodbourne Cl LYMN SO41 ... 227 H7
Rodfield La RWIN SO21 ... 29 G5
Rodlease La LYMN SO41 ... 202 C6
Rodney Cl BKME/WDN BH12 ... 219 L8 1
LSOL/BMARY PO13 ... 209 G2
Rodney Dr CHCH/BSGR BH23 ... 238 E2
Rodney Rd ENEY PO4 ... 211 K3
Rodney Wy HORN PO8 ... 140 F2
Rodway WIMB BH21 ... 192 A4
Rodwell Cl NBNE BH10 ... 220 A2
Roebuck Av FHAM PO15 ... 160 B3
Roebuck Cl CHAM PO6 ... 187 K1 3
NMIL/BTOS BH25 ... 225 M5
Roeshot Crs CHCH/BSGR BH23 ... 224 C7
Roewood Cl FAWY SO45 ... 180 A5 2
Roewood Rd FAWY SO45 ... 180 A5
Rogate Gdns
FHAM/PORC PO16 ... 162 A7
Roger Penny Wy FBDG SP6 ... 98 F5
Rogers Cl ELGH SO50 ... 82 D2
GPORT PO12 ... 209 M2
Rogers Md HISD PO11 ... 189 K5
Rogers Rd ELGH SO50 ... 82 D4
Roker Wy ELGH SO50 ... 83 G7
Roland Cl HORN PO8 ... 140 F2
Rollestone Rd FAWY SO45 ... 179 M5
Rolls Dr SBNE BH6 ... 238 A4
Roman Cl CHFD SO53 ... 81 K1
Roman Dr ROWN SO16 ... 106 D1
Roman Gdns FAWY SO45 ... 155 H7 1
Roman Gv FHAM/PORC PO16 ... 186 B2
Roman Landing SELS PO20 ... 215 J6
Roman Rd BDST BH18 ... 217 J4
FAWY SO45 ... 155 G6
FAWY SO45 ... 179 M2
ROWN SO16 ... 80 D7
RWIN SO21 ... 54 F3
Romans' Rd WINC SO23 ... 26 E2
Roman Wy FAWY SO45 ... 155 H7
HAV PO9 ... 165 G6
Romford Rd HLER SO31 ... 158 B8
Romill Cl WEND SO18 ... 108 A5
Romney Cl NBNE BH10 ... 220 C5 2
Romney Rd NBNE BH10 ... 220 C4
Romsey Av FHAM/PORC PO16 ... 161 L8
HSEA PO3 ... 211 M2
Romsey Cl ELGH SO50 ... 81 M5
Romsey Rd ELGH SO50 ... 81 M5
FUFL SO22 ... 2 C8
HORN PO8 ... 116 B6
LYND SO43 ... 151 K2
ROMY SO51 ... 76 D4
ROMY SO51 ... 103 K3
ROWN SO16 ... 105 J3
RSAL SP5 ... 47 G4
TOTT SO40 ... 102 E8
Romyns Ct FHAM/STUB PO14 ... 6 E6
Rookcliff Wy LYMN SO41 ... 242 B4
Rookery Av FHAM PO15 ... 159 G1
HLER SO31 ... 158 F1
Rookery La FBDG SP6 ... 71 L7
The Rookery EMRTH PO10 ... 166 E7
Rookes Cl HORN PO8 ... 140 F2
Rookes La LYMN SO41 ... 228 B6
Rook Hill Rd CHCH/BSGR BH23 ... 239 G2
Rookley HLER SO31 ... 157 G1
Rooksbridge FAWY SO45 ... 155 G5 3
Rooksbury Cft HAV PO9 ... 165 L3 5
Rooks Down Rd FUFL SO22 ... 26 C3
Rooksway Gv
FHAM/PORC PO16 ... 161 J8
Rookwood Cl ELGH SO50 ... 82 A2 2
Rookwood La SELS PO20 ... 215 L4
Rookwood Rd SELS PO20 ... 215 L6
Rookwood Vw WVILLE PO7 ... 139 K3
Roosevelt Crs BWD BH11 ... 219 M2
Rope Hl LYMN SO41 ... 202 B7
Ropers La UPTN BH16 ... 232 C1
Ropley Cl ITCH SO19 ... 132 E8 2
Ropley Rd HAV PO9 ... 165 M3
LTDN BH7 ... 237 H1
Rosamund Av WIMB BH21 ... 192 C7
Roscrea Cl SBNE BH6 ... 238 A4 1
Roscrea Dr SBNE BH6 ... 238 A4
Rosebank Cl ROWN SO16 ... 105 K3
Rosebay Cl ELGH SO50 ... 109 H2 4
Rosebay Ct WVILLE PO7 ... 164 D3 3
Rosebery Av CHAM PO6 ... 187 L1
Rosebery Cl VWD BH31 ... 145 G3
Rosebery Crs ELGH SO50 ... 82 A2
Rosebery Rd BOSC BH5 ... 236 F3 4
Rosebud Av
MOOR/WNTN BH9 ... 220 E6 5
Rosebury Av FAWY SO45 ... 155 L7
Rose Cl FAWY SO45 ... 155 L6 5
HEND SO30 ... 109 H8
Rosecrae Cl
NMIL/BTOS BH25 ... 225 K4 2
Rose Crs PLE BH15 ... 233 L2
Rosedale Av ROMY SO51 ... 78 F1
Rosedale Cl
CHCH/BSGR BH23 ... 238 D2 5
FHAM/STUB PO14 ... 159 K8
Rose Gdns MOOR/WNTN BH9 ... 220 E6
Rose Hl HORN PO8 ... 140 E2
Rosehill Cl CHCH/BSGR BH23 ... 197 M7 2
Rosehill Dr CHCH/BSGR BH23 ... 197 M7
Roselands HEND SO30 ... 108 C8 3
HORN PO8 ... 140 E3
Roselands Cl ELGH SO50 ... 83 G5
Roselands Gdns PTSW SO17 ... 106 F6
Roseleigh Dr TOTT SO40 ... 129 J2
Rosemary Gdns
BKME/WDN BH12 ... 234 A1
FHAM PO15 ... 135 H8
HEND SO30 ... 134 A3
Rosemary La PSEA PO1 ... 12 C2 4
Rosemary Rd
BKME/WDN BH12 ... 234 B1
Rosemary Wy HORN PO8 ... 140 F4
Rosemoor Gv CHFD SO53 ... 53 G7
Rosemount Rd WBNE BH4 ... 235 G6
Rosendale Rd CHFD SO53 ... 81 J4 1
Rose Rd SHAM SO14 ... 106 F8
TOTT SO40 ... 129 L2
The Rosery GPORT PO12 ... 10 E9
Rosetta Rd ENEY PO4 ... 211 M4
Rosewall Rd ROWN SO16 ... 105 L5
Rosewarne Ct WINC SO23 ... 2 F5
Rosewood LSOL/BMARY PO13 ... 185 J7
Rosewood Gdns HORN PO8 ... 116 B3
NMIL/BTOS BH25 ... 225 K4
TOTT SO40 ... 130 E7
Rosina Cl WVILLE PO7 ... 140 F8
Roslin Rd TWDS BH3 ... 235 K1
Roslin Rd South TWDS BH3 ... 235 J1
Rosoman Rd ITCH SO19 ... 132 D4
Rossan Av HLER SO31 ... 182 B1
Ross Gdns ROWN SO16 ... 105 M6
WIMB BH21 ... 219 G3 1
Rossington Av WEND SO18 ... 132 D1
Rossington Wy WEND SO18 ... 132 D1
Rossley Cl CHCH/BSGR BH23 ... 224 C6
Rosslyn Cl NBAD SO52 ... 79 M4
Rossmore Rd
BKME/WDN BH12 ... 219 G8
Ross Rd RGWD BH24 ... 147 G7
Ross Wy LSOL/BMARY PO13 ... 208 D1
Rostron Cl WEND SO18 ... 107 M5 2
Rosyth Rd WEND SO18 ... 132 D1
Rotary Cl WIMB BH21 ... 192 D1
Rotary Ct HLER SO31 ... 156 F2
Rothbury Cl ITCH SO19 ... 132 E4 1
TOTT SO40 ... 104 C7
Rothbury Pk
NMIL/BTOS BH25 ... 225 M6 2
Rotherbank Farm La LISS GU33 ... 36 E2
Rother Cl EPSF GU31 ... 64 B4
WEND SO18 ... 108 A7
Rothercombe La PSF GU32 ... 62 F3
Rother Dl ITCH SO19 ... 133 J5
Rotherfield Rd
CHCH/BSGR BH23 ... 224 E7
SBNE BH6 ... 237 G5 1
Rother La EPSF GU31 ... 66 D7
Rotherwick Cl HAV PO9 ... 165 M3
Rothesay Dr CHCH/BSGR BH23 ... 239 K1
Rothesay Rd GPORT PO12 ... 209 L1
TWDS BH3 ... 235 H2
Rothsbury Dr CHFD SO53 ... 81 G2
Rothschild Cl ITCH SO19 ... 132 C8
Rothville Pl CHFD SO53 ... 53 G6 2
Rothwell Cl CHAM PO6 ... 162 E7 3

Rotterdam Dr
CHCH/BSGR BH23 .... 238 C1
Roughdown La FAWY SO45 ...... 180 A7
Roumelia La BOSC BH5 .... 236 D4
The Roundabouts LISS GU33 .. 36 F3
Roundcopse FAWY SO45 .... 155 C5
Round Hl FBDG SP6 .... 97 L7
Roundhaye Rd BWD BH11 ..... 219 K3
Roundhill Cl WEND SO18 ...... 107 M7
Roundhouse Dr TOTT SO40 .... 128 C7
Roundhouse Meadow
EMRTH PO10 .... 190 E1
Roundhuts Ri WINC SO23 ..... 3 M7
Roundway WVILLE PO7 .... 140 D8
Routs Wy ROWN SO16 .... 105 K1
Rowallan Av
LSOL/BMARY PO13 .... 184 F7
Rowan Av HORN PO8 .... 140 F6
Rowan Cl BPWT SO32 .... 112 A4
CHCH/BSGR BH23 .... 224 B8
HLER SO31 .... 133 K8
LSOL/BMARY PO13 .... 208 D3
LYMN SO41 .... 200 F7
RGWD BH24 .... 169 H4
ROMY SO51 .... 79 H2
ROWN SO16 .... 105 L5
TOTT SO40 .... 129 H2
Rowan Dr CFDH BH17 .... 217 J7
CHCH/BSGR BH23 .... 224 B8
VWD BH31 .... 144 F4
Rowan Gdns HEND SO30 ..... 134 B2
Rowan Rd HAV PO9 .... 165 M5
The Rowans TOTT SO40 ...... 130 D7
Rowan Wy FHAM/STUB SO14 . 160 A8
Rowbarrow Cl CFDH BH17 .... 218 C6
Rowborough Rd WEND SO18 . 107 L8
Rowbury Rd HAV PO9 .... 165 H2
Rowden Cl ROMY SO51 ...... 76 D1
Rowe Ashe Wy HLER SO31 ... 158 D5
Rowena Rd SBNE BH6 .... 237 L3
Rowes La LYMN SO41 .... 229 M1
Rowhay La BPWT SO32 ...... 84 B3
Rowhill Dr FAWY SO45 ...... 155 C5
Rowin Cl HISD PO11 .... 214 B6
Rowland Av PLE BH15 .... 233 K3
Rowland Rd CHAM PO6 ...... 162 C7
FHAM PO15 .... 6 E4
Rowlands Av WVILLE PO7 .... 140 C7
Rowlands Castle Rd
HORN PO8 .... 141 K2
Rowlands Cl CHFD SO53 ..... 80 F1
Rowlands Hl BH21 .... 192 A3
Rowlett Rd LYMN SO41 ...... 228 C5
Rowley Cl HEND SO30 .... 109 L8
Rowley Dr HEND SO30 .... 109 L8
Rowlings Rd FUFL SO22 ..... 16 C5
Rowner Cl LSOL/BMARY PO13 . 185 G2
Rowner Rd LSOL/BMARY PO13 . 185 G8
Rowner Rd LSOL/BMARY PO13 . 184 F7
Rownhams Cl ROWN SO16 .... 105 K2
Rownhams La NBAD SO52 .... 79 L3
ROMY SO51 .... 79 L7
ROWN SO16 .... 105 L1
Rownhams Rd CHAR BH8 ..... 221 C5
HAV PO9 .... 165 H3
NBAD SO52 .... 79 M5
ROWN SO16 .... 105 L6
Rownhams Rd North
ROWN SO16 .... 105 L3
Rownhams Wy ROWN SO16 .. 105 K2
Rowse Cl ROMY SO51 .... 50 E7
The Row RSAL SP5 .... 73 K1
Row Wood La
LSOL/BMARY PO13 .... 184 F7
Royal Crescent Rd SHAM SO14 . 5 J6
Royal Gdns HAV PO9 .... 141 L7
Royal Ga ENEY PO4 .... 211 M6
Royal Oak Rd NBNE BH10 ... 220 A3
Royal Sovereign Av
FHAM/STUB SO14 .... 184 D7
Royal Wy WVILLE PO7 ...... 164 E1
Royce Cl SELS PO20 .... 215 L7
Royce Wy SELS PO20 ...... 215 L7
Royden La LYMN SO41 ...... 202 B5
Roydon Cl FUFL SO22 ...... 26 C3
Roy's La BPWT SO32 .... 113 H6
Royster Cl CFDH BH17 ..... 218 A7
Royston Av ELGH SO50 ..... 81 M3
Royston Cl PTSW SO17 ..... 107 C6
Royston Dr WIMB BH21 .... 192 B3
Royston Cl NMIL/BTOS BH25 . 225 M8
Rozelle Rd PSTN BH14 ..... 234 B4
Rubens Cl NMIL/BTOS BH25 . 225 L4
Ruby Rd ITCH SO19 .... 132 E2
Rudd La ROMY SO51 .... 50 F1
Rudgwick Cl
FHAM/PORC PO16 .... 161 M8
Rudmore Sq NEND PO2 ...... 187 G8
Ruffield Cl FUFL SO22 ..... 16 B6
Rufford Cl ELGH SO50 ..... 81 M2
Rufford Gdns SBNE BH6 .... 237 K3
Rufus Cl CHFD SO53 .... 53 K8
ROWN SO16 .... 105 J2
Rufus Gdns TOTT SO40 ..... 129 G1
Rugby Rd CFDH BH17 ...... 217 L7
SSEA PO5 .... 13 L3
Rumbridge Gdns TOTT SO40 . 129 L1
Rumbridge St TOTT SO40 ... 129 K2
Runnymede FHAM PO15 ..... 160 B4
HEND SO30 .... 108 C7
Runnymede Av BWD BH11 ... 219 H2
Runton Rd BKME/WDN BH12 . 234 E3
The Runway CHCH/BSGR BH23 . 239 G1
Rushall La WIMB BH21 ...... 216 E4
Rushcombe Wy WIMB BH21 . 217 H2
Rushes Rd PSF GU32 .... 63 K4
The Rushes TOTT SO40 ..... 130 D6
Rushfield Cl LISS GU33 .... 36 E5
Rushford Warren
CHCH/BSGR BH23 .... 238 E4
Rushington Av TOTT SO40 .. 129 K2
Rushington La TOTT SO40 .. 129 J3
Rushmere La HORN PO8 .... 139 H1
Rushmere Rd SBNE BH6 .... 237 H1
Rushton Crs TWDS BH3 .... 235 L2
Ruskin Av MOOR/WNTN BH9 . 220 F5
Ruskin Rd ELGH SO50 ...... 81 M3

ENEY PO4 .... 211 L4
Ruskin Wy HORN PO8 ...... 140 D4
Rusland Cl CHFD SO53 ..... 81 G1
Russell Cl LSOL/BMARY PO13 . 208 D2
Russell Cotes Rd BMTH BH1 . 15 G7
Russell Dr CHCH/BSGR BH23 . 238 C2
ROMY SO51 .... 21 J8
Russell Gdns RGWD BH24 ... 169 M3
UPTN BH16 .... 232 B4
Russell Pl FHAM/PORC PO16 . 7 J5
PTSW SO17 .... 107 C7
Russell Rd HAV PO9 .... 8 F1
LSOL/BMARY PO13 .... 208 D3
WINC SO23 .... 3 H3
Russell St GPORT PO12 .... 209 L2
SHAM SO14 .... 5 H5
Russel Rd EPSF GU31 ...... 63 M6
Russel Rd NBNE BH10 ..... 220 A2
LYMN SO41 .... 228 D6
Russet Cl FERN BH22 ...... 194 B2
Russett Cl BPWT SO32 ..... 112 A4
Rustan Cl ELGH SO50 ...... 83 J6
HEND SO30 .... 133 M2
Rutland Gdns HLER SO31 ... 133 L7
Rutland Rd CHCH/BSGR BH23 . 222 D7
MOOR/WNTN BH9 .... 220 F8
Rutland Wy WEND SO18 .... 107 M7
Ruxley Cl FAWY SO45 ...... 180 A4
Ryall Dr CFDH BH17 .... 218 B7
Ryan Cl FERN BH22 .... 194 A1
Ryan Gdns FERN BH22 ..... 194 A1
Rydal Cl CHAM PO6 .... 162 F7
CHCH/BSGR BH23 .... 222 B4
Rydal Rd GPORT PO12 ..... 185 L8
Ryde Pl LSOL/BMARY PO13 .. 208 L4
Ryde Ter SHAM SO14 ...... 5 K5
Rye Cl NBAD SO52 .... 80 E2
Ryecroft FHAM/STUB PO14 .. 159 G6
HAV PO9 .... 9 K4
Ryecroft Av BWD BH11 .... 219 J3
Rye Dl TOTT SO40 .... 129 G5
Ryedown La ROMY SO51 .... 77 H4
Ryefield Cl EPSF GU31 ..... 64 B5
Rye Paddock La FAWY SO45 . 180 T4
Rylandes Ct ROWN SO16 ... 105 L5

S

Sabre Rd EMRTH PO10 ...... 190 E5
Sackville St SSEA PO5 ..... 13 G4
Saddle Cl WIMB BH21 ...... 193 G2
Saddlers Cl ELGH SO50 .... 81 M2
Sadlers La FAWY SO45 ..... 155 L7
Sadlers Wk EMRTH PO10 ... 166 E8
Saffron Dr CHCH/BSGR BH23 . 223 M8
Saffron Wy BWD BH11 ..... 219 H5
FHAM PO15 .... 135 H8
Sage Cl WVILLE PO7 .... 164 E2
Sages La ALTN GU34 ...... 33 H3
Sailor's La BPWT SO32 ..... 86 B1
St Agatha's Rd HLER SO31 .. 157 L4
St Alban's Av CHAR BH8 ... 236 A1
St Alban's Crs CHAR BH8 .. 236 A1
St Alban's Rd CHAR BH8 ... 236 A1
HAV PO9 .... 165 L4
SHAM SO14 .... 5 K1
St Aldhelm's Cl CCLF BH13 . 234 E5
St Aldhelm's Rd CCLF BH13 . 234 E4
St Andrew Cl HORN PO8 ... 116 B6
St Andrews Cl NBAD SO52 . 79 K3
ROMY SO51 .... 50 C2
St Andrews Pk ELGH SO50 . 109 H2
St Andrew's Rd CHAM PO6 . 164 D8
GPORT PO12 .... 10 F4
HISD PO11 .... 213 M6
SHAM SO14 .... 5 H1
SSEA PO5 .... 13 J5
WIMB BH21 .... 217 L3
St Anne's Av SBNE BH6 .... 237 K3
St Annes Cl FUFL SO22 .... 26 B3
St Anne's Gdns ITCH SO19 . 132 C6
LYMN SO41 .... 228 B5
St Anne's Gv
FHAM/STUB SO14 .... 184 D1
St Annes La BPWT SO32 ... 136 B1
St Anne's Rd ITCH SO19 ... 132 C6
UPTN BH16 .... 232 A1
St Ann's Crs GPORT PO12 .. 209 L2
St Ann's Rd HORN PO8 .... 141 C1
St Anthony's Rd WCLF BH2 . 14 E2
St Aubin's Av ITCH SO19 ... 132 E3
St Aubin's Pk HISD PO11 .. 213 H5
St Aubyns Ct PLE BH15 .... 233 G6
St Aubyns La RGWD BH24 .. 147 J7
St Augustine Gdns
PTSW SO17 .... 107 J7
St Augustine Rd ENEY PO4 . 211 K5
St Augustin's Rd WCLF BH2 . 14 E1
St Austell Cl ELGH SO50 ... 82 D5
St Barbara Wy NEND PO2 .. 187 K4
St Barbe Cl ROMY SO51 .... 78 F2
St Bartholomew's Gdns
SSEA PO5 .... 13 K5
St Blaize Rd ROMY SO51 ... 51 G8
St Bonnet Dr BPWT SO32 .. 85 H8
St Brelades Av
BKME/WDN BH12 .... 219 H7
St Catherines WIMB BH21 . 192 B3
St Catherine's Rd ELGH SO50 . 81 M3
HISD PO11 .... 213 G5
SBNE BH6 .... 237 K5
WEND SO18 .... 107 K7
WINC SO23 .... 27 G2
St Catherines Wy LTDN BH7 . 222 F8
St Catherine's Vw
HEND SO30 .... 133 L2
St Catherines Wy
FHAM/PORC PO16 .... 161 J7
St Chad's Av NEND PO2 .... 187 J6
St Christopher Av
FHAM/PORC PO16 .... 7 K2
St Christopher's Av NBAD SO52 . 79 L4
St Christopher's Rd HAV PO9 . 165 G5
St Clair Rd CCLF BH13 .... 245 K2

St Clares Av HAV PO9 ..... 165 H1
St Clements Cl ROMY SO51 . 50 D8
St Clements Gdns BMTH BH1 . 236 C3
St Clement's Rd BMTH BH1 . 236 C3
PLE BH15 .... 234 A1
St Clement St WINC SO23 .. 2 F8
St Colman's Av CHAM PO6 . 163 L8
St Cross Rd WINC SO23 ... 26 D5
St Cuthberts Av HLER SO31 . 158 F4
St Cuthberts La HLER SO31 . 158 F4
St David's Cl TOTT SO40 ... 104 B7
St Davids Rd HLER SO31 ... 158 D5
HORN PO8 .... 116 B3
SSEA PO5 .... 13 K4
UPTN BH16 .... 232 A1
St Denys PTSW SO17 ...... 107 G7
PTSW SO17 .... 107 G7
St Edmund Cl
FHAM/STUB PO14 .... 158 F7
St Edmund's Rd ROWN SO16 . 106 A8
St Edward's Rd GPORT PO12 . 10 F4
HLER SO31 .... 156 F1
SSEA PO5 .... 13 G6
St Elizabeth's Av WEND SO18 . 132 F1
St Evox Cl ROWN SO16 .... 105 L3
St Faith's Cl GPORT PO12 .. 10 C2
St Faith's Rd PSEA PO1 .... 211 H2
WINC SO23 .... 26 E3
St Francis Av WEND SO18 .. 108 A8
St Francis Cl FAWY SO45 ... 206 C1
St Francis Ct NEND PO2 .... 187 J4
St Francis Pl HAV PO9 ..... 165 J5
St Francis Rd FAWY SO45 .. 206 C1
GPORT PO12 .... 11 G9
St Gabriel's Rd WEND SO18 . 132 F1
St George Cl HLER SO31 ... 133 K7
St Georges Av CHAR BH8 .. 236 B1
BKME/WDN BH12 .... 218 F8
HAV PO9 .... 9 K4
St Georges Cl
CHCH/BSGR BH23 .... 197 M8
CHAR BH8 .... 221 G8
CHCH/BSGR BH23 .... 224 B8
St Georges Crs FBDG SP6 .. 97 L6
St George's Dr FERN BH22 . 194 A4
St George's Rd CHAM PO6 . 163 K8
ENEY PO4 .... 211 L6
FBDG SP6 .... 97 L6
HISD PO11 .... 213 H5
HLER SO31 .... 158 D5
PSEA PO1 .... 12 C3
St Georges Sq PSEA PO1 .. 12 D2
St Georges St SHAM SO14 . 5 G4
WINC SO23 .... 3 G7
St George's Wy PSEA PO1 . 12 D2
St Giles Cl WINC SO23 .... 3 K9
St Giles Wy HORN PO8 .... 116 B6
St Helena Gdns WEND SO18 . 107 L5
St Helena Wy
FHAM/PORC PO16 .... 162 A8
St Helen's Cl ENEY PO4 .... 211 K6
St Helen's Pde ENEY PO4 .. 13 M9
St Helens Rd GPORT PO12 . 209 J5
HISD PO11 .... 213 H5
St Helier Rd BKME/WDN BH12 . 219 H4
St Hellen's Rd CHAM PO6 .. 164 B8
St Hermans Rd HISD PO11 . 214 A6
St Hilda Av HORN PO8 .... 116 B6
St Hubert Rd HORN PO8 ... 116 B6
St Ives End La RGWD BH24 . 169 J3
St Ives Gdns WCLF BH2 .... 14 F2
St Ives Pk RGWD BH24 .... 169 L3
St Ives Wd RGWD BH24 ... 169 M3
St James Cl HORN PO8 .... 116 B4
PLE BH15 .... 233 G7
St James' La FUFL SO22 ... 2 D8
St James's Rd EMRTH PO10 . 166 D8
HEND SO30 .... 108 C6
LYMN SO41 .... 201 L7
WIMB BH21 .... 193 L2
St James's St WSHM SO15 . 106 B7
St James's Park Rd
ROWN SO16 .... 106 B6
St James's Sq BOSC BH5 ... 236 F3
St James's St PSEA PO1 .... 12 E1
St James' Ter FUFL SO22 .. 2 E8
St James' Vls WINC SO23 .. 2 E9
St James Wy
FHAM/PORC PO16 .... 162 B8
St John's Av WVILLE PO7 .. 164 C4
St John's Cl GPORT PO12 .. 10 E1
HISD PO11 .... 213 J5
ROWN SO16 .... 105 K1
WIMB BH21 .... 192 B4
St Johns Ct TOTT SO40 .... 130 D7
St Johns Dr TOTT SO40 .... 130 C7
St John's Gdns
MOOR/WNTN BH9 .... 220 D7
St Johns Glebe ROWN SO16 . 105 L1
St John's Hl WIMB BH21 ... 192 B3
St John's Rd BOSC BH5 .... 236 C4
CHAM PO6 .... 163 J8
CHCH/BSGR BH23 .... 237 M2
ELGH SO50 .... 82 A4
EMRTH PO10 .... 167 G7
HAV PO9 .... 165 G4
HEND SO30 .... 133 L4
HLER SO31 .... 158 F6
NMIL/BTOS BH25 .... 225 L1
PLE BH15 .... 233 J4
WINC SO23 .... 3 K7
St John's St FAWY SO45 ... 155 L4
WINC SO23 .... 3 J8
St Just Cl FERN BH22 ..... 193 M5
St Lawrence Rd ELGH SO50 . 81 M4
SHAM SO14 .... 5 J6
St Ledger's Pl BMTH BH1 .. 236 C2
St Ledger's Rd CHAR BH8 .. 236 C1
St Leonard's Av HISD PO11 . 213 L5
St Leonards Cl FHAM PO15 . 159 J5
St Leonards Rd CHAR BH8 .. 236 A2
LYMN SO41 .... 203 M8
St Leonards Wy RGWD BH24 . 168 B6
St Lukes Cl HEND SO30 .... 109 H7
St Luke's Rd GPORT PO12 .. 209 L2

TWDS BH3 .... 235 L1
St Margaret's Av
CHCH/BSGR BH23 .... 237 M2
St Margaret's Cl WEND SO18 . 132 F1
St Margarets La
FHAM/STUB PO14 .... 159 J7
St Margarets Rd HISD PO11 . 213 L5
ROWN SO16 .... 106 B4
St Mark's Cl GPORT PO12 .. 10 D9
St Marks Rd LYMN SO41 ... 227 M5
BWD BH11 .... 219 M5
GPORT PO12 .... 10 D9
NEND PO2 .... 187 H7
St Martin's Cl ROWN SO16 . 105 K5
WINC SO23 .... 3 K7
St Mary Gv LYMN SO41 .... 226 E6
St Mary's Av GPORT PO12 . 10 D7
St Mary's Cl
CHCH/BSGR BH23 .... 197 M8
RSAL SP5 .... 73 L3
WINC SO23 .... 17 H3
St Mary's Pl SHAM SO14 .. 5 H3
St Mary's Rd CHAR BH8 ... 236 C2
ELGH SO50 .... 82 C4
FERN BH22 .... 194 A3
HISD PO11 .... 213 K5
HLER SO31 .... 157 G2
LISS GU33 .... 36 E4
PSEA PO1 .... 211 J2
SHAM SO14 .... 5 H1
St Mary's Ter RWIN SO21 .. 54 F2
St Mary St FUFL SO22 .... 26 C3
SHAM SO14 .... 5 J4
St Matthews Cl SHAM SO14 . 5 H1
St Matthew's Rd CHAM PO6 . 163 K8
FUFL SO22 .... 2 D8
St Merrin's Cl NBNE BH10 . 220 A4
St Michaels Cl FAWY SO45 . 232 D5
VWD BH31 .... 144 D3
St Michaels Ct CHAM PO6 . 162 F7
St Michael's Gdns WINC SO23 . 2 F8
St Michael's Gv
FHAM/STUB PO14 .... 6 F8
FHAM/STUB PO14 .... 184 D1
St Michael's Rd HAV PO9 .. 165 G5
HLER SO31 .... 158 D6
PSEA PO1 .... 12 F3
St Michael's St SHAM SO14 . 4 F5
St Michaels Wy HORN PO8 . 116 B6
St Monica Rd ITCH SO19 ... 132 E5
St Nicholas WINC SO23 ... 17 G2
St Nicholas Av
LSOL/BMARY PO13 .... 209 G1
St Nicholas' Rd HAV PO9 .. 165 G5
St Nicholas St PSEA PO1 ... 12 D5
St Osmund's Rd PSTN BH14 . 234 B5
St Patrick's La LISS GU33 .. 37 H3
St Paul's HI FUFL SO22 .... 2 E6
St Paul's La BMTH BH1 .... 15 J4
St Paul's Pl BMTH BH1 .... 15 J4
St Pauls Rd BMTH BH1 .... 15 J5
HLER SO31 .... 158 C2
SSEA PO5 .... 12 F3
St Pauls Rbt BMTH BH1 ... 15 G6
St Peter's Av HISD PO11 ... 190 A6
St Peter's Gv SSEA PO5 .... 13 J5
St Peter's Rd BMTH BH1 .. 14 F5
HISD PO11 .... 190 A6
PSF GU32 .... 63 L5
PSTN BH14 .... 233 M4
St Peters Rbt BMTH BH1 .. 15 G6
St Peter's Sq EMRTH PO10 . 166 D8
St Peter's St BPWT SO32 .. 85 H8
St Peter St WINC SO23 .... 3 G7
St Philip's Wy WEND SO18 . 132 F1
St Piran's Av HSEA PO3 ... 211 L1
St Ronan's Av ENEY PO4 .. 13 M7
St Ronan's Rd ENEY PO4 .. 13 M7
St Sebastian Crs
FHAM/PORC PO16 .... 7 K1
St Simon Cl HLER SO31 ... 158 F5
St Simon's Rd SSEA PO5 .. 13 K8
St Stephens La VWD BH31 . 144 E2
St Stephen's Rd FUFL SO22 . 2 B3
NEND PO2 .... 187 J8
WCLF BH2 .... 14 C4
St Stephen's Wy WCLF BH2 . 14 E4
St Swithin Cl BPWT SO32 .. 85 G8
St Swithin's Cl ROMY SO51 . 51 J7
St Swithun's Rd BMTH BH1 . 15 K3
NEND PO2 .... 187 K6
St Swithun's Rd South
BMTH BH1 .... 15 K4
St Swithun St WINC SO23 . 2 F9
St Theresas Cl HAV PO9 ... 165 J5
St Thomas Av HISD PO11 .. 213 H5
St Thomas Cl FHAM/PORC PO16 . 7 J2
St Thomas Pk LYMN SO41 . 228 B4
St Thomas's Cl NBNE BH10 . 220 B6
St Thomas's Rd GPORT PO12 . 185 M8
St Thomas St LYMN SO41 . 228 B5
PSEA PO1 .... 12 C5
St Thomas St WINC SO23 .. 2 F9
St Tristan Cl HLER SO31 ... 158 F5
St Ursula Gv SSEA PO5 .... 13 J5
St Valerie Rd GPORT PO12 . 10 D7
WCLF BH2 .... 14 C4
St Vigor Wy RWIN SO21 ... 54 F2
St Vincent Crs HORN PO8 .. 140 F2
St Vincent Rd GPORT PO12 . 209 M2
SSEA PO5 .... 13 J5
St Vincent St SSEA PO5 ... 12 F3
St Winifred's Rd ROWN SO16 . 106 B6
WCLF BH2 .... 14 E2
Salcombe Av HSEA PO3 .... 187 L7
Salcombe Cl CHFD SO53 ... 81 G4
Salcombe Crs TOTT SO40 .. 129 J2
Salcombe Rd TOTT SO40 ... 129 J2

WSHM SO15 .... 130 F1
Salcot Rd WINC SO23 ...... 3 G3
Salem St WSHM SO15 ..... 106 B7
Salerno Dr GPORT PO12 .... 10 B5
Salerno Pl PLE BH15 ...... 232 C6
Salerno Rd NEND PO2 ..... 187 H4
ROWN SO16 .... 106 B4
Salet Wy WVILLE PO7 ..... 140 F7
Salisbury Rd ELGH SO50 ... 82 A4
Salisbury Rd BOSC BH5 .... 236 D4
CHAM PO6 .... 187 L1
CHCH/BSGR BH23 .... 222 F2
ENEY PO4 .... 211 K6
FBDG SP6 .... 97 M6
PSTN BH14 .... 234 B3
PTSW SO17 .... 106 F5
RGWD BH24 .... 122 E7
ROMY SO51 .... 49 K8
RSAL SP5 .... 44 D7
TOTT SO40 .... 104 D7
Salisbury St FBDG SP6 .... 97 L7
WIMB BH21 .... 94 D8
Salisbury Ter
LSOL/BMARY PO13 .... 208 D3
Salmon Dr ELGH SO50 ..... 82 E6
FERN BH22 .... 194 A3
Salterns Av ENEY PO4 .... 211 M3
Salterns Cl HISD PO11 .... 214 A5
Salterns Est FHAM/PORC PO16 . 7 K9
Salterns La FAWY SO45 ... 180 F4
FHAM/PORC PO16 .... 184 F1
HISD PO11 .... 213 M5
HLER SO31 .... 157 L2
Salterns Rd FHAM/STUB PO14 . 183 M8
PSTN BH14 .... 235 M5
Salterns Wy PSTN BH14 ... 234 B4
Salter Rd CCLF BH13 ..... 245 G5
Saltgrass La LYMN SO41 ... 242 F6
Saltings La UPTN BH16 ... 232 A2
The Saltings CHAM PO6 ... 188 C1
HAV PO9 .... 189 K2
Salt La BPWT SO32 .... 57 K5
Saltmarsh La HISD PO11 .. 213 J3
Saltmarsh Rd SHAM SO14 . 5 K5
Saltmead PTSW SO17 ..... 107 J7
Salt Meat La GPORT PO12 . 210 B2
Salvia Cl WVILLE PO7 ..... 164 E2
Salwey Rd HEND SO30 .... 134 B3
Samber Cl LYMN SO41 .... 228 A4
Sampan Cl HLER SO31 .... 158 C7
Samples Wy CFDH BH17 ... 218 D8
Sampson Rd
FHAM/STUB PO14 .... 184 D2
PSEA PO1 .... 210 D2
Samson Cl LSOL/BMARY PO13 . 209 H1
Samson Rd PLE BH15 ..... 232 C5
Samuel Rd PSEA PO1 ..... 211 L2
Sancreed Rd BKME/WDN BH12 . 234 D1
Sandbanks Rd PLE BH15 .. 233 L5
PLE BH15 .... 233 M5
Sandbourne Rd CCLF BH13 . 235 G7
PLE BH15 .... 233 J4
WBNE BH4 .... 235 H7
Sandcroft Cl GPORT PO12 . 209 J5
Sandecotes Rd PSTN BH14 . 234 B5
Sanderling Rd ENEY PO4 .. 212 A3
The Sanderlings HISD PO11 . 213 L6
Sandford Av GPORT PO12 . 209 H4
Sandford Cl MOOR/WNTN BH9 . 221 G5
Sandford Wy BDST SO18 .. 217 K5
Sandhill La LSOL/BMARY PO13 . 208 E1
Sandhills Cl CFDH BH17 ... 218 B6
Sandhurst Dr WIMB BH21 .. 168 E1
Sandhurst Rd WSHM SO15 . 131 K2
San Diego Rd GPORT PO12 . 209 L4
Sandisplatt
FHAM/STUB PO14 .... 160 A8
Sandle Copse FBDG SP6 ... 97 L5
Sandleford Rd HAV PO9 ... 165 H1
Sandleheath Rd FBDG SP6 . 96 E8
Sandlewood Cl HORN PO8 . 116 B3
TOTT SO40 .... 104 D8
Sandmartin Cl
NMIL/BTOS BH25 .... 240 E1
Sandown Cl GPORT PO12 .. 209 H5
Sandown Rd CHAM PO6 ... 187 J1
CHCH/BSGR BH23 .... 238 D2
WSHM SO15 .... 106 A7
Sandpiper Cl CFDH BH17 .. 217 K7
HORN PO8 .... 140 E1
TOTT SO40 .... 130 C7
Sandpiper Rd ROWN SO16 . 105 M3
Sandpit La LYMN SO41 .... 230 C4
Sandport Gv
FHAM/PORC PO16 .... 185 M1
Sandringham Cl
MOOR/WNTN BH9 .... 220 F4
NBAD SO52 .... 80 E4
Sandringham Gdns
MOOR/WNTN BH9 .... 220 F4
Sandringham La PSEA PO1 . 13 L1
Sandringham Rd
FHAM/STUB PO14 .... 159 M8
PSEA PO1 .... 13 L1
PSF GU32 .... 63 L4
PSTN BH14 .... 234 A5
WEND SO18 .... 107 K7
Sandsbury La PSF GU32 ... 63 G3
Sandy Cl EPSF GU31 ...... 64 B5
Sandycroft HLER SO31 .... 158 B8
Sandy Down LYMN SO41 .. 201 M4
Sandy Field Crs HORN PO8 . 140 C5
Sandyhurst Cl CFDH BH17 . 218 A7
Sandy La BPWT SO32 ..... 111 H7
CHCH/BSGR BH23 .... 222 C6
ELGH SO50 .... 83 G6
EPSF GU31 .... 64 B5
LISS GU33 .... 37 K5
LYND SO43 .... 151 K4
MIDH GU29 .... 67 M8
NBAD SO52 .... 80 A3
RGWD BH24 .... 169 K4
ROMY SO51 .... 50 F5
RSAL SP5 .... 73 K1
SBNE BH6 .... 237 G3
UPTN BH16 .... 216 A2

VWD BH31 .... 144 E2
WIMB BH21 .... 144 C6
Sandy Mead Rd CHAR BH8 .... 221 K7
Sandy Plot CHCH/BSGR BH23 .... 223 C7
Sandy Wy NBNE BH10 .... 220 C5
Sanross Cl FHAM/STUB PO14.... 183 L7
Sapphire Cl WVILLE PO7 ...... 164 E1
Sapphire Rdg WVILLE PO7 ...... 164 E1
Saracen Cl LYMN SO41 .... 228 A7
Saracens Rd CHFD SO53 .... 81 L1
Sarah Cl LTDN BH7 .... 221 M8
Sarah Sands Cl
CHCH/BSGR BH23 .... 223 H8
Sark Rd BKME/WDN BH12 ...... 219 H8
Sarnia Ct ROWN SO16 .... 105 K5
Sarum Av FERN BH22 .... 168 C4
Sarum Cl FUFL SO22 .... 26 B1
Sarum Rd CHFD SO53 .... 81 K2
FUFL SO22 .... 2 A8
FUFL SO22 .... 25 J1
Sarum St PLE BH15 .... 233 G7
Sarum Vw FUFL SO22 .... 26 A2
Sarum Wk LYMN SO41 .... 228 B2
Satchell Cl HLER SO31 .... 157 L5
Saturn Cl ROWN SO16 .... 105 L4
Saulfland Dr
CHCH/BSGR BH23 .... 224 B8
Saulfland Pl
CHCH/BSGR BH23 .... 224 B8
Saunders La ROWN SO51 .... 49 K3
Saunders Ms ENEY PO4 .... 211 M6
Savernake Cl
LSOL/BMARY PO13 .... 185 H6
ROMY SO51 .... 51 G7
Saville Cl ELGH SO50 .... 82 C3
GPORT PO12 .... 10 A5
Saville Gdns FHAM/PORC PO16.... 6 F1
Sawyer Cl FUFL SO22 .... 16 B7
Saxholm Cl ROWN SO16 .... 106 C2
Saxholm Dl ROWN SO16 .... 106 C2
Saxholm Wy ROWN SO16 .... 106 C2
Saxley Ct HAV PO9 .... 165 C2
Saxonbury Rd SBNE BH6 .... 237 K2
Saxon Cl FHAM/PORC PO16 ...... 161 M7
HLER SO31 .... 158 C7
HORN PO8 .... 116 B4
Saxonford Rd
CHCH/BSGR BH23 .... 239 H1
Saxon Gdns HEND SO30 .... 133 L3
Saxonhurst RSAL SP5 .... 72 F1
Saxonhurst Cl NBNE BH10 ...... 220 C3
Saxonhurst Gdns
NBNE BH10 .... 220 C4
Saxonhurst Rd NBNE BH10 ...... 220 B4
Saxon King Gdns SBNE BH6 .... 238 A4
Saxon Pl LYMN SO41 .... 228 B2
Saxon Rd FAWY SO45 .... 180 D6
WINC SO23 .... 3 C5
WSHM SO15 .... 4 A2
Saxon Wy FBDG SP6 .... 121 L3
ROMY SO51 .... 79 C1
Sayers Rd ELGH SO50 .... 82 C6
Scafell Av FHAM/STUB PO14 ...... 6 B8
Scallows La ROMY SO51 .... 76 C3
Scantabout Av CHFD SO53 ...... 81 K1
Scant Road (West) RCCH PO18.... 167 M6
Scarf Rd CHFD PO17 .... 233 L1
Scholars' Wk CHAM PO6 .... 188 B4
School Cl CHFD SO53 .... 81 C3
LYMN SO41 .... 228 A6
School Hl WPST SO32 .... 113 H2
School La BWD BH11 .... 219 H8
CHCH/BSGR BH23 .... 198 C4
CHFD SO53 .... 80 B7
EMRTH PO10 .... 166 F3
HLER SO31 .... 157 H7
LISS GU33 .... 36 E4
LYMN SO41 .... 202 B8
LYMN SO41 .... 228 C4
LYMN SO41 .... 242 D2
MIDH GU29 .... 67 J7
PLE BH15 .... 233 H3
PSF GU32 .... 63 M2
RCCH PO18 .... 118 E6
RCCH PO18 .... 191 K1
RGWD BH24 .... 169 L3
WIMB BH21 .... 168 D1
WINC SO23 .... 17 C3
WVILLE PO7 .... 139 H3
School Rd BPWT SO32 .... 112 C6
CHCH/BSGR BH23 .... 198 C4
FAWY SO45 .... 180 C5
GPORT PO12 .... 185 K7
HAV PO9. .... 8 D5
HLER SO31 .... 133 L8
ROMY SO51 .... 51 H7
ROMY SO51 .... 76 C6
RSAL SP5 .... 73 L4
RSAL SP5 .... 75 H8
RWIN SO21 .... 54 E2
TOTT SO40 .... 129 L2
WHAM PO17 .... 136 F5
Schooner Wy HLER SO31 .... 158 C7
HSEA PO3 .... 212 A2
The Scimitars
FHAM/STUB PO14 .... 183 M5
Scivier's La BPWT SO32 .... 84 B6
Scotland Cl ELGH SO50 .... 83 K6
Scotland La RSAL SP5 .... 74 F1
Scotney Ct HAV PO9 .... 165 M2
Scott Cl BKME/WDN BH12 ...... 219 K7
FHAM/STUB PO14 .... 184 A4
RWIN SO21 .... 54 F8
Scotter Rd ELGH SO50 .... 82 C5
LTDN BH7 .... 237 G3
Scott Rd BKME/WDN BH12 .... 219 K8
ELGH SO50 .... 81 L6
HSEA PO3 .... 187 K3
ITCH SO19 .... 132 D7
PSEA PO1 .... 210 D2
Scott's Gn CHCH/BSGR BH23 .... 223 K8
Scotts Hills La
CHCH/BSGR BH23 .... 238 C1
Scratchface La HAV PO9 .... 164 F6
WVILLE PO7 .... 164 C6
Scullards La SHAM SO14 .... 4 F3
Seabird Wy FHAM/PORC PO16 .... 7 K9

Seabourne Pl BOSC BH5 .... 237 G3
Seabourne Rd BOSC BH5 .... 237 G4
Seabreeze Wy LYMN SO41 ...... 241 M2
Seacombe Gn ROWN SO16 ...... 105 J4
Seacombe Rd CCLF BH13 ...... 245 G5
Sea Crest Rd
LSOL/BMARY PO13 .... 208 D3
Seacroft Av NMIL/BTOS BH25.... 225 J8
Seafield Cl NMIL/BTOS BH25 .... 240 E1
Seafield Dr SBNE BH6 .... 237 K2
Seafield Park Rd
FHAM/STUB PO14 .... 183 M7
Seafield Rd CHCH/BSGR BH23.... 239 H2
FHAM/PORC PO16 .... 185 M1
HSEA PO3. .... 187 L7
NMIL/BTOS BH25 .... 225 J8
ROWN SO16 .... 105 J6
SBNE BH6 .... 237 J4
Seafields EMRTH PO10 .... 166 C8
Seaford Cl HLER SO31 .... 133 K7
Sea Front HISD PO11 .... 213 K6
Seagarth La ROWN SO16 ...... 106 C3
Seager's Ct PSEA PO1 .... 12 B5
Sea Grove Av HISD PO11 ...... 213 L6
Seagrove Rd NEND PO2 ...... 187 H7
Seagull La EMRTH PO10 .... 166 D7
Seagull Rd CHAR BH8 .... 221 C7
The Seagulls
LSOL/BMARY PO13 .... 208 E4
Sea Kings FHAM/STUB PO14 .... 183 M6
Sea La LSOL/BMARY PO13 ...... 184 A8
Seaman's La LYND SO43 ...... 126 F4
Seamead FHAM/STUB PO14 .... 184 A8
Seamoor La CCLF BH13 .... 235 C5
Seamoor Rd CCLF BH13 ...... 235 C5
WBNE BH4 .... 235 C5
Searles Hl RWIN SO21 .... 54 F2
Sea Rd BOSC BH5. .... 236 D4
ITCH SO19 .... 132 B4
LYMN SO41 .... 242 D4
NMIL/BTOS BH25 .... 225 J8
SBNE BH6 .... 237 L5
Seaton Av HSEA PO3 .... 187 L8
Seaton Cl CHCH/BSGR BH23 .... 224 F8
FHAM/STUB PO14. .... 184 A8
LYMN SO41 .... 228 C3
WEND SO18 .... 108 B7
Seaton Rd CHCH/BSGR BH23.... 224 F8
Seatown Cl CFDH BH17 .... 218 E7
Seaview Av FHAM/PORC PO16 .... 162 C7
CHAM PO6 .... 164 A8
Seaview Rd CHCH/BSGR BH23 .... 225 C7
HISD PO11 .... 214 A5
NMIL/BTOS BH25 .... 240 C1
Seaward Av NMIL/BTOS BH25 .... 240 D1
SBNE BH6 .... 237 C4
Seaward Dr SELS SO20 .... 215 L7
Seaward Rd FAWY SO45 .... 155 M5
ITCH SO19 .... 132 C4
Seaway NMIL/BTOS BH25 ...... 225 M8
Seaway Av CHCH/BSGR BH23 .... 239 H2
Seaway Crs ENEY PO4 .... 212 A4
Seaway Gv FHAM/PORC PO16.... 186 A2
Seawinds LYMN SO41 .... 241 M3
Sebastian Gv WVILLE PO7 ...... 140 E8
Second Av CHAM PO6. .... 188 C1
EMRTH PO10 .... 167 H8
HAV PO9 .... 9 J3
WSHM SO15. .... 130 B1
Second Marine Av
NMIL/BTOS BH25 .... 240 C2
Second St FAWY SO45 .... 156 C8
Sedbergh Rd ROWN SO16 ...... 105 J7
Sedgefield Cl CHAM PO6 ...... 162 D8
TOTT SO40 .... 104 B8
Sedgeley Gv GPORT PO12 ...... 185 L8
Sedgemead HLER SO31 .... 156 F3
Sedgewick Cl
LSOL/BMARY PO13 .... 185 C8
Sedgewick Rd ELGH SO50 ...... 82 C5
ITCH SO19 .... 133 C3
Sedley Cl SSEA PO5 .... 13 J4
Sedgley Rd MOOR/WNTN BH9 .... 220 C8
Segars La RWIN SO21 .... 54 E3
Segensworth Rd FHAM PO15.... 159 K5
Selangor Av EMRTH PO10 ...... 166 B7
Selborne Av HAV PO9 .... 165 H3
WEND SO18 .... 108 B8
Selborne Cl PSF GU32 .... 63 M3
Selborne Gdns GPORT PO12 .... 10 B3
Selborne Pl FUFL SO22 .... 26 C3
Selbourne Dr ELGH SO50 ...... 81 M4
Selbourne Rd HAV PO9 .... 8 D5
TOTT SO40 .... 104 C8
Selbourne Ter PSEA PO1 .... 13 M2
Selby Cl BDST BH18 .... 217 L5
Seldon Cl FUFL SO22 .... 26 A4
Seldown La PLE BH15 .... 233 J3
Seldown Br PLE BH15 .... 233 J3
Seldown La PLE BH15 .... 233 J3
Seldown Rd PLE BH15 .... 233 J3
Selfridge Av SBNE BH6 .... 238 A5
Selfridge Cl SBNE BH6 .... 238 A5
Selhurst Wy ELGH SO50 .... 83 H7
Seliot Cl PLE BH15 .... 233 J3
Selkirk Cl WIMB BH21 .... 192 C7
Sellwood Rd HLER SO31 .... 157 G2
Sellwood Wy
NMIL/BTOS BH25 .... 225 H8
Selsdon Av ROMY SO51 .... 51 C8
Selsey Av ENEY PO4 .... 211 L6
GPORT PO12 .... 185 K3
Selsey Cl HISD PO11 .... 214 D6
ROWN SO16 .... 105 K6
Selsmore Av HISD PO11 ...... 214 A6
Selsmore Rd HISD PO11 ...... 213 L5
Selworth La BPWT SO32 .... 113 C5
Selworthy Cl PSTN BH14 ...... 233 M6
Selwyn Gdns ELGH SO50 ...... 83 H6
Sengana Cl HEND SO30 .... 134 B2
Senlac Rd ROMY SO51 .... 79 G1
Sennen Pl CHAM PO6 .... 186 E1
Sentinel Cl WVILLE PO7. .... 140 F7
Seps 4 Rd FAWY SO45 .... 180 A4
September Cl HEND SO30 ...... 108 C2
Serle Cl TOTT SO40. .... 128 F7

Serle Gdns TOTT SO40 .... 129 H2
Sermon Rd FUFL SO22 .... 16 A7
Serpentine Rd
FHAM/PORC PO16 .... 7 J2
PLE BH15 .... 233 H5
SSEA PO5 .... 12 F8
SSEA PO5 .... 13 G7
Setley Gdns CHAR BH8 .... 221 J5
Setters Cl RWIN SO21 .... 54 E8
Set Thorns Rd LYMN SO41 ...... 201 C6
Settle Cl ROWN SO16 .... 106 A8
Settlers Cl PSEA PO1 .... 211 H2
Sevenoaks Dr LTDN BH7 ...... 221 L8
Sevenoaks Rd CHAM PO6 ...... 163 J8
Severals Rd MIDH GU29 .... 67 L8
Severn Cl CHAM PO6. .... 162 F7
FHAM/PORC PO16 .... 161 L8
Severn Rd FERN BH22 .... 194 E2
ROWN SO16 .... 105 K8
Severn Wy HEND SO30 .... 108 C7
Seward Ri ROMY SO51 .... 51 H8
Seymour Cl CHFD SO53 .... 81 K3
NEND PO2 .... 211 H1
TOTT SO40 .... 104 B7
Seymour La NBAD SO52 .... 79 L4
Seymour Rd
LSOL/BMARY PO13 .... 208 D4
RGWD BH24 .... 146 F7
ROWN SO16 .... 106 B5
Shackleton Rd
LSOL/BMARY PO13 .... 185 H8
Shackleton Sq
CHCH/BSGR BH23 .... 197 M7
Shadwell Rd NEND PO2 .... 187 J6
Shaftesbury Av CHFD SO53 .... 81 H4
PTSW SO17 .... 107 G7
WVILLE PO7 .... 164 B4
Shaftesbury Cl FERN BH22 ...... 168 D6
Shaftesbury Rd CHAR BH8 ...... 236 B2
FERN BH22 .... 168 D7
PLE BH15 .... 233 J5
SSEA PO5 .... 13 G7
Shaftesbury St FBDG SP6 ...... 97 K7
Shaftsbury Rd GPORT PO12 .... 11 G4
Shaggs Meadow LYND SO43 .... 151 K3
Shakespeare Av HORN PO8 .... 140 C5
Shakespeare Gdns HORN PO8 .... 116 C4
Shakespeare Rd ELGH SO50 .... 81 L3
PSEA PO1 .... 211 J2
SBNE BH6 .... 237 J1
WIMB BH21 .... 192 A2
Shalbourne Rd GPORT PO12 .... 209 L1
Shalcombe HLER SO31 .... 157 G1
Shaldon Cl ROWN SO16 .... 106 A4
Shaldon Rd HAV PO9 .... 165 M2
Shales Rd WEND SO18 .... 132 F1
Shallow La LYMN SO41 .... 202 B8
The Shallows FBDG SP6 .... 98 B1
Shambehurst La HEND SO30 .... 109 H7
Shamblehurst La
North BPWT SO32 .... 109 J5
Shamblehurst La South
HEND SO30 .... 109 H8
Shamrock Cl GPORT PO12 ...... 11 J4
Shamrock Rd ITCH SO19 ...... 132 B5
Shamrock Wy FAWY SO45 ...... 155 L3
Shanklin Crs WSHM SO15 ...... 106 C7
Shanklin Rd ENEY PO4 .... 13 M4
WSHM SO15 .... 106 C6
Shannon Cl FHAM PO15. .... 6 A3
Shannon Rd
FHAM/STUB PO14 .... 183 M4
FHAM/STUB PO14 .... 184 D3
Shannon Wy CHFD SO53 .... 81 G3
Shapland Av BWD BH11 .... 219 J3
Shappen Hill La RGWD BH24 .... 172 D6
Shapton Cl FAWY SO45 .... 179 M4
Shapwick Rd PLE BH15 .... 232 F7
Shard Cl VWD BH31 .... 144 E2
Sharf Rd BKME/WDN BH12 .... 234 F1
Sharlands Cl BDST BH18 .... 217 M5
Sharon Rd HEND SO30 .... 108 B6
Sharpley Cl FBDG SP6. .... 97 K5
Sharpness Cl
FHAM/STUB PO14 .... 160 A8
Sharps Cl HSEA PO3 .... 187 M5
Sharps Rd HAV PO9 .... 165 M3
Sharvells Rd LYMN SO41 .... 242 B3
Shavard La BPWT SO32 .... 87 J3
Shaves La NMIL/BTOS BH25. .... 225 L3
Shaw Cl TOTT SO40 .... 129 H1
WEND SO18 .... 107 M6
Shawfield Rd HAV PO9 .... 9 H6
Shawford Cl ROWN SO16 ...... 106 D4
TOTT SO40 .... 128 F1
Shawford Gdns CHAR BH8 .... 221 H6
Shawford Gv HAV PO9 .... 165 C3
Shawford Rd CHAR BH8. .... 221 H5
RWIN SO21 .... 54 E2
Shaw Rd RGWD BH24 .... 147 C6
Sheardley La BPWT SO32 .... 87 L8
Shearer Rd PSEA PO1 .... 211 J1
Shear Hl EPSF GU31 .... 64 A3
Shears Brook Cl
CHCH/BSGR BH23 .... 197 M7
Shears Rd ELGH SO50 .... 82 D5
Shearwater Av
FHAM/PORC PO16 .... 161 J8
Shearwater Cl
LSOL/BMARY PO13 .... 184 F6
Shearwater Dr CHAM PO6 ...... 188 D1
Sheep Pond La BPWT SO32 ...... 86 F5
Sheep St PSF GU32 .... 63 L5
Sheepwash La SELS SO20 ...... 215 M5
WVILLE PO7 .... 139 K8
Sheepwells Av ENEY PO4 ...... 211 M4
Sheffield Rd PSEA PO1 .... 13 L1
Shelbourne Cl CHAR BH8 ...... 236 B2
Shelbourne Rd CHAR BH8 ...... 236 B2
Sheldrake Gdns LYMN SO41 .... 226 F4
ROWN SO16 .... 106 A3
Sheldrake Rd
CHCH/BSGR BH23 .... 238 F3
Shelford Rd ENEY PO4 .... 211 M3
Shellcroft HLER SO31 .... 158 B8
Shelley Av CHAM PO6 .... 162 C7
Shelley Cl BMTH BH1 .... 236 D3

CHCH/BSGR BH23 .... 239 H1
FUFL SO22 .... 2 A6
RGWD BH24 .... 169 J3
Shelley Gdns BMTH BH1 ...... 236 D3
HORN PO8 .... 140 D5
Shelley La ROMY SO51 .... 77 K7
Shelley Rd BMTH BH1 .... 236 D3
ELGH SO50 .... 81 L7
ITCH SO19 .... 133 H2
PSTN BH14 .... 234 C3
TOTT SO40 .... 104 C6
Shelley Rd East BMTH BH1 .... 236 D3
Shelton Rd SBNE BH6 .... 237 H2
Shenley Cl FHAM PO15. .... 160 A6
Shepards Cl FHAM/STUB PO14 .... 160 A8
Shepherd Cl CHCH/BSGR BH23 .... 224 D7
Shepherds Cl FUFL SO22 ...... 26 A4
TOTT SO40 .... 127 M2
Shepherds Hey Rd TOTT SO40 .... 104 A5
Shepherds Hl RGWD BH24 .... 146 A2
Shepherds La RGWD BH24 .... 145 L2
RWIN SO21 .... 53 L2
Shepherds Purse Cl
HLER SO31 .... 158 D6
Shepherds Rd TOTT SO40. .... 127 M2
WINC SO23 .... 3 M7
ROWN SO16 .... 105 H3
Sheppard Cl HORN PO8 .... 140 C2
Shepton Br BROC SO42 .... 177 M3
Sherborn Crs CFDH BH17 ...... 218 D7
Sherborne Ct ELGH SO50 ...... 81 L2
Sherborne Dr FERN BH22 ...... 194 B4
Sherborne Rd PTSW SO17 ...... 107 G6
Sherborne Wy HEND SO30 .... 134 A2
Sherfield Av HAV PO9 .... 165 L3
Sherfield Cl CHAR BH8 .... 221 H6
Sherfield English La
ROMY SO51 .... 76 B2
RSAL SP5 .... 76 A3
Sherfield English Rd RSAL SP5.... 76 A5
Sheridan Cl FUFL SO22 .... 26 B3
ITCH SO19 .... 133 G3
Sheridan Gdns HLER SO31 .... 135 C8
TOTT SO40 .... 129 H1
Sheringham Rd
BKME/WDN BH12 .... 234 E3
CHAM PO6 .... 163 H7
Shermin's Bank
CHCH/BSGR BH23 .... 238 D3
Sherrin Cl PLE BH15 .... 233 J3
Sherringham Cl FAWY SO45 .... 180 F5
Sherwood Av FERN BH22 ...... 194 A5
HEND SO30 .... 134 A4
PSTN BH14 .... 233 L6
Sherwood Cl
CHCH/BSGR BH23 .... 237 L1
LISS GU33. .... 36 F1
ROWN SO16 .... 106 D5
Sherwood Dr VWD BH31 ...... 144 E2
Sherwood Gdns HLER SO31 .... 158 C4
Sherwood Rd CHFD SO53 ...... 53 K7
GPORT PO12 .... 10 D3
Sherwood Wy FAWY SO45 ...... 206 C1
Shetland Cl CHAM PO6 .... 163 K7
TOTT SO40 .... 85 H6
Shetland Ri HLER SO31 .... 158 F2
Shillinglee WVILLE PO7 .... 164 C5
Shillingstone Dr
MOOR/WNTN BH9 .... 220 F5
Shillito Rd BKME/WDN BH12 .... 234 C3
Shingle Bank Dr LYMN SO41 .... 242 C4
Shipbuilding Rd PSEA PO1 ...... 210 D1
Shipcote La BPWT SO32 .... 85 H6
Ship Leopard St PSEA PO1 ...... 12 C2
Shipley Rd RWIN SO21 .... 54 F1
Shipstal Cl UPTN SO16 .... 232 B4
Shire Cl HLER SO31 .... 158 F1
HORN PO8 .... 140 F7
Shires Cl RGWD BH24 .... 170 E4
Shires Copse SBNE BH6 .... 237 L5
Shires Md VWD BH31 .... 144 E2
The Shires HEND SO30 .... 133 L2
Shirley Av ENEY PO4 .... 212 A4
WSHM SO15 .... 106 A8
Shirley Cl CHCH/BSGR BH23.... 197 M7
FERN BH22 .... 168 C6
Shirley High St ROWN SO16.... 106 A8
Shirley Holms LYMN SO41 .... 201 K7
Shirley Park Rd ROWN SO16 .... 106 A8
Shirley Rd BKME/WDN BH12 .... 234 A2
MOOR/WNTN BH9 .... 220 F7
SSEA PO5 .... 13 L8
WSHM SO15. .... 106 B8
Shoe La BPWT SO32 .... 84 E2
Sholing Ct HAV PO9 .... 165 H2
Sholing Rd ITCH SO19 .... 132 C5
Shooters Hill Cl ITCH SO19 .... 132 F5
Shoot Hl WHAM PO17 .... 138 B5
Shoot La LSOL/BMARY PO13 .... 184 E8
Shop La HLER SO31 .... 133 J5
Shore Av HSEA PO3 .... 211 M2
UPTN BH16 .... 232 B2
Shore Cl UPTN BH16 .... 232 B2
Shore Crs BPWT SO32 .... 111 J1
Shorefield Crs LYMN SO41 ...... 242 B3
Shorefield Rd LYMN SO41 ...... 241 M2
TOTT SO40 .... 130 D6
Shorefield Wy LYMN SO41 ...... 242 B3
Shore Gdns UPTN BH16 ...... 232 A2
Shorehaven CHAM PO6 .... 162 D8
Shore La BPWT SO32 .... 111 J1
UPTN BH16 .... 232 A3
Shore Rd CCLF BH13 .... 245 J2
FAWY SO45 .... 155 M4
PSTN BH14 .... 245 J1
Shorewell HLER SO31 .... 157 G1
Short Cl BKME/WDN BH12 .... 219 L8
Short Hl ROMY SO51 .... 51 H7
Short Rd FHAM/STUB PO14 .... 183 L6
Short Rw PSEA PO1 .... 210 E2
Shorts Cl CHCH/BSGR BH23 .... 223 G7
Shorts Rd ELGH SO50 .... 83 C6
Shotterfield Ter LISS GU33 ...... 36 E4
Shottsford Rd PLE BH15 .... 233 H3
Shotts La LYMN SO41 .... 229 G4
Shraveshill Cl TOTT SO40 .... 104 C7

CHCH/BSGR BH23 .... 239 H1
FUFL SO22 .... 2 A6
RGWD BH24 .... 169 J3
Shrubbery Cl
FHAM/PORC PO16 .... 186 A1
The Shrubbery GPORT PO12 .... 209 K1
Shrubb's Av LYMN SO41 .... 228 C4
Shrubbs Hill Gdns
LYND SO43 .... 151 K4
Shrubbs Hill Rd LYND SO43 .... 151 K4
Shrubland Cl WEND SO18 ...... 108 A3
Sibland Cl FHAM/STUB PO14 .... 6 A8
The Sidings HLER SO31 .... 157 H3
RSAL SP5 .... 44 F7
Sidlesham Cl HISD PO11 .... 214 D6
Sidmouth Av HSEA PO3 .... 187 L8
Silchester Cl WCLF BH2. .... 14 E3
Silchester Rd HSEA PO3 .... 211 M1
Silkin Gdns TOTT SO40 .... 129 H2
Silkstead La HAV PO9 .... 165 K2
Silkstead La RWIN SO21 .... 53 L8
Sillen La FBDG SP6. .... 68 F5
Silver Birch Av
FHAM/STUB PO14. .... 6 C7
Silver Birch Cl
BKME/WDN BH12 .... 234 F4
LISS GU33 .... 36 F4
Silver Birches HLER SO31 ...... 133 K8
Silverdale Cl BDST BH18 ...... 217 J4
Silverdale Crs FBDG SP6 .... 121 L2
Silverdale Dr WVILLE PO7 ...... 140 A6
Silverdale Rd WSHM SO15 .... 131 J1
Silver Hl WINC SO23 .... 3 H8
Silverlock Cl NEND PO2 .... 187 H8
Silversands Gdns HISD PO11 .... 213 M6
Silvers End FAWY SO45 .... 155 L7
Silver St CHCH/BSGR BH23 .... 238 A2
LYMN SO41 .... 226 D4
LYND SO43 .... 151 H3
SSEA PO5 .... 12 F5
Silvers Wd TOTT SO40 .... 104 B7
Silverthorne Wy WVILLE PO7 .... 140 B8
Silvertrees EMRTH PO10 ...... 166 D6
Silver Wy CHCH/BSGR BH23 .... 224 C8
Silverwood Cl FUFL SO22 ...... 26 C3
WIMB BH21 .... 192 B6
Silvester Rd HORN PO8 .... 140 C6
Silwood Cl FUFL SO22 .... 2 B4
Simmonds Cl PLE BH15 .... 233 J3
Simmons Cl HEND SO30 .... 109 H8
Simmons Gn HISD PO11 .... 214 A5
Simnel St SHAM SO14 .... 4 F5
Simon Wy WEND SO18 .... 133 J1
Simpson Cl FHAM/PORC PO16.... 162 A8
Simpson Rd NEND PO2 .... 187 G7
Sinah La HISD PO11 .... 213 C5
Sinclair Rd ROWN SO16 .... 105 M3
Singleton Dr NBNE BH10 ...... 220 A6
Singleton Gdns HORN PO8 .... 116 C4
Singleton Wy TOTT SO40 ...... 104 A8
Sir Christopher Cl
FAWY SO45 .... 155 M4
Sirdar Rd PTSW SO17 .... 107 H5
Sir Galahad Rd NBAD SO52 .... 80 E2
Sir George's Rd WSHM SO15 .... 131 H2
Sir Lancelot Cl NBAD SO52 .... 80 E2
Siskin Cl BPWT SO32 .... 84 F8
FERN BH22 .... 193 M1
ROWN SO16 .... 105 M3
Siskin Gv WVILLE PO7 .... 164 C3
Sissinghurst Cl ITCH SO19 ...... 132 E7
Sissinghurst Rd
FHAM/PORC PO16 .... 185 M1
Six Oaks Rd NBAD SO52 ...... 79 M3
Sixpenny Cl
BKME/WDN BH12 .... 234 E1
HLER SO31 .... 158 E7
Sixth Av CHAM PO6 .... 163 J8
Sizer Wy FAWY SO45 .... 154 F5
Skew Rd WHAM PO17 .... 162 A6
Skinner St PLE BH15 .... 233 H7
Skipper Wy LSOL/BMARY PO13 .... 208 D3
Skipton Cl BDST BH18 .... 217 L6
Skipton Rd CHFD SO53 .... 81 J4
Sky End La LYMN SO41 .... 226 E6
Skylark Mdw FHAM PO15 ...... 159 K3
Skys Wood Rd NBAD SO52 .... 80 C1
Slab La ROMY SO51 .... 76 C5
RSAL SP5 .... 72 F1
Slade Cl LYMN SO41 .... 226 E5
Slade La EPSF GU31 .... 65 H4
Slades Farm Rd NBNE BH10 .... 220 A7
Slades Hl FAWY SO45 .... 180 D6
Slade's La NBNE BH10 .... 220 A8
Slater Cl TOTT SO40 .... 104 A8
Sleepbrook Cl VWD BH31 ...... 144 C2
Sleepers Delle Gdns FUFL SO22 .... 26 D2
Sleepers Hl FUFL SO22 .... 26 C2
FUFL SO22 .... 26 C2
Sleepers Hill Gdns FUFL SO22 .... 26 C2
Slepe Crs BKME/WDN BH12 .... 219 K8
Slindon Cl HORN PO8 .... 116 C3
Slindon St PSEA PO1 .... 13 H1
Slingsby Cl PSEA PO1 .... 12 F5
Slinn Rd CHCH/BSGR BH23.... 238 D1
Slipper Rd EMRTH PO10 ...... 190 E1
Slip Wy PLE BH15 .... 233 G6
Sloane Av FAWY SO45 .... 180 A4
Sloane Ct FAWY SO45 .... 180 B4
Sloane Pk BPWT SO32 .... 136 B1
Sloe Tree Cl HLER SO31 ...... 159 G6
Smallcutts Av EMRTH PO10 .... 167 H7
Smeaton St NEND PO2 .... 187 G6
Smeeton Rd
LSOL/BMARY PO13 .... 208 D2
Smith Cl FAWY SO45 .... 180 D6
Smithe Cl ELGH SO50 .... 81 M5
Smithfield Pl
MOOR/WNTN BH9 .... 220 D7
Smith Gv HEND SO30 .... 134 A3
Smith La EMRTH PO10 .... 191 G7
Smith's Fld ROMY SO51 .... 50 F7
Smiths La BPWT SO32. .... 111 L8
Smithson Cl
BKME/WDN BH12 .... 220 A8
Smith St GPORT PO12 .... 10 D3
Smithy La NMIL/BTOS BH25. .... 225 L2
The Smithy WVILLE PO7 .... 139 J4

Smugglers La North
CHCH/BSGR BH23 .... **224** A8
Smugglers La South
CHCH/BSGR BH23 .... **224** C8
Smugglers Wood Rd
CHCH/BSGR BH23 .... **224** A7
Smythe Rd *WVILLE* SO19 .... **133** H5
Snailing La *LISS* GU33 .... **36** A2
Snail's La *RGWD* BH24 .... **146** E6
Snakemoor La *BPWT* SO32 ...... **109** K3
Snapdragon Cl *HLER* SO31 ...... **158** D6 🔟
Snape Cl *LSOL/BMARY* PO13 ... **185** C8 🔟
Snellgrove Cl *TOTT* SO40 .... **104** B6
Snellgrove Pl *TOTT* SO40 .... **104** B6 🔟
Snooks La *LYMN* SO41 .... **228** F2
Snowberry Crs *HAV* PO9 .... **165** M5
Snowdon Dr *FHAM/STUB* PO14 .... **6** C8
Snowdon Rd *WBNE* BH4 .... **235** H4
Snowdrop Gdns
CHCH/BSGR BH23 .... **223** M7
Soake Rd *WVILLE* PO7 .... **139** M5
Soalwood La *PSF* GU32 .... **34** E7
Soberton Rd *CHAR* BH8 .... **236** C1
HAV PO9 ....
Soldridge Cl *HAV* PO9 .... **165** M2 🔟
Solent Av *ITCH* SO19 .... **133** J2
LYMN SO41 .... **228** D5
Solent Cl *CHFD* SO53 .... **81** K2
LYMN SO41 .... **228** D5
Solent Dr *FAWY* SO45 .... **155** K6
HISD PO11 .... **213** K6
HLER SO31 .... **182** B2
NMIL/BTOS BH25 .... **240** F1
Solent Mdw *HLER* SO31 .... **157** L7
Solent Rd *CHAM* PO6 .... **164** A8
CHCH/BSGR BH23 .... **224** F6
FAWY SO45 .... **155** J8
FHAM/STUB PO14 .... **183** L7
HAV PO9 .... **8** C5
SBNE BH6 .... **237** M5
Solent Vw *FHAM/PORC* PO16 .... **161** M7
Solent Wy *BROC* SO42 .... **179** G3
BROC SO42 .... **204** F1
FHAM/STUB PO14 .... **183** L7
GPORT PO12 .... **11** J7
GPORT PO12 .... **209** J3
HAV PO9 .... **8** A7
HSEA PO3 .... **212** B2
LSOL/BMARY PO13 .... **208** E5
LYMN SO41 .... **242** E6
PSEA PO1 .... **12** G4
SHAM SO14 .... **5** G7
Solly Cl *BKME/WDN* BH12 ...... **234** D1
Solomons La *BPWT* SO32 ...... **111** L6
Solomon Wy *PLE* BH15 .... **232** C6
Solona Cl *CHFD* SO53 .... **81** L1 🔟
Somborne Dr *HAV* PO9 .... **165** K3
Somerby Rd *PLE* BH15 .... **233** J2
Somerford Av
CHCH/BSGR BH23 .... **223** M8
Somerford Cl *ITCH* SO19 ...... **132** E2 🔟
Somerford Rd
CHCH/BSGR BH23 .... **238** E1
Somerford Wy
CHCH/BSGR BH23 .... **238** E1
Somerley Rd
MOOR/WNTN BH9 .... **235** H1
Somerley Vw *RGWD* BH24 ...... **146** E8 🔟
Somers Cl *FUFL* SO22 .... **26** C3
Somerset Av *WEND* SO18 ...... **133** L5
Somerset Crs *CHFD* SO53 ...... **81** H5
Somerset Rd
CHCH/BSGR BH23 .... **237** K1
LTDN BH7 .... **236** E3
PTSW SO17 .... **107** H6
SSEA PO5 .... **13** K9
Somerset Ter *WSHM* SO15 ...... **130** F2
Somers Rd *SSEA* PO5 .... **13** K3
Somers Rd North *PSEA* PO1 .... **13** K1
Somerton Av *WEND* SO18 ...... **132** F1
Somerton Cl
NMIL/BTOS BH25 .... **226** B5 🔟
Somervell Cl *GPORT* PO12 ...... **10** D8
Somervell Dr *FHAM/PORC* PO16 .... **7** G2
Somerville Rd *RGWD* BH24 ...... **147** C8
WCLF BH2 .... **14** B6
Sonnet Wy *WVILLE* PO7 .... **140** F8 🔟
Sopers La *CFDH* BH17 .... **217** L7
CHCH/BSGR BH23 .... **237** M2
Sopley Cl *NMIL/BTOS* BH25 ...... **225** H8
Sopley Ct *HAV* PO9 .... **165** M2 🔟
Sopwith Cl
CHCH/BSGR BH23 .... **239** G2 🔟
Sopwith Crs *WIMB* BH21 .... **192** C6
Sopwith Wy *HLER* SO31 .... **134** C8
Sorrel Cl *ROMY* SO51 .... **51** H7
WVILLE PO7 .... **164** C2
Sorrel Dr *FHAM* PO15 .... **159** H1
Sorrel Gdns *WIMB* BH21 .... **217** K6
Sorrell Cl *HLER* SO31 .... **158** D6
Sorrell Wy *CHCH/BSGR* BH23 .... **223** M8
South Acre *EPSF* GU31 .... **93** G5
Southampton Hl
FHAM/STUB PO14 .... **159** K7
Southampton Rd *BROC* SO42 .... **201** L3
CHAM PO6 .... **162** D8
ELGH SO50 .... **81** M8
FAWY SO45 .... **155** L5
FBDG SP6 .... **98** A7
FHAM PO15 .... **159** G3
FHAM/PORC PO16 .... **7** J4
FHAM/PORC PO16 .... **159** H6
LYMN SO41 .... **228** B3
LYND SO43 .... **152** A2
RGWD BH24 .... **146** E8
ROMY SO51 .... **78** F2
TOTT SO40 .... **127** M1
Southampton St
WSHM SO15 .... **131** K2 🔟
South Av *FAWY* SO45 .... **180** C5
NEND PO2 .... **187** J4
NMIL/BTOS BH25 .... **225** M6
South Baddesley Rd
LYMN SO41 .... **228** F4
South Bay *EMRTH* PO10 .... **190** E5
Southbourne Av *CHAM* PO6 .... **187** M1
EMRTH PO10 .... **166** F8
FAWY SO45 .... **180** A4

Southbourne Coast Rd
SBNE BH6 .... **237** K5
Southbourne Gv *SBNE* BH6 ...... **237** G4
Southbourne Overcliff Dr
SBNE BH6 .... **237** H5
SBNE BH6 .... **237** G3
Southbrook Cl *CFDH* BH17 ...... **218** E6
HAV PO9 .... **8** E8
Southbrook Rd *HAV* PO9 .... **8** E8
South Charford Dro *FBDG* SP6 .... **71** M4
Southcliff
LSOL/BMARY PO13 .... **208** C1 🔟
Southcliffe Rd
CHCH/BSGR BH23 .... **239** G2
NMIL/BTOS BH25 .... **225** H8
Southcliff Rd *SHAM* SO14 ...... **131** L1
South Cliff Rd *WCLF* BH2 ...... **14** E8
South Cl *GPORT* PO12 .... **10** B7
HAV PO9 .... **9** G6
ROMY SO51 .... **51** H7 🔟
Southcote Rd *BMTH* BH1 .... **15** L3
South Ct *HLER* SO31 .... **157** J6
Southcroft Rd *GPORT* PO12 .... **10** A1
South Cross St *GPORT* PO12 .... **11** K3
Southdown Rd *CHAM* PO6 ...... **163** L8
HORN PO8 .... **116** B5
RWIN SO21 .... **54** C2
South Downs Wy *BPWT* SO32 .... **58** F8
EPSF GU31 .... **93** K7
HORN PO8 .... **90** B5
NARL SO24 .... **29** J4
PSF GU32 .... **88** D1
RWIN SO21 .... **27** J2
WVILLE PO7 .... **113** M4
Southdown Vw *WVILLE* PO7 .... **140** A6
Southdown Wy *FERN* BH22 ...... **168** D7
South Dr *ROMY* SO51 .... **54** A5
South East Crs *ITCH* SO19 ...... **132** A5
South East Rd *ITCH* SO19 ...... **132** A5
South End Cl *RWIN* SO21 ...... **53** G2
Southend La *BPWT* SO32 .... **113** J8
Southern Av *FERN* BH22 .... **168** E7
Southern Gdns *TOTT* SO40 ...... **129** J1
Southernhay Rd *VWD* BH31 .... **144** F7
Southern La *NMIL/BTOS* BH25 .... **225** K8
Southern Oaks
NMIL/BTOS BH25 .... **225** K7
Southern Rd *HEND* SO30 .... **108** C8
LYMN SO41 .... **228** B4
SBNE BH6 .... **237** H4
WSHM SO15 .... **4** C3
Southey Rd
CHCH/BSGR BH23 .... **223** K8
CHCH/BSGR BH23 .... **238** E1 🔟
Southfield *RGWD* BH24 .... **170** E2 🔟
Southfield Ms *RGWD* BH24 ...... **170** E2 🔟
Southfields Cl *BPWT* SO32 ...... **85** H8
South Front *SHAM* SO14 .... **5** H3
South Gv *LSOL/BMARY* PO13 .... **208** D3
Southgate St *WINC* SO23 .... **2** F8
South Haven Cl *UPTN* BH16 .... **232** A4
South Hl *BPWT* SO32 .... **86** F8
FBDG SP6 .... **121** L2
Southill Gdns
MOOR/WNTN BH9 .... **220** F7
Southill Rd *BKME/WDN* BH12 .... **234** B2
MOOR/WNTN BH9 .... **220** F7
South Kinson Dr *BWD* BH11 .... **219** L4
Southlands *LYMN* SO41 .... **228** A6
Southlands Av *SBNE* BH6 ...... **237** L4
WIMB BH21 .... **217** H2
South La *EMRTH* PO10 .... **167** J5
EPSF GU31 .... **91** J4
HORN PO8 .... **116** A3
RSAL SP5 .... **101** H1
Southlawns Wk
NMIL/BTOS BH25 .... **225** K7
Southlea Av *SBNE* BH6 .... **237** L3
Southleigh Gv *HISD* PO11 ...... **213** K4
Southleigh Rd *EMRTH* PO10 .... **166** D5
HAV PO9 .... **9** J5
South Ldg *FHAM* PO15 .... **159** M7
Southmead Rd *FHAM* PO15 ...... **6** B5
South Millers Dl *CHFD* SO53 .... **81** G1
South Mill Rd *WSHM* SO15 ...... **130** D1
Southmoor La *HAV* PO9 .... **8** B8
South Pde *FAWY* SO45 .... **211** H7
South Park Rd
BKME/WDN BH12 .... **219** L8
South Pl *LSOL/BMARY* PO13 .... **208** E4
South Rd *BMTH* BH1 .... **236** D5
CHAM PO6 .... **162** E6
CHAM PO6 .... **188** B1
HISD PO11 .... **213** K5
HORN PO8 .... **116** B7
PSEA PO1 .... **211** J1
PTSW SO17 .... **107** H8
WHAM PO17 .... **162** E2
WIMB BH21 .... **217** H1
Southsea Ter *SSEA* PO5 .... **12** F6
South Sp *CHAM* PO6 .... **162** F6
South St *ELGH* SO50 .... **81** M8
EMRTH PO10 .... **166** D8
FAWY SO45 .... **155** L5
FHAM/STUB PO14 .... **159** K8
GPORT PO12 .... **11** J4
HAV PO9 .... **8** F6
LYMN SO41 .... **228** A6
RSAL SP5 .... **40** A1
SSEA PO5 .... **12** F5 🔟
South Sway La *LYMN* SO41 .... **201** L3
South Ter *PSEA* PO1 .... **12** C1 🔟
South Trestle Rd *FAWY* SO45 .... **181** G3
South Vw Pl *WCLF* BH2 .... **14** D7
South View Pl *WCLF* BH2 ...... **14** G7
South View Rd
CHCH/BSGR BH23 .... **237** M2
FUFL SO22 .... **26** A5
WSHM SO15 .... **106** D9
Southville Rd *BOSC* BH5 ...... **237** G3 🔟
Southway *FHAM* PO15 .... **159** J5
Southways *FHAM/STUB* PO14 .... **184** B6
South Weirs *BROC* SO42 ...... **201** H1

South West Coast Pth
SWGE BH19 .... **245** G8
South Western Crs
PSTN BH14 .... **234** A5
Southwick Av
FHAM/STUB PO14 .... **184** E2 🔟
Southwick Cl *FUFL* SO22 ...... **16** C4 🔟
Southwick Ct
FHAM/STUB PO14 .... **184** E2 🔟
Southwick Hill Rd *CHAM* PO6 .... **163** J7
Southwick Pl *SBNE* BH6 .... **237** H1 🔟
Southwick Rd *CHAM* PO6 ...... **163** G6
SBNE BH6 .... **237** H2
WHAM PO17 .... **137** G5
WVILLE PO7 .... **139** J4
Southwood Av
CHCH/BSGR BH23 .... **224** E7
SBNE BH6 .... **237** H4
Southwood Cl
CHCH/BSGR BH23 .... **224** E7
FERN BH22 .... **194** A3
South Wood Gdns *HLER* SO31 .... **158** D5
Southwood Rd *HISD* PO11 ...... **214** A6
NEND PO2 .... **187** J4
Sovereign Cl *LTDN* BH7 ...... **221** K8 🔟
HEND SO30 .... **134** B2
Sovereign Crs
FHAM/STUB PO14 .... **158** E7
Sovereign Dr *ENEY* PO4 ...... **212** B3 🔟
HEND SO30 .... **134** B2
Sovereign La *WVILLE* PO7 ...... **164** C5
Sovereign Wy *ELGH* SO50 ...... **81** L2
Sowden Cl *HEND* SO30 .... **133** M1
Sowley La *LYMN* SO41 .... **229** L3
The Spain *PSF* GU32 .... **63** K5
Spalding Rd *ITCH* SO19 .... **133** H3
Spaniard's La *ROMY* SO51 ...... **78** E3
Sparkford Cl *FUFL* SO22 .... **26** D2
LTDN BH7 .... **221** M8 🔟
Sparkford Rd *FUFL* SO22 ...... **26** D2
Spa Rd *SHAM* SO14 .... **4** F4
Sparrow Cl *HORN* PO8 .... **140** D4
Sparrow Ct
LSOL/BMARY PO13 .... **208** D1 🔟
Sparrow Sq *ELGH* SO50 .... **81** J6
Sparrowgrove *RWIN* SO21 ...... **54** B4
Sparsholt Cl *HAV* PO9 .... **165** G3
Sparsholt Rd *ITCH* SO19 .... **132** D3
RWIN SO21 .... **25** G5
Spartan Cl *EMRTH* PO10 .... **190** E4
FHAM/STUB PO14 .... **184** A3
Spartina Dr *LYMN* SO41 .... **228** C2
Speakers Corner Rbt
SHAM SO14 .... **5** G4
Spear Rd *SHAM* SO14 .... **106** F8
Specks La *ENEY* PO4 .... **211** L4
Speedwell Cl *HLER* SO31 ...... **158** D6 🔟
Speedwell Dr
CHCH/BSGR BH23 .... **223** M8 🔟
Speggs Wk *HEND* SO30 .... **134** A2
Speltham Hl *WVILLE* PO7 ...... **114** C6
Spencer Cl *HISD* PO11 .... **213** L5 🔟
Spencer Ct *FHAM/STUB* PO14 .... **184** C7
Spencer Dr *LSOL/BMARY* PO13 .... **208** D3
Spencer Gdns *HORN* PO8 ...... **140** C5
Spencer Rd *BMTH* BH1 .... **15** M3
CCLF BH13 .... **234** D8
ELGH SO50 .... **81** K6
EMRTH PO10 .... **166** C4
ENEY PO4 .... **211** K6
ITCH SO19 .... **133** H2
NMIL/BTOS BH25 .... **225** L5
Spenlow Cl *NEND* PO2 .... **187** H8 🔟
Spenser Cl *HLER* SO31 .... **158** B8 🔟
Spetisbury Cl
MOOR/WNTN BH9 .... **220** F5
Spicer La *BWD* BH11 .... **219** J3
Spicer's Hl *TOTT* SO40 .... **129** K3
Spicer St *PSEA* PO1 .... **211** G2
Spicer's Wy *TOTT* SO40 .... **129** J2
Spicewood *FHAM* PO15 .... **6** C4
Spinacre *NMIL/BTOS* BH25 ...... **225** M8
Spindle Cl *HAV* PO9 .... **9** L1
WIMB BH21 .... **217** K6
Spindle Warren *HAV* PO9 ...... **9** L1
Spindlewood Cl
NMIL/BTOS BH25 .... **225** L7 🔟
ROWN SO16 .... **106** F2
Spindlewood Wy *TOTT* SO40 .... **130** D8
Spinnaker Cl *HISD* PO11 ...... **213** J4 🔟
LSOL/BMARY PO13 .... **209** H1 🔟
Spinnaker Dr *NEND* PO2 ...... **187** H4
Spinnaker Gra *HISD* PO11 ...... **190** A4
Spinnaker Vw *CHAM* PO6 ...... **164** F7
Spinners *FERN* BH22 .... **168** C7 🔟
Spinney Cl *HORN* PO8 .... **140** C5
RGWD BH24 .... **169** H4
Spinney Dl *FAWY* SO45 .... **155** M6
Spinney Gdns *FAWY* SO45 ...... **155** M6 🔟
Spinneys La *FERN* BH22 .... **194** B3
The Spinney *ELGH* SO50 .... **82** F6
FHAM/PORC PO16 .... **161** K7
HORN PO8 .... **140** E2
LSOL/BMARY PO13 .... **185** H7 🔟
NARL SO24 .... **31** H3
RGWD BH24 .... **169** H2
ROWN SO16 .... **106** C2
RWIN SO21 .... **54** B1
TOTT SO40 .... **104** B7
WVILLE PO7 .... **139** K5
Spinney Wk *WEND* SO18 ...... **107** L5
Spinney Wy *NMIL/BTOS* BH25 .... **225** L2
Spitfire End *WINC* SO23 ...... **17** J8 🔟
Spitfire Loop *ELGH* SO50 ...... **107** L1
Spitfire Wy *HLER* SO31 .... **157** K6
Spithead Av *GPORT* PO12 ...... **210** A7
Spittlefields *RGWD* BH24 ...... **170** F1
Spouts La *ROMY* SO51 .... **76** C2
Springbank Rd *LTDN* BH7 ...... **221** K8
Spring Cl *ELGH* SO50 .... **83** H6
ITCH SO19 .... **132** D3
VWD BH31 .... **144** D3
Spring Crs *PTSW* SO17 .... **107** J3
Springcroft
LSOL/BMARY PO13 .... **184** F3
Springdale Av *BDST* BH18 ...... **217** K3
Springdale Gv *WIMB* BH21 ...... **217** J4
Springdale Rd *BDST* BH18 ...... **217** L3 🔟
WIMB BH21 .... **217** H4

Springfield Av
CHCH/BSGR BH23 .... **222** B6
FAWY SO45 .... **180** A4
SBNE BH6 .... **237** M4
Springfield Cl *HAV* PO9 .... **164** F6
LYMN SO41 .... **228** D5
VWD BH31 .... **144** D3
Springfield Crs *PSTN* BH14 .... **234** A4
RSAL SP5 .... **73** J3
Springfield Dr *TOTT* SO40 ...... **129** J2 🔟
Springfield Gdns
NMIL/BTOS BH25 .... **226** B6 🔟
Springfield Gv *FAWY* SO45 .... **180** A4
Springfield Rd *PSTN* BH14 ...... **233** M3
VWD BH31 .... **144** D3
Springfields *RWIN* SO21 .... **54** E7
Springfield Wy
FHAM/STUB PO14 .... **184** A7
Springford Cl *ROWN* SO16 ...... **106** A5
Springford Crs *ROWN* SO16 .... **106** A5
Springford Gdns *ROWN* SO16 .... **106** A4
Springford Rd *ROWN* SO16 ...... **106** A5
Spring Garden La *GPORT* PO12 .... **11** H2
Spring Gdns *BKME/WDN* BH12 .... **234** C3
EMRTH PO10 .... **166** D8
NBAD SO52 .... **79** L3
PSEA PO1 .... **12** F2 🔟
Spring Gv *HLER* SO31 .... **133** L7
Springhill Rd *CHFD* SO53 ...... **81** H2
Spring Hills *ITCH* SO19 .... **133** G4
Spring La *BPWT* SO32 .... **112** A3
ELGH SO50 .... **82** C5
NMIL/BTOS BH25 .... **226** B6
RWIN SO21 .... **54** E7
Springles La *FHAM* PO15 ...... **159** H3
Spring Pl *ROMY* SO51 .... **78** D3 🔟
Spring Rd *BMTH* BH1 .... **15** M2
FAWY SO45 .... **155** L4
HLER SO31 .... **158** D2
ITCH SO19 .... **132** D2
LYMN SO41 .... **228** E5
Spring St *PSEA* PO1 .... **13** G1
The Spring *WVILLE* PO7 ...... **139** K5
Spring V *BPWT* SO32 .... **111** M4
HORN PO8 .... **140** F4
Springvale Av *LTDN* BH7 ...... **221** K8
WINC SO23 .... **17** G2
Springvale Rd *WINC* SO23 ...... **17** G2 🔟
Springwater Cl *BWD* BH11 ...... **219** L5 🔟
Springwater Rd *BWD* BH11 .... **219** L5
Springwood Av *WVILLE* PO7 .... **164** D2
Spruce Av *WVILLE* PO7 .... **164** E1
Spruce Cl *CFDH* BH17 .... **217** J7
ITCH SO19 .... **133** J3
Spruce Dr *ITCH* SO19 .... **133** J3
TOTT SO40 .... **104** A8
Spur Cl *WIMB* BH21 .... **193** G2 🔟
Spurgeon Rd *LTDN* BH7 .... **237** G2
Spur Hill Av *PSTN* BH14 ...... **234** C5
Spurlings Rd *WHAM* PO17 ...... **161** H4
Spur Rd *CHAM* PO6 .... **163** K8
PSTN BH14 .... **234** C4
WVILLE PO7 .... **164** C1
The Spur *GPORT* PO12 .... **10** A8
WHAM PO17 .... **136** D1
The Square *EMRTH* PO10 ...... **166** F5 🔟
ELGH SO50 .... **93** G4
FAWY SO45 .... **180** F5 🔟
LYMN SO41 .... **228** A5
PSF GU32 .... **63** L5
ROMY SO51 .... **49** G4
WHAM PO17 .... **136** C1
WINC SO23 .... **3** G8
Squaray Cl *RSAL* SP5 .... **72** E2
Squires Wk *ITCH* SO19 .... **133** G1
Squirrel Cl *ELGH* SO50 .... **82** E6 🔟
Squirrel Dr *ITCH* SO19 .... **132** E5
Squirrels Cl
CHCH/BSGR BH23 .... **222** B6 🔟
Squirrels Wk *FAWY* SO45 ...... **155** K6
Stable Cl *FHAM/STUB* PO14 .... **159** H6
Stacey Cl *BKME/WDN* BH12 .... **234** B1
Stacey Ct *HAV* PO9 .... **165** H1
Stacey Gdns *CHAR* BH8 .... **221** K6
Stafford Rd *BMTH* BH1 .... **15** H5
PSF GU32 .... **63** L3
SSEA PO5 .... **13** G6
Staff Rd *ROMY* SO51 .... **22** M3
Stagbrake Cl *SHAM* SO14 ...... **163** H8
Stag Cl *ELGH* SO50 .... **82** E6
NMIL/BTOS BH25 .... **226** B6
Stagshorn Rd *HORN* PO8 ...... **141** G1 🔟
Stags La *RWIN* SO21 .... **55** M3
Stagswood *VWD* BH31 .... **144** B2
Stag Wy *FHAM* PO15 .... **160** B3
Stainer Rd *ITCH* SO19 .... **133** G3
Staith Cl *ITCH* SO19 .... **133** G3
Stakes Hill Rd *WVILLE* PO7 .... **164** C1
Stakes La *BPWT* SO32 .... **84** D6
BPWT SO32 .... **85** L1
Stakes Rd *WVILLE* PO7 .... **164** B4
Stalbridge Dr *FERN* BH22 ...... **194** B4
Stalham Rd *BKME/WDN* BH12 .... **234** C1
Stallard Cl *EMRTH* PO10 .... **166** C4
Stallards La *RGWD* BH24 ...... **170** D1
Stalybridge Cl *HLER* SO31 ...... **158** C2
Stamford Av *HISD* PO11 .... **213** J5
Stamford St *SBNE* BH6 .... **237** J3
Stamford Wy *ELGH* SO50 ...... **83** H7 🔟
Stamshaw Rd *NEND* PO2 ...... **187** H7
Stanbridge La *ROMY* SO51 ...... **50** A5
Stanbridge Rd *HAV* PO9 .... **165** M4
Standard Wy *FHAM/PORC* PO16 .... **7** M1
Standen Rd *ROWN* SO16 .... **105** H3
Standford St *SHAM* SO14 ...... **5** K4 🔟
Stanfield Rd *BKME/WDN* BH12 .... **234** C1
FERN BH22 .... **194** A2
MOOR/WNTN BH9 .... **220** C8
Stanford Cl *CHAM* PO6 .... **163** H8
Stanford Ct *HAV* PO9 .... **165** M3 🔟
Stanford Ri *LYMN* SO41 .... **200** F6
Stanhope Rd *PSEA* PO1 .... **13** G1
Stanier Wy *HEND* SO30 .... **109** H3
Stanley Av *HSEA* PO3 .... **187** M8

Stanley Cl *FHAM* PO15 .... **6** C5
GPORT PO12 .... **185** L7
VWD BH31 .... **144** E5
Stanley Green Rd *PLE* BH15 .... **233** H3
Stanley La *SSEA* PO5 .... **13** H7
Stanley Rd *BMTH* BH1 .... **15** L2
CHCH/BSGR BH23 .... **224** E8
EMRTH PO10 .... **166** E4
FAWY SO45 .... **180** B4
LYMN SO41 .... **228** D6
NEND PO2 .... **187** G7
PLE BH15 .... **233** H7
PTSW SO17 .... **107** H7
TOTT SO40 .... **104** C7
Stanley St *SSEA* PO5 .... **13** H7
Stanmore La *FUFL* SO22 .... **26** B2
Stannington Cl
NMIL/BTOS BH25 .... **225** M6 🔟
Stannington Crs *TOTT* SO40 .... **104** E8
Stannington Wy *TOTT* SO40 .... **104** E8
Stanpit *CHCH/BSGR* BH23 ...... **238** D3
Stanstead Rd *HAV* PO9 .... **142** A6
Stanstead Rd *ELGH* SO50 ...... **81** L4
Stansted Crs *HAV* PO9 .... **165** M2
Stansted Rd *SSEA* PO5 .... **13** K4
Stanswood Rd *FAWY* SO45 ...... **206** F4
Stanton Rd *NBNE* BH10 .... **220** A6
PSF GU32 .... **63** K4
WSHM SO15 .... **130** D1
Stanwater La *MIDH* GU29 ...... **67** H4
Stapehill Crs *WIMB* BH21 ...... **192** F3
Stapehill Rd *WIMB* BH21 ...... **193** K3
Staple Ash La *PSF* GU32 ...... **62** B1
Staple Cl *WVILLE* PO7 .... **140** B7
Staple Close La *PLE* BH15 ...... **233** H2
Staplecross La
CHCH/BSGR BH23 .... **223** H8
Stapleford Av *FERN* BH22 ...... **194** D2
Stapleford Cl *ROMY* SO51 ...... **51** G6
Stapleford La *BPWT* SO32 ...... **109** L3
Staplehurst Cl *ITCH* SO19 ...... **132** E8
Staplers Reach
LSOL/BMARY PO13 .... **184** F7
Stapleton Rd *HSEA* PO3 ...... **187** L8 🔟
Staplewood La *TOTT* SO40 ...... **130** B7
Stares Cl *LSOL/BMARY* PO13 .... **209** G1
Starina Gdns *WVILLE* PO7 ...... **140** F8
Starlight Farm Cl *VWD* BH31 .... **144** E1 🔟
Starling Sq *ELGH* SO50 .... **81** J6 🔟
Station Ap *BDST* BH18 .... **217** L4
PSEA PO1 .... **12** C2
Station Cl *WHAM* PO17 .... **136** E4
Station Hl *ELGH* SO50 .... **82** A5
HEND SO30 .... **135** G1
HLER SO31 .... **157** M1
WINC SO23 .... **2** F6 🔟
Station La *CHFD* SO53 .... **81** H2
Station Rd *BPWT* SO32 .... **111** H1
BPWT SO32 .... **113** H1
CHAM PO6 .... **188** A2
CHCH/BSGR BH23 .... **224** C5
CHCH/BSGR BH23 .... **237** M1
EPSF GU31 .... **63** L4
FBDG SP6 .... **121** K2
FERN BH22 .... **168** B5
FHAM/PORC PO16 .... **162** B8
GPORT PO12 .... **209** K1
HISD PO11 .... **213** J4
HLER SO31 .... **156** F3
HSEA PO3 .... **187** L8
ITCH SO19 .... **132** E5
LISS GU33 .... **36** E4
LYMN SO41 .... **200** F6
NMIL/BTOS BH25 .... **225** L6
PSF GU32 .... **60** B4
PSF GU32 .... **63** K4
PSTN BH14 .... **234** A5
RGWD BH24 .... **199** J2
ROMY SO51 .... **78** D3
ROWN SO16 .... **104** F3
VWD BH31 .... **144** B1
WHAM PO17 .... **136** E4
WIMB BH21 .... **192** B5
WINC SO23 .... **2** E6
WSHM SO15 .... **105** H8
Station Rd North *TOTT* SO40 .... **129** L2 🔟
Station Rd South
TOTT SO40 .... **129** M1 🔟
Station St *LYMN* SO41 .... **228** D4
PSEA PO1 .... **13** G1
Station Ter *WIMB* BH21 .... **192** B4
Station Yd *FBDG* SP6 .... **121** J2
Staunton Av *HISD* PO11 .... **213** H5
Staunton Rd *PSEA* PO1 .... **211** G2
Staunton St *PSEA* PO1 .... **211** G2
Staunton Wy *HAV* PO9 .... **8** C2
HAV PO9 .... **165** G5
HORN PO8 .... **90** E8
Stead Cl *HISD* PO11 .... **213** M5
Stedham La *MIDH* GU29 ...... **67** M3
Stedman Rd *BOSC* BH5 .... **237** G3 🔟
Steele Cl *CHFD* SO53 .... **81** J4
Steels Dro *FBDG* SP6 .... **98** D1
Steels La *FBDG* SP6 .... **96** B4
Steel St *SSEA* PO5 .... **12** F5
Steep *FHAM/PORC* PO16 ...... **162** A7 🔟
Steeple Cl *CFDH* BH17 .... **218** B5
Steepleton Rd *BDST* BH18 ...... **218** A3
Steeple Wy *FHAM/STUB* PO14 .... **159** M5
Steerforth Cl *NEND* PO2 ...... **211** H1
Steinbeck Cl *FHAM* PO15 ...... **135** G8
Stein Rd *EMRTH* PO10 .... **167** H6
Stem La *NMIL/BTOS* BH25 ...... **225** J3
Stenbury Wy *HLER* SO31 ...... **157** G1
Stenhurst Rd *PLE* BH15 .... **233** K2 🔟
Stephen Langton Dr
BWD BH11 .... **219** H3 🔟
Stephen Martin Gdns
FBDG SP6 .... **97** K6 🔟
Stephen Rd *FHAM* PO15 ...... **6** F5
Stephens Cl *GPORT* PO12 ...... **10** C8 🔟
Stephenson Rd *TOTT* SO40 .... **104** C6
Stephenson Wy *HEND* SO30 .... **109** G5
Steplake Rd *ROMY* SO51 ...... **76** C1

Step Ter *FUFL* SO22 ...... 2 D7
Sterte Av *PLE* BH15 ...... 233 C4
Sterte Cl *PLE* BH15 ...... 233 H4
Sterte Rd *PLE* BH15 ...... 233 H4
Steuart Rd *WEND* SO18 ...... 132 B1
Stevenson Crs *PSTN* BH14 ...... 234 C5
Stevenson Rd *SBNE* BH6 ...... 237 M5 ⬛
Stevensons Cl *WIMB* BH21 ...... 192 A4
Steventon Rd *WEND* SO18 ...... 133 G1
Stewart Cl *CHAR* BH8 ...... 15 M1
Stewart Rd *CHAR* BH8 ...... 236 A2
Stewarts Gn *WVILLE* PO7 ...... 114 B5
Stewarts Wy *FERN* BH22 ...... 194 C1
Stibbs Wy *CHCH/BSGR* BH23 ...... 198 A2
Stillmore Rd *BWD* BH11 ...... 219 H5
Stinchar Dr *CFDH* SO53 ...... 80 F3
Stinsford Cl *MOOR/WNTN* BH9 ...... 220 F4
Stinsford Rd *BWD* BH17 ...... 218 B7
Stirling Av *WVILLE* PO7 ...... 164 D1
Stirling Cl *NMIL/BTOS* BH25 ...... 225 M5
   TOTT SO40 ...... 104 F8
Stirling Crs *HEND* SO30 ...... 109 H7
   TOTT SO40 ...... 104 F8
Stirling Rd *MOOR/WNTN* BH9 ...... 235 K1
Stirling St *NEND* PO2 ...... 187 H4
Stirling Wy *CHCH/BSGR* BH23 ...... 239 G2
Stirrup Cl *UPTN* BH16 ...... 232 C1
   WIMB BH21 ...... 193 G2
Stoborough Dr *BDST* BH18 ...... 217 L6 ⬛
Stockbridge Cl *CFDH* BH17 ...... 218 F6 ⬛
   HAV PO9 ...... 165 M3 ⬛
Stockbridge Rd *FUFL* SO22 ...... 2 C5
   ROMY SO51 ...... 50 B1
Stocker Pl
   LSOL/BMARY PO13 ...... 185 H6 ⬛
Stockers Av *FUFL* SO22 ...... 2 A3
Stockheath La *HAV* PO9 ...... 8 C2
Stockheath Rd *HAV* PO9 ...... 165 K4
Stockheath Wy *HAV* PO9 ...... 165 K5
Stockholm Dr *HEND* SO30 ...... 134 A3 ⬛
Stockley Cl *FAWY* SO45 ...... 180 A5 ⬛
Stocks La *ALTN* GU34 ...... 32 F7
   BPWT SO32 ...... 87 M4
Stockton Cl *HEND* SO30 ...... 134 B1 ⬛
Stoddart Av *ITCH* SO19 ...... 132 C2
Stodham La *EPSF* GU31 ...... 36 D8
   LISS GU33 ...... 36 D6
Stoke Common Rd *ELGH* SO50 ...... 82 C3
Stoke Gdns *GPORT* PO12 ...... 10 F4
Stoke Hts *ELGH* SO50 ...... 83 G5
Stoke Park Rd *ELGH* SO50 ...... 82 D4
Stoke Rd *GPORT* PO12 ...... 10 C7
   ROWN SO16 ...... 105 M7
   WINC SO23 ...... 3 H1
Stokes Av *PLE* BH15 ...... 233 H6
Stokesay Cl *FAWY* SO45 ...... 155 L8 ⬛
Stokes Bay Rd *GPORT* PO12 ...... 209 H6
Stoke Wood Cl *ELGH* SO50 ...... 83 G6 ⬛
Stoke Wood Rd *TWDS* BH3 ...... 235 L1
Stonechat Cl *EPSF* GU31 ...... 64 B6
Stonechat Dr *TOTT* SO40 ...... 104 A8
Stonechat Rd *HORN* PO8 ...... 140 C2
Stone Crop Cl *HLER* SO31 ...... 158 C7
Stonecroft Cl *WIMB* BH21 ...... 217 J6 ⬛
Stone Gdns *CHAR* BH8 ...... 221 L6
Stoneham Cemetery Rd
   WEND SO18 ...... 107 L4
Stoneham Cl *PSF* GU32 ...... 63 J4
   ROWN SO16 ...... 107 J3 ⬛
Stoneham La *ELGH* SO50 ...... 81 K8
   ROWN SO16 ...... 107 J3
Stoneham Pk *PSF* GU32 ...... 63 J4
Stoneham Wy *ELGH* SO50 ...... 107 K3
Stonehills *FAWY* SO45 ...... 181 C6
   GPORT PO12 ...... 10 F4 ⬛
Stone La *GPORT* PO12 ...... 10 F5 ⬛
Stoneleigh Av *LYMN* SO41 ...... 226 D4
Stoneleigh Cl
   FHAM/PORC PO16 ...... 161 M8 ⬛
Stoners Cl *LSOL/BMARY* PO13 ...... 184 F5
Stone Sq *HAV* PO9 ...... 165 K4
Stone St *SSEA* PO5 ...... 12 F5
Stoney La *FUFL* SO22 ...... 2 A2
Stony La *CHCH/BSGR* BH23 ...... 222 F6
   FBDC SP6 ...... 95 M4
   PSEA PO1 ...... 210 E2
Stony La South
   CHCH/BSGR BH23 ...... 238 B2
Stonymoor Cl *FAWY* SO45 ...... 180 A5
Stopples La *LYMN* SO41 ...... 226 D4
Storrington Rd *HORN* PO8 ...... 116 C3
Story La *BDST* BH18 ...... 217 M4
Stourbank Rd
   CHCH/BSGR BH23 ...... 237 M2
Stourcliffe Av *SBNE* BH6 ...... 237 H6
Stour Cl *PSF* GU32 ...... 63 K6
   WEND SO18 ...... 107 M5
   WIMB BH21 ...... 193 H4
Stourcroft Dr
   CHCH/BSGR BH23 ...... 222 B6
Stourfield Rd *BOSC* BH5 ...... 237 C4
Stourpaine Rd *CFDH* BH17 ...... 218 C2
Stour Rd *CHAR* BH8 ...... 236 C2
   CHCH/BSGR BH23 ...... 237 M1
Stourvale Av
   CHCH/BSGR BH23 ...... 222 B8
Stourvale Gdns *CHFD* SO53 ...... 80 F1
Stourvale Pl *BOSC* BH5 ...... 237 G3 ⬛
Stourvale Rd *SBNE* BH6 ...... 237 G3
Stour Valley Wy *FERN* BH22 ...... 194 D3
   MOOR/WNTN BH9 ...... 221 G2
   SBNE BH6 ...... 237 K1
   WIMB BH21 ...... 192 A4
Stour Wy *CHCH/BSGR* BH23 ...... 222 B6
Stourwood Av *SBNE* BH6 ...... 237 H4
Stourwood Rd *SBNE* BH6 ...... 237 J4
Stouts La *CHCH/BSGR* BH23 ...... 197 M7
Stowe Cl *HEND* SO30 ...... 109 J7
Stowe Rd *ENEY* PO4 ...... 211 M4
Stradbrook *LSOL/BMARY* PO13.. 184 F1
Stragwyne Cl *NBAD* SO52 ...... 79 L2 ⬛
The Straight Mile *ROMY* SO51 ...... 51 K7
Strand *SHAM* SO14 ...... 5 G4
Strand St *PLE* BH15 ...... 233 C4
The Strand *HISD* PO11 ...... 214 A7
Stratfield Dr *CFDH* SO53 ...... 53 G7 ⬛

Stratfield Pl
   NMIL/BTOS BH25 ...... 225 J5 ⬛
Stratford Pl *ELGH* SO50 ...... 82 A4 ⬛
   LYMN SO41 ...... 228 B3
Stratford Rd *WVILLE* PO7 ...... 140 E8
Strathmore Dr *VWD* BH31 ...... 144 F2
Strathmore Rd *GPORT* PO12 ...... 11 H5
   NBNE BH10 ...... 220 E4
Stratton Cl *CHAM* PO6 ...... 163 G8
Stratton Rd *MOOR/WNTN* BH9 .. 221 G4
   WINC SO23 ...... 3 K9
   WSHM SO15 ...... 106 B7
Strawberry Hl *HLER* SO31 ...... 158 D5
Streamleaze
   FHAM/STUB PO14...... 159 G7
Street End *NBAD* SO52 ...... 80 A3
Streets La *RGWD* BH24 ...... 171 G4
The Street *MIDH* GU29 ...... 67 K7
   RSAL SP5 ...... 46 F4
Strettons Copse *LIPH* GU30...... 38 E5
Stride Av *HSEA* PO3...... 211 M2
Strides La *RGWD* BH24 ...... 170 D1
Strides Wy *TOTT* SO40 ...... 128 F1
Strode Gdns *RGWD* BH24 ...... 169 M3
Strode Rd *NEND* PO2 ...... 187 G6
Strongs Cl *ROMY* SO51 ...... 51 G8 ⬛
Stroud Cl *WIMB* BH21 ...... 192 E2
Strouden Av *CHAR* BH8 ...... 220 F7
Strouden Ct *HAV* PO9 ...... 165 H1
Stroud End *PSF* GU32 ...... 63 G4
Strouden Rd
   MOOR/WNTN BH9 ...... 220 E7
Stroud Gdns
   CHCH/BSGR BH23 ...... 238 D2 ⬛
Stroud La *CHCH/BSGR* BH23 ...... 238 D2
Stroudley Av *CHAM* PO6 ...... 188 A2
Stroudley Wy *HEND* SO30 ...... 109 J6
Stroud Park Av
   CHCH/BSGR BH23 ...... 238 D1
Stroudwood La *BPWT* SO32 ...... 83 M5
   RWIN SO21 ...... 83 M3
Stroudwood Rd *HAV* PO9 ...... 165 L5
Struan Ct *RGWD* BH24 ...... 169 L2
Struan Dr *RGWD* BH24 ...... 169 L2
Struan Gdns *RGWD* BH24 ...... 169 K2
Stuart Cl *FHAM/STUB* PO14 ...... 184 A6
   UPTN BH16 ...... 232 A1
Stuart Crs *FUFL* SO22 ...... 26 D3
Stuart Rd *CHCH/BSGR* BH23 ...... 224 F8
Stubbington Gn
   FHAM/STUB PO14 ...... 184 A5
Stubbington La
   FHAM/STUB PO14 ...... 184 A8
Stubbington Wy *ELGH* SO50 ...... 83 J7
Stubbs Dro *HEND* SO30 ...... 134 B1
Stubbs Rd *ITCH* SO19 ...... 133 G6 ⬛
Stuckton Rd *FBDC* SP6 ...... 97 M8
Studland Cl *ROWN* SO16 ...... 105 J7
Studland Dr *LYMN* SO41 ...... 242 A3
Studland Rd
   LSOL/BMARY PO13 ...... 208 C2
   ROWN SO16 ...... 105 J7
   WBNE BH4 ...... 235 H7
Studley Av *FAWY* SO45 ...... 180 A5
Studley Cl *CHCH/BSGR* BH23 ...... 225 C8
Studley Ct *NMIL/BTOS* BH25 ...... 225 H8 ⬛
Sturminster Rd
   MOOR/WNTN BH9 ...... 220 F4 ⬛
Sudbury Rd *CHAM* PO6 ...... 163 H8
Suetts La *BPWT* SO32 ...... 111 L1
Suffolk Av *CHCH/BSGR* BH23 ...... 222 D6
   WSHM SO15 ...... 131 H1
Suffolk Cl *CHFD* SO53 ...... 81 H6
   WIMB BH21 ...... 193 G2 ⬛
Suffolk Dr *CHFD* SO53 ...... 81 H6
   FHAM PO15 ...... 158 F1
   HLER SO31 ...... 158 F1
Suffolk Rd *ENEY* PO4 ...... 211 L5
   WCLF BH2 ...... 14 A5
Suffolk Rd South *WBNE* BH4 ...... 14 A4
Sullivan Cl *CHAM* PO6 ...... 162 C8
Sullivan Rd *ITCH* SO19 ...... 133 H5 ⬛
Sullivan Wy *WVILLE* PO7 ...... 164 C1
Sultan Rd *EMRTH* PO10 ...... 166 D7
   NEND PO2 ...... 211 G1
Sumar Cl *FHAM/STUB* PO14...... 184 B3
Summercroft Wy *FERN* BH22 ... 168 C5
Summer Fld *WIMB* BH21 ...... 192 E4
Summerfield Cl
   CHCH/BSGR BH23 ...... 223 G6 ⬛
Summerfield Gdns
   ROWN SO16 ...... 107 J3 ⬛
Summerfield Rd *SELS* SO20...... 215 L6
Summerfields
   FHAM/STUB PO14...... 158 F7
   LTDN BH7 ...... 236 E1
Summer Flds *VWD* BH31 ...... 144 D4
Summerhill Rd *HORN* PO8 ...... 140 D5
Summerlands Rd *ELGH* SO50 ...... 83 H6
Summer La *BROC* SO42 ...... 179 J7
Summerleigh Wk
   FHAM/STUB PO14 ...... 184 B3 ⬛
Summers Av *BWD* BH11 ...... 219 M2
Summers La *CHCH/BSGR* BH23.. 223 H7
Summers St *SHAM* SO14 ...... 131 M2
Summertrees Ct
   NMIL/BTOS BH25 ...... 226 B4
Summit Wy *WEND* SO18 ...... 107 L7
Sunbeam Wy *GPORT* PO12 ...... 10 F6
Sunbury Ct *FHAM* PO15 ...... 160 C4
Sunderland Dr
   CHCH/BSGR BH23 ...... 239 G1 ⬛
Sunderton La *HORN* PO8 ...... 116 A4
Sundew Cl *CHCH/BSGR* BH23 ... 224 A7
   NMIL/BTOS BH25 ...... 226 B4 ⬛
Sundew Rd *WIMB* BH21 ...... 217 J6
Sundridge Cl *CHAM* PO6 ...... 163 J8
Sunningdale *FAWY* SO45 ...... 155 K6
Sunningdale Cl *ELGH* SO50 ...... 82 E6 ⬛
   LSOL/BMARY PO13 ...... 185 G7 ⬛
Sunningdale Crs *NBNE* BH10... 220 D4
Sunningdale Gdns
   WEND SO18 ...... 132 F1 ⬛
Sunningdale Rd
   FHAM/PORC PO16 ...... 186 B1
   HSEA PO3...... 211 L2

Sunnybank Rd *WIMB* BH21 ...... 192 F2
Sunnydown Rd *FUFL* SO22 ...... 25 M5
Sunnyfield Ri *HLER* SO31 ...... 133 L7 ⬛
Sunnyfield Rd
   NMIL/BTOS BH25 ...... 225 L8
Sunnyheath *HAV* PO9 ...... 165 J4
Sunny Hill Rd
   BKME/WDN BH12 ...... 234 C3
Sunnyhill Rd *SBNE* BH6 ...... 237 G3
Sunnylands Av *SBNE* BH6 ...... 237 J4
Sunnymead Dr *WVILLE* PO7 ...... 140 A6
Sunnymoor Rd *BWD* BH11 ...... 219 L7
Sunnyside Rd
   BKME/WDN BH12 ...... 234 C2
Sunny Wk *PSEA* PO1 ...... 12 B1
Sunny Wy *TOTT* SO40 ...... 129 K1 ⬛
Sunridge Cl *BKME/WDN* BH12... 234 F2
Sunset Av *TOTT* SO40 ...... 104 D8
Sunset Rd *TOTT* SO40 ...... 104 D8
Sunshine Av *HISD* PO11 ...... 213 M6 ⬛
Sun St *PSEA* PO1 ...... 12 D2 ⬛
Sunvale Cl *ITCH* SO19 ...... 132 F5
Sunwood Rd *HAV* PO9 ...... 165 H3
Surbiton Rd *ELGH* SO50 ...... 82 A3
Surrey Cl *CHCH/BSGR* BH23 ...... 222 D6
   TOTT SO40 ...... 129 H3
Surrey Gdns *WBNE* BH4 ...... 235 H4
Surrey Rd *BKME/WDN* BH12 ...... 234 F3
   CHFD SO53 ...... 81 H5
   ITCH SO19 ...... 132 B6
   WBNE BH4 ...... 235 H4
Surrey Rd South *WBNE* BH4 ...... 235 H4
Surrey St *PSEA* PO1 ...... 13 G1
Sussex Border Pth
   EMRTH PO10 ...... 190 D5
   EPSF GU31 ...... 92 E3
   HAV PO9 ...... 142 B4
   HORN PO8 ...... 117 H4
   LISS GU33 ...... 37 L2
Sussex Gdns *MOOR/WNTN* BH9 ... 220 F4
Sussex Pl *SSEA* PO5 ...... 13 G6 ⬛
Sussex Rd *CHFD* SO53 ...... 81 J5
   EPSF GU31 ...... 63 M6
   SHAM SO14 ...... 5 J3
   SSEA PO5 ...... 13 G6
Sussex St *WINC* SO23 ...... 2 F7
Sutherland Av *BDST* BH18 ...... 217 J3
   ROMY SO51 ...... 51 G7 ⬛
Sutherland Rd *ENEY* PO4 ...... 13 M5
   ROWN SO16 ...... 105 L3
Sutherlands Ct *CHFD* SO53 ...... 81 H2 ⬛
Sutherlands Wy *CHFD* SO53 ...... 81 H1
Sutton Cl *CFDH* BH17 ...... 218 E6
   HORN PO8 ...... 140 B5
   HSEA PO3...... 187 M4
Sutton Gdns *WINC* SO23 ...... 3 G7
Sutton Pl *BROC* SO42 ...... 175 L7 ⬛
Sutton Rd *HORN* PO8 ...... 140 B5
   MOOR/WNTN BH9 ...... 220 F7
   TOTT SO40 ...... 104 C7
Swale Dr *CHFD* SO53 ...... 80 F1
Swallow Cl *CFDH* BH17 ...... 217 K8
   HAV PO9 ...... 9 J1
   TOTT SO40 ...... 128 F2
Swallow Ct
   LSOL/BMARY PO13 ...... 208 D1 ⬛
Swallow Dr *LYMN* SO41 ...... 242 E4
Swallow Sq *ELGH* SO50 ...... 81 J6 ⬛
Swanage Cl *ITCH* SO19 ...... 132 C5
Swanage Rd
   LSOL/BMARY PO13 ...... 208 C2
Swan Cl *EMRTH* PO10 ...... 166 E8
   HLER SO31 ...... 158 B1
Swancote *FHAM/PORC* PO16 ...... 161 K8
Swan La *WINC* SO23 ...... 2 F6
Swanley Cl *ELGH* SO50 ...... 81 M3
Swan Md *RGWD* BH24 ...... 171 G2
Swanmore Av *ITCH* SO19 ...... 132 F5
Swanmore Cl *FUFL* SO22 ...... 16 C4
   LTDN BH7 ...... 237 G1 ⬛
Swanmore Rd *BPWT* SO32...... 111 L1
   HAV PO9 ...... 165 H1
   LTDN BH7 ...... 237 G1
Swansbury Dr *CHAR* BH8 ...... 221 L6
Swan St *PSF* GU32 ...... 63 K5
Swanton Gdns *CHFD* SO53 ...... 81 G1
Swanwick La *HLER* SO31 ...... 134 B8
Swanwick Shore Rd
   HLER SO31 ...... 158 B1 ⬛
Swanwick Rd *HAV* PO9 ...... 165 L4
Sway Cl *HAV* PO9 ...... 165 M3 ⬛
Sway Gdns *CHAR* BH8...... 221 H6
Sway Rd *BROC* SO42 ...... 201 K1
   LYMN SO41 ...... 227 J3
   NMIL/BTOS BH25 ...... 225 M2
Swaything Rd *HAV* PO9 ...... 165 H2
   HEND SO30 ...... 108 A6
The Sweep *RGWD* BH24 ...... 170 D1 ⬛
Sweetbriar Gdns
   WVILLE PO7 ...... 164 D3 ⬛
Sweethills Crs *HLER* SO31 ...... 134 F8
Sweyns Lease *BROC* SO42 ...... 204 A2
Swift Cl *CFDH* BH17 ...... 217 K8
   ELGH SO50 ...... 81 J6
   FUFL SO22 ...... 26 C3
   HORN PO8 ...... 140 E1
Swift Gdns *ITCH* SO19 ...... 132 B7
Swift Hollow *ITCH* SO19 ...... 132 B7 ⬛
Swift Rd *EMRTH* PO10 ...... 190 E5
   ITCH SO19 ...... 132 B7
Swinburn Gdns *HORN* PO8 ...... 140 D4
Swincombe Ri *WEND* SO18 ...... 108 A7
Swiss Rd *WVILLE* PO7 ...... 164 C1
Swivelton La *WHAM* PO17 ...... 161 L5
Sword Cl *GPORT* PO12 ...... 209 J6
   HORN PO8 ...... 116 A3
Swordfish Dr
   CHCH/BSGR BH23 ...... 239 G1 ⬛
Sword Sands Rd *HSEA* PO3 ...... 212 A1
Sycamore Av *CHFD* SO53 ...... 53 H7
Sycamore Cl *CFDH* BH17 ...... 217 K7
   CHCH/BSGR BH23 ...... 222 B8 ⬛
   FHAM/STUB PO14 ...... 159 G7 ⬛
   HLER SO31 ...... 133 K8
   HORN PO8 ...... 140 C5
   LSOL/BMARY PO13 ...... 185 J7 ⬛

Sycamore Dr *FAWY* SO45 ...... 179 M3
Sycamore Rd *BPWT* SO32 ...... 85 K8
   FAWY SO45 ...... 155 K5
   LYMN SO41 ...... 226 D4
   ROWN SO16 ...... 105 M6
Sydenham Ter *PSEA* PO1 ...... 13 K2
Sydling Cl *CFDH* BH17 ...... 218 F6
Sydmanton Cl *ROMY* SO51 ...... 78 F2 ⬛
Sydmonton Ct *HAV* PO9 ...... 165 M2 ⬛ ⬛
Sydney Av *HLER* SO31 ...... 157 J5
Sydney Rd *BDST* BH18 ...... 217 L5
   CHCH/BSGR BH23 ...... 222 C7
   ELGH SO50 ...... 82 C4
   GPORT PO12 ...... 10 F3
   WSHM SO15 ...... 106 A7
Syers Rd *LISS* GU33 ...... 36 E4
Sylmor Gdns
   MOOR/WNTN BH9 ...... 220 E6
Sylvan Av *ITCH* SO19 ...... 133 G2
Sylvan Cl *LYMN* SO41 ...... 226 F6
   RGWD BH24 ...... 169 H4
Sylvan Dr *NBAD* SO52 ...... 79 L4
Sylvan La *HLER* SO31 ...... 157 L6
Sylvan Rd *BKME/WDN* BH12 ...... 234 A2
   CHFD SO53 ...... 81 H5
   ITCH SO19 ...... 132 B6
   WBNE BH4 ...... 235 H4
Sylvan Rd South *WBNE* BH4 ...... 235 H4
The Sylvans *FAWY* SO45 ...... 155 H5 ⬛
Sylvan Vw *WVILLE* PO7 ...... 164 D2
Sylvia Crs *TOTT* SO40 ...... 104 D7
Sylvia Rd *ROMY* SO51 ...... 79 G1
Symes Rd *PLE* BH15 ...... 232 C4
   ROMY SO51 ...... 79 G1
Symonds Cl *CHFD* SO53 ...... 81 J4
Symonds St *WINC* SO23 ...... 3 G9
Sywell Crs *HSEA* PO3...... 187 M4

T

Tadburn Cl *CHFD* SO53 ...... 81 J3
   ROMY SO51 ...... 78 F1 ⬛
Tadburn Rd *ROMY* SO51 ...... 78 F2
Tadden Wk *BDST* BH18 ...... 217 K6
Tadfield Rd *ROMY* SO51 ...... 78 F1
Tagdell La *HORN* PO8 ...... 115 L8
Tait Cl *CFDH* BH17 ...... 233 K1
Tait Pl *LSOL/BMARY* PO13 ...... 185 H7
Talbot Cl *SHAM* SO14 ...... 5 K1 ⬛
Talbot Av *TWDS* BH3 ...... 235 K1
Talbot Cl *HAV* PO9 ...... 165 G5
   ROWN SO16 ...... 106 E4
Talbot Dr *BKME/WDN* BH12 ...... 219 M8
   CHCH/BSGR BH23 ...... 224 D6
Talbot Hill Rd
   MOOR/WNTN BH9 ...... 220 D8
Talbot Mdw
   BKME/WDN BH12 ...... 219 M8
Talbot Ms *NBNE* BH10 ...... 219 M7 ⬛
Talbot Ri *NBNE* BH10 ...... 220 A7
Talbot Rd *ENEY* PO4 ...... 13 M4
   FAWY SO45 ...... 155 H7
   HAV PO9 ...... 8 A1
   MOOR/WNTN BH9 ...... 220 B8
Talland Rd *FHAM/STUB* PO14 ... 158 F7
Tamar Cl *FERN* BH22 ...... 194 E3
   FHAM/PORC PO16 ...... 161 L7
Tamar Down *WVILLE* PO7 ...... 164 E1
Tamar Gv *FAWY* SO45 ...... 155 J5
Tamarisk Cl *ENEY* PO4 ...... 212 A5
   FHAM/STUB PO14 ...... 184 A7 ⬛
   WVILLE PO7 ...... 164 E3 ⬛
Tamarisk Rd *HEND* SO30 ...... 133 M1
Tamarisk Gdns *WEND* SO18 ...... 107 K8
Tamella Rd *HEND* SO30 ...... 134 C2
Tammys Turn
   FHAM/STUB PO14 ...... 159 M8 ⬛
Tamorisk Dr *TOTT* SO40 ...... 129 G2
Tamworth Rd *HSEA* PO3 ...... 211 L2
   LTDN BH7 ...... 236 E3 ⬛
Tanfield La *WHAM* PO17 ...... 136 D5
Tanfield Pk *WHAM* PO17 ...... 136 D5
Tangier Cl *BPWT* SO32 ...... 110 E1
Tangier Rd *HSEA* PO3 ...... 211 L1
Tanglewood
   FHAM/PORC PO16 ...... 7 G1
   TOTT SO40 ...... 130 E7 ⬛
Tanglewood Cl *WVILLE* PO7 ...... 164 A4 ⬛
Tangmere Cl
   CHCH/BSGR BH23 ...... 239 G2
Tangmere Dr *ROWN* SO16 ...... 105 L4
Tangyes Cl *FHAM/STUB* PO14 ... 184 B5
Tanhouse Cl *HEND* SO30 ...... 134 A3
Tanhouse La *HEND* SO30 ...... 134 B3
Tan Howse Cl *LTDN* BH7 ...... 221 M8
Tankerdale La *PSF* GU32 ...... 36 B8
Tankerton Cl *CHAM* PO6 ...... 163 J8 ⬛
Tankerville Rd *ITCH* SO19 ...... 132 B5
Tanner's Brook Wy
   WSHM SO15 ...... 130 D2
Tanners La *FBDG* SP6 ...... 96 K5
   FHAM/STUB PO14 ...... 184 C2
   LYMN SO41 ...... 229 L4
   ROMY SO51 ...... 49 J8
   WVILLE PO7 ...... 139 K3
Tanner's Rdg *WVILLE* PO7 ...... 164 C5
Tanners Rd *NBAD* SO52 ...... 79 M4
The Tanners
   FHAM/STUB PO14 ...... 159 G7 ⬛
Tanner St *WINC* SO23 ...... 3 H8
Tansy Cl *WVILLE* PO7 ...... 164 E2
Tansy Meadow *NBAD* SO52 ...... 80 E4 ⬛
The Tanyards *CHFD* SO53 ...... 53 G7 ⬛
Taplin Dr *HEND* SO30 ...... 109 H8
Taplings Cl *FUFL* SO22 ...... 2 A1
   FUFL SO22 ...... 16 C5
Taplings Rd *FUFL* SO22 ...... 2 A1
Taranto Rd *ROWN* SO16 ...... 106 B4
Tarbery Crs *HORN* PO8 ...... 141 G1
Target Rd *NEND* PO2 ...... 187 G5
Tarius Cl *LSOL/BMARY* PO13 ...... 185 H7
Tarleton Rd *CHAM* PO6 ...... 162 F7
Tarn Dr *CFDH* BH17 ...... 217 K7
Tarn Ri *HORN* PO8 ...... 116 B6
Tarrant Cl *CFDH* BH17 ...... 218 C6
Tarrant Gdns *HAV* PO9 ...... 8 B1
Tarrant Rd *MOOR/WNTN* BH9 ... 220 F5

Tasman Cl *CHCH/BSGR* BH23 ... 222 D8
   SHAM SO14 ...... 5 K8
Taswell Rd *SSEA* PO5 ...... 13 K8
Tatchbury La *TOTT* SO40 ...... 103 L7
Tate Rd *WSHM* SO15 ...... 105 H8
   FAWY SO45 ...... 155 H8
Tates Rd *FAWY* SO45 ...... 155 M6 ⬛
Tatnam Rd *PLE* BH15 ...... 233 H4
Tattenham Rd *BROC* SO42 ...... 175 K8
Tattershall Crs
   FHAM/PORC PO16 ...... 185 M1
Tatwin Cl *ITCH* SO19 ...... 133 H3
Tatwin Crs *ITCH* SO19 ...... 133 H3
Taunton Dr *WEND* SO18 ...... 132 F1
Tavells Cl *TOTT* SO40 ...... 130 C7
Tavell's La *TOTT* SO40 ...... 130 C7
Taverner Cl *PLE* BH15 ...... 233 J6 ⬛
Taverners Cl *ITCH* SO19 ...... 133 H5
Tavistock Cl *ROMY* SO51 ...... 51 G7 ⬛
Tavistock Gdns *HAV* PO9 ...... 9 J5
Tavy Cl *CHFD* SO53 ...... 81 G2
Taw Dr *CHFD* SO53 ...... 81 G1
Tawny Owl Cl
   FHAM/STUB PO14 ...... 183 M4 ⬛
Taylor Dr *CHAR* BH8 ...... 221 H4
Taylor's Buildings *PLE* BH15 ... 233 H7 ⬛
Teachers Wy *FAWY* SO45 ...... 179 M4 ⬛
Teal Cl *FHAM/PORC* PO16 ...... 161 K8
   HISD PO11 ...... 213 M5
   TOTT SO40 ...... 129 G1 ⬛
Teasel Wy *FERN* BH22 ...... 168 C7
Teazle Cl *EPSF* GU31 ...... 64 B6
Tebourba Dr *GPORT* PO12 ...... 10 C6
Tebourba Wy *WSHM* SO15 ...... 130 D1
Tedder Cl *BWD* BH11 ...... 219 M5
Tedder Gdns *BWD* BH11 ...... 219 M5
Tedder Rd *BWD* BH11 ...... 219 M5
   LSOL/BMARY PO13 ...... 185 H5
   WEND SO18 ...... 107 M8
Tedder Wy *TOTT* SO40 ...... 129 H1
Teddington Rd *ENEY* PO4 ...... 211 L4
Tees Cl *CHFD* SO53 ...... 80 F1
Teg Down Meads *FUFL* SO22 ... 16 A7
Teignmouth Rd *GPORT* PO12 ... 209 K1
   HSEA PO3...... 187 L8
Telegraph La *EPSF* GU31 ...... 93 K6
Telegraph Rd *HEND* SO30 ...... 108 D8
Telephone Rd *ENEY* PO4 ...... 13 M3
Telford Gdns *HEND* SO30 ...... 109 J6 ⬛
Telford Rd *NEND* PO2 ...... 187 J5
Teme Crs *ROWN* SO16 ...... 105 K8
Teme Rd *ROWN* SO16 ...... 105 K8 ⬛
Tempest Av *WVILLE* PO7 ...... 140 E8
Templar Cl *BKME/WDN* BH12 ... 219 K7
Templars Mede *CHFD* SO53 ...... 81 G5
Templars Wy *NBAD* SO52 ...... 80 E4
Templecombe Rd *ELGH* SO50 ... 82 E7
Temple Gdns *ITCH* SO19 ...... 132 D6 ⬛
Temple La *PSF* GU32 ...... 61 J8
Templemere
   FHAM/STUB PO14 ...... 184 A1
Temple Rd *ITCH* SO19 ...... 132 D6
   LISS GU33 ...... 36 F2
Templeton Cl *NEND* PO2 ...... 187 J5 ⬛
Temple St *PSEA* PO1 ...... 211 G2
Tenby Cl *WEND* SO18 ...... 107 M8
Tenby Dr *CHFD* SO53 ...... 80 F4
Tench Wy *ROMY* SO51 ...... 50 E8
Tennyson Cl *BPWT* SO32 ...... 85 K8
   FAWY SO45 ...... 179 M3 ⬛
Tennyson Crs *WVILLE* PO7 ...... 140 B7
Tennyson Gdns
   FHAM/PORC PO16 ...... 7 G4
Tennyson Rd *ELGH* SO50 ...... 81 L6
   MOOR/WNTN BH9 ...... 220 D6
   NEND PO2 ...... 187 K8
   PSTN BH14 ...... 233 M5
   PTSW SO17 ...... 107 G8
   TOTT SO40 ...... 104 C6
   WIMB BH21 ...... 192 A2
Tensing Cl *FHAM/PORC* PO16 ...... 7 G1
Tensing Rd *CHCH/BSGR* BH23 ... 238 D1
Tenterton Av *ITCH* SO19 ...... 132 F5
Terence Av *CFDH* BH17 ...... 218 A7 ⬛
Terence Rd *WIMB* BH21 ...... 217 G3
Terminus Ter *SHAM* SO14 ...... 5 J6
Tern Cl *FAWY* SO45 ...... 155 M6
Tern Ct *SBNE* BH6 ...... 237 J2
Terrace Rd *WCLF* BH2 ...... 14 D6
Terrier Cl *HEND* SO30 ...... 109 H5
Terrington Av
   CHCH/BSGR BH23 ...... 224 C7
Terriote Cl *CHFD* SO53 ...... 81 H1
Terwick La *EPSF* GU31 ...... 66 D8
Testbourne Av *TOTT* SO40 ...... 129 H1
Testbourne Cl *TOTT* SO40 ...... 129 H1
Testbourne Rd *TOTT* SO40 ...... 129 H1
Test Cl *PSF* GU32 ...... 63 K7
Testcombe Rd *GPORT* PO12 ...... 10 D6
Testlands Av *ROWN* SO16 ...... 105 J2
Test La *ROWN* SO16 ...... 105 G6
Test Rd *SHAM* SO14 ...... 131 M8
Test Wy *ROMY* SO51 ...... 49 M6
   TOTT SO40 ...... 104 F7
Testwood Av *TOTT* SO40 ...... 104 C6
Testwood Crs *TOTT* SO40 ...... 104 C6
Testwood La *TOTT* SO40 ...... 104 E7
Testwood Pl *TOTT* SO40 ...... 104 E7
Testwood Rd *HAV* PO9 ...... 165 H3 ⬛
   WSHM SO15 ...... 130 F2
Tethering Dro *FBDG* SP6 ...... 73 J5
Tetney Cl *ROWN* SO16 ...... 105 K5
Teviot Rd *CHFD* SO53 ...... 80 F3
Tewkesbury Av *FHAM* PO15 ...... 160 A5
   GPORT PO12 ...... 209 L1
Tewkesbury Cl *CHAM* PO6 ...... 163 H8
Texas Dr *FUFL* SO22 ...... 26 A6
Thackeray Rd *PTSW* SO17 ...... 107 G8
Thames Cl *FERN* BH22 ...... 194 E2
   WEND SO18 ...... 108 A1
Thames Dr *FHAM* PO15 ...... 160 B6
Thamesmead Cl
   CHCH/BSGR BH23 ...... 209 K1 ⬛
Thames Ms *PLE* BH15 ...... 233 G7 ⬛
Thames St *PLE* BH15 ...... 233 G7
Thatchers La
   CHCH/BSGR BH23 ...... 197 K6
   LYMN SO41 ...... 203 G3

Theatre Ms *SSEA* PO5 .... 13 K7
The Itchen Br *ITCH* SO19 .... 5 M6
Theobold Rd
  CHCH/BSGR BH23 .... 195 L8
Theseus Rd *LSOL/BMARY* PO13... 208 B1
Thetchers CI
  NMIL/BTOS BH25 .... 225 M3
Thetford Gdns *CHFD* SO53 .... 80 F1
Thetford Rd
  BKME/WDN BH12 .... 234 E3
The Thicket
  FHAM/PORC PO16 .... 161 L8
  LSOL/BMARY PO13 .... 185 J7
  ROMY SO51 .... 79 H2
  SSEA PO5 .... 13 J6
  WVILLE PO7 .... 164 B6
Third Av *CHAM* PO6 .... 163 J8
  HAV PO9 .... 9 H3
  WSHM SO15 .... 130 D2
Thirlmere *ELGH* SO50 .... 81 L6
Thirlmere CI
  FHAM/STUB PO14 .... 184 B4
Thirlmere Rd *ROWN* SO16 .... 105 K6
Thirlstane Firs *CHFD* SO53 ...... 81 G4
Thistlebarrow Rd *LTDN* BH7 ... 236 D2
Thistledown *HORN* PO8 .... 140 F3
Thistledowne Gdns
  EMRTH PO10 .... 166 F8
Thistle Rd *HEND* SO30 .... 133 M2
  NBAD SO52 .... 80 E3
Thomas CI *TOTT* SO40 .... 129 H2
Thomas Lewis Wy
  PTSW SO17 .... 107 G8
Thomas Rd *NBAD* SO52 .... 79 M4
Thompson's La *RWIN* SO21 .... 83 L1
  WVILLE PO7 .... 139 G3
Thoresby Ct
  NMIL/BTOS BH25 .... 225 J5
Thornbrake Rd *GPORT* PO12 ..... 11 H5
Thornbury Av *FAWY* SO45 .... 180 C8
  WSHM SO15 .... 131 J1
Thornbury CI
  FHAM/STUB PO14 .... 160 A8
Thornbury Hts *CHFD* SO53 .... 53 L7
Thornbury Rd *SBNE* BH6 .... 237 M4
Thornbury Wd *CHFD* SO53 .... 53 L7
Thorncliffe CI *NEND* PO2 .... 187 K4
Thorn CI *ELGH* SO50 .... 81 M3
  EPSF GU31 .... 64 B6
Thorncombe CI *CFDH* BH17 ..... 218 C4
Thorncroft Rd *PSEA* PO1 .... 13 M2
Thorndike CI *ROWN* SO16 .... 105 M6
Thorne CI *VWD* BH31 .... 144 C1
Thorness CI *ROWN* SO16 .... 105 H1
Thorney CI *FHAM/STUB* PO14 .... 6 A8
Thorney Old Pk *EMRTH* PO10 ... 191 F4
Thorney Rd *EMRTH* PO10 .... 190 F3
Thornfield Dr
  CHCH/BSGR BH23 .... 224 D7
Thorngate Wy *GPORT* PO12 ...... 11 K3
Thornham La *EMRTH* PO10 ...... 190 F2
Thornham Rd
  NMIL/BTOS BH25 .... 226 B5
Thornhill Av *ITCH* SO19 .... 133 H2
Thornhill CI *FAWY* SO45 .... 180 D6
Thornhill Park Rd *WEND* SO18 .. 133 H1
Thornhill Rd *FAWY* SO45 .... 180 D6
  ROWN SO16 .... 106 C4
Thorni Av *FHAM* PO15 .... 160 A5
Thornleigh Rd *ITCH* SO19 .... 132 C6
Thornley Rd *NBNE* BH10 .... 220 B4
Thorn Rd *CFDH* BH17 .... 218 A5
Thorns La *LYMN* SO41 .... 230 D1
Thornton Av *HLER* SO31 .... 158 A7
Thornton Rd *GPORT* PO12 ...... 185 M8
Thornton CI *CHAM* PO6 .... 163 M6
  WIMB BH21 .... 217 G3
Thorncroft Av *ITCH* SO19 .... 132 K7
Thorold Rd *CHFD* SO53 .... 53 K7
  WEND SO18 .... 107 K7
Three Acre Dr
  NMIL/BTOS BH25 .... 225 K8
Three Acres *WVILLE* PO7 .... 139 L5
Three Castles Pth *RWIN* SO21 ... 17 H4
Three Cross Rd *WIMB* BH21 ..... 168 C2
Threefield La *SHAM* SO14 .... 5 L5
Three Horse Shoes La
  ALTN GU34 .... 32 D6
Three Oaks *ITCH* SO19 .... 133 J3
Three Tun CI *PSEA* PO1 .... 12 D7
Thresher CI *HORN* PO8 .... 141 C7
Throop CI *CHAR* BH8 .... 221 L7
Throop Rd *CHAR* BH8 .... 221 J4
Throopside Av
  MOOR/WNTN BH9 .... 221 H4
Thrush Rd *BKME/WDN* BH12 .... 219 G2
Thrush Wk *HORN* PO8 .... 140 C4
Thruxton Rd *HAV* PO9 .... 165 G3
Thurbern Rd *NEND* PO2 .... 187 J6
Thurmell CI *HEND* SO30 .... 134 A4
Thurmond Crs *FUFL* SO22 .... 26 B2
Thurmond Rd *FUFL* SO22 .... 26 B2
Thursby Rd *CHCH/BSGR* BH23... 224 D6
Thurston CI *CHFD* SO53 .... 81 J1
Thwaite Rd *BKME/WDN* BH12 ... 235 G4
Thyme Av *FHAM* PO15 .... 135 H8
Tides Reach *WEND* SO18 .... 107 J2
Tichborne Gv *HAV* PO9 .... 165 H3
Tichborne Rd *ELGH* SO50 .... 81 L8
  WEND SO18 .... 108 C8
Tichborne Wy
  LSOL/BMARY PO13 .... 185 H7
Tickleford Dr *ITCH* SO19 .... 132 F7
Tickner Rd *HEND* SO30 .... 134 B3
Ticonderoga Gdns *ITCH* SO19 ... 132 C7
Tidemill CI *CHCH/BSGR* BH23... 222 E8
Tides Wy *TOTT* SO40 .... 130 D6
Tideway Gdns *ENEY* PO4 .... 212 A4
Tidworth Rd *HAV* PO9 .... 165 K4
Tiffany CI *LYMN* SO41 .... 226 D4
Tiffield CI *HSEA* PO3 .... 188 A4
Tilbrook Rd *WSHM* SO15 .... 105 M8
Tilburg Rd *CHCH/BSGR* BH23... 238 C1
Tilden Rd *RWIN* SO21 .... 54 B3
Tilebarn La *BROC* SO42 .... 201 K2
Tilford Rd *HORN* PO8 .... 140 D2
Tillington Gdns *HORN* PO8 ..... 116 C4
Tilmore Gdns *PSF* GU32 .... 63 L3
Tilmore Rd *PSF* GU32 .... 63 L3

Timberlane *WVILLE* PO7 .... 164 B4
Timberley La *RSAL* SP5 .... 73 M2
Timberly CI *FAWY* SO45 .... 180 A4
The Timbers *FHAM* PO15 .... 160 A7
Timor CI *HLER* SO31 .... 134 F8
Timothy CI *NBNE* BH10 .... 220 B3
Timpson Rd *PSEA* PO1 .... 211 J2
Timsbury Crs *HAV* PO9 .... 8 C1
Timsbury Dr *ROWN* SO16 .... 105 J6
Timson CI *TOTT* SO40 .... 129 G2
Tincleton Gdns
  MOOR/WNTN BH9 .... 220 F4
Tindale Rd *ROWN* SO16 .... 105 K6
Tinker Aly *ELGH* SO50 .... 107 M1
Tinneys CI *RSAL* SP5 .... 73 J4
Tintagel Wy *CHAM* PO6 .... 186 F1
Tintern CI *CHAM* PO6 .... 162 D7
Tintern Gv *WSHM* SO15 .... 4 C1
Tintern Rd *GPORT* PO12 .... 10 D3
Tipner Gn *NEND* PO2 .... 187 G5
Tipner La *NEND* PO2 .... 186 F5
Tipner Rd *NEND* PO2 .... 187 G6
Tipper La *EPSF* GU31 .... 93 G5
Tiptree CI *ELGH* SO50 .... 81 M3
Tisted CI *HAV* PO9 .... 165 M3
Titchfield HI *FHAM/STUB* PO14... 159 L8
Titchfield La *FHAM* PO15 .... 136 A8
  WHAM PO17 .... 136 A7
Titchfield Park Rd *FHAM* PO15... 159 H5
Titchfield Rd
  FHAM/STUB PO14 .... 183 L1
Tithe Barn *LYMN* SO41 .... 228 C3
Tithelands La *NARL* SO24 .... 31 L4
The Tithe *WVILLE* PO7 .... 139 K5
Tithewood CI *CHFD* SO53 .... 53 C6
Titus Gdns *WVILLE* PO7 .... 140 E8
Tivoli CI *CHFD* SO53 .... 81 L1
Toby St *PSEA* PO1 .... 211 C2
Todber CI *BWD* BH11 .... 219 H5
Tokar St *ENEY* PO4 .... 211 L6
Tokio Rd *HSEA* PO3 .... 187 L7
Tollefrey Gdns *NBAD* SO52 ...... 80 E2
Tollard CI *BKME/WDN* BH12 ..... 219 J8
Tollbar Wy *HEND* SO30 .... 108 F8
Tollerford Rd *CFDH* BH17 ...... 218 B6
Tollgate *CHFD* SO53 .... 81 H6
Tollgate Rd *HLER* SO31 .... 134 B8
Tolpuddle Gdns
  MOOR/WNTN BH9 .... 220 F4
Tolstoi Rd *PSTN* BH14 .... 233 M2
Toms La *RGWD* BH24 .... 123 L8
Tonbridge St *SSEA* PO5 .... 13 H7
Tonge Rd *BWD* BH11 .... 219 M2
Tonnant CI
  FHAM/STUB PO14 .... 184 B7
Toogoods Wy *ROWN* SO16 ..... 105 J3
Toomer CI *FAWY* SO45 .... 180 D6
Toothill Rd *ROMY* SO51 .... 79 H7
Topaz Gv *WVILLE* PO7 .... 140 F8
Topiary Gdns *HLER* SO31 .... 158 F4
Top La *RGWD* BH24 .... 170 E1
Torbay Rd *PSTN* BH14 .... 234 B5
Torberry Dr *EPSF* GU31 .... 64 A6
Torch CI *ELGH* SO50 .... 83 G4
Tor CI *FHAM/PORC* PO16 .... 161 J7
Torcross CI *ITCH* SO19 .... 132 C6
Torfrida Ct *ENEY* PO4 .... 212 A5
Tormead *FAWY* SO45 .... 155 K5
Tornay Gv *NBAD* SO52 .... 79 L4
Toronto PI *GPORT* PO12 .... 10 F2
Toronto Rd *NEND* PO2 .... 211 J1
Torquay Av *GPORT* PO12 ...... 185 L8
  WSHM SO15 .... 106 B8
Torque CI *ITCH* SO19 .... 133 J4
Torre CI *ELGH* SO50 .... 81 M2
Torridge Gdns *WEND* SO18 .... 108 A5
Torrington CI *ITCH* SO19 ...... 132 E4
Torrington Rd *NEND* PO2 ...... 187 J5
Tortworth CI *FHAM/STUB* PO14... 6 A8
Tor Wy *EPSF* GU31 .... 63 M5
Torwood Gdns *ELGH* SO50 ...... 82 E6
Tosson CI *ROWN* SO16 .... 105 K8
Tote La *MIDH* GU29 .... 67 K2
Totland CI *ROWN* SO16 .... 105 K8
Totland Rd *CHAM* PO6 .... 187 J1
  LSOL/BMARY PO13 .... 185 G6
Totmel Rd *CFDH* BH17 .... 218 E6
Totnes CI *ELGH* SO50 .... 81 L3
Totnes Rd *NBAD* SO52 .... 79 L5
Tottenham Rd *PSEA* PO1 .... 211 J2
Totton By-pass *TOTT* SO40 .... 129 L2
Tournerbury La *HISD* PO11 ..... 213 L4
Tourney Rd *BWD* BH11 .... 219 H2
Tower CI *GPORT* PO12 .... 209 H5
Tower Gdns *HAV* PO9 .... 189 K2
Tower La *ELGH* SO50 .... 82 B6
  WIMB BH21 .... 192 B2
Tower PI *HEND* SO30 .... 108 C7
Tower Rd *BMTH* BH1 .... 236 D3
  CCLF BH13 .... 235 G7
  ENEY PO4 .... 211 K5
  WINC SO23 .... 2 F6
Tower Rd West *CCLF* BH13 ..... 234 F7
Towers Farm *WIMB* BH21 ..... 217 H1
Tower St *EMRTH* PO10 .... 166 E8
  PSEA PO1 .... 12 B5
  WINC SO23 .... 2 F6
Towers Wy *WIMB* BH21 .... 217 H1
Towngate Br *PLE* BH15 .... 233 H6
Town Hall Rd *HAV* PO9 .... 8 F5
Townhill Wy *WEND* SO18 .... 107 M7
Town La *EPSF* GU31 .... 64 A3
Town Quay *SHAM* SO14 .... 4 F7
Townsend CI *BWD* BH11 .... 219 H4
Townsend Rd *FBDG* SP6 .... 68 D2
Townsville Rd
  MOOR/WNTN BH9 .... 220 F6
Towpath Md *ENEY* PO4 .... 212 A4
Toynbee CI *ELGH* SO50 .... 81 M5
Toynbee Rd *ELGH* SO50 .... 81 M5
Tozer CI *BWD* BH11 .... 219 K6
Trafalgar CI *CHFD* SO53 .... 81 G3
Trafalgar Ct *FHAM/STUB* PO14 ... 184 D1
Trafalgar Rd
  MOOR/WNTN BH9 .... 235 L1

Trafalgar Sq *GPORT* PO12 ...... 10 E1
Trafalgar St *WINC* SO23 .... 2 F8
Trafalgar Wy *FAWY* SO45 ..... 155 M7
Trafford Wy *ELGH* SO50 .... 83 G7
Trampers La *WHAM* PO17 ...... 137 L7
Tranby Rd *ITCH* SO19 .... 132 C4
Tranmere CI *ENEY* PO4 .... 211 M5
Tranmere Rd *ENEY* PO4 .... 211 M5
Treadwheel Rd *HORN* PO8 ..... 141 L2
Treagore Rd *TOTT* SO40 .... 104 B7
Trearnan Rd *ROWN* SO16 ...... 105 L8
Treble CI *FUFL* SO22 .... 26 A4
Tredegar Rd *ENEY* PO4 .... 211 K5
Treebys CI *CHCH/BSGR* BH23... 223 H7
Treeside Av *TOTT* SO40 .... 129 L1
Treeside Rd *WSHM* SO15 ...... 106 B8
Tree Side Wy *WVILLE* PO7 ..... 140 C7
Trefoil CI *WVILLE* PO7 .... 164 D1
Trefoil Wy *CHCH/BSGR* BH23... 224 A8
Tregaron Av *CHAM* PO6 .... 187 M1
Tregonwell Rd *WCLF* BH2 .... 14 D6
Treloar Rd *HISD* PO11 .... 214 C7
Treloyhan CI *CHFD* SO53 .... 81 J4
Tremona Rd *ROWN* SO16 ...... 106 A5
Trenley CI *FAWY* SO45 .... 180 A5
Trent CI *WEND* SO18 .... 107 L7
Trent Wy *FERN* BH22 .... 194 E2
  LSOL/BMARY PO13 .... 208 D2
Tresillian Gdns *WEND* SO18 .... 108 A6
Tresillian Wy
  CHCH/BSGR BH23 .... 224 F6
Trevis Rd *ENEY* PO4 .... 212 A4
Trevone CI *TOTT* SO40 .... 129 J3
Trevor CI *ENEY* PO4 .... 13 M6
Trevose CI *CHFD* SO53 .... 81 J4
  LSOL/BMARY PO13 .... 185 G7
Trevose Crs *CHFD* SO53 .... 81 J4
Trevose Wy *FHAM/STUB* PO14 ... 158 F7
Triangle La *FHAM/STUB* PO14 ... 183 J4
The Triangle *RSAL* SP5 .... 47 G4
  WCLF BH2 .... 14 C6
Tribe Rd *GPORT* PO12 .... 10 D2
Tricketts La *FERN* BH22 .... 194 D2
Trigon Rd *PLE* BH15 .... 233 J1
Trimaran CI *HLER* SO31 .... 158 C7
Trimaran Rd *HLER* SO31 .... 158 C7
Trimm's Dro *FBDG* SP6 .... 72 D8
Trinidad Crs
  BKME/WDN BH12 .... 219 G8
Trinity CI *GPORT* PO12 .... 11 K4
Trinity Gn *GPORT* PO12 .... 11 L4
Trinity Rd *BMTH* BH1 .... 15 H4
  SHAM SO14 .... 5 H1
Trinity St *FHAM/PORC* PO16 ..... 7 J3
  WINC SO23 .... 3 J7
Tristan CI *FAWY* SO45 .... 207 J1
Triumph CI *FHAM* PO15 .... 160 A8
Triumph Rd *FHAM/STUB* PO14 ... 184 D3
Troak CI *CHCH/BSGR* BH23 .... 223 J8
Trojan Wy *WVILLE* PO7 .... 164 D5
Troon Crs *CHAM* PO6 .... 164 A7
Troon Rd *WIMB* BH21 .... 217 L3
Trosnant Rd *HAV* PO9 .... 8 C2
Trotton Rd *EPSF* GU31 .... 66 C8
Trotts La *TOTT* SO40 .... 130 A4
Trowbridge CI *ROWN* SO16 .... 105 K2
Truman Rd *BWD* BH11 .... 219 M2
Truro CI *ELGH* SO50 .... 82 D5
Truro Rd *CHAM* PO6 .... 162 D8
Truscott Av
  MOOR/WNTN BH9 .... 235 M1
Trussell CI *FUFL* SO22 .... 2 A1
Trussell Crs *FUFL* SO22 .... 2 A1
Tuckers La *PLE* BH15 .... 232 E7
Tucks CI *CHCH/BSGR* BH23 .... 197 L7
Tuckton CI *SBNE* BH6 .... 237 J4
Tuckton Rd *SBNE* BH6 .... 237 J4
Tudor Av *EMRTH* PO10 .... 166 C4
Tudor CI *FBDG* SP6 .... 121 L3
  FHAM/PORC PO16 .... 161 M7
  HISD PO11 .... 213 K6
  LSOL/BMARY PO13 .... 185 H8
  TOTT SO40 .... 104 B8
Tudor Ct *FHAM/STUB* PO14 .... 184 D1
  PLE BH15 .... 233 K2
Tudor Crs *CHAM* PO6 .... 187 K2
Tudor Gdns *HEND* SO30 .... 133 L3
Tudor Rd *BDST* BH18 .... 217 M4
Tudor Wood CI *ROWN* SO16 ... 106 E4
Tuffin CI *ROWN* SO16 .... 105 H3
Tukes Av *LSOL/BMARY* PO13 ... 184 F4
Tulip Gdns *HAV* PO9 .... 165 G6
  HLER SO31 .... 158 D5
Tulip Rd *ROWN* SO16 .... 107 H4
Tumulus CI *ITCH* SO19 .... 133 K4
Tunstall Rd *CHAM* PO6 .... 163 H7
  ITCH SO19 .... 133 J4
Tunworth Ct *HAV* PO9 .... 165 M3
Tuppenny La *EMRTH* PO10 ..... 167 G8
Turbary CI *BKME/WDN* BH12 ... 219 J8
Turbary Ct *UPTN* BH16 .... 217 G8
Turbary Park Av *BWD* BH11 ... 219 K5
Turbary Rd *BKME/WDN* BH12... 234 C1
  FERN BH22 .... 194 D1
Turks La *PSTN* BH14 .... 233 M7
Turlin Rd *UPTN* BH16 .... 232 B4
Turnberry CI
  CHCH/BSGR BH23 .... 237 M2
Turner Av *LSOL/BMARY* PO13 ... 185 J7
Turners Farm Crs
  LYMN SO41 .... 226 E6
Turnpike Down *WINC* SO23 ...... 3 M7
Turnpike Wy *HEND* SO30 ...... 133 L2
Turnstone Gdns *ROWN* SO16 ... 106 A3
Turnworth CI *BDST* BH18 ...... 218 A4
Turtle CI *FHAM/STUB* PO14 .... 183 M4
Tuscan Wk *CHFD* SO53 .... 81 M5
Tuscany Wy *WVILLE* PO7 .... 140 F8
The Tussocks *TOTT* SO40 ...... 130 D6
Tutland Rd *NBAD* SO52 .... 79 L4
Tutor CI *HLER* SO31 .... 157 K5
Tutts La *ROMY* SO51 .... 76 D4
Tweedale Rd
  MOOR/WNTN BH9 .... 221 G5

Tweed CI *CHFD* SO53 .... 80 F1
Tweed La *LYMN* SO41 .... 202 B8
Twemlow Av *PSTN* BH14 .... 233 L6
Twiggs End CI *HLER* SO31 ..... 158 D4
Twiggs La *TOTT* SO40 .... 154 A3
Twin Oaks CI *BDST* BH18 ...... 217 M5
Twyford Av *NEND* PO2 .... 187 H7
  WSHM SO15 .... 106 B7
Twyford CI *CHAR* BH8 .... 221 H6
Twyford Rd *ELGH* SO50 .... 82 A2
Twyford Wy *CFDH* BH17 .... 218 E6
Twynham Av
  CHCH/BSGR BH23 .... 237 M2
Twynham CI *RSAL* SP5 .... 72 E2
Twynham Rd *SBNE* BH6 .... 237 L4
Twynhams HI *BPWT* SO32 ..... 111 M8
Tylers CI *LYMN* SO41 .... 228 B3
The Tyleshades *ROMY* SO51 .... 78 F2
Tyne CI *CHFD* SO53 .... 80 F3
Tynedale CI *CHFD* SO53 .... 185 K8
  MOOR/WNTN BH9 .... 221 H2
Tyneham Av *BKME/WDN* BH12... 218 F8
Tyne Wy *HEND* SO30 .... 108 D6
Tyrell Rd *CHFD* SO53 .... 81 H1
Tyrell Gdns *CHAR* BH8 .... 221 L6
Tyrrells La *RGWD* BH24 .... 172 C4
Tyrrells Ct *CHCH/BSGR* BH23 ... 197 M8
Tyseley Rd *SSEA* PO5 .... 13 H3
Tytherley Gn *CHAR* BH8 .... 221 H6
Tytherley Rd *WEND* SO18 ...... 108 B8

U

Uddens Dr *WIMB* BH21 .... 193 J2
Ullswater Av *WEND* SO18 ...... 108 A7
Ullswater Rd *ROWN* SO16 ...... 105 K7
  WIMB BH21 .... 192 A6
Undercliff Dr *BMTH* BH1 .... 15 H4
Underclliff Rd *BOSC* BH5 .... 236 C5
Underdown Av *WVILLE* PO7 .... 164 B6
Undershore *LYMN* SO41 .... 229 H2
Underwood CI *CFDH* BH17 ..... 217 M7
  ROWN SO16 .... 106 C4
Underwood Rd *ELGH* SO50 ..... 82 C4
  ROWN SO16 .... 106 D4
Unicorn Rd *LSOL/BMARY* PO13... 208 B1
  PSEA PO1 .... 210 F2
Union La *BPWT* SO32 .... 86 F6
Union PI *PSEA* PO1 .... 211 H2
Union Rd *HAV* PO9 .... 8 D4
  SHAM SO14 .... 131 M2
Union St *FHAM/PORC* PO16 ..... 7 M6
  PSEA PO1 .... 12 D1
  WINC SO23 .... 3 J7
University Crs *PTSW* SO17 ..... 107 G5
University Pkwy *ROWN* SO16 ... 80 B7
University Rd *PTSW* SO17 ...... 106 F5
Unwin CI *ITCH* SO19 .... 132 B7
Upham St *BPWT* SO32 .... 84 B4
Uphill Rd *FUFL* SO22 .... 16 A3
Upland La *LISS* GU33 .... 35 M1
Uplands Av *NMIL/BTOS* BH25 ... 225 L8
Uplands CI *FERN* BH22 .... 168 E8
Uplands Crs *FHAM/PORC* PO16... 7 J3
Uplands Rd *CHAM* PO6 .... 164 A7
  CHAR BH8 .... 221 H6
  FERN BH22 .... 168 D6
  FUFL SO22 .... 2 D1
  HAV PO9 .... 142 A6
  WVILLE PO7 .... 139 G6
Uplands Wy *PTSW* SO17 .... 106 F6
Uplyme CI *CFDH* BH17 .... 218 C6
Upper Arundel St *PSEA* PO1 .... 13 H1
Upper Banister St
  WSHM SO15 .... 131 K2
Upper Barn Copse *ELGH* SO50 ... 83 C5
Upper Bere Wd *WVILLE* PO7 ... 164 D1
Upper Brook Dr *HLER* SO31 ... 158 C5
Upper Brook St *WINC* SO23 ...... 3 G7
Upper Brownhill Rd
  ROWN SO16 .... 105 L5
Upper Bugle St *SHAM* SO14 ..... 4 F5
Upper Church Rd
  LYMN SO41 .... 227 K4
Upper Cornaway La
  FHAM/PORC PO16 .... 161 M8
Upper Crabbick La *WVILLE* PO7... 139 G3
Upper Crescent Rd *NBAD* SO52 ... 79 L4
Upper Deacon Rd *ITCH* SO19 ... 132 F2
Upper Golf Links Rd
  BDST BH18 .... 217 M3
Upper Gordon Rd
  CHCH/BSGR BH23 .... 224 E7
Upper Heyshott *EPSF* GU31 .... 63 M5
Upper High St *FUFL* SO22 .... 2 E5
Upper Hinton Rd *BMTH* BH1 .... 14 F6
Upper House Ct *WHAM* PO17 ... 136 E5
Upper Lamborough La
  NARL SO24 .... 30 C1
Upper Market St *ELGH* SO50 .... 82 C4
Upper Mead *ELGH* SO50 .... 83 J6
Upper Moors Rd *ELGH* SO50 ... 54 E7
  RWIN SO21 .... 54 E8
Upper Mt *LISS* GU33 .... 36 D5
Upper Mullin's La *FAWY* SO45 ... 155 J5
Upper New Rd *HEND* SO30 ..... 108 C7
Upper Northam CI
  HEND SO30 .... 133 L2
Upper Northam Dr
  HEND SO30 .... 133 J2
Upper Northam Rd
  HEND SO30 .... 133 L1
Upper Norwich Rd *WCLF* BH2 ... 14 D6
Upper Old St
  FHAM/STUB PO14 .... 183 L5
Upper Piece *WVILLE* PO7 ...... 139 J5
Upper Rd *BKME/WDN* BH12 .... 234 B2
Upper St Helens Rd
  HEND SO30 .... 133 M4
Upper Shaftesbury Av
  PTSW SO17 .... 107 G5
Upper Shirley Av *WSHM* SO15... 106 B7
Upper Spinney *HLER* SO31 ..... 158 A8
Upper Terrace Rd *WCLF* BH2 .... 14 D6

Upper Toothill Rd *ROWN* SO16 ... 79 K7
Upper Wardown *EPSF* GU31 .... 64 A4
Upper Weston La *ITCH* SO19 ... 132 E6
Upper Whf *FHAM/PORC* PO16 ..... 7 L7
Uppleby Rd *BKME/WDN* BH12... 234 B3
Upton CI *HAV* PO9 .... 165 H1
  UPTN BH16 .... 232 B1
Upton Ct *UPTN* BH16 .... 232 B1
Upton Crs *ROWN* SO16 .... 105 H1
Upton Grey CI *FUFL* SO22 ...... 16 C5
Upton Heath Est *UPTN* BH16 ... 232 A1
Upton Rd *CFDH* BH17 .... 232 D1
Upton Wy *BDST* BH18 .... 217 J5
Upwey Av *PLE* BH15 .... 232 D5
Utrecht Ct *CHCH/BSGR* BH23 ... 238 C1

V

Vadne Gdns *GPORT* PO12 ..... 209 M2
Vaggs La *LYMN* SO41 .... 226 C2
Vale Dr *WEND* SO18 .... 107 L7
Vale Gv *GPORT* PO12 .... 209 L1
Valencia CI
  CHCH/BSGR BH23 .... 222 B4
Valentine Av *ITCH* SO19 .... 133 G5
Valentine CI *FHAM* PO15 .... 160 A5
Valentine Ct *WVILLE* PO7 ...... 140 E8
Valerian CI *ELGH* SO50 .... 109 H2
Valerian Rd *HEND* SO30 .... 134 A2
Vale Rd *BMTH* BH1 .... 236 C4
  PSTN BH14 .... 234 D4
  RSAL SP5 .... 73 J2
  WINC SO23 .... 27 G2
The Vale *FAWY* SO45 .... 155 K5
  HLER SO31 .... 158 F6
  HORN PO8 .... 116 B7
  SSEA PO5 .... 13 H8
Valetta Pk *EMRTH* PO10 ...... 166 C8
Valetta Rd *EMRTH* PO10 ...... 191 H7
Valette Rd *MOOR/WNTN* BH9 ... 220 E5
Valiant Gdns *NEND* PO2 .... 187 H4
Valiant Rd *EMRTH* PO10 ...... 191 H7
Valiant Wy *CHCH/BSGR* BH23... 239 G1
Valley CI *CHCH/BSGR* BH23 .... 222 C5
  RSAL SP5 .... 73 J2
  RWIN SO21 .... 54 E8
  WVILLE PO7 .... 164 A5
Valleydene *FAWY* SO45 .... 155 K6
Valley HI *FUFL* SO22 .... 16 B3
Valley La *CHCH/BSGR* BH23 ... 198 C4
Valley Park Dr *HORN* PO8 ..... 116 C5
Valley Rd *HLER* SO31 .... 158 C4
Valley Rd *CHAR* BH8 .... 221 K5
  CHFD SO53 .... 81 H1
  FUFL SO22 .... 16 A3
  TOTT SO40 .... 129 K3
The Valley *FUFL* SO22 .... 26 C2
Valley Vw *BKME/WDN* BH12 ... 235 C1
Valley Wk *BPWT* SO32 .... 57 H6
Vallis CI *PLE* BH15 .... 233 J7
Valsheba Dr *FHAM/STUB* PO14... 183 M7
Vanburgh Wy *CHFD* SO53 .... 53 G7
Vanguard HI *FUFL* SO22 .... 16 B2
Vanguard Rd *CHAR* BH8 .... 221 J7
  PLE BH15 .... 233 H6
  WEND SO18 .... 107 M8
Vanstone Rd
  LSOL/BMARY PO13 .... 185 H8
Vardy CI *ITCH* SO19 .... 133 H5
Varna Rd *WSHM* SO15 .... 131 G3
Varos CI *GPORT* PO12 .... 209 L2
Varsity Rd *EMRTH* PO10 .... 191 H7
Vaudrey CI *WSHM* SO15 .... 106 B7
Vaughan CI *ITCH* SO19 .... 133 J3
Vaughan Rd *FAWY* SO45 .... 155 G4
Vauxhall Wy *PSF* GU32 .... 63 K5
Veal's La *TOTT* SO40 .... 154 F1
Vear's La *RWIN* SO21 .... 54 F1
Vecta CI *CHCH/BSGR* BH23 .... 239 H2
Vectis Rd *GPORT* PO12 .... 209 J5
  NMIL/BTOS BH25 .... 240 C1
Vectis Wy *CHAM* PO6 .... 187 K1
Velder Av *ENEY* PO4 .... 211 L3
Vellan Ct *ROWN* SO16 .... 105 H7
Velmore Rd *CHFD* SO53 .... 81 G4
Velsheda Rd *FAWY* SO45 ...... 155 L3
Velvet Lawn Rd
  NMIL/BTOS BH25 .... 225 K8
Venator PI *WIMB* BH21 .... 192 A2
Venerable Rd
  FHAM/STUB PO14 .... 184 E3
Vengeance Rd
  LSOL/BMARY PO13 .... 208 C1
Venice CI *WVILLE* PO7 .... 140 E8
Venning Av *BWD* BH11 .... 219 J3
Ventnor Rd *ENEY* PO4 .... 13 M4
  LSOL/BMARY PO13 .... 184 F5
Ventnor Wy *FHAM/PORC* PO16... 161 J7
Ventry CI *CCLF* BH13 .... 234 E4
Ventura PI *UPTN* BH16 .... 232 C2
Venture CI *ROWN* SO16 .... 80 D7
Verbena Crs *HORN* PO8 .... 140 F4
Verbena Wy *HEND* SO30 .... 134 D2
Verdon Av *HLER* SO31 .... 157 J5
Verger CI *FHAM/STUB* PO14 ... 159 C5
Verity Crs *CFDH* BH17 .... 218 E7
Vermont CI *ROWN* SO16 .... 106 E4
Vernalls CI *NBNE* BH10 .... 220 B4
Vernalls Gdns *NBNE* BH10 .... 220 B3
Verne Rd *VWD* BH31 .... 144 E3
Verney CI *BWD* BH11 .... 219 M5
Verney Rd *BWD* BH11 .... 219 L5
Vernham Rd *FUFL* SO22 .... 16 C3
Verno La *CHCH/BSGR* BH23 ... 224 D4
Vernon Av *ENEY* PO4 .... 211 L4
Vernon CI *GPORT* PO12 .... 10 C3
Vernon HI *BPWT* SO32 .... 85 H6
Vernon Rd *GPORT* PO12 .... 10 D2
  HSEA PO3 .... 187 L6
Verona Av *SBNE* BH6 .... 237 J5
Verona Rd *CHFD* SO53 .... 81 K1
Verulam PI *BMTH* BH1 .... 14 F5
Verulam Rd *PLE* BH15 .... 233 L4
  SHAM SO14 .... 131 M1

Verwood Crs SBNE BH6 ... 237 M4
Verwood Rd HAV PO9 ... 165 M2 12
RGWD BH24 ... 145 L7
WIMB BH21 ... 144 D7
Veryan FHAM PO15 ... 6 C6
Vespasian Rd WEND SO18 ... 132 B1
Vespasian Wy CHFD SO53 ... 81 K2
Vesta Wy CHFD SO53 ... 81 K1
Vetch Cl CHCH/BSGR BH23 ... 223 M8
Vian Cl LSOL/BMARY PO13 ... 185 G4
Vian Rd WVILLE PO7 ... 164 B2
Vicarage Dr HEND SO30 ... 133 M3
Vicarage Gdns LYMN SO41 ... 226 E6 2
Vicarage La BPWT SO32 ... 112 B2
FHAM/STUB PO14 ... 184 A5
LYMN SO41 ... 226 E6
TOTT SO40 ... 103 G7
WVILLE PO7 ... 114 C5
Vicarage Pk RSAL SP5 ... 73 J2
Vicarage Rd
MOOR/WNTN BH9 ... 220 C7
PLE BH15 ... 233 H3
RSAL SP5 ... 73 M3
TOTT SO40 ... 130 D7
VWD BH31 ... 144 D2
Vicarage Wy
CHCH/BSGR BH23 ... 223 H6
Vice La ROMY SO51 ... 101 M4
Viceroy Rd ITCH SO19 ... 132 E5
Vickers Cl CHAR BH8 ... 221 M6
Vickery Wy CHCH/BSGR BH23 ... 223 J8
Victena Rd ELGH SO50 ... 83 H6
Victoria Av HISD PO11 ... 213 K5
MOOR/WNTN BH9 ... 220 C7
WVILLE PO7 ... 163 M5
Victoria Cl HLER SO31 ... 158 E7
WIMB BH21 ... 217 H4
Victoria Crs BKME/WDN BH12 ... 234 C2
Victoria Gdns FBDG SP6 ... 97 J7
FERN BH22 ... 194 B2
RGWD BH24 ... 170 E2 7
Victoria Gld HLER SO31 ... 157 G3
Victoria Gv SSEA PO5 ... 13 K6
Victoria Park Rd
MOOR/WNTN BH9 ... 220 C7
Victoria Pl BMTH BH1 ... 15 M1
GPORT PO12 ... 10 F4 5
LYMN SO41 ... 228 C6
Victoria Rd BKME/WDN BH12 ... 234 B3
BMTH BH1 ... 15 M2
BPWT SO32 ... 85 G8
CHCH/BSGR BH23 ... 238 D3
ELGH SO50 ... 82 A3
EMRTH PO10 ... 166 C7
FBDG SP6 ... 97 J7
FERN BH22 ... 194 B2
HISD PO11 ... 189 K6
HLER SO31 ... 156 E2
ITCH SO19 ... 132 B7 5
LYMN SO41 ... 242 A4
PSEA PO1 ... 210 D2
WINC SO23 ... 2 F5
WVILLE PO7 ... 164 C1 1
Victoria Rd North SSEA PO5 ... 13 L3
Victoria Rd South SSEA PO5 ... 13 J7
Victoria Sq LSOL/BMARY PO13 ... 208 C2
Victoria St GPORT PO12 ... 11 G2
PSEA PO1 ... 211 G1
SHAM SO14 ... 5 L2
Victor Rd EMRTH PO10 ... 191 H7
HSEA PO3 ... 211 K1 1
Victor St WSHM SO15 ... 106 B8 2
Victory Av HORN PO8 ... 140 E2
Victory Cl CHFD SO53 ... 81 G3
Victory Crs WSHM SO15 ... 130 F2 1
Victory Gn NEND PO2 ... 187 G6 1
Victory Rd FHAM/STUB PO14 ... 184 B6
PSEA PO1 ... 12 C2 6
WSHM SO15 ... 130 F2
Victory Sq WSHM SO15 ... 130 F2 2
Viewside Cl WIMB BH21 ... 217 G3
Viking Cl FAWY SO45 ... 180 D8
FHAM/STUB PO14 ... 183 M5
ROWN SO16 ... 105 K3
SBNE BH6 ... 237 M4
The Vikings ROMY SO51 ... 79 G1 5
Viking Wy CHCH/BSGR BH23 ... 238 F3
HORN PO8 ... 116 B5
SBNE BH6 ... 237 M4
Villa Gdns WVILLE PO7 ... 140 C8
Village Cl FHAM/STUB PO14 ... 184 A6
Village Rd GPORT PO12 ... 10 B7
Village St PSF GU32 ... 64 A2
Ville De Paris Rd
FHAM/STUB PO14 ... 184 E3
Villette Cl CHCH/BSGR BH23 ... 222 E7
Villiers Rd FAWY SO45 ... 155 K8
SSEA PO5 ... 13 H8
WSHM SO15 ... 131 G1
Vimoutiers Ct FBDG SP6 ... 97 K7 2
Vince Cl BWD BH11 ... 219 M3
Vincent Av ROWN SO16 ... 106 B6
Vincent Cl NMIL/BTOS BH25 ... 225 L6
Vincent Gv FHAM/PORC PO16 ... 186 A1
Vincent Rd NMIL/BTOS BH25 ... 225 K5
WSHM SO15 ... 106 B8
Vincent's Gv WSHM SO15 ... 106 B8 5
Vincent St WSHM SO15 ... 106 A8
Vincent's Wk SHAM SO14 ... 5 G4
Vine Bank WEND SO18 ... 108 B8
Vine Cl HLER SO31 ... 158 B5
LTDN BH7 ... 236 F1
Vine Coppice WVILLE PO7 ... 164 C4
Vine Farm Cl
BKME/WDN BH12 ... 220 A8 5
Vine Farm Rd
BKME/WDN BH12 ... 219 M8
Vinegar Hl LYMN SO41 ... 242 C3
Vineries Cl WIMB BH21 ... 192 D2
The Vineries WIMB BH21 ... 192 D2
Vine Rd ROWN SO16 ... 105 M5
Vinery Gdns ROWN SO16 ... 106 A6
Vinery Rd ROWN SO16 ... 106 B6 1
Vineside LSOL/BMARY PO13 ... 185 J7
Vineyard Cl ITCH SO19 ... 132 B5
The Vineyards NBAD SO52 ... 79 M4
Viney Av ROMY SO51 ... 51 G8
Viney Rd LYMN SO41 ... 228 C7
Vinnells La PSF GU32 ... 60 C1
Vinneys Cl CHCH/BSGR BH23 ... 223 G6
Vinson Rd LISS GU33 ... 36 F4
Violet Av FHAM/STUB PO14 ... 183 M6
Violet Cl NBAD SO52 ... 80 F2
Violet La NMIL/BTOS BH25 ... 225 L4
Violet Rd ROWN SO16 ... 106 F4
Virginia Cl BKME/WDN BH12 ... 234 B1 1
Virginia Park Rd GPORT PO12 ... 209 K2
Viscount Dr CHCH/BSGR BH23 ... 239 G2
Viscount Wk BWD BH11 ... 219 H2
WIMB BH21 ... 219 G3
Vita Rd NEND PO2 ... 187 J5
Vitre Gdns LYMN SO41 ... 228 C6
Vivash Rd PSEA PO1 ... 13 L2 4
Vixen Cl FHAM/STUB PO14 ... 183 M6
Vixen Wk NMIL/BTOS BH25 ... 225 M3
Vokes Cl ITCH SO19 ... 132 F3
Vulcan Cl WSHM SO15 ... 130 D2
Vulcan Rd EMRTH PO10 ... 191 H7
WSHM SO15 ... 130 D2
Vyse La SHAM SO14 ... 4 F6 2

W

Wade Court Rd HAV PO9 ... 9 G6
Wade La HAV PO9 ... 9 G8
Wadham Rd NEND PO2 ... 187 H6
Wadhurst Gdns ITCH SO19 ... 132 E8
Wadhurst Rd HEND SO30 ... 134 A2
The Wad SELS PO20 ... 215 K7
Wagtail Dr NMIL/BTOS BH25 ... 225 K6 5
Wagtail Rd HORN PO8 ... 140 E2
Wagtail Wy FHAM/PORC PO16 ... 161 K8
Wainscott Rd ENEY PO4 ... 211 L6
Wainsford Cl LYMN SO41 ... 227 M5
Wainsford Plantation
LYMN SO41 ... 227 J8 2
Wainsford Rd LYMN SO41 ... 227 J6
Wainwright Cl CHAM PO6 ... 188 A2
Wait End Rd WVILLE PO7 ... 164 C2
Wakefield Av FHAM/PORC PO16 ... 6 F1
NBNE BH10 ... 220 C3
Wakefield Ct WEND SO18 ... 107 M7 5
Wakefield Rd WEND SO18 ... 107 M7
Wakefords Wy HAV PO9 ... 165 M2
Wakely Gdns BWD BH11 ... 219 L3 2
Wakely Rd BWD BH11 ... 219 M3
Walberton Av CHAM PO6 ... 163 L8
Walburton Wy HORN PO8 ... 116 C4
Walcheren Pl PLE BH15 ... 232 B5
Walcott Av CHCH/BSGR BH23 ... 222 D7
Waldegrave Cl ITCH SO19 ... 132 B7 4
Walden Gdns HORN PO8 ... 140 F1
Walden Rd NEND PO2 ... 187 G6
Walditch Gdns CFDH BH17 ... 218 C6
Waldon Gdns WEND SO18 ... 108 A6 5
Waldren Cl PLE BH15 ... 233 J6
Wales St WINC SO23 ... 3 J7
Walford Cl WIMB BH21 ... 192 A2
Walford Rd CHAM PO6 ... 163 G8
Walhampton Hl LYMN SO41 ... 228 D3
Walker Gdns HEND SO30 ... 109 H7
Walker Pl LSOL/BMARY PO13 ... 185 H7 4
Walker Rd NEND PO2 ... 187 H6
Walkers Cl ELGH SO50 ... 83 J6 5
Walkers La North FAWY SO45 ... 180 D7
Walker's La South FAWY SO45 ... 206 D1
Walkford La NMIL/BTOS BH25 ... 225 H5
Walkford Rd CHCH/BSGR BH23 ... 225 G6
Walkford Wy
CHCH/BSGR BH23 ... 224 F7 2
Walkwood Av LTDN BH7 ... 221 M8
Wallace La BROC SO42 ... 204 A2
Wallace Rd BDST BH18 ... 217 L5
ITCH SO19 ... 132 D7 5
NEND PO2 ... 187 H8
Wallington Ct
FHAM/STUB PO14 ... 184 D2 1
Wallington Dr CHFD SO53 ... 52 F8
Wallington Hl FHAM/PORC PO16 ... 7 L4
Wallington Rd NEND PO2 ... 187 K7
Wallington Shore Rd
FHAM/PORC PO16 ... 7 M4
Wallington Wy
FHAM/PORC PO16 ... 7 L4
Walliscott Rd BWD BH11 ... 219 L7
Wallisdean Av
FHAM/STUB PO14 ... 6 E8
HSEA PO3 ... 211 M1
Wallisdown Rd
BKME/WDN BH12 ... 219 H6
Wallis Gdns WVILLE PO7 ... 140 C7
Wallis Rd NBNE BH10 ... 219 M7
WVILLE PO7 ... 140 C7
Walmer Cl ELGH SO50 ... 81 M1
Walmer Rd PSEA PO1 ... 13 M2
Walnut Av WEND SO18 ... 107 K3
Walnut Cl CHFD SO53 ... 53 H6
NMIL/BTOS BH25 ... 225 K5
ROWN SO16 ... 105 L7
Walnut Dr FHAM/STUB PO14 ... 183 M6
Walnut Gv FUFL SO22 ... 26 B3
ROWN SO16 ... 105 L8
Walnut Tree Cl HISD PO11 ... 213 K5 1
Walnut Tree Dr EMRTH PO10 ... 167 J5
Wainwright Gdns HEND SO30 ... 109 H5
Walpole La HLER SO31 ... 158 C1
Walpole Rd BMTH BH1 ... 236 C3
FUFL SO22 ... 26 B3
GPORT PO12 ... 11 H3
Walsall Rd HSEA PO3 ... 211 L2
Walsford Rd WBNE BH4 ... 235 H3
Walsingham Cl CHAM PO6 ... 163 H7 5
Walsingham Dene LTDN BH7 ... 221 K8
Walsingham Gdns WEND SO18 ... 107 M5
Waltham Cl BPWT SO32 ... 86 F6
FHAM/PORC PO16 ... 162 A6
Waltham Crs ROWN SO16 ... 106 A4
Waltham Rd LTDN BH7 ... 237 G1
Waltham St SSEA PO5 ... 12 F3 5
Walton Cl GPORT PO12 ... 10 D4
WVILLE PO7 ... 164 C3
Walton Ct FHAM PO15 ... 160 B4
Walton Pl FUFL SO22 ... 26 C3
Walton Rd CHAM PO6 ... 188 A2
GPORT PO12 ... 10 D4
ITCH SO19 ... 133 H4 5
NBNE BH10 ... 220 A6
PLE BH15 ... 233 M2
Waltons Av FAWY SO45 ... 180 B4
Wandesford Pl GPORT PO12 ... 185 L7
Wangfield La BPWT SO32 ... 110 B7
Wansbeck Cl CHFD SO53 ... 81 G3 2
Wanstead Cl RGWD BH24 ... 146 F8
Warbler Cl HORN PO8 ... 140 E1
ROWN SO16 ... 106 A2
UPTN BH16 ... 216 F8
Warblington Av HAV PO9 ... 9 K5
Warblington Cl CHFD SO53 ... 81 G5 3
Warblington Rd EMRTH PO10 ... 190 C1
Warblington St PSEA PO1 ... 12 D4
Warborne La LYMN SO41 ... 228 E1
Warbrook Ct HAV PO9 ... 165 M3 13
Warburton Cl ITCH SO19 ... 133 J4 1
Warburton Rd CFDH BH17 ... 218 C8 3
ITCH SO19 ... 133 H3
Ward Crs EMRTH PO10 ... 166 E5
Warden Cl HEND SO30 ... 108 C7 6
Wardens Cl HISD PO11 ... 213 K3
Wardle Rd ELGH SO50 ... 82 C1
Ward Rd ENEY PO4 ... 211 L6
Wardroom Rd NEND PO2 ... 186 F7
Wareham Rd WIMB BH21 ... 216 F5
Warfield Av WVILLE PO7 ... 164 C1
Warfield Crs WVILLE PO7 ... 164 C1
Warland Wy WIMB BH21 ... 217 J1
Warlock Cl ITCH SO19 ... 133 H5 5
Warmwell Cl CFDH BH17 ... 218 D6
Warnes La RGWD BH24 ... 172 D6
Warnford Cl GPORT PO12 ... 10 B4
Warnford Crs HAV PO9 ... 165 H3
Warnford Rd LTDN BH7 ... 237 G1
Warren Av CHCH/BSGR BH23 ... 238 E3
CHFD SO53 ... 81 K3
ENEY PO4 ... 211 M3
HSEA PO3 ... 187 L4
ROWN SO16 ... 105 M6
Warren Cl CHFD SO53 ... 81 K3
HISD PO11 ... 213 G4
RGWD BH24 ... 170 B3
ROWN SO16 ... 105 M6
Warren Crs ROWN SO16 ... 105 M6
Warren Dr RGWD BH24 ... 170 B2
Warren Edge Cl SBNE BH6 ... 237 L5 3
Warren Edge Rd SBNE BH6 ... 237 L5
Warren La BROC SO42 ... 205 H8
PSF GU32 ... 35 H3
RGWD BH24 ... 170 B3
RWIN SO21 ... 28 D8
Warren Pk LYMN SO41 ... 241 M2
Warren Pl TOTT SO40 ... 104 B6
Warren Rd LISS GU33 ... 36 F1
PSTN BH14 ... 234 C4 1
WBNE BH4 ... 235 G6
WINC SO23 ... 3 M6
Warren Side EPSF GU31 ... 93 G5
Warrens La RSAL SP5 ... 44 D4
The Warren FAWY SO45 ... 179 M3
Warrior Cl CHFD SO53 ... 81 G4
Warrys Cl FAWY SO45 ... 155 L8
Warsash Cl HAV PO9 ... 165 J2 6
Warsash Gv
LSOL/BMARY PO13 ... 185 G6 7
Warsash Rd FHAM/STUB PO14 ... 159 J7
HLER SO31 ... 158 B7
Warspite Cl NEND PO2 ... 187 H4
Warton Cl BROC SO42 ... 204 A2
Warwick Av NMIL/BTOS BH25 ... 225 M5
Warwick Cl CHFD SO53 ... 80 F4 4
LSOL/BMARY PO13 ... 208 E4
WINC SO23 ... 3 G3
Warwick Crs SSEA PO5 ... 13 H4
Warwick Rd LTDN BH7 ... 236 F3
PSTN BH14 ... 234 B5 1
TOTT SO40 ... 104 E8 1
WSHM SO15 ... 106 C6
Wasdale Cl HORN PO8 ... 116 B6
Washbrook Rd CHAM PO6 ... 163 H8
Washington Av BMTH BH1 ... 236 C2
Washington Rd EMRTH PO10 ... 166 D7
NEND PO2 ... 187 H8
Watcombe Rd SBNE BH6 ... 237 J3
Waterbeech Dr HEND SO30 ... 109 H8 6
Waterberry Dr WVILLE PO7 ... 140 A7
Waterditch Rd
CHCH/BSGR BH23 ... 223 K5
Waterford Cl LYMN SO41 ... 228 D5
Waterford Cl PSTN BH14 ... 233 M6 2
Waterford Gdns
CHCH/BSGR BH23 ... 239 M1
Waterford La LYMN SO41 ... 228 D5
Waterford Pl
CHCH/BSGR BH23 ... 239 M1
Waterford Rd
CHCH/BSGR BH23 ... 224 F8
NMIL/BTOS BH25 ... 226 A5
Waterhouse La WSHM SO15 ... 130 F2 3
Waterhouse Wy WSHM SO15 ... 130 F1
Water La FAWY SO45 ... 155 J6
SBNE BH6 ... 237 J1
TOTT SO40 ... 104 C8
WINC SO23 ... 3 J7
Waterlock Gdns ENEY PO4 ... 212 B4
Waterloo Cl HORN PO8 ... 140 B5
Waterloo Rd CFDH BH17 ... 218 A8
GPORT PO12 ... 11 H9
HAV PO9 ... 8 F3
LYMN SO41 ... 228 D4
MOOR/WNTN BH9 ... 235 L1
WIMB BH21 ... 216 F2
WSHM SO15 ... 131 G2
Waterloo St SSEA PO5 ... 13 H3
Waterloo Ter WSHM SO15 ... 131 K2
Waterloo Wy RGWD BH24 ... 170 E2 6
Watermain Rd RGWD BH24 ... 195 L3
Watermans La FAWY SO45 ... 155 J7
Watermead Rd CHAM PO6 ... 188 C1 1
Watermill Rd
CHCH/BSGR BH23 ... 222 E8
Water's Edge HEND SO30 ... 133 M2
Waters Edge Gdns
EMRTH PO10 ... 166 D8
Watersedge Rd CHAM PO6 ... 162 E8 2
Waters Gn BROC SO42 ... 175 L6 2
Waters Green Ct BROC SO42 ... 175 L6 3
Watership Dr RGWD BH24 ... 171 H2
Waterside CHCH/BSGR BH23 ... 238 E4
FAWY SO45 ... 155 K3
Waterside Cl RGWD BH24 ... 146 F7
Waterside Gdns
FHAM/PORC PO16 ... 161 H7 1
Waterside La
FHAM/PORC PO16 ... 186 C2
Waterside Rd ROMY SO51 ... 50 F7 4
Watersmeet
FHAM/PORC PO16 ... 184 F2
The Waters WHAM PO17 ... 160 C3
Waterston Cl CFDH BH17 ... 218 B7 2
Water Tower Rd BDST BH18 ... 218 A4
Waterworks Rd CHAM PO6 ... 164 B8
PSF GU32 ... 63 M2
RWIN SO21 ... 54 B4
Watery La CHCH/BSGR BH23 ... 223 L7
Watkin Rd BOSC BH5 ... 236 E4
HEND SO30 ... 109 K6 1
Watley Cl ROWN SO16 ... 105 J3
Watley La RWIN SO21 ... 55 G2
Watson Wk TOTT SO40 ... 129 G1 3
Watton Cl CHAR BH8 ... 221 L6
Watton La BPWT SO32 ... 87 J6
Watton Rd FAWY SO45 ... 180 A5
Watts Cl ROWN SO16 ... 105 K6
Watts Rd HEND SO30 ... 134 A1
PSEA PO1 ... 211 H1
Wavell Av CFDH BH17 ... 217 L7
Wavell Rd BWD BH11 ... 219 M4
LSOL/BMARY PO13 ... 185 H5
WEND SO18 ... 132 E1
Wavell Wy FUFL SO22 ... 26 B3
Wavendon Av
NMIL/BTOS BH25 ... 225 J8
Waveney Cl
LSOL/BMARY PO13 ... 208 D2 5
Waveney Gn ROWN SO16 ... 105 K7
Waverley Av HLER SO31 ... 157 G2
Waverley Cl FBDG SP6 ... 97 L5
ROMY SO51 ... 51 G7 6
Waverley Ct HLER SO31 ... 157 G3 2
Waverley Crs PLE BH15 ... 233 J3
Waverley Gv ENEY PO4 ... 13 L8
Waverley Rd CHAM PO6 ... 164 A8
FBDG SP6 ... 97 L5
NMIL/BTOS BH25 ... 225 M6
SSEA PO5 ... 13 L7
WSHM SO15 ... 4 A1
Wayfarer Cl ENEY PO4 ... 212 A3 5
HLER SO31 ... 158 D7
Wayfarers LSOL/BMARY PO13 ... 209 H1
Wayfarer's Wk BPWT SO32 ... 58 B7
HAV PO9 ... 165 G6
HORN PO8 ... 89 K6
NARL SO24 ... 58 A3
WVILLE PO7 ... 163 M6
Waylands Pl HEND SO30 ... 133 L4
Wayman Rd WIMB BH21 ... 217 J2 2
Wayne Rd BKME/WDN BH12 ... 234 A2
Waynflete Cl BPWT SO32 ... 85 H8
Waynflete Pl FUFL SO22 ... 26 C2 2
Wayside HLER SO31 ... 134 B8
Wayside Cl LYMN SO41 ... 242 C3
Wayside Rd RGWD BH24 ... 169 J7
SBNE BH6 ... 237 K4
Wayte St CHAM PO6 ... 187 K1
Waytown Cl CFDH BH17 ... 218 B7
Weald Cl HLER SO31 ... 158 E4
Weardale Rd CHFD SO53 ... 81 J4
Weavers Cl FERN BH22 ... 168 C7 2
Weavers Gn HAV PO9 ... 9 L1
Weavers Pl CHFD SO53 ... 53 G8
Weavills Rd ELGH SO50 ... 82 F6
Webb Cl HISD PO11 ... 213 L6
Webb La HISD PO11 ... 213 L6
Webb Rd FHAM/PORC PO16 ... 186 B2
Webbs Cl RGWD BH24 ... 169 H2
Webbs Gn BPWT SO32 ... 113 G5
Webburn Gdns WEND SO18 ... 107 M5 3
Webster Rd FUFL SO22 ... 16 A7
Webster Rd
MOOR/WNTN BH9 ... 220 E5 4
Wedgewood Cl FAWY SO45 ... 180 A4
FHAM/STUB PO14 ... 184 A6 1
Wedgewood Gdns
CHCH/BSGR BH23 ... 198 A7 2
Wedgewood Wy WVILLE PO7 ... 140 C6
Wedgwood Dr PSTN BH14 ... 233 M6
Wedmore Cl FUFL SO22 ... 25 M5
Weeke Cl RSAL SP5 ... 72 C1 1
Weeke Manor Cl FUFL SO22 ... 2 A3
Welbeck Av PTSW SO17 ... 107 G6
Welch Rd ENEY PO4 ... 13 M8
GPORT PO12 ... 209 L1
Welch Wy ROWN SO16 ... 105 K3
Welchwood Cl HORN PO8 ... 140 D2
Weldon Av BWD BH11 ... 219 J3
Welland Gdns WEND SO18 ... 108 A6
Welland Gn ROWN SO16 ... 105 K8
Welland Rd WIMB BH21 ... 192 B4
Wellands Rd LYND SO43 ... 151 K3 3
Wellbrooke Gdns CHFD SO53 ... 81 G1
Well Cl NMIL/BTOS BH25 ... 225 K7
Well Copse Cl HORN PO8 ... 116 B7
Wellers Cl TOTT SO40 ... 128 F1
Wellesley Av
CHCH/BSGR BH23 ... 239 G1
Wellesley Cl WVILLE PO7 ... 164 C1
Welles Rd CHFD SO53 ... 81 J2
Well House Cl FBDG SP6 ... 71 G5
Well House La FUFL SO22 ... 16 D3
Wellington Av
CHCH/BSGR BH23 ... 239 H1
WEND SO18 ... 132 F1
Wellington Cl FAWY SO45 ... 155 H7
HORN PO8 ... 141 H2
Wellington Gv
FHAM/PORC PO16 ... 186 A1
Wellington Pk HEND SO30 ... 108 F7
Wellington Rd CHAR BH8 ... 15 G1
PSTN BH14 ... 234 B5
WEND SO18 ... 107 J6
Wellington St SSEA PO5 ... 13 G3
Wellington Wy WVILLE PO7 ... 164 C1 2
Well La BPWT SO32 ... 112 A1
FBDG SP6 ... 98 D6
HLER SO31 ... 157 L6
PLE BH15 ... 233 H4
Well Meadow HAV PO9 ... 165 J2
Wellowbrook Cl CHFD SO53 ... 80 F2 2
Wellow Cl HAV PO9 ... 8 B1
WEND SO18 ... 133 G1
Wellow Dro ROMY SO51 ... 76 D1
Wellow Gdns
FHAM/STUB PO14 ... 159 G6
Wellow Wood Rd ROMY SO51 ... 48 C8
Wellsfield SELS PO20 ... 215 L7
Wellsmoor FHAM/STUB PO14 ... 159 G5
Wells Pl ELGH SO50 ... 81 M6
Wellswood Gdns HAV PO9 ... 142 A5
Wellsworth La HAV PO9 ... 142 A5
Wembley Gv CHAM PO6 ... 187 L2 1
Wendover Cl
NMIL/BTOS BH25 ... 225 K7 4
Wendover Rd HAV PO9 ... 8 C3
Wensley Gdns EMRTH PO10 ... 166 D5
Wentwood Gdns
NMIL/BTOS BH25 ... 226 B6
Wentworth Av BOSC BH5 ... 236 F4
Wentworth Cl BOSC BH5 ... 236 F5
Wentworth Dr BDST BH18 ... 217 L3
CHCH/BSGR BH23 ... 237 L2 2
HORN PO8 ... 140 F1
Wentworth Gdns
FAWY SO45 ... 180 B6 1
ITCH SO19 ... 132 F7 1
Wentworth Gra FUFL SO22 ... 26 D2
Wentworth Gv FAWY SO45 ... 180 B5
Wescott Wy BWD BH11 ... 219 J4 2
Wesermarsch Rd HORN PO8 ... 140 E4
Wesley Cl CHAR BH8 ... 15 M1
ITCH SO19 ... 133 H4
Wesley Gv HSEA PO3 ... 187 K5
Wesley Rd PSTN BH14 ... 234 B3
WIMB BH21 ... 192 B3
WINC SO23 ... 17 H1
Wessex Av NMIL/BTOS BH25 ... 225 L6
Wessex Cl CHCH/BSGR BH23 ... 239 H1
FAWY SO45 ... 180 D7
Wessex Dr FUFL SO22 ... 2 C2
Wessex Est RGWD BH24 ... 146 F8
Wessex Gdns
FHAM/PORC PO16 ... 185 M1
ROMY SO51 ... 79 G1
Wessex La WEND SO18 ... 107 J4
Wessex Rd HORN PO8 ... 116 B5
PSTN BH14 ... 233 M5
RGWD BH24 ... 146 F8
Wessex Wy CHAR BH8 ... 221 L7
RWIN SO21 ... 54 F8
WBNE BH4 ... 235 G4
WCLF BH2 ... 14 C4
West Ashling Rd RCCH PO18 ... 167 M5
West Av WIMB BH21 ... 144 B8
West Bargate SHAM SO14 ... 4 F4 1
West Battery Rd NEND PO2 ... 186 F7
Westbeams Rd LYMN SO41 ... 200 F6
Westborn Rd
FHAM/PORC PO16 ... 7 K5
Westbourne Av EMRTH PO10 ... 166 E6
FAWY SO45 ... 180 A4
Westbourne Cl EMRTH PO10 ... 166 E6 1
WBNE BH4 ... 235 H5
Westbourne Crs PTSW SO17 ... 106 E7
Westbourne Park Rd
WBNE BH4 ... 235 G6
Westbourne Rd EMRTH PO10 ... 166 E5
NEND PO2 ... 187 K8
Westbroke Gdns ROMY SO51 ... 50 E7 3
Westbrook Cl HLER SO31 ... 158 E3
Westbrooke Cl HORN PO8 ... 140 E2
Westbrook Gv WVILLE PO7 ... 164 B3
Westbrook Rd
FHAM/PORC PO16 ... 186 B2
Westbrook Wy WEND SO18 ... 107 K4 3
Westbury Cl CHAM PO6 ... 162 F7 6
CHCH/BSGR BH23 ... 223 L1
CHCH/BSGR BH23 ... 224 B7
NMIL/BTOS BH25 ... 225 L8
Westbury Ct HEND SO30 ... 134 A3
Westbury Rd RGWD BH24 ... 170 F1
WSHM SO15 ... 130 D1
West Butts St PLE BH15 ... 233 G6 3
Westby Rd BOSC BH5 ... 236 D4
Westcliff Cl LSOL/BMARY PO13 ... 208 C1
West Cliff Gdns WCLF BH2 ... 14 C8
West Cliff Rd WBNE BH4 ... 235 H6
WCLF BH2 ... 14 C7
West Cl LYMN SO41 ... 227 M6
VWD BH31 ... 144 B2
West Common FAWY SO45 ... 206 B1
Westcot Rd FAWY SO45 ... 179 M5 3
Westcroft Pk BDST BH18 ... 218 A4
Westcroft Rd GPORT PO12 ... 10 A1
Westdown Rd BWD BH11 ... 219 L3
West Downs Cl
FHAM/PORC PO16 ... 160 E4
West Dr ELGH SO50 ... 82 C4
West End Cl FUFL SO22 ... 2 D7
Westend Rd ITCH SO19 ... 132 E1
WEND SO18 ... 108 B8
West End Rd HEND SO30 ... 133 K4
WEND SO18 ... 107 M8
West End Ter FUFL SO22 ... 2 D7
Westerham Cl CHAM PO6 ... 163 J8
Westerham Rd CCLF BH13 ... 235 G5
Westering ROMY SO51 ... 51 H7 2
ROMY SO51 ... 51 H8 3
Westerley Cl HLER SO31 ... 158 C7 5
Western Av CCLF BH13 ... 234 D6
EMRTH PO10 ... 166 B8
NBNE BH10 ... 220 B4
NMIL/BTOS BH25 ... 225 H8
Western Cl NBNE BH10 ... 220 B3
Western District Cut
WSHM SO15 ... 131 H1 1
Western Esp SHAM SO14 ... 4 D2
Western Pde EMRTH PO10 ... 190 C1
SSEA PO5 ... 12 F6
Western Rd CCLF BH13 ... 234 E8
CHAM PO6 ... 187 J2
CHFD SO53 ... 53 K7

FHAM/PORC PO16 ...... 7 J6
FUFL SO22 ...... 2 D6
HAV PO9 ...... 8 C3
HEND SO30 ...... 108 C7
LISS GU33 ...... 36 E4
LYMN SO41 ...... 228 B4
Western Wy FHAM/PORC PO16 ...... 7 H6
GPORT PO12 ...... 209 J3
Westfield Av FHAM/STUB PO14 ...... 6 E7
HISD PO11 ...... 213 J5
Westfield Cl ELGH SO50 ...... 109 H1
HLER SO31 ...... 157 J6
Westfield Common
HLER SO31 ...... 157 H6 [1]
Westfield Crs CHFD SO53 ...... 81 H5
Westfield Dr BPWT SO32 ...... 112 C6
Westfield Dro NARL SO24 ...... 29 M8
Westfield Gdns
CHCH/BSGR BH23 ...... 223 M7
Westfield Rd CHFD SO53 ...... 81 H5
ENEY PO4 ...... 211 L5
FUFL SO22 ...... 16 A3
GPORT PO12 ...... 10 B2
LYMN SO41 ...... 228 D6
SBNE BH6 ...... 237 K4
TOTT SO40 ...... 104 E1
WSHM SO15 ...... 130 E1
Westgate FHAM/STUB PO14 ...... 184 A7
Westgate Pk WBNE BH4 ...... 235 G5
Westgate St SHAM SO14 ...... 4 F6
Westgrove FBDG SP6 ...... 97 K7 [3]
Westham Cl CFDH BH17 ...... 218 C5
West Haye Rd HISD PO11 ...... 214 B7
West Hayes LYMN SO41 ...... 228 D5
Westheath Rd BDST BH18 ...... 217 M4
West Hill Dr FAWY SO45 ...... 155 K3
FUFL SO22 ...... 2 C7
West Hill Pk FUFL SO22 ...... 2 B7
West Hill Pl WCLF BH2 ...... 14 C5
West Hill Rd WCLF BH2 ...... 14 C7
West Hoe La BPWT SO32 ...... 85 L1
West Horton La ELGH SO50 ...... 82 E7
West Howe Cl BWD BH11 ...... 219 L4 [2]
Westland Dr WVILLE PO7 ...... 164 C4
Westland Gdns GPORT PO12 ...... 10 C6
Westlands Ct
CHCH/BSGR BH23 ...... 197 L8
Westlands Gv
FHAM/PORC PO16 ...... 186 A1
West La HISD PO11 ...... 213 J3
LYMN SO41 ...... 227 J7
NBAD SO52 ...... 79 K3
Westley Cl FUFL SO22 ...... 2 A4
Westley Gv FHAM/STUB PO14 ...... 6 E7
Westman Rd FUFL SO22 ...... 2 A2
West Marlands Rd SHAM SO14 ...... 4 F2
Westmead Cl HISD PO11 ...... 213 H5
West Meade LIPH GU30 ...... 38 E6
Westminster Rd LYMN SO41 ...... 242 H4
Westminster Gdns
FHAM/STUB PO14 ...... 159 C5 [6]
Westminster Ga FUFL SO22 ...... 26 A3
Westminster Rd CCLF BH13 ...... 235 G7
Westminster Rd East
CCLF BH13 ...... 235 G7
West Moors Rd FERN BH22 ...... 194 B1
WIMB BH21 ...... 168 C1
Westmorland Wy CHFD SO53 ...... 81 K3
Weston Av ENEY PO4 ...... 211 M4
Weston Cl ITCH SO19 ...... 132 C7
Weston Crs WEND SO18 ...... 133 C1
Weston Dr BMTH BH1 ...... 15 K5
Weston Grove Rd ITCH SO19 ...... 132 B6
Weston La ITCH SO19 ...... 132 C7
PSF GU32 ...... 63 G8
ROWN SO16 ...... 104 F4
Weston Rd ELGH SO50 ...... 81 M5
EPSF GU31 ...... 63 M5
WIMB BH21 ...... 192 D1 [6]
West Overcliff Dr WBNE BH4 ...... 235 H6
Westover La RGWD BH24 ...... 170 B2
Westover Rd BMTH BH1 ...... 14 F4
HSEA PO3 ...... 187 M4
LYMN SO41 ...... 242 C4
ROWN SO16 ...... 105 G4
West Park Dr FBDG SP6 ...... 96 C3
West Park Rd WSHM SO15 ...... 4 E2
West Quay Rd PLE BH15 ...... 233 G6
WSHM SO15 ...... 4 D3
Westridge PTSW SO17 ...... 107 G7
West Rd BOSC BH5 ...... 236 F3 [1]
CHCH/BSGR BH23 ...... 197 L8
EMRTH PO10 ...... 166 C4
FAWY SO45 ...... 155 H7
HEND SO30 ...... 133 K2
ITCH SO19 ...... 132 C6
LYMN SO41 ...... 241 M3
SHAM SO14 ...... 5 J1
WHAM PO17 ...... 162 C2
Westrow Gdns WSHM SO15 ...... 131 J1
Westrow Rd WSHM SO15 ...... 131 J1
West Strd SELS PO20 ...... 215 J8
West St BPWT SO32 ...... 113 G3
EMRTH PO10 ...... 166 D8
FAWY SO45 ...... 155 K3
FBDG SP6 ...... 97 K7
FHAM/PORC PO16 ...... 7 L6
FHAM/PORC PO16 ...... 162 B8
West View Rd
CHCH/BSGR BH23 ...... 238 C4
PLE BH15 ...... 233 H4
Westward Rd HEND SO30 ...... 109 H4
West Wy BDST BH18 ...... 217 K5
LYMN SO41 ...... 228 A6
MOOR/WNTN BH9 ...... 220 D4
Westway FHAM PO15 ...... 159 J5
West Way Cl
MOOR/WNTN BH9 ...... 220 F7 [2]
Westway Vw ROWN SO16 ...... 105 G4
Westways CHAM PO6 ...... 164 D8
Westways
FHAM/STUB PO14 ...... 184 B6

Westways Cl ROWN SO16 ...... 105 J3 [1]
Westwood Av FERN BH22 ...... 194 A2
Westwood Cl EMRTH PO10 ...... 166 E5
Westwood Gdns CHFD SO53 ...... 53 K8
Westwood Rd HLER SO31 ...... 156 F1
LYND SO43 ...... 151 K2
NEND PO2 ...... 187 J4
PTSW SO17 ...... 106 E8
Westwood Vw NARL SO24 ...... 30 D7
Wetherby Cl CFDH BH17 ...... 217 L6
Wetherby Gdns TOTT SO40 ...... 104 B8
Wetherdown EPSF GU31 ...... 63 N5
Weyhill Cl FHAM/PORC PO16 ...... 162 A7
HAV PO9 ...... 165 H3 [3]
Weyman's Av NBNE BH10 ...... 220 A2
Weymans Dr NBNE BH10 ...... 220 A2
Weymouth Av GPORT PO12 ...... 185 K8
Weymouth Rd PSTN BH14 ...... 234 B3
Whaddon Cha
FHAM/STUB PO14 ...... 183 M6
Whaddon Cl HAV PO9 ...... 165 G2
Whaddon La RWIN SO21 ...... 55 M7
Whale Island Wy NEND PO2 ...... 187 G7
Whalesmead Cl ELGH SO50 ...... 82 E7
Whalesmead Rd ELGH SO50 ...... 82 E7
Whaley Rd NEND PO2 ...... 186 F7
Wharf Cl BKME/WDN BH12 ...... 234 D2
Wharfdale Rd
BKME/WDN BH12 ...... 234 C2
WBNE BH4 ...... 235 H4
Wharf Hl WINC SO23 ...... 27 G2
Wharf Rd NEND PO2 ...... 187 G8
Wharncliffe Gdns
CHCH/BSGR BH23 ...... 239 M1
Wharncliffe Rd BMTH BH1 ...... 236 C4
CHCH/BSGR BH23 ...... 239 M1
ITCH SO19 ...... 132 B5
Whartons La TOTT SO40 ...... 129 C4
Whatleigh Cl PLE BH15 ...... 233 H7
Wheat Cl NBAD SO52 ...... 80 E2
Wheatcroft Dr WEND SO18 ...... 108 A7 [2]
Wheatcroft Rd
LSOL/BMARY PO13 ...... 208 D2
Wheatear Dr EPSF GU31 ...... 64 B5 [3]
Wheatears Dr ROMY SO51 ...... 76 D5
Wheatland Cl FUFL SO22 ...... 26 C3
Wheatlands FHAM/STUB PO14 ...... 159 G4
Wheatlands Av HISD PO11 ...... 214 C7
Wheatlands Crs HISD PO11 ...... 214 C7 [3]
Wheaton Rd LTDN BH7 ...... 236 F3
Wheatsheaf Ct HEND SO30 ...... 133 M2 [2]
Wheatsheaf Dr HORN PO8 ...... 140 B5
Wheatstone Rd ENEY PO4 ...... 13 M6
Wheeler Cl GPORT PO12 ...... 209 M2
Wheelers La BWD BH11 ...... 219 G3
Wheelers Wk FAWY SO45 ...... 180 C3
Wherwell Ct HAV PO9 ...... 165 M3 [10]
Whichers Cl HAV PO9 ...... 141 M8
Whichers Gate Rd HAV PO9 ...... 141 M8
Whimbrel Cl ENEY PO4 ...... 212 A3
Whinchat Cl FHAM PO15 ...... 160 A4
ROWN SO16 ...... 106 A2
Whincroft Cl FERN BH22 ...... 194 C1
Whincroft Dr FERN BH22 ...... 194 C2
Whinfield Rd FAWY SO45 ...... 155 J7
Whinwhistle Rd ROMY SO51 ...... 77 G6
Whippingham Cl CHAM PO6 ...... 163 H8
Whistler Cl ITCH SO19 ...... 133 G5
Whistlers Cl CHCH/BSGR BH23 ...... 197 M7
Whitaker Crs LYMN SO41 ...... 228 A5
Whitby Av BDST BH18 ...... 217 L6
Whitby Cl CHCH/BSGR BH23 ...... 222 B4 [2]
Whitby Crs BDST BH18 ...... 217 L6
Whitby Rd LYMN SO41 ...... 242 A4
Whitchurch Cl TOTT SO40 ...... 129 J1 [2]
Whitcombe Cl TOTT SO40 ...... 129 J1 [2]
Whitcombe Gdns HSEA PO3 ...... 211 K2
White Barn Crs LYMN SO41 ...... 226 E5
Whitebeam Cl
FHAM/STUB PO14 ...... 6 C7
HORN PO8 ...... 141 G3 [4]
RWIN SO21 ...... 54 F8
White Beam Ri HORN PO8 ...... 116 B3
Whitebeam Rd NEND SO30 ...... 134 B2
Whitebeam Wy NBAD SO52 ...... 79 M3
VWD BH31 ...... 144 F3
Whitechimney Rw
EMRTH PO10 ...... 166 F5
Whitecliff Crs PSTN BH14 ...... 233 M6
Whitecliff Av HSEA PO3 ...... 211 L1
Whitecliff Rd PSTN BH14 ...... 233 L6
White Cliff Rd PSTN BH14 ...... 233 M6
White Cloud Pk ENEY PO4 ...... 211 K5 [4]
Whitecross Cl CFDH BH17 ...... 218 C5
Whitecross Gdns NEND PO2 ...... 187 K5
Whitedell La WHAM PO17 ...... 161 H4
White Dirt La HORN PO8 ...... 116 A6
White Farm Cl NBNE SO40 ...... 220 B8
Whitefield Rd FAWY SO45 ...... 180 A5
NMIL/BTOS BH25 ...... 225 L5
PSTN BH14 ...... 233 M6
White Gates BPWT SO32 ...... 110 A3
Whitehall CHCH/BSGR BH23 ...... 238 A3
Whitehart Rds RGWD BH24 ...... 147 G8 [6]
Whitehaven
FHAM/PORC PO16 ...... 185 M1
HORN PO8 ...... 141 H2
White Heather Ct
FAWY SO45 ...... 155 L3
Whitehorn Dr RSAL SP5 ...... 75 J8
White Horse La WVILLE PO7 ...... 139 L2
Whitehouse Gdns PSF GU32 ...... 63 K3
White House Gdns
WSHM SO15 ...... 130 E2
Whitehouse Rd WIMB BH21 ...... 192 B6

White Knights
NMIL/BTOS BH25 ...... 240 E1
White Ladies Cl HAV PO9 ...... 9 G5
Whitelands CHCH/BSGR BH23 ...... 198 B5
White La RWIN SO21 ...... 26 F8
Whitelaw Rd WSHM SO15 ...... 130 F1
Whiteleaf La WVILLE PO7 ...... 114 B1
Whitelegg Wy NBNE BH10 ...... 220 C3
Whiteley La FHAM PO15 ...... 159 K4
HLER SO31 ...... 135 G7
Whiteley Wy FHAM PO15 ...... 159 H2
Whitemoor La TOTT SO40 ...... 103 K4
Whitemoor Rd BROC SO42 ...... 175 H6
Whitenap Cl ROMY SO51 ...... 79 G2
Whitenap La ROMY SO51 ...... 79 H2
White Rd ELGH SO50 ...... 82 C4
Whites Hl RWIN SO21 ...... 55 L4
Whiteshoot RSAL SP5 ...... 73 L4
Whiteshoot Hl RSAL SP5 ...... 73 K4
Whiteshute La WINC SO23 ...... 26 D4
Whites La FAWY SO45 ...... 180 F5 [10]
Whitestone Cl ROWN SO16 ...... 105 L8 [3]
White Swan Rd PSEA PO1 ...... 12 F2
Whitethorn Rd HISD PO11 ...... 213 M5 [1]
Whitewater Ri FAWY SO45 ...... 155 K6
Whiteways WIMB BH21 ...... 192 C2
The White Wy BPWT SO32 ...... 58 E6
Whitfield Pk RGWD BH24 ...... 169 M3
Whithedwood Av WSHM SO15 ...... 106 C8
Withers La BROC SO42 ...... 204 A2
Whitley Cl EMRTH PO10 ...... 166 F3
Whitley Rd HORN PO8 ...... 140 D2
Whitley Wy NMIL/BTOS BH25 ...... 225 M3
Whitsbury Cl CHAR BH8 ...... 221 H6 [8]
Whitsbury Rd FBDG SP6 ...... 97 L5
HAV PO9 ...... 165 L3
Whitstable Rd CHAM PO6 ...... 163 J8
Whittington Cl FAWY SO45 ...... 155 J8
Whittington St EMRTH PO10 ...... 166 D8
Whittle Av FHAM PO15 ...... 159 G3
Whittle Rd WIMB BH21 ...... 193 K1
Whittles Wy PLE BH15 ...... 233 G6
Whitwell HLER SO31 ...... 157 G1 [7]
Whitwell Rd ENEY PO4 ...... 13 L1
Whitworth Cl GPORT PO12 ...... 10 D3
Whitworth Crs WEND SO18 ...... 107 J8
Whitworth Rd GPORT PO12 ...... 10 D3
NEND PO2 ...... 187 K8
WEND SO18 ...... 107 J8
Whyte Cl FAWY SO45 ...... 179 M5
Whyteways ELGH SO50 ...... 81 L4
Wick Cl NMIL/BTOS BH25 ...... 225 J6
Wick Dr NMIL/BTOS BH25 ...... 225 J6
Wicket Rd NBNE BH10 ...... 220 A4
The Wicket FAWY SO45 ...... 155 K6
Wickfield Av
CHCH/BSGR BH23 ...... 238 A2
Wickfield Cl
CHCH/BSGR BH23 ...... 238 A2 [8]
Wickham Dr WIMB BH21 ...... 217 H4
Wickham Rd BPWT SO32 ...... 112 F4
FHAM/PORC PO16 ...... 7 J1
WHAM PO17 ...... 160 F4
Wickham St PSEA PO1 ...... 12 C1
Wick La CHCH/BSGR BH23 ...... 238 A3
RSAL SP5 ...... 43 M8
SBNE BH6 ...... 237 M3
Wicklea Rd SBNE BH6 ...... 238 A4
Wicklow Dr CHFD SO53 ...... 80 F3
Wickmeads Rd SBNE BH6 ...... 237 M3 [2]
Wickor Cl EMRTH PO10 ...... 166 E6
Wickor Wy EMRTH PO10 ...... 166 D5
Wicor Mill La
FHAM/PORC PO16 ...... 185 M2
Wicor Pth FHAM/PORC PO16 ...... 186 C2
Widbury Rd LYMN SO41 ...... 228 A6
Widden Cl LYMN SO41 ...... 200 F6
Widdicombe Av PSTN BH14 ...... 234 D6
Widecombe Dr FAWY SO45 ...... 155 J4
Wide La ELGH SO50 ...... 107 L1
WEND SO18 ...... 107 K3
Wide Lane Cl BROC SO42 ...... 175 K7 [2]
Widgeon Cl GPORT PO12 ...... 209 M1
ROWN SO16 ...... 106 A2
Widget Cl BWD BH11 ...... 219 M6
Widlers La BPWT SO32 ...... 84 D2
Widley Ct FHAM/STUB PO14 ...... 184 D2
Widley Court Dr CHAM PO6 ...... 187 L1
Widley Gdns WVILLE PO7 ...... 164 B5
Widley Rd CHAM PO6 ...... 163 K6
NEND PO2 ...... 187 G6
Widley Wk CHAM PO6 ...... 163 K6
Widworthy Dr BDST BH18 ...... 217 K3
Wield Cl HAV PO9 ...... 165 G4
Wigan Crs HAV PO9 ...... 164 F6
Wight Wk FERN BH22 ...... 194 C6
Wilberforce Cl FUFL SO22 ...... 26 B3 [3]
Wilberforce Rd GPORT PO12 ...... 11 G9
SSEA PO5 ...... 13 G5 [3]
Wild Arum Wy NBAD SO52 ...... 80 C3
Wildburn Cl TOTT SO40 ...... 104 B6
Wild Cherry Wy NBAD SO52 ...... 80 F2 [3]
Wilde Cl TOTT SO40 ...... 129 H1 [1]
Wildern Cl HLER SO31 ...... 158 D5 [2]
Wildern La HEND SO30 ...... 109 G8
Wilderton Rd CCLF BH13 ...... 234 E5
Wilderton Rd West
CCLF BH13 ...... 234 E4
Wildfell Cl CHCH/BSGR BH23 ...... 222 E7
Wildown Gdns SBNE BH6 ...... 237 L5
Wildown Rd SBNE BH6 ...... 237 M5
Wild Ridings FHAM/STUB PO14 ...... 159 M4
Wild Rose Crs HLER SO31 ...... 158 C6
Wilfred Rd BOSC BH5 ...... 236 E4
Wilkins Cl HORN PO8 ...... 116 A4
Wilkinson Dr CHAR BH8 ...... 221 K4
Wilks Cl ROWN SO16 ...... 105 H3
Willersley Cl CHAM PO6 ...... 163 G7
William Cl CHCH/BSGR BH23 ...... 224 E6
FHAM/STUB PO14 ...... 184 B7
William Macleod Wy
ROWN SO16 ...... 105 M3
William Price Gdns
FHAM/PORC PO16 ...... 7 J3
William Rd LTDN BH7 ...... 236 E1
LYMN SO41 ...... 228 C3 [8]

Williams Cl FAWY SO45 ...... 180 B5
LSOL/BMARY PO13 ...... 209 H1
Williams Rd HSEA PO3 ...... 187 M5
William St SHAM SO14 ...... 5 M1
Willis Av NBAD SO52 ...... 80 A4
Willis Rd GPORT PO12 ...... 11 K3
PSEA PO1 ...... 13 G1
ROWN SO16 ...... 105 J3
Willis Wy CFDH BH17 ...... 233 G2
Willis Waye WINC SO23 ...... 17 H3
Willow Av FBDG SP6 ...... 97 K6
Willow Cl HAV PO9 ...... 9 G5
HEND SO30 ...... 108 D6 [1]
RGWD BH24 ...... 169 H4
UPTN BH16 ...... 232 C3
Willow Ct ROWN SO16 ...... 105 M5
Willowdale Cl PSF GU32 ...... 62 E4
Willowdene Cl HAV PO9 ...... 164 F4
NMIL/BTOS BH25 ...... 226 A5
Willow Dr CHCH/BSGR BH23 ...... 237 M3
RGWD BH24 ...... 170 E3
TOTT SO40 ...... 130 D8
WIMB BH21 ...... 193 G2
Willow Gdns EMRTH PO10 ...... 166 E4
NBAD SO52 ...... 79 L3
Willow Gn RWIN SO21 ...... 54 F8
Willow Gv ELGH SO50 ...... 83 J6
Willow Herb Cl HLER SO31 ...... 158 C5
Willow La CHCH/BSGR BH23 ...... 198 B5
Willow Md CHAR BH8 ...... 221 H4
Willow Pk PSTN BH14 ...... 233 L5
Willow Pl GPORT PO12 ...... 10 F1
Willow Rd BPWT SO32 ...... 111 K1
LISS GU33 ...... 36 A3
The Willows NMIL/BTOS BH25 ...... 225 M8
WVILLE PO7 ...... 139 J4
Willow Tree Av HORN PO8 ...... 140 F6
Willow Tree Gdns
FHAM/STUB PO14 ...... 6 C7
Willow Tree Ri BWD BH11 ...... 219 M6
Willow Tree Wk ITCH SO19 ...... 132 F5
Willow Wy
CHCH/BSGR BH23 ...... 237 M3 [3]
FERN BH22 ...... 194 B1
Willow Wood Rd HISD PO11 ...... 213 L5 [3]
Wills Cl WIMB BH21 ...... 217 H4
Wills Rd BKME/WDN BH12 ...... 234 E3
Wills Wy ROMY SO51 ...... 78 F2
Willwood Cl CFDH BH17 ...... 218 C5 [2]
Wilmer Rd ELGH SO50 ...... 81 M6
Wilmington Cl WEND SO18 ...... 107 L5
Wilmot Cl ELGH SO50 ...... 82 D3
Wilmott Cl GPORT PO12 ...... 10 A2
Wilmott La GPORT PO12 ...... 10 A2
Wilmur Crs PLE BH15 ...... 233 K2
Wilson Gv SSEA PO5 ...... 13 K5
Wilson Rd BMTH BH1 ...... 236 C3
NEND PO2 ...... 187 G6
PSTN BH14 ...... 234 B4
Wilson St SHAM SO14 ...... 5 L1
Wilton Av WSHM SO15 ...... 131 J2
Wilton Cl CHCH/BSGR BH23 ...... 222 B7
Wilton Crs WSHM SO15 ...... 106 C7
Wilton Dr HORN PO8 ...... 140 C7
Wilton Gdns
NMIL/BTOS BH25 ...... 225 K5 [6]
WSHM SO15 ...... 106 C7
Wilton Pl SSEA PO5 ...... 13 H7
Wilton Rd LTDN BH7 ...... 236 E3
WSHM SO15 ...... 106 C7
Wilton Ter SSEA PO5 ...... 13 J7 [8]
Wiltshire Gdns
CHCH/BSGR BH23 ...... 197 K8
Wiltshire Rd
CHCH/BSGR BH23 ...... 197 K8
CHFD SO53 ...... 81 J5
Wiltshire St SSEA PO5 ...... 12 F3
Wilverley Av CHAR BH8 ...... 221 K6
HAV PO9 ...... 165 L4
Wilverley Pl FAWY SO45 ...... 180 C7
Wilverley Rd BROC SO42 ...... 175 K7
NMIL/BTOS BH25 ...... 199 K5
Wimbledon Pk Rd SSEA PO5 ...... 13 K8
Wimble La WVILLE PO7 ...... 140 C7
Wimborne Rd BWD BH11 ...... 219 M2
ENEY PO4 ...... 211 L4
MOOR/WNTN BH9 ...... 220 B4
NBNE BH10 ...... 220 E4
PLE BH15 ...... 233 H2
TWDS BH3 ...... 235 L1
UPTN BH16 ...... 216 B4
WCLF BH2 ...... 14 F3
WIMB BH21 ...... 192 C2
Wimborne Rd East FERN BH22 ...... 194 B2
WIMB BH21 ...... 193 L2
Wimborne Rd West
WIMB BH21 ...... 192 E4
Wimpole St PSEA PO1 ...... 13 H2
Wimpson Gdns ROWN SO16 ...... 105 L7
Wimpson La ROWN SO16 ...... 105 K8
Wincanton Wy WVILLE PO7 ...... 140 F7
Winchcombe Rd CHAM PO6 ...... 162 F7
Winchester By-pass
WINC SO23 ...... 17 J2
Winchester Hl ROMY SO51 ...... 51 G8
Winchester Rd BPWT SO32 ...... 84 C1
BPWT SO32 ...... 109 K5
CHFD SO53 ...... 81 J3
ELGH SO50 ...... 83 H4
NEND PO2 ...... 187 J3
NMIL/BTOS BH25 ...... 226 A3
PSF GU32 ...... 62 A3
ROMY SO51 ...... 51 J7 [2]
ROWN SO16 ...... 105 M7
RWIN SO21 ...... 54 C1
WHAM PO17 ...... 136 C3
Winchester St HEND SO30 ...... 109 M8
WSHM SO15 ...... 131 K2
Winchester Wy TOTT SO40 ...... 129 G3 [2]
Winchfield Cl ITCH SO19 ...... 132 E8 [3]
Winchfield Crs HAV PO9 ...... 165 G2
Wincombe Cl FERN BH22 ...... 194 B5 [3]
Wincombe Rd FERN BH22 ...... 194 B4
Windbury Rd ROWN SO16 ...... 105 K6
Windermere Av
FHAM/STUB PO14 ...... 184 B4
ROWN SO16 ...... 105 J6
Windermere Gdns TOTT SO40 ...... 104 D8

Windermere Rd NEND PO2 ...... 187 K5
TWDS BH3 ...... 235 M2
WEND SO18 ...... 108 A7
Windfield Dr ROMY SO51 ...... 51 G8 [2]
Windham Rd BMTH BH1 ...... 15 L2
Windmill Cl HORN PO8 ...... 116 B3
LYMN SO41 ...... 242 C3
RGWD BH24 ...... 169 K4
Windmill Copse FAWY SO45 ...... 155 K7 [6]
Windmill Fld WVILLE PO7 ...... 139 L4
Windmill Gv FHAM/PORC PO16 ...... 185 M2
Windmill La HLER SO31 ...... 133 L6
RGWD BH24 ...... 170 B4
Windover Cl ITCH SO19 ...... 133 G2
Windrush Gdns WVILLE PO7 ...... 164 B1
Windrush Rd ROWN SO16 ...... 105 K7
Windrush Wy FAWY SO45 ...... 155 L5
Windsor Cl LYMN SO41 ...... 226 C4
RGWD BH24 ...... 169 K3
Windsor Ct ELGH SO50 ...... 82 C4 [2]
Windsor Ga ELGH SO50 ...... 81 M2
Windsor Rd BOSC BH5 ...... 236 D4
CHAM PO6 ...... 187 K1
CHCH/BSGR BH23 ...... 222 B8
FHAM/PORC PO16 ...... 186 B1
GPORT PO12 ...... 10 D3
PSF GU32 ...... 63 L5
PSTN BH14 ...... 234 A5
WVILLE PO7 ...... 140 B6
Windsor Wy FBDG SP6 ...... 121 L2
Windwhistle La RSAL SP5 ...... 45 L1
Winfield Wy EMRTH PO10 ...... 166 D4 [1]
Winfrith Crs
BKME/WDN BH12 ...... 219 J8
Winfrith Wy ROWN SO16 ...... 105 J3
Wingate Dr ITCH SO19 ...... 132 F3
Wingate Rd TOTT SO40 ...... 104 C8
Wingfield Av
CHCH/BSGR BH23 ...... 224 B7
PLE BH15 ...... 233 J2
Wingfield St PSEA PO1 ...... 211 H1
Wingrove Rd TOTT SO40 ...... 129 C5 [2]
Winifred Cl ELGH SO50 ...... 83 H5 [2]
Winifred Rd PLE BH15 ...... 233 K3
WVILLE PO7 ...... 140 C3
Winkle St SHAM SO14 ...... 4 F7
Winkton Cl CHCH/BSGR BH23 ...... 223 G5
HAV PO9 ...... 8 B1
Winnall Cl WINC SO23 ...... 3 M1
Winnall Manor Rd WINC SO23 ...... 3 M7
Winnall Valley Rd WINC SO23 ...... 3 L6
Winnards Cl FERN BH22 ...... 194 C6
Winnards Pk HLER SO31 ...... 158 B5
Winnham Dr
FHAM/PORC PO16 ...... 161 L7
Winnington FHAM PO15 ...... 160 B4
Winn Rd PTSW SO17 ...... 106 F8
Winscombe Av HORN PO8 ...... 140 E6
Winsford Av ELGH SO50 ...... 82 F7
Winsford Cl
CHCH/BSGR BH23 ...... 224 B7 [2]
ELGH SO50 ...... 82 F7 [1]
HAV PO9 ...... 165 H3 [3]
Winsley Av SBNE BH6 ...... 237 H4
Winsor Cl HISD PO11 ...... 214 B7
Winsor La TOTT SO40 ...... 103 J8
Winsor Rd TOTT SO40 ...... 127 M1
TOTT SO40 ...... 129 L2
Winspit Cl PLE BH15 ...... 232 D5
Winstanley Rd NEND PO2 ...... 187 G2
ROWN SO16 ...... 105 H3
Winston Av BKME/WDN BH12 ...... 234 F2
Winston Churchill Av SSEA PO5 ...... 13 H5
Winston Cl ELGH SO50 ...... 81 M4
HISD PO11 ...... 213 J5
ROWN SO16 ...... 105 L6
Winstone Crs NBAD SO52 ...... 79 K3
Winston Gdns
BKME/WDN BH12 ...... 234 F2
Winston Rd MOOR/WNTN BH9 ...... 220 D3
Winston Wy RGWD BH24 ...... 146 F8
Winterbourne Rd
CHAM PO6 ...... 162 D7 [2]
PLE BH15 ...... 233 J4
ROMY SO51 ...... 51 F7 [2]
Winterhayes Cl CFDH BH17 ...... 218 C5
Winterhill Rd CHAM PO6 ...... 163 H8
Winter Rd ENEY PO4 ...... 211 L5
Winters Cl FAWY SO45 ...... 180 B5
Winters Hl BPWT SO32 ...... 84 D8
Winterslow Dr HAV PO9 ...... 165 J2 [7]
Winters Rd BPWT SO32 ...... 111 M8
Winton Cl LYMN SO41 ...... 228 D5 [1]
Winton Rd NEND PO2 ...... 187 K6
NMIL/BTOS BH25 ...... 225 M3
Wisbech Wy LYMN SO41 ...... 226 D5
Wisborough Rd SSEA PO5 ...... 13 K7
Wishart Gdns
MOOR/WNTN BH9 ...... 220 F3
Wish Pl SSEA PO5 ...... 13 L7
Wisteria Dr VWD BH31 ...... 145 G4
Wisteria Gdns HAV PO9 ...... 165 M4
Witchampton Cl HAV PO9 ...... 165 L3 [4]
Witchampton Rd BDST BH18 ...... 217 K6
Witham Cl CHFD SO53 ...... 80 F2
Witherbed La FHAM PO15 ...... 159 J4
Withermoor Rd
MOOR/WNTN BH9 ...... 220 C8
Withies La LSOL/BMARY PO13 ...... 185 H8
Withingham Rd CCLF BH13 ...... 234 C5
Withy Cl ROMY SO51 ...... 50 E8 [3]
Witley RGWD BH24 ...... 147 G8 [4]
ROWN SO16 ...... 105 L3
Witt Rd ELGH SO50 ...... 83 H6
Witts Hl WEND SO18 ...... 107 M8
Witt's La LYMN SO41 ...... 227 M6
Woburn Cl ELGH SO50 ...... 81 M2
Woburn Rd ROWN SO16 ...... 106 A3
Wode Cl HORN PO8 ...... 116 B5
Wodehouse Rd ITCH SO19 ...... 133 C4

Woking Rd PSTN BH14 ...... 234 B4
Wolfe Cl CHCH/BSGR BH23 ...... 238 D1
  FUFL SO22 ...... 26 B3
Wollaston Rd SBNE BH6 ...... 237 L5
Wollaton Rd FERN BH22 ...... 194 A5
Wollstonecraft Rd
  BOSC BH5 ...... 236 E5
Wolseley Rd BKME/WDN BH12 ...... 234 C2
  WSHM SO15 ...... 131 G1
Wolsey Wy LYMN SO41 ...... 242 C3
Wolterton Rd
  BKME/WDN BH12 ...... 234 F3
Wolverley Ct ROWN SO16 ...... 106 C5
Wolverton Rd HAV PO9 ...... 165 J3
  LTDN BH7 ...... 236 E3
  SHAM SO14 ...... 5 K1
Wolvesey Pl CHFD SO53 ...... 80 F4
Wonston Rd HAV PO9 ...... 165 M2
Wonston Rd ROWN SO16 ...... 106 A4
Woodacre Gdns FERN BH22 ...... 194 C4
Wood Barn Rd FHAM PO15 ...... 6 A5
Woodberry La EMRTH PO10 ...... 166 D1
  HAV PO9 ...... 142 B7
Woodbourne Cl FHAM PO15 ...... 6 A6
  LISS GU33 ...... 36 F4
Woodbury Av CHAR BH8 ...... 221 K6
  HAV PO9 ...... 8 E7
  PSF GU32 ...... 63 K3
Woodbury Cl
  CHCH/BSGR BH23 ...... 222 C5
Woodbury Gv HORN PO8 ...... 140 D3
Wood Cl ITCH SO19 ...... 133 G5
Woodcock La LYMN SO41 ...... 226 E5
Woodcocks Crs LTDN BH7 ...... 236 F1
Woodcot Crs HAV PO9 ...... 165 L2
Woodcote Dr UPTN BH16 ...... 232 A2
Woodcote La BPWT SO32 ...... 84 F1
  FHAM/STUB PO14 ...... 184 E6
Woodcote Rd PTSW SO17 ...... 107 H5
Woodcroft La HORN PO8 ...... 140 D3
Woodend
  MOOR/WNTN BH9 ...... 235 K1
Wood End Rd RGWD BH24 ...... 171 J3
Wood End Wy NBAD SO52 ...... 80 F1
Wooden House La LYMN SO41 ...... 242 F6
Wooderson Cl ELGH SO50 ...... 83 G5
Woodfern FBDG SP6 ...... 98 C6
Woodfield Av CHAM PO6 ...... 164 C7
Woodfield Dr FUFL SO22 ...... 26 A2
Woodfield Gdns
  CHCH/BSGR BH23 ...... 224 B7
Woodfield Park Rd
  EMRTH PO10 ...... 166 F7
Woodfield Rd RGWD BH24 ...... 219 L3
Woodford Cl RGWD BH24 ...... 170 F1
Woodford Rd BMTH BH1 ...... 15 L4
Woodgason La HISD PO11 ...... 190 A7
Wood Glade Cl TOTT SO40 ...... 130 D7
Woodgreen Av HAV PO9 ...... 8 B2
Woodgreen Dr BWD BH11 ...... 219 H4
Woodgreen Rd FUFL SO22 ...... 16 C4
Woodhall Wy FHAM PO15 ...... 6 D1
Woodhayes Av
  CHCH/BSGR BH23 ...... 224 C6
Woodhouse La HAV PO9 ...... 142 A4
  HEND SO30 ...... 109 K8
  HORN PO8 ...... 141 L2
Woodhouse Rd HORN PO8 ...... 141 K1
Woodington Cl HAV PO9 ...... 165 L2
Woodington Rd ROMY SO51 ...... 77 H4
Woodlake Cl FHAM BH17 ...... 218 B7
Woodland Av BOSC BH5 ...... 236 F4
Woodland Cl ROMY SO51 ...... 77 G6
  WEND SO18 ...... 133 H1
Woodland Dro RWIN SO21 ...... 54 F5
Woodland Ms HEND SO30 ...... 108 C7
Woodlands
  FHAM/PORC PO16 ...... 161 H6
Woodlands Av EMRTH PO10 ...... 166 D1
  PLE BH15 ...... 232 D5

Woodlands Cl
  CHCH/BSGR BH23 ...... 197 L8
  CHFD SO53 ...... 53 J6
  FAWY SO45 ...... 155 J7
  HLER SO31 ...... 158 D2
  HYDE SO45 ...... 209 G2
Woodlands Ct FAWY SO45 ...... 155 J7
Woodlands Crs PLE BH15 ...... 232 E5
Woodlands Dr HLER SO31 ...... 157 H2
Woodlands Dro TOTT SO40 ...... 128 D5
Woodlands La HISD PO11 ...... 213 J3
  LISS GU33 ...... 37 G6
  RCCH PO18 ...... 143 J6
Woodlands Rd BROC SO42 ...... 201 K1
  NMIL/BTOS BH25 ...... 240 D1
  TOTT SO40 ...... 128 C4
The Woodlands WINC SO23 ...... 17 H2
Woodlands St PSEA PO1 ...... 211 J2
Woodlands Wy HAV PO9 ...... 165 K4
  HLER SO31 ...... 133 K8
  NBAD SO52 ...... 79 K4
  NMIL/BTOS BH25 ...... 225 M2
  RGWD BH24 ...... 169 K4
  WSHM SO15 ...... 106 E8
Woodland Vw HLER SO31 ...... 133 K8
  HORN PO8 ...... 140 D2
Woodland Wk BOSC BH5 ...... 236 F4
  FERN BH22 ...... 194 D1
Woodland Wy
  CHCH/BSGR BH23 ...... 224 B8
  LYMN SO41 ...... 242 B4
Wood La BWD BH11 ...... 219 J2
  LYMN SO41 ...... 242 B4
  NARL SO24 ...... 31 J3
  WHAM PO17 ...... 162 E1
Woodlane Cl NARL SO24 ...... 31 J3
Wood Lawn Cl
  NMIL/BTOS BH25 ...... 225 K8
Woodlea Cl FUFL SO22 ...... 2 C2
Woodlea Gdns HEND SO30 ...... 108 D7
Woodlea Wy ROMY SO51 ...... 52 E6
Woodleaze Cl BDST BH18 ...... 217 M2
Woodleigh Cl HAV PO9 ...... 166 A5
Woodley Cl ROMY SO51 ...... 51 H6
Woodley Gdns LYMN SO41 ...... 228 B3
Woodley Rd ROMY SO51 ...... 50 F7
Woodley Rd GPORT PO12 ...... 11 G4
  ITCH SO19 ...... 132 B5
Woodley Wy ROMY SO51 ...... 51 H6
Woodlinken Cl VWD BH31 ...... 144 F4
Woodlinken Dr VWD BH31 ...... 144 F4
Woodlinken Wy VWD BH31 ...... 144 F4
Wood Ldg TOTT SO40 ...... 104 A7
Woodmancote La
  EMRTH PO10 ...... 167 J4
Woodmancote Rd ENEY PO4 ...... 211 L4
Woodmill La WEND SO18 ...... 107 J5
Woodmoor Cl TOTT SO40 ...... 130 E7
Woodpath SSEA PO5 ...... 13 H6
Woodpecker Cl HAV PO9 ...... 9 J4
  VWD BH31 ...... 144 D3
Woodpecker Copse
  HLER SO31 ...... 158 F5
Woodpecker Dr CFDH BH17 ...... 217 J8
  FUFL SO22 ...... 16 B6
  TOTT SO40 ...... 130 C7
Woodpecker Wy ELGH SO50 ...... 81 J6
Woodrow WVILLE PO7 ...... 139 J4
Woodrush Crs HLER SO31 ...... 158 C6
Woodsedge WVILLE PO7 ...... 164 E3
Woodside LSOL/BMARY PO13 ...... 184 F3
  ROWN SO16 ...... 80 D6
Woodside Av ELGH SO50 ...... 81 L3
  LYMN SO41 ...... 228 C7
Woodside Cl FERN BH22 ...... 194 C2
  TOTT SO40 ...... 130 C7
Woodside Crs ROWN SO16 ...... 80 C6

Woodside Gdns TOTT SO40 ...... 129 C6
Woodside La LYMN SO41 ...... 228 C6
Woodside Rd BOSC BH5 ...... 237 C4
  ELGH SO50 ...... 81 K4
  FERN BH22 ...... 194 C2
  NBAD SO52 ...... 79 L4
  PSTN BH14 ...... 234 B5
  PTSW SO17 ...... 107 G8
Woodside Wy HEND SO30 ...... 133 L3
Woodstock Av HORN PO8 ...... 140 E3
Woodstock Cl FHAM PO15 ...... 6 C5
  HEND SO30 ...... 134 B3
Woodstock Dr PTSW SO17 ...... 106 F7
Woodstock La RGWD BH24 ...... 170 E2
Woodstock Rd
  CHCH/BSGR BH23 ...... 223 H6
  GPORT PO12 ...... 11 G4
  HAV PO9 ...... 165 G6
  PSTN BH14 ...... 233 M6
Woods View Rd
  MOOR/WNTN BH9 ...... 220 B8
Woodthorpe Gdns HLER SO31 ...... 158 D2
Woodvale FHAM PO15 ...... 6 A4
Woodvale Gdns
  NMIL/BTOS BH25 ...... 226 A4
Woodview Cl ROWN SO16 ...... 106 F2
Woodville Dr PSEA PO1 ...... 12 E5
Woodville Rd FAWY SO45 ...... 180 F5
  HAV PO9 ...... 164 F6
Woodward Cl GPORT PO12 ...... 10 A4
Woofferton Rd CHAM PO6 ...... 162 E7
Woolbeding La MIDH GU29 ...... 67 L3
Woolfield La ALTN GU34 ...... 34 A5
  PSF GU32 ...... 34 B6
Woolford Cl FUFL SO22 ...... 26 B2
Woolmer Cl HAV PO9 ...... 165 M3
Woolmer La RGWD BH24 ...... 146 D6
Woolmer St EMRTH PO10 ...... 166 C4
Woolner Av CHAM PO6 ...... 163 L8
  PSF GU32 ...... 63 L4
Wool Rd BKME/WDN BH12 ...... 218 F8
Wools Br RGWD BH24 ...... 169 G2
Woolsbridge Rd RGWD BH24 ...... 169 J4
Woolslope Cl FERN BH22 ...... 168 C7
Woolslope Gdns FERN BH22 ...... 168 D7
Woolslope Rd FERN BH22 ...... 168 C7
Woolston Rd HAV PO9 ...... 165 G2
  HLER SO31 ...... 132 F8
Woolven Cl PSTN BH14 ...... 233 M3
Woolwich Cl HLER SO31 ...... 133 K6
Wooton La LSOL/BMARY PO13 ...... 208 E4
Wootton HLER SO31 ...... 157 C1
Wootton Farm Rd
  NMIL/BTOS BH25 ...... 199 J6
Wootton Gdns BMTH BH1 ...... 15 C5
Wootton Mt BMTH BH1 ...... 15 H5
Wootton Rough
  NMIL/BTOS BH25 ...... 199 M8
Wootton St CHAM PO6 ...... 187 K1
Worbarrow Gdns
  BKME/WDN BH12 ...... 219 G8
Worcester Pl ITCH SO19 ...... 132 F6
  LYMN SO41 ...... 228 D6
Wordsworth Av CHAM PO6 ...... 162 C7
  CHAR BH8 ...... 221 J7
Wordsworth Cl BPWT SO32 ...... 85 K8
  FUFL SO22 ...... 2 B6
Wordsworth Pl HLER SO31 ...... 134 F7
Wordsworth Rd ROWN SO16 ...... 106 B7
Worgret Rd PLE BH15 ...... 233 J1
Workhouse La PSF GU32 ...... 61 J7
Workman's La HLER SO31 ...... 182 C3
Workshop Rd WVILLE PO7 ...... 162 E6
Worldham Rd HAV PO9 ...... 165 M2
Worrell Dr BKME/WDN BH12 ...... 219 G8
Worsley Rd SSEA PO5 ...... 13 H6
Worsley St ENEY PO4 ...... 211 L6
Worthing Av GPORT PO12 ...... 185 K8
Worthing Rd SSEA PO5 ...... 13 K8
Worthington Crs PSTN BH14 ...... 233 M5
Worthy Ct HAV PO9 ...... 165 M3

Worthy La WINC SO23 ...... 2 F5
Worthy Rd NMIL/BTOS BH25 ...... 225 L5
  WINC SO23 ...... 3 G3
Wortley Rd CHCH/BSGR BH23 ...... 239 M1
Wraxhall Cl CFDH BH17 ...... 218 B7
Wraysbury Park Dr
  EMRTH PO10 ...... 166 D4
Wren Cl CHCH/BSGR BH23 ...... 239 G3
  FUFL SO22 ...... 26 C3
  NMIL/BTOS BH25 ...... 225 K6
  RGWD BH24 ...... 171 G2
Wren Crs BKME/WDN BH12 ...... 235 G3
Wren Gdns FBDG SP6 ...... 121 M2
Wren Rd ELGH SO50 ...... 81 K7
Wren Wy FHAM/PORC PO16 ...... 161 K8
Wrexham Gr HORN PO8 ...... 116 A6
Wright's Hl ITCH SO19 ...... 132 E6
Wroxham Rd
  BKME/WDN BH12 ...... 234 E3
Wryneck Cl ROWN SO16 ...... 106 A2
Wyatts Cl WIMB BH21 ...... 217 H2
Wyatts La WIMB BH21 ...... 217 G2
Wyborn Cl HISD PO11 ...... 213 L6
Wych La LSOL/BMARY PO13 ...... 184 F4
Wychwood Cl WCLF BH2 ...... 14 D3
Wychwood Dr FAWY SO45 ...... 206 C1
  WCLF BH2 ...... 14 E2
Wychwood Gv CHFD SO53 ...... 53 K8
Wycliffe Rd MOOR/WNTN BH9 ...... 220 D8
  WEND SO18 ...... 107 M7
Wycote Rd LSOL/BMARY PO13 ...... 184 F4
Wyeford Cl HAV PO9 ...... 165 M2
Wyelands Av WIMB BH21 ...... 193 H3
Wykeham Cl CFDH BH17 ...... 218 C8
  ROWN SO16 ...... 106 D4
Wykeham Fld WHAM PO17 ...... 136 E5
Wykeham Pl FUFL SO22 ...... 26 C3
  LYMN SO41 ...... 228 C5
Wykeham Rd HLER SO31 ...... 156 F2
  NEND PO2 ...... 187 J7
Wylde Green La LISS GU33 ...... 36 F5
Wylds La PSF GU32 ...... 63 H8
Wyllie Rd NEND PO2 ...... 187 J4
Wylye Cl WEND SO18 ...... 108 A5
Wymering La CHAM PO6 ...... 163 J8
Wymering Manor Cl
  CHAM PO6 ...... 163 J8
Wymering Rd NEND PO2 ...... 187 J8
Wyncombe Rd BOSC BH5 ...... 237 C3
Wyndcliffe Rd ENEY PO4 ...... 13 M6
Wyndham Cl
  CHCH/BSGR BH23 ...... 224 F6
  HORN PO8 ...... 140 F4
Wyndham Ms PSEA PO1 ...... 12 D5
Wyndham Pl WSHM SO15 ...... 4 D1
Wyndham Rd
  CHCH/BSGR BH23 ...... 224 F6
  PSTN BH14 ...... 234 A5
Wynford Rd
  MOOR/WNTN BH9 ...... 220 E4
  PSTN BH14 ...... 234 B5
Wynne Cl BDST BH18 ...... 217 K4
Wynter Cl LTDN BH7 ...... 236 E1
Wynter Rd WEND SO18 ...... 108 A8
Wynton Wy FHAM PO15 ...... 160 A5
Wynyards Gap NBAD SO52 ...... 79 L4
Wyre Cl CHFD SO53 ...... 81 G2
Wyvern Cl BKME/WDN BH12 ...... 234 C1
  CHFD SO53 ...... 81 G2

Y

Yaldhurst Ct HAV PO9 ...... 165 M2
Yaldhurst La LYMN SO41 ...... 227 M4
Yapton St PSEA PO1 ...... 13 G1
Yarborough Rd SSEA PO5 ...... 13 G6
Yardlea Cl HAV PO9 ...... 141 M7
Yardley Cl HSEA PO3 ...... 188 A4
Yardley Rd HEND SO30 ...... 133 M3

Yarmouth Cl
  BKME/WDN BH12 ...... 234 F3
Yarmouth Gdns WSHM SO15 ...... 106 A7
Yarmouth Rd
  BKME/WDN BH12 ...... 234 E2
Yarrell Md LYMN SO41 ...... 227 M4
Yarrells Cl UPTN BH16 ...... 232 B2
Yarrells La UPTN BH16 ...... 232 B2
Yarrow Cl CHCH/BSGR BH23 ...... 223 M8
Yarrow Rd BKME/WDN BH12 ...... 218 E8
Yarrow Wy HLER SO31 ...... 158 C6
Yateley Cl HAV PO9 ...... 165 G3
Yaverland HLER SO31 ...... 157 C2
Yeatminster Rd CFDH BH17 ...... 218 D6
Yelverton Av FAWY SO45 ...... 155 L7
Yelverton Rd WCLF BH2 ...... 14 E5
Yeo Ct ENEY PO4 ...... 212 A5
Yeomans Fld RCCH PO18 ...... 167 M7
Yeomans Rd CHAR BH8 ...... 221 J5
Yeomans Wy CHAR BH8 ...... 221 J5
  TOTT SO40 ...... 104 E8
Yeovil Cha WEND SO18 ...... 108 A8
Yeovilton Cl LYMN SO41 ...... 227 J7
Yerville Gdns LYMN SO41 ...... 226 D5
Yew La NMIL/BTOS BH25 ...... 226 A4
Yew Rd WEND SO18 ...... 107 M8
Yewside LSOL/BMARY PO13 ...... 185 J7
The Yews HORN PO8 ...... 141 H1
Yewtree Cl FAWY SO45 ...... 155 L8
Yew Tree Cl ELGH SO50 ...... 83 H5
  HEND SO30 ...... 133 M2
  WIMB BH21 ...... 192 A3
Yew Tree Dr FHAM PO15 ...... 135 G8
  HLER SO31 ...... 158 F1
Yew Tree Gdns WVILLE PO7 ...... 139 J4
Yewtree La ROWN SO16 ...... 105 H5
Yew Tree Pl LISS GU33 ...... 36 F4
Yew Tree Rd HISD PO11 ...... 189 L8
Yoells Crs HORN PO8 ...... 140 D2
Yoells La HORN PO8 ...... 140 D2
Yokesford Hl ROMY SO51 ...... 50 D3
Yonge Cl ELGH SO50 ...... 82 A5
York Av NMIL/BTOS BH25 ...... 225 M5
York Buildings SHAM SO14 ...... 5 G4
York Cl BDST BH18 ...... 217 L6
  CHCH/BSGR BH23 ...... 237 L1
  ELGH SO50 ...... 109 J1
  NBAD SO52 ...... 79 K4
  PSF GU32 ...... 63 J5
  SHAM SO14 ...... 132 A2
  TOTT SO40 ...... 104 F8
York Crs LSOL/BMARY PO13 ...... 208 E4
York Dro RSAL SP5 ...... 75 H8
  WEND SO18 ...... 132 F1
Yorke St SSEA PO5 ...... 12 F4
Yorke Wy HLER SO31 ...... 157 J5
York Gdns FHAM/PORC PO16 ...... 186 B2
York Pl LTDN BH7 ...... 236 F3
  PSEA PO1 ...... 210 F2
York Rd BMTH BH1 ...... 15 K4
  CFDH BH17 ...... 217 L7
  ELGH SO50 ...... 81 M7
  WSHM SO15 ...... 131 G1
Yorkwood LISS GU33 ...... 36 E4
Youngs Rd BWD BH11 ...... 219 L3
Yves Ms SSEA PO5 ...... 13 J7

Z

Zamek Cl BWD BH11 ...... 219 L3
Zetland Rd CHAM PO6 ...... 188 B1
Zeus La WVILLE PO7 ...... 164 D5
Zinnia Cl NBNE BH10 ...... 220 C6

Index - featured places

Abbey Chiropractic Clinic
  ROMY SO51 ...... 78 D1
Abbey Mead Surgery
  ROMY SO51 ...... 78 C1
Abbotswood Junior School
  TOTT SO40 ...... 129 H1
ABC Cinema
  BMTH BH1 ...... 14 F6
Abraham Gallery
  SSEA PO5 ...... 13 H4
Acorn Business Centre
  CHAM PO6 ...... 163 H8
Ad Astra County First School
  CFDH BH17 ...... 218 C7
Adeline Road Surgery
  BOSC BH5 ...... 236 D4
Admiral Lord Nelson School
  HSEA PO3 ...... 187 M7
Albany Business Centre
  WHAM PO17 ...... 160 F1
Alderman Quilley
  Secondary School
  ELGH SO50 ...... 81 L7
Aldermoor Health Centre
  ROWN SO16 ...... 106 B4
Alderney Middle School
  BKME/WDN BH12 ...... 219 H1
Allington Manor
  Business Centre
  ELGH SO50 ...... 108 D1
All Saints C of E Primary School
  RSAL SP5 ...... 47 G3
All Saints Community
  Primary School
  WINC SO23 ...... 27 G1
Alma Road Surgery
  PTSW SO17 ...... 106 F8
Alma Road Surgery
  ROMY SO51 ...... 78 D1
The Alpha Business Park
  SHAM SO14 ...... 131 M1

Alverstoke C of E Junior School
  GPORT PO12 ...... 10 C6
Alverstoke County
  Infant School
  GPORT PO12 ...... 10 C8
Amey Industrial Estate
  PSF GU32 ...... 63 K5
A M F Bowling
  ITCH SO19 ...... 132 D2
A M F Bowling
  PSEA PO1 ...... 13 H1
Ampfield Primary School
  ROMY SO51 ...... 52 B4
Anchor Business Centre
  CHFD SO53 ...... 81 G2
Andover Road Retail Park
  FUFL SO22 ...... 2 E5
The Andrew Isaacs Practice
  BMTH BH1 ...... 15 J4
Anne Dale County Junior &
  Infant School
  FHAM/STUB PO14 ...... 184 A6
Apple Industrial Estate
  FHAM PO15 ...... 159 G3
Applemore College
  FAWY SO45 ...... 155 G6
Applemore Recreation Centre
  FAWY SO45 ...... 155 G5
Arch Farm Industrial Estate
  FBDG SP6 ...... 97 K5
The Arnewood Practice
  NMIL/BTOS BH25 ...... 225 L3
Arnewood School
  NMIL/BTOS BH25 ...... 225 K7
The Art Gallery
  EMRTH PO10 ...... 166 H4
Art Space School
  PSEA PO1 ...... 211 G1
Arundel Court Junior &
  Infant School
  PSEA PO1 ...... 211 H2

Ashdown School
  CFDH BH17 ...... 218 C7
Ashley County Infant School
  NMIL/BTOS BH25 ...... 226 B5
Ashley Heath Industrial Estate
  WIMB BH21 ...... 169 G1
Ashley Junior School
  NMIL/BTOS BH25 ...... 226 A5
Ashurst Hospital
  TOTT SO40 ...... 128 F7
Associated Football Club
  TOTT SO40 ...... 104 F8
Atherley House Surgery
  WSHM SO15 ...... 131 H2
The Atherley School
  ROWN SO16 ...... 105 G2
Avenue Clinic
  WSHM SO15 ...... 131 K2
Avenue Shopping Centre
  WCLF BH2 ...... 14 D5
Avonbourne Girls School
  CHAR BH8 ...... 236 F1
Avon Castle
  RGWD BH24 ...... 170 B5
Avonlea Preparatory School
  RGWD BH24 ...... 146 F8
Awbridge County School
  ROMY SO51 ...... 49 J3
Baddesley Park Industrial Estate
  NBAD SO52 ...... 80 A4
Baden Powell & St Peters
  C of E (VC) School
  PSTN BH14 ...... 234 A5
Badger Farm Surgery
  FUFL SO22 ...... 26 B4
Ballard College
  NMIL/BTOS BH25 ...... 225 L5
Ballard Lake
  Preparatory School
  NMIL/BTOS BH25 ...... 225 L4

Banister School
  WSHM SO15 ...... 131 K1
Bargate Museum
  SHAM SO14 ...... 5 G4
Bargate Shopping Centre
  SHAM SO14 ...... 5 G4
Barncroft Infant School
  HAV PO9 ...... 165 H4
Barncroft Junior School
  HAV PO9 ...... 165 G4
Barratt Industrial Park
  PTSW SO17 ...... 159 G3
Bartley C of E Middle School
  TOTT SO40 ...... 127 M1
Barton Peveril College
  ELGH SO50 ...... 81 L7
Barton Surgery
  NMIL/BTOS BH25 ...... 225 L7
Bassett Green Junior School
  ROWN SO16 ...... 107 G4
Baycroft School
  FHAM/STUB PO14 ...... 184 B6
Bay House School
  GPORT PO12 ...... 209 J6
BBC South TV & Radio Solent
  WSHM SO15 ...... 4 E1
The Bear Museum
  EPSF GU32 ...... 63 L6
Bearwood County
  Primary School
  WIMB BH21 ...... 219 G2
Beaucroft School
  WIMB BH21 ...... 192 C2
Beaufort Road Surgery
  SBNE BH6 ...... 237 H3
Beaulieu CP School
  BROC SO42 ...... 178 D7
Bedales School
  PSF GU32 ...... 63 K1

Bedenham County
  Junior & Infant School
  LSOL/BMARY PO13 ...... 185 H5
Beechwood Middle School
  WEND SO18 ...... 132 D1
Belbins Business Park
  ROMY SO51 ...... 50 F5
Belgrave Industrial Estate
  PTSW SO17 ...... 107 H6
Bellemoor Secondary School
  ROWN SO16 ...... 106 C6
Berrywood Primary School
  HEND SO30 ...... 109 J7
Bethany C of E (VA)
  Junior School
  BMTH BH1 ...... 236 C3
Bevois Town Primary School
  SHAM SO14 ...... 131 L1
Bicknell Boys
  Residential School
  LTDN BH7 ...... 236 F1
Bidbury Junior & Infant School
  HAV PO9 ...... 8 A2
Birchwood Medical Centre
  CFDH BH17 ...... 217 K8
Bishops Waltham County
  Infant School
  BPWT SO32 ...... 85 J8
Bitterne C of E First School
  ITCH SO19 ...... 132 D1
Bitterne C of E Infant School
  ITCH SO19 ...... 132 D1
Bitterne Health Centre
  ITCH SO19 ...... 132 D1
Bitterne Leisure Centre
  ITCH SO19 ...... 132 E1
Bitterne Manor
  Primary School
  ITCH SO19 ...... 132 B1
Bitterne Middle School
  ITCH SO19 ...... 132 D2

Bitterne Park Clinic
  WEND SO18 .... 107 K8
Bitterne Park Junior &
  Infant School
  WEND SO18 .... 107 J6
Bitterne Park
  Secondary School
  WEND SO18 .... 107 K6
Bitterne Park Surgery
  WEND SO18 .... 107 K8
Blackbrook Business Park
  FHAM PO15 .... 6 C5
Blackfield Health Centre
  FAWY SO45 .... 180 B6
Blackfield Junior &
  Infant School
  FAWY SO45 .... 180 C7
Blue Fish Zoo
  BMTH BH1 .... 14 E6
The Boatyard Industrial Estate
  FHAM/PORC PO16 .... 7 H8
The Bold Gallery
  CHCH/BSGR BH23 .... 238 A1
Boscombe Dental
  Health Centre
  BOSC BH5 .... 236 E3
Boscombe Manor
  Medical Centre
  BOSC BH5 .... 236 E4
Bosmere Junior School
  HAV PO9 .... 8 C3
Botley Junior & Infant School
  HEND SO30 .... 134 E1
Botley Park Hotel &
  Country Club
  BPWT SO32 .... 109 L6
Boundary Oak School
  WHAM PO17 .... 160 F3
The Bourne Community College
  EMRTH PO10 .... 167 G7
Bournemouth Borough Council
  BMTH BH1 .... 15 K5
Bournemouth Business Centre
  BMTH BH1 .... 15 J4
Bournemouth College
  BMTH BH1 .... 15 M4
Bournemouth County Council
  BMTH BH1 .... 15 J4
Bournemouth County Court
  BMTH BH1 .... 15 H4
Bournemouth
  International Airport
  CHCH/BSGR BH23 ...... 195 K8
Bournemouth
  Magistrates Court
  BMTH BH1 .... 15 H5
Bournemouth Mosque
  MOOR/WNTN BH9 .... 220 D8
The Bournemouth
  Nuffield Hospital
  BMTH BH1 .... 15 J4
Bournemouth & Poole College
  BMTH BH1 .... 15 H5
Bournemouth & Poole College
  BMTH BH1 .... 15 J5
Bournemouth & Poole College
  PSTN BH14 .... 233 L3
Bournemouth & Poole
  College of Further Education
  PSTN BH14 .... 233 L4
Bournemouth School for Boys
  CHAR BH8 .... 221 G7
Bournemouth School for Girls
  CHAR BH8 .... 221 G6
Bournemouth Sports Club
  CHCH/BSGR BH23 ...... 195 G7
Bournemouth University
  BKME/WDN BH12 .... 220 A8
Bournemouth University
  BMTH BH1 .... 15 J5
Bournemouth University
  BMTH BH1 .... 15 K5
Boveridge House School
  WIMB BH21 .... 95 H6
Boyatt Shopping Centre
  ELGH SO50 .... 81 M3
Boyatt Wood Surgery
  ELGH SO50 .... 81 L3
Braemore C of E
  Primary School
  FBDG SP6 .... 72 A8
Braishfield CP School
  ROMY SO51 .... 51 J2
Bramshaw Golf Club
  LYND SO43 .... 101 M7
Branksome Heath
  Middle School
  BKME/WDN BH12 .... 234 B2
Bransgore Primary School
  CHCH/BSGR BH23 .... 198 A8
Breamore House
  FBDG SP6 .... 71 M5
Brickfield Trading Estate
  CHFD SO53 .... 81 G3
Brickyards Industrial Estate
  PSF GU32 .... 35 M7
Bridge Gallery
  WSHM SO15 .... 131 K2
Bridgemary Community School
  LSOL/BMARY PO13 .... 185 G6
The Bridge Shopping Centre
  PSEA PO1 .... 13 K1
Broad Chalke Primary School
  RSAL SP5 .... 40 B1
Broadlands House
  ROMY SO51 .... 78 D3
Broadstone First School
  BDST BH18 .... 217 M4
Broadstone Middle School
  BDST BH18 .... 218 A3
Brockenhurst College
  BROC SO42 .... 175 L6
Brockenhurst Primary School
  BROC SO42 .... 175 K7
Brockhurst County
  Infant School
  GPORT PO12 .... 209 K1
Brockhurst County
  Junior School
  GPORT PO12 .... 209 L2
Brockhurst Medical Centre
  GPORT PO12 .... 209 K1

Brokenhurst Manor Golf Club
  BROC SO42 .... 201 J2
Brompton Gallery
  SHAM SO14 .... 5 H2
Brookes Hill Industrial Estate
  TOTT SO40 .... 104 A4
Brookfield Secondary School
  HLER SO31 .... 158 C4
Brookwood Industrial Estate
  ELGH SO50 .... 81 L5
The Brownhill Surgery
  CHFD SO53 .... 81 J1
Brownsea Open Air Theatre
  CFDH BH17 .... 217 L8
Brune Park Community School
  LSOL/BMARY PO13 .... 185 J8
Buckholme School
  PSTN BH14 .... 233 M4
Buckland Medical Centre
  NEND PO2 .... 187 H8
The Burgate School
  FBDG SP6 .... 97 L5
Burgess Road Surgery
  ROWN SO16 .... 107 H4
Buriton Business Park
  EPSF GU31 .... 91 H1
Buriton CP School
  EPSF GU31 .... 91 J3
Burley CP School
  RGWD BH24 .... 172 E6
Burley Golf Club
  RGWD BH24 .... 172 F5
Burrfields Retail Park
  HSEA PO3 .... 187 M7
Burridge Social & Sports Club
  HLER SO31 .... 134 F6
Bursledon C of E
  Junior & Infant School
  HLER SO31 .... 133 L8
Bursledon Windmill Museum
  HLER SO31 .... 133 L6
Burton Primary School
  CHCH/BSGR BH23 .... 223 G5
Business Centre
  SHAM SO14 .... 5 J7
The Business Centre
  RSAL SP5 .... 73 J1
Byngs Business Park
  WVILLE PO7 .... 139 M6
By Pass Football Club
  ROMY SO51 .... 78 E2
Cadnam Surgery
  TOTT SO40 .... 127 L1
Calmore County Junior & Infant
  School
  TOTT SO40 .... 104 B6
Calmore Industrial Estate
  TOTT SO40 .... 104 D6
Calmore Sports Club
  TOTT SO40 .... 103 M6
Calshot Castle
  FAWY SO45 .... 181 M7
Cameleon Theatre
  WSHM SO15 .... 131 H2
Campbell Surgery
  SSEA PO5 .... 13 K5
Cams Hill School
  FHAM/PORC PO16 .... 161 J8
Canada House Business Centre
  NMIL/BTOS BH25 .... 226 A6
Canford Heath First School
  CFDH BH17 .... 233 K1
Canford Heath Middle School
  CFDH BH17 .... 233 J1
Canford School
  WIMB BH21 .... 192 E6
Cantell Secondary School
  ROWN SO16 .... 106 F4
The Canute Surgery
  ITCH SO19 .... 132 C5
The Carpet Gallery
  WBNE BH4 .... 235 H5
Carter Community School
  PLE BH15 .... 232 E6
Carvers Trading Estate
  RGWD BH24 .... 170 E1
Castle County Primary School
  FHAM/PORC PO16 .... 186 B1
Castle Court School
  ROWN SO16 .... 105 K4
Catherine Corbett Clinic
  HAV PO9 .... 8 F3
Catherington C of E
  Controlled Infant School
  HORN PO8 .... 116 A7
The Cedar School
  ROWN SO16 .... 105 K4
Central Business Park
  BMTH BH1 .... 15 M2
Central Trading Estate
  SHAM SO14 .... 5 L3
Centurion Industrial Park
  SHAM SO14 .... 132 A1
Chamberlayne Park School
  ITCH SO19 .... 132 E7
Chandlers Ford Infant School
  CHFD SO53 .... 81 J1
Charles Dickens Junior &
  Infant School
  PSEA PO1 .... 211 H2
Chawton House Surgery
  LYMN SO41 .... 228 C5
Chesil Theatre
  WINC SO23 .... 3 J9
Chevron Business Park
  FAWY SO45 .... 179 M2
Christchurch Infant School
  CHCH/BSGR BH23 .... 237 M1
Christchurch Junior School
  CHCH/BSGR BH23 .... 237 L1
Christchurch Medical Centre
  HAV PO9 .... 166 A5
Christchurch Ski &
  Leisure Centre
  CHCH/BSGR BH23 .... 195 M5
Christ the King RC
  Primary School
  BWD BH11 .... 219 L3
Churchers College
  EPSF GU31 .... 63 M4
Churchers College Junior School
  PSF GU32 .... 63 K5

Churchill Yard Industrial Estate
  WVILLE PO7 .... 140 C7
City Business Centre
  WINC SO23 .... 3 G5
City Grove Trading Estate
  ELGH SO50 .... 81 K4
City Industrial Park
  WSHM SO15 .... 4 C3
City Museum
  PSEA PO1 .... 12 E5
City Museum & Art Gallery
  PSEA PO1 .... 12 E5
City Offices
  WINC SO23 .... 3 H8
The City of Portsmouth
  Boys School
  NEND PO2 .... 187 J4
The City of Portsmouth
  Girls School
  PSEA PO1 .... 211 J2
City of Portsmouth Sports Club
  NEND PO2 .... 187 H5
Civil Service Sports Ground
  ENEY PO4 .... 211 K3
Civil Service Sports Ground
  HSEA PO3 .... 187 L5
Clanfield Junior School
  HORN PO8 .... 116 A1
Clanfield Surgery
  HORN PO8 .... 116 B4
Clayfields Sports Centre
  FAWY SO45 .... 155 H4
Cliffdale Primary School
  NEND PO2 .... 187 K6
The Club House
  LISS GU33 .... 37 K4
Cluster Industrial Estate
  HSEA PO3 .... 211 L3
The Coast Clinic
  FAWY SO45 .... 180 F5
Colden Common
  Primary School
  RWIN SO21 .... 54 E7
College Art School
  WINC SO23 .... 26 C2
College Park Infant School
  NEND PO2 .... 187 K6
Collingwood Business Park
  FHAM/STUB PO14 .... 184 F2
Commercial Business Centre
  CHFD SO53 .... 81 H2
Compton All Saints
  C of E Primary School
  RWIN SO21 .... 26 C8
Compton & Upmarden
  C of E Primary School
  RCCH PO18 .... 118 E6
Continental Ferry Port
  NEND PO2 .... 187 G8
Copnor Infant School
  HSEA PO3 .... 187 L7
Copnor Junior School
  NEND PO2 .... 187 K7
Copythorne First School
  TOTT SO40 .... 103 G6
Corfe Hills School
  WIMB BH21 .... 217 K2
Corhampton Golf Club
  BPWT SO32 .... 86 D4
Cornerways Surgery
  RGWD BH24 .... 169 J4
Corpus Christie School
  BOSC BH5 .... 236 E3
Corpus Christi RC
  Primary School
  NEND PO2 .... 187 H7
Cosham Health Centre
  CHAM PO6 .... 187 K1
Cottage Grove Primary School
  SSEA PO5 .... 13 H5
County and Magistrates Court
  PSEA PO1 .... 13 G3
Courthill First School
  PSTN BH14 .... 234 C4
Court Lane Junior &
  Infant School
  CHAM PO6 .... 187 L1
Cowplain School
  HORN PO8 .... 140 C6
Cranewater Junior School
  ENEY PO4 .... 13 M7
Crescent Primary School
  ELGH SO50 .... 81 M5
The Crestwood
  Community School
  ELGH SO50 .... 81 L3
Crofton School
  FHAM/STUB PO14 .... 184 C6
The Crookhorn
  Community School
  WVILLE PO7 .... 164 D4
Crow Arch Lane
  Industrial Estate
  RGWD BH24 .... 170 E3
Cumberland Business Centre
  SSEA PO5 .... 13 K2
Cumberland Infant School
  ENEY PO4 .... 211 L5
Cupernham County
  Junior & Infants School
  ROMY SO51 .... 51 G7
Curdridge Primary School
  BPWT SO32 .... 110 C7
Cutlers Gallery
  BMTH BH1 .... 14 F5
David Hart Business Centre
  RSAL SP5 .... 44 D8
Dawkins Business Centre
  PLE BH15 .... 232 C5
D Day Museum
  SSEA PO5 .... 211 G7
Deacon Trading Estate
  ELGH SO50 .... 82 B6
Dean Court (Bournemouth FC)
  LTDN BH7 .... 236 E2
Deanery Campus
  SHAM SO14 .... 5 J5
Dean Farm Estate
  WHAM PO17 .... 160 E3
Delta Business Park
  FHAM/PORC PO16 .... 184 F1

Denmead Health Centre
  WVILLE PO7 .... 139 J3
Denmead Infant School
  WVILLE PO7 .... 139 L4
Denmead Junior School
  WVILLE PO7 .... 139 K4
Derby Road Surgery
  NEND PO2 .... 187 H7
Devonshire Infant School
  ENEY PO4 .... 211 M4
Devonshire Infant School
  ENEY PO4 .... 13 M4
Devonshire Practice
  ENEY PO4 .... 211 M5
Discover Bible School
  WSHM SO15 .... 131 G2
Dockyard Apprentice
  Exhibition
  PSEA PO1 .... 12 B1
Dorset County Council
  BMTH BH1 .... 15 H4
Dorset County Council
  FERN BH22 .... 194 B3
Dorset County Council
  WIMB BH21 .... 193 K1
Dorset County Council
  WIMB BH21 .... 192 A3
Dorset Health Authority
  FERN BH22 .... 194 B3
Dorset Healthcare NHS Trust
  WEND SO18 .... 133 G1
Dorset Magistrates Court
  BMTH BH1 .... 15 G4
Dorset Medical Centre
  SHAM SO14 .... 5 G2
Down House
  RSAL SP5 .... 45 J8
Downton C of E Primary School
  RSAL SP5 .... 44 D8
Downton County
  Secondary School
  RSAL SP5 .... 72 D1
Downton Industrial Estate
  RSAL SP5 .... 44 D8
Dr Hughes & Partners
  RCWD BH24 .... 170 D1
Dr Munroe & Partners
  TOTT SO40 .... 104 E8
Droxford Junior School
  BPWT SO32 .... 86 F7
Droxford Primary School
  BPWT SO32 .... 86 F7
Dunhurst School
  PSF GU32 .... 63 K2
Dunwood Manor Golf Club
  ROMY SO51 .... 49 J6
Durley Primary School
  BPWT SO32 .... 109 M2
Durlston Court School
  NMIL/BTOS BH25 .... 240 F1
Eagle House School
  PSTN BH14 .... 233 M3
East Dorset Area
  Health Authority
  FERN BH22 .... 194 B3
Eastern Industrial Centre
  CHAM PO6 .... 188 A2
East Hants District Council
  PSF GU32 .... 63 K5
Eastleigh Borough Council
  ELGH SO50 .... 81 L5
Eastleigh College of Further
  Education
  ELGH SO50 .... 81 M6
Eastleigh Football Club
  ELGH SO50 .... 107 K1
Eastleigh Health Centre
  ELGH SO50 .... 81 M5
Eastleigh Museum
  ELGH SO50 .... 81 M6
Eastleigh Rugby Club
  ELGH SO50 .... 82 B5
East Meon Controlled
  Primary School
  PSF GU32 .... 61 J7
Eastney Health Centre
  ENEY PO4 .... 211 L5
Eastney Swimming Baths
  ENEY PO4 .... 212 A6
Easton Lane Business Park
  WINC SO23 .... 3 L6
East Shore School
  HSEA PO3 .... 211 M2
East Street Shopping Centre
  SHAM SO14 .... 5 H4
Ebblake Industrial Estate
  RGWD BH24 .... 145 H4
Eling County Infant School
  TOTT SO40 .... 129 L2
Elmhurst Business Park
  GPORT PO12 .... 10 F3
Elmrise Junior & Infant School
  BWD BH11 .... 219 K4
Elson County Infant School
  GPORT PO12 .... 185 L8
Elson County Junior School
  GPORT PO12 .... 185 L8
Embley Park School
  ROMY SO51 .... 77 K2
Emsworth Museum
  EMRTH PO10 .... 166 D7
Emsworth Primary School
  EMRTH PO10 .... 166 C7
Emsworth Surgery
  EMRTH PO10 .... 166 D8
English Gallery
  HAV PO9 .... 142 A6
Enterprise Industrial Estate
  HORN PO8 .... 116 B8
The Epiphany School
  MOOR/WNTN BH9 .... 220 F4
Fairfield Infant School
  HAV PO9 .... 9 G4
Fairisle Junior & Infant School
  ROWN SO16 .... 105 K4
Fairlands Montessori School
  BPWT SO32 .... 136 C1
Fair Oak Junior &
  Infant School
  ELGH SO50 .... 83 J7
Fairway Business Centre
  HSEA PO3 .... 188 A5

Fareham Borough Council
  FHAM PO15 .... 159 H3
Fareham Borough Council
  FHAM/PORC PO16 .... 185 L1
Fareham Borough Council
  FHAM/PORC PO16 .... 7 K5
Fareham College
  FHAM/STUB PO14 .... 6 D6
The Fareham Gallery
  FHAM/PORC PO16 .... 7 J6
Fareham Leisure Centre
  FHAM/PORC PO16 .... 7 H4
Fareham Megabowl
  FHAM/STUB PO14 .... 184 F3
Fareham Park C of E
  Controlled Junior School
  FHAM PO15 .... 160 A5
Fareham Park Infant School
  FHAM PO15 .... 160 A5
Far Horizons Gallery
  PSF GU32 .... 63 K5
Fawley Business Centre
  FAWY SO45 .... 180 E5
Fawley County First School
  FAWY SO45 .... 180 E5
Fenwick Hospital
  LYND SO43 .... 151 J2
Ferndown First School
  FERN BH22 .... 194 A3
Ferndown Medical Centre
  FERN BH22 .... 194 B3
Ferndown Middle School
  FERN BH22 .... 193 M3
Ferndown Sports Centre
  FERN BH22 .... 193 M2
Ferndown Town Council
  FERN BH22 .... 194 A2
Ferndown Upper School
  FERN BH22 .... 193 M2
Fernhurst Junior School
  ENEY PO4 .... 211 K4
Fernside Business Park
  WIMB BH21 .... 193 L1
Fish Farm
  RSAL SP5 .... 44 F5
Flanders Industrial Park
  HEND SO30 .... 109 G8
Fleming Park Leisure Centre
  ELGH SO50 .... 81 K5
Flying Bull Junior &
  Infant School
  NEND PO2 .... 187 H8
Fordingbrdge Junior &
  Infant School
  FBDG SP6 .... 97 L5
Fordingbridge Hospital
  FBDG SP6 .... 97 L7
Forest Edge School
  TOTT SO40 .... 129 J1
Forest End Surgery
  WVILLE PO7 .... 164 B1
Forest Gate Surgery
  TOTT SO40 .... 129 G1
Forestside Medical Practice
  FAWY SO45 .... 155 J8
Fort Brockhurst
  LSOL/BMARY PO13 .... 185 K7
Fort Cumberland
  ENEY PO4 .... 212 C5
Forton Road Surgery
  GPORT PO12 .... 209 L2
Fort Wallington
  Industrial Estate
  FHAM/PORC PO16 .... 161 H6
Foundry Lane Middle & Primary
  School
  WSHM SO15 .... 106 A8
Foxhills County First School
  TOTT SO40 .... 129 H1
Freeground Junior &
  Infant School
  HEND SO30 .... 134 B2
Freemantle Business Centre
  WSHM SO15 .... 131 G3
Friarsgate Medical Centre
  WINC SO23 .... 3 H8
Frobisher Industrial Centre
  ROMY SO51 .... 50 C7
Front Lawn GM Junior School
  HAV PO9 .... 165 K2
Front Lawn Infant School
  HAV PO9 .... 165 K3
Froxfield Endowed
  Controlled Infant School
  PSF GU32 .... 34 D6
Fryern Junior & Infant School
  CHFD SO53 .... 81 K2
The Fryern Surgery
  CHFD SO53 .... 81 K1
The Futcher School
  CHAM PO6 .... 164 A8
The Gallery
  LYMN SO41 .... 200 F7
The Gallery
  SSEA PO5 .... 13 H7
Gasholders
  SHAM SO14 .... 5 K2
Gatcombe Park Infant School
  NEND PO2 .... 187 K4
George & Dragon Surgery
  EMRTH PO10 .... 166 F5
George Street School
  Branch Clinic
  PSEA PO1 .... 211 K1
Glenfield Infant School
  WEND SO18 .... 132 D1
Glenhurst School
  HAV PO9 .... 9 G4
Glenmoor School for Girls
  NBNE BH10 .... 220 B7
Glenwood School
  EMRTH PO10 .... 166 C7
Goldfield Gallery
  BPWT SO32 .... 113 H7
Goldfield Gallery
  PSEA PO1 .... 12 D5
Goldsmith Infant School
  ENEY PO4 .... 13 M5
Gomer County Junior &
  Infant School
  GPORT PO12 .... 209 L5

Goodway Sea School
GPORT PO12 ..... 185 L8
Goodwyn Gallery
PSEA PO1 ..... 13 L1
Gordleton Industrial Estate
LYMN SO41 ..... 227 K3
Gosport Health Centre
GPORT PO12 ..... 10 C4
Gosport Ice Rink
LSOL/BMARY PO13 ..... 185 J7
Gosport Museum
GPORT PO12 ..... 11 K3
Gosport War Memorial Hospital
GPORT PO12 ..... 10 C4
Grange Comprehensive School
CHCH/BSGR BH23 ..... 223 C4
Grange County Junior & Infant School
LSOL/BMARY PO13 ..... 209 G1
Grange Farm Business Park
BPWT SO32 ..... 111 H8
Gravatom Business Centre
BPWT SO32 ..... 85 G8
Greatbridge Business Park
ROMY SO51 ..... 50 C7
Greenacres School
FUFL SO22 ..... 2 E3
The Gregg School
WEND SO18 ..... 107 M5
Greggs School
PTSW SO17 ..... 106 F7
Grey Welles Surgery
HAV PO9 ..... 165 K4
Group Surgery
ROWN SO16 ..... 107 L4
Grove Medical Practice
WSHM SO15 ..... 131 C1
Gudge Heath Surgery
FHAM PO15 ..... 6 B2
Gundrymoor Trading Estate
WIMB BH21 ..... 168 D3
Gurdwara Sikh Temple
SHAM SO14 ..... 131 L2
Hadleigh Practice
WIMB BH21 ..... 217 G4
Hale Primary School
FBDG SP6 ..... 73 H1
Hall of Aviation
SHAM SO14 ..... 5 K6
Halterworth CP School
ROMY SO51 ..... 79 H1
Hamble County Primary School
HLER SO31 ..... 157 J4
Hamble County Secondary School
HLER SO31 ..... 157 J4
Hambledon Cricket Club
WVILLE PO7 ..... 114 D3
Hambledon Infant School
WVILLE PO7 ..... 114 C5
Hambrook Business Centre
RCCH PO18 ..... 167 M4
Hammond County Junior & Infant School
FHAM/STUB PO14 ..... 184 A6
Hammond Industrial Estate
FHAM/STUB PO14 ..... 184 B7
Hampreston Primary School
WIMB BH21 ..... 193 J5
Hampshire County Council
ELGH SO50 ..... 82 A5
Hampshire County Council
ELGH SO50 ..... 81 K5
Hampshire County Council
FHAM/PORC PO16 ..... 7 K4
Hampshire County Council
GPORT PO12 ..... 11 G4
Hampshire County Council
HAV PO9 ..... 9 G5
Hampshire County Council
LYMN SO41 ..... 228 C4
Hampshire County Council
RGWD BH24 ..... 170 E2
Hampshire County Council
TOTT SO40 ..... 129 K4
Hampshire County Council
WINC SO23 ..... 2 E7
Hampshire County Cricket Club
WSHM SO15 ..... 106 E8
Hampshire Gallery
BMTH BH1 ..... 15 H4
Hamwic College
SHAM SO14 ..... 5 H4
Hamworthy Community Clinic
PLE BH15 ..... 232 D5
Hamworthy First School
PLE BH15 ..... 232 E7
Hamworthy Middle School
PLE BH15 ..... 232 E7
Hanway Group Practice
NEND PO2 ..... 187 J7
Hanway Surgery
PSEA PO1 ..... 211 H1
Harbridge School
RGWD BH24 ..... 122 B8
Hardley School
FAWY SO45 ..... 180 A3
Harefield Clinic
WEND SO18 ..... 132 E1
Harefield Junior & Infant School
WEND SO18 ..... 108 A8
Harestock Infant School
FUFL SO22 ..... 16 C5
Harrison County Primary School
FHAM/PORC PO16 ..... 7 K4
Hart Plain Infant School
HORN PO8 ..... 140 C6
Hart Plain Junior School
WVILLE PO7 ..... 140 C6
Haselworth County Primary School
GPORT PO12 ..... 10 F5
Havant Business Centre
HAV PO9 ..... 8 A6
Havant College
HAV PO9 ..... 8 D1
Havant Leisure Centre
HAV PO9 ..... 8 E2

Havant Museum
HAV PO9 ..... 8 F5
Havant Retail Park
HAV PO9 ..... 164 F7
Havant Rugby Football Club
HAV PO9 ..... 8 A2
Havant Sports Club
HAV PO9 ..... 8 E3
Havant Town Football Club
HAV PO9 ..... 165 L3
Havant War Memorial Hospital
HAV PO9 ..... 8 D3
Hayeswood County First School
WIMB BH21 ..... 192 E2
Hayling Billy Business Centre
HISD PO11 ..... 213 H4
Hayling Island Health Centre
HISD PO11 ..... 213 L5
Haymoor Middle School
FBDG BH17 ..... 218 C7
Hayward Business Centre
HAV PO9 ..... 165 M5
Hazel Wood First School
TOTT SO40 ..... 129 G1
Headlands Business Park
RGWD BH24 ..... 146 E6
Heatherlands First School
BKME/WDN BH12 ..... 234 C3
Heathfield Infant & Middle School
ITCH SO19 ..... 133 G6
Heathfield School
FHAM/STUB PO14 ..... 160 A8
Heathlands Primary School
BWD BH11 ..... 219 L5
Hedge End Business Centre
HEND SO30 ..... 109 G8
Hedge End Retail Park
HEND SO30 ..... 133 L1
Hedge End Town Council
HEND SO30 ..... 133 M2
Henbury View First School
WIMB BH21 ..... 217 G2
Henry Beaufort School
FUFL SO22 ..... 16 D5
Henry Cort Community School
FHAM PO15 ..... 159 M5
The Heritage Centre & Museum
TOTT SO40 ..... 129 M2
Herne County Junior School
EPSF GU31 ..... 63 M4
The Herne Farm Leisure Centre
EPSF GU31 ..... 63 M4
Highbury College
CHAM PO6 ..... 187 L3
Highbury College
PSEA PO1 ..... 13 H1
Highbury College of Technology
PSEA PO1 ..... 210 F2
Highbury Primary School
CHAM PO6 ..... 187 L2
Highcliffe Castle Golf Club
CHCH/BSGR BH23 ..... 239 K1
Highcliffe County Junior School
CHCH/BSGR BH23 ..... 224 E7
Highcliffe GM Comprehensive School
CHCH/BSGR BH23 ..... 224 B7
Highcliffe Medical Centre
CHCH/BSGR BH23 ..... 224 D8
Highcroft Industrial Estate
HORN PO8 ..... 116 B8
Highfield C of E (A) Primary School
PTSW SO17 ..... 106 F6
Highgrove Industrial Park
HSEA PO3 ..... 187 M5
Highlands Medical Centre
FHAM PO15 ..... 160 A5
Highlands Medical Centre
FHAM PO15 ..... 6 A2
Hightown Industrial Estate
RGWD BH24 ..... 170 F2
Hightown Primary School
ITCH SO19 ..... 133 J4
Hillbourne First School
CFDH BH17 ..... 217 L6
Hillbourne Middle School
CFDH BH17 ..... 217 L6
Hill House School
LYMN SO41 ..... 202 B7
Hill Lane Surgery
WSHM SO15 ..... 131 J1
Hill Park Clinic
FHAM PO15 ..... 6 D1
Hillside County First School
VWD BH31 ..... 144 E1
Hillside Industrial Estate
HORN PO8 ..... 116 B8
Hill View First School
NBNE BH10 ..... 220 C5
Hill View Junior School
NBNE BH10 ..... 220 C5
Hiltingbury County Junior & Infant School
CFDH SO53 ..... 53 H7
Hindu Temple
SHAM SO14 ..... 131 M2
Hiscock Gallery
SSEA PO5 ..... 13 H7
H M Coroners Court
BMTH BH1 ..... 15 H4
HMS Victory
PSEA PO1 ..... 210 D2
Holbrook County Junior & Infant School
LSOL/BMARY PO13 ..... 185 G5
Holbrook Recreation Centre
LSOL/BMARY PO13 ..... 185 J7
Holbury County JMI School
FAWY SO45 ..... 180 A5
Hollybrook First School
ROWN SO16 ..... 106 C5
Hollybrook Middle School
ROWN SO16 ..... 106 C5
Hollycombe School
LIPH GU30 ..... 38 F4

Holy Family RC Primary School
ROWN SO16 ..... 105 H6
Homefield School
CHCH/BSGR BH23 ..... 223 C4
Homeopathic Surgery
NMIL/BTOS BH25 ..... 240 E1
Homewood Chiropractic Health Centre
FHAM/PORC PO16 ..... 7 K4
Hook with Warsash Primary School
HLER SO31 ..... 158 B8
Hordle C of E GM Primary School
LYMN SO41 ..... 226 E5
Hordle House School
LYMN SO41 ..... 241 M3
Horndean C of E Junior School
HORN PO8 ..... 141 G1
Horndean Community School
HORN PO8 ..... 140 F1
Horndean Football Club
HORN PO8 ..... 140 F1
Horndean Health Centre
HORN PO8 ..... 141 H1
Horndean Infant School
HORN PO8 ..... 141 G1
Housndown School
TOTT SO40 ..... 129 K4
Hulbert Junior School
WVILLE PO7 ..... 164 D2
Hunter Simmonds Gallery
CCLF BH13 ..... 235 G4
Hyde (C of E Controlled) Primary School
FBDG SP6 ..... 123 H3
Hythe CP School
FAWY SO45 ..... 155 L4
Hythe Medical Centre
FAWY SO45 ..... 155 K6
Imax Cinema
BMTH BH1 ..... 14 F7
International Centre & Leisure Pool
WCLF BH2 ..... 14 E8
Isambard Brunel Junior School
NEND PO2 ..... 187 J8
Isle of Wight Car Ferry Terminal
PSEA PO1 ..... 12 C4
Itchen College
ITCH SO19 ..... 132 E3
Jellicoe Theatre
PSTN BH14 ..... 233 L3
J M L Trading Estate
WVILLE PO7 ..... 4 C2
Jubilee Business Centre
WVILLE PO7 ..... 140 C8
Jubilee Surgery
FHAM/STUB PO14 ..... 159 K8
Kanes Hill Primary School
ITCH SO19 ..... 133 J2
Keble Memorial Primary School
RWIN SO21 ..... 53 G2
Kelseys Doctors Surgery
LISS GU33 ..... 36 E4
King Alfred College
FUFL SO22 ..... 2 B8
King Alfreds College of Higher Education
FUFL SO22 ..... 2 C9
King Edward VI School
WSHM SO15 ..... 106 D8
King Richard School
CHAM PO6 ..... 162 D8
Kings Copse Primary School
HEND SO30 ..... 134 A3
Kings Junior School
SBNE BH6 ..... 237 L3
Kingsland Market
SHAM SO14 ..... 5 H3
Kingsleigh First School
NBNE BH10 ..... 220 A5
Kingsleigh Junior School
NBNE BH10 ..... 220 A5
Kingsleigh Secondary School
NBNE BH10 ..... 220 A5
Kings Park Primary School
BMTH BH1 ..... 236 D2
The Kings Primary School
HEND SO30 ..... 108 C5
Kings School
ELGH SO50 ..... 83 G7
Kings School
FUFL SO22 ..... 26 A2
Kings Theatre
SSEA PO5 ..... 13 K6
Kingsworthy Primary School
WINC SO23 ..... 17 H2
Kin Hon Clinic
SSEA PO5 ..... 12 F3
Kinson Primary School
BWD BH11 ..... 219 M3
Knightwood Primary School
NBDE SO52 ..... 80 E1
Lacey Lodge School
HSEA PO3 ..... 211 M2
Lake Road Health Centre
PSEA PO1 ..... 211 J2
Landford C of E Primary School
RSAL SP5 ..... 75 J4
Langdown County Infants School
FAWY SO45 ..... 155 M6
Langdown County Junior School
FAWY SO45 ..... 155 M5
Langrish CP School
PSF GU32 ..... 62 F5
Langside School
BKME/WDN BH12 ..... 219 L8
Langstone Infant School
HSEA PO3 ..... 211 L2
Langstone Junior School
HSEA PO3 ..... 211 L1
Lankhills School
WINC SO23 ..... 2 F4
Lansdowne Clinic
BMTH BH1 ..... 15 H2
Lee on Solent Health Centre
LSOL/BMARY PO13 ..... 208 C2

Lee-on-the-solent Infant School
LSOL/BMARY PO13 ..... 208 D3
Lee-on-the-solent Junior School
LSOL/BMARY PO13 ..... 208 D3
Leesland C of E Infant School
GPORT PO12 ..... 10 E3
Leesland C of E Junior School
GPORT PO12 ..... 10 E3
Leigh House Hospital
CHFD SO53 ..... 53 G8
Leisure Centre
HAV PO9 ..... 8 F2
Leisure Centre
SHAM SO14 ..... 131 L2
Lido Sports Club
WINC SO23 ..... 3 G5
Lilliput First School
PSTN BH14 ..... 234 B8
Liner Industrial Estate
WSHM SO15 ..... 131 G2
Linwood School
MOOR/WNTN BH9 ..... 235 M1
Liss Business Centre
LISS GU33 ..... 36 D3
Liss County Infant & Junior School
LISS GU33 ..... 36 E5
Littledown Leisure Centre
LTDN BH7 ..... 221 L8
Little Green School
RCCH PO18 ..... 118 D4
Lockerley C of E (A) Primary School
ROMY SO51 ..... 20 F7
Locksheath County Infants & Primary School
HLER SO31 ..... 158 E7
Locks Road Surgery
HLER SO31 ..... 158 E7
Lockswood Surgery
HLER SO31 ..... 158 E7
Longbridge Industrial Park
SHAM SO14 ..... 5 K6
Longdown Estates
TOTT SO40 ..... 129 M3
Longfleet C of E VC Combined School
PLE BH15 ..... 233 K4
Longspee School
CFDH BH17 ..... 233 J1
Lordshill Health Centre
ROWN SO16 ..... 105 L4
L S U College of Higher Education
WSHM SO15 ..... 131 K1
Lucia Foster Welch College
SHAM SO14 ..... 5 J6
Ludlow Infant School
ITCH SO19 ..... 132 C5
Ludlow Middle School
ITCH SO19 ..... 132 C4
Lulworth Business Centre
TOTT SO40 ..... 104 D6
Lydlynch County First School
TOTT SO40 ..... 129 J1
Lymington Community Hospitals
LYMN SO41 ..... 228 C4
Lymington County Junior & Infant School
LYMN SO41 ..... 228 B4
Lymington Hospital
LYMN SO41 ..... 228 B4
Lymington Recreation Centre
LYMN SO41 ..... 228 A5
Lyndhurst Infant School
LYND SO43 ..... 151 K3
Lyndhurst Junior School
NEND PO2 ..... 187 K7
Lyndhurst Surgery
LYND SO43 ..... 151 K3
Lytchett Minster Upper School
UPTN BH16 ..... 216 C8
Magpies Sports Club
WIMB BH21 ..... 144 D8
Mainline Business Centre
LISS GU33 ..... 36 E4
Malmesbury Park School
CHAR BH8 ..... 236 A2
Malmesbury Park School
CHAR BH8 ..... 15 J1
Malvern Business Centre
ROWN SO16 ..... 106 C6
Manor Infant School
FAWY SO45 ..... 180 A3
Manor Infant School
PSEA PO1 ..... 211 J1
Manor Road Surgery
VWD BH31 ..... 144 C2
Mansbridge Primary School
WEND SO18 ..... 107 K4
Mansel Infant & Junior Schools
ROWN SO16 ..... 105 J6
Maple Business Park
WIMB BH21 ..... 193 K1
Marchwood C of E Infant School
TOTT SO40 ..... 130 C8
Marchwood Junior School
TOTT SO40 ..... 130 D7
Marchwood Priory Hospital
TOTT SO40 ..... 154 E1
Maritime Museum
BROC SO42 ..... 205 H4
Marlands Shopping Centre
SHAM SO14 ..... 4 F3
The Martin Kemp Welch School
BKME/WDN BH12 ..... 219 H8
Marwell Zoological Park
RWIN SO21 ..... 55 L8
Marycourt Co-educational School
GPORT PO12 ..... 10 D9
Mary Rose Exhibition
PSEA PO1 ..... 12 B1
Mary Rose Ship Hall
PSEA PO1 ..... 210 D2
Mason Manor Primary School
ROWN SO16 ..... 105 L8

Mayfield Gallery
MOOR/WNTN BH9 ..... 220 D6
Mayflower Theatre
WSHM SO15 ..... 4 D1
Mayville High School
SSEA PO5 ..... 13 K8
Meadowlands Infant School
HORN PO8 ..... 140 C3
Meadowlands Junior School
HORN PO8 ..... 140 C3
Medina Primary School
CHAM PO6 ..... 187 J1
Mengham Infant School
HISD PO11 ..... 213 L4
Mengham Junior School
HISD PO11 ..... 213 L4
Meoncross School
FHAM/STUB PO14 ..... 184 B4
Meon Infant School
ENEY PO4 ..... 211 M4
Meon Junior School
ENEY PO4 ..... 211 M3
Meonstoke School
BPWT SO32 ..... 87 H4
Meon Valley Golf & Country Club
BPWT SO32 ..... 111 J8
Meon Valley Police Station
BPWT SO32 ..... 85 J8
Merdon Junior School
CHFD SO53 ..... 81 J1
Meredith Infant School
NEND PO2 ..... 187 J8
Meridian TV Studios
SHAM SO14 ..... 132 A2
Middle Park Medical Centre
HAV PO9 ..... 165 G4
Milford C of E School
LYMN SO41 ..... 242 D2
Millbrook Clinic
ROWN SO16 ..... 105 K8
Millbrook Community School
ROWN SO16 ..... 105 K5
Millbrook Secondary School
ROWN SO16 ..... 105 K5
Millbrook Trading Estate
WSHM SO15 ..... 130 C1
Millers Dale Surgery
CHFD SO53 ..... 53 G8
Millhouse Business Centre
ITCH SO19 ..... 132 B4
Millstream Trading Estate
RGWD BH24 ..... 170 D3
Milton Park Infant School
ENEY PO4 ..... 211 M4
Milton Park Junior School
ENEY PO4 ..... 211 M4
M L S College
BMTH BH1 ..... 14 E5
Monks Brook Industrial Park
CHFD SO53 ..... 81 G3
Moordown C of E Primary School
MOOR/WNTN BH9 ..... 220 D7
Moorgreen Hospital
HEND SO30 ..... 108 E6
Moorings Way Infant School
ENEY PO4 ..... 212 A2
Moorlands College
CHCH/BSGR BH23 ..... 222 F2
Moorlands Infant School
WEND SO18 ..... 107 M7
Morelands Primary School
WVILLE PO7 ..... 164 C6
Moreton House School
PSF GU32 ..... 63 K5
Morgans Vale & Woodfalls Primary School
RSAL SP5 ..... 73 J1
Mortimers Farm Industrial Estate
ROMY SO51 ..... 103 K2
Mottisfont Abbey
ROMY SO51 ..... 21 L5
Mottisfont Club House
ROMY SO51 ..... 21 K6
Mountbatten Business Centre
WSHM SO15 ..... 4 B1
Mountbatten Secondary School
ROMY SO51 ..... 79 H2
The Mount Hospital
ELGH SO50 ..... 82 C3
Mount Pleasant Industrial Estate
SHAM SO14 ..... 131 M1
Mount Pleasant Junior School
SHAM SO14 ..... 131 M1
Moyles Court School
RGWD BH24 ..... 147 G2
Mudeford County Primary School
CHCH/BSGR BH23 ..... 238 D2
Mudeford Junior School
CHCH/BSGR BH23 ..... 238 E2
Muscliff C Primary School
MOOR/WNTN BH9 ..... 221 G5
Music Gallery
MOOR/WNTN BH9 ..... 220 F8
National Motor Museum
BROC SO42 ..... 178 D6
National Museum of Artillery
WHAM PO17 ..... 161 M5
Natural Sciences Museum
ENEY PO4 ..... 211 K7
Nelson Industrial Park
HEND SO30 ..... 109 G7
Nethercliffe School
FUFL SO22 ..... 2 D5
Netley Abbey Infant School
HLER SO31 ..... 156 F1
Netley Court School
HLER SO31 ..... 156 F3
Netley Marsh C of E Controlled Infant School
TOTT SO40 ..... 128 E1
Neville Lovett Community School
FHAM/STUB PO14 ..... 6 E8
Newbridge Junior School
NEND PO2 ..... 211 K1
New Forest District Council
NMIL/BTOS BH25 ..... 225 L6

New Forest District Council
  RGWD BH24 .... 170 D2
New Forest Golf Club
  LYND SO43 .... 151 M2
New Forest Museum &
  Visitors Centre
  LYND SO43 .... 151 L3
Newlands Infant &
  Middle School
  ROWN SO16 .... 105 K7
New Milton Junior School
  NMIL/BTOS BH25 .... 225 L7
New Milton Recreation Centre
  NMIL/BTOS BH25 .... 225 K6
New Milton Sports Club
  NMIL/BTOS BH25 .... 226 A5
New Milton Town Council
  NMIL/BTOS BH25 .... 225 L6
New Theatre Royal
  PSEA PO1 .... 12 F2
The Newton Health Clinic
  SHAM SO14 .... 131 L2
Newtown Soberton
  County Primary School
  WHAM PO17 .... 137 M2
Nightingale County
  Junior & Infant School
  ELGH SO50 .... 81 J7
Nightingale Surgery
  ROMY SO51 .... 50 F8
Nomansland & Hamptworth
  C of E Primary School
  RSAL SP5 .... 75 C8
Northam Business Centre
  SHAM SO14 .... 132 A4
Northam Primary School
  SHAM SO14 .... 5 L1
North Baddesley County Infants
  School
  NBAD SO52 .... 80 A4
North Baddesley Junior School
  NBAD SO52 .... 80 A4
Northbrook Industrial Estate
  ROWN SO16 .... 106 B6
Northern County
  Junior & Infant School
  FHAM/PORC PO16 .... 162 J4
Northern Parade Clinic
  NEND PO2 .... 187 J4
Northern Parade Infant School
  NEND PO2 .... 187 J5
Northern Parade Junior School
  NEND PO2 .... 187 J5
Northview Gallery
  HLER SO31 .... 134 A8
Norwood CP School
  ELGH SO50 .... 81 M5
Nova Business Park
  NMIL/BTOS BH25 .... 225 J6
Nuffield Theatre
  PTSW SO17 .... 106 F5
Nursling C of E Primary School
  ROWN SO16 .... 105 J3
Nursling Industrial Estate
  ROWN SO16 .... 105 C5
Oakdale South Road
  Middle School
  PLE BH15 .... 233 J3
Oakfield Primary School
  TOTT SO40 .... 104 D8
Oaklands Community School
  ROWN SO16 .... 105 J8
Oaklands RC School
  WVILLE PO7 .... 164 D3
Oak Lodge School
  FAWY SO45 .... 155 C8
Oakmead College of
  Technology
  BWD BH11 .... 219 K3
Oakwood First School
  ROWN SO16 .... 106 A3
Oakwood Junior School
  ROWN SO16 .... 106 A3
Oatlands House Health Clinic
  ROWN SO16 .... 106 B6
Oceanographic Centre
  SHAM SO14 .... 5 K8
Odeon Cinema
  BMTH BH1 .... 14 F6
Odeon Cinema
  NEND PO2 .... 187 H7
Odeon Cinema
  WSHM SO15 .... 4 D4
Oil Refinery
  FAWY SO45 .... 180 D4
O Jays Industrial Park
  HSEA PO3 .... 187 L6
Old Anchor Inn Surgery
  ELGH SO50 .... 82 K6
Old Dames School
  FBDC SP6 .... 73 L4
Oldfield Gallery
  SSEA PO5 .... 13 H5
The Old Fire Station Surgery
  ITCH SO19 .... 132 C5
Old Hambledonians Cricket Club
  HORN PO8 .... 89 K6
Olivers Battery Primary School
  FUFL SO22 .... 26 B5
On Line School
  WSHM SO15 .... 131 K2
Orchard County Infant & Junior
  School
  FAWY SO45 .... 155 J6
Orchard Lea Junior &
  Infant Schools
  FHAM PO15 .... 160 C4
Orion Business Centre
  WEND SO18 .... 107 K3
The Osborn Clinic
  FHAM/PORC PO16 .... 7 L5
Osborne Practice Surgery
  SSEA PO5 .... 13 C7
Otterbourne Primary School
  RWIN SO21 .... 54 A6
Our Lady & St Joseph RC
  Primary School
  LYMN SO41 .... 228 D4
Owslebury CP School
  RWIN SO21 .... 55 M4
Padnell Infant School
  HORN PO8 .... 140 E6

Padnell Junior School
  HORN PO8 .... 140 F5
Palace House
  BROC SO42 .... 178 C7
Palmerston Business Park
  FHAM/STUB PO14 .... 184 E1
Park Community School
  HAV PO9 .... 165 G3
Park Gate Business Centre
  HLER SO31 .... 158 F2
Park Gate Junior School
  HLER SO31 .... 158 F3
Park House Primary School
  HAV PO9 .... 165 G3
Parklands Business Park
  WVILLE PO7 .... 139 K5
Park Lane Medical Centre
  HAV PO9 .... 165 H5
Parkstone Grammar
  School for Girls
  CFDH BH17 .... 217 M8
Parkway Retail Park
  BMTH BH1 .... 15 J2
Parley First School
  FERN BH22 .... 194 B5
The Pascoe Practice
  PSEA PO1 .... 12 E4
Paulsgrove Industrial Centre
  CHAM PO6 .... 162 F8
Paulsgrove Primary School
  CHAM PO6 .... 162 F8
Pavilion
  BMTH BH1 .... 15 G3
Pavilion Theatre
  BMTH BH1 .... 14 E6
Pavillion Theatre
  BMTH BH1 .... 14 F7
Peacock Trading Estate
  ELGH SO50 .... 81 L3
Peel Common County
  Junior & Infant School
  LSOL/BMARY PO13 .... 184 E6
Pegham Industrial Park
  FHAM PO15 .... 159 M2
Penhale Infant School
  PSEA PO1 .... 13 M1
Pennington County
  Junior & Infant School
  LYMN SO41 .... 228 A5
Peter Dyer Gallery
  SSEA PO5 .... 13 H7
Petersfield Business Park
  PSF GU32 .... 63 J5
Petersfield Community
  Hospital
  PSF GU32 .... 63 K5
Petersfield County
  Infant School
  EPSF GU31 .... 63 L5
Petersfield Golf Club
  PSF GU32 .... 36 B8
Petersfield Rugby Football Club
  EPSF GU31 .... 64 C4
Petersfield School
  PSF GU32 .... 63 K6
Petersfield Swimming Pool
  EPSF GU31 .... 63 L5
Petersfield Town Council
  EPSF GU31 .... 63 M5
Petersfield Town Football Club
  EPSF GU31 .... 63 M4
Petersgate Infant School
  HORN PO8 .... 116 B4
Peter Symonds College
  FUFL SO22 .... 2 E4
Phoenix Industrial Park
  ELGH SO50 .... 82 B6
Pier Theatre
  BMTH BH1 .... 14 F8
Pilgrims School
  WINC SO23 .... 3 H9
Pipers Wood Industrial Park
  WVILLE PO7 .... 140 A8
Pitmore School
  CHFD SO53 .... 53 L8
Plaza Theatre
  ROMY SO51 .... 78 E1
Pokesdown Primary School
  BOSC BH5 .... 237 G3
The Polygon School
  WSHM SO15 .... 131 J2
Poole Grammar School
  CFDH BH17 .... 218 B6
Poole Road Medical Centre
  WBNE BH4 .... 14 A6
Poole Technical High School
  PLE BH15 .... 233 H4
Portcastrian R F C
  SBNE BH6 .... 237 K2
Portchester Castle
  FHAM/PORC PO16 .... 186 C3
Portchester
  Community School
  FHAM/PORC PO16 .... 186 A1
Portchester Health Centre
  FHAM/PORC PO16 .... 162 A8
Portchester School
  LTDN BH7 .... 236 F1
Portsdown Group Practice
  WVILLE PO7 .... 164 C5
Portsmouth City Council
  CHAM PO6 .... 187 J1
Portsmouth City Council
  CHAM PO6 .... 163 K8
Portsmouth City Council
  CHAM PO6 .... 162 F7
Portsmouth City Council
  HAV PO9 .... 165 K4
Portsmouth City Council
  PSEA PO1 .... 211 J1
Portsmouth City Council
  PSEA PO1 .... 12 D5
Portsmouth City Council
  SSEA PO5 .... 13 G6
Portsmouth City Council
  SSEA PO5 .... 13 H2
Portsmouth City Council
  SSEA PO5 .... 13 J5
Portsmouth County Court
  PSEA PO1 .... 13 G2
Portsmouth Crown Court
  PSEA PO1 .... 13 G3

Portsmouth Grammar School
  PSEA PO1 .... 12 E4
Portsmouth High School
  SSEA PO5 .... 12 F6
Portsmouth Natural
  Health Centre
  SSEA PO5 .... 12 F4
Portsmouth Rugby
  Football Club
  HSEA PO3 .... 187 L4
Portsmouth Sixth Form
  College
  HSEA PO3 .... 212 A1
Portswood Primary School
  PTSW SO17 .... 107 H6
Portswood Road Surgery
  PTSW SO17 .... 107 G7
Poulner Junior & Infant School
  RGWD BH24 .... 147 G6
The Practice Doctors Surgery
  FHAM/PORC PO16 .... 7 H5
Premier Business Park
  FHAM/STUB PO14 .... 6 C7
Priestlands County
  Secondary School
  LYMN SO41 .... 228 A5
Priets House Museum
  WIMB BH21 .... 192 A4
Princes Mead School
  RWIN SO21 .... 17 K2
Princess Anne Hospital
  ROWN SO16 .... 106 A5
Priory C of E VA
  Primary School
  CHCH/BSGR BH23 .... 238 A2
Priory School
  SSEA PO5 .... 13 L3
Private Medical Centre
  BMTH BH1 .... 15 C5
Purbrook Cricket Club
  WVILLE PO7 .... 163 M4
Purbrook Junior &
  Infant School
  WVILLE PO7 .... 164 B3
Purbrook Park School
  WVILLE PO7 .... 164 B5
Queen Alexandra Hospital
  CHAM PO6 .... 163 J7
Queens Enclosure
  Primary School
  WVILLE PO7 .... 140 E7
Queens Road Surgery
  NEND PO2 .... 187 J8
Rachel Madocks School
  HORN PO8 .... 140 B4
Rake C of E Controlled
  First School
  LISS GU33 .... 37 L3
Ranvilles Junior & Infant School
  FHAM/STUB PO14 .... 160 A8
Red Barn County
  Primary School
  FHAM/PORC PO16 .... 161 M8
Redbridge Community School
  ROWN SO16 .... 105 J8
Redbridge Primary School
  ROWN SO16 .... 105 J8
Red Funnel Ferry Terminal
  SHAM SO14 .... 4 F7
Red Gallery
  SSEA PO5 .... 13 J7
Red House Museum & Gardens
  CHCH/BSGR BH23 .... 238 A2
Redlands County
  Primary School
  FHAM/PORC PO16 .... 7 H9
Red Lodge School
  ROWN SO16 .... 106 D4
Redlynch C of E
  Primary School
  RSAL SP5 .... 73 M3
Redwood Park School
  CHAM PO6 .... 187 M2
Regents Park Girls School
  ROWN SO16 .... 105 M8
Regents Park Surgery
  WSHM SO15 .... 106 A8
Regional Film Theatre
  SHAM SO14 .... 5 J8
Rex Industrial Estate
  CHFD SO53 .... 81 H3
Richard Martin
  Gallery & Bookshop
  GPORT PO12 .... 11 K4
Riders Junior & Infant School
  HAV PO9 .... 165 H3
Ridgemede Junior School
  BPWT SO32 .... 85 J3
Ridgeway House
  Special School
  ITCH SO19 .... 132 C3
Ringwood C of E Infant School
  RGWD BH24 .... 170 E1
Ringwood County
  Junior School
  RGWD BH24 .... 170 E2
Ringwood Recreation Centre
  RGWD BH24 .... 170 E1
Ringwood School
  RGWD BH24 .... 170 E1
Ringwood Town Council
  RGWD BH24 .... 170 E2
Ringwood Trading Estate
  RGWD BH24 .... 170 E2
Ringwood Waldorf School
  RGWD BH24 .... 169 M2
River Park Leisure Centre
  WINC SO23 .... 3 H5
Riverside Business Park
  LYMN SO41 .... 228 D4
Riverside Close Surgery
  LISS GU33 .... 36 D4
Riverside School
  WVILLE PO7 .... 164 D5
Robert King Gallery
  SSEA PO5 .... 13 J5
Rogate C of E Controlled School
  EPSF GU31 .... 65 L4
Romsey Abbey C of E
  Primary School
  ROMY SO51 .... 78 C1

Romsey County Junior School
  ROMY SO51 .... 50 F8
Romsey Cricket Club
  ROMY SO51 .... 78 E2
Romsey Hospital
  ROMY SO51 .... 78 F1
Romsey Industrial Estate
  ROMY SO51 .... 50 D7
Romsey Infant School
  ROMY SO51 .... 78 E1
Romsey Rugby Football Club
  ROMY SO51 .... 78 E2
The Romsey School
  ROMY SO51 .... 50 D8
Romsey Sports Centre
  ROMY SO51 .... 78 E2
Rookesbury Park School
  WHAM PO17 .... 137 H4
Rowmans House
  Industrial Estate
  ROWN SO16 .... 105 K2
Rowner County Infant School
  LSOL/BMARY PO13 .... 185 H7
Rowner County Junior School
  LSOL/BMARY PO13 .... 185 H7
Rowner Health Centre
  LSOL/BMARY PO13 .... 185 G8
Rowner Swimming Centre
  LSOL/BMARY PO13 .... 209 G2
Royal Hampshire
  County Hospital
  FUFL SO22 .... 2 B8
Royal Hampshire
  Regiment Museum
  WINC SO23 .... 2 F8
Royal Hospital Haslar
  GPORT PO12 .... 11 K7
Royal Marines Museum
  ENEY PO4 .... 211 M6
Royal Naval Museum
  PSEA PO1 .... 12 A1
Royal Navy Submarine Museum
  Offices
  GPORT PO12 .... 11 L6
Royal South Hants Hospital
  SHAM SO14 .... 131 L2
Royal Winchester Golf Club
  FUFL SO22 .... 26 A1
Rushcombe County
  First School
  WIMB BH21 .... 217 H2
Rushington Business Park
  TOTT SO40 .... 129 J3
Russell Cotes Art
  Gallery & Museum
  BMTH BH1 .... 15 G7
Russell Hicks & Temple
  ROMY SO51 .... 78 D1
St Albans C of E
  Primary School
  HAV PO9 .... 165 L5
St Aldhelms C of E
  Combined School
  BKME/WDN BH12 .... 234 F2
St Andrews Surgery
  ELGH SO50 .... 81 M6
St Annes School
  LSOL/BMARY PO13 .... 208 C1
St Anns Hospital
  CCLF BH13 .... 245 K2
St Anthonys RC Primary School
  FHAM/STUB PO14 .... 159 H6
St Barbe Museum
  LYMN SO41 .... 228 C4
St Bedes C of E Primary School
  WINC SO23 .... 3 H6
St Catherines RC Primary School
  WIMB BH21 .... 192 C1
St Catherines Road
  Junior School
  ELGH SO50 .... 81 M3
St Christophers Hospital
  FHAM/PORC PO16 .... 7 L2
St Christophers School
  WEND SO18 .... 107 K8
St Clements C of E School
  BMTH BH1 .... 236 C3
St Cuthmans School
  MIDH GU29 .... 67 K2
St Denys Primary School
  PTSW SO17 .... 107 H7
St Edmunds Catholic School
  PSEA PO1 .... 13 J1
St Edward
  Comprehensive School
  PLE BH15 .... 233 L1
St Edwards School
  ROMY SO51 .... 47 M7
St Faiths Primary School
  WINC SO23 .... 26 E3
St Francis Primary School
  NBAD SO52 .... 80 E3
St Francis School
  FHAM/STUB PO14 .... 160 A7
St Georges Beneficial C of E
  Primary School
  PSEA PO1 .... 12 D2
St Georges Business Centre
  PSEA PO1 .... 12 D2
St Georges Catholic Boys School
  ELGH SO50 .... 107 H2
St Georges Hospital
  LYMN SO41 .... 242 B4
St Georges Industrial Estate
  ENEY PO4 .... 211 L3
St Georges University
  School of Medicine
  WINC SO23 .... 3 G1
St Ives CP School
  RGWD BH24 .... 169 L3
St James C of E Primary School
  EMRTH PO10 .... 166 C1
St James C of E Primary School
  LTDN BH7 .... 237 G3
St James C of E (VC)
  First School
  FBDC SP6 .... 121 J1
St James Hospital
  ENEY PO4 .... 211 M3
St James Primary School
  HEND SO30 .... 108 E6

St Johns Cathedral
  PSEA PO1 .... 210 F2
St Johns Cathedral
  Primary School
  PSEA PO1 .... 13 K1
St Johns C of E Infant School
  HLER SO31 .... 159 K6
St Johns C of E Primary School
  GPORT PO12 .... 209 M1
St Johns C of E
  Primary School
  HAV PO9 .... 141 M8
St Johns College
  SSEA PO5 .... 13 J6
St Johns School
  WIMB BH21 .... 192 B4
St John the Baptist School
  BPWT SO32 .... 111 K6
St Josephs RC School
  BKME/WDN BH12 .... 234 D1
St Josephs RC School
  CHCH/BSGR BH23 .... 223 L8
St Judes Catholic
  Primary School
  FHAM/STUB PO14 .... 6 C6
St Judes C of E Primary School
  PSEA PO1 .... 12 E5
St Katherines C of E
  Primary School
  SBNE BH6 .... 238 A4
St Leonards Hospital
  RGWD BH24 .... 169 G7
St Lukes C of E School
  MOOR/WNTN BH9 .... 220 D8
St Lukes C of E School
  SSEA PO5 .... 13 H2
St Lukes Surgery
  HEND SO30 .... 109 C8
St Marks C of E County
  Infant School
  CHCH/BSGR BH23 .... 224 D7
St Marks C of E Junior School
  WSHM SO15 .... 131 H1
St Marks C of E Primary School
  NBNE BH10 .... 220 A7
St Marys C of E Primary School
  SHAM SO14 .... 5 J2
St Marys C of E Primary School
  SHAM SO14 .... 5 K2
St Marys College
  WEND SO18 .... 107 K8
St Marys First School
  FERN BH22 .... 168 B5
St Marys Hospital
  HSEA PO3 .... 211 L2
St Marys RC Primary School
  GPORT PO12 .... 10 C1
St Marys RC School
  PLE BH15 .... 233 K3
St Marys Surgery
  SHAM SO14 .... 5 J3
St Michaels C of E School
  WCLF BH2 .... 14 B6
St Michaels Middle School
  WIMB BH21 .... 192 C1
St Monica Infant School
  ITCH SO19 .... 132 E5
St Monica Middle School
  ITCH SO19 .... 132 E5
St Patricks RC Primary School
  ITCH SO19 .... 132 C5
St Pauls Hospital
  FUFL SO22 .... 2 E6
St Pauls RC Primary School
  CHAM PO6 .... 162 F8
St Peter's Church
  BMTH BH1 .... 14 F6
St Peters School
  FUFL SO22 .... 26 A3
St Peters School
  LTDN BH7 .... 221 M8
St Peters School
  SBNE BH6 .... 237 L4
St Swithuns RC Primary School
  SSEA PO5 .... 13 M8
St Swithuns School
  RWIN SO21 .... 17 J3
St Swithun Wells RC
  Primary School
  CHFD SO53 .... 81 J3
St Thomas Clinic
  LYMN SO41 .... 228 B5
St Thomas Mores RC
  Primary School
  HAV PO9 .... 8 A1
St Vincent College
  GPORT PO12 .... 10 F1
St Walburgas RC Primary School
  MOOR/WNTN BH9 .... 220 F6
Salterns School
  TOTT SO40 .... 104 F8
The Sanatorium
  Canford School
  WIMB BH21 .... 192 E7
Sandleheath Industrial Estate
  FBDC SP6 .... 97 G5
Sandle Manor School
  FBDC SP6 .... 97 J6
Sarisbury Green C of E
  Primary School
  HLER SO31 .... 158 C3
Sarisbury Infant School
  HLER SO31 .... 158 C4
Sarum Road Hospital
  FUFL SO22 .... 26 B1
Saxon Shore Infant School
  CHAM PO6 .... 162 C8
Scantabout Primary School
  CHFD SO53 .... 81 L1
Scaplens Court Museum
  PLE BH15 .... 233 G7
Shakespeare Business Centre
  ELGH SO50 .... 82 A4
Shakespeare County
  Infant School
  ELGH SO50 .... 81 M4
Shamblehurst CP School
  HEND SO30 .... 109 H8
Sharps Copse Junior &
  Infant School
  HAV PO9 .... 165 M3

Shawcross Industrial Park
  HSEA PO3 .... **187** L3
Sheet CP School
  PSF GU32 .... **64** A2
Shelley Museum
  BOSC BH5 .... **236** E4
Shepherds Down School
  RWIN SO21 .... **54** B2
Sherborne House School
  CHFD SO53 .... **53** J8
Shirley Business Park
  WSHM SO15 .... **131** L5
Shirley First & Middle School
  WSHM SO15 .... **106** B7
The Shirley Health Centre
  WSHM SO15 .... **131** L5
Shirley Swimming Pool
  WSHM SO15 .... **131** L5
Shirley Warren Primary School
  ROWN SO16 .... **105** M6
Sholing First School
  ITCH SO19 .... **132** E4
Sholing Girls School
  ITCH SO19 .... **132** E4
Sholing Infants School
  ITCH SO19 .... **132** E3
Sholing Middle School
  ITCH SO19 .... **132** E3
Sidings Industrial Estate
  HLER SO31 .... **157** H3
Sikh Temple
  SSEA PO5 .... **13** J4
Simcoe Clinic
  WSHM SO15 .... **131** J1
Sinclair First & Junior School
  ROWN SO16 .... **105** M3
Siskin County Junior &
  Infant School
  LSOL/BMARY PO13 .... **209** H4
Slades Farm Special School
  NBNE BH10 .... **220** B4
Solent Business Centre
  WSHM SO15 .... **130** F4
Solent Industrial Centre
  WSHM SO15 .... **131** G4
Solent Industrial Estate
  HEND SO30 .... **109** G4
Solent Infant School
  CHAM PO6 .... **164** B8
Solent Junior School
  CHAM PO6 .... **164** B8
Solent Peoples Theatre
  ITCH SO19 .... **133** G5
Somerford County
  Infant School
  CHCH/BSGR BH23 .... **238** D1
Somerford County
  Junior School
  CHCH/BSGR BH23 .... **238** D1
Somers Park Primary School
  SSEA PO5 .... **13** J2
Somers Town Health Centre
  SSEA PO5 .... **13** J3
Sopley CP School
  CHCH/BSGR BH23 .... **197** G7
Southampton Airport Parkway
  Station
  ELGH SO50 .... **107** L2
Southampton Central Mosque
  SHAM SO14 .... **131** M2
Southampton City College
  SHAM SO14 .... **5** J4
Southampton City Council
  PTSW SO17 .... **107** H6
Southampton City Council
  ROWN SO16 .... **106** A7
Southampton City Council
  ROWN SO16 .... **106** C3
Southampton City Council
  ROWN SO16 .... **105** H4
Southampton City Council
  SHAM SO14 .... **5** J2
Southampton City Council
  SHAM SO14 .... **5** K3
Southampton City Council
  SHAM SO14 .... **4** F5
Southampton City Council
  SHAM SO14 .... **4** F6
Southampton City Council
  WSHM SO15 .... **4** C2
Southampton Football Club
  WSHM SO15 .... **131** J2
Southampton
  General Hospital
  ROWN SO16 .... **106** A5
Southampton
  Institute & Millais Gallery
  WSHM SO15 .... **5** G1
Southampton
  Magistrates Court
  WSHM SO15 .... **131** J2
Southampton & New Forest
  Magistrates Courts
  WSHM SO15 .... **4** D1
Southampton Sports Centre
  ROWN SO16 .... **106** C4
Southampton Sports Club
  ROWN SO16 .... **105** H6
Southampton
  Technical College
  SHAM SO14 .... **5** M5
Southampton University
  ROWN SO16 .... **80** B7
South Baddesley C of E Primary
  School
  LYMN SO41 .... **229** H2
Southbourne County
  Junior & Infant School
  EMRTH PO10 .... **167** J8
Southbourne Surgery
  EMRTH PO10 .... **167** J8
Southdown School
  RWIN SO21 .... **54** B2
The South Downs College
  WVILLE PO7 .... **164** E5
Southern Electric Museum
  CHCH/BSGR BH23 .... **238** A1
South Hants Country Club
  WHAM PO17 .... **137** L7
Southlands School
  LYMN SO41 .... **228** C1

South Parade Pier
  PSEA PO1 .... **211** J7
Southsea Castle Museum
  SSEA PO5 .... **211** G7
Southsea Infant School
  SSEA PO5 .... **13** L7
South West Health Authority
  HEND SO30 .... **133** M4
Southwick Park
  Naval Recreation Centre
  WHAM PO17 .... **162** E3
Spectrum Sports Club
  SBNE BH6 .... **237** H4
Spitfire Court Surgery
  SHAM SO14 .... **5** M6
Springdale First School
  BDST BH18 .... **217** J4
Springfield School
  CHAM PO6 .... **188** A1
Springhill RC Primary School
  WSHM SO15 .... **131** J2
Stag Business Park
  RGWD BH24 .... **170** E3
Stakes Hill Infant School
  WVILLE PO7 .... **164** D2
Stakes Lodge Surgery
  WVILLE PO7 .... **164** E2
Stamshaw Infant School
  NEND PO2 .... **187** H6
Stamshaw Junior School
  NEND PO2 .... **187** G5
Stamshaw & Tipner
  Leisure Centre
  NEND PO2 .... **187** G5
Stanbridge Earls School
  ROMY SO51 .... **50** A5
Stanley Green First School
  PLE BH15 .... **233** H2
Stanmore Primary School
  FUFL SO22 .... **26** D3
Stanton Industrial Estate
  WSHM SO15 .... **130** E1
Stapehill Abbey
  WIMB BH21 .... **193** J3
Station Theatre
  HISD PO11 .... **213** H4
Staunton Park
  Community School
  HAV PO9 .... **165** M1
Stedham CP School
  MIDH GU29 .... **67** J7
Steep School
  PSF GU32 .... **63** K1
Stephen's Castle
  VWD BH31 .... **120** E8
Stoke Gallery
  GPORT PO12 .... **10** F5
Stoke Park County
  Junior School
  ELGH SO50 .... **82** D5
Stoke Park Infant School
  ELGH SO50 .... **82** D6
Stokewood Surgery
  ELGH SO50 .... **82** F6
Stourfield First School
  SBNE BH6 .... **237** J2
Stroud School
  ROMY SO51 .... **51** K8
Summerbee First School
  CHAR BH8 .... **221** G7
Summerbee Junior School
  CHAR BH8 .... **221** G7
Summerbee Secondary School
  CHAR BH8 .... **221** H7
Sunnyside Doctors Surgery
  PSEA PO1 .... **13** L1
Sun Valley Business Park
  WINC SO23 .... **3** M5
Super Bowl
  BMTH BH1 .... **15** G5
Super Bowl
  WSHM SO15 .... **130** D1
Superstore
  BMTH BH1 .... **15** J3
Superstore
  SHAM SO14 .... **4** E2
Superstore
  SHAM SO14 .... **4** E3
Surrey House First School
  ITCH SO19 .... **133** G5
Surrey House Health Centre
  ITCH SO19 .... **133** G5
Swanmore Business Park
  BPWT SO32 .... **111** L3
Swanmore C of E School
  BPWT SO32 .... **112** A2
Swanmore County
  Secondary School
  BPWT SO32 .... **111** M3
Swan Street Surgery
  PSF GU32 .... **63** K5
Swanwick Business Park
  HLER SO31 .... **158** B1
Sway Park Industrial Estate
  LYMN SO41 .... **200** F7
Sway St Lukes Primary School
  LYMN SO41 .... **200** F6
Swaythling Clinic
  PTSW SO17 .... **107** H5
Swaythling Primary School
  PTSW SO17 .... **107** G5
Sylvan First School
  BKME/WDN BH12 .... **234** A2
Synagogue
  BMTH BH1 .... **15** G5
The Synagogue
  PTSW SO17 .... **131** K1
Talbot Heath School
  WBNE BH4 .... **235** H3
Talbot House
  Preparatory School
  MOOR/WNTN BH9 .... **220** C8
Talbot School
  BKME/WDN BH12 .... **219** M8
Talisman Business Centre
  HLER SO31 .... **158** F2
Tankerville School
  ELGH SO50 .... **82** A5
Tanners Brook Infant School
  ROWN SO16 .... **130** D1
Tanners Brook Junior School
  ROWN SO16 .... **130** D1

Tatchbury Manor House
  TOTT SO40 .... **103** L7
Tatchbury Mount Hospital
  TOTT SO40 .... **103** M6
Tauntons College
  WSHM SO15 .... **106** D7
Terminus Industrial Estate
  PSEA PO1 .... **13** J2
Test Vale Surgery
  TOTT SO40 .... **104** E8
Test Valley Business Centre
  TOTT SO40 .... **105** G6
Testwood School
  TOTT SO40 .... **104** E7
Thornden School
  CHFD SO53 .... **53** L8
Thorney County
  Primary School
  EMRTH PO10 .... **190** E5
Thornhill Clinic
  ITCH SO19 .... **133** H3
Thornhill First School
  ITCH SO19 .... **133** G3
Thornhill Junior School
  ITCH SO19 .... **133** G3
Thornhill Park Surgery
  ITCH SO19 .... **133** H2
Three Legged Cross Country
  First School
  WIMB BH21 .... **144** C7
Tiptoe CP School
  LYMN SO41 .... **200** B8
Titchfield County
  Primary School
  FHAM/STUB PO14 .... **159** K7
Totton College
  TOTT SO40 .... **129** J3
Totton College
  TOTT SO40 .... **104** C8
Totton Recreation Centre
  TOTT SO40 .... **104** C8
Tower Industrial Estate
  ELGH SO50 .... **82** B6
Townhill Infant School
  WEND SO18 .... **107** M6
Townhill Middle School
  WEND SO18 .... **107** M6
Townhill Park Health Clinic
  WEND SO18 .... **107** M6
Townhill Surgery
  WEND SO18 .... **108** A5
The Toynbee School
  CHFD SO53 .... **81** J3
Treadgold Museum
  PSEA PO1 .... **12** D1
Trinidad First School
  BKME/WDN BH12 .... **219** G8
Trinity Business Centre
  TOTT SO40 .... **104** D6
Trinity Industrial Estate
  WSHM SO15 .... **130** D1
Trojans Sports Club
  ELGH SO50 .... **107** H1
Tudor House Museum
  SHAM SO14 .... **4** F5
Turlin Moor First School
  UPTN BH16 .... **232** B4
Turlin Moor Middle School
  UPTN BH16 .... **232** B4
Turnpike Business Park
  FHAM/PORC PO16 .... **7** K3
Turnpike Gallery
  PSF GU32 .... **63** L5
Two Riversmeet
  Leisure Centre
  CHCH/BSGR BH23 .... **238** B2
Twyford C of E
  Primary School
  RWIN SO21 .... **54** E2
Twyford School
  RWIN SO21 .... **54** F2
Twyford Surgery
  RWIN SO21 .... **54** E7
Twynham
  Comprehensive School
  CHCH/BSGR BH23 .... **237** M2
United Services
  Cricket Ground
  PSEA PO1 .... **12** D3
United Services Rugby Club
  PSEA PO1 .... **12** E2
University of Portsmouth
  ENEY PO4 .... **211** M4
University of Portsmouth
  HISD PO11 .... **212** D4
University of Portsmouth
  PSEA PO1 .... **13** K2
University of Portsmouth
  PSEA PO1 .... **12** D1
University of Portsmouth
  PSEA PO1 .... **12** D4
University of Portsmouth
  PSEA PO1 .... **12** E2
University of Portsmouth
  PSEA PO1 .... **12** E3
University of Portsmouth
  SSEA PO5 .... **13** G3
University of Portsmouth
  SSEA PO5 .... **13** H4
University of Portsmouth
  SSEA PO5 .... **12** F6
University of Southampton
  PTSW SO17 .... **107** G5
University of Southampton
  ROWN SO16 .... **106** E5
University Practice
  SSEA PO5 .... **12** F4
Upham School
  BPWT SO32 .... **84** D3
Uplands County
  Primary School
  FHAM/PORC PO16 .... **7** G2
Uplands School
  PSTN BH14 .... **234** B5
Upton Health Centre
  UPTN BH16 .... **232** B1
Venture Industrial Park
  LSOL/BMARY PO13 .... **185** H5
Vermont School
  ROWN SO16 .... **106** D4
Verwood C of E First School
  VWD BH31 .... **144** C3

Verwood C of E School
  VWD BH31 .... **144** C3
Verwood Industrial Estate
  VWD BH31 .... **144** F2
Verwood Leisure Centre
  VWD BH31 .... **144** D2
Verwood Sports Centre
  VWD BH31 .... **144** E2
Verwood Town Council
  VWD BH31 .... **144** D1
Victoria Cottage Hospital
  EMRTH PO10 .... **166** D8
Victoria Park
  Swimming Centre
  PSEA PO1 .... **12** F1
Victor Street Surgery
  WSHM SO15 .... **106** A7
Victory Business Centre
  PSEA PO1 .... **13** L2
Victory Retail Park
  PSEA PO1 .... **211** G1
Victory Trading Estate
  HSEA PO3 .... **187** M6
Village Medical Practice
  FERN BH22 .... **168** B6
The Vine School
  BPWT SO32 .... **110** C8
Vintage Motorcycle Museum
  NMIL/BTOS BH25 .... **225** J3
Virgin Cinemas
  SHAM SO14 .... **5** J7
Wallisdean County
  Infant School
  FHAM/STUB PO14 .... **6** D7
Wallisdean County
  Junior School
  FHAM/STUB PO14 .... **6** E7
Waltham Business Park
  BPWT SO32 .... **111** M4
Warblington School
  HAV PO9 .... **9** J4
War Memorial Hospital
  LYMN SO41 .... **242** D4
Warren Avenue
  Industrial Estate
  ENEY PO4 .... **211** M3
Warren Park Primary School
  HAV PO9 .... **165** H1
Warrior Business Centre
  CHAM PO6 .... **188** C1
Waterfront Garden Surgery
  FAWY SO45 .... **155** L3
Waterfront Museum
  PLE BH15 .... **233** G7
Waterloo Industrial Estate
  HEND SO30 .... **109** G7
The Waterloo School
  WVILLE PO7 .... **164** C1
Waterlooville Football Club
  WVILLE PO7 .... **140** C8
Waterlooville Health Centre
  WVILLE PO7 .... **140** B6
The Waterside Health Centre
  FAWY SO45 .... **155** L6
Waterside School
  FHAM/PORC PO16 .... **186** F5
Webb Peploe House Surgery
  LYMN SO41 .... **228** C5
Weeke CP School
  FUFL SO22 .... **2** A2
Wellington Sports Club
  ELGH SO50 .... **107** J1
Wellow County
  Primary School
  ROMY SO51 .... **76** E5
Wentworth College
  BOSC BH5 .... **236** F4
Wessex Nuffield Hospital
  CHFD SO53 .... **53** L7
Wessex Nuffield Hospital
  ELGH SO50 .... **82** A5
Wessex Regional
  Health Authority
  HEND SO30 .... **109** G7
Wessex Superbowl
  CHAM PO6 .... **164** E7
Westbourne County
  Primary School
  EMRTH PO10 .... **166** F4
Westbourne Galleries
  CCLF BH13 .... **235** G5
Westbourne Surgery
  EMRTH PO10 .... **166** F5
West Cliff Medical Centre
  WCLF BH2 .... **14** C8
West End Surgery
  HEND SO30 .... **108** D6
Western Community Hospital
  ROWN SO16 .... **105** M7
Western Downland
  Primary School
  FBDG SP6 .... **96** C4
Western Downland School
  FBDG SP6 .... **70** E7
Western Primary School
  FUFL SO22 .... **2** B6
Westfield Junior School
  CHAM PO6 .... **162** C8
The Westgate School
  FUFL SO22 .... **2** C5
West Hill Park School
  FHAM/STUB PO14 .... **159** J8
Westlands Medical Centre
  FHAM/PORC PO16 .... **186** A1
West Meon Controlled
  Primary School
  PSF GU32 .... **60** A3
West Moors Group Practice
  FERN BH22 .... **168** B6
West Moors Middle School
  FERN BH22 .... **168** D7
Weston Park Boys School
  ITCH SO19 .... **132** F7
Weston Park First School
  ITCH SO19 .... **132** E7
Weston Park Junior School
  ITCH SO19 .... **132** E7
Weston Shore First School
  ITCH SO19 .... **132** D8
Westover Gallery
  BMTH BH1 .... **14** F6

Westover Primary School
  HSEA PO3 .... **187** M8
West Quay Retail Park
  WSHM SO15 .... **4** D3
West Quay Shopping Centre
  SHAM SO14 .... **4** E3
West Wittering
  Parochial School
  SELS PO20 .... **215** K7
Westwood Business Park
  TOTT SO40 .... **104** E6
Whiteley County
  Primary School
  FHAM PO15 .... **159** G1
The Whiteley Surgery
  HLER SO31 .... **134** F8
Whiteparish Surgery
  RSAL SP5 .... **47** G5
Wickham C of E
  Controlled Primary School
  WHAM PO17 .... **136** D3
Wickham Park Golf Club
  WHAM PO17 .... **136** C4
Wickham Riding School
  WHAM PO17 .... **137** J6
Wickham Surgery
  WHAM PO17 .... **136** E4
Wick 1 Industrial Estate
  NMIL/BTOS BH25 .... **225** J5
Wick 2 Industrial Estate
  NMIL/BTOS BH25 .... **225** J6
Wicor County Primary School
  FHAM/PORC PO16 .... **161** L8
Wildern Clinic
  HEND SO30 .... **134** A1
The Wildern School
  HEND SO30 .... **134** A1
Wildground County
  Infant School
  FAWY SO45 .... **155** K7
Wildground County
  Junior School
  FAWY SO45 .... **155** K7
William Gilpin C of E
  Primary School
  LYMN SO41 .... **202** D7
Willments Industrial Estate
  ITCH SO19 .... **132** B3
Wimbledon Park Sports Centre
  SSEA PO5 .... **13** K8
Wimborne Industrial Estate
  WIMB BH21 .... **192** A3
Wimborne Junior &
  Infant School
  ENEY PO4 .... **211** L4
Winchester
  Agricultural Museum
  WINC SO23 .... **3** G5
Winchester City Museum
  WINC SO23 .... **3** G8
Winchester College
  WINC SO23 .... **26** F2
The Winchester Gallery
  ROWN SO16 .... **106** D5
Winchester Lawn Tennis Club
  FUFL SO22 .... **2** B3
Winchester Recreation Centre
  WINC SO23 .... **3** H6
Winchester Rugby Football Club
  WINC SO23 .... **3** J4
Winchester School of Art
  WINC SO23 .... **3** J6
Winnall CP School
  WINC SO23 .... **3** L7
Winnall Farm Industrial Estate
  WINC SO23 .... **3** K6
The Wishing Well Gallery
  CHCH/BSGR BH23 .... **197** M7
The Wishing Well Gallery
  RGWD BH24 .... **172** E5
Wolvesey Palace
  WINC SO23 .... **3** H9
Woodhill Preparatory School
  CHFD SO53 .... **81** J1
Woodhills School
  HEND SO30 .... **134** D1
Woodlands Community School
  WEND SO18 .... **108** C8
Wool House Maritime Museum
  SHAM SO14 .... **4** F6
Woolsbridge Industrial Estate
  WIMB BH21 .... **168** F2
Woolsbridge Small
  Business Centre
  WIMB BH21 .... **168** E2
Woolston First School
  ITCH SO19 .... **132** C6
Woolston School
  ITCH SO19 .... **132** D5
Wordsworth Infant School
  WSHM SO15 .... **106** B7
Wykeham House School
  FHAM/PORC PO16 .... **7** M5
Wykeham Industrial Estate
  WINC SO23 .... **3** L4
Wynford Farm Industrial Estate
  ROMY SO51 .... **50** E4
The Wyvern Community Secondary
  School
  ELGH SO50 .... **83** H7
Yarrells Preparatory School
  UPTN BH16 .... **232** A1
Yeoman Industrial Park
  TOTT SO40 .... **105** G6